THE PROBLEMS OF JURISPRUDENCE

THE PROBLEMS *of* JURISPRUDENCE

Richard A. Posner

Harvard University Press
Cambridge, Massachusetts
London, England

First Harvard University Press paperback edition, 1993

Library of Congress Cataloging-in-Publication Data

Posner, Richard A.
   The problems of jurisprudence / Richard A. Posner.
      p.   cm.
   Includes bibliographical references.
   ISBN 0–674–70875–X (alk. paper) (cloth)
   ISBN 0–674–70876–8 (paper)
   1. Jurisprudence.   I. Title.
K230.P665P76   1990   89–26781
340—dc20   CIP

In Memoriam
Paul M. Bator

Contents

PART V. JURISPRUDENCE WITHOUT FOUNDATIONS

Preface

By "jurisprudence" I mean the most fundamental, general, and theoretical plane of analysis of the social phenomenon called law. For the most part it deals with problems, and uses perspectives, remote from the daily concerns of legal practitioners: problems that cannot be solved by reference to or by reasoning from conventional legal materials; perspectives that cannot be reduced to legal doctrines or to legal reasoning. Many of the problems of jurisprudence cross doctrinal, temporal, and national boundaries.

"Philosophy" is the name we give to the analysis of fundamental questions; thus the traditional definition of jurisprudence as the philosophy of law, or as the application of philosophy to law, is prima facie appropriate. Problems of jurisprudence include whether and in what sense law is objective (determinate, impersonal) and autonomous rather than political or personal; the meaning of legal justice; the appropriate and the actual role of the judge; the role of discretion in judging; the origins of law; the place of social science and moral philosophy in law; the role of tradition in law; the possibility of making law a science; whether law progresses; and the problematics of interpreting legal texts.

All these are examples of what may be termed "wholesale" problems of jurisprudence, to distinguish them from such "retail" problems as the philosophical pros and cons of forbidding abortion or capital punishment, or of imposing tort liability for failing to rescue a stranger. The retail problems are no less worthy than the wholesale ones, nor even less fundamental in a useful sense; they are only narrower. The line is as indistinct as it is unimportant, and it will be crossed frequently in this book—for example, to discuss in Chapter 5 both the state of mind required for criminal liability and the distinction between voluntary and involuntary confessions; in Chapter 6 the problem of legal proof; in

Chapter 9 affirmative action; in Chapter 11 abortion; in Chapter 15 free speech. Yet I shall suggest that philosophy has less to contribute to the retail problems of jurisprudence than to the wholesale ones (see last section of Chapter 11).

The principal tools that I use in dealing with both the wholesale and the retail problems of jurisprudence are those of analytical philosophy, the study of "normative problems about reasons and reasoning" (L. Jonathan Cohen, *The Dialogue of Reason: An Analysis of Analytical Philosophy* 11, 1986). Although moral and political philosophy figure as well in my analysis, the emphasis on the analytical approach places the question of law's objectivity at center stage. I want to make clear at the outset that I am a consumer rather than a producer of philosophy. I seek neither to compete with professional philosophers nor to take sides in philosophical debates, but only to mine philosophy for insights useful to law. At times, though, this requires me to indicate which among competing philosophical positions on a question I find more persuasive.

The spirit in which I approach the problems of jurisprudence is that of the epitaph that William Butler Yeats composed for his tombstone:

> Cast a cold eye
> On life, on death.
> Horseman, pass by!

"Cold" for Yeats is not the coldness of indifference or hostility, for we read in "The Wild Swans at Coole" of swans that "lover by lover, / They paddle in the cold / Companionable streams or climb the air." It is the cold of detachment—a clear-eyed, no-nonsense, but passionate detachment, as in these lines from "The Fisherman":

> 'Before I am old
> I shall have written him one
> Poem maybe as cold
> And passionate as the dawn.'

I try to examine the problems of jurisprudence with the coldness recommended by Yeats, and hence without the piety and cant that are *de rigueur* in many discussions of law. I defend a jurisprudence that is critical of formalism (less pejoratively, of traditional legalism) and that has affinities with legal realism, shorn however of the left-of-center politics characteristic of that movement and its offspring. It is a jurisprudence that, like legal realism, draws on the philosophy of pragmatism (though not only on that philosophy) but that, unlike some versions of legal realism, seeks to demythologize law without either denigrating or diabolizing it.

I have tried to keep the presentation as simple as possible, with a minimum of legal and philosophical jargon. There is no reason why the fascinating subject of jurisprudence should be the exclusive preserve of the handful of academic lawyers who specialize in it. It should be of interest to all lawyers and law students—and also to the increasing number of philosophers, economists, political scientists, sociologists, psychologists, and historians interested in law and justice. Because this is a book not about the scholarship of jurisprudence but about the problems which that scholarship addresses, the reader should not expect a comprehensive exegesis of the classics of jurisprudence. Nor do I discuss *all* the problems of jurisprudence, although I touch on enough of them to warrant titling the book as I have. At times the touch is light, however, and perhaps the implicit title is *The Problems of Jurisprudence as I See Them*.

My interest in jurisprudence goes back a number of years. In the 1970s I began writing about Bentham's attack on Blackstone, about the normative foundations of economic analysis of law, about law's roots in revenge, and about corrective justice. Since becoming a judge in 1981, I have, naturally, become fascinated by the issue of objectivity in adjudication, and it occupies center stage in this book. The approach I take to the issue is sketched in "The Jurisprudence of Skepticism," 86 *Michigan Law Review* 827 (1988), and I reprint portions of that article in this book along with portions of several other articles: "The Concept of Corrective Justice in Recent Theories of Tort Law," 10 *Journal of Legal Studies* 187 (1981), © 1981 The University of Chicago; "Lawyers and Philosophers: Ackerman and Others," 1981 *American Bar Foundation Research Journal* 231, © 1981 American Bar Foundation; "Wealth Maximization Revisited," 2 *Notre Dame Journal of Law, Ethics and Public Policy* 85 (1985), © 1985 Thomas J. White Center on Law & Government, University of Notre Dame; "The Decline of Law as an Autonomous Discipline: 1962–1987," 100 *Harvard Law Review* 761 (1987), copyright © 1987 The Harvard Law Review Association; "Legal Formalism, Legal Realism, and the Interpretation of Statutes and the Constitution," 37 *Case Western Reserve Law Review* 179 (1987), copyright © 1987 Case Western Reserve University; "The Law and Economics Movement," 77 *American Economic Review Papers and Proceedings* 1 (May 1987), copyright American Economic Association 1987; "Conventionalism: The Key to Law as an Autonomous Discipline?" 38 *University of Toronto Law Journal* 333 (1988), © University of Toronto Press 1988; "Conservative Feminism," 1989 *University of Chicago Legal Forum* 191, © 1989 The University of Chicago. The book is largely new, however, and its previously published components appear here heavily revised and rearranged.

Selections from "A Coat," "The Fisherman," and "Under Ben Bulben" are reprinted with permission of Macmillan Publishing Company from *Collected Poems of W. B. Yeats,* copyright 1916, 1919 by Macmillan Publishing Company, renewed 1944, 1947, by Bertha Georgie Yeats and copyright 1940 by Georgie Yeats, renewed 1968 by Bertha Georgie Yeats, Michael Butler Yeats, and Anne Yeats.

I am more than usually indebted for help in bringing this book to its present form. Ricardo Barrera, James Taggart, Catherine Van Horn, Darren Fortunato, Laura Neebling, Adam Pritchard, Barbara Smith, Steven Hetcher, and Philip Clark provided excellent research assistance. Ronald Allen, Dennis Black, Steven Burton, Frank Easterbrook, William Eskridge, Robert Ferguson, David Friedman, Robert Fullinwider, Linda Hirschman, Stephen Holmes, David Luban, Stephen McAllister, Eric Posner, Margaret Radin, Eva Saks, George Stigler, Stephen Stigler, David Strauss, Lloyd Weinreb, Robin West, and an anonymous reader for the Harvard University Press made valuable comments on the manuscript; so did participants in the University of Chicago's Seminar for Contemporary Social and Political Theory and in the University of Maryland's Legal Theory Workshop. The extensive and provocative comments of Lawrence Lessig, Frank Michelman, and Martha Minow require a special acknowledgment, as do Albert Alschuler's valiant efforts, through comments and correspondence, to save me from error; the comments, support, guidance, and wise counseling of Michael Aronson, General Editor at the Harvard University Press; and the sensitive and meticulous copyediting of Elizabeth Gretz. The philosophers Daniel Brudney, Jonathan Cohen, Jules Coleman, Michael Corrado, and Russell Hardin were kind enough to read parts or all of the manuscript and point out errors in it; Brudney's comments resulted in substantial changes in several chapters. To Ronald Allen and Steven Burton I owe an additional debt for helpful conversations on the subject matter of the book, while to Cass Sunstein I owe a particularly large debt for extensive comments, and numerous conversations, that resulted in major revisions.

My last acknowledgment is to the late Paul Bator, who in a review of an earlier book of mine called me "a captive of a thin and unsatisfactory epistemology" ("The Judicial Universe of Judge Richard Posner," 52 *University of Chicago Law Review* 1146, 1161 [1985]). I found this an arresting accusation and one with considerable merit, and it stimulated me to examine the problems of jurisprudence in greater depth than I had ever expected to. In addition, conversations with Professor Bator on the subject matter of the book helped to shape its themes and avert many pitfalls.

THE PROBLEMS OF JURISPRUDENCE

Introduction
The Birth of Law and
the Rise of Jurisprudence

Jurisprudence addresses the questions about law that an intelligent lay-person of speculative bent—not a lawyer—might think particularly interesting. What is law? A system of rules? Of rules plus judicial dis-cretion? Of principles? Or is it just organized public opinion? Is it a thing, entity, or concept at all—and if not, does this make the original question ("What is law?") meaningless? Where does law come from? Can there be law without lawyers and judges? Is there progress in law? How do we know when a legal question has been answered cor-rectly? What is "knowledge" of law knowledge of? What conditions are necessary or sufficient to make law objective? Should law even try to be objective? Can legal findings of fact ever be verified? Is there really a distinct form of *legal* reasoning or is it identical to some other form, such as moral or economic reasoning? Is law an autonomous discipline? How, if at all, does it differ from politics? Does the criminal law presuppose the existence of minds? Of free will? Does the case for pro-tecting free speech depend on the existence of truth? Is objective inter-pretation of statutes and constitutions a chimera? What is the purpose of law? How do we identify a well-functioning legal system? Is law a sci-ence, a humanity, or neither? If a law is sufficiently vicious does it cease to be law? Does "law" mean the same thing in all these questions and, if not, what is the range of meanings of the word? A practicing lawyer or a judge is apt to think questions of this sort at best irrelevant to what he does, at worst naive, impractical, even childlike (how high is up?).[1]

1. Compare with the questions listed above such lawyers' questions as: Can the doctrine of pendent jurisdiction be used to add a party to a case or just to add a claim? Does the replacement of contributory by comparative negligence imply the demise of the doctrine of last clear chance? Can a person who returns a lost article to its owner claim the reward posted for its return if he didn't know about the reward? Does allowing a federal magistrate

To question the point of asking such questions is valid; I hope to show that there is a point.

When I entered Harvard Law School as a student thirty years ago, the emphasis in legal education was heavily practical, in the sense of anti-theoretical. (It is only slightly less so today.) I recall vividly the questions with which my first-year courses began. In torts it was whether an assault, to be actionable at law, requires a touching of the victim. The vehicle for discussing this question was a fourteenth-century case in which the defendant had swung at a tavernkeeper with an axe and missed.[2] In property the opening question was the meaning of "adverseness" in the doctrine of adverse possession. A person who occupies land in the honest but mistaken belief that it is his can by passage of time acquire a good title, but only if his possession is adverse to the "true" owner: a tenant, whose possession is not adverse to his landlord, does not acquire ownership of the premises he rents, no matter how long he has rented them. In contracts we examined the difference between liquidated damages—an estimate made in the contract itself of how much the promisee is likely to lose in the event of a breach—and penalties. Liquidated-damages clauses are enforceable, penalty clauses not. And in civil procedure we examined the difference between "substance" and "procedure." The federal rules of civil procedure authorize a litigant to require his adversary to undergo a medical examination if the adversary's physical condition is pertinent to the litigation, as it often will be in a personal-injury case. The question in the case we read was whether the rule is substantive, and consequently outside the congressional authorization for rules of procedure, or procedural, and hence within it.[3]

This way of studying law, which involves beginning the study *in*

---

to preside over a jury trial in a case where federal jurisdiction is based on diversity of citizenship violate Article III of the Constitution? These questions are quite *general* by lawyers' standards, but they are not jurisprudential questions in my sense. They are not general enough, they are not fundamental, and they are not—and perhaps cannot usefully be—approached from the standpoint of philosophy.

I do not suggest that the word "jurisprudence" has an established meaning; it does not. See, for example, R. H. S. Tur, "What Is Jurisprudence?" 28 *Philosophical Quarterly* 149 (1978). I use the word to mean the set of issues in or about law that philosophy can illuminate.

2. I. de S. & Wife v. W. de S., Y. B. Liber Assisarum, 22 Edw. 3, f. 99, pl. 60 (1348 or 1349); for text and discussion, see my book *Tort Law: Cases and Economic Analysis* 13–16 (1982).

3. Sibbach v. Wilson & Co., 312 U.S. 1 (1941).

medias res, taking the structure of the legal system and the principal rules of law for granted, and treating cases decided in different eras as if all had been decided yesterday (rather than treating old cases as historical curiosities), remains an invaluable method of professional instruction. It conveys to the student the texture of legal practice, and it does so more coherently and efficiently than would an apprenticeship system of legal training. It inducts the students into the folkways of the profession. It drills them in the critical use of logic—an essential though sometimes overworked technique of legal analysis. It teaches them to think on their feet. It instills—again more efficiently than would alternative systems of training—essential lessons, such as that legal language often differs from lay language (the legal meanings of "assault," "adverse," "substance," "procedure," and "penalty" are all counterintuitive), that—a related point—legal meanings are heavily dependent on context ("procedure," notoriously, has many different legal meanings), that many rules of law must be inferred from—they are not stated clearly, or usably, in—judicial decisions, and that at its margins law is far more plastic than the lay public believes. A layperson is apt to think that the answer to every legal question is contained in a book somewhere, and that all one has to know is where to look. The law student soon learns better.

These lessons, background, and competences, and the "Socratic" method by which they are imparted, continue to supply essential preparation for the practice of law—broadly conceived to include judging and other law functions as well as practice in a law firm—at the high level of skill that many American practitioners display. But the concern of this book is not with—more precisely, not at—the practice level of law; and it should be apparent that the pedagogic approach just described is not oriented to asking and answering the kind of questions with which I began, unless the teacher is Socrates himself. The relationship between a conventional legal education and doing jurisprudence is much like that between learning a language and doing linguistics.

The general, fundamental, and deeply problematic character of the questions with which I began mark them as philosophical. To practical people, however, including judges and lawyers and even many law professors, philosophy is an exasperating subject. Philosophers seem preoccupied with questions that no one with a modicum of common sense and a living to earn would waste a minute on, such as: How do we know that any other person has a mind, when we can never observe it? How can we prove that the sun will rise tomorrow, or that no zebras wear overcoats in the wilds—or can we? How even in principle can ideas, which have no spatio-temporal locus, affect bodies? If you are in a room that is locked from the outside but do not know it, and while it is locked you decide not to leave, are you exercising free will in making this decision or are you "acting" under compulsion? How do you know you are not a brain in a vat, being fed impressions of an external world by a mad scientist? I ask nonphilosophical readers to suspend their disbelief, for I hope to show that questions such as these, remote as they may seem not only from common sense but from common law (and every other sort of law), can shed light on the perennial problems of jurisprudence. Meanwhile, Bertrand Russell's eloquent defense of philosophy is worth pondering:

> The man who has no tincture of philosophy goes through life imprisoned in the prejudices derived from common sense, from the habitual beliefs of his age or his nation, and from convictions which have grown up in his mind without the co-operation or consent of his deliberate reason. To such a man the world tends to become definite, finite, obvious; common objects rouse no questions, and unfamiliar possibilities are contemptuously rejected. As soon as we begin to philosophize, on the contrary, we find . . . that even the most everyday things lead to problems to which only very incomplete answers can be given. Philosophy, though unable to tell us with certainty what is the true answer to the doubts which it raises, is able to suggest many possibilities which enlarge our thoughts and free them from the tyranny of custom. Thus, while diminishing our feeling of certainty as to what things are, it greatly increases our knowledge as to what they may be; it removes the somewhat arrogant dogmatism of those who have never travelled into the region of liberating doubt, and it keeps alive our sense of wonder by showing familiar things in an unfamiliar aspect.[4]

The Origins of Law and Jurisprudence

To understand the problems of jurisprudence—even to understand why there are such problems—it is necessary to know a little about the origins of law, itself a jurisprudential question when pursued in a speculative fashion.[5] The ultimate source of these problems lies in the divi-

---

4. *The Problems of Philosophy* 156–157 (1912). "Philosophy, beginning in wonder, as Plato and Aristotle said, is able to fancy everything different from what it is. It sees the familiar as if it were strange, and the strange as if it were familiar. It can take things up and lay them down again. Its mind is full of air that plays round every subject. It rouses us from our native dogmatic slumber and breaks up our caked prejudices." William James, *Some Problems of Philosophy: A Beginning of an Introduction to Philosophy* 7 (1911).

5. Such questions are the domain of historical jurisprudence, the field made famous by Savigny, Maine, and Holmes. See the interesting discussion in Edwin W. Patterson, "His-

sion of labor. Even the simplest society has norms, tacit or explicit, that evolve from the needs of the society before there are judges or other officials.[6] The fact that norms precede formal legal systems is, no doubt, one cause of belief in "natural law." In its strongest form, this term, which we will encounter many times, denotes the idea that there is a body of suprapolitical principles that underwrite "positive law," meaning law laid down by courts, legislatures, or other state organs. When a customary norm is violated to someone's injury in a simple, "prelegal" society, the instinct of the victim or his family to take revenge is activated. Tacit norms enforced by the threat of revenge are the rudimentary form of a legal system; or, if one prefers, a forerunner to it, for it is unimportant from a practical standpoint whether one calls a system of enforcing customary norms through revenge "law" or "prelaw." What is important is that the grave drawbacks of a revenge system[7] make it intolerable except in the smallest or most primitive societies. There are huge advantages to having specialists in the creation and enforcement of norms, and as soon as society can afford them these specialists emerge.

The history of law in forms recognizable to us (that is, of publicly declared and enforced norms) is to a significant degree one of increasing specialization in the performance of legal tasks. In the first stage after the pure system of private revenge, a chief or king, or perhaps even a popular assembly, will legislate and adjudicate as undifferentiated aspects of governing. Examples are Agamemnon in Euripides' *Hecuba,* Creon in *Antigone,* and the jury that tried and condemned Socrates.[8] Gradually these functions are hived off to specialists, but even before

---

torical and Evolutionary Theories of Law," 51 *Columbia Law Review* 681 (1951). For recent contributions see Peter Stein, "The Tasks of Historical Jurisprudence," in *The Legal Mind: Essays for Tony Honoré* 293 (Neil MacCormick and Peter Birks eds. 1986); Stein, *Legal Evolution: The Story of an Idea* (1980); Stein, "Adam Smith's Jurisprudence—Between Morality and Economics," 64 *Cornell Law Review* 621 (1979); E. Donald Elliott, "The Evolutionary Tradition in Jurisprudence," 85 *Columbia Law Review* 38 (1985); Herbert Hovenkamp, "Evolutionary Models in Jurisprudence," 64 *Texas Law Review* 645 (1985).

6. For an interesting discussion, from a philosophical perspective, of the emergence of norms, see Gilbert Harman, *The Nature of Morality: An Introduction to Ethics* 110–111 (1977).

7. Discussed in my books *The Economics of Justice,* pt. 2 (1981), and *Law and Literature: A Misunderstood Relation,* ch. 1 (1988).

8. The trial and condemnation of Socrates (see Thomas C. Brickhouse and Nicholas D. Smith, *Socrates on Trial* 24–37 [1989]) by a jury of hundreds, with no professional judges, no deliberations, and no possibility of appeal, illustrates the limitations of popular justice. So does the inability of even a modern jury to administer any but the simplest remedies. Injunctions and other equitable remedies had to await the appearance of professional judges.

that happens the system of social control will stand in marked contrast to that of a prelegal culture, where the victim is both the adjudicator and the enforcer.

As soon as law enforcement is handed over to officials, however, an "agency problem" arises: What is to guarantee that officials will act in the interest of victims? What is to prevent legal specialists from becoming a professional caste with goals that diverge sharply from social need and popular understanding? How, in other words, is law to be kept human but not too human, too personal, too subjective, capricious? How does an official even find out what happened in the case presented for decision, when he will not have been a participant in the events giving rise to the dispute?

The underlying problem is the general one, central to political theory, of securing competent and responsible rulers. The traditional focus of political theory has been on the overtly political branches of government—the legislature and the executive. The focus of Anglo-American legal theory has been on the individuals who resolve disputes over the application of legal norms and who often in the course of doing so modify, refine, or elaborate those norms—the judges. The position of the judge, as a person called on to resolve a dispute in a manner almost certain to harm one party and benefit the other, is inherently precarious. We can see this by comparing his position with that of the doctor. The doctor is not usually helping one person at the expense of another (an exception is triage), and therefore no one has much incentive to interfere with his work or to challenge his competence. But it is natural for a powerful person who finds himself in a dispute with a weak one to try to use his power to influence the outcome; and it is equally natural for judges, at least the strong-minded ones, to want to prevent interference that puts them in the sway of the powerful. There have been times when and places where such interference was common and made a mockery of law. In a modern society the threat is more likely to come from an interest group or from public opinion than from an individual, but in any case it is not trivial and continues to affect the way in which judges and their defenders in the legal community think about law.

The issue of judicial independence has a private as well as a social aspect. Independence is something judges want the way academics want tenure. Judges do not want to be handmaidens of the powerful. But if independence means only that judges decide cases as they like without pressure from other officials, it is not obvious that an independent judiciary is in the public interest; the people may be exchanging one set of tyrants for another. Where will judges look for guidance once they have achieved independence from rank political interference? Will they merely act as politicians exempt from the usual political constraints, or will they be hemmed in somehow by professional norms? Is there a body of objective norms (either "positive law" or "natural law") or a set of analytic methods ("legal reasoning") that can be used to ensure that judicial decisions will be objective, determinate, impersonal? If not, are judges reduced to ruling by fiat made impressive by the hieratic stagecraft of judging—the raised bench, the robes, the oaths, the jargon and rhetoric?

The answers may depend on what is meant by "objective." If we stress the first two syllables and insist that a judicial decision, to be more than fiat, must correspond to something that is really "out there," we shall be forced to choose between natural law in a strong sense and the legal nihilist's view that law is simply the will of the judges. We may be forced to a similar pass even if, rejecting ontological objectivity (objectivity as correspondence to an external reality), we use "objective" in a weaker sense, which is the scientific sense, of replicable. A finding is objective in this sense if different investigators, not sharing the same ideological or other preconceptions (except—maybe a big "except"— that they would have to share the scientific worldview), would be bound to agree with it. (Hence the association of objectivity with both impersonality and determinacy—and sometimes I use all three terms synonymously.) Although I call this the scientific sense of objectivity, its applications are not limited to science; there are many nonscientific propositions that persons of diverse ideology can agree on. The problem for law is that there is little tendency for inquirers who hold different ideologies to converge on the answers to difficult legal questions. Not all legal questions are difficult, of course; and one of the points I shall be emphasizing is that there really are easy legal questions—many of them. But naturally the focus of professional attention is on the difficult ones. And only if we are content to define "objective" in a third sense (which I shall sometimes call the "conversational" sense), as merely reasonable—that is, as not willful, not personal, not (narrowly) political, not utterly indeterminate though not determinate in the ontological or scientific sense, but as amenable to and accompanied by persuasive though not necessarily convincing explanation—will we be able to locate, with respect to difficult legal questions, a middle ground between the natural lawyer's view and the legal nihilist's view.

Although my focus is on judges, judicial independence is desired almost as much by lawyers. To demonstrate professionalism and justify judicial independence, judges have evolved (with much help from lawyers, of course) technical concepts and methods that in turn support the lawyers' claim to a monopoly of representing persons involved in legal disputes. The proposition that law is strongly objective and therefore impersonal, and concomitantly that law is autonomous and professional, provides the most easily understood raison d'être of the lawyer and the law professor as well as of the judge and helps explain the frequency with which practicing lawyers and academic lawyers, as well as judges, make exaggerated claims for the proposition.

The division of labor is not the only historical movement that has made the issue of objectivity central to jurisprudence. Another is the growing efficacy of law in society. There have been—to overschematize—three stages in that growth. In the first, symbolized in modern times by the Soviet Constitution of 1936, law is largely aspirational—a set of norms that look good on paper but are not enforced, because the courts are co-opted or overawed by other forces in the society. In the second stage, which in this country spans the approximate period 1800 to 1960, judges achieve genuine independence and their decrees are obeyed, but the profession pays little attention to the actual system for "delivery" of legal services, litigation is costly and cumbersome, and as a result much of the law on the books is as dead a letter as in the first stage. In the third stage, which is the stage the United States is in now, the focus of professional concern shifts to the law in action, and great efforts are made—as by subsidizing the legal expenses of indigent criminal defendants, excluding illegally obtained evidence from criminal trials, relaxing the limitations on standing to sue, facilitating class actions, requiring prisons to have law libraries, and making losing defendants pay the plaintiffs' attorney's fees—to ensure that legal rights can actually, dependably, be enforced.[9] In this stage, which is also associated with a growth in "claims consciousness,"[10] the legal system becomes immensely costly, intrusive, and politically controversial. The stakes in the age-old struggle for judicial independence seem greater

---

9. See, for example, *Innovations in the Legal Services* (Erhard Blankenburg ed. 1980). The growing penetration of law in American life is the theme of Lawrence M. Friedman, *Total Justice* (1985).

10. See the interesting discussion in William L. F. Felstiner, Richard L. Abel, and Austin Sarat, "The Emergence and Transformation of Disputes: Naming, Blaming, Claiming . . . ," 15 *Law and Society Review* 631 (1980–81). The three stages can coexist. That is, at a given moment one field of law might be in stage 1, another in stage 2, and another in stage 3. For example, antitrust law reached stage 3 long before civil rights law did; employment discrimination law may not yet have reached stage 3; public international law may not have reached stage 1. Recent years may have seen a slight recession from stage 3 in some areas of American law.

than ever, and the problems of jurisprudence are correspondingly magnified.

A Short History of Jurisprudence

The question where the judges get the norms they apply arises early. Consider its presentation in *Antigone,* written in the fifth century B.C. Creon, the ruler of Thebes, decrees that Polynices, who died in a traitorous attack on the city, shall as punishment be denied the honorable burial that had been given to Eteocles, Polynices' brother, who died defending the city against the traitor. Creon's reasoning is civic and instrumental; he wants to safeguard the state and, to that end, to deter treason by making the punishment for it as horrible as possible. Antigone, the sister of Eteocles and Polynices, defends a rival concept, law as conformity to the dictates of nature,[11] which requires her to arrange a proper burial for her brother, traitor though he was.

These opposed concepts of law receive parallel formulations in the *Republic.* The civic or political concept is expressed by Thrasymachus: "if one reasons correctly, one will come to agree that the just [*dikaion*] is the same thing everywhere—whatever is to the profit or advantage [*sumpheron*] of the mightier [*kreittonos*]."[12] If all Thrasymachus had meant was that law bends to the whims of powerful individuals, he would have been describing not a concept of law but the fact of lawlessness. But what he actually meant, I think, was that law is, and by implication should be, the expression of the values of the dominant groups in society.[13] He was stating the case for the uncompromising form of legal positivism that teaches that (political) might makes (legal) right, and that nothing else can do so. Against this Socrates proposed a conception

---

11. This is "natural law" in its literal sense—a concept also prominent in *Oedipus Tyrannus.* On the natural law tradition, and particularly its modern shift away from nature, see Lloyd L. Weinreb, *Natural Law and Justice* (1987); Weinreb, "The Natural Law Tradition: Comments on Finnis," 36 *Journal of Legal Education* 501 (1986); cf. Robert P. George, "Recent Criticism of Natural Law Theory," 55 *University of Chicago Law Review* 1371 (1988); Russell Hittinger, *A Critique of the New Natural Law Theory* (1987). A still serviceable introduction to natural law thinking is A. P. d'Entrèves, *Natural Law: An Introduction to Legal Philosophy* (1951).

12. *Platonis Opera,* vol. 4, p. 339a (Ioannes Burnet ed. 1902) (*Politeia,* Bk. I, 11. 2–4). The translation is my own.

13. There is much disagreement, though, over the precise meaning of Thrasymachus's concept of justice. See Kimon Lycos, *Plato on Justice and Power: Reading Book I of Plato's "Republic"* (1987), and references cited there.

of justice as something that man discovers rather than creates—that exists literally apart from him, in the Heaven of Forms.

Much of jurisprudence simply rings changes on the disagreement between Creon and Antigone, Thrasymachus and Socrates;[14] it will be apparent on which side we can expect to find most lawyers. In the seventeenth century we find James I asking Edward Coke, the Chief Justice of England, why James is not competent to deliver legal judgments: law is founded on reason, and his reasoning powers are as good as the judges'. Coke could not challenge either premise, but replied that the reason on which law was founded was a species of "artificial reason" that only a person trained and experienced in law could exercise.[15] Coke's reply encapsulated three elements of the orthodox lawyer's view of law: that law is reason, not fiat; that it is a special sort of reason and not just common sense, applied moral philosophy, or policy analysis; and, a related point, that only lawyers know it. Law so conceived resembles Socrates' Form of Justice in that it exists apart from the political organs of government, as the preserve of a professional caste, and more fundamentally because of its "formalism," its independence from the world of fact. But Coke's is not a natural law concept—at least not explicitly. To Coke the law is not a body of ethical or religious principles that subtends, inspires, and is available to criticize specific judgments. If it were, King James's competence to render judgments could not be questioned—not by Coke, anyway. Law is the body of doctrines developed by judges and expressed or implied in their judicial opinions.

This concept of law is not only distinct from but in tension with that of Socrates, whom I have placed first in Coke's ancestral line. Socrates' belief in natural law carried with it a disdain for sophistry—that is, for legal reasoning, criticized by Socrates in Plato's *Gorgias* and exemplified by common law judges such as Coke. Lawyers' tricks do not sit comfortably with natural law in the strong form urged by Socrates. Further marring the symmetry of my classification, James I, whom I have grouped with Antigone and Socrates against Creon and Thrasymachus, could be thought a sort of Creon, with a natural law twist (the *divine right of kings*). We begin to see an association of legal positivism with

14. Throughout, "Socrates" refers to the character in Plato's dialogues, not the historical Socrates, whose view of law and justice may well have differed from that attributed to him by Plato in the late dialogues, including the *Republic* and (possibly) *Gorgias*.

15. Prohibitions del Roy, 12 Co. Rep. 63, 65, 77 Eng. Rep. 1342, 1343 (1608). See Gerald J. Postema, *Bentham and the Common Law Tradition,* ch. 1 (1986). Coke was speaking of the common law—law made by judges as a by-product of deciding cases—rather than of statute law.

legal formalism, as in Coke, and natural law with legal realism (conceived as antiformalism), as in James I and perhaps in Socrates; these associations blur the more familiar association of positivism with realism (Thrasymachus, Creon) and natural law with formalism (Blackstone and also to a degree Coke, as we are about to see). This terminology will become clearer as we proceed, although one of the things I hope to show in this book is that we can live quite happily without such terminology. The following matrix presents the basic permutations:

	Natural law	Positive law
Legal formalism	Blackstone	Coke
Legal realism	James I	Thrasymachus

Coke provided a foil for Hobbes, who argued that law is the command of the sovereign.[16] Although this concept of law resembles Thrasymachus's (not to mention James I's), the dispute between Hobbes and Coke might appear to be merely over the locus of sovereignty in resolving legal disputes: is it in the king or in the judges? The appearance is misleading. Coke would not be likely to question the sovereignty of James I so frontally. His point was merely that the judges, by virtue of their training and experience, have privileged access to a body of authoritative norms. Yet it is a subversive point after all, for it implies that the judges are expositors of natural law, in the sense of law that is authoritative yet does not emanate from "the sovereign." Although this does not quite make them competing sovereigns with the king, it does compromise the king's sovereignty. That is what troubled Hobbes and set him against Coke.

In the next century, Blackstone made the natural law implications of Coke's legalism explicit in the course of painting an admiring picture of the artificial reason of the English common law in all its doctrinal and institutional intricacies.[17] Although conscious both of the utilitarian function of the common law and of its most conspicuous imperfections,

16. See *Leviathan*, pt. II, ch. 26 (1651); see also Hobbes, *A Dialogue between a Philosopher and a Student of the Common Laws of England* (Joseph Cropsey ed. 1971), and Huntington Cairns, *Legal Philosophy from Plato to Hegel*, ch. 7 (1949). For a discussion of how Matthew Hale played Coke to Hobbes (that is, answered Hobbes as Coke would have done if he had still been alive), see J. H. Hexter, "Thomas Hobbes and the Law," 65 *Cornell Law Review* 471 (1980).

17. William Blackstone, *Commentaries on the Laws of England* (4 vols., 1765–1769).

including the excessive severity of many criminal punishments and the arbitrary limitations on trial procedure (for example, the parties to a suit could not testify as witnesses, or criminal defendants be represented by counsel), Blackstone tried to give the common law a transcendental aura. He argued that the common law was rooted in Saxon customary law, which was itself natural law—specifically, the law of God as it had been perceived by human reason in clearer-sighted times. Blackstone gave the common law, in other words, a natural law pedigree. As a concomitant, he downplayed the creative role of judges, calling them the "oracles" of the law. By depicting them as unmediating transmitters of divinely originating commands, this metaphor placed the judges at a far remove from politicians and statesmen. But judges are not unmediated transmitters. Only lawyers can understand them; lawyers translate the oracular discourse for the laity.

Blackstone provided a natural target for Jeremy Bentham. Acutely conscious of the many dysfunctional features of eighteenth-century law, Bentham wanted to refashion the law—and quickly, too—into an instrument for maximizing the greatest happiness of the greatest number. Coke's professionalism (the "artificial reason") and Blackstone's incrementalism, traditionalism, and transcendentalism were obstacles to this program. In combination, these "isms" implied that the common law should not or even could not (without impiety) be changed to conform to the greatest-happiness principle—not soon, anyway—or, at the very least, that any change must be agreeable to the legal profession. The profession might not be sympathetic to the greatest-happiness principle, and in any event had a vested interest in the status quo—a fusty, barnacled, superstitious, reactionary status quo, it seemed to Bentham.[18] Bentham not only made penetrating criticisms of specific legal rules and institutions (while willfully failing to appreciate the strengths of the common law system) but deployed a version of legal positivism most damaging to Blackstone's transcendental pretensions. He showed that much of Blackstone's conceptual apparatus consisted of transparent and unworthy fictions.[19] There was nothing "natural," universal, or tran-

18. On the conflict between Bentham and Blackstone, see *The Economics of Justice*, note 7 above, ch. 1; Postema, note 15 above, pt. 2. The character of Bentham's jurisprudence is most fully displayed in his posthumous treatise *Of Laws in General* (H. L. A. Hart ed. 1970).

19. Such as the oneness of man and woman in marriage: as explained by one of Bentham's successors in the activity of debunking legal fictions, in an essay originally published in 1870, "At law husband and wife lie under certain incapacities in respect to one another. They are not subject to these incapacities *because* they are one person, but *as if* they were one person. These incapacities aside, the law regards them as twain, because they *are*

scendental about law. It was the creation of distinctly earthbound political authorities—legislators and, at the time, especially judges.

Erroneously believing that he had found in rule by representative legislatures the answer to the practical question of how to get government to dedicate itself to the greatest-happiness principle, Bentham wanted to shift the center of legal rule making from the courts to a suitably reformed Parliament, which he hoped would draft detailed codes covering every area of law and would thereby minimize judicial discretion. The judges would be minor bureaucrats rather than politicians parading in phony oracular colors—minor because the codes would be drafted in ordinary language and so require no professional training to decipher and because they would be so comprehensive that judges would have no scope for legislating in the guise of filling gaps left by legislators.

Bentham's is the most comprehensive scheme for making law a true and complete expression of popular sovereignty. This may seem to make him a Creon, Thrasymachus, James I, or Hobbes, albeit with a democratic twist—and the twist is an accident of Bentham's mistaken belief that a popular sovereign would adopt the greatest-happiness principle; if an enlightened despot could have been trusted to do the same, Bentham would have favored, as indeed was his original impulse, vesting all sovereign powers in the despot. Yet with the contingent, almost fortuitous, character of Bentham's attachment to democratic politics acknowledged, it still is the case that he differs importantly from Creon, Thrasymachus, and (less clearly) James I. For at the root of his jurisprudence is not a merely civic or political concept, such as "what's good for Thebes," but the greatest-happiness principle—as sovereign and imperative a norm to a utilitarian as nature is to a natural lawyer.

Even if Parliament had taken up Bentham's invitation to codify the law, the essential elements of the orthodox view would have survived. The judges would have exchanged a divine for a secular overseer but would still have had to possess substantial professional skills, as Continental judges do notwithstanding the extensive codification of law on the Continent. Bentham did not understand this because he thought language purely referential and transparent to reality.[20] This view led

---

twain." Nicholas St. John Green, "Proximate and Remote Cause," in Green, *Essays and Notes on the Law of Tort and Crime* 31, 32 (1933) (emphasis in original—as throughout this book unless otherwise indicated).

20. See James Steintrager, *Bentham* 22–28 (1977). The idea is captured in one of Holmes's aphorisms: "We must think things not words." "Law in Science and Science in Law," 12 *Harvard Law Review* 443, 460 (1899). In other words, all words are names.

him to suppose that a legal code could be drafted that would establish an undistorted path of communication between the legislators on the one hand and the judges and citizens on the other and would make the interpretation and application of law mechanical—a task for low-level civil servants.

Bentham's idea of the law as utilitarian has a significance that transcends the debates between natural law and positivism and between formalism and realism. Rejecting on the one hand every moralism (except utilitarianism itself) as a foundation for law, and on the other hand every merely emotive, traditional, rhetorical, or (in short) unreflective and unsystematic approach to law, Bentham sought to place law on a scientific footing—to make it a practical human instrument for the achievement of definite social ends.[21] In this limited but important respect Bentham is the originator of the pragmatic concept of law advocated in this book.

Despite Bentham's promptings, neither the English Parliament nor American legislatures showed much taste for codification. Throughout the nineteenth century and well into this one, therefore, most Anglo-American law was still common law. Bentham's onslaught, however, together with the steady diminution in religious belief among the educated classes, had left the intellectual foundations of the orthodox view in disarray. If the common law did not come from God, where did it come from? It was one thing to speak of "natural law" when nature was conceived to be the expression of divine love or order, and quite another to find universal legal norms in Darwinian nature, red in tooth and claw. The natural law project has never recovered from what Nietzsche called the death of God (at the hands of Darwin). If not from God or nature, where could the common law have come but from the judges themselves? That would make them legislators—unelected ones, to boot. Many of our states confronted this possibility head on, by making their judiciaries elective. But this experiment merely undermined judicial independence and encouraged the perception (at times self-perception) of judges as nothing more than legislators in robes (if that: until late in the nineteenth century, most American judges did not wear robes). Despite its persistence, the concept of an elective judiciary is generally and correctly regarded as a failure.

Into the breach stepped the American legal formalists, of whom the best known today is Dean Christopher Columbus Langdell of the Harvard Law School. On one level the formalists were Platonists, believing

21. See Nancy L. Rosenblum, *Bentham's Theory of the Modern State*, ch. 3 (1978).

that there existed a handful of permanent, unchanging, indispensable principles of law imperfectly embodied in the many thousands of published judicial opinions, and that the goal of legal reasoning was to penetrate the opinions to the principles. That is the flavor of Langdell's own scholarship.[22] On another—more interesting but not sharply distinct—level the formalists had reconceived law as an inductive science. (In this they had been anticipated, however, by Francis Bacon.)[23] The reports of appellate decisions were the data from which the principles of the common law could be inferred—principles such as that a promise is not legally enforceable unless supported by consideration, or that liability in tort requires proof of blameworthy conduct. Once these principles were brought to light the correct outcome of a case could be deduced. Thus the principles could be used both to show that outliers in the sample of appellate cases from which the principles had been derived had been decided incorrectly and to guide the decision of new cases. Although man-made, the principles could minimize judicial discretion, just as Blackstone's divinely originated common law had been thought to. And although these principles did not have divine backing they had something almost as good—the power of scientific induction and the verdict of time.

The orthodox view had been reinstated in secular, scientific dress. But the challenge remained of explaining just how the creation of legal principles as by-products of judicial decision making could confer on them a political legitimacy equivalent to that of legislative rules. The use of induction to derive principles from cases left a gap between "is" and "ought," and the verdict of time could easily be questioned in a period when social conditions were changing rapidly.

As Bentham had taken on Blackstone, so it fell to Holmes to take on the heirs of Blackstone. Three features of formalism repelled Holmes. The first was its conceptualism and scientism. Formalism considered law a set of principles and legal reasoning a branch of exact inquiry, a

---

22. See, for example, the preface to C. C. Langdell, *A Selection of Cases on the Law of Contracts* (1871).

23. See Paul H. Kocher, "Francis Bacon on the Science of Jurisprudence," 18 *Journal of the History of Ideas* 3, 7 (1957). The formalists acknowledged Bacon's priority. See Perry Miller, *The Life of the Mind in America: From the Revolution to the Civil War* 159 (1965). As Miller's book makes clear, Langdell's approach was not original even in America. Formalism had become the American legal profession's orthodoxy before the Civil War. See id., ch. 3 ("The Science of the Law"), especially pp. 159–163; also M. H. Hoeflich, "Law and Geometry: Legal Science from Leibniz to Langdell," 30 *American Journal of Legal History* 95, 112–121 (1986).

source of apodictic certainty. Second and closely related was the static quality of formalism, its penchant for treating the cases from which the principles of law are inferred as a set of data having no chronological dimension and the principles themselves as timeless, like the propositions of Euclidean geometry.[24] The third objectionable feature of formalism, combining the first two, was the separation of law from life. A formal system like geometry is a system of relations among ideas, not between ideas and physical reality; the formalists' induction was from judicial opinions, not from the problems and practices of social life. (And most of the opinions in which the American formalists found clues to the principles of law were not even American, but English.) Holmes's outlook was severely though imperfectly pragmatic.[25] There are no conceptual entities; the meaning of an idea lies not in its definition, its Form, its relation to other ideas, but rather in its consequences in the world of fact. By the same token there are no legal principles in an interesting sense. There is merely the fact that if you do thus and so, eventually the sheriff will show up at your door and take away some of your property to satisfy a legal judgment against you, and if you resist him the police or, if necessary, the army will be summoned to crush your resistance. As it is unlikely that any of this rough stuff would ensue from violating a precept discovered by a law professor in his library, it must be that the force of the state is deployed in the name of law for concrete political reasons. The rules of law are the systematized and coercive embodiment of the salient opinions of the most powerful groups in society and therefore change as those opinions and groups change.

But Holmes, unlike Thrasymachus, did not believe that legal doctrines are *merely* decrees, reflecting the whims of a tyrant or the caprice of public opinion. Holmes was writing at a time when there was a professional judiciary. Legal doctrines have an intellectual structure and to some extent a life of their own (or at least judges have lives of their own), independent of the political forces that give the doctrines their weight and direction. To paraphrase Hamlet, the political forces rough hew the law but the judges shape it. A man of the century of Darwin, Spencer, Hegel, Marx, and Nietzsche, Holmes thought that the best

24. See Thomas C. Grey, "Langdell's Orthodoxy," 45 *University of Pittsburgh Law Review* 1 (1983).

25. As we shall see in Chapter 7, Holmes's outlook resembles that of his contemporary and acquaintance Charles Sanders Peirce, the founder of pragmatism, but is by no means "orthodoxly pragmatist," assuming there could be such a thing. Also, it is unclear to what extent Holmes was influenced by Peirce and to what extent by their common *Zeitgeist*. See Thomas C. Grey, "Appendix: Holmes and the Pragmatists," in Grey, "Holmes and Legal Pragmatism," 41 *Stanford Law Review* 787, 864 (1989).

judge was the one who shaped the law to conform most closely to, even to anticipate, the desires of the dominant groups in the community, which is to say, who jumped on history's bandwagon.

Holmes's *The Common Law* (1881) is an extended paean to judges' skill in adapting common law doctrines to changes in durable public opinion, which reflects social need and power. The book points out, for example, that when law was merely a substitute for revenge, legal doctrines were designed to give victims of the kinds of wrong that engender a thirst for revenge a remedy approximating what would have been considered necessary to slake that thirst before there were legal remedies. When revenge fell out of favor and other goals, such as deterrence and compensation, came to the fore, the old doctrines were ingeniously adapted to the new goals. Consider the law of deodands. A deodand is an inanimate object that causes a death. In ancient law, deodands were treated as criminals, and destroyed. This behavior was consistent with law's roots in revenge. If you are hurt, you will want to lash out at whoever—or, if you cannot locate the precise line between animate and inanimate objects, whatever—hurt you. Thus a tree that fell on a person and killed him was a deodand and had to be destroyed. All this eventually became dysfunctional but, as Holmes explained, the old law of deodands turned out to have a new use. The victim of a maritime accident may encounter great difficulty in trying to obtain legal redress directly against the owner of the ship that did the harm, because the owner may live far away, quite possibly in a foreign jurisdiction. By analogy to the law of deodands, why not treat the ship itself as the wrongdoer, and hence let the victim sue the ship in the first port in which it berths after the accident? Until the suit is resolved, the ship will not be allowed to leave the port unless the ship's owner or master posts a bond. In this way the victim can obtain and collect a judgment without traveling to the owner's domicile. Admiralty law adopted this approach and still follows it.

Holmes did not believe that the evolution of the law was complete. Indeed, a great believer in evolution in all spheres, he did not consider human biological evolution complete, and looked with apparent favor on eugenic breeding of human beings.[26] He thought it likely that political power would shift to the working class and that crime might come

---

26. See, for example, Buck v. Bell, 274 U.S. 200 (1927); Letter to Harold Laski of May 12, 1927, in *Holmes-Laski Letters,* vol. 2, p. 942 (Mark DeWolfe Howe ed. 1953) ("I wrote and delivered a decision [*Buck v. Bell*] upholding the constitutionality of a state law for sterilizing imbeciles the other day—and felt that I was getting near to the first principle of real reform").

to be considered a disease rather than blameworthy conduct. He thought it inevitable and on the whole desirable that law would change to accommodate these shifts in power and opinion—that it would, for example, become more favorable to labor unions—and he did not think the shift should be impeded by adherence to principles derived from judicial opinions.[27] His tolerant attitude toward federal and state legislation challenged under the Constitution reflected his view that law should not be an obstacle to social change. The exception that he made for governmental action that restricts freedom of speech was consistent, because it was the opponents of social change who wanted to stifle free speech.

Holmes's jurisprudential views are scattered among thousands of judicial opinions, letters, academic writings, occasional pieces, and even anecdotes. It would be remarkable if views so presented were consistent, and they are not.[28] But they are more consistent than they may seem to be, as a brace of examples will help show. The first is Holmes's belief in an "objective" theory of contractual liability (indeed, of liability generally, including criminal liability): a party to a contract may be bound to a contractual undertaking that neither party intended but that seems implied by the words of the contract. The second example is Holmes's rejection of the doctrine of unconstitutional conditions: he thought that since a person has no right to be a police officer (or any other type of public employee), an officer cannot complain if the police department has a rule denying its employees free speech. The greater power—the power not to hire—includes the lesser power to condition employment on the employee's agreeing to surrender his constitutional rights. The objective theory of contract followed directly for Holmes from his rejection of occult, immaterial entities; another person's mind is closed to us (and what is the mind made of, anyway?), so intentions should not figure in the determination of legal duties. The rejection of the doctrine of unconstitutional conditions followed from Holmes's belief that law registers the balance of political power, a belief that led Holmes always to look for the source of power and to make law follow it. Power—closely related to physical force as it is (for Holmes, power *meant* the ability to

27. See, for example, Gitlow v. New York, 268 U.S. 652, 673 (1925) (dissenting opinion): "If, in the long run, the beliefs expressed in proletarian dictatorship are destined to be accepted by the dominant forces of the community, the only meaning of free speech is that they should be given their chance and have their way."

28. As powerfully argued, although with some exaggeration (owing I think to the author's lack of sympathy for his subject), in Robert W. Gordon, "Holmes' *Common Law* as Legal and Social Science," 10 *Hofstra Law Review* 719 (1982).

mobilize force in support of one's desires)—is an attractive concept to someone who wants a material, nonmoral ground for legal obligations.[29]

Holmes's idea of law as a superstructure is more important than the specific base that he found when he burrowed beneath it. Whether the base is power or, what is closely related in a democratic society, dominant public opinion—or even some social or ethical objective, such as maximizing social wealth or utility (and Holmes flirted with that possibility, too)—Holmes's approach invites the student of law to seek an explanation for its rules and outcomes, its doctrines and institutions, outside the law itself, at least as "law" is conventionally defined. This search continues to be an important part of legal theory.

I have dwelt on Holmes at such length because his jurisprudential ideas are so fascinating and fruitful; he remains the leading figure in American jurisprudence. But of course the history of jurisprudence did not end with Holmes. Benjamin Cardozo in the next generation consolidated many of Holmes's insights in an important book, *The Nature of the Judicial Process* (1921)—a clear exposition, as we shall see, of a mature pragmatic jurisprudence. Holmes and Cardozo, along with John Chipman Gray and Roscoe Pound—but particularly Holmes—had laid the foundations for the "legal realist" movement, which flourished in the 1920s and 1930s.[30] I shall pass over the realists. Given the similarity

29. "I believe that force, mitigated so far as may be by good manners, is the *ultima ratio*, and between two groups that want to make inconsistent kinds of world I see no remedy except force." Letter to Sir Frederick Pollock of Feb. 1, 1920, in *Holmes-Pollock Letters* 36 (Mark DeWolfe Howe ed. 1961).

30. On legal realism, see Robert Samuel Summers, *Instrumentalism and American Legal Theory* (1982); Alan Hunt, *The Sociological Movement in Law*, ch. 3 (1978); Andrew Altman, "Legal Realism, Critical Legal Studies, and Dworkin," 15 *Philosophy and Public Affairs* 205–214 (1986); Charles M. Yablon, "Law and Metaphysics," 96 *Yale Law Journal* 613, 615–624 (1987); Edward A. Purcell, Jr., *The Crisis of Democratic Theory: Scientific Naturalism and the Problem of Value*, ch. 9 (1973). For Cardozo's gentle but penetrating criticism of the excesses of legal realism, see "Jurisprudence," in *Selected Writings of Benjamin Nathan Cardozo: The Choice of Tycho Brahe* 7 (Margaret E. Hall ed. 1947). The term "realist" is unfortunate. The legal realists were not scientific realists (who are "idealists" in the lay sense, because they believe in the existence of a world behind sense data—an invisible world). As emphasized by Summers, they were pragmatists, in all the varied hues of that term.

Legal realism is largely an American phenomenon. The English legal tradition is highly formalist, the Continental heavily imbued with natural law thinking well summarized in Peter Goodrich, *Reading the Law: A Critical Introduction to Legal Method and Techniques* 6–8 (1986). The reason for the Continental affection for natural law may be the greater importance of legislatures vis-à-vis courts in the Continental tradition than in the Anglo-American. In the Continental system the judges' docility can usually be assumed (for an important exception—German judges in the Weimar republic—see Chapter 7), and the focus

of their views to Holmes's, and the emphasis I place in this book on pragmatic jurisprudence, this may seem a surprising omission. But it is more postponement than omission; I refer to realism, and more frequently to its current epigone, critical legal studies, in subsequent chapters. If I seem nevertheless to slight legal realism, this may be because I have difficulty understanding what is original in it. At least about the large questions of jurisprudence that are the focus of this book, the legal realists had little to say that Holmes and Cardozo had not said earlier.

Holmes's relationship to modern legal positivism[31] deserves comment. In the influential positivist view expounded by H. L. A. Hart in his book *The Concept of Law* (1961), the law is the set of rules laid down by legislators, judges, and other authorized lawgivers. When the rules run out or fail to fit (as they often do), the judges have discretion to modify, trim, or extend them as may be necessary to make them cover the case at hand. Alternatively—but it comes to the same thing—one of the rules that compose the law is a jurisdictional rule authorizing judges to exercise discretion whenever there is a gap or ambiguity in the substantive rules. In this view the judge is, as Holmes put it, an interstitial legislator.

Holmes argued that law is a prediction of what the judges will do

---

shifts to the principles that ought to guide an enlightened legislature. The differences in actual behavior between Anglo-American judges on the one hand and Continental judges on the other should not be exaggerated, however. See Konrad Zweigart and Hein Kötz, *Introduction to Comparative Law*, vol. 1, pp. 278–280 (2d rev. ed., Tony Weir trans., 1987).

31. Another unfortunate choice of words, since positivism in law is not at all the same thing as positivism in philosophy. Positivism in law can mean either that legal obligation does not depend on moral obligation, and therefore the expression "immoral law" is not an oxymoron, or (the stronger version of legal positivism) that law can emanate *only* from judges and other duly authorized government officials, that ethical obligation alone cannot create a legal obligation. See Jules L. Coleman, "Negative and Positive Positivism," in Coleman, *Markets, Morals, and the Law* 3 (1988); see also David Lyons, "Moral Aspects of Legal Theory," 7 *Midwest Studies in Philosophy* 223 (1982). Either way the important thing is that positive law is not necessarily grounded in or vetted by natural law.

Positivism in philosophy is the idea that only perceptible things are real: succinctly, "seeing is believing." Ian Hacking, *Representing and Intervening: Introductory Topics in the Philosophy of Natural Science* 63 (1983). This metaphysical notion shares with legal positivism only a distrust of vague entities—see Deryck Beyleveld and Roger Brownsword, *Law as a Moral Judgment* 4–7 (1986)—though that is something; and as Gordon, note 28 above, at 722–726, argues, Holmes was, at times anyway, a scientific positivist (or, as it is often called, a logical positivist or logical empiricist) as well as a legal one. For powerful criticism of legal positivism, see Lon L. Fuller, *The Law in Quest of Itself* (1940). As a final wrinkle, notice that positive analysis is frequently contrasted with normative analysis, the former being descriptive (but not necessarily positivistic!) and the latter prescriptive; I shall examine this usage in Chapter 12.

when confronted with a specific set of facts. I discuss this view at greater length in Chapter 7 and for now merely note its consistency with the more conventional positivist view of the judge as rule applier and, on occasion, rule modifier or creator. On either view, law is the activity of licensed persons, the judges, rather than a body of concepts (rules, principles, whatever). Judges employ discretion to change rules, and discretion is not "principled," although it may be bounded by principles. Indeed, to speak of "employing discretion" may be too grand. Judges change rules, period. In the end the law is what the judges do with your case.

The idea of judicial discretion—a blank space or black box, not the solution to the problem of deciding cases when the rules run out but merely the name of the problem—is, no matter how fancied up, a source of unease to the legal profession. If, much of the time, and certainly in the most interesting cases, judges are legislators, why are they not subject to the same political—today, democratic—controls as legislators? Two of the best-known modern answers are those of Hart and Sacks[32] and of Dworkin.[33] Hart and Sacks argued that the judge is a legislator with a difference—his training, the procedures he follows, and the traditions of legal reasoning entitle us to repose greater confidence in his probity and competence. They also believed, however, that ordinary legislators—the members of Congress and of state legislatures—were scrupulous and reasonable, like judges, which if true made a possible convergence of the judicial and legislative powers less worrisome in any event.

Hart and Sacks were writing in a period of political and legal consensus, including general satisfaction with the burst of legislative activity during the New Deal. In such a period their message was convincing; it is no longer. Dworkin's answer to the question of whether the judge is an undemocratic legislator, offered as it was after the consensus had collapsed, was bound to seem less convincing from the start. The considerations that judges are entitled to use in deciding whether to create or modify a rule Dworkin names "principles" and makes a part of law itself—in fact the major part. Rather than use notions of public policy to change or create law, judges, in Dworkin's view, interpret principles to discover the law applicable to the case at hand. The principles take

---

32. See Henry M. Hart, Jr., and Albert Sacks, *The Legal Process: Basic Problems in the Making and Application of Law* (tentative ed. 1958).

33. See Ronald Dworkin, *Taking Rights Seriously* (1977); *A Matter of Principle* (1985); *Law's Empire* (1986).

the place of the Form of Justice or the law of God. Yet as Dworkin acknowledges, they do not compose a consistent whole. They include such frequently warring precepts as that no person shall be allowed to profit from his own wrongdoing and that promises shall be obeyed, thus placing the judge in a quandary as to how to approach a suit for breach of an illegal contract. They also include vague norms, such as treat like cases alike, to which both sides to a legal dispute may be able to appeal with equal plausibility. Nevertheless Dworkin claims that every legal question has a right and a wrong answer; that is, an answer given by law and an answer contrary to law. This conclusion is an organic component of his theory rather than a baroque addition to it. If there could be two right answers to a legal question the judge would have room to exercise discretion; maybe, indeed, he would *have* to exercise discretion, and then the law would be determined by extralegal considerations. We would have come full circle to positivism: the law would be the will of the judges or other officials.

Yet defining law as broadly as Dworkin does provides no escape. When law is defined to include, under the rubric of "principle," the ethical and political norms that judges use to decide the most difficult cases, decision according to law and decision according to political preference become difficult, sometimes impossible, to distinguish in a society as morally heterogeneous as ours. Dworkin does distinguish between policy and principle, and he argues that only the latter is a fit foundation for and limitation on judicially declared rights. The argument is unconvincing, the distinction arbitrary, the principles merely the policies that commend themselves to Dworkin's brand of political liberalism. And such is the malleability of "principles" and the associated term "rights" that judges widely regarded as lawless become in Dworkin's view paragons of lawfulness if the observer shares the judges' political preferences, while conventionally lawful judges become exemplars of lawlessness because they disregard principles that, however political they may look, are actually part of law. The timid judge, the judge who hesitates to innovate, the judge who thinks it the business of legislatures rather than of judges to legislate—to Dworkin *he* is the lawless judge.

The irony of Dworkin's project is that the more broadly law is defined, the less rather than the more secure the "rule of law" becomes. Law loses distinctness—merging first with morals, and then, when it is recognized that society is morally diverse, with politics and hence no-law. If law includes a broad swatch of political principles, then judges can do politics and say with a good conscience that they are doing law.

"Right" and "wrong" become epithets bestowed on the legal analyst's political friends and enemies. The significance of Dworkin as an apologist for an "activist" judiciary and the association, as in Bentham, of legal positivism with hostility to an active judiciary become transparent.[34]

Dworkin is correct that judges do not automatically become lawless when they bring moral and political values into their decision making, but he is incorrect in thinking that value-laden judicial decisions can be confidently pronounced right or wrong. Without social, cultural, and political homogeneity, a legal system is not able to generate demonstrably right, or even professionally compelling, answers to difficult legal questions, whether from within the legal culture or by reference to moral or other extralegal norms—the traditional province of natural law. For without either nature, or a political, social, and moral community so monolithic that the prevailing legal norms are "natural" in the sense of taken for granted, natural law can be but a shadow of its former self—can be but a name for the considerations that influence law even though not prescribed by a legislature or other official body.

Lately Dworkin has been emphasizing the interpretive character of law. Even in a novel case, he argues, the judge is not making a new rule but interpreting a legal tradition. Yet we shall see that the concept of interpretation need not, and in the most difficult cases will not, limit judicial discretion. Moreover, the American legal tradition is now so rich, variegated, conflicted, and ambivalent that a strand of it can easily be found to support either side in difficult cases. Dworkin has created a rich vocabulary for masking discretionary, political decision making by judges.

34. Making the title of Dworkin's latest book—"Law's *Empire*"—significant in a way perhaps not intended, since, as Frank Michelman reminds me, Dworkin may simply have meant to echo Harrington's slogan, "an empire of laws and not of men." James Harrington, *The Commonwealth of Oceana,* in *The Political Works of James Harrington* 155, 171 (J. G. A. Pocock ed. 1977). The relation between Dworkin's jurisprudence and his defense of liberal judicial activism is discussed in Ken Kress, "The Interpretive Turn," 97 *Ethics* 834, 844–846 (1987). For representative criticisms of Dworkin's enterprise, see J. L. Mackie, "The Third Theory of Law," in Mackie, *Persons and Values: Selected Papers,* vol. 2, p. 132 (Joan Mackie and Penelope Mackie eds. 1985); Altman, note 30 above, at 232–234; Lawrence A. Alexander and Michael D. Bayles, "Hercules or Proteus? The Many Theses of Ronald Dworkin," 5 *Social Theory and Practice* 267 (1980); Stanley C. Brubaker, "Reconsidering Dworkin's Case for Judicial Activism," 46 *Journal of Politics* 503 (1984); Drucilla L. Cornell, "Institutionalization of Meaning, Recollective Imagination, and the Potential for Transformative Legal Interpretation," 136 *University of Pennsylvania Law Review* 1135 (1988); Weinreb, *Natural Law and Justice,* note 11 above, at 117–122.

A Preview of the Book

I began the previous section by contrasting a strong positivist (Thrasymachus) and a strong natural lawyer (Plato's Socrates). This terminology identifies one difference between the two contending schools of jurisprudence that I have been discussing: the moral difference or, equivalently, the difference in political theory. But there is also an epistemic difference. Most though not all legal positivists are skeptical about the claim that law is objective and autonomous. Law to them is too close to politics for that. So while "strong" natural lawyers tend to be the true believers in law, legal positivists tend to be legal skeptics. But these correlations are not necessary. A legal positivist who believed that the methods of legal reasoning enabled the sovereign's commands to be infallibly understood and applied by judges would be a moral but not an epistemic skeptic—that is, he would be skeptical about whether law was good but not about whether it was determinate—while a natural lawyer who believed that the methods of legal reasoning often were incapable of discovering moral truth would be an epistemic but not a moral skeptic. (Plato appears to have believed that the methods of legal reasoning *obscure* moral truth.) That is why a positivist can be a legal formalist and a natural lawyer a legal realist; the former conjunction is in fact common.[35] Holmes flirted with formalist positivism, especially in his "objective" theory of contractual (and statutory) interpretation. And notice that while the formalist who is also a positivist believes that *at root* law is "all politics," he believes that *in application* it is nonpolitical, because the judge is not exercising discretion. This posture lets the jurist disdain politics and natural law in the same breath.

For that matter, a natural lawyer can be a positivist—Coke, and maybe Dworkin in his recent writings, which emphasize interpretation, fit this bill. And maybe a formalist can be a realist. Economic analysis of law is a formalist edifice erected on a realist base, so one is not surprised to find that it has been criticized as formalist by antiformalists and as realist by antirealists. And to the extent that the economic analyst seeks to shape law to conform to economic norms, economic analysis of law has a natural law flavor.

These conflations reveal the poverty of labels but do not entirely obliterate the fact that, for more than two millennia, the field of jurisprudence has been fought over by two distinct though variegated

---

35. For an example, see Rolf Sartorius, "Social Policy and Judicial Legislation," 8 *American Philosophical Quarterly* 151 (1971).

groups. One contends that law is more than politics and in the hands of skillful judges yields—at least at certain times, in stable conditions—correct answers to even the most difficult legal questions. The other contends that law is politics through and through and that judges exercise broad discretionary authority. On the side of law as an objective entity and autonomous discipline we have the distinguished lineage of Antigone, Socrates, Coke, Blackstone, Langdell, Hart-Sacks, and Dworkin; let us call them the "Legalists." On the side of law as politics, or law as the will of the stronger, or law as the activity of licensed professionals (judges, legislators, and so on), we have the equally distinguished lineage of Creon, Thrasymachus, James I, Hobbes, Bentham, Holmes, and H. L. A. Hart; let us call them the "Skeptics." This division, which resembles William James's distinction between the "tender-minded" and the "tough-minded," is imperfect; Socrates is a particularly poor fit. And the lists are radically incomplete. From the Skeptics I have omitted, to note just a few examples, not only John Austin, the great nineteenth-century expositor of Hobbes's command theory of law, and the distinguished jurisprude Ambrose Bierce, whose *Devil's Dictionary* succinctly defines "lawful" as "compatible with the will of a judge having jurisdiction,"[36] but also the members of the critical legal studies movement—heirs to the legal realists.[37] Contemporary Legalists less exotic than Dworkin include, again to note just a few, Charles Fried, Walter Berns, and Michael Oakeshott.[38] Legalists advance positions that are more congenial to the legal profession than those of the Skeptics, but perhaps also more humane and more edifying; it is to Legalists such as Coke and Blackstone that we owe many of the distinctive Anglo-

36. *The Collected Writings of Ambrose Bierce* 289 (1946).

37. See Mark Kelman, *A Guide to Critical Legal Studies* (1987); Goodrich's fine book, cited in note 30 above; *The Politics of Law: A Progressive Critique* (David Kairys ed. 1982); Mark Tushnet, "Critical Legal Studies: An Introduction to Its Origins and Underpinnings," 36 *Journal of Legal Education* 505 (1986). For criticism of critical legal studies, see Martin Krygier, "Critical Legal Studies and Social Theory—A Response to Alan Hunt," 7 *Oxford Journal of Legal Studies* 26 (1987); William Ewald, "Unger's Philosophy: A Critical Legal Study," 97 *Yale Law Journal* 665 (1988); Joseph Isenbergh, "Why Law?" 54 *University of Chicago Law Review* 1117 (1987).

38. See Fried, "The Artificial Reason of the Law or: What Lawyers Know," 60 *Texas Law Review* 35 (1981); Berns, *Taking the Constitution Seriously* (1987); Oakeshott, "The Rule of Law," in Oakeshott, *On History, and Other Essays* 119 (1983). Fried represents a school of thought that I call neotraditionalism and discuss in Chapter 14. Critical legal studies is discussed *passim*, but particularly in Chapters 1, 4, 8, and 13. Other recent tendencies in legal theory that bear on the issues I discuss in this book, including feminism (see Chapter 13) and law and economics (Chapter 12), are also examined in due course.

American liberties enshrined in the Bill of Rights and the Fourteenth Amendment. The Skeptics, other than H. L. A. Hart, are a bit scary, although attempts to link them with fascism and other horrors[39] are misconceived and indeed flavored with hysteria. Yet while the Skeptics are too skeptical and too positivist, they have, I believe, a better grip on the realities of law.

The rest of this book is devoted to exploring the basic issues debated by the two groups and the issues that grow out of those issues. I shall argue against "artificial reason," against Dworkin's "right-answer" thesis, against formalism, against overarching conceptions of justice such as "corrective justice," "natural law," and "wealth maximization"—though not against modest versions of these normative systems—but also against "strong" legal positivism (see note 31). I shall argue for an "activity" theory of law—the theory that underlies Holmes's prediction theory; for behaviorism and therefore against "rich" conceptions of mentalism, intentionality, and free will; for the critical as distinct from constructive use of logic; for the idea that the judge's proper aim in difficult cases is a reasonable result rather than a demonstrably right one; and for a concept of the judge as a responsible agent rather than as a conduit of decisions made elsewhere in the political system. More, I shall argue for objectivity as a cultural and political rather than epistemic attribute of legal decisions, for balancing rule-of-law virtues against equitable and discretionary case-specific considerations, for making law more receptive to science—but with due awareness of the irremediably authoritarian character of law, which limits the scope for a scientific ethos in law—and for a consequentialist theory of interpretation. I shall argue in short for a functional, policy-saturated, nonlegalistic, naturalistic, and skeptical,[40] but decidedly not cynical, conception of the legal process; in a word (although, I fear, an inadequate word), for a *pragmatic* jurisprudence.

This is no invention of mine. Holmes, Cardozo, and the realists were pragmatists, although Holmes incompletely so; and legal pragmatism has its contemporary defenders as well, although they will disagree with much of my argument.[41] That argument, I add, is both positive and

---

39. Attempts well discussed in Purcell, note 30 above, ch. 9.

40. I mean "skepticism" in its lay sense rather than in its philosophical sense: that is, skepticism as attitude rather than as metaphysics. See Michael Williams, "The Elimination of Metaphysics," in *Fact, Science and Morality: Essays on A. J. Ayer's "Language, Truth, and Logic"* 9, 14–16 (Graham Macdonald and Crispin Wright eds. 1986).

41. See, for example, Summers, note 30 above; Daniel A. Farber, "Legal Pragmatism and the Constitution," 72 *Minnesota Law Review* 1331 (1988); the perspectivist approach

norinative—that is, both descriptive and evaluative. I argue that American law really is, and also should be, pragmatic, and that it can be improved by greater awareness of its pragmatic character.

I use "pragmatic" in its philosophical rather than its lay sense, to refer to the theories of the American pragmatist philosophers—notably Peirce, James, Dewey, Mead, Kuhn, and Rorty—and of the European philosophers, notably Wittgenstein and Habermas, who have espoused similar views.[42] There is enormous diversity within this group. There

---

taken by Martha Minow in her article "The Supreme Court, 1986 Term: Foreword, Justice Engendered," 101 *Harvard Law Review* 10 (1987); and Grey's fine article "Holmes and Legal Pragmatism," note 25 above. A good older discussion of pragmatic jurisprudence, emphasizing (as do both Grey and I) John Dewey's brand of pragmatism, is Edwin W. Patterson, "Pragmatism as a Philosophy of Law," in *The Philosophy of the Common Man: Essays in Honor of John Dewey to Celebrate His Eightieth Birthday* 172 (1940); also in Patterson, *Jurisprudence: Men and Ideas of the Law,* ch. 17 (1953). Summers's book has a more historical, and less philosophical, emphasis than mine and focuses more than I do on the legal realists. Farber's article contains a particularly good reply to Dworkin's criticisms of legal pragmatism, which appear in *Law's Empire,* note 33 above, at 151–164 (see also index references in *Law's Empire* under "Pragmatism"). See 72 *Minnesota Law Review* at 1343–1347. Dworkin uses the term "pragmatism" strictly in its lay, "what works" sense; thus "the pragmatist thinks judges should always do the best they can for the future, in the circumstances, unchecked by any need to respect or secure consistency in principle with what other officials have done or will do." *Law's Empire,* note 33 above, at 161. This is not an interesting or even coherent version of pragmatism, implying as it does that a pragmatic judge is an ad hoc decision maker having no appreciation for the benefits of consistency with precedent and of fidelity to statutory and constitutional texts. This is tantamount to saying that a pragmatic judge ignores all systemic as distinct from case-specific consequences of his decisions; nothing in pragmatism warrants, or indeed permits, so truncated a conception of the judicial task.

42. On the revival of interest in pragmatic philosophy, see *Anti-Foundationalism and Practical Reasoning: Conversations between Hermeneutics and Analysis* (Evan Simpson ed. 1987); Richard Rorty, *Contingency, Irony, and Solidarity* (1989); Rorty, *Consequences of Pragmatism (Essays 1972–1980)* (1982), esp. pp. 160–166; Cornel West, *The American Evasion of Philosophy: A Genealogy of Pragmatism* (1989); Hilary Putnam and Ruth Anna Putnam, "William James's Ideas," 8 *Raritan,* Winter 1989, at 27; Richard H. King, "'In Other Words': The Philosophical Writings of Richard Rorty," 19 *Journal of American Studies* 95 (1985); Joseph Margolis, *Pragmatism without Foundations: Reconciling Realism and Relativism* (1986) (vol. 1 of his trilogy *The Persistence of Reality*); *Pragmatism: Its Sources and Prospects* (Robert J. Mulvaney and Philip M. Zeltner eds. 1981). For background, see John E. Smith, *Purpose and Thought: The Meaning of Pragmatism* (1978); David A. Hollinger, *In the American Province: Studies in the History and Historiography of Ideas,* ch. 2 (1985); H. S. Thayer, *Meaning and Action: A Critical History of Pragmatism* (1968). Although Richard Rorty is the best-known modern American pragmatist—and his essay "The Priority of Democracy," in *The Virginia Statute for Religious Freedom: Its Evolution and Consequences in American History* 257 (Merrill D. Peterson and Robert C. Vaughan eds. 1988), is a particularly good introduction to pragmatism—I reject Rorty's Romantic, antiscientific brand of pragmatism. See Chapter 12. And I have very little sympathy for most of Habermas's views.

are also close links between its members and a variety of other philosophers who are not usually called pragmatists. Among these are Emerson, Nietzsche, and Popper; utilitarians (who like pragmatists are strongly instrumentalist), such as Bentham; British empiricists, such as Hume, Mill (also a utilitarian, of course), and Russell; and such contemporary analytic philosophers as Quine and Davidson.[43] Not only is it difficult to tell when one has strayed across the boundaries that separate pragmatism from neighboring philosophical traditions, but the core of pragmatism, if there is such a thing, is too variform to make pragmatism a single philosophy or philosophical school in a useful sense. It lacks the unity of such schools as logical positivism—another neighbor of, and rival to, pragmatism. To say that one is a pragmatist is to say little. The brand of pragmatism that I like emphasizes the scientific virtues (open-minded, no-nonsense inquiry), elevates the process of inquiry over the results of inquiry, prefers ferment to stasis, dislikes distinctions that make no practical difference—in other words, dislikes "metaphysics"—is doubtful of finding "objective truth" in any area of inquiry, is uninterested in creating an adequate philosophical foundation for its thought and action, likes experimentation, likes to kick sacred cows, and—within the bounds of prudence—prefers shaping the future to maintaining continuity with the past. So I am speaking of an attitude rather than a dogma; an attitude whose "common denominator" is "a future-oriented instrumentalism that tries to deploy thought as a weapon to enable more effective action."[44] Most of this book is concerned with attacking the dogmas and letting pragmatism emerge as the natural alternative.

Some quotations from Cardozo's *The Nature of the Judicial Process* will give a flavor of pragmatic jurisprudence and will sound some themes explored in the chapters below. "The final cause of law," writes Cardozo, "is the welfare of society" (p. 66). So much for the formalist idea, whose scientistic provenance and pretensions are evident, of law as a body of immutable principles. Cardozo does not mean, however, that in (for example) judging the constitutional validity of statutes the judges "are free to substitute their own ideas of reason and justice for those of the men and women whom they serve. Their standard must be an objective one"—but objective in a pragmatic sense, which is not the

43. On the relation between pragmatism and British empiricism, see A. J. Ayer, *The Origins of Pragmatism: Studies in the Philosophy of Charles Sanders Peirce and William James* (1968).

44. West, note 42 above, at 5.

sense of correspondence with an external reality. For, he writes, "in such matters, the thing that counts is not what I believe to be right. It is what I may reasonably believe that some other man of normal intellect and conscience might reasonably look upon as right" (p. 89).

Legal rules are to be viewed in instrumental terms, implying contestability, revisability, mutability. "Few rules in our time are so well established that they may not be called upon any day to justify their existence as means adapted to an end. If they do not function, they are diseased. If they are diseased, they need not propagate their kind. Sometimes they are cut out and extirpated altogether. Sometimes they are left with the shadow of continued life, but sterilized, truncated, impotent for harm" (pp. 98–99). "I sometimes think we worry ourselves overmuch about the enduring consequences of our errors . . . In the endless process of testing and retesting, there is a constant rejection of the dross" (p. 179); "the tide rises and falls, but the sands of error crumble" (p. 177).

Law is forward-looking. This is implicit in an instrumental concept of law—which is the pragmatic concept of law, law as the servant of human needs. "Not the origin, but the goal, is the main thing. There can be no wisdom in the choice of a path unless we know where it will lead . . . The rule that functions well produces a title deed to recognition . . . The final principle of selection for judges . . . is one of fitness to an end" (pp. 102–103). The reference to "title deed" is particularly noteworthy; it is a rebuke to formalists who require that law to be valid be "pedigreed" by being shown to derive from some authoritative source.

Where does the judge turn for the knowledge that is needed to weigh the social interests that shape the law? "I can only answer that he must get his knowledge . . . from experience and study and reflection; in brief, from life itself" (p. 113). This is vague, but points in the right direction. The judge is not merely an interpreter of legal materials. He is not only a finder but also a maker of law: John Marshall "gave to the constitution of the United States the impress of his own mind; and the form of our constitutional law is what it is, because he moulded it while it was still plastic and malleable in the fire of his own intense convictions" (pp. 169–170).

One purpose of this book is to extend these insights and bring them up to date.

The book is in five parts, with the first four concentrating on the major attempts to give law a satisfactory philosophical foundation and the last exploring antifoundationalist approaches. Part I focuses on the epistemology of law. The central questions are what is legal reasoning and to what extent can it produce knowledge and not merely opinion or belief? I examine the role of exact inquiry (logical or scientific) in law and find it to be limited; the role of rules in law is correlatively limited. I then discuss legal reasoning as a branch of practical reasoning, conceived as the diverse set of reasoning methods (embracing intuition, authority, analogy, deliberation, interpretation, tacit knowing, subjecting propositions to the test of time, and much else) that people use when logic and science run out. Although these methods often generate determinate results in law, there are occasions—and these the cruces of legal evolution—when they do not, and then judicial decision is based perforce on policy, politics, social vision, "values," even "prejudice" (in Gadamer's sense of prejudgment). Decisions so based are not easily determined to be "right" or "wrong"; the vocabulary of apodictic certainty is misplaced. Perhaps the highest aspiration of the judge is reasonableness in adjudication.

Part II looks at the same questions from a different angle—the ontological. Epistemology and ontology are closely related, the former dealing with what we can know, the latter with what there is to know. The less there is to know, the harder it is to know much. Yet it is possible to believe, for example, that there are moral "reals" (for example, Platonic Forms) but that we have no way of discovering them, and conversely that there are no moral "reals" but that objective knowledge of moral duties is possible, perhaps through consensus or through convention. Part II asks, What are the "objects" of legal inquiry? In what sense do law, and even fact, "exist"? I do not question only obviously problematic entities, such as intent. With the aid of a variety of examples, including criminal intent, coerced confessions, legal fact-finding, judicial behavior, and the debate over the question of what law is, I argue that legal inquiry is hampered by the elusive character of many of the entities that appear to be central to it. Legal thought cannot be made objective by being placed in correspondence with the "real" world. It owes whatever objectivity it has to cultural uniformity rather than to metaphysical reality or methodological rigor.

Part III takes up in much greater detail than in Part I the question of interpretation, which is sometimes thought the key to objectivity in law—not only statutory and constitutional law but also common law, that is, law overtly made by judges. I argue that the term "interpretation" is so elastic (in part because the concept or activity of interpretation serves so many different functions) that it often is a fig leaf covering judicial discretion rather than a guide to decision making. This is not to say that all legal texts are inscrutable—far from it. Most such texts communicate a straightforward, readily decipherable message. But for those that do not, neither the theory nor the practice of "interpretation" provides objective footing for a legal judgment. We might do better to discard the term and concentrate instead on comparing the practical consequences of proposed applications of a legal text in cases where its meaning is unclear.

Part IV, switching the emphasis from metaphysics (Parts I and II) and hermeneutics (Part III) to moral and political philosophy, examines a variety of overarching concepts of justice that could be used to channel legal inquiry. The concepts range from corrective justice and wealth maximization to the feminist ethic of care and the romantic yearnings of radical communitarians, with intermediate stops at egalitarianism, natural rights, and civic republicanism. The first two of these approaches, at least, have significant roles to play in channeling legal inquiry, but neither one (nor both together) can close the open area of judicial decision making all the way. The other approaches are vulnerable to disabling criticisms. Both in endorsing a significant role for corrective justice and in urging only a limited role for wealth maximization, this book modifies some of my previously published views.

Part V examines efforts to find alternatives to *systems,* whether novel or traditional, of jurisprudence. (The last chapter of Part IV paves the way, by recasting the wealth-maximization approach to law in pragmatic terms.) The first chapter in this part examines the "back to basics" movement that I call neotraditionalism, which draws on Aristotle and Burke for a jurisprudence that emphasizes prudence and professional tradition rather than deduction from first principles. I argue that neotraditionalism is no more directive than are the modes of interdisciplinary inquiry to which it is offered as an alternative. The final chapter gathers together proposals of my own that are scattered throughout the book and defends the case for a new pragmatist jurisprudence, one similar in some respects to neotraditionalism yet distinct from and in part opposed to it.

As should be evident from even so bare a summary, the questions that give structure to the book are whether, in what sense, and to what extent the law is a source of objective and determinate, rather than merely personal or political, answers to contentious questions. Recurring to the three senses of objectivity—the ontological, the scientific (replicable, convergent), and the conversational—my argument is that the first is out of the question in most legal cases; the second is sometimes attainable, but given the attitudes of and the constraints on the legal profession, and the character of the problems that it deals with, often not; and the third is attainable—but that isn't saying much. The conversational method is, by definition, inconclusive in difficult cases when society is heterogeneous. But this is to speak redundantly, for it is cultural, social, and political heterogeneity that makes cases difficult. Contemporary American law is, then, strongly objective in easy cases, weakly objective in difficult ones, but rarely either highly determinate or merely political. The only way to make it more objective is to make the courts and the legislatures more homogeneous, culturally and politically. There would be costs to doing this even if it were feasible. There would also be costs to making the courts and the legislatures more heterogeneous; for one, the law would become more political, which would damage rule-of-law virtues that are genuine, indeed precious (though limited), social goods.

Extreme positions are more fun, but in jurisprudence the true as well as the good is to be found between the formalistic and "realistic" extremes depicted by Mencken:

> The average American judge . . . [has] no more give and take in his mind than you will find in the mind of a terrier watching a rathole. He converts the law into a series of rubber-stamps, and brings them down upon the scalped skulls of the just and unjust alike. The alternative to him, as commonly conceived, is quite as bad—an uplifter in a black robe, eagerly gulping every new brand of Peruna that comes out, and converting his pulpit into a sort of soap-box.[45]

My position may seem boringly centrist, but it will provoke both the true centrists in the profession, who want very much to believe that law is autonomous and apolitical, and the political activists who want to move the law sharply to the left or to the right. It will be criticized by the Left as authoritarian and complacent, and by the Right as cynical and amoral. It may appear to be merely old-fashioned legal realism with a conservative twist abhorrent to the realists, but that would not be an accurate characterization. Unlike Holmes and other legal (and logical) positivists, I do not believe that legal questions can be partitioned into those that can be answered with certainty and those that cannot be answered by rational methods at all but depend on the will or caprice or politics of the judge. I am also not a "strong" legal positivist, as Holmes was; indeed, I resist the effort to dichotomize positive and natural law. My position owes more to philosophical pragmatism than did the realist movement. If I had to choose I would range myself on the side of the Skeptics, but the pragmatic approach may enable the conflict

---

45. H. L. Mencken, "Mr. Justice Holmes," in *The Vintage Mencken* 189, 195 (Alistair Cooke ed. 1955) (essay first published in 1932).

between Legalists and Skeptics to be transcended. I repeat that legal positivists who believe that the sovereign's commands are readily interpretable are formalists, at least in the sense of believers in right answers to all or virtually all legal questions. I am not a formalist.

Although I shall recur from time to time to Holmes, Dworkin, H. L. A. Hart, and other jurisprudes, I shall not undertake a detailed examination of the texts or arguments of the warring schools, whose positions I have sketched—and with a broad brush—merely to give the reader a sense of the terrain that the rest of the book will explore. And while the quest, unsuccessful though I believe it must prove in the end, for grounds on which to reaffirm confidently law's objectivity and autonomy gives structure to the book, that search is indeed skeleton rather than flesh. I urge readers to attend to the particulars of my analysis rather than merely to its direction and conclusion. If, having done so, they still conclude that the ratio of destructive to constructive criticism is too high, I ask them to ponder Voltaire's reply when he was taken to task for offering no substitute for Christianity, which he had attacked: "Je vous délivre d'une bête féroce, et vous me demandez par quoi je la remplace!"[46]

46. "I save you from a ferocious beast and you ask me what I replace it with!"

PART I

THE EPISTEMOLOGY OF LAW

1 ∽

Law as Logic, Rules, and Science

This chapter begins the inquiry into whether and to what degree law is objective, impersonal, determinate: whether, in other words, it is an external (though not necessarily an effective—that is a separate question) constraint on judges; in an earlier diction that has come to seem naive, whether judges find rather than make law. I offer a moderately skeptical answer, in two steps. First, many important questions of law, though certainly not all and maybe only a tiny fraction (but one rich in landmark and seminal cases), cannot be answered by the use of the methods of legal reasoning, in part because those methods are not powerful when viewed as tools for construction rather than merely for criticism. Second, when legal reasoning runs out and the judge has to appeal to policies, preferences, values, morals, public opinion, or whatever else may be necessary to answer a legal question in a way satisfactory to himself and his colleagues, it will often mean that the answer is indeterminate. If, to anticipate subsequent discussion, "truth is what would emerge as the result of unconstrained inquiry pursued indefinitely,"[1] then indeterminacy is the state where unconstrained inquiry is—interminable: where there is no light at the end of the tunnel. That is often the case in law.

The first half of my thesis denies Coke's "artificial reason" but is consistent with the possibility that legal outcomes can be made determinate by methods of analysis that owe nothing to legal training or experience. The second half denies that every legal question *has* a right answer, whatever sources or procedures are appealed to. The artificial-reason thesis reflects nostalgia for a lost sense of the law's autonomy, the right-

---

1. Joseph Rouse, *Knowledge and Power: Toward a Political Philosophy of Science* 7 (1987). This is not a satisfactory definition of truth—as we shall see in Chapter 3, there are no satisfactory definitions of truth—but it is a useful *criterion* of truth.

answer thesis nostalgia for lost certitudes. I disagree with both theses, but I also disagree with the radical skepticism that equates law to politics (and hence a judge to a legislator or other politician), regards all legal analysis as bunk, all legal questions as indeterminate. Although "politics" is a word of many meanings, some of which overlap "law," it is not true that what a judge does is indistinguishable from what a legislator or an executive-branch official does.

So I face two ways in this chapter, as throughout the book. I defend my middle position primarily by attacking the extremes, particularly the right-answer / artificial-reason extreme because that is the more plausible and influential one. Whether the reader who is persuaded by my arguments thinks I have shown that the glass is half full or half empty will depend on the reader's conception of how objective, impersonal, and determinate law must be to deserve the name of law—which is not to say, however, to deserve the citizen's respect. Law can be highly objective and impersonal, yet thoroughly unjust. The inquiry into justice is postponed to later chapters, but the tradeoff between formal and substantive justice should be kept in mind from the start.

To decide how people, judges specifically, might acquire true beliefs about legal questions will require consideration of the various methods by which nonlawyers acquire true beliefs about nonlegal questions, as well as consideration of the use of such methods by lawyers and judges. The methods can be divided into two broad classes, exact inquiry and practical reason. The first will occupy us in this chapter.

The Syllogism and Other Methods of Logic

I begin with the apt and famous (though, as we shall have occasion to notice, nonstandard) syllogism: "All men are mortal; Socrates is a man; therefore Socrates is mortal." The validity of the argument—not the truth of the conclusion, which depends on the truth of its premises—seems utterly compelling. But that is only because the conclusion that Socrates is mortal is contained in the first premise, the definition of "man." That premise says, in effect, here is a box, labeled "men," with a bunch of things in it, every one of which is "mortal." The second premise tells us that the things in the box have name tags and that one of the tags says "Socrates." When we pluck Socrates out of the box we know he is mortal because the only things in it are mortals. We are merely taking out what we put in.

We thus find the syllogism's validity compelling by virtue of a metaphor, the metaphor of the box. (It may seem odd that one's confidence in the validity of logic should be bolstered by a metaphor—yet this is a clue to the limitations of logic and the cognitive importance of metaphor.) As we move away from the simplest, most transparent examples of logical reasoning, such as the syllogism, the nature and cogency of such reasoning become less perspicuous. We think that the proposition $2 + 2 = 4$ is true by definition in much the same sense that the proposition that Socrates is mortal is true by definition. But because it is not clear in the numerical example what the container and the thing contained are, the metaphor of inclusion is no longer available to reassure us of the compelling quality of logical reasoning. And as soon as we begin to ask complicated mathematical questions, such as whether every even number is the sum of two odd prime numbers (as 16, for example, is the sum of 13 and 3), we enter a realm in which no mechanical or apodictic decision procedure is available and the questions are as difficult, uncertain, and inaccessible to lay understanding as the most difficult questions about the empirical as distinguished from the conceptual, the definitional, world. Indeed, it has proved impossible to reduce mathematics to logic.[2] But we can set these problems to one side and stick with the simplest forms of logical reasoning, for with rare exceptions they are the only ones lawyers use.

So compelling and familiar is syllogistic reasoning that lawyers and judges, ever desirous of making their activity seem as objective as possible, try hard to make legal reasoning seem as syllogistic as possible.[3] The overuse of the syllogism is the defining characteristic of the brand

---

2. See, for example, Alvin I. Goldman, *Epistemology and Cognition* 34–35 (1986); Gregory J. Chaitin, "Randomness in Arithmetic," *Scientific American,* July 1988, at 80; Ernest Nagel and James R. Newman, *Gödel's Proof* (1958).

3. On the use of the syllogism in legal reasoning, see, for example, Steven J. Burton, *An Introduction to Law and Legal Reasoning,* ch. 3 (1985); Neil MacCormick, *Legal Reasoning and Legal Theory* 19–52 (1978); Vincent A. Wellman, "Practical Reasoning and Judicial Justification: Toward an Adequate Theory," 57 *University of Colorado Law Review* 45, 64–80 (1985); also A. G. Guest, "Logic in the Law," in *Oxford Essays in Jurisprudence* 176 (A. G. Guest ed. 1961). On logical reasoning in general, Carl Wellman, *Challenge and Response: Justification in Ethics,* ch. 1 (1971), is particularly helpful, and on the subject matter of this chapter generally, see Gidon Gottlieb, *The Logic of Choice: An Investigation of the Concepts of Rule and Rationality,* chs. 1 and 2 (1968).

Three terminological points to bear in mind: First, by "logic" I mean deductive and mathematical logic, not systematic thinking in general or specialized logics such as inductive logic. I do discuss induction but not under the rubric of logic. Second, in the term "syllogism" I include the enthymeme, a syllogism with an implicit premise. Legal reasoning is in fact more often enthymematic than syllogistic in the strict sense. Third, a syllogism can have more than two premises; and again this is characteristic of most syllogistic reasoning in law.

of legal formalism attacked by Holmes. But today when used pejoratively, "formalism" is more likely to refer to an exaggerated belief in the transparency of statutory or constitutional language and hence in the possibility of definitely correct answers to difficult interpretive questions than to the overuse of the syllogism. When used nonpejoratively, formalism can refer to a strong—but perhaps justifiably strong—belief in the possibility of obtaining right answers to legal questions by means of conventional methods of legal analysis, mainly the careful reading of texts to find the rules in them, followed by deduction from the rules to the outcome of the particular case.[4] Or formalism can refer simply to the use of logic to reason from premises to legal conclusions.

The most useful sense of this protean term, however, derives from the contrast between form and substance—form referring to what is internal to law, substance to the world outside of law, as in the contrast between formal and substantive justice. The autonomy and objectivity of law are secured by confining legal analysis to the formal level, the level requiring only an exploration of the relations among legal ideas. Autonomy and objectivity are threatened when the legal outcome depends on facts about the world, which might be the facts of a dispute or the social or ethical facts relevant to creating or interpreting a rule. Since logical reasoning is the exploration of relations between concepts, the relation between the form-substance sense of formalism and the logico-mathematical sense should be plain.

Formalism comes in both natural law and legal positivist varieties. The only prerequisite to being a formalist is having supreme confidence in one's premises and in one's methods of deriving conclusions from them. The natural law formalist is certain about the principles of justice and the power of logic to derive specific case outcomes from those

---

4. See Frederick Schauer, "Formalism," 97 *Yale Law Journal* 509 (1988); Neil MacCormick and Ota Weinberger, *An Institutional Theory of Law: New Approaches to Legal Positivism* 115–144 (1986); James G. Wilson, "The Morality of Formalism," 33 *UCLA Law Review* 431 (1985); Robert Samuel Summers, *Instrumentalism and American Legal Theory* 137–159 (1982). Schauer advocates what he calls "presumptive formalism" (see also Schauer, "Is the Common Law Law?" 77 *California Law Review* 455, 470 [1989])—a preference for sticking with rules unless they produce palpably absurd or outrageous results. The *reason* for the presumption is not fully explained but presumably is the value of certainty and predictability. This invites consideration of an alternative approach—identifying classes of rules in which certainty is particularly important and confining the presumption to them. The distinct question, not examined by Schauer, is the *feasibility* of formalism, whether presumptive or absolute; this is one of the questions addressed in the present chapter. For exemplary criticism of legal formalism, see Judith N. Shklar, *Legalism: Law, Morals, and Political Trials* 33–36 (1964).

premises; the positive law formalist is certain that the law consists only of legislative or other official commands that, read carefully, yield demonstrably correct results in all cases. Either approach spares the lawyer or judge from a messy encounter with empirical reality. There are not only natural law formalists and positive law formalists but also natural law realists and positive law realists. Most natural lawyers are formalists, though; and while most legal positivists are realists, there are plenty of positive law formalists. It is a safe bet that a majority of legal professionals are formalists.

Formalism contains a built-in bias against legal change; this is a clue to the breadth and durability of its appeal. The most secure premise for deducing the outcome of a new case is the decision of the most recent case that had essentially the same facts, so that the rule expressed or implied in that case fits the new one like a glove (another comfortable metaphor). As a result, people who are defending the legal status quo— whether it is a liberal status quo or a conservative one—tend to assume a formalist stance. But so, paradoxically, do the people attacking the status quo.[5] Having the burden of persuasion, they want to show that their "revisionist" position is compelled by logic, is the authentic original position, that the defenders of the status quo are not merely wrong but demonstrably, irrefutably, and newly wrong—for example, because the precedents on which the defenders rely are invalid deductions from a more authoritative premise, such as the text of the Constitution. The rhetorical power of formalism makes discourse about law more formalistic than the actualities of the judicial process warrant.

I have been stressing the syllogism (including the enthymeme), but of course lawyers employ other elementary forms of logic as well, such as the principle that a proposition cannot be both true and false or that if two things are identical to a third they are identical to each other. Lawyers also use the language of logic where, strictly speaking, it does not belong. Most judges (myself included) would say without hesitation that it would be illogical to read into a speed-limit statute an implied exception for BMWs (as distinct from one for police cars or ambulances). Yet this is using "illogical" as a synonym for "clearly wrong."

---

5. An important exception, however, consists of those legal realists who attacked the very idea that there were legal rules, those for whom every new case created new law. The legacy of these realists is the Federal Rules of Civil Procedure, which do not require the plaintiff to plead his case in terms of preexisting legal pigeonholes. See, for example, Judith Resnik, "Failing Faith: Adjudicatory Procedure in Decline," 53 *University of Chicago Law Review* 494, 502–503 (1986); Note, "Plausible Pleadings: Developing Standards for Rule 11 Sanctions," 100 *Harvard Law Review* 630, 644–647 (1987).

A harmless usage unless taken literally, it misconceives the domain of logic. Logic has nothing to do with the question, easy though it may be to answer. The question is one of statutory interpretation, and we shall see that interpretation, although it sometimes yields reasonably certain answers, is not a method of logic. Given the purpose of the statute, there is no reason to exclude BMWs. But the rejection of the exception becomes a logical conclusion only *after* a rule has been extracted from the statute by a process that is not itself one of logic.

It is similarly misleading to suggest that logic informs in a helpful way the idea of treating like things alike—an idea of great resonance for law (equal justice under law, equal protection of the laws, equality before the law, one law for rich and poor, and so forth). Although a natural extension of the logical propositions that things are identical to themselves and that two things identical to a third are identical to each other, the idea is empty without specification of the criteria for "likeness," and in law those criteria are political.[6] The legal principle of equal treatment distinguishes those differences between litigants that may properly be considered in the allocation of legal benefits and burdens, such as differences in skill and effort, from those that, sometimes or always, may not be, such as differences in religion, race, social class, income, or relationship to the judge. The principle has nothing interesting to do with the avoidance of contradiction except insofar as it forbids completely arbitrary—"irrational"—classifications (like the exception for BMWs), as distinct from vicious, invidious, or politically intolerable ones that may be perfectly rational, at least to the classifiers. But irrational classifications are rare.

Rules, Standards, and Discretion

Despite the critical tone of the previous section, most legal questions *are* resolved syllogistically. A legal rule has the form of the major premise of a syllogism. For example: no contract is enforceable without consideration; the contract in suit has no consideration; therefore the contract is not enforceable. By a process not itself syllogistic or otherwise deductive, judges extract rules from statutes and previous decisions and then use them as premises to decide cases syllogistically. Are wages income? Is marriage to one's sister valid? Is murder excused if the victim consents

6. See Peter Westen, "The Empty Idea of Equality," 95 *Harvard Law Review* 537 (1982); Westen, "The Meaning of Equality in Law, Science, Math, and Morals: A Reply," 81 *Michigan Law Review* 604 (1983).

in advance? Is it illegal to drive sixty miles an hour in a forty-mile zone? Is Illinois entitled to have three U.S. senators? These and many other legal questions are answered deductively by the application of clear and uncontested rules to facts determined or conceded. The reason such questions do not figure largely in legal debate, and indeed lie almost beneath the professional horizon, is that they are too simple to be a likely subject of litigation or even to require legal counseling. This makes it easy in doing jurisprudence—too easy—to forget about such questions and suppose that all legal questions are indeterminate. (There is a missing link here: questions might have determinate answers without those answers' being *logically* entailed. But that is a subject taken up in later chapters.) Not only are many legal questions determinate in the approximate sense of logical determinacy; they are the very ones that loom largest in the thinking of ordinary people about law. Most laypeople demand of the law only that it tell them the rules they must live by, and they are therefore more likely than lawyers to think of law as determinate, constraining. A big part of legal training, especially at the elite law schools, is exploration of the law's indeterminacies, and it creates an outlook remote from that of the average person and indeed from that of many lawyers. Another reason that laypersons have a more vivid sense of the law's determinacy than do lawyers is that lawyers, sometimes with a guilty conscience, *tell* the laity (I mean laypersons in general – not clients!) that the law is determinate.

We must distinguish between the validity of a syllogism and its soundness—that is, its power to yield a true conclusion. Soundness depends not only on the validity of the particular syllogism but also on the truth of the premises.[7] This is not a problem with the syllogism about Socrates, because no one is likely to question that all men are mortal or that Socrates was a man. (*Why* no one is likely to question the first premise is not so clear as one might think, and will be discussed later.) But with rules of law, the truth of the major and minor premises is often contestable. To begin with, establishing the minor premise—in other words, finding the facts—is often difficult; and finding facts is not a process of logic. How difficult depends in part on the rule's generality. Compare the two basic liability regimes for injuries caused by accident:

---

7. The importance of the distinction between validity and soundness is shown by the fact that a syllogism can have a true conclusion even though both its premises are false: "All Spartans are wise; Socrates is a Spartan; therefore Socrates is wise." This syllogism—at once valid and unsound—illustrates the limitations of syllogisms as devices for reasoning to the truth.

strict liability and negligence. Under the former the injurer is liable if he caused the accident, and usually it will be pretty straightforward to determine whether he did cause it. Under negligence the injurer is liable only if he could have avoided the accident by exercising due care. Even if "due care" is defined quite precisely, for example as taking precautions that cost less than the expected cost of the accidents they would prevent, there may be difficulty determining whether this precondition of liability has been established.

A rule, such as negligence, that requires a relatively broad factual inquiry to establish the minor premise is often called a "standard" to distinguish it from the simpler sort of rule in which the minor premise states a single fact. This is not to say that the simpler sort of rule is always simpler to apply. The single fact may be difficult to determine or may not really be a fact ("wages" in my earlier example of an "easy" case); or the rule may be ambiguous. I suppress these complications for now, along with most of the trade-offs between rules and standards,[8] in order to focus on one point. A rule suppresses potentially relevant circumstances of the dispute (could the injurer have avoided the accident at reasonable cost?), while a standard gives the trier of fact—the judge or jury—more discretion because there are more facts to find, weigh, and compare. The rule engenders tension with the social policies that underlie it and that may be achieved only imperfectly when the rule is applied without regard to the particular circumstances of the dispute. The standard solves *that* problem—the problem of achieving substantive justice rather than merely formal justice—but, by vesting broad discretion in the officials applying it, it opens the way to abuse. (The solution may thus be illusory.) The more flexible the criteria, the more difficult it will be for an observer to determine when the officials have applied them intelligently and impartially. Rules create pressure for ad hoc exceptions, but standards could be thought the very institutionalization of the ad hoc exception. In a regime of standards, the principles or policies that in a regime of rules would determine the content of the rules are used to determine the outcome of particular cases.

Even if officials do not abuse the broad discretion that a regime of

8. See Isaac Ehrlich and Richard A. Posner, "An Economic Analysis of Legal Rulemaking," 3 *Journal of Legal Studies* 257 (1974); Anthony I. Ogus, "Quantitative Rules and Judicial Decision Making," in *The Economic Approach to Law* 210 (Paul Burrows and Cento G. Veljanovski eds. 1981); Colin S. Diver, "The Optimal Precision of Administrative Rules," 93 *Yale Law Journal* 65 (1983); Pierre Schlag, "Rules and Standards," 33 *UCLA Law Review* 379 (1985); cf. Duncan Kennedy, "Form and Substance in Private Law Adjudication," 89 *Harvard Law Review* 1685 (1976).

standards gives them, standards have the disadvantage of making it harder to predict the outcome of a legal dispute—there are more variables, which makes litigation more likely and also makes it harder for people to plan and to conduct their affairs. Uncertainty is a source of cost and disutility and is increased by substituting standards for rules. A conspicuous—virtually a defining—characteristic of legal realism, critical legal studies, and feminist jurisprudence is depreciation of the benefits of rules in reducing uncertainty. Their slogan might be William Blake's dictum that "To Generalize is to be an Idiot. To Particularize is the Alone Distinction of Merit."[9] Yet no one really believes this. No one thinks, for example, that the rule that school buses must stop, look, and listen at railroad crossings even if the warning gate is up is necessarily inferior to a standard that would require the driver merely to exercise due care in the circumstances. The rule guards against a lapse of judgment by the bus driver, and this gain may well outweigh the cost in minuscule delay from stopping every time.

The general point illustrated by this example is that rules economize on information. The fact that the application of a standard requires the adjudicator to have more information than the application of a rule implies that the ratio of standards to rules will be greater, the lower the costs to courts of assimilating information. Perhaps over a long period of time there has been a general if irregular increase in the ability of courts to handle information; if so, this might explain what appears to be a historical shift in the balance between rules and standards, in favor of the latter.[10] Since syllogistic reasoning plays a smaller role in determining the outcome of a dispute governed by a standard than one governed by a rule, we may have a clue to the widely perceived decline (welcomed in some quarters, deplored in others) of legal formalism.

A bigger danger to the idea that law can be made determinate by syllogistic logic impends when we switch our focus from the minor premise—the facts—to the major premise—the rule itself. The source of

9. "Annotations to Sir Joshua Reynolds's Discourses," in *The Complete Writings of William Blake* 445, 451 (Geoffrey Keynes ed. 1958).

10. See my book *The Economics of Justice*, chs. 6 and 7 (1981). It is not a steady progression. There was a movement from standards to rules in English law in the nineteenth century, see Ogus, note 8 above, at 216–217; there is more use of strict liability in tort law today than there was thirty years ago (although for reasons largely unrelated to a desire to make law simpler and more certain); and the recently promulgated Federal sentencing guidelines curtail the traditional discretion of judges in deciding how long a sentence to give a convicted defendant within the limits set by the legislature. Indeed, there is a growing sense that the legal system has gone too far in the direction of substituting standards for rules and is due for retrenchment.

the danger is not, as one might think, that rules have exceptions. That in itself is not problematic, provided the exceptions are themselves rules, as normally they will be. The statute of limitations in Illinois for bringing suit on a written contract is ten years. One exception is if the defendant misled the plaintiff into thinking he had more than ten years to sue. The main rule will get us as far as concluding that if a plaintiff waits more than ten years to bring suit on a written contract, the defendant will have a prima facie defense that the statute of limitations has run. We may then have to start over and consider whether the plaintiff has rebutted the defense by establishing the applicability of one of the exceptions. But as each exception is itself a rule, and a rule that cleanly defeats the main rule, the plaintiff has only to prove the exception's minor premise (for example, that the defendant had in fact misled him) to establish that the suit is timely.

The problems with governance by rule lie elsewhere; they are familiar but deserve emphasis. One is that the domain of a rule may be uncertain, and then judges will continually have to decide whether to apply the rule to situations not foreseen, or at least left open, when the rule was laid down. Rules make dichotomous cuts in continuous phenomena. A rule that punishes breaking and entering at night more severely than breaking and entering in daytime is perfectly clear at the semantic level, but by disregarding the actual relation between day and night (one of imperceptible blending) the rule fails to track the reality being described, creating ambiguity in application. The more general point is that legal rules frequently treat as referential words (like "day" and "night") that do not have a definite referent. The First Amendment forbids Congress to establish "religion" or interfere with its free exercise. Religious organizations also are exempt from state property taxes, and contributions to religious organizations are tax deductible. But what is "religion"? The word does not denote some closed or definite set of practices or objects or entities. In the absence of a legislative definition judges have to decide what the word *shall* mean for legal purposes, not what it does mean.

The decisions that judges are required to make in fitting rules to facts can be described either as interpretation or as the making of ad hoc exceptions and adjustments, in effect the continual remaking of the rules. Practically these are the same but judges prefer the first formulation, the interpretive, because it casts them in a less creative, and therefore less usurpative-seeming, role.

The older the rule, and the more dynamic the activity governed by it (that is, the greater the change over time in the activities to which the rule refers), the more pressure there will be on the judges to make ad hoc exceptions and ad hoc extensions. Indeed, the more dynamic the regulated activity, the less amenable it will be to governance by rules at all, as distinct from standards. The choice in international trade theory between fixed and floating exchange rates provides an analogy. Many economists believe that fixed exchange rates mask rather than contain underlying economic changes, resulting in a substitution of abrupt for smooth adjustments. There may be analogous consequences when rules are chosen over standards to govern variegated and changing activities.

Another problem with rules is that inconsistent rules may be applicable to the same activity. Here logic reasserts its claims. Logically inconsistent rules cannot be applied to the same activity. The judge has a duty to eliminate the inconsistency. But logic does not tell him which rule to discard.

Many legal rules, moreover, are judge-made, and they can be judge-unmade. The common law is a vast collection of judge-made rules, and much of statutory and constitutional law also consists of judge-made rules, loosely tethered to debatable interpretations of ambiguous enactments. The estoppel exception to the statute of limitations is judge-made, and the judges could unmake it if persuaded that such an exception was unnecessary in the case of a long statute of limitations and produced too much uncertainty and litigation. As long as either the rule or its exceptions are contestable, the neat logical pattern of rule and exception will not resolve all cases even if the rule is both clear and consistent with all related rules. Adherence to a rule is, as Wittgenstein famously explained in Part I of *Philosophical Investigations,* not a dictate of logic; the rule does not tell you when to follow it.

We thus have the paradox that a legal question might be at once determinate and indeterminate: determinate because a clear rule covers it, indeterminate because the judge is not obligated to follow the rule. This makes a legal rule a little like a natural law. And it supports Holmes's view that the law is really just a prediction of what judges *will* do with a given set of facts, because the judges are not *bound* by the rules to do anything.

Finally, decision according to rule is not inherently more objective than decision according to standard; the principled and the ad hoc are not, in law, as polar as the terms connote. Consider the following choices for a regime to govern First Amendment challenges to offensive art: a rule immunizing all such art from censorship or other regulation; a rule giving such art no protection; and a standard requiring the judges to "balance"—employing weights inevitably influenced by their personal values—offensiveness against artistic quality and to authorize censorship when the balance inclines decisively against the artist. Each of these choices has as much, or as little, grounding in the text and history of the First Amendment, and in considerations of institutional competence, as any of the others. If one of the two rules (which happen to be opposites) is adopted instead of the standard, decisions will appear to be strongly objective because logically deducible. But the appearance will fade as soon as the contestability of the premise is noticed, enabling the observer to see that the decisions are no more objective in an ultimate sense than those made under the more frankly ad hoc regime of the balancing test. Rules mask—they do not eliminate and may not even reduce—the role of the subjective and the political in the formation of legal rights and duties.

As we become more realistic about rules, their advantages vis-à-vis standards begin to dim. The principal advantages are curtailing official discretion—the discretion of the officials who administer the rules, but not of those who make them—and reducing uncertainty about legal rights and duties. These advantages depend, however, on having rules that are relatively few and simple, relatively immutable, and clear in both statement and application, and these are ideals that a system of legal rules rarely attains. Even if the rules are clear, moreover, they may be so numerous that the people subject to them cannot learn them; then their clarity is delusive. Standards that capture lay intuitions about right behavior (for example, the negligence standard) and that therefore are easy to learn may produce greater legal certainty than a network of precise but technical, nonintuitive rules covering the same ground. Notoriously, legalistic rules are traps for the unwary. And many judges sense this.

The school bus example shows, however, that it would be a mistake to denounce rules *tout court,* or to expect or desire judges to subvert them at every turn. Realism about rules includes, moreover, a recognition that judges consider stability valuable and therefore often refuse to reexamine rules to make ad hoc exceptions to them even when confronted by powerful claims of substantive justice. But judges' reasons for generally sticking by rules have little if anything to do with logic and often are not "reasons" at all. Without going so far as to argue that a judge's decisions are influenced by his digestion, or that judges who are sticklers for rules have an "authoritarian personality" and would benefit from psychoanalysis,[11] I suggest that differences in temperament are indeed

---

11. See Jerome Frank, *Law and the Modern Mind* (1930). The first part of his conjecture, about the authoritarian personality, is more persuasive than the second—that such personalities are amenable to psychotherapy.

responsible for much of the evident difference among judges in willingness to interpret rules flexibly, recognize exceptions freely, transmute rules into standards willingly, and cede discretion to juries and to lower-court judges comfortably.[12] Some judges have greater tolerance for untidiness, even disorder, than others. They see law as exploration and dialogue rather than as governance and hierarchy. Such judges may be highly sensitive to the particulars of each case, which is good, but insufficiently sensitive to the costs (mainly hidden) of legal uncertainty. Other judges are uncomfortable about assuming responsibility for decisions. They want to think that they are just carrying out the orders of other people (legislators, the founding fathers, higher or earlier judges). There are well-known dangers with the deferential posture[13]—but the Promethean judge is no prize either. These differences in judicial outlook and behavior reflect different judgments and life experiences, but they are also temperamental in the sense that they are deeply rooted in the judge's psyche and therefore resistant to experience.

Let us look a little more closely at the character of legal rules, before turning again to logic and formalism. The contestability of legal rules stands in contrast to that of two other kinds of rules, the rules of games and the rules of language. Although the rules of a game are changed from time to time, it is unthinkable (in a "serious" game) to change a rule during the game. Tennis players are not overheard saying to the referee, "It's true my ball landed behind the baseline, but if one thought about the matter carefully one would have to conclude that the baselines are too shallow and should be extended, so my ball ought not be deemed out of bounds." There is of course an open area in a game, an area left to the strategy and tactics of the players. The rules do not determine the game's outcome. But they constrain the players' play and by

12. For some evidence, see Philip E. Tetlock, Jane Bernzweig, and Jack L. Gallant, "Supreme Court Decision Making: Cognitive Style as a Predictor of Ideological Consistency of Voting," 48 *Journal of Personality and Social Psychology* 1227 (1985); see also Chapters 4 and 5 of this book. Admittedly the jury example is equivocal. A formalist might want to cede discretion to juries in order to avoid having to exercise it himself. Jury discretion is a licensed area of lawlessness in law, the existence of which permits the judge to decide all issues with certainty in the (diminished) sphere in which he is the decisionmaker. Notice how a conservative formalist, distrustful of juries but eager to divest himself of discretion, might feel torn on this issue.

13. See Stanley Milgram, *Obedience to Authority: An Experimental View* (1974), finding that highly obedient people, by casting themselves as the instruments of another, tend to slough off responsibility for their actions, however egregious those actions may be. One is put in mind of Churchill's epithet for the German soldiery in World War II: "lethal sheep."

doing so *make* it a game and not a free-for-all. And the rules that do this are fixed, definite, and at least in the course of the game, immutable.[14]

Legal rules likewise are enabling as well as repressive. Just as the rules of chess enable a subtle and challenging game to be played, rather than simply imposing irksome and repressive constraints on the players, so (for example) the rules of property law facilitate investment and transacting, the rules of contract law enable the making of commitments to buy and sell that unfold over time rather than being performed at the same instant, and the rules of criminal law enable people to go about their business unarmed and without guards. But these rules do not so completely define the activities which they enable or facilitate that those activities lose their purpose if the rules are changed while the activities are in progress. A chess player who announces in the middle of the game that he will not allow his rook to be captured by his opponent's queen, because queens have too much power in chess, might just as well sweep all the pieces from the board; and it would make not the slightest difference whether the umpire agreed with him, or whether the player waited until he lost the game and then asked the umpire to order it replayed under rules reflecting a more equitable distribution of power among the pieces. These sorts of appeals are allowed in law, however.

Therefore, paradoxical as it may seem, the duty to play by the rules is more imperative in games than in law; for in law the rules may be up for grabs. Not all of them, of course; not even most of them. Yet judges do have a limited license to "disobey" rules by changing them in midcourse.[15] We could eliminate the paradox by saying that every time the judges break a rule they are doing so in order to comply with a higher-level rule, or that if judges are somehow licensed to break rules this shows that what they are doing is not really breaking rules. But this

---

14. So we might contrast normative rules with a "rule of thumb" rule that guides but does not constrain play; such a rule corresponds to a recipe in cooking. For a useful typology of rules, see David K. Lewis, *Convention: A Philosophical Study* 100–107 (1969).

Counterparts in law to the principle of not changing the rules *in medias res* include "stare decisis" ("stand by what has been decided"—that is, follow precedent) and "law of the case" (in general, courts will not change the applicable rules of law during the course of a lawsuit); res judicata, which (to oversimplify) prevents the relitigation of a claim between the same parties, provides a more distant analogy. Stare decisis is far from rigid; law of the case is flexible too, although less so than stare decisis. Moreover, the doctrine of law of the case is not that the court will refrain from changing the applicable law between the dispute giving rise to the lawsuit and the decision resolving the dispute, but only that it will refrain from changing that law between the first decision in the case and subsequent decisions.

15. See Mortimer R. Kadish and Sanford H. Kadish, *Discretion to Disobey: A Study of Lawful Departures from Legal Rules* 85–91 (1973).

would just be word play and would not change the fact that judges with some frequency decide to discard or to change what until then had seemed a valid rule. They may have good reasons to do this, but compliance with a higher-level rule is not a good reason; it is merely a fancy way of stating the conclusion.

A better analogy to rules of law may be "rules" of how to win a game. I mentioned strategy and tactics in chess. A related but simpler example is skiing. The beginner learns various rules about turning, stopping, and the like, but he is "allowed" to break them when skiing and often he has to, to avoid falling. The rules are really guides, and maybe this is what rules of law are to judges. A further analogy is to the labor practice known as "working to rule." The workers decide to comply fully with every job rule—and the result is a disastrous slowdown, because the rules were not meant to be obeyed to the letter. The judge who takes rules too seriously may be a bureaucratic stickler.

Still another analogy to rules of law is "law" in its scientific rather than legal or moral sense. If a nonconforming instance is found, and it cannot be ascribed to mistakes in observation or experimental procedure, the law has to be changed; a scientific law is descriptive, not prescriptive. Similarly, if the judges decide not to apply a rule but instead to act contrary to it, in effect they have forced a change in the rule, as within broad limits they are licensed to do.

The principal difference, so far as is relevant here, between law and science on the one hand, and games on the other, is that law and science are concerned with right results, while the function of the rules of a game is to provide a framework for comparing and appraising the contestants' performance in the game. Law, however, unlike science, is concerned not only with getting the result right but also with stability, to which it will frequently sacrifice substantive justice. In short, all three activities—law, science, and game playing—have different purposes, and these purposes affect the attitude of the "players" toward obedience to rules.

Language resembles law in that its rules are mutable and change in use, but language is more stable. Because no one (except the French Academy!) is specifically authorized to change language rules, they tend to change at the glacial pace typical of customs. The judicial system, being hierarchical within each jurisdiction, has the power to change the law of the jurisdiction abruptly. That the judiciary seldom exercises the power—and therefore may not *really* possess it, because of political constraints on judges—does not make legal outcomes the result of a logical process. Those outcomes may be predictable because of the known propensity of the judges to stick by the existing rules—the propensity called stare decisis. But because those rules are subject to reexamination, the predictable outcomes are not compelled by logic. The analogy is to the Socrates syllogism if spoken by the lexicographical dictator in *Nineteen Eighty-Four* (O'Brien), who could have redefined "man" and "mortal" at a stroke of the pen.

Another feature common to law and language is that both are, in a sense, beyond right and wrong. Our language is full of errors that are no longer subject to being corrected. For example, the collective noun "pease," a word parallel to "wheat" and preserved in the nursery rhyme "pease porridge hot," was long ago misunderstood to be a plural noun, so "pea" was "inferred" to be the singular and "peas" was constructed to be the "regular" plural. Hamlet's phrase "more honored in the breach," referring to a custom more honorable to avoid than to follow— the specific referent was excessive drinking—has been misread to refer to a custom that is not observed, and this error, like "pea" and "peas" is a secure, an unshakable, part of our language. Because law, like language, values stability, legal mistakes, too, can become sanctified by time and usage.

All this is not to deny that there are legal rules in a useful sense. I have no quarrel with H. L. A. Hart's classic statement:

> We promise to visit a friend the next day. When the day comes it turns out that keeping the promise would involve neglecting someone dangerously ill. The fact that this is accepted as an adequate reason for not keeping the promise surely does not mean that there is no rule requiring promises to be kept, only a certain regularity in keeping them. It does not follow from the fact that such rules have exceptions incapable of exhaustive statement, that in every situation we are left to our discretion and are never bound to keep a promise. A rule that ends with the word 'unless . . .' is still a rule.[16]

And one might add that the fact that a rule is not eternal does not mean that it is not a rule while it lasts.

But it is significant that Hart's example is described from the standpoint of people subject to rules rather than from that of the rule makers. The "we" in the example are not the people who made or can unmake the rule that promises should be kept. From the perspective of persons subject to the rules, the fact that rules have fuzzy edges or may be changed does not make them nonbinding. But from the standpoint of the rulers, rules may be so much putty. The rulers may have complete,

16. *The Concept of Law* 136 (1961).

or at least extensive, discretion to repeal or revise or "interpret" the rules; this is one reason why sophisticated members of the legal profession are more aware of legal indeterminacy than are laypeople. In Hart's example, the rule about keeping promises is just there. There is no mention of its creation, and this omission obscures the fact that the people who create rules have a different relationship to them than do the people who are penalized if they disobey them and have no power to revise or repeal them. The sanctions for not enforcing a rule are not the same, and normally are not as severe, as those for not obeying a rule.

We like to think of judges as being under the law, that is, as being ruled rather than ruling. But besides the point just made about the different sanctions for nonenforcement and noncompliance, judges can, within broad limits, change the rules, particularly those of the common law and of constitutional law. This power is consistent with the fact that rules do not have to be pellucid, definite, or incapable of revision or repeal in order to bind in a meaningful sense the persons subject to them. It is merely that the judges are not subject to the rules in the same sense—which is not to deny, however, that even judge-made rules carry weight with judges, that is, that there really is a policy, although a flexible one, of adhering to precedent, in order both to stabilize law and to economize on judges' time.[17]

Mention of legal stability brings us face to face once again with the limitations of logic in law. The appearance of stability is highly sensitive to the interval over which a body of rules is examined. At any moment the law as a whole is relatively stable, because only a few rules are on the agenda of change. But expand the time period, and the picture changes. The bodies of rules that make up such otherwise disparate fields as tort law, constitutional law, and antitrust law have changed greatly over the last century, almost entirely as a result of changes in judge-made rules. The process by which the judges have changed these rules—or, more bluntly, have created the rules under which we now live—is not a logical process, not a matter of correcting errors in syllogistic reasoning made by their predecessors. To pick one of many possible examples, the vast expansion in tort liability in this century cannot be explained in terms of logic. It may have to do with a sense that accidents are more readily avoidable by potential injurers than was once the

17. For acknowledgment of this point from an unexpected source, see Duncan Kennedy, "Freedom and Constraint in Adjudication: A Critical Phenomenology," 36 *Journal of Legal Education* 518 (1986). The "weight" metaphor should not be taken literally, evoking as it does an exact force—gravity—which has no close counterpart in judicial incentives or constraints.

case (and perhaps less avoidable by potential victims), or with a greater capacity of courts to process cases, or with a fall in the costs to accident victims of bringing suit, or with a growing enthusiasm for social insurance; it may have to do above all with a drive toward making law more efficacious—the "stage 3" in the growth of law discussed in the Introduction. Logic doesn't enter. It doesn't enter into the law's cycling between generous and niggardly protection of criminal defendants' rights, or between generous and niggardly protection of patent owners' rights, or between generous and niggardly protection of employers' rights.

When judges and lawyers do use logic, they use the simplest methods. Formal logic is rarely taught in law schools or encountered in judicial opinions, briefs, or law review articles. (Not too much should be made of this, however. Formal logic is rarely found outside books and articles on logic. I am not advocating formal notation for judicial opinions.) The closest thing to formal logic in law is the use by economic analysts of mathematical models of legal rules; the model of these models is Learned Hand's formula, which defines negligence in a simple algebraic formula.[18] As for the syllogism, it should be apparent by now that it is an unhelpful template for legal reasoning. Its function is to demonstrate the validity of a reasoning process rather than to establish the truth of the outcome of the process. It is used not to prove that Socrates is mortal—for no one doubts that—but to demonstrate a logical relation, as would be clearer if we substituted A for man (men), B for mortal, and C for Socrates.[19] Logic, like mathematics, explores relations between ideas rather than correspondence to facts. The legal system cannot be indifferent to issues of empirical truth.

Despite appearances, it is not my intention to disparage the use of logic in law. Even in difficult cases it plays a role, a *critical* role. Bertrand Russell put the basic point well: "Logical errors are, I think, of greater practical importance than many people believe; they enable their per-

18. United States v. Carroll Towing Co., 159 F.2d 169, 173 (2d Cir. 1947) (B < PL, meaning that if the burden to the injurer of avoiding the accident was less than the loss if the accident occurred discounted [that is, multiplied] by the probability that it would occur, the injurer is negligent). Compare American Hospital Supply Corp. v. Hospital Products Ltd., 780 F.2d 589, 593 (7th Cir. 1986), and see generally William M. Landes and Richard A. Posner, *The Economic Structure of Tort Law* (1987).

19. The fact that A stands for two different words in the Socrates syllogism is a clue to its nonstandard status, on which see Willard Van Orman Quine, *Methods of Logic* 107, 259–267 (4th ed. 1982). In contrast, the syllogism "All Greeks are dark-haired; all Cretans are Greeks; therefore all Cretans are dark-haired" causes no difficulty when put in the form "All A are B; all C are A; therefore all C are B."

petrators to hold the comfortable opinion on every subject in turn. Any logically coherent body of doctrine is sure to be in part painful and contrary to current prejudices. The dialectic method—or, more generally, the habit of unfettered discussion—tends to promote logical consistency, and is in this way useful. But it is quite unavailing when the object is to discover new facts."[20] The qualification in the last sentence is, as we shall see in the next section, highly relevant.

Here is an example of how logic can be used critically in law. The Supreme Court has held that the Constitution does not forbid a state to make sodomy between consenting homosexual adults a crime.[21] The Court emphasized the long history of criminalizing such conduct, implying that conduct long punished criminally cannot find shelter in the concept of "privacy" that the Court has claimed to have discovered in the Constitution, no matter how private the conduct is. But, if so, then the Court's earlier decisions, which *Bowers v. Hardwick* does not purport to overrule, holding that women cannot be forbidden to have abortions or married or unmarried couples to practice contraception, seem unsound, for those practices too had long been forbidden. So there is a potential inconsistency in the majority opinion. The dissenting Justices likewise ignored a potential inconsistency in their position. They treated homosexual sodomy as no different in any relevant respect from heterosexual sex acts, and in particular from heterosexual sodomy. If there is *no* socially or legally pertinent difference between homosexual and heterosexual activity, a state that refuses to recognize homosexual marriage is discriminating arbitrarily. None of the dissenting Justices was willing to confront, let alone embrace, this implication of their stated position. If, as I suspect, these Justices do not believe that the Constitution requires the recognition of homosexual marriage, then they do not really believe that homosexual sodomy is relevantly identical to heterosexual sodomy.

Logic will not decide the most difficult cases. Logic the destroyer is not logic the creator. To show that an opinion is illogical is not to show that the outcome is incorrect—a particularly pertinent observation when both the majority and the dissenting opinions in a case are illogical. Maybe the earlier privacy decisions should have been overruled in *Bowers;* or maybe homosexual marriage should be legalized. If propositions A and B are inconsistent, one of them has to go, but logic will not tell you which one. It can, however, kick the props out from under

20. *A History of Western Philosophy* 93 (1945).
21. Bowers v. Hardwick, 478 U.S. 186 (1986).

many of the arguments offered in cases and put pressure on the opponents to argue anew, and specifically to bring into the open the premises necessary to resolve the inconsistencies, for I am not denying the possibility that the inconsistencies I have identified might be dispelled in a fuller analysis.[22] The very importance of the critical use of logic in law, however, should help us to understand why lawyers and judges overuse logic. Law attracts and rewards people who are good at handling informal logic (not formal logic—the logic of lemmas and the predicate calculus and the like; that attracts a different kind of mind), and not all of them are content to use their logical skills to refute other lawyers' and judges' arguments. They want to make law as well as criticize law, and to do so with the tools they know best, the tools of simple logic.

All this emphasis on judges and litigation may bore or irritate lawyers who specialize in fields in which litigation is not the central focus. There are many such fields, and they tend to get short shrift in books of Anglo-American jurisprudence; they will in this one. The judge is a more problematic figure than the lawyer who negotiates a lease or other contract against a background of settled and slowly changing law or the arbitrator who decides a dispute arising from such a contract. But there is one field in which litigation is not the focus of practice yet jurispru-

---

22. The omission of essential premises is of a piece with the generally evasive character of the *Bowers* opinions, which, while mentioning traditional disapproval and sporadic persecution of homosexuals, disregard such potentially relevant facts as that (1) sodomy laws are no longer enforced in this country (there was an arrest but no prosecution in *Bowers* itself); (2) in the United States and Western Europe male homosexuals were at the time *Bowers* was decided the principal known carriers, as well as victims, of the virus that causes the ghastly disease AIDS, although their role as transmitters of the virus may be declining relative to that of drug addicts; (3) there is widespread revulsion among heterosexuals toward specific sexual practices of homosexuals and toward the flaunting of those practices and of the life style associated with them; (4) a visible and significant number of male homosexuals are highly promiscuous (this is connected with point 2), although the number has diminished in response to the AIDS epidemic; (5) the biological and psychiatric question of whether and if so to what extent sexual orientation is voluntary is unresolved; (6) homosexuals appear to be above average in education, income, and artistic and intellectual creativity; (7) they are increasingly assertive politically; (8) societies differ greatly in their attitudes toward homosexuality, with some being tolerant. For discussion and references, see Michael Ruse, *Homosexuality: A Philosophical Inquiry* (1988). I am far from certain of the exact bearing of all these facts, but I have difficulty understanding a responsible judge's failing to consider them in trying to decide whether the Constitution should be construed to limit public regulation of homosexual sex acts. Of course, the Justices may have thought about these things—may even have discussed them among themselves (though I doubt that)—but decided not to include them in the opinions. A prudent Court, I believe, would have dismissed the case as moot in view of the state's decision not to prosecute the plaintiff, and not have decided the merits.

dential problems highly pertinent to this chapter abound, and that is federal taxation. Tax legislation and regulations issue with such frequency and in such volume from Congress and the Treasury Department that the judicial function of filling gaps in legislative and related texts is rarely employed. Yet the price of this approach is high, and should give pause to those inclined to agree with Bentham that the problem of judicial legitimacy could be solved by codification. Carefully drafted though they typically are, tax statutes and regulations by their very precision and exactitude create loopholes that lawyers are quick to exploit for their clients. The loopholes incite amendatory legislation or regulation. The result is a structure with fewer unintended loopholes than generally supposed, but it is a structure of immense complexity. Whether it is a net improvement on a simpler structure that would make greater use of the courts to plug loopholes is anyone's guess.

The experience with taxation, an institution that conservatives do not admire, casts a sidelight on the position of Hayek and his followers that the rule of law implies governance by clear rules, known to all in advance and not subject to change through judicial interpretation, which operates retroactively.[23] A society in as much ferment as ours needs a mechanism for legal change, and it is not obvious that the combination that predominates in federal income taxation—extremely detailed statutory specifications with frequent amendments and continuous executive rule making—is always to be preferred to judicial administration of flexible standards. It is odd that conservatives in the libertarian tradition should want to expand the legislative and administrative roles in our society.

Joseph Isenbergh has mounted a strong attack on the judge-made doctrine of tax law that authorizes the tax collector to disregard the form of a transaction and penetrate to its substance in an effort to prevent the

---

23. See, for example, F. A. Hayek, *The Constitution of Liberty,* ch. 10 (1960); Hayek, *Law, Legislation, and Liberty,* vol. 1 (1973); Norman P. Barry, *Hayek's Social and Economic Philosophy,* ch. 5 (1979); James M. Buchanan, "Good Economics—Bad Law," 60 *Virginia Law Review* 483 (1974); Buchanan, "Contractarian Political Economy and Constitutional Interpretation," 78 *American Economic Review Papers and Proceedings* 135 (May 1988); Randy E. Barnett, "Foreword: Can Justice and the Rule of Law Be Reconciled?" 11 *Harvard Journal of Law and Public Policy* 597 (1988). Hayek's hostility to legal standards is related to the extreme skepticism of the school of "Austrian economics," of which he is the preeminent exponent, regarding the reliability of information generated by government rather than by markets. Standards, as I have noted, require more information to administer than rules, and in that sense imply a potentially more intrusive role for government than regulation by rules does. The "Austrian" position resembles that of the advocates of formal, or procedural, justice (such as Lon Fuller), whose position I discuss in Chapters 7 and 11.

exploitation of unintended loopholes in tax statutes and regulations.[24] After reviewing a number of cases in which he believes the "substance over form" doctrine has been misapplied, Isenbergh concludes that "more parsing of the statute and specific transactions and less concern with how to save the world from manipulative taxpayers would have led to sounder holdings in all these cases" (p. 879). From there Isenbergh moves to larger ground and argues for what he describes as a formalistic approach to interpretation in general. "Hard grappling with the facts of a case and the inner workings of a statute, although both difficult and intellectually admirable, is frequently passed off as a trivial or excessively 'formal' exercise. For one who has gotten that far, the slogan of 'substance over form' is as good a means as any to clear the intellectual landscape for an inquiry about the 'larger' nature of the statute itself. The latter exercise is in fact quite easy, requiring only the assertion of a statutory purpose that encapsulates one's own tastes, either generally or regarding the transaction under scrutiny" (id.). Why do judges adopt such an approach? Isenbergh has already given an answer that might have seemed sufficient: judges are sometimes lazy, and they are often at sea when dealing with complex commercial transactions. Now he adds: "Judges have aspirations. Little attention is drawn to those who hew narrowly to technical rules. The painstaking process of examining transactions and statutes to determine whether they concord promises little glory. In a society that has always looked to courts for strokes of statesmanship, it is easy enough to understand a judge's temptation to cut through, rather than unravel, the Gordian knot" (p. 882).[25] So at the root of the "substance over form" doctrine lies—judicial ambition (in *tax law?*). And "on the whole, law professors do not help much either. It is their wont to decry 'formalism' and glorify the ends of 'policy' in the resolution of disputes" (id.).

Isenbergh is not a consistent formalist. He derides "the enshrinement of substance over form" as a "'maxim' of statutory construction. As with its older relatives . . . it is harder and harder to know which way it will cut when it surfaces" (p. 879). The canons of statutory construction are the main props of formalistic reasoning in statutory cases. Nor does the approach that Isenbergh favors—careful scrutiny of the details

24. "Musings on Form and Substance in Taxation," 49 *University of Chicago Law Review* 859, 863–884 (1982). Subsequent page references to this article appear in the text. For a warmer view of the doctrine, see Marvin A. Chirelstein, "Learned Hand's Contribution to the Law of Tax Avoidance," 77 *Yale Law Journal* 440 (1968).

25. The metaphor is not well chosen. The Gordian knot *couldn't* be untied—it had to be cut, as only Alexander the Great understood.

of the transaction, mastery of the inner workings of the statute, rejection of broad generalizations offered as easy formulas for decision—seem equivalent to formalism in any clear sense of that much-abused term. The approach does not entail denial that there are unintended tax loopholes and that courts should try to close them. Yet Isenbergh does not merely criticize the intellectually lazy style in which many judges perform that office. He also criticizes the result, as in the famous case of *Gregory v. Helvering*.[26]

Mrs. Gregory was the sole owner of a corporation that owned certain assets which she wanted to sell. If they were either sold directly or distributed to and then sold by her, there would be a large tax; for example, the distribution of assets to her directly would be treated as a dividend equal in amount to the value of the assets and would be taxable in that amount as ordinary income to her. So she formed a new corporation, also wholly owned by her, to which she had the old corporation transfer the assets in question. She then dissolved the new corporation, three days after having created it; received the assets as a liquidating dividend; and then sold them. Because the distribution of the assets to her had literally been pursuant to a "plan of reorganization," and because a liquidating dividend issued pursuant to such a plan is not a taxable dividend, she claimed to be liable only for a tax on the capital gain she reaped when she sold the assets. The Supreme Court held that the "reorganization" had been a sham and therefore Mrs. Gregory was not entitled to treat the distribution of assets pursuant to it as a liquidating dividend exempt from ordinary income tax.

Isenbergh argues that the decision is wrong. The statute defined a reorganization as a change in corporate form (for example, dissolution) that complied with certain technicalities, all of which Mrs. Gregory had observed. There was thus no fact to which a court could refer in order to decide whether a reorganization conforming to the statutory definition was invalid; there was only the concept of reorganization that had been created by the statute. This reasoning, quintessentially formalist, treats the tax statute as having created a conceptual world, like the set of real numbers or the theorems of Euclid, having no necessary correspondence to the world of fact. To Isenbergh, reorganization is not a transaction in the world, by which a firm advances the business interests of its owners; it is a paper shuffle danced to the tune played by the statute. Ignored is the purpose of exempting the gains incident to changes in corporate structure from taxation: to facilitate reorganiza-

26. 293 U.S. 465 (1935), discussed at pp. 866–870 of Isenbergh's article.

tions viewed as purposive business transactions, rather than to encourage the empty transaction in which Mrs. Gregory engaged—a transaction the sole purpose and (had it succeeded) effect of which were to beat taxes.[27] We now understand "hard grappling . . . with the inner workings of a statute" to preclude judicial consideration of the consequences of alternative statutory interpretations.[28]

My disparagement of legal formalism, in its specific guise as rule by rules, may seem music to the ears of left-wing critics of liberalism, who see any compromise with the strictest formalist conception of law as signifying a crisis of liberalism.[29] I disagree with them,[30] while granting that they can cite Hayek and other conservatives in support of their position. It is desirable to minimize the discretion of officials, including judges, but undesirable as well as impossible to eliminate official discretion altogether. It seems obvious that legislators have, and must have, discretion.[31] And if, rather than attempting the impossible by specifying in advance every imaginable exception to every rule of conduct laid down by them, they leave it to the courts to create (perhaps within specified bounds) exceptions on an ad hoc basis, this is a detail about the division of labor among the branches of government rather than an abandonment of the concept of the liberal state. Even if responsibility for formulating basic rules of conduct is left mainly to the courts, as was

27. As explained by the committee reports in the House and Senate, Congress had "adopted the policy of exempting from tax the gain from exchanges made in connection with a reorganization, in order that ordinary business transactions will not be prevented." S. Rep. No. 398, 68th Cong., 1st Sess. 14–15 (1924); H.R. Rep. No. 179, 68th Cong., 1st Sess. 13 (1924).

28. The Irish Supreme Court, in the recent case of *McDermott v. McGrath,* rejected the "substance over form" doctrine for Irish tax law; and the Irish parliament seems unable to figure out a legislative method of plugging the loophole created by the decision. See George Guttman, "Irish Supreme Court Upholds Tax Avoidance Scheme," 40 *Tax Notes,* July 25, 1988, at 349, 350.

29. See, for example, Duncan Kennedy, "Legal Formality," 2 *Journal of Legal Studies* 351 (1973); Roberto Mangabeira Unger, *Knowledge and Politics,* ch. 2 (1975); Mark Kelman, *A Guide to Critical Legal Studies,* ch. 1 (1987); Terry Eagleton, *William Shakespeare* 35–58 (1986).

30. See my book *Law and Literature: A Misunderstood Relation* 105–109 (1988); also Nancy L. Rosenblum, *Another Liberalism: Romanticism and the Reconstruction of Liberal Thought* 38–42 (1987).

31. Obvious to me, anyway. But Hayek belongs to the school of political thought, German in origin (see Leonard Krieger, *The German Idea of Freedom: History of a Political Tradition* [1957], esp. pp. 46–125) that stresses limited government rather than popular government; and the more government is limited, the less discretion legislators have. See my article "The Constitution as an Economic Document," 56 *George Washington Law Review* 4, 21–22 (1987).

done in England and America until this century, this does not make liberalism a lie. Were England and America *less* liberal, in the classical sense of the word, during the heyday of the common law than they are in the era of the welfare state? A *system* of untrammeled official discretion would be inconsistent with the premises of the liberal state, prominent among which is the rule of law—the concept of a "government of laws, not men." But pockets of discretion are not inconsistent with liberalism. We do not have an "illiberal" system merely because judges use discretion to decide difficult cases, juries sometimes nullify criminal statutes, and the executive branch can pardon criminals without giving reasons. The liberal state has always been a mixture of rule and discretion, and the issue should be whether we get a better mixture under liberalism than we would get in the sorts of regime preferred by its critics. But even to state the issue this way is to take labels too seriously. It should not matter whether our legal system is called "liberal." The practical question is whether it is better than a system with even more rules and less discretion or a system with even more discretion, more standards, and fewer rules.[32]

Having criticized legal formalism at such length I should make clear that I am not opposed to all formalism. Mathematics is a formalist discipline; so is logic; so are much painting, sculpture, architecture, and literature. Economics has its formalist side; my work in economic analysis of law has been described both as formalist and as antiformalist.[33] Abstracting from particulars is an essential part of science; so in a sense all science, not just economic science, is formalist. All this merely illustrates the poverty of categorization (a typically formalist defect!). The prestige of true formalisms is part of the reason so many judges and legal scholars aspire to make law a formalist discipline.

Scientific Observation

After logic the most rigorous and objective methods of extending our knowledge involve systematic empirical inquiry, using either controlled experiments or "natural" experiments that can be statistically verified.

32. For good illustrations of lawyers' "label anxiety"—specifically the anxiety of modern welfare-state liberals to preserve the "liberal" label for themselves in the face of the radical Left's effort to attach the "liberal" label to the advocates of laissez-faire—see Ronald Dworkin, *Law's Empire* 440–444 (1986); Richard H. Fallon, Jr., "What Is Republicanism, and Is It Worth Reviving?" 102 *Harvard Law Review* 1695 (1989).

33. Compare Wilson, note 4 above, at 481, with Louis Menand, "Objection Overruled," *New Republic,* March 13, 1989, at 31.

Although these methods of inquiry provide only tentative support for propositions, and the "truths" they demonstrate (or at least lead people to accept) often are transitory, the scientific method is for most people in modern society the model of objective inquiry—such has been the success of science in altering both our worldview and our world.

Scientific method plays little role in legal reasoning. Parties to lawsuits lack the time and money necessary to conduct scientific experiments or other scientific studies. The relevant data are often difficult or impossible to obtain. Legal decisions may depend on predictions of extremely long-term consequences, such as the effect of abortion or capital punishment on attitudes toward the sanctity of life, and large-scale social experiments designed to test such predictions are rarely feasible, would take too long, or would raise insuperable ethical questions. Lawyers and judges (not to mention jurors) are not trained in the scientific method. The trial is not modeled on scientific inquiry. As we shall see in the next chapter, authority and hierarchy play a role in law that would be inimical to scientific inquiry. And many legal doctrines are too entrenched to adjust rapidly to changes in scientific understanding. (There is no principle of stare decisis in scientific inquiry.) Society is unable or at least unwilling to allow legal judgments either to be deferred until the results of patient scientific research are available or to be changed the minute a legal doctrine becomes scientifically obsolete.

One could perhaps *imagine* law on the model of a science—say, physics. Academic lawyers, corresponding to physicists, would from time to time discover scientific laws that govern a legal system, such as the less certain law is, the lower the settlement rate will be. Practicing lawyers and judges, corresponding to electrical engineers, would embody these discoveries in the "machinery" of justice, which already contains devices, such as the pretrial conference, for fostering settlement by reducing uncertainty about the outcome of trial. Innovations would be evaluated by comparing their actual as distinct from their anticipated effects.[34] An objection to the "social engineering" metaphor is that it seems to invite lawyers to remake our world, but we can avoid this implication by focusing on the role of the engineer as one who implements scientific discoveries. On the theoretical or "scientific" plane, society decides that burglary should be punished more heavily when it

34. The notion of using the scientific method to guide social reform is quintessentially pragmatic. See, for example, George H. Mead, "The Working Hypothesis in Social Reform," 5 *American Journal of Sociology* 367, 369–371 (1899).

takes place at night than when it takes place during the daytime. The social engineer's job is to find a feasible, though necessarily an arbitrary, way of distinguishing between day and night. The need to make dichotomous cuts in continuous phenomena shows why law can never be—and should never aspire to be—an elegant field; and in this too it resembles engineering.

Another way to make the point is to note that both professions care critically about the application of theories, which requires working with people and materials as well as with designs and implies a concern with stability, often at the expense of elegance. The redundancies that engineers build into structures and machines to reduce the probability of failure correspond (though only very roughly) to the reluctance of legal professionals to countenance abrupt changes and daring departures in law. The engineer's preference for a tried-and-true process or product over one embodying a more exciting technology has its counterpart in rules limiting the reopening of legal judgments on the basis of newly discovered evidence or new arguments. A related respect in which lawyers are like engineers is that they try *very* hard to avoid making mistakes. Mistakes in law as in engineering are more likely to have dramatic and immediate real-world consequences (the loss of a case or collapse of a building, for example) than would a scientific or a mathematical error.

Some progress toward recasting the law in a genuinely rather than merely analogically scientific-technological mold is visible. This progress is due largely to the efforts of economists and economically minded lawyers. Economics, including the branch known as economic analysis of law, or "law and economics," really is a science, though an immature one (see Chapter 12). The practitioners of law and economics are trying with some success to use the methods and results of economics to improve our understanding of law and assist in its reform. Further progress on this front can be expected. But in part because the scientific fields, such as economics and psychology, upon which a science of law would have to build *are* immature, and in part because of the institutional factors noted above, the day is far distant when law can take its place among the sciences. As with science, so with engineering: engineering marvels are more easily determined to be such than are legal ones, progress in engineering is more dramatic than in law, and the methods of engineers are less problematic than those of lawyers.

Am I pressing the distinction between the technical and legal realms too hard? Is exact inquiry really all that exact? The reader may bridle at my serene equation of exact inquiry with science. Not only is it unconventional (outside of the philosophy of science) to treat logic, mathematics, and statistics as branches of science;[35] but even natural science (leave aside economics, psychology, and other social sciences) is not always, perhaps not typically, as rigorous, exact, and certain as the term "exact inquiry" connotes.[36] Many scientific theories, including natural selection and the "big bang," cannot be verified by experimentation or by any other method of exact observation.[37] Many have been proved false after having been universally accepted; examples are Euclidean geometry as a theory of spatial relations, the geocentric universe, Newton's laws of motion, and the luminiferous ether. Many scientific theories—some philosophers of science think all—are temporary or ad hoc constructs to explain phenomena that might be explained in other ways. Many yield results that are only weakly supported.[38]

35. But not incorrect. See, for example, W. V. Quine, "Success and Limits of Mathematization," in Quine, *Theories and Things* 148 (1981). It is true that logic and mathematics deal with entities (such as number) whose ontology is more questionable than that of such scientific entities as atoms and electromagnetic radiation—in what sense does a number "exist"? But the tendency of both logical and mathematical inquiries to converge, and the role of logic and science in successful scientific theories, are grounds for believing that logical and mathematical inquiries yield "truth." In contrast, ethical, literary, and legal inquiries neither exhibit a strong tendency toward convergence nor play a role in successful scientific theorizing.

36. For an excellent introduction to the philosophy and methodology of science, see David Oldroyd, *The Arch of Knowledge: An Introduction to the History of the Philosophy and Methodology of Science* (1986).

37. Yet it would be a mistake to infer from this point, as the Louisiana legislature did in insisting upon the teaching in its public schools of "creation science," that "evolution is not a scientific 'fact,' since it cannot actually be observed in a laboratory. Rather, evolution is merely a scientific theory or 'guess.'" Edwards v. Aguillard, 107 S. Ct. 2573, 2598 (1987) (dissenting opinion). What a curious collocation of religious faith with extreme scientific positivism! Imagine the fix that religion would be in if its defenders were required to provide laboratory confirmation of miracles. On the status of evolution as scientific theory, see Michael Ruse, *Philosophy of Biology Today*, ch. 1 (1988); Florian von Schilcher and Neil Tennant, *Philosophy, Evolution, and Human Nature* 91–105 (1984). On the debate over "creation science," see *Science and Creationism* (Ashley Montagu ed. 1984).

38. The frequent mistakes, and frequently shoddy methods, even of modern science are painstakingly recounted in David Faust, *The Limits of Scientific Reasoning* (1984). From the Left come charges that ideology shapes the direction, and sometimes even the outcome, of scientific research. See, for example, Rouse, note 1 above; Bruno Latour and Steve Woolger, *Laboratory Life: The Social Construction of Scientific Facts* (1979); *Feminist Approaches to Science* (Ruth Bleier ed. 1986). These criticisms must be kept in perspective. None of these writers contends that such propositions as that the blood circulates or that tuberculosis is caused by bacteria or that the sun is millions of miles from the earth are just twentieth-century myths, no truer than the views the ancient Greeks held on these matters; or that the "Aryan physics" of Nazi Germany had as much truth value as the physics practiced by Einstein. See Rom Harré, *Varieties of Realism: A Rationale for the Natural Sciences* (1986);

The basic problems concerning the objectivity of science are three. The first is the sheer diversity, indeed indefinability, of science, which makes it impossible to survey the entire field, let alone to reduce it to a single methodology or tight set of methodologies. The second, little discussed nowadays in academic circles, is that millions of highly intelligent people selectively disbelieve in science, and who is to gainsay them?[39] The third problem is that it is unclear how a scientific theory can ever be validated.[40] Suppose one deduces from theory A a hypothesis that event X will be observed under certain conditions; and X *is* observed, which supports A. But the observation will equally support A + B (A might be the theory that the blood circulates, B that human beings have souls), or C (any other theory from which a hypothesis predicting X can be derived logically). Realistically, in order for X to support A + B or C rather than just A, there would have to be an argument that B or C was related to A. But such arguments are not difficult to make. An indefinite number of theories, many of them plausible, will be consistent with a given set of observations, and the choice among the plausible theories is likely to be made on utilitarian or practical grounds, such as simplicity and fruitfulness, rather than on epistemic ones.

Moreover, the observations relied on to "confirm" the theory may be ambiguous. "Controlled" experiments suppress features of the natural environment that are deemed irrelevant, in order to isolate the effect of the variable under investigation. But the experimenter may err in the design of the experiment. One of the excluded features may be the real cause of the phenomenon observed, and the independent variable that the experimenter wanted to test and that he found to have causal significance may just be a correlate of the omitted variable.

Alan D. Beyerchen, *Scientists under Hitler: Politics and the Physics Community in the Third Reich,* ch. 7 (1977). Moreover, the sense in which such refuted scientific theories as the Euclidean theory of space or Newton's laws of motion are "false" is a rather special one; for most purposes, including most technological purposes, they are true ("true enough"). (More on "truth" in Chapter 3.) For a succinct summary of the case for scientific realism, see Richard N. Boyd, "How to Be a Moral Realist," in *Essays on Moral Realism* 181, 188–189 (Geoffrey Sayre-McCord ed. 1988). The antirealist case is well argued in Andrew Pickering, *Constructing Quarks: A Sociological History of Particle Physics* (1984).

39. "I believe that every human being has two human parents; but Catholics believe that Jesus only had a human mother." Ludwig Wittgenstein, *On Certainty* 32e (G. E. M. Anscombe and G. H. von Wright eds. 1969) (¶239). Among these believers are a number of distinguished scientists. See, for example, R. J. Berry, "What to Believe about Miracles," 322 *Nature* 321 (1986).

40. See, for example, Clark Glymour, *Theory and Evidence* 29–48, 110–290 (1980).

The problem is not solved by trying to go from data to theory, that is, by induction. As Hume pointed out centuries ago, to discover that whenever we observe datum A we also observe datum B will *habituate* us to expect B when we see A but will give us no *rational* basis for expecting the pattern to continue.[41] Even seeing the sun rise every day does not give one a warranted confidence that it will continue to do so—any more than waking up every morning gives one a warranted confidence that one will live forever—unless one has a theory of what is causing the sun to rise. But as just noted, it is unclear that theories can be proved by confirmation. An indefinite number of theories, many contradictory, will yield the prediction that the sun will continue to rise every day, and each of these theories will thus be confirmed repeatedly. Theories can be falsified, but if we agree therefore with Popper that the mark of a scientific theory is that it is falsifiable but not verifiable (see Chapter 3), we are driven to the odd conclusion that all scientific theory is conjecture and no inductions are reliable.

All that this discussion demonstrates, however, is the existence of unsolved problems in the philosophy of science, not the existence of deep problems with science.[42] Although every bit of what we now believe about the nature of the universe may eventually be overthrown, in the meantime "science reveals hidden mysteries, predicts successfully, and works technological wonders."[43] Airplanes designed not by trial and error but by applying scientific theories "verified" in wind-tunnel experiments actually fly. As this example[44] shows, progress in science is compatible with the conjectural character of human knowledge. Even if the theories upon which our notions of flight are based are someday falsified or superseded, planes designed in accordance with those theories will fly; we are in no danger of being thrown back to the Wright brothers' time. As this example shows, we have only to describe knowledge in "know how" rather than "know that" terms to see that scientific knowledge has indeed grown steadily. Our atomic theory may ultimately be

41. For a good modern discussion, see Haim Gaifman, "On Inductive Support and Some Recent Tricks," 22 *Erkenntnis* 5 (1985).

42. For a good discussion, see Arthur Fine, "Unnatural Attitudes: Realist and Instrumentalist Attachments to Science," 95 *Mind* 149 (1986).

43. W. V. O. Quine, "Natural Kinds," in *Naturalizing Epistemology* 31, 43 (Hilary Kornblith ed. 1985).

44. Which is from Paisley Livingston, *Literary Knowledge: Humanistic Inquiry and the Philosophy of Science* 74–75 (1988).

shown to be as off base as Democritus's; but that we know how to do more things than Democritus and other ancient Greek scientists knew how to do—for example, we know how to make an atomic bomb—is beyond question. Natural laws that engineers make use of in building things are more reliable than the scientific theories that are formulated to explain those laws.

One might be tempted to argue in like vein that even though every legal rule we live by may someday be overthrown, meanwhile the system of rules is as certain, as useful, as well established as the existing body of scientific knowledge. Some parts of law—for example, the rule that murder is criminal—are *more* solidly established than some parts of science. But it would be a mistake to conclude that because the epistemological foundations of science are less secure than they once seemed (even as science has become an ever more reliable fount of knowledge), fields with even weaker epistemological foundations, such as law, yield, on average, knowledge comparable in reliability to scientific knowledge. The methods by which scientific knowledge is created and, if not verified, at least temporarily supported and transformed into useful gadgetry are by and large not available to law, not yet anyway.

Even if in good pragmatist fashion we forget about foundations, accept the broadest possible definition of science, and agree with Richard Rorty to withhold the name of science from a method of belief formation only "if force is used to change belief . . . [or] we can discern . . . [no] connection with our ability to predict and control,"[45] we shall not confuse law with science. Prediction and control are precisely what science gives us and philosophy, politics, and law do not—except (in the case of politics and law) with the aid of force.

To summarize, if science does establish certainty, still its methods and domain are so different from those of law that the exactitude of science cannot be translated into exactitude in law, while if science does not establish certainty, then it cannot be used as a foundation for or model of legal certainty. In either event we must look elsewhere for the grounds of that certainty. But is there an elsewhere? Logical positivists

45. Rorty, "Is Natural Science a Natural Kind?" in *Construction and Constraint: The Shaping of Scientific Rationality* 49, 72 (Ernan McMullin ed. 1988). It may be hard to see how we can "predict and control" physical phenomena if we do not have a grip on reality, but this argument for scientific realism is weakened by the fact that many refuted theories have had excellent predictive properties, including Ptolemaic cosmology, which is still usable for navigating by the stars.

would say no. They believe[46] that propositions, to be meaningful, must be either analytic, in the sense in which propositions in logic or mathematics are analytic (true by definition or something akin to definition), or verifiable by observation; propositions neither analytic nor verifiable are merely emotive.[47] On this view most legal propositions are either emotive or deduced from emotive propositions. This conclusion if correct would warrant a radical skepticism about the objectivity of law, but it would be correct only if exact inquiry were the only path to truth.

Suppose we go to the opposite extreme and accept the increasingly widespread view that the objectivity and certainty of the scientific method were greatly exaggerated by previous generations of philosophers of science—including the logical positivists themselves, whose skepticism about nonverifiable nonanalytic propositions was the obverse of their passionate faith in science.[48] Would this argue *a fortiori* for the indeterminacy of law? Not necessarily. Observing that science is successful despite the lack of epistemological foundations as solid as once believed, we might conclude that law could be successful even if its foundations are likewise less solid than once believed. (Indeed, in either field, the quest for foundations may be misconceived.) This possibility can be

46. Perhaps I should use the past tense; philosophers consider logical positivism thoroughly discredited. But discredited philosophies are revenants (recent examples are social contractarianism, Aristotelianism, and pragmatism—all of which were widely considered discredited thirty years ago); and the attitudes that motivated logical positivism continue to be influential. The methodology of economics, we shall see in Chapter 12, has a logical-positivist flavor.

47. The best introduction to logical positivism remains A. J. Ayer, *Language, Truth, and Logic* (rev. ed. 1946), but the best brief summary is more than two hundred years old: "If we take in our hand any volume; of divinity or school metaphysics, for instance; let us ask, *Does it contain any abstract reasoning concerning quantity or number?* No. *Does it contain any experimental reasoning concerning matter of fact and existence?* No. Commit it then to the flames: for it can contain nothing but sophistry and illusion." David Hume, *An Enquiry Concerning Human Understanding* 165 (3d ed., P. H. Nidditch ed., 1975) (§12, pt. 3). Remember that logical positivism and legal positivism are not the same thing, although Holmes for one subscribed to both.

48. Clifford Geertz, *Local Knowledge: Further Essays in Interpretive Anthropology* 162–163 (1983), gives a dramatic example of how, viewed from the inside, physics lacks the purity and certainty that laypeople associate with it. He is quoting a physicist who says that "physics is like life; there's no perfection. It's never all sewed up. It's all a question of better, better yet, and how much time and interest do you really have in it . . . A theory isn't right and wrong. A theory has a sort of sociological position that changes as new information comes in. 'Is Einstein's theory correct?' You can take a poll and have a look. Einstein is rather 'in' right now. But who knows if it is 'true'? . . . Nobody said anything about Truth. Perhaps Truth is 'out.' One thinks, 'Well, this idea looks bad for or looks good for general relativity.'"

glimpsed in the following comparison between induction in science and in law:

> Sometimes an observation or measurement in the experiment turns out to have been faulty, and so the report of what occurred was incorrect. Sometimes a hidden variable was interfering with the action of the controlled variables in the experiment, so that factors other than those reported were influencing the result. In either of these two types of case the replicability of the experiment would be unreliable. And in a third type of case the experiment is satisfactorily replicable, but the hypothesis is treated as an idealization to which the real world only conforms under an unrealizable *ceteris paribus* condition. Similarly a supposed legal precedent may be discounted in one or other of three analogous ways. Sometimes the previous case may be shown to have been wrongly decided, or to have been heard by a judge whose decisions are not binding in the instant case, so that the alleged precedent lacks authority. Sometimes the previous case had features that were significantly different from those of the instant case, so that the alleged precedent is irrelevant. And sometimes the conclusion is that the principles underlying the law would be best codified by our establishing a new nexus of legal roles and relations which would not quite accord at every point with relevant precedents.[49]

The analogy is fine; and maybe it is more than analogy—maybe induction is induction, a universal method of reasoning, as inescapable in law as in science. But neither the fact that lawyers, like scientists, use induction, nor the intriguing suggestion that scientists, like lawyers, are judgmental rather than mechanical in their use of induction—that is, in the weight they attach to "precedents," viewed as confirming instances—makes law scientific in an interesting sense. What is missing from law are penetrating and rigorous theories, counterintuitive hypotheses that are falsifiable but not falsified (and so are at least tentatively supported), precise instrumentation, an exact vocabulary, a clear separation of positive and normative inquiry, quantification of data, credible controlled experiments, rigorous statistical inference, useful technological by-products, dramatic interventions with measurable consequences, and above all and subsuming most of the previous points, objectively testable—and continually retested—hypotheses. In law there is the blueprint or shadow of scientific reasoning, but no edifice.

This conclusion may seem to overemphasize the observational aspect of science. Science is not only exact observation but also the search for

49. L. Jonathan Cohen, *The Dialogue of Reason: An Analysis of Analytical Philosophy* 98 (1986).

unity in multiplicity (and finding it, most dramatically in the physics of Newton and of Einstein). Science thus has its Platonic as well as its Aristotelian aspect. And law certainly has the former. But this does not make law scientific, or even half-scientific, any more than the shared characteristic of abstraction makes a legal rule a scientific law. The quest for unity in multiplicity is not unique to science. It is also the project of theology and of metaphysics, modes of inquiry that differ from science in declining to subject their theories to the fires of empirical testing — and that is all the difference in the world. In this critical respect law is closer to theology and to metaphysics than to science. Lawyers are not only quick but unashamed to make emphatic assertions on matters of fact (for example, the role of the religion clauses of the First Amendment in preserving religious pluralism in the United States) without attempting, desiring, or even being willing to subject those assertions to an empirical test.

If we redescribe "science" as merely (but not trivially) the idea, practice, and ethics of systematic, disinterested inquiry[50]—in essence, an attitude of respect for fact—we may seem to be setting before the lawyer, judge, and law professor an eminently attainable as well as highly worthwhile ideal. We can then begin to see more clearly how cases might be the counterpart to scientific data and a potential basis therefore for inferring lawlike behavior in the scientific, not legal, sense of "law." We can note the parallel between, on the one hand, the scientist's deduction of consequences from a scientific theory and attempt to discover those consequences in nature and, on the other hand, the judge's comparison of the implications of a legal doctrine with social reality. Of course there is a vast gulf between scientific aspiration and scientific achievement, but the more interesting point, to be explored below, is that practices deeply woven in the fabric of law may place even the aspiration beyond law's reach.

50. A typically pragmatist conception. See, for example, Rorty, note 45 above.

2 ∽

Legal Reasoning as Practical Reasoning

What Is Practical Reason?

Set against the methods of exact inquiry are those of "practical reason." Unfortunately the term lacks a standard meaning. It is most often used to denote the methods ("deliberation" and "practical syllogism" are the key expression here) that people use to make a practical or ethical choice, such as whether to go to the theater, or whether to lie to an acquaintance.[1] Practical reason in this sense is action-oriented, in contrast to the methods of "pure reason" by which we determine whether a proposition is true or false, an argument valid or invalid. Practical reason involves setting a goal—pleasure, the good life, whatever—and choosing the means best suited to reaching it.

The term is also used, notably by the academic lawyers whom I call "neotraditionalists" and discuss in Chapter 14, to denote a methodology for reaching conclusions that relies heavily on the traditions in the particular field of inquiry or endeavor and is actually suspicious of what we usually think of as reason, including, in some versions of traditionalism, practical reason in the first sense. Both of these usages have good Aristotelian credentials. I am going to use the term in a third sense, which overlaps the others and also is Aristotelian. Found mainly in Aristotle's discussions of induction, dialectic, and rhetoric, it denotes the methods

---

1. For illustrative discussions, see *Practical Reasoning* (Joseph Raz ed. 1978); Anthony Kenny, *Will, Freedom, and Power,* ch. 5 (1975); David P. Gauthier, *Practical Reasoning: The Structure and Foundations of Prudential and Moral Arguments and Their Exemplification in Discourse* (1963); Michael E. Bratman, *Intention, Plans, and Practical Reason* (1987); M. T. Thornton, "Aristotelian Practical Reason," 91 *Mind* 57 (1982). This is the sense in which Vincent Wellman uses "practical reasoning" in his project of constructing a jurisprudence of practical reason. See "Practical Reasoning and Judicial Justification: Toward an Adequate

by which people who are not credulous form beliefs about matters that cannot be verified by logic or exact observation.[2]

The first usage, which conceives of practical reason as the methodology for deciding what to *do,* might seem more appropriate than the third usage to a worldly activity like law. But my focus is on the judicial decision, especially the appellate decision, which is action of a sort but contemplative action. The judge is not deciding what to do in *his* life; he is deciding what the litigants should have done in their lives, and the litigants and society demand a statement of reasons. But this is not correct either; actually the judge is in the uncomfortable position of having both to act and to offer convincing reasons for acting. He does not have the luxury of the pure thinker, who can defer coming to a conclusion until the evidence gels.

I have been taken to task for ignoring the substantial literature that treats law as a form of practical reason in the first sense, the doer sense.[3] I admit that it is a sense relevant to law, but I am unable to find the content in this literature. Granted that the judge needs analytical methods that will issue in action—what then? The "then" is exploring the resources for decision making that people use when they are in a hurry, or lack the skills or resources for patient, disinterested mathematical or scientific research, or are dealing with a question not amenable to logical or scientific inquiry. And that brings me immediately to practical reason in my sense.

Theory," 57 *University of Colorado Law Review* 45, 87–115 (1985). See also John Ladd, "The Place of Practical Reason in Judicial Decision," in *Nomos VII: Rational Decision* (Carl J. Friedrich ed. 1964); and note 3 below.

2. It is hard to find a compendious modern discussion of these methods, but some useful references are Stephen Edelston Toulmin, *The Uses of Argument* (1958); *Practical Reasoning in Human Affairs: Studies in Honor of Chaim Perelman* (James L. Golden and Joseph J. Pilotta eds. 1986); Ch. Perelman, *The Idea of Justice and the Problem of Argument,* chs. 10–13 (1963); H. H. Price, *Belief* (1969); D. S. Clarke, Jr., *Practical Inferences* (1985); James L. Kinneavy, *A Theory of Discourse* 236–255 (1971); Ronald Beiner, *Political Judgment* 72–97 (1983); Larry Arnhart, *Aristotle on Political Reasoning: A Commentary on the "Rhetoric"* 141–162 (1981); Stephen N. Thomas, *Practical Reasoning in Natural Language* (2d ed. 1981); Larry Wright, *Better Reasoning: Techniques for Handling Argument, Evidence, and Abstraction* (1982). The principal sources in Aristotle are the *Prior Analytics,* the *Posterior Analytics,* the *Topics,* and the *Rhetoric.* A neglected masterpiece of the genre is Cardinal Newman's *Grammar of Assent.* Finally, on the many pitfalls of practical reasoning, see Richard Nisbett and Lee Ross, *Human Inference: Strategies and Shortcomings of Social Judgment* (1980).

3. See Steven J. Burton, "Judge Posner's Jurisprudence of Skepticism," 87 *Michigan Law Review* 710, 720–723 (1988). The literature to which Burton refers is illustrated by Robert Alexy, *A Theory of Legal Argumentation: The Theory of Rational Discourse as Theory of Legal Justification,* pt. c (1989). Alexy also discusses interpretation and other methods of practical reason in my sense, but the discussion is exceedingly abstract.

Practical reason in this sense is not a single analytical method or even a family of related methods. It is a grab bag that includes anecdote, introspection, imagination, common sense, empathy, imputation of motives, speaker's authority, metaphor, analogy, precedent, custom, memory, "experience," intuition, and induction (the expectation of regularities, a disposition related both to intuition and to analogy). There is duplication in this list, so in a sense the list is too long. And some of the entries are questionable—either because they straddle the line between exact inquiry and practical reason (induction, for example), or because they belong to the logic of discovery rather than of justification, which limits their utility to judges. Some of the entries can be viewed not as belonging to a domain distinct from exact inquiry but instead as approximations to exact inquiry (but of course that means they are *not* exact). Many of the inferences we draw with the aid of practical reason, whether in everyday life, literary criticism, or legal analysis, are based on crude forms of hypothesis testing, parallel to scientific inquiry though not close to it.

In another sense, however, my list is too short, because some of the entries are multiple rather than single. Consider "intuition." The brain imposes structure on our perceptions, so that, for example, we ascribe causal significance to acts without being able to observe—we never do observe—causality. This "faculty of induction," to which I alluded in Chapter 1, is one sense of intuition. In a different and more colloquial sense intuition is the sort of inarticulate awareness that I discuss in the next chapter under the heading of "tacit knowing." Finally, and most interesting, intuition is the body of our bedrock beliefs: the beliefs that lie so deep that we do not know how to question them; the propositions that we cannot help believing and that therefore supply the premises for reasoning.[4]

Miscellaneous and unrigorous it may be, but practical reason is our principal set of tools for answering questions large and small. Maybe our only set. Logic almost always, and scientific experimentation often, are methods of justification rather than of discovery. (Mathematics is both.) But as this book is greatly concerned with methods of justification available to judges, I take no comfort in the fact that logic and experiments, so rarely usable to decide difficult legal cases, are for the most part *merely* methods of justification rather than of inquiry. We shall see that many methods of practical reason are also better at generating conclusions or guiding behavior than at providing justifications. They

4. See L. Jonathan Cohen, *The Dialogue of Reason: An Analysis of Analytical Philosophy* 73–117 (1986).

too, therefore, let the judge down when it comes time to write the opinion explaining his decision.

Sometimes, it is true, practical reason yields as high a degree of certainty as do logical demonstrations. An example of a proposition that is not analytic or verifiable and also not as a practical matter falsifiable, and yet is certain, is that no human being has ever eaten an adult elephant in one sitting.[5] This is the sort of example that philosophers like to give in order to show that logical positivism is false, but in so doing they also show why it refuses to stay dead. Logical positivism may be wrong but it is inescapable, because it points, however exaggeratedly, to something real and important—that in areas not susceptible of logical demonstration or empirical verification our knowledge is likely to be meager and insecure. Not many of the propositions we are interested in establishing are as certain as that no one has ever eaten an adult elephant in one sitting or that cats don't grow on trees—and both these propositions, though not themselves verifiable, are known to be true only by virtue of scientific investigations, from which it is possible to infer with some confidence that the earth's biological repertoire has never permitted either phenomenon. Without science, these would be purely inductive propositions, and we would be uneasy about them, just as we would be uneasy about the proposition that "none of the people living today existed at the time of Newton"[6] if we had no scientific theory explaining why human cells cannot renew themselves indefinitely.

Here is a more difficult question for practical reason: How do we know that objects continue to exist when no one is looking at them? One answer is pragmatic: Who cares? It makes no difference whether objects continue to exist when no one is looking at them. Another, suggested by Wittgenstein, is that our certainty that objects continue to exist when no one is looking at them is greater than any ground that could be given for this belief.[7] Put differently, if one doubts the existence

5. The example is from Peter D. Klein, *Certainty: A Refutation of Skepticism* 122 (1981). See also Hilary Putnam, "Philosophers and Human Understanding," in Putnam, *Realism and Reason* 184, 185–186 (vol. 3 of his *Philosophical Papers*). Putnam's example is that cats don't grow on trees; the same example appears in Ludwig Wittgenstein, *On Certainty* 36e (G. E. M. Anscombe and G. H. von Wright eds. 1969) (¶282).

6. Haim Gaifman, "On Inductive Support and Some Recent Tricks," 22 *Erkenntnis* 5, 13 (1985).

7. See Wittgenstein, note 5 above, at 17e (¶111); Alan R. White, "Common Sense: Moore and Wittgenstein," 40 *Revue internationale de philosophie* 313 (1986); R.W. Newell, *Objectivity, Empiricism, and Truth*, ch. 4 (1986). If (this is the central example in *On Certainty*) you asked me whether I had a right hand, I would not, except in extraordinary circumstances—perhaps after an accident—*look* at my right hand to verify that I still had it.

of the external world one just is not playing our game. Less politely, one is nuts; the premise of an external world is constitutive of rationality in much the same way that scientific induction—whose validity also is not demonstrable—is. Suppose a person "based all his major decisions on visions of the future he has when asleep. Furthermore, he has always been wrong. When we point out this fact to him, he replies that he does not care because he has just had a vision that assured him that all his future visions will be accurate. Would we not, *on this basis,* judge him to be irrational?"[8]

Bertrand Russell, however, tried to *reason* (albeit practically) to the conclusion that unobserved objects exist:

> The way in which simplicity comes in from supposing that there really are physical objects is easily seen. If the cat appears at one moment in one part of the room, and at another in another part, it is natural to suppose that it has moved from the one to the other, passing over a series of intermediate positions. But if it is merely a set of sense-data, it cannot have ever been in any place where I did not see it; thus we shall have to suppose that it did not exist at all while I was not looking, but suddenly sprang into being in a new place. If the cat exists whether I see it or not, we can understand from our own experience how it gets hungry between one meal and the next; but if it does not exist when I am not seeing it, it seems odd that appetite should grow during non-existence as fast as during existence. And if the cat consists only of sense-data, it cannot be *hungry,* since no hunger but my own can be a sense-datum to me. Thus the behavior of the sense-data which represent the cat to me, though it seems quite natural when regarded as an expression of hunger, becomes utterly inexplicable when regarded as mere movements and changes of patches of colour, which are as incapable of hunger as a triangle is of playing football.[9]

Russell's argument was more persuasive before the invention of the motion picture and the development of quantum theory, and it relies heavily on a criterion whose relation to truth is obscure: simplicity.

Here is another difficult question, one we shall come back to in Chapter 5, that only practical reason can answer, though again not well. How do we know that there are other minds, since we can never observe another person's mind but only words, actions, brain waves, and other physical phenomena? We use a combination of introspection, observation, and induction. We know (never mind how) that we ourselves have minds, which enable us to do things such as plan and con-

---

8. Brian Skyrms, *Choice and Chance: An Introduction to Inductive Logic* 44 (1966).
9. *The Problems of Philosophy* 23 (1912).

ceal, and we observe that other people appear to do the same things, which—since they seem at least grossly similar to us in other ways—argues that they possess similar mental equipment. But this method of inquiry will not tell us whether animals, some of which also plan and conceal, but in more rudimentary and predictable ways than we, and which do not appear to speak, also have minds, or whether a newborn human infant has a mind. And there is an ambiguity in the concept of mind. When we say of people that they have minds, it is unclear to what extent we are attempting to denote a thing and to what extent we are merely using a shorthand expression for our ignorance of motives, our own and others'.

Of particular importance for law, practical reason can answer some *ethical* questions with a high degree of certainty. It is almost as certain that killing people for pure sport is evil as it is that cats don't grow on trees. Of course, a hundred years from now this particular ethical certitude (which may well depend on man's being a "social animal"—a condition that conceivably could change) may be overthrown; but then a hundred years from now it may be possible to grow cats on trees.[10] Not only can practical reason yield the occasional ethical certainty; logic and science cannot. This point is overlooked in Arthur Leff's influential skeptical writings on law. To show the futility of normative discourse in law, Leff asserts the impossibility of establishing in a secular age even the most elementary moral propositions: "There is today no way of 'proving' that napalming babies is bad except by asserting it (in a louder and louder voice), or by defining it as so."[11] The example is mawkish and incomplete; the morality of "napalming babies" may depend on whether it is an inevitable accident in a just war, a readily avoidable accident in such a war, or a deliberate act of terrorization in an injust war.[12] But forget all that; the pertinent point is Leff's misunderstanding of the nature of knowledge. The quoted passage assumes that the only things we really know are the things that have been proved. Yet if a proof is deductive, the conclusion of the proof will be true (other than by accident) only if the premises are true and the deduction is valid; and

10. Will we still call them cats when that happens? I think so; test-tube babies are human, after all. But the question of how much and what kinds of change are consistent with continued identity is a profound one.

11. Arthur Allen Leff, "Economic Analysis of Law: Some Realism about Nominalism," 60 *Virginia Law Review* 451, 454 (1974). See also Leff, "Unspeakable Ethics, Unnatural Law," 1979 *Duke Law Journal* 1229.

12. Leff no doubt had in mind the Vietnam War, and no doubt thought it an injust war.

the premises are not the result, but the beginning, of the proof. If the premises are the result of another proof, this simply pushes the quest for certainty back a step. The ultimate premise has to be an intuition—something we cannot help believing—rather than the conclusion of an earlier proof. If a proof is inductive rather than deductive—and if you believe in inductive "proofs"—its validity depends on the accuracy and number of observations and on the principles of scientific induction, and hence ultimately on our intuitions about perception, causality, and regularity. Our most confident knowledge, therefore, is intuitive, because intuitions lie at the base of all our proofs and reasoning and because it is always possible to make a mistake in the process of proof itself (as by omitting premises). So the fact that we cannot *prove* that napalming babies is bad does not imply that we cannot *know* that it is bad. In fact our intuition that wanton killing is bad is as strong as many of the intuitions on which our knowledge of the empirical world is founded, and stronger than many conclusions of proofs. Difficulties arise only when different people have different and inconsistent moral intuitions regarding the issue at hand. This problem, which is obscured by the tautological character of so many moral propositions (we know murder is wrongful because the word "murder" means deliberate *and unjustified* killing), is a serious one, but it has nothing to do with the idea, which is false, that knowledge is limited to what can be proved.

Let me change Leff's example. You and I are driving; you are the driver and I the passenger. A child appears in the middle of the road, and you turn to me and say, "Should I try to avoid killing the child?" This question would mark you as crazy, just as if you told me that you had discussed this book with Plato last night. So at some level there is epistemological parity between science and morals. Of course, it may not be the interesting level.

If practical reason can yield knowledge about metaphysical, scientific, and ethical issues, not always but sometimes, why not sometimes about law as well? Then just because the methods of exact inquiry are rarely usable by judges it would not follow that most judicial decisions were willful or arbitrary, in the sense of determined by the judge's personality or temperament, by class bias ("politics"), or by the flip of a coin.[13] The

13. Notice that anyone who did believe in the radical indeterminacy of judicial decision making would think it exceedingly perverse that judges should ever impose sanctions (as they routinely do) for the filing of frivolous cases. See Sanford Levinson, "Frivolous Cases: Do Lawyers Really Know Anything at All?" 24 *Osgoode Hall Law Journal* 353 (1986).

argument that most judicial decisions are of that character is not well supported.[14] Not only is its theoretical base (Leff-tist skepticism) weak; its empirical support is shallow. It depends heavily on an impression of rampant indeterminacy that is a result of sampling bias. A sample of cases litigated to judgment will be biased in favor of uncertainty because when the outcome is clear the parties will usually settle the case before trial. Even within this biased sample, not *all* cases will be uncertain. Many cases are litigated *à outrance* not because the case is difficult but because the parties or their lawyers are obtuse or stubborn or because of acrimony arising from the underlying dispute or from the litigation itself. But when a litigated case is easy, the judges often decide it without a published opinion, so the universe of reported appellate cases is heavily weighted in favor of difficult cases. And this is above all true of the Supreme Court's decisions, which crowd the horizon of many academic lawyers to the virtual exclusion of decisions by other courts. Yet, while not all cases are difficult, many are; and while some of these can be resolved by logic, science, or practical reason, a considerable residue of cases is left—and those the very ones the profession cares the most about—against which logic and science will be unavailing and practical reason will break its often none-too-sturdy lance. Moreover, the methods of practical reason necessary to resolve the difficult case may not be methods of *legal* reasoning in a distinctive sense.

Law uses many methods of practical reason. This chapter discusses the two that have received the most attention: reliance on authority and reasoning by analogy. In both the concept of precedent plays a key role. I make two main arguments. The first is that authority plays a different role in law than in science, being essentially political in the former and epistemic in the latter, and indeed that the law's heavy though necessary reliance on authority retards the emergence of a scientific ethos in law. The second is that reasoning by analogy is not a distinctively legal method of reasoning, and may reduce to basing decision on all available information including information contained in previous decisions.

14. As pointed out in John Stick, "Can Nihilism Be Pragmatic?" 100 *Harvard Law Review* 332 (1986); Lawrence B. Solum, "On the Indeterminacy Crisis: Critiquing Critical Dogma," 54 *University of Chicago Law Review* 462 (1987); Joan C. Williams, "Critical Legal Studies: The Death of Transcendence and the Rise of the New Langdells," 62 *New York University Law Review* 429, 471–495 (1987); Brian Langille, "Revolution without Foundation: The Grammar of Scepticism and Law," 33 *McGill Law Journal* 451 (1988); Ken Kress, "Legal Indeterminacy," 77 *California Law Review* 283 (1989).

Authority

In an age not only of science but of hostility to almost all forms of authority, it is easy to forget how many of our beliefs, including scientific ones, are based on authority rather than on investigation.[15] An example is the proposition that (roughly speaking) the earth revolves around the sun. Neither an observable nor a readily inferable fact (unlike the roundness of the earth), it is simply the theory that best organizes the data. Few of us have a first-hand acquaintance with the data or can replicate the reasoning that connects them with the theory. Common sense and intuition support the discredited geocentric theory. We believe in the heliocentric theory only because scientists are unanimous in believing it and because we are taught to defer to scientific consensus on matters classified as scientific (unless it collides with our religious beliefs!), of which the earth's revolution is today one. Of course such deference is, by and large, a very sensible policy; it has survival value. It is not merely blind obedience, especially since what is to be classified as a scientific question is jointly determined by the scientific and lay communities.

"Authority" means something else in law. Legal decisions are authoritative not when they command a consensus among lawyers, corresponding to a consensus among scientists, but when they emanate from the top of the judicial hierarchy. The only parallel between this sort of political authority and the intellectual authority to which laypeople defer in forming scientific beliefs is that judicial decisions made at the top of the hierarchy are somewhat more likely to be correct than those of judges lower down. The higher judges are more carefully selected (on average, not in every instance, of course) and have a broader view as well as the benefit of the lower judges' thoughts on the case and additional briefing and argument by the lawyers. But this presumption of superior correctness is weak. And even if all the judges up and down the line agree, their decisions have much less intrinsic persuasiveness than unanimous scientific judgments have, because judges' methods of inquiry are so much feebler than scientists' methods. (Does anyone doubt, as Justice Robert Jackson once remarked, that if there were a

15. For good discussions, see Richard T. De George, *The Nature and Limits of Authority,* ch. 3 (1985); W. V. Quine and J. S. Ullian, *The Web of Belief* 54–63 (2d ed. 1978); Price, note 2 above, lecture 5; Putnam, note 5 above, at 186; C. A. J. Coady, "Testimony and Observation," 10 *American Philosophical Quarterly* 149 (1973). For discussions of authority in law, see note 35 below.

court above the Supreme Court a large fraction of the Supreme Court's decisions would be reversed?)[16] This is why the legal profession would look askance at a judge who cultivated a close personal relationship with the members of the court above him in the hope that a better understanding of their values and beliefs would enable him to predict their decisions more accurately. Society does not have such confidence in the superior wisdom of the higher judges that it wants their judicial inferiors to abdicate all independent judgment.

Another reason not to place too much weight on the fact that many judicial decisions are unanimous (even in the Supreme Court)[17] is that few judges will write or even note a dissent in every case in which they disagree with the majority. And sometimes when a case is indeterminate but not highly charged ideologically, some, maybe most, members of the court will lack a powerful conviction about how it should be decided and will defer to a colleague who does have such a conviction—without necessarily agreeing in any strong sense with him. Finally, while there is very little explicit vote trading in appellate courts, judges do make efforts to minimize disagreement with each other and as a result will on occasion go along with the strongly expressed conviction of a colleague, even if their impulse is to disagree.[18] This is particularly likely within factions of a factionalized court.

Admittedly it is a legal convention—though one not fully shared by the rest of the community or even by the entire legal profession—that a decision foursquare in accord with a recent decision by the highest court of the jurisdiction is "correct" by virtue of its conformity to authority. But it is a weak convention. A lawyer who loses a case in the Supreme Court, a judge who is reversed by the Court, a law professor commenting on the Court's latest (and let us say unanimous) decision—none of these is speaking nonsense, or even violating professional etiquette, if he says the decision is wrong. Our legal discourse is not so positivistic that one is forbidden to appeal to a "higher law" even after the oracles of the law have spoken; nor need the appeal be couched in such terms. Even when the latest decision is admitted to be "on all fours" with a string of earlier ones, it is possible to argue that it is incorrect because

16. Brown v. Allen, 344 U.S. 443, 540 (1953) (concurring opinion).

17. For the statistics on how many, see Frank H. Easterbrook, "Agreement among the Justices: An Empirical Note," 1984 *Supreme Court Review* 389.

18. For an empirical study of the extent to which recorded dissents understate disagreement among judges, see Justin J. Green, "Parameters of Dissensus in Shifting Small Groups," in *Judicial Conflict and Consensus: Behavioral Studies of American Appellate Courts* 139 (Sheldon Goldman and Charles M. Lamb eds. 1986).

those decisions were wrong too. (Yet in another and equally valid sense, judges usually are correct to follow precedent.) Vast areas of established jurisprudence are weakly grounded, in the sense of resting on highly contestable precedents; and indeed a common symptom of formalist discourse is to treat a decision as a *reason* for, rather than as the source of, the holding for which the decision is cited, as if the decision were a theorem in Euclid or the outcome of a scientific experiment rather than a political act.

The feet-of-clay problem is conspicuous in the common law. A decision may be authoritative by virtue of a previous decision that is authoritative by virtue of a decision previous to it and so on until one reaches the first decision in the chain of precedent—but what then? That decision cannot be validated by reference to binding precedent. It was a policy decision, which is to say a political decision although usually not a partisan political decision.

The political foundations of precedent are important to emphasize lest we be tempted to draw an analogy between decision according to precedent and the conservative epistemic procedure summed up in Quine's (and before him William James's) notion of a web of belief. When a discovery in logic or mathematics or science is made that we accept as true and that is at variance with our existing beliefs, we do not chuck out *all* the old beliefs; instead we try to fit the new discovery into our belief system in the way that will cause the least perturbation in the system. We try—it is the efficient procedure—to accommodate the new discovery by adjusting the periphery of our epistemic system rather than by changing the core. (Nonliteral interpretation of Genesis is an example.) In a superficially similar sense, the law tries to accommodate doctrine to altered conditions with as little change as possible; this is one way of describing stare decisis, the policy of generally abiding by precedent. All that the comparison shows, however, is that at a sufficiently high level of abstraction there are many analogies between science and law (and abstraction is one of them, as I said in the last chapter). At the operational level there are few. The law does not cling to the old verities because it is an efficient epistemic strategy to give ground slowly in areas of apparently warranted certitude, but because stability of legal obligation is an important social policy. The legal core is not a body of principles validated by scientific method or by robust common sense; it is a set of policy decisions, some made long ago under different social conditions. To give up, in the face of anomalies, *Marbury v. Madison,* or *Erie R. R. v. Tompkins,* or the "right of privacy" decisions on which the dissenting Justices in *Bowers v. Hardwick* relied would not cause the same epistemic wrench as giving up the proposition that $2 + 2 = 4$ or that all men are mortal.

Authority in intellectual matters is best understood as a transmission belt that carries news of scientific or other intellectual discovery to persons lacking the time or background to verify the discovery themselves and that also authenticates the discovery for them. Authority in law is different. Judicial decisions are authoritative because they emanate from a politically accredited source rather than because they are agreed to be correct by individuals in whom the community reposes an absolute epistemic trust. The trappings of judicial authority—the robe, the elaborate deference, the solemn rhetoric, and so forth—are clues to the political nature of that authority. Another clue is the doctrine of precedent itself, which in one sense is a refusal to correct errors—a posture that would be thought bizarre in scientific inquiry.

The hierarchical structure of a legal system and the desire for stability that is encapsulated in the doctrine of stare decisis may advance "justice" in a variety of senses, by making judicial decisions more acceptable to the lay public and by reducing uncertainty, but they impede the search for truth. Justification in a scientific sense involves mounting, meeting, and overcoming challenges.[19] Beliefs that are not challenged tend to be weakly grounded—especially when challenge is actively discouraged. Systems of thought that emphasize hierarchy, tradition, authority, and precedent disvalue the kind of critical inquiry that tests belief and advances knowledge, and as a result the truths that such systems accept are not robust. This is notoriously true of religion, an activity in which the perceived costs of free inquiry are often very high.[20] It is also true of law, and is one reason that the scientific attitude is not at home in the legal enterprise.

19. See, for example, Carl Wellman, *Challenge and Response: Justification in Ethics* 128, 167 (1971). In John Dewey's words, "In every instance, from passing query to elaborate scientific undertaking, the art of knowing criticizes a belief which has passed current as genuine coin, with a view to its revision. It terminates when freer, richer and more secure objects of belief are instituted as goods of immediate acceptance . . . Starting from one good, treated as apparent and questionable, and ending in another which is tested and substantiated, the final act of knowing is acceptance and intellectual appreciation of what is significantly conclusive." *Experience and Nature* 428–429 (1929). Of course this is an idealized picture of science; real science contains examples of appeals to authority in approximately the legal sense. See David L. Hull, *Science as a Process: An Evolutionary Account of the Social and Conceptual Development of Science* 374 (1988).

20. See, for example, Douglas Laycock and Susan E. Waelbroeck, "Academic Freedom and the Free Exercise of Religion," 66 *Texas Law Review* 1455, 1456–1458 (1988), discussing how much academic freedom is optimal for the Catholic Church.

To be blunt, the *ultima ratio* of law is indeed force—precisely what is excluded by even the most latitudinarian definitions of rationality. Rationality "is *simply* a method of being open and curious, and of relying on persuasion rather than force."[21] Law is not characteristically "open and curious," and it relies on force as well as on persuasion. If you ask how we know that Venus exerts a gravitational pull on Mars, the answer is that the people who study these things agree it does. If you ask how we know that the Fourteenth Amendment forbids the states to prohibit certain abortions, the answer is that the people who have the political power to decide the issue—namely, the Justices of the Supreme Court—have so determined by majority vote.

The example of abortion brings to light another important difference between authority in science and authority in law. In general, the more scientists, textbooks, and so on that endorse a scientific proposition the more warranted we are in accepting it. But the more cases that endorse a proposition the shakier it may be. Remember that people are unlikely to litigate a dispute if the judicial outcome is certain. If an issue keeps being relitigated this may be because the litigants are uncertain whether the court will stick to its position, or because they cannot believe the court could have meant what it said, or because they think the court is susceptible to pressure. The court's reaffirmation of its position in the face of repeated challenges may show that the position is robust, but alternatively may be the prelude to the abandonment of the position.

All this said, there are many judicial decisions—and many legal propositions not requiring judicial endorsement—that not only all judges but all lawyers would agree were correct. Laypersons are entitled to accept those decisions and propositions as "authoritative" in the approximate sense that scientific consensus is authoritative for laypersons. And there are many questions about which scientists disagree, although not too much should be made of this. Scientists have procedures that enable them to answer questions with a high degree of confidence and then move on to other and more difficult questions, so that while at any moment the scientific community is full of controversy there is a sense that scientific knowledge is growing continuously. That sense is missing in law. We do not think, for example, that although the question whether and to what extent the Constitution should be interpreted to protect sexual freedom is undoubtedly a difficult one, the legal community will eventually answer it and move on to other questions. The

---

21. Richard Rorty, "Is Natural Science a Natural Kind?" in *Construction and Constraint: The Shaping of Scientific Rationality* 49, 71 (Ernan McMullin ed. 1988).

question may eventually cease to be troubling, but not because it will have been answered to the satisfaction of all reasonable persons. It is not a question but a profound social problem. We cope with, we manage, we outgrow—but we rarely solve—such problems. This lack of closure, of convergence,[22] of progressivity—the sheer interminability of so much legal debate—makes the problem of legal indeterminacy fundamentally different from that of scientific or mathematical indeterminacy. Another difference is that the scientific community itself largely determines the field of its inquiries; it is not forced to butt its head against a stone wall.[23] Judges decide virtually all issues society flings at them, however intractable the issues may be. Occasionally the judges will balk, notably in cases raising "political questions." But this is a term of art (and one decreasingly invoked); many conventionally justiciable legal disputes are political to their core. Formalists seek to constrict the range of justiciable issues, while prudentialists in the style of the late Alexander Bickel want the courts to postpone as long as possible intervening in highly charged political issues; I noted in Chapter 1 that *Bowers v. Hardwick* would have provided an apt occasion for ducking a hot issue in the name of prudence. But judges rarely heed such advice nowadays, and anyway they do not escape politics when they draw their horns in for political reasons,[24] just as they do not escape politics when they use political reasoning to create a rule that thereafter can be applied deductively, mechanically.

I therefore question David Brink's suggestion that we can appeal to the example of science to demonstrate that changes in legal rules are consistent with law's being determinate.[25] The suggestion is, however, based on a plausible criticism of what used to be the standard philosophical account of meaning. In that account the meaning of a word is given by its definition (the identifying properties conventionally associated with it) and in turn determines the extension, or reference, of the

22. The proposition that science is "converging" on the "truth" is, like other versions of scientific realism, controversial. See, for example, Ian Hacking, *Representing and Intervening: Introductory Topics in the Philosophy of Natural Science* 55–57 (1983). It is not essential to my argument.

23. See Richard W. Miller, *Fact and Method: Explanation, Confirmation, and Reality in the Natural and the Social Sciences* 133–134 (1987). Of course social and political factors play a role in guiding scientific research; but only in totalitarian societies are scientists forced to do research that they consider scientifically barren.

24. See Jan G. Deutsch, "Neutrality, Legitimacy, and the Supreme Court: Some Intersections between Law and Political Science," 20 *Stanford Law Review* 169 (1968).

25. See David O. Brink, "Legal Theory, Legal Interpretation, and Judicial Review," 17 *Philosophy and Public Affairs* 105 (1988).

word (the things it names). The standard account implies that modern scientists know no more about the "atom" than Democritus did, because they define the word differently and therefore it has a different extension. This is implausible; what is "out there" also affects the meaning of the word.[26] Therefore, Brink argues, we should not be troubled by the fact that the words "cruel and unusual punishments" meant something different to the authors of the Eighth Amendment from what they mean to us; we simply know more about cruel and unusual punishments than they did. But though it seems reasonably clear, at least to one of scientific-realist bent, that the universe contains objects of the sort that Democritus was groping for and that modern scientists have a much better grip on, it is unclear that our social universe contains objects or entities—cruel and unusual punishments—toward which both the authors of the Eighth Amendment and modern judges and scholars were (are) groping. Punishments there were and are, but the characterizing of them as cruel and unusual is an act that has no close counterpart in physics. The physical environment contributes to scientific meaning; the counterpart contribution of reality to legal meaning is unclear. Not always: for example, there *are* monopolies "out there," and thanks to the progress of economic science we know more about them than the framers of the Sherman Act did. Whether there are cruel and unusual punishments out there—whether they are more than unstable local cultural artifacts—may be doubted. I do not mean to depreciate the legal prohibition, or to contend that there are no applications of it that would command a consensus among lawyers and judges, or to deny that there are scientific questions on which no consensus has formed. But the quest for the meaning of the Eighth Amendment is not in my view fruitfully described as a quest for greater knowledge of what has always been sitting out there in some political or social counterpart of physical space. I add that even my Sherman Act example is ambiguous, since we are not *sure* that the Act's framers were trying to talk about what we call a monopoly.

The "incommensurability" thesis inspired by the work of Thomas Kuhn is pertinent. In its most radical form[27] the thesis denies that there is scientific progress, by asserting that every scientific revolution involves a change in the frame of reference rather than an advance along a common path. The implication is that for Aristotle, Ptolemy, the

26. See Hilary Putnam, *Representation and Reality* 12–14, 32, 36 (1988).

27. To which Kuhn himself does not subscribe. See Thomas S. Kuhn, *The Structure of Scientific Revolutions* 169–170, 198–207 (2d ed. 1970).

medieval Christian church, and even modern sailors, the sun and the other heavenly bodies *do* revolve around the earth, because that is the simplest and most fruitful cosmology for their purposes. I am dubious. The ambitions of the geocentric school went beyond helping navigators; the geocentric theory was a refutable theory of the structure of the universe, and has been refuted. But the same cannot be said of the "theory" of cruel and unusual punishments held by nineteenth-century judges. It is not a theory that has been falsified as we have learned more about punishment.

The idea that what passes as linear progress actually involves a succession of incommensurable frames of reference has greater application to legal and moral issues than to scientific ones. In a traditional Indian frame of reference suttee makes perfectly good sense; in a Western frame of reference it is barbaric. Neither translation nor mediation between these frames of references seems possible.[28] The issue of capital punishment can be debated fruitfully among persons who believe that deterrence is the dominant consideration in designing a system of punishments, because such persons occupy the same frame of reference. Whether it can be debated fruitfully among persons who disagree about the values at stake in a criminal justice system or who attach radically different weights to those values is unclear.

Reasoning by Analogy

The heart of legal reasoning as conceived by most modern lawyers is reasoning by analogy. This method of practical reason has an impeccable Aristotelian pedigree,[29] but no definite content or integrity; it denotes an unstable class of disparate reasoning methods. This is an important point, not a quibble. With formal logic playing no role in legal reasoning, reasoning by analogy is the principal candidate for a method that

28. This is the answer given by moral relativism, the pros and cons of which are the subject of a vast literature well represented by *Relativism: Interpretation and Confrontation* (Michael Krausz ed. 1989). The issue between the relativists and the absolutists is well stated in Gilbert Harman, "Is There a Single True Morality?" in id. at 363.

29. As noted in what is still the authoritative treatment of reasoning by analogy in law: Edward H. Levi, *An Introduction to Legal Reasoning* 1 n. 2 (1949). See also Martin P. Golding, *Legal Reasoning* 44–49, 102–111 (1983). For compendious philosophical treatments of analogy, see Hilary Putnam, *The Many Faces of Realism: The Paul Carus Lectures* 73–75 (1987); Quine and Ullian, note 15 above, at 90–95. The fallacious quality of much reasoning by analogy is well discussed in Monroe C. Beardsley, *Thinking Straight: Principles of Reasoning for Readers and Writers* 125 (3d ed. 1966) (§11), and in Brian Barry, "On Analogy," 23 *Political Studies* 86 (1975).

will set lawyers apart from everyday reasoners. Informal logic is an important method of reasoning and lawyers can take pride in being good at it. But in part because logic is more often a critical than a constructive tool in law, lawyers who recognize the limitations of logic (not all do) aspire to being good at more than logic, and the "more" is often said to be reasoning by analogy.

Aristotle gives the following example: "If then we wish to prove that [for the Athenians] to fight with the Thebans is an evil, we must assume that to fight against neighbours is an evil. Conviction of this is obtained from similar cases, e.g., that the war against the Phocians was an evil to the Thebans. Since then to fight against neighbours is an evil, and to fight against the Thebans is to fight against neighbours, it is clear that to fight against the Thebans is an evil."[30] Hardly.[31] If the war with the Phocians was an evil to the Thebans, the Thebans must have lost. Why shouldn't the Athenians be optimistic about beating proven losers who probably are in a weakened state? Aristotle's example seems, in fact, either nonsense or induction. It is nonsense if taken to mean that if two things (a war of Athenians against Thebans and a war of Thebans against Phocians) have one property in common (warring against neighbors), they probably have every other property in common (such as experiencing an evil) as well. That is like saying that if A and B have dark hair, and A is a woman, B is probably a woman too. Aristotle's example is induction if taken to mean that experience shows that people who start wars against their neighbors lose—so Athens had better watch out. Induction will often suggest some regularity, some "law," such as that water boils at 212° Fahrenheit or that it is easier to start a war than to stop one, and then we cast about for a theory that might explain why and by doing so might help us avoid false predictions, such as that water will boil at 212° on a mountaintop.

Even without a theory we often reason inductively, with more or less reliability depending on the circumstances. I have owned Volvo automobiles (a total of four) since 1963, and I have been generally satisfied with them. I infer from this experience that if I replace my present Volvo with a new one I probably will be satisfied with the new one too. The prior purchases are "precedents" or "analogies" that create a certain like-

30. *Prior Analytics*, Bk. II, §24, in *The Complete Works of Aristotle: The Revised Oxford Translation*, vol. 1, p. 110 (Jonathan Barnes ed. 1984) (p. 68, col. b, l. 37, to p. 69, col. a, l. 19, of the original Greek text).

31. See Ricardo Miguel Barrera, "Legal Reasoning according to Edward H. Levi: An Epistemological Critique" (unpublished seminar paper, University of Chicago Law School, Jan. 12, 1988).

lihood that I will be satisfied if I buy another Volvo the next time I am in the market for a car. This may be a sensible method of reasoning, and it is hardly touched by the lively philosophical debate, begun by Hume and not yet resolved, over the validity of induction (for one must not confuse philosophical and practical doubts about induction, the latter being the sort of doubt that can land you in the madhouse). But common-sense, practical, everyday induction—well illustrated by the inferential procedure of a baby who burns himself on a stove—is a bit low-keyed to be the core of legal reasoning in a sense flattering to the legal procession.

Can we fancy up our account of induction by speaking of scientific induction instead?[32] If reasoning by analogy is actually induction, maybe there is something to the nineteenth-century formalists' idea that law is an inductive science (see Introduction). If careful study of court cases revealed that promises were never enforced unless there were both an offer and an acceptance, we would infer a rule or principle, corresponding to a law of nature. However, the forms of science may be present where the spirit is absent. Judges and law professors have a freedom in their inductive procedures that would be highly destructive in science. This is the freedom to reject an observation as normatively unsound.[33] It is as if a scientist could say, "I know that the orbit of Mercury is anomalous in Newtonian cosmology, but I shall ignore that ugly fact because it would be nobler if that orbit were different." Or, "I shall deem it to be different." Or, "I shall change it." Judges often and law professors always are free to reject anomalous decisions; they are not imperatively required to reconsider their theories in order to accommodate anomalies. The pressure both to theorize and to adjust theory to observations is correspondingly relaxed.

A related but deeper problem with the "inductive science" concept of law is that the existence of a pattern, although it may create an expectation that it *will* be followed in the future, cannot show that it *should* be followed. The fact that no promise had ever been enforced without both an offer and an acceptance would not be a reason for refusing to enforce the next promise that lacked one or both elements. The inductive method can isolate the common element in the previous cases but cannot establish its indispensability, just as a rule does not create an obli-

32. Recall Cohen's comparison of scientific and legal induction, in Chapter 1; see also Cohen, note 4 above, at 71–72.

33. A point noted by Francis Bacon, the great scientific-legal inductivist. See Paul H. Kocher, "Francis Bacon on the Science of Jurisprudence," 18 *Journal of the History of Ideas* 3, 20 (1957).

gation to follow it. Finally, the deepest problem with scientific induction is also a problem with legal induction. Generalizing from observations is perilous. Water will boil at a lower temperature than 212° Fahrenheit at the top of a mountain, some wars against neighbors are won by the aggressor, and some Volvos are lemons. Likewise, the fact that ten cases have been decided one way does not prove that the next case, which is bound not to be identical in every respect to any of the previous ones, should be decided the same way too. The selection bias in litigation figures importantly here. Cases identical in all conceivably relevant respects to a string of previous cases are likely to be settled out of court (or never to arise in the first place) rather than to be litigated to the appellate level. Legal induction is likely to fail in just the cases where it is needed.

I have suggested that reasoning by analogy is actually induction, yet the way in which lawyers purport to reason by analogy is often, and misleadingly, syllogistic (technically, enthymematic) rather than inductive. The property lawyer who says that oil and gas are analogous to rabbits, deer, and other wild animals is really proposing that the rule governing property rights in such animals—the "rule of capture"—is an instance of a more general rule that subsumes oil and gas: the rule that there are no nonpossessory property rights in fugitive resources. The problem is then to justify the general rule, which cannot be done either syllogistically or analogically.

There is still another sense in which lawyers and other practical reasoners can be said to reason by analogy. Analogies, viewed simply as instances similar to the problem at hand (examples, anecdotes) rather than as steps in a logical demonstration or even as the pieces in a regular pattern (the Volvo and contract examples) on which an inductive inference might be based, provide a fund of ideas and information on which to draw in deciding what to do. It is common sense that before a staff officer formulates a plan for a military campaign he consider "precedent" in the form of similar campaigns in the past; maybe that is all Aristotle meant by his military example. Previously decided cases supply lawyers and judges with a wealth of facts, reasons, and techniques pertinent to how a new case should be decided. (Admiralty's use of the deodand analogy is a dramatic example.) Cases are vicarious experiences.

The use of cases as informative analogies must be distinguished from their use as authorities, that is, from the policy of decision according to precedent. All analogies are, from the user's standpoint, precedents— that is, things that go before—whether or not they are authoritative.

Paying attention to precedents thus does not commit one to stare decisis; the issues of authority and analogy are distinct. The use of analogy, example, anecdote—and hence of "precedent" in the nonauthoritative sense—is inevitable in fields where theory is weak, as it is in military science, in advertising, in law, and in many other fields of human endeavor. I merely question whether reasoning by analogy, when distinguished from logical deduction and scientific induction on the one hand and stare decisis on the other, deserves the hoopla and reverence that members of the legal profession have bestowed on it. Obviously if one has a case that raises for the first time the question whether automobile manufacturers should be liable for negligence to their ultimate consumers,[34] one will want to find out what previous cases said about similar questions of liability, such as the liability of drug manufacturers to the ultimate consumers of drugs. That is not a reasoning procedure special to law; it is like asking other owners of Volvos what their experience has been or seeing how other city-states have fared in wars against their neighbors. And one can conduct such canvasses with only the vaguest sense (it need not even be conscious) of what counts as "similar" or "analogous" instances, although a judgment of similarity or analogy presupposes some, and possibly extensive, categorization. But unless a precedent is authoritative in the sense of announcing a major premise that cannot be questioned, it can be a source only of data that are anecdotal in character or of reasons, considerations, values, policies.

The qualification in the last sentence needs to be emphasized: a previous case may be authoritative by virtue of stare decisis.[35] And the more precedents there are on a particular point the stronger the tug of stare decisis *may* be (recall the qualification noted in the preceding section). But counting cases to determine the force of stare decisis is not reasoning by analogy; it is weighing authority. These are different—even opposed—methods of appealing to a previous case, and it is remarkable that lawyers and judges run them together so often. When cases are

---

34. MacPherson v. Buick Motor Co., 217 N.Y. 382, 111 N.E. 1050 (1916)—Cardozo's classic manipulation of precedent—discussed in Levi, note 29 above, at 9–24.

35. For illuminating discussions of precedents as authorities, see Frederick Schauer, "Precedent," 39 *Stanford Law Review* 571 (1987); Charles W. Collier, "Precedent and Legal Authority: A Critical History," 1988 *Wisconsin Law Review* 771; Max Radin, "Case Law and Stare Decisis: Concerning *Präjudizienrecht in Amerika,*" 33 *Columbia Law Review* 199 (1933). Schauer emphasizes, as do I, the close parallels between the use of precedent in law and its use in everyday life. See especially 39 *Stanford Law Review* at 602–604. On logical conundrums created by decision according to precedent, see Laurence Goldstein, "Some Problems about Precedent," 43 *Cambridge Law Journal* 88 (1984), and references cited there.

viewed as experiences rather than as authorities, reasoning by analogy is a method of undermining legal certitude (at least initially) rather than of establishing it—a method by which established principles are subjected to continual retesting in the crucible of new cases. If the principles survive the tests, they are strengthened; the analogy to fallibilist theories of science should be apparent. But the new cases are tests, not mere instantiations, of the principles. When as in this example we think of law on the model of science, we challenge rather than celebrate law's hierarchical and authoritarian character. We come to see law as an uneasy compromise between science, where inquiry is sovereign, and theology, where authority is sovereign.

In defense of reasoning by analogy it is tempting to point out that human beings have an innate capacity for recognizing patterns, an innate standard of similarity.[36] This is what enables us to recognize faces after an interval and objects seen from a new angle. A set of cases can compose a pattern. But when lawyers or judges differ on what pattern it composes, their disagreement cannot be resolved either by an appeal to an intuitive sense of pattern or by the methods of scientific induction.

Nor will it do to emphasize the importance of analogy in the workings of the scientific—or the legal—imagination.[37] To see one problem as being like another that has already been solved is indeed to place the new problem on the road to solution. But here the difference between a logic of discovery and one of justification kicks in; analogy belongs to the former rather than to the latter. It is one thing to see oil and gas as analogous to rabbits and foxes, and another to justify the same (or different) legal treatment. To take a scientific example, suppose there is a form of radiation that is powerful enough to destroy a malignant tumor but that will also destroy the tissues through which it passes en route to the tumor. By analogy to the case of an attacking force that splits into small groups, which enables the fortress to be attacked from all sides at once, the tumor can be treated safely and effectively by directing low-intensity beams on it from different directions, so that it receives a

36. See Howard Margolis, *Patterns, Thinking, and Cognition: A Theory of Judgment* (1987) (esp. pp. 113–114); W. V. O. Quine, "Natural Kinds," in *Naturalizing Epistemology* 31 (Hilary Kornblith ed. 1985).

37. For examples from science, see Andrew Pickering, *Constructing Quarks: A Sociological History of Particle Physics* 12, 407 (1984); Mary Hesse, *Revolutions and Reconstructions in the Philosophy of Science,* ch. 4 (1980). The use of numbers for counting and other computation is in a sense reasoning by analogy. And there are important examples in philosophy as well, Plato's cave being only the best known; we shall encounter another example in Chapter 11, in connection with Judith Jarvis Thomson's views on abortion.

higher dose of radiation than do any of the tissues through which the beams pass.[38] The analogy is fine; but it is not *evidence* for the efficacy of the medical treatment and would not be cited in a paper writing up the discovery. It does not belong to the logic of justification.

The mere assertion of an analogy may, it is true, have persuasive force in a psychological sense. Metaphors are often persuasive in that sense, and they are a form of analogy. Metaphor is also a form of redescription—an effort to change the way things look—and such efforts are important to intellectual change, including, as I shall note in Chapter 4, doctrinal change in law. But judges aspire to more than rhetorically effective, emotionally compelling, or even perspective-altering expression—and will not be comforted to be told that much of their reasoning is metaphoric—just as they aspire to more than the ability to decide cases on sound but inarticulable grounds.

The limitations of reasoning by analogy are but highlighted when it is praised as a method of making sure that judges take only one step at a time, that is, create law incrementally.[39] First, the admonition does not help the judge decide whether to take each step; it merely licenses him to take small steps. Second, a series of small steps can add up to a giant stride, and although on the one hand moving incrementally gives judges a chance to stop as soon as experience demonstrates the error of their ways, on the other hand it may conceal from them the magnitude of the change they are cumulatively effecting. The latter tendency may well dominate, given the limited feedback that judicial decision makers receive (see Chapter 3). Third, there is no metric for determining the social, political, or economic "distance" between a prior, "analogous" case and the present case. The judge who analogizes oil and gas to rabbits and foxes may think he is taking a small step; actually he is impeding the efficient exploitation of valuable resources.[40] Fourth and related, argument by analogy and the closely related technique of the

38. See John H. Holland et al., *Induction: Processes of Inference, Learning, and Discovery* 289–295 (1986).

39. See Joseph Raz, *The Authority of Law: Essays on Law and Morality* 180–210 (1979).

40. The "rule of capture," on which see Howard R. Williams and Charles J. Meyers, *Oil and Gas Law*, vol. 1, §§203.1, 204.4 (1988), makes sense when applied to things that are not scarce, such as rabbits and foxes in the period when the rule was developed. It makes no sense when applied to scarce resources, such as oil and gas. By not allowing rights to future use to be obtained, the rule creates an incentive to exploit the resource as quickly as possible—which is too quickly. See, for example, Richard J. Pierce, Jr., "State Regulation of Natural Gas in a Federally Deregulated Market: The Tragedy of the Commons Revisited," 73 *Cornell Law Review* 15, 20–23 (1987).

legal fiction are often used to disguise change as continuity, making it difficult to evaluate or even to understand legal development.[41]

The last point illustrates the rhetorical function of citing previous cases in a judicial decision. Or, rather, rhetorical functions; citations of previous cases are also used to disguise fiat as reason, to establish propositions not in dispute and therefore not in need of support, and as sources from which to quote general language that either is truistic or is contradicted by general language in other cases, which the opinion does not cite. Case citations often are used, in other words, to make an opinion look more solid than it really is.[42] But my main point, which I will illustrate with an example of Neil MacCormick's,[43] is that reasoning by analogy, even when it is not rhetorical—or enthymematic, or fallacious, or purely ornamental—is not actually a method of *reasoning,* that is, of connecting premises to conclusions. MacCormick discusses a case in which the plaintiff, despite the absence of contractual or other understandings, was suing to recoup the expenses he had incurred in saving the defendant's property. The court had previously allowed such recoveries when life rather than property was in jeopardy; the question now was whether to decide the property case for the plaintiff too, by analogy to the life-saving case. To answer such a question intelligently requires not skill at spotting analogies but the ability to identify the considerations behind allowing such recoveries when life is at stake, to appraise the force of these considerations when only property is at stake, and to bring to bear any other relevant considerations. Suppose the earlier cases had rested on the idea that the defendant, if asked before the emergency that endangered his life whether he would be willing to reimburse the expenses of someone who saved him, surely would have replied, "Of course!" The question would then be how plausible such an imputation of promissory intent was when something of lesser value to the owner than life was at stake. The earlier cases would be sources of information useful in deciding the present case, but the decision would require a fresh ethical or policy judgment.

The distinction between legal precedent as information and as authority may seem to overlook the fact that the values, considerations, policies, and ethical insights found in previous decisions of the same or a

---

41. See my book *Law and Literature: A Misunderstood Relation* 2–4 (1988).

42. On the manipulative character of judicial rhetoric, see Peter Goodrich, *Legal Discourse: Studies in Linguistics, Rhetoric, and Legal Analysis,* pt. 2 (1987); also *Law and Literature: A Misunderstood Relation,* note 41 above, ch. 6.

43. From his book *Legal Reasoning and Legal Theory* 161–163 (1978).

coequal or a higher court are entitled to greater weight—are more authoritative—in the decision of the present case than are the values, considerations, and so forth that might be gleaned from other sources. But is it more than habit and indolence that causes lawyers and judges to look for the ethical and political materials of judgment in previous decisions rather than in scholarly literature, statistical compendia, and everyday experience? Well, it is a little more; the blinkered vision that results may conduce to greater stability in law, which is a good, although not an unqualified one. And the millions of pages of reported cases do contain much information and ethical insight. But they also contain vast amounts of misinformation and obsolete ethics, and there are no reliable techniques for winnowing the wheat from the chaff.

A careful study would, I predict, show that judges who know more about a particular field of law are less deferential toward precedent than equally able (and no more "restrained") judges who know less about the same field. This is so even when the greater knowledge of the specialist judge is due simply to a deeper immersion in the case law rather than to a study of nonlegal sources of wisdom as well. That immersion will bring to light conflicts among the precedents that will undermine the claim of any single one to be authoritative. A field of law looks less tidy to a specialist than to a generalist. A related but weaker hypothesis is that a specialized court will be less deferential to precedent and therefore less (rather than, as generally believed, more) predictable than a generalist court. It is a weaker hypothesis because the precedents to which the specialized court will be asked to defer will for the most part be its own precedents, the product of specialists rather than of generalists.

A specialist court should not be censured for paying less attention to precedent than the generalist court does. Precedent is only one source of information on which to base judgment, and the specialist court has additional sources that the generalist court lacks. Against this it can be argued that in seeking sources of guidance the judge is looking not only for relevant experience but also for relevant commitments, and these are more likely to be found in judicial opinions than in statistical compilations or academic commentary. But the question is the role of precedent in cases where there is no previous decision squarely on point. Why must dicta (that is, the nonauthoritative parts of the judicial opinion) be given more weight than the considered views of scholars who may have spent years studying the particular legal problem involved, or of social scientists who may have spent a professional lifetime in systematic study of the pertinent social realities, merely because the judge is an official?

Even if judges should not feel limited to previous cases in seeking guidance in deciding novel ones, it can be argued that they should not stray outside the bounds of conventional moral and political opinion in their society—and therefore that an American judge is not to decide cases on the basis of the ethics of Marx or Nietzsche, but is to stay within the circle marked out by the values that have already gained a footing in our legal traditions. I wonder. How does a new value get into the legal tradition? By legislation or constitutional enactment only? Can a judge never be the first person to bring a new value, a new political or ethical insight, into the law?

I am not arguing that academic or other extrajudicial texts should have the same authority that judicial decisions have. A judicial holding normally will trump even a better-reasoned academic analysis because of the value that the law places on stability, a value often though not always promoted by sticking by what has been decided. I am arguing only that when there is no holding, when there are only dicta, their weight ought to be determined by their intrinsic merit rather than by their official source. A possible counterargument is that the core of distinctively legal reasoning lies precisely in distinguishing between precedent as authority (holding) and precedent as information (dictum). Precedents can be read broadly or narrowly, and deciding which course to follow in a particular case is often said to be central to the art of lawyering and judging. Maybe, but this has nothing to do with logical or quasi-logical deduction, or even with the handling of analogies. If, read as narrowly as possible, a precedent dictates the decision of a later case, that decision will be a decision based on precedent. If, read that narrowly, the precedent does not control the later case, but the court in the later case chooses to read the precedent more broadly so that it will control, the key to the decision is precisely that choice, a choice not dictated by precedent—a choice as to what the precedent *shall* be. Once the choice has been made, the precedent, viewed as authority rather than example, drops out of the picture. There is no practical difference between on the one hand treating a case as one of "first impression," and on the other hand subsuming it under a previous case after first deciding as a matter of discretion to read the previous case broadly enough to enable the subsumption.[44]

---

44. Hume's discussion of reasoning by analogy in law is thus unexpectedly apt to contemporary American law—as well as pungent: "If direct laws and precedents be wanting, imperfect and indirect ones are brought in aid; and the controverted case is ranged under them by analogical reasoning and comparisons, and similitudes, and correspondencies, which are often more fanciful than real. In general, it may safely be affirmed that jurisprudence is, in this respect, different from all the sciences; and that in many of its nicer

The more narrowly a precedent is interpreted, the less force it has as rule, so that the choice between broad and narrow interpretations of precedent is a choice between more and less dependence on rules relative to standards and implicates the considerations examined in Chapter 1. Those considerations have nothing to do with logic or with reasoning analogically. This is not to deny that they are weighty considerations. Since rules are a necessary component of a rational legal system and precedents are an important source of rules in the Anglo-American legal system, it would be senseless always to read precedents in the narrowest possible manner; there would be no judge-made rules. Suppose that a previous case—involving, let us say, an interpretation of the estoppel defense to the statute of limitations—is "on all fours" with the present one except that in the earlier one the plaintiff had been left-handed and in the present one the plaintiff is right-handed. Could the previous case be "confined" to left-handed plaintiffs? It could not—but only because there is no consideration of policy or ethics that would justify so narrow an interpretation. So, not only does the decision whether to read a precedent narrowly or broadly have nothing to do with logical or analogical reasoning; even ascertaining the lower bound of reading narrowly is independent of these methods of reasoning.

That the distinction between holding and dictum is not hard and fast is shown by the inability of courts to agree on an operational definition of these terms.[45] The reasons for reading a previous decision narrowly are multitudinous, and their weight will determine how much of a previous decision is deemed holding, how much dictum. The reasons include the later court's possession of additional information; the earlier court's lack of considered attention to the issue in question, maybe because it was peripheral to the case before that court; the later court's disagreement with the earlier court's analysis (as opposed to outcome—

---

questions, there cannot properly be said to be truth or falsehood on either side. If one pleader bring the case under any former law or precedent, by a refined analogy or comparison; the opposite pleader is not at a loss to find an opposite analogy or comparison: and the preference given by the judge is often founded more on taste and imagination than on any solid argument. Public utility is the general object of all courts of judicature; and this utility too requires a stable rule in all controversies; but where several rules, nearly equal and indifferent, present themselves, it is a very slight turn of thought which fixes the decision in favour of either party." *An Enquiry Concerning Human Understanding* 308–309 (3d ed., P. H. Nidditch ed., 1975) (App. 3).

45. See discussion in United States v. Crawley, 837 F.2d 291 (7th Cir. 1988); also Peter Goodrich, *Reading the Law: A Critical Introduction to Legal Method and Techniques* 72–73 (1986).

for then the later court would incontestably be rejecting the holding of the previous case rather than anything that could be described as merely dictum); the earlier court's use of overboard language inadvertently encompassing the issue in the present case; the relative unimportance of having fixed rules in the particular field of law involved in the case; and, in short, virtually anything that might make the previous decision an unsuitable or dispensable guide to decision of the present one. The absence of all or most of these considerations would argue for a broad reading. All are considerations of policy, and they happen not to lend themselves to a neat formulaic or algorithmic definition.

This discussion bears on the issue of the proper weight to be given dicta in comparison with unofficial sources of wisdom. The decision to classify a part of an earlier opinion as dictum is a decision to treat it as relatively nonweighty in the present case. This opens the door to consideration of other sources of guidance. And were it more generally recognized that at least in difficult cases—but they are disproportionately represented in litigation—the main significance of precedents is as information rather than as authority, as challenging instances rather than as confirming ones, judges and lawyers might make greater use than they do of nonlegal and comparative materials, which are important sources of information but not of authority. Modern judicial opinions do cite nonlegal materials, sometimes promiscuously, but the vast majority of these citations reflect the reading of the law clerks rather than of the judges. The preoccupation with precedent as authority may be one of the causes of American judges' insensitivity to the ways in which foreign legal systems deal with problems similar to ours, since foreign decisions have no authority in an American court except in the rare case where a question of foreign law is presented.[46] Too many of our judicial opinions contain unexamined assumptions, conventional and perhaps shallow pieties, and confident assertions bottomed on prejudice and folklore.[47]

---

46. Maybe Professor Glendon's brilliant study of foreign approaches to the abortion question will help us overcome our provincialism. See Mary Ann Glendon, *Abortion and Divorce in Western Law* 10–62 (1987). An interesting proposal for upgrading the authority of social science findings in law is made in two articles by Laurens Walker and John Monahan: "Social Science Research in Law: A New Paradigm," 43 *American Psychologist* 465 (1988), and "Social Facts: Scientific Methodology as Legal Precedent," 76 *California Law Review* 877 (1988).

47. Here is a typical example of judicial certitude: "No better instrument has been devised for arriving at truth than to give a person in jeopardy of serious loss notice of the case against him and opportunity to meet it. Nor has a better way been found for generating the feeling, so important to a popular government, that justice has been done." Joint Anti-Fascist Refugee Comm. v. McGrath, 341 U.S. 123, 171–172 (1951) (Frankfurter, J., con-

The point to be particularly emphasized is that in a system of precedent it is the later court that has the whip hand, not the earlier court, the court that created the precedent. The later court decides whether to read the earlier decision broadly or narrowly and, if it cannot be narrowed sufficiently to distinguish the present case, whether to overrule it. That court has the power, and it also has more information, just by virtue of coming later. The decision of how much weight to give the earlier precedent—whether to apply it at all, and if so how broadly—is a pragmatic decision in which the uncertainty that will be created by a too casual attitude toward past decisions—and the additional work that such an attitude will create for the courts both by requiring more time on each case and, as a result of the greater uncertainty, engendering more cases—are compared with the increased risk of error that an uncritical view of past decisions will create. (This discussion contains an echo of Chapter 1; the balance is much like that which must be struck in deciding whether to follow a rule or create an exception.) Reasoning by analogy is not a technique for striking the balance.

A Note on Legal Education

Searching the past for relevant experience and considerations, which I contend is the essence of legal reasoning by analogy, is an important and worthy dimension of practical reason. But it is so ordinary—a word I use not as a pejorative but merely to indicate the remoteness of reasoning by analogy from an inferential technique that might have to be taught, as statistical inference or formal logic has to be taught—that one is led to wonder in just what sense the highly inductive, case-oriented, analogy-saturated "Socratic" method of legal instruction actually teaches reasoning at all, beyond honing the student's skills in identifying contradictions.[48] That is an important qualification—but is

---

curring) (footnote omitted). The only supports offered for these emphatic and nonobvious propositions are a quotation from a speech of Daniel Webster and a quotation from an English judicial opinion. The style suggests a dogmatic rather than an inquiring mind. It is a characteristic judicial style.

48. The "Socratic" method is well discussed in William C. Heffernan, "Not Socrates, But Protagoras: The Sophistic Basis of Legal Education," 29 *Buffalo Law Review* 399 (1980); William Epstein, "The Classical Tradition of Dialectics and American Legal Education," 31 *Journal of Legal Education* 399 (1981); John O. Cole, "The Socratic Method in Legal Education: Moral Discourse and Accommodation," 35 *Mercer Law Review* 867 (1984); Edwin W. Patterson, "The Case Method in American Legal Education: Its Origins and Objectives," 4 *Journal of Legal Education* 1 (1951). A reader of Plato's dialogues will notice genuine

identifying contradictions all that "thinking like a lawyer" comes to? The "Socratic" method familiarizes the student with legal materials, most of them written in the profession's standard style, which exaggerates the uniqueness and the power of the analytical methods that lawyers and judges use. And it imbues the student with that style, at the same time training him to exploit, by means of logic wielded as a critical tool, the indeterminacies in legal materials. To recur to an earlier "analogy," what law school teaches on the methodological side is a language rather than a method of reasoning: a culture, a vocabulary, a set of representative texts and problems. Courses in foreign languages do not claim to teach methods of reasoning.

I have no desire to belittle conventional legal training (which in any event is not all that modern law schools offer). Without it a tedious apprenticeship would be required to equip a person to practice law and would not do so as well. One should recognize, however, the similarity of conventional legal training to the apprenticeship system that preceded and for a long time coexisted with it. The immersion in judicial opinions and other legal materials that is the hallmark of a legal education provides the student from the outset with a simulacrum of practice; he is like an airline pilot training on a simulator. The teacher throws questions at him as would a senior partner and the student answers them by "researching" the legal materials placed before him by the casebook editors.[49]

---

affinities between the method of Socrates depicted in the dialogues and the "Socratic" method of law school instruction. Both Socrates and the Socratic law school professor identify spokesmen of recurrent fallacies and demonstrate by sharp questioning that the spokesmen are deeply confused; by a process of refuting fallacious approaches the true approach emerges. The methods are particularly close when, as is common, the law professor finds a Thrasymachus among his students who thereafter serves as the spokesman for the "law as politics" school. Of course there are also many differences between the two methods, having to do with the difference in subject matters, the difference in the social relationship between the Socratic figure and the other participants in the dialogue, and the ultimate objectives of the exercise.

49. Veblen exaggerated, yet had the kernal of a good point, when he said: "In point of substantial merit the law school belongs in the modern university no more than a school of fencing or dancing. This is particularly true of the American law schools . . . and it is more particularly true the more consistently the 'case method' is adhered to. These schools devote themselves with great singleness to the training of practitioners, as distinct from jurists; and their teachers stand in a relation to their students analogous to that in which the 'coaches' stand to the athletes. What is had in view is the exigencies, expedients and strategy of successful practice; and not so much a grasp of even those quasi-scientific articles of metaphysics that lie at the root of the legal system. What is required and inculcated in the way of a knowledge of these elements of law is a familiarity with their strategic use." Thorstein Veblen, *The Higher Learning in America* 211 (1918).

The cases studied in law school provide not only glimpses of the rules and rhetoric of law but also a kind of surrogate experience of life, and of the particular slices of life (such as crimes, breaches of contract, and racial discrimination) that the lawyer is most likely to encounter in his career at the bar. But I repeat that these voluminous case materials are not a reliable guide to the social phenomena depicted in them.[50] The immersion in cases that is so characteristic of both legal education and legal practice may be less a source of strength than a brute necessity indicative of weakness—a stopgap pending better (more scientific, empirical, interdisciplinary) legal theory rather than a superior alternative to such theory.

This question could itself be examined empirically. If conventional lawyerly experience increases the power of legal analysis, we might expect a judge's performance (something more readily, though not easily, measurable than the performance of a practicing lawyer, by counting citations to the judge's opinions and the number and percentage of his cases that are reversed)[51] to vary systematically with the nature of his experience before appointment to the bench. We might also expect judges having greater experience as practicing lawyers to outperform judges with less such experience, other things (such as education) being equal.

The most important thing that law school imparts to its students is a feel for the outer bounds of permissible legal argumentation at the time when the education is being imparted. (Later those bounds will change, of course.) What "thinking like a lawyer" means is not the use of special analytic powers but an awareness of approximately how plastic law is at the frontiers—neither infinitely plastic, as a Thrasymachus might think, nor rigid and predetermined, as many laypersons think—and of the permissible "moves" in arguing for, or against, a change in the law. It is neither method nor doctrine, but a repertoire of acceptable arguments and a feel for the degree and character of doctrinal stability, or, more generally, for the contours of a professional culture—a professional culture lovable to some, hateful to others.[52]

50. For a court to use Blackstone as authority for the proposition "that natural bonds of affection lead parents to act in the best interests of their children," as in Parham v. J. R., 442 U.S. 584, 602 (1979), is legal reasoning at its most provincial.

51. It should be apparent from earlier discussion why reversal rates cannot be the only measure of judicial performance (just as the best baseball hitter is not the one who strikes out the least). In making this point I admit to vocational bias.

52. Science is a culture too, but a culture of unforced inquiry in a way that law is not.

3 ⤎

Other Illustrations of
Practical Reasoning in Law

Interpretation

If a neighbor, seeing your house on fire, phones you and says, "Your house is on fire," you had better be able to decode the message. To do so you will need a certain linguistic competence, of course—a competence in the comprehension and manipulation of symbols. But you will also need to know something about the speaker's seriousness and reliability, that is, about character, capacity, and intentions. The process of understanding is thus not a logical process, although lawyers and judges often pretend it is, but a matter of understanding people, practices (such as living in houses), and the physical environment (the consequences of fire)— forms of understanding that depend on sharing the same basic life experiences. Alternatively, it is an imaginative process enabled by this sharing. We understand a message by putting ourselves in the speaker's shoes.[1] We imagine that we are seeing a house burn and telling the owner about it, and the congruence between the speaker's intentions and our imaginative reconstruction—the success of the latter—is what enables the communication to succeed. The role of imagination in understanding is one reason you can decode the sentence, "I'll eat my hat," as ironic (another is that it is a well-known idiom). You know you'd never try

---

1. This is not to say that the listener must be able to re-create in his mind an image in the speaker's mind. Suppose, to borrow an example from Gerald MacCallum (based on Wittgenstein—see *The Blue and Brown Books* 3 [1958]), that you ask your assistant to fetch you all the ashtrays he can find for a meeting at which there will be many smokers but you don't know how many (an example that rather dates MacCallum's fine article). It would be idiotic of him to return empty-handed, with the excuse that he was not sure which of the ashtrays he had seen were the ones you had in your mind when you dispatched him on

to eat a hat (even though it's smaller than an elephant), and you assume that I am enough like you in this regard not to try either.[2]

The difference between a logical proposition and a communication can be clarified with the aid of the syllogism "All men are mortal" from Chapter 1. Its conclusion—that Socrates is mortal—is a logical proposition. But if you say to me, "Socrates is mortal," your statement is a communication, and to grasp its meaning I will need to know a lot more than the rules of logic and the contents of the dictionary. The statement may have no intended meaning; you may be a parrot repeating what you heard, without comprehension. I may misunderstand the reference: you may be referring to your pet gerbil, "Socrates," rather than to its Athenian namesake. There may be confusion about the meaning of particular words: by "mortal" you may mean "fallible" rather than bound to die. There may be uncertainty about the mood of the utterance: by emphasizing the first word and pitching the third word higher you may be expressing skepticism about the proposition rather than warranting its truth.

As the last example suggests, the danger of misunderstanding a spoken communication is reduced by the fact that the speaker's inflection and facial expression help dispel ambiguities in his words; it is almost as if inflection and facial expression were additional words. Although inflection does not always dispel ambiguity—it can inject ambiguity, just as additional words can—a listener can seek clarification from the speaker. The potential for misunderstanding a written communication is usually greater. Not always: documents often are drafted at leisure, with special care taken to achieve clarity. But the potential for misunderstanding is great if the document, however carefully written, was written by someone who has since died or by a committee (all of whose members may be dead, too), or is in a foreign language, or was written hundreds of years ago. Interpreting the Constitution involves all these problems except translation from a foreign language—and in some respects eighteenth-century English *is* a foreign language. Even interpreting recently enacted statutes can be a daunting task, because the authors may not have foreseen and addressed—or may have foreseen and decided not to address—the question of meaning or application that

---

the errand. See MacCallum, "Legislative Intent," in *Essays in Legal Philosophy* 237, 256–257 (Robert S. Summers ed. 1968). The visual imagery in my fire example is thus inessential.

2. MacCallum's example of the fallacy of literal-mindedness has the assistant complying with the request to fetch all the ashtrays he can find by ripping some off the walls and stealing others. See id. at 256–257.

has arisen. This last point helps show why the interpretation of judicial opinions is a less serious problem for judges than the interpretation of statutes is. If the previous opinion did not address a question, that is a good reason for not treating the opinion as authoritative on the question and for seeking the answer elsewhere.

Whether one thinks of success in communication as being dependent on the sender's and the recipient's experience of the same relevant practices (such as "smoking" and "getting things" in MacCallum's examples in notes 1 and 2) or on the recipient's exercise of imagination—and these may come to the same thing—the social *distance* between sender and recipient is critical. Normally a person can readily understand what he himself is saying (even if it is complex), because he already is, as it were, in his own shoes. Yet when he reads something he wrote many years ago, at a time when he may have been in a sense a different person, his attempt at imaginative reconstruction may fail. Old married couples understand each other's fragmentary utterances better than a stranger would, because married people grow to be alike by sharing the same experiences (and also by tailoring language to their precise communication needs—the analogy is to customizing a word processor's formats). It is the same with identical twins, with people who have been brought up together, and with people educated in the same way. The closer knit the community that includes the speaker and his audience, the easier the interpretive task. Equivalently, the more homogeneous the interpretive community, the lower the costs of overcoming the inevitable "noise" in the channels of communication: another illustration of the importance of cultural homogeneity in fixing meaning and thereby securing what passes for objectivity.

One can see why the idea that understanding is imaginative reconstruction rather than simple decoding was a Romantic idea:[3] the Roman-

---

3. Notably Schleiermacher's. See Richard E. Palmer, *Hermeneutics: Interpretation Theory in Schleiermacher, Dilthey, Heidegger, and Gadamer* 84-97 (1969). But it is older; it was Vico's idea before it was Schleiermacher's (see, for example, R. G. Collingwood, *The Idea of History* 65 [1946]), and Aristotle's before it was Vico's. And in between Aristotle and Vico was the English judge Edmund Plowden—see Eyston v. Studd, 2 Plow. 459, 467 (1574), discussed in Warren Lehman, "How to Interpret a Difficult Statute," 1979 *Wisconsin Law Review* 489—not to mention the earlier English judges discussed in Theodore F. T. Plucknett, *Statutes and Their Interpretation in the First Half of the Fourteenth Century* (1922). See Harold Dexter Hazeltine, "General Preface," in id. at v, xxii. Aristotle himself had applied the idea to law: "All law is universal but about some things it is not possible to make a universal statement which will be correct. In those cases, then, in which it is necessary to speak universally, but not possible to do so correctly, the law takes the usual case, though it is not ignorant of the possibility of error. And it is none the less correct; for the error is

tics were trying to break down the barriers between individuals. But the idea has only limited utility for the modern judge, particularly in constitutional interpretation. The modern judge has little in common with the draftsmen of the Constitution. It is futile for him to try to put himself in their place in order to figure out whether they would have wanted to strike down laws forbidding abortions, sodomy, antitakeover statutes, affirmative action, the special-prosecutor law, or laws authorizing the censorship of student newspapers or pornographic videocassettes. The relevant practices are not ones we share with the framers. They did not have the experiences we have, they did not know what we know (and we have forgotten much of what they knew), and we haven't a clue to how they would have fitted our experiences to their values. Even the interpretive community that consists of the members of a recent legislature and the judges asked to interpret the legislature's enactments is not at all like one person, a married couple, or a group of friends chatting over lunch.[4]

The Romantic ideal of an imaginative coalescence between writer and reader, when transposed to the legal setting, may be not only impossibly strenuous but unnecessarily so. Even though the hypostatization of a "legislative intent"—a group mind, when even the concept of a single mind is problematic (see Chapter 5)—is an insult to philosophy, statutes and constitutional provisions are purposive utterances. And often their purposes can be discerned from text and context (including what the draftsmen may have said about the text in a committee report or hearings, or in floor debate) and used to answer an interpretive question in

---

not in the law nor in the legislator but in the nature of the thing . . . [Therefore] it is right, when the legislator fails us and has erred by over-simplicity, to correct the omission—to say what the legislator himself would have said had be been present, and would have put into his law if he had known." *Nicomachean Ethics*, Bk. V, §10, in *The Complete Works of Aristotle: The Revised Oxford Translation*, vol. 2, pp. 1795–1796 (Jonathan Barnes ed. 1984) (p. 1137, col. b, ll. 12–24 of the Greek text); to similar effect see *Rhetoric*, Bk. I, §13, in id., vol. 2, p. 2188 (p. 1374 of the Greek text, col. a, ll. 18–36; col. b). See also Raymond B. Marcin, "*Epieikeia:* Equitable Lawmaking in the Construction of Statutes," 10 *Connecticut Law Review* 377 (1978). Jeremy Bentham, *Of Laws in General* 164–165 (H. L. A. Hart ed. 1970), contains an interesting reformulation of Aristotle's point.

4. A problem that Hart and Sacks elided in their influential version of interpretation as imaginative reconstruction by assuming that the legislators are just like the judges. "A court should try to put itself in imagination in the position of the legislature which enacted the measure . . . It should assume, unless the contrary unmistakably appears, that the legislature was made up of reasonable persons pursuing reasonable purposes reasonably." Henry M. Hart, Jr., and Albert M. Sacks, *The Legal Process: Basic Problems in the Making and Application of Law* 1414–1415 (tentative ed. 1958).

a way that advances the cooperative purpose set on foot by the enactment. It may not be necessary to "enter" a legislator's "mind" in order to understand and follow the command in a legislative enactment. It may, however, be necessary to project in the imagination the consequences of alternative interpretations; and the interpretation that has, all things considered, the better consequences may by virtue of that fact be the "correct" interpretation.

The fact that interpretation is a mysterious process, distinct from logic and scientific observation, is not in itself a challenge to law's objectivity. The process by which scientists choose which hypotheses to test, the process Charles Sanders Peirce called "abduction," is mysterious too, but we know it works, because we can verify the results. We can often verify the results of communication as well. If I send out invitations to a party at a specific time and address, I am hypothesizing that the recipients (or some of them) will appear at that time and that address. If they do, the hypothesis is supported, and with it the theory of workable communication from which it is derived. But the type of communication that we call a statute or a constitution cannot be verified, a problem that produces the multiplicity of insecure approaches to statutory interpretation explored in Chapters 9 and 10.

Means-End Rationality

The weatherman has forecast rain, and I must decide whether to take an umbrella when I leave the house. I will consider (very rapidly, perhaps unconsciously) the probability that the forecast is correct, the discomfort of being rained on, the bother of carrying the umbrella, and the probability of losing it. This type of analysis, called cost-benefit analysis by economists and means–end rationality (sometimes "deliberation") by philosophers of practical reason, is important in every department of thought and certainly in legal reasoning. The choice between alternative legal rules often depends on deciding which makes a closer fit with some underlying goal; we saw this in discussing interpretation. But the decisional process is policy or ethical analysis rather than anything unique to law. When the goal is agreed on and it is clear which of two alternative rules, interpretations, or applications is better suited to achieving it, then what I am calling policy or ethical analysis will conduce to a determinate outcome—which is fine but does not identify a distinctive method of *legal* reasoning.

Consider the old jurisprudential chestnut about whether the beneficiary in a will who kills his testator should be permitted to inherit.[5] The case is sometimes analyzed as a conflict between the principle that donative intentions should be honored and the principle that no one should be allowed to profit from his own wrongdoing.[6] An alternative approach dissolves the conflict and demonstrates both the utility of means-end rationality in legal reasoning and the close relationship between it and imagination, the essential faculty for exploring alternative possible states of the world.[7] The approach is to ask whether if the testator had thought about the possibility of being murdered by his heir he would have added to his will a clause disinheriting the murderer. (Notice the analogy to the method used in the preceding chapter to determine whether someone who saves another's life or property should be entitled to reimbursement of his expenses by the rescued person.) Almost certainly the testator would have included such a clause, so his donative intentions are honored by forbidding the heir to inherit, and there is no conflict between legal principles. (This is "imaginative reconstruction" writ small.) This conclusion, although highly satisfactory, owes nothing to legal reasoning in any distinct sense. Another alternative approach, also illustrative of means-end rationality, asks whether disinheriting the murderer is a suitable adjunct to the other sanctions for murder. Either approach provides a framework for answering such further questions as whether the heir should be disinherited if he killed the testator accidentally rather than deliberately.

I have treated the murdering-heir problem as one of adjusting two competing principles of common law, but the analysis of *Riggs* itself (note 5) is complicated by the fact that the murderer was the beneficiary under a will rather than an heir in the technical sense, that is, one who inherits if there is no will. The victim had complied with all the statutory formalities for a bequest, and the statute contained no provision invalidating bequests to a testator's murderer. In order to rule against the murderer the court had to interpret the statute as containing an implied provision to that effect. More realistically, what the court did was to graft an exception onto the statute, the better to carry out in proper Aristotelian fashion—the majority opinion in *Riggs* cites Aristo-

---

5. The best known of the murdering-heir cases is Riggs v. Palmer, 115 N.Y. 506, 22 N.E. 188 (1889).

6. See, for example, Ronald Dworkin, *Law's Empire* 15-20 (1986); and for criticism, Charles Silver, "Elmer's Case: A Legal Positivist Replies to Dworkin," 6 *Law and Philosophy* 381 (1987).

7. For a good discussion of the imaginative dimension of deliberation, see John Dewey, *Human Nature and Conduct: An Introduction to Social Psychology* 189-209 (1922).

tle's discussion of *epieikeia* (equity)—the desires the legislators would have had regarding the question if they had foreseen it.

Vincent Wellman has argued that the fitting of means to ends is, and rightly so, *the* method of justification used in law. Fidelity to precedent is just another consideration—another policy or principle—to be placed in the balance in deciding whether a particular outcome would be a suitable means to the judicial end.[8] So far, so good. But Wellman believes he has identified what is at once a distinctive and an adequate form of legal reasoning, when actually what he has done is describe the making of policy judgments under conditions of often radical uncertainty. Because such judgments, made under such conditions, are unreliable, one is not surprised to find him acknowledging that his theory of law as practical reason "denies that legal statements are true or false."[9] His article illustrates both halves of my thesis: that legal reasoning is not special and that it often does not yield determinate outcomes.

Given the identity of means-end rationality to cost-benefit analysis and the close relationship noted in Chapter 1 between logical reasoning and economic models, such as Learned Hand's formula for negligence, one can understand why economics has made such inroads into law in recent years: the implicit structure of much legal reasoning is economic. The resistance to this development is understandable too. Lawyers and judges are reluctant to admit the degree to which legal reasoning is pervaded by policy considerations, economic or otherwise. Rupert Cross said that "when a judge does consider the pros and cons of each party's case [in a case not ruled by precedent], there is no recognized name for the reasoning."[10] The disconcerting characteristic of this analytic method that dare not speak its name is that different judges are apt to weigh the pros and cons differently.

Even logic can be subsumed under means-end rationality. The lawyer's critical use of logic is a method of promoting consistency. Consistency is valued—logic is valued—because it helps with fitting means to ends. Such fitting is the core of rationality, and logic and rationality are closely related. Unfamiliar though the term is to most lawyers and judges, means-end rationality is closer to the center of the legal enterprise than logic, a term much bandied about by the profession. Or than

8. See Vincent A. Wellman, "Practical Reasoning and Judicial Justification: Toward an Adequate Theory," 57 *University of Colorado Law Review* 45, 87-115 (1985).

9. Id. at 108.

10. *Precedent in English Law* 194 (3d ed. 1977). The full title of Cross's book is pertinent; as we shall see in the next chapter, English judges do not need to make policy judgments as often as American judges.

reasoning by analogy. The key step in deciding whether the rule of capture should be extended from rabbits and foxes to oil and gas, or whether the salvor's right to a reward from life salvage should be extended to property salvage, is to extract a goal from the previous cases or from other sources and then determine which decision in the new case will promote that goal most effectively and at least cost.

I have classified means-end rationality under practical reason, but an alternative classification, which would group interpretation, analogy, and authority together with logic, and exact observation together with means-end rationality, will help us distinguish between formalistic and pragmatic reasoning. The lawyer's hope for the methods in the first group is that they will enable using existing knowledge to answer a new question *with minimal investigation of the new question.* If all A's are B's, and C is an A, then we can conclude that C is a B without examining C to see whether it is a B. Or, if we interpret a statute to forbid X conduct, then to decide whether the statute applies to Y all we need to determine is whether Y is an instance of X, and we may be able to determine this with only a superficial examination of Y. If we had great confidence in reasoning by analogy, we might decide that oil and gas are subject to the rule of capture without knowing anything more about them than that they flow rather than sit quietly in one place. In contrast, means-end rationality and exact observation entail direct scrutiny of the new question, although existing knowledge provides the indispensable jumping-off point for that scrutiny. The two groups of reasoning methods thus differ with respect to willingness to confront the new question on its own terms rather than to insist on answering it exclusively on the basis of old experience. The first group is backward-looking, in the manner of Blackstone, the second forward-looking, in the manner of Bentham. Lawyers tend to be backward-looking. That is why they tend to value precedent as authority, rather than as testing instance: as a reason to act, rather than as information potentially useful in deciding how to act.

Tacit Knowing

Philosophers as different from each other as Michael Polanyi and Gilbert Ryle have emphasized that some of our most complex thinking is tacit, unconscious.[11] The mathematical formula for adjusting one's weight on

11. See, for example, Michael Polanyi, "The Logic of Tacit Inference," in Polanyi, *Knowing and Being: Essays* 138 (Marjorie Grene ed. 1969); Michael Polanyi and Harry

a bicycle to keep from falling is highly complex, yet without knowing the formula people learn to ride bicycles. People follow the incredibly intricate rules of language use (going far beyond what is taught in the name of grammar or syntax or vocabulary) without having any conscious knowledge of those rules, leading Noam Chomsky, Jerry Fodor, and others to conclude that people must have a substantial innate facility for language. Many distinguished writers "write with their pen," and the examples are not limited to literature.[12] So much "thinking" is unconscious that the very concept of "mind" becomes problematic.

Tacit knowledge is important in legal reasoning. Lawyers develop a feel, not fully articulable, for what types of argument are in the legal ballpark, and what are not ("thinking like a lawyer," again). A comparison can be drawn to the native English speaker who corrects the learner's description of a "red large barn." The native speaker is unlikely to be aware of any rule governing the order of adjectives; "red large barn" just doesn't sound right to him. There are plenty of logical "moves" in law that just don't sound right to the experienced lawyer.

One also speaks of lawyers who have "good judgment"—some ineffable compound of caution, detachment, imagination, and common sense. But that is a different phenomenon. Sagacity and judgment owe little to legal training and experience (and much to age), being qualities that are brought to bear on legal methods, materials, and experiences rather than created by them. Young lawyers do not have better judgment than persons of similar age and intelligence in other walks of life.

The fundamental difficulty with using the concept of tacit knowledge to defend a view of law as determinate or legal reasoning as distinctive is that unless the possession of such knowledge is stipulated (as in my language example, in which a native English speaker is defined vis-à-vis a novice as one who knows the tacit rules of English), it can be gauged only by observing the uses to which it is put. We measure the bicycle rider's tacit knowledge by watching him ride; if he keeps falling down,

---

Prosch, *Meaning* 46-65 (1975); Gilbert Ryle, *The Concept of Mind,* ch. 2 (1949) (emphasizing the difference between "knowing how" and "knowing that"). But cf. John Searle, *Minds, Brains, and Science* 51-52 (1984).

12. I give some examples of unconscious literary creativity in my book *Law and Literature: A Misunderstood Relation* 231-232 (1988). Wittgenstein said that when he sat down to write philosophy he had no idea what he was going to say. See *Culture and Value* 17e (G. H. von Wright ed. 1980). Here is the testimony of another distinguished philosopher: "it is only as I write that I discover what I think, and this is almost never what I thought when I began." Donald Davidson, "Postscript to Replies," in *Essays on Davidson: Actions and Events* 253 (Bruce Vermazen and Merrill B. Hintikka eds. 1985).

we conclude that he lacks it. What are the counterparts in law to the rider who keeps his balance and the rider who keeps falling down? The market for legal services provides some criteria for evaluating the performance of practicing lawyers, but the criteria are imperfect because information about causality is sparse; surprisingly little is known about successful technique in law. Enough is known, however, to make clear that skill in legal reasoning, as measured for example by law-school exams, is only a part of that technique, so that observing successful lawyers in action provides incomplete and often misleading evidence of skill at legal reasoning. The evaluation of judicial performance is also difficult, which in turn makes it difficult to determine which judges are well endowed with the requisite tacit knowledge and which poorly endowed.

The underlying problem is that so little is known about the consequences of legal decisions. Not only are the usual methods of scientific verification unavailable but so are the commonplace observations and experiences that enable us to correct our everyday behavior, whether in riding a bicycle, changing a fuse, or assembling a piece of equipment. Common sense cannot answer the question whether the preservation of political or religious freedom requires a broad reading of the First Amendment, or whether the exclusionary rule is needed as an adjunct to the tort remedies against unreasonable police searches.[13] Often when people have difficulty evaluating the output of a process they evaluate its inputs instead. This may be one reason for the emphasis placed by employers (particularly academic employers) on the lawyer's formal credentials. It is easier to determine whether a lawyer did well in law school than whether he is a good lawyer. But it is difficult to monitor even the inputs into judging, let alone its outputs. In this country, judges usually are middle-aged when first appointed to the bench and their academic performance many years earlier is an uncertain predictor of their judicial performance, though not a worthless one. A disproportionate though very small number of distinguished judges have been stellar law students (examples that come immediately to mind are Brandeis, Frankfurter, and Friendly), but some stellar law students have turned out to be undistinguished judges, and in any event it would be a mistake to stock the bench exclusively from the ranks of the academically gifted,

---

13. On the difficulty of evaluating the consequences of law, see, for example, Gerald N. Rosenberg, "Protecting Fundamental Liberties: The Constitution in Context" (unpublished paper, University of Chicago, Department of Political Science, 1988); Richard A. Posner, "The Constitution as an Economic Document," 56 *George Washington Law Review* 4, 27-31 (1987).

even if this were politically feasible. It would deprive the bench of necessary diversity. Academic prowess to one side, we do not know what readily observable traits predict excellent performance in a judge, and only in part is this due to divergent opinions as to what an excellent judge is.

This discussion bears on the question whether law is an autonomous discipline. Perhaps, even if the lawyer's analytical tools are no different from those of everyday life, they can be so sharpened by training and experience as to yield a qualitatively distinct product. The analogy would be to the difference between an amateur musician and a professional one. But it is not a close analogy. We can distinguish between the two musicians by listening to them play; how do we distinguish between lawyers and ordinary reasoners as far as analytical power is concerned? Obviously lawyers are much more comfortable with legal questions. But many questions can be cast as either legal or political (or ethical, or policy) questions—abortion, for example. How do we decide whether it is best to formulate them as legal questions and thus give them to lawyers to decide?

Although of only limited applicability to questions of legal justification, the concept of tacit knowledge does offer a partial antidote to skepticism about the judicial process. When discussing the process, judges and lawyers, including law professors, often seem to ascribe to judges unrealistic capacities for reflection, detachment, and analysis—capacities inconsistent with the conditions under which judges work and with the criteria by which they are selected. As a description of the conscious thoughts of judges this talk is indeed unrealistic and inflated—but so would be a "model" of the bike rider that showed him making continuous mathematical calculations to avoid losing his balance. By virtue of background, training, and experience both judicial and pre-judicial—in part simply by virtue of being a member of society—a judge may be capable of making judgments that can be modeled in highly complex terms even though they are not the terms in which the judge thinks.[14]

14. Compare John Dewey: "Long brooding over conditions, intimate contact associated with keen interest, thorough absorption in a multiplicity of allied experiences, tend to bring about those judgments which we then call 'intuitive'; but they are true judgments, because they are based on intelligent selection and estimation, with solution of a problem as the controlling standard." *How We Think: A Restatement of the Relation of Reflective Thinking to the Educative Process* 124 (1933). And compare J. H. Hexter's contrast (paraphrasing Coke and Hale) between the common lawyer's immersion in and long study of particulars, leading to "erudite experienced alertness," with the logician's "analytical deductive efficiency." "Thomas Hobbes and the Law," 65 *Cornell Law Review* 471, 485 (1980).

So there may be great judicial decisions—yet we may be unable to determine which ones they are!

This last observation recalls the distinction between the formation and the justification of beliefs, decisions, and actions. Tacit knowing is a way of deciding to (or how to) do something, but it is not a way of justifying the decision or action. The only justification is in the doing or, as in my language example, in the saying. In correcting the word order in "red large barn" you don't *defend* the rule that an adjective of size precedes one of color, and probably you are not even aware that there is such a rule. You just say it correctly. When we speak of legal reasoning we normally have in mind the articulation of the principles and other considerations that show that a decision is correct. Such articulation cannot exhibit or give proof of tacit knowing.

Submitting to the Test of Time

An underestimated device of practical reason is to subject a proposition to the test of time and to accept it if it passes. Though particularly important in aesthetic evaluation,[15] the test also figures in the evaluation of factual (including scientific) and even legal propositions. It is a refinement of the idea that whatever most people think is probably true. The idea itself is unhelpful even if we think "truth" a meaningful and useful concept. Most people are ignorant about most matters, and history is littered with examples of consensus on matters of fact that we now know—or think we know—are false. But the longer a widespread belief persists, surviving changes in outlook and culture and advances in knowledge, the likelier it is to be correct; the intergenerational consensus is more reliable (you can't fool all of the people all of the time). Much of our stock of commonsense knowledge and elementary moral beliefs is validated in this and no other way.

The test of time is a commonsense idea; certainly this is how it was presented by its first influential expositor, Samuel Johnson, and by such important successors as George Orwell.[16] But it also has an interesting

15. See Anthony Savile, *The Test of Time: An Essay in Philosophical Aesthetics* (1982); *Law and Literature,* note 12 above, ch. 2. And for its use in law, see Edwin W. Patterson, "Historical and Evolutionary Theories of Law," 51 *Columbia Law Review* 681, 685 (1951). Patterson cites Dewey and James, which suggests the congeniality of the test of time to pragmatist philosophy.

16. See Johnson, "Preface to the Plays of Shakespeare," in *Samuel Johnson: Selected Poetry and Prose* 299, 300 (Frank Brady and W. K. Wimsatt eds. 1977); David Hume, "Of the Standard of Taste," in Hume, *Essays: Moral, Political, and Literary* 226, 231-233 (Eugene F.

philosophical, scientific, and economic provenance. It can be seen to rest on the pragmatic idea that, with the debatable exception of elementary logical and mathematical truths, consensus is the only *operational* concept of truth that we have. This is not to equate truth with consensus. That would be a big mistake. It is not misusing the word "true" to say that "everyone except me believes the proposition *p*, but *p* is not true." Indeed, it would stifle inquiry to suppose that when consensus was achieved, truth had been found. The challenging of settled beliefs is an essential spur to intellectual progress. And this implies that settled beliefs are often false, as of course they are. To equate truth to consensus would imply that the earth once was flat, and now is round; that the sun used to revolve around the earth but now the earth revolves around the sun. Taken literally, it would imply that if humanity were destroyed, the heliocentric theory would cease to be true.[17] There is equal paradox,

---

Miller ed 1985); Orwell, "Lear, Tolstoy, and the Fool," in *The Collected Essays, Journalism and Letters of George Orwell,* vol. 4, pp. 287, 290 (Sonia Orwell and Ian Angus eds. 1968); and other references in *Law and Literature,* note 12 above, at 71-74. For a recent criticism of the test of time in literature, see Barbara Herrnstein Smith, *Contingencies of Value: Alternative Perspectives for Critical Theory* 47-53 (1988). She argues, for example, that since Homer means nothing to most people in Africa, its survival in Western culture must be due to its fulfilling culturally specific functions. Granted—but the question is why Homer, rather than *The Egyptian Book of the Dead* or *The Epic of Gilgamesh?* Is it *just* racism, as a reader of Martin Bernal, *Black Athena: The Afroasiatic Roots of Classical Civilization,* vol. 1, *The Fabrication of Ancient Greece, 1785-1985* (1987), might infer? Or is there not something genuinely "in" the Homeric epics that makes them so resonant in Western culture even after more than two and a half millennia? Smith's work is part of a growing school of "canon bashing" that raises issues which range too far afield to be discussed here. For another example of the school, see Jane Tompkins, "Masterpiece Theater: The Politics of Hawthorne's Literary Reputation," 36 *American Quarterly* 617 (1984).

17. A paradox ignored in Peirce's formulation: "The opinion which is fated to be ultimately agreed to by all who investigate, is what we mean by the truth." "How to Make Our Ideas Clear," in *Collected Papers of Charles Sanders Peirce,* vol. 5, pp. 248, 268 (Charles Hartshorne and Paul Weiss eds. 1934). William James's formulation—truth is what is useful to believe—also leads to serious paradoxes. See Bertrand Russell, "William James's Conception of Truth," in Russell, *Philosophical Essays* 127 (1910). But Peirce's fuller statement— "The real, then, is that which, sooner or later, information and reasoning would finally result in, and *which is therefore independent of the vagaries of me and you*" ("Some Consequences of Four Incapacities," in *Collected Papers of Charles Sanders Peirce,* above, vol. 5, pp. 156, 186; emphasis added)—is convergent with more common notions of truth, which likewise stress observer independence, that is, objectivity in one of its stronger senses. See, for example, Hilary Putnam, *Representation and Reality* 109 (1988) ("it is a property of truth that whether a sentence is true is logically independent of whether a majority of the members of the culture *believe* it to be true"). Peirce's stress on the long run was related to his view that scientific induction is a form of statistical sampling. The larger the sample, the more reliable the findings based on it.

however, in using current opinion as the criterion of truth, and thus in saying that the earth is round because our present methods of validating propositions show it to be round although future methods may show otherwise. This is equivalent to saying that the earth *really* is round today but a century from now we may know better—quite a confused statement.

Pragmatists believe that truth is what free inquiry—unforced, undistorted, and uninterrupted—would eventually discover about the objects of inquiry.[18] Since the process of inquiry never ends, this implies that truth always lies beyond our horizon: it is there, but we aren't. The pragmatic concept of truth is related to the test of time, but complexly. The pragmatic concept is forward-looking; truth is the destination we have not yet arrived at, but under the right conditions we can hope to arrive there eventually. The test of time is backward-looking; some of our beliefs are true, and they are probably the ones that, having survived the longest, command the most robust consensus. But the two approaches are at one in referring truth to a process of belief formation that unfolds over time. In so doing they depart from normal usage, in which "truth" and "belief" are sharply distinguished (see note 17). So what? It might be well to forget about "truth" and speak only of justified or, better (because weaker), warranted belief (and this is the tendency in pragmatist thought), recognizing that there is no way to distinguish in practice between truth and what one cannot help believing, and noting that consensus is a legitimate though highly fallible method of justification.

This is a skeptical posture but not of an anguished or radical cast. If absolute truth is not in the cards we should not be upset when we fail to find it. It is not as if we shall be left without any moorings in what we call reality. The pragmatist's skepticism is not the skepticism that doubts the existence of a world external to human sensation or even the existence of (as distinct from the knowability of) truth. We may agree that the earth is "real," that it is either round or not round, and that, if it is round today, almost certainly it was round 2,500 years ago, when the consensus view was that it was flat. Today's consensus is strongly

---

18. See preceding footnote, and also Richard Rorty, "Is Natural Science a Natural Kind?" in *Construction and Constraint: The Shaping of Scientific Rationality* 49, 71 (Ernan McMullin ed. 1988); Carl Wellman, *Challenge and Response: Justification in Ethics* (1971); William M. Sullivan, "After Foundationalism: The Return to Practical Philosophy," in *Anti-Foundationalism and Practical Reasoning: Conversations between Hermeneutics and Analysis* 21 (Evan Simpson ed. 1981).

supported by the kinds of evidence that we have good reason to find persuasive (note the element of circularity in this method of validation, though). We rate the probability that we are right and the ancients wrong on this question very high. Closer to truth we cannot come, so why worry?

There is reason to worry. Views that many people regard as preposterous display remarkable tenacity, yet this is not taken as evidence of their truth. That a majority of the American people believe (though often without full conviction) in magic, miracles, and astrology, and that these beliefs are thousands of years old, has no persuasive force with disbelievers, who regard the believers as ignorant and credulous. This is an example of refusal to abide by the test of time, and more broadly of persistent deviation between belief and reality, consensus and truth. Yet although it is a weak method of determining truth, the test of time is not negligible. It helps repair the deficiencies of consensus as a criterion of truth. Precisely because consensus is a provisional, uncertain, mutable criterion, the broader the consensus on a particular matter the greater its reliability. Time enables the consensus to be broadened; it enlarges the franchise. It also enlarges or multiplies our perspectives, which is vital if, like Nietzsche and Wittgenstein, we hold a perspectival theory of truth, which by emphasizing the extent to which a person's outlook is shaped by his culture and historical situation denies our ability to achieve a God's-eye view.

An economic and biological metaphor is an alternative to the electoral metaphor for the test of time: in this construction the test of time subjects ideas to a competitive or Darwinian test, which makes any consensus that emerges more convincing (comparison shopping across the centuries). We think a competitive economy more likely to meet consumer needs than a centrally managed one, a decentralized scientific community in a society committed to freedom of speech and expression more conducive to accurate scientific judgments than a scientific community that is subject to censorship or that operates under tight governmental control—although evolution in business and in science is not powered by the same blind and random process that is at work in biological evolution.[19] When expressed in the biological metaphor the test of time can be seen to be implicit in Popper's philosophy of science—the highly

19. This is a historically important distinction. The *mindlessness* of biological evolution is the most arresting aspect of Darwinism. The wonder is not that man evolved from the lower animals but that he did so without its being planned.

influential, though flawed,[20] culmination of the fallibilist tradition whose earlier exponents include Bacon and Mill. Competitive and evolutionary in character, Popper's philosophy teaches that the best methodological rule is to "try out, and aim at, bold theories, with great informative content; and then let those bold theories compete, by discussing them critically and by testing them severely."[21] The more tests they survive, the more confidence we can have that they are a close approximation to truth. And the process of severe and thorough testing takes time. Newton's laws of motion, until Einstein, had survived repeated tests triumphantly.

The test of time becomes especially important for objectivity in law if, giving up on the attempt to discover a distinctive methodology of legal reasoning, we describe the lawyer's and the judge's reasoning as the "art" of social governance by rules[22] (which may be just a fancy term for tacit knowledge). When we reflect on the fact that law schools do

20. For illustrative criticism, see Hilary Putnam, "The 'Corroboration' of Theories," in Putnam, *Mathematics, Matter, and Method* 250 (2d ed. 1979) (vol. 1 of his *Philosophical Papers*). Popper's notion of testing hypotheses that have the *least* antecedent probability seems particularly questionable; and since there is an infinite number of such hypotheses, his implied research program is highly inefficient. (Granted, it would not be a sound research strategy to test only the hypotheses that are consistent with existing knowledge. Confirmation of those hypotheses—the likeliest outcome of such a strategy—would add nothing to our knowledge and would narcotize rather than stimulate our inquiring faculties.) Peirce may have been on the right track in suggesting that we are able to choose promising hypotheses to test because our minds, being themselves the products of nature, have an intuitive grasp of the principles of nature. See Nicholas Rescher, *Peirce's Philosophy of Science: Critical Studies in His Theory of Induction and Scientific Method* (1978). This is the project of what is now called evolutionary or Darwinian epistemology. See, for example, Florian von Schilcher and Neil Tennant, *Philosophy, Evolution, and Human Nature,* ch. 3 (1984); Michael Ruse, *Taking Darwin Seriously: A Naturalistic Approach to Philosophy,* ch. 5 (1986).

For a nice summary of Popper's philosophy of science, see David Oldroyd, *The Arch of Knowledge: An Introduction to the History of the Philosophy and Methodology of Science,* ch. 8 (1986); also David Miller, "Falsification versus Inductivism," in *Applications of Inductive Logic* 109 (L. Jonathan Cohen and Mary Hesse eds. 1980). The Darwinian interpretation of Popper's philosophy of science is stressed in Peter Munz, *Our Knowledge of the Growth of Knowledge: Popper or Wittgenstein?* (1985), and criticized in Ruse, above, at 61–65. For a thorough exploration of Peirce's philosophy of science, see Christopher Hookway, *Peirce,* chs. 2, 7–9 (1985); also W. B. Gallie, *Peirce and Pragmatism* (1966).

21. "The Problem of Induction," in *Popper Selections* 101, 112 (David Miller ed. 1985). This "challenge theory" of truth parallels John Stuart Mill's influential theory of free speech, which emphasizes the tenuous moorings of beliefs that are not subjected to the test of controversy. See *On Liberty,* ch. 2 (1859). The parallel is not surprising; Mill like Popper was a fallibilist.

22. An approach suggested by the late Paul Bator in conversation and in unpublished talks.

not teach a distinctive analytic method, on the prominent role of rhetoric in judicial opinions, and on the low voltage of the methods of legal
reasoning, we may be led to agree that law is indeed better regarded as
an art (or more humbly as a craft, or as a skill such as riding a bicycle
or speaking a foreign language)[23] than as a system of disciplined inquiry
whose results can be justified in quasi-scientific terms. But just as art is
ineffable, so is its critique. Art cannot be reduced to a set of analytic
procedures; no more can art criticism. If law is an art, what can be the
criteria for a "correct" legal decision? The very word becomes a misnomer. We ask not whether a work of art is correct but whether it is
beautiful, meaningful, stirring, enriching. Since these words are inap-
posite to legal rulings, an aesthetic view of law is hard to imagine. But
it would in any event require a wrenching alteration in our vocabulary
of legal evaluation.

It is dizzying to see the autonomy and objectivity of law defended
first by treating law as a branch of logic and then by treating it as a form
of art. Yet the incongruity is only apparent; the fact that logic always
and art often are formalist disciplines illustrates the tenacity of formalism in legal thought.

So inconclusive is evaluative criticism of art, and so striking are the
vicissitudes of artistic taste,[24] that the test of time is the only criterion of
aesthetic excellence that can be depended on to silence most doubters.
The more we model law on art, therefore, the more we shall be drawn
to the test of time as the criterion of legal soundness. It is in fact a component of "traditionary" theories of precedent (Hale and Blackstone),[25]
and it also has a role to play in the concept of precedent presented in
Chapter 2. One thing that can solidify a precedent—that can make it
authoritative (or more authoritative) rather than just a source of information—is its endorsement by many judges over a substantial period of
time. Other things being equal, a conclusion to which a number of different individuals have come—a conclusion (better, a hypothesis) that
has survived continual retesting—is entitled to more deference than the

23. Either the craft or the skill metaphor is preferable to the art metaphor, the last suggesting as it does a preoccupation with elegance and other formal properties and an indifference to consequences in the world.

24. For an illuminating case study, see Bruno S. Frey and Werner W. Pommerehne, "Is
Art Such a Good Investment?" 91 *Public Interest,* Spring 1988, at 79.

25. See Charles M. Gray, "Editor's Introduction," in Matthew Hale, *The History of the
Common Law of England* xi, xxxiv (1971); Gerald J. Postema, "Some Roots of Our Notion
of Precedent," in *Precedent in Law* 9, 18–20 (Laurence Goldstein ed. 1987). Compare the
discussion of tradition sanctified by time in Paul Veyne, *Did the Greeks Believe in Their
Myths? An Essay in the Constitutive Imagination,* ch. 1 (1988).

conclusion of a single individual. So time can help stabilize legal doctrine. Notice that, from this perspective, the more diverse the judiciary, the more its rulings invite unforced agreement, ungrudging deference.

But the test of time does not really respond to the needs of the legal system in a dynamic society. First, the test is after the fact: it does not tell the judge how to write an opinion that will survive. Second, all but one decision in a chain of precedent may have relied uncritically on the first decision, since acquiescence in precedent may reflect a desire for stability rather than agreement with the outcome of the earlier case. Third, the very thing that gives a chain of precedent its strength—its length over time—may in a changing society signal obsolescence. Fourth, most of the rulings that interest the profession are too recent to be evaluated by their survival properties. We can use the test to criticize the Dred Scott decision, *Lochner,* and the early free-speech cases, but possibly even *Brown v. Board of Education,* and certainly *Roe v. Wade,* are too recent to be adjudged good or bad by reference to their survival. *Swift v. Tyson* (see Chapter 14) had a "run" of a century.

A final point is that a case can accrete authority over time regardless of its merit or even the judges' desire for stability and economy in decision making. It can do this by engendering reliance the protection of which is more important than getting the law just right,[26] or by fostering the organization of an interest group that has sufficient political muscle to prevent the case from being overruled. These possibilities, especially the second, bring to the fore a serious objection to the test of time: its failure to distinguish among methods of creating consensus. As Peirce and Holmes liked to point out, killing dissenters is a time-honored method of creating consensus, but not one calculated to get us closer to the truth. When the test of time is conceived in Darwinian terms, this point is obscured because genocide is *the* method of competition in nature. Yet, practically speaking, the longer a belief persists, the likelier it is to be true, rather than to have persisted merely because rival beliefs were repressed. Historically, repression has not proved to be effective on other than a temporary basis; the truth will out. Still, the marketplace analogy is closer than the biological one. Competition can be depended upon to bring about the socially desired price and output

26. An example is the reaffirmation, in Flood v. Kuhn, 407 U.S. 258 (1971), of the anomalous and outdated decision holding that major league baseball did not affect interstate commerce and therefore was not subject to the federal antitrust statutes. See Federal Baseball Club v. National League, 259 U.S. 200 (1922). Noting the social interest in the protection of reliance is another way of making the earlier point that stare decisis reflects a desire for stability as well as a respect for the thinking of other people (the earlier judges).

only if competitors are forbidden to employ certain tactics, including violence, fraud, and collusion. Similarly, the test of time is a reliable method of establishing truth only if the process of inquiry is guaranteed to operate without significant political distortions, and this condition is not satisfied in the legal area because judicial decisions become rallying points for political coalitions.

The problem goes deeper. The sensible emphasis in law on hierarchy, continuity, and stability sets up a tension with the search for truth. Imagine arguing that scientists should be drawn from a common social and educational background, because then they will be more likely to agree. Applied to judges this is not a ridiculous argument, although I am not convinced by it. Stability *is* a desirable quality of law; and because legal reasoning does not have the power to secure agreement that formalists ascribe to it, legal stability is more likely to be achieved if the judges are like-minded, and they are more likely to be like-minded if they are socially and educationally homogeneous. But the more homogeneous they are, the less robust will their conclusions be in an epistemic, though not necessarily in a political or social, sense. In law, truth is traded off against other valued goods, and rightly so. That is not the scientific ideal.

Recall the distinction made in the Introduction among ontological, scientific, and conversational objectivity. The first is in play when there is something "out there" to which our concepts correspond, the second when observations are replicable so that all observers can be brought to unforced agreement on what it is they are observing. These senses of objectivity are related; the fact that scientists of diverse background and politics will agree with each other on most scientific questions, even though their agreement is not coerced, suggests there is something "out there" that is compelling agreement; scientific consensus argues for scientific realism. Objectivity in its third sense, which refers to bringing about agreement on nonverifiable propositions through methods of inquiry that are not exact (replicable), is usually weak. Not always: the proposition that the unrestricted killing of human beings is wrong commands the sort of broad and unforced consensus that makes it seem "objectively" correct, although it neither has a referent nor is the fruit of exact inquiry. Such instances do not, however, predominate in the areas of primary interest to the legal profession. Yet law needs agreement in order to avoid social chaos, and it does not scruple to coerce the necessary agreement through a variety of political and rhetorical methods ranging from judicial hierarchy to the licensure of lawyers to formalist opinion writing to the enforcement of judgments by sheriffs, marshals, and if need be soldiers.[27] Force is always in the background. Compare the Soviet Union's use (diminishing, one hopes) of psychiatric hospitals to imprison dissidents with the practice in our country, where commitments for insanity are hedged about with many procedural restrictions and administered on a decentralized basis. The difference is that between coercive and competitive objectivity. Yet coercive objectivity is and must be an element of law even in a liberal society such as the United States. As Justice Robert Jackson put it, "we act in these matters not by authority of our competence but by force of our commissions."[28]

Still another factor that limits the usefulness of the test of time for law is the absence of a feedback mechanism. (Astrology may be a parallel case. Astrologers are careful to keep their predictions vague, so that falsification is difficult.) The test of time is related to the idea of trial and error. Scientists—in Popper's conception, which is broadly pragmatist, of science—try one theory after another, confront each one with data, discard the ones that the data falsify, and by this process continuously enlarge scientific knowledge. Artists, too, try one thing after another; most of their innovations are rejected, but some survive, and those that do seem robust because of their power to command the interest of diverse audiences. Unlike the case of science, however, one is never confident that a rejected artist or art form will stay rejected; there is a continual rediscovery of forgotten authors, painters, composers.[29] It is much the same in law. Except for a handful of dramatic examples such as the Dred Scott and *Plessy* decisions, competitive or survivalist notions rarely bring about decisive rejections of legal innovations. This observation is related to the hierarchical character of judicial systems, which limits the scope for competition among precedents. Long after the demise of *Swift v. Tyson* and *Lochner v. New York,* of privity of contract in personal-injury cases, of strict liability in collision cases, of fact pleading, and so on almost without end, discarded doctrines continue to enlist distinguished champions, who cannot be silenced effectively by pointing to the rejection of their views in the legal marketplace. And I am

27. Cf. Sabina Lovibond, *Realism and Imagination in Ethics* 172–175 (1983), on "coercive objectivity"; and notice the twist that the present discussion gives to Austin's theory of law (following Hobbes) as the *command* of the sovereign, on which see Russell Hardin, "Sanction and Obligation," 68 *Monist* 403 (1985).

28. West Virginia State Board of Education v. Barnette, 319 U.S. 624, 640 (1943).

29. I am overdrawing the contrast between science and art. For Copernicus may be said to have revived Aristarchus, nuclear physics to have revived pre-Socratic atomic theory, and modern genetics to have rediscovered Mendel.

speaking of champions *within* the legal community, that is, within the community of recognized experts; it is as if some distinguished scientists believed in astrology.

But this is to paint too bleak a picture, and it is time to begin restoring perspective. There is a limited competitive process in law; it corresponds to the competitive process in science summarized in the idea of unforced inquiry. The world contains a vast number of legal systems, and comparisons are possible. Of particular significance is the large number of separate legal systems in the United States, the consequence of our federal system of government. Here the competitive relationship is direct. A legal system is one of the public services that each state offers to its residents and to the people and firms who do business with them. If the system is poor—the judges corrupt or incompetent, the laws archaic or cumbrous or unenforced, the courts biased, expensive, or impacted by delay—the state will lose residents and trade. (In principle, "voting with one's feet" is also possible at the national level, but emigration is much more costly than moving to another part of the same country and therefore provides a much weaker constraint on a legal system.) Here at last is a feedback mechanism that might enable legal performance to be monitored and improved. Unfortunately, judicial competition among states is weak, both because political systems frequently are unresponsive to the interests of the citizenry and because law is only one (and, needless to say, an unstudied) factor in decisions regarding migration and trade.

Yet if we go back far enough—to trial by battle, for example, or prosecution for witchcraft—we can find plenty of legal practices that no one defends anymore. These practices have decisively flunked the competitive process implicit in the test of time, although more because of the rise of science than because of any ability of law to purge itself of prejudice and superstition. And a number of legal practices that were innovations in their time have passed the test of time. They include the trust, the counterclaim, estates in land, the concept of estoppel, powers of attorney, the recording of titles, the prohibition of torture, the subjection of senior government officials to the rule of law, habeas corpus (however overextended the current American practice may be), the final-judgment rule, summary judgment, burden of proof, concepts of standing to sue, of ripeness, and of justiciability generally, the publication of judicial opinions (including dissents), impoundment, the injunction, the administrative agency, the receivership, rescission, restitution, arbitration, and many more. Some of these, though, seem a bit commonplace; and even such durable innovations as the canons of statutory construction, tort liability for accidents, the civil jury, cross-examination, pretrial discovery, the exclusionary rule, the privilege against compulsory self-incrimination, limited liability, and punitive damages are vigorously questioned. Some of these innovations, moreover, have changed so much since they were new—the jury, for example—that it is unclear what it means to say they have survived. While it is reasonably certain that law has progressed since the eighteenth century, there is a perfectly good argument to be made—not a conclusive argument, but not an easily refutable one either—that law, taking all its consequences into account (including the opportunity costs of the human resources that have been sucked into the legal profession), has regressed in the United States since 1960. Like legal questions that do not get into court because they can be decided deductively, legal practices and institutions that have been validated by functioning smoothly over a long period of time refute extreme versions of legal skepticism but do not justify complacency about the power of legal reasoning either to solve the tough problems, whether doctrinal or institutional, in law or to establish the law's progressivity.

The situation would be improved if law committed itself to a simple functionalism or consequentialism. Suppose the sole goal of every legal doctrine and institution was a practical one. The goal of a new bankruptcy statute, for example, might be to reduce the number of bankruptcies and lower interest rates. The operation of the statute would be evaluated in terms of these goals, and if the statute failed to fulfill them it would be repealed. Law really would be a method of social engineering, and its structures and designs would be susceptible of objective evaluation, much like the projects of civil engineers. This would be a triumph of pragmatism. And not the first triumph for pragmatism in law. Consider the fate of the rule of capture. Much as in scientific investigation and engineering implementation, analogy (from rabbits and other wild animals) was used to generate a hypothesis—that the rule of capture would provide an efficient property-rights regime for oil and gas. The hypothesis was tested by observing the performance of the rule of capture as applied to oil and gas. The hypothesis flunked the test and was rejected: the rule of capture was superseded by statutes requiring unitization and other methods of imparting incentives for efficient development.[30]

30. See Howard R. Williams and Charles J. Meyers, *Oil and Gas Law,* vol. 6, §§905, 912 (1988).

But law is not ready to commit itself to concrete, practical goals across the board. Legal innovations are often defended by reference to intangibles such as the promotion of human dignity, the securing of justice and fairness, and the importance of complying with the ideals or intentions of the framers of the Constitution or of statutes. These goals are too nebulous for progress toward achieving them to be measured. So even when it is apparent that ballyhooed legal innovations have had costly, unintended, and unforeseen consequences, their defenders may be able to fend off proposals for repeal by invoking unquantifiable benefits, as well as by rallying whatever interest groups have coalesced around the innovation. Having done consulting for a manufacturer of buses before I became a judge, I can attest that bus manufacturers are among the most enthusiastic supporters of judicial decrees that require the busing of schoolchildren to achieve public-school integration. As we shall see in Chapter 14, many recent legal innovations in American law appear to have miscarried; that is why I said that the cause of legal justice may actually have suffered from the hectic "reforms" of the recent past. But it cannot be proved that these innovations have miscarried, because their goals are too vague to allow a cost-benefit or means-end evaluation; as a result, the record of apparent failure does not emit a clear signal for change.

4 ❦

Legitimacy in Adjudication

The Problem of Rational Prejudgment

We have seen that when the methods available to the legal reasoner for making, criticizing, or justifying legal decisions are examined coldly, we see that they are not always distinctively legal and not always very objective, even when a relaxed, pragmatic approach to objectivity is taken. These points may seem to have potentially serious implications for the legitimacy of the judicial enterprise. I think they do, but I must deal with the counterargument that, provided the reasons ranged on either side of a legal dispute are not of exactly equal weight, the judge can always decide in favor of the party who has the stronger case in a technical legal sense. The judge need never resort to personal values, preferences, or politics, even if the stronger case is not overpowering. If this is true, then all the judge needs to avoid the problems discussed at such length in the preceding chapters is a pair of blinders!

Metaphor can mislead. It is unclear what exactly it means to "weigh" arguments and, therefore, whether the process of decision in the face of conflicting arguments can be conceived in mechanically computational terms. Even if it can be, it is the wrong approach for a judge to follow. A person should not surrender deeply held beliefs on the basis of a weak argument just because he cannot at the moment find a stronger one in defense of those beliefs. Intuition, itself a method of practical reason, has its claims, and establishes presumptions that the other methods of practical reason may not always be able to overcome.[1] Granted, intu-

1. See Richard Nisbett and Lee Ross, *Human Inference: Strategies and Shortcomings of Social Judgment* 167–169 (1980); Gilbert Harman, *Change of View: Principles of Reasoning* 35–41 (1986). I am using "intuition" here in the second sense in which I defined it at the beginning of Chapter 2; so defined, it is closely related to tacit knowledge, to Gadamer's

ition should rule only in close cases; that is a requirement of the rule of law. But those cases are the focus of professional attention. It would be cold comfort to a defender of law's objectivity to be told that only close cases are indeterminate. Moreover, whether a case is close may depend in part on the strength of the judge's intuition. He may feel that legal doctrine has gone seriously awry, without being able fully to articulate the sources of his unease. So the category of close cases is ill defined.

To make the point differently, the preconceptions that judges bring to cases are not extraneous and impertinent foreign matter. The tabula rasa is not the judicial ideal. Society does not want judges to act as umpires of debating contests or as referees of controversies in law reviews. Many considerations are out of bounds to the judge (various partisan and personal reactions to a lawsuit or the litigants), but they do not include a disinterested conviction that a case really ought to be decided one way even though the lawyer urging the other way has stronger arguments. The upshot, however, is that it will often be extremely difficult to determine whether a legal decision is correct or incorrect. Intuition is inarticulate, disinterest is not objectivity, and the judge's disinterested intuition will often not be verifiable or falsifiable by experience. So what began as an argument for law's objectivity—the possibility of going with the balance of the arguments—turns out to be another argument against it. The irony is deepened when we reflect that intuition in the sense used here is similar to tacit knowing, a method of practical reason that defenders of law's objectivity invoke as a substitute for logic and science without realizing that the more reliance they place on tacit knowing to determine legal outcomes, the more difficult they make the task of justifying those outcomes. For tacit knowing is private and inarticulate, justification public and articulate.

Consensus

The power of legal reasoning to generate determinate case outcomes could perhaps be saved by turning law into something else—economics perhaps, or some ethical or political doctrine that might yield definite solutions to ethical or political problems. But no branch of the human-

---

emphasis on "prejudice" as an essential component of interpretation (see Hans-Georg Gadamer, *Truth and Method* 238–267 [1975]), and to the Bayesian statistician's concept of priors, on which see Chapter 6 of this book. For endorsement of that view from an unexpected source, see Henry J. Friendly, "Reflections of a Lawyer—Newly Turned Judge," 71 *Yale Law Journal* 218, 233–234 (1961).

ities or the social sciences, applied to such rebarbative materials as those thrown up in litigated disputes, is likely to achieve determinacy in the close case; in any event the arguments for transforming law into another branch of social thought could not be based on legal reasoning. The broader point is that either there is a strong political consensus that determines legal doctrine or there is not—and a fragmented political and ethical discourse will no more yield determinate outcomes than legal reasoning will. To sound a recurrent note in this book, consensus is a necessary condition for legal objectivity in all but the weakest sense.

Not much comfort can be taken from the fact that there are *some* areas of political consensus; it only seems that they must guarantee a sphere of legal determinacy. There is, to begin with, something odd about using political agreement to ground epistemological confidence. The point is related to an observation about the pragmatists, especially Habermas. Their view that "truth is what would emerge as the result of unconstrained inquiry pursued indefinitely . . . partially transforms the epistemological problem of distinguishing true from false (warranted from unwarranted, or rational from irrational) beliefs into the political problem of distinguishing free inquiry from inquiry constrained and distorted by the exercise of power."[2] The idea that political interference with the process of inquiry must be prevented is less troublesome than the idea that objectivity in law depends on the happenstance that a political consensus has formed around the premises of judicial analysis. What is political consensus but a polite name for the will of the stronger? What, therefore, are judges who render "objective" decisions but people who deduce the implications of the power relations in society?

These rhetorical questions are overheated, however, apart from the fact that judges need not prescribe so confining a role for themselves— although if they do not, their claim to be engaged in an objective reasoning process is weakened. Even if every law may be said in some sense to reflect dominant public opinion—even if ultimately might makes legal right—it does not follow that all law is amoral. Causes and justifications need not coincide. There would be no law against murder if

---

2. Joseph Rouse, *Knowledge and Power: Toward a Political Philosophy of Science* 7, 18–19 (1987). The proposition that inquiry can be distorted by "power" is ambiguous. If all this means is that political interference with the marketplace in ideas can distort inquiry, fine. But if it means also or instead that the advantages conferred by the possession of wealth can distort inquiry, implying that unforced inquiry may require either redistributing wealth or continually intervening in the marketplace of ideas, it is troublesome—which is not to say it necessarily is wrong; I shall give an example in Chapter 6 of a situation in which inequality of resources can indeed distort legal inquiry.

the dominant groups in society did not desire it, yet that law promotes the general welfare (as do many other civil and criminal laws, a few examples being the laws for the making and enforcing of contracts, for the protection of intellectual property, and for the prevention and redress of fraud and negligence) and no judge need be ashamed of enforcing it.[3]

The evidence for the inconclusiveness of legal reasoning is not merely aprioristic. Controversy—which appears to be on the rise—over the politics of judicial appointees is one datum. Another is the trappings of the judicial process—the impressive courtroom, with the judge sitting at an elevated bench and in uniform, and addressed with honorifics unusual in democratic society: all a conscious effort to make law more impressive than it would be if treated purely as a method of rational inquiry. That the point is indeed to impress the litigants and the public, rather than the judges, is suggested by the fact that judges do not wear robes when actually deliberating or making their decisions; and sitting behind a raised bench and being addressed with exaggerated deference are hardly humbling experiences for a judge.

Here is another datum on the inconclusiveness of judicial reasoning.[4] American judges today are subject to exquisitely refined and elaborate rules on disqualification for conflict of interest. The tiniest potential conflict is disqualifying. This would make no sense if legal reasoning (including the resolution of factual disputes) were as transparent and reproducible as scientific reasoning and experimentation, for then an erroneous decision would be perceived and corrected and the judge ridiculed or removed for having yielded to temptation. The legal system must lack confidence in its ability to detect judicial errors. Consistent with this point, the rules on conflict of interest have been growing stricter in lockstep with the decline of consensus in law and the concomitant growth in judicial discretion. The weaker the consensus, the more difficult it is for judges to fix the premises of decision and, by so doing, to make legal reasoning approximate logical deduction. Because legal reasoning is more (only?) cogent when there is a consensus concerning the relevant political and social values, conflict of interest rules are less

---

3. On how norms emerge, see Robert Axelrod, "An Evolutionary Approach to Norms," 80 *American Political Science Review* 1095, 1108–1109 (1986); J. L. Mackie, "Co-Operation, Competition, and Moral Philosophy," in Mackie, *Persons and Values: Selected Papers,* vol. 2, p. 152 (Joan Mackie and Penelope Mackie eds. 1985); F. A. Hayek, *Law, Legislation, and Liberty,* vol. 1, pp. 72–81 (1973); Edna Ullmann-Margalit, *The Emergence of Norms* (1977).

4. Well discussed in John Leubsdorf, "Theories of Judging and Judge Disqualification," 62 *New York University Law Review* 237 (1987) (esp. pp. 249–250, 261).

needed in that setting to prevent bias from operating. The English judiciary is more homogeneous than ours, enabling greater agreement on premises and hence greater reliance on genuinely syllogistic legal reasoning. We would therefore expect the English conflict of interest rules to be less strict than ours, and so they are, although the difference is small.[5] We would also expect English law to be more certain than American law, and this is the general impression, although it would be nice to be able to move beyond impressions.

The immediate causes of the decline in consensus in our law are several. One is the growth of statutory and constitutional law relative to common law. As we shall see in Chapter 8, it is only superficially that the common law can be said to have a structure more logical than that of statutory or constitutional law; but what is true is that statutory and constitutional law has expanded into area after area of intense political controversy, an expansion unparalleled in the common law sphere. Other causes of the decline in legal consensus are a rise in the diversity of the legal profession since the 1950s, a concomitant decline in political consensus nationwide, and the increase in litigation,[6] which has multiplied judges and precedents and in particular has made adjudication by the Supreme Court less determinate. The Court's capacity for decision making is essentially fixed, but the Court is selecting from an ever-richer population of cases, and as a result an increasing fraction of the cases it decides are difficult rather than easy ones. And as the court of last resort it cannot be, or at least has chosen not to be, ruled by precedent—which is another reason that so large a fraction of the cases it decides are difficult. Moreover, as the ratio of decisions by the Supreme Court to decisions by lower courts shrinks, lower courts are increasingly deprived of authoritative precedent to guide their decision making; so more of their cases fall in the open area, too.

The decline in legal consensus has deeper causes. Hierarchy and other forms of authority often weaken as peoples become wealthier; at least that seems to be the lesson of American, perhaps of world, history since

5. See Shimon Shetreet, *Judges on Trial: A Study of the Appointment and Accountability of the English Judiciary*, pt. 5 (1976) (esp. pp. 308–309); *de Smith's Judicial Review of Administrative Action*, ch. 5 (4th ed., J. M. Evans ed., 1980).

6. That increase has been enormous, especially in the federal courts, in the last three decades. For statistics to mid-1983, see my book *The Federal Courts: Crisis and Reform*, ch. 3 (1985). The increase has continued since, as documented in the annual reports of the Director of the Administrative Office of the U.S. Courts.

World War II.[7] With wealth come freedom, independence, and mobility, and *pari passu* a loosening of familial and community bonds. Judges, like other authority figures, are trusted less, respected less, unthinkingly deferred to less—another cause of more stringent rules against judicial conflicts of interest. People stand on their rights more and an immediate effect is more litigation, which can lead to greater indeterminacy by the path just sketched. With the decline of authority and the rise of independent thinking a society also becomes morally heterogeneous,[8] to the point where people within the same political community may come to inhabit incommensurable moral universes. That is the situation in this country today with respect to the abortion controversy and the reason the controversy seems to admit of no rationally demonstrable resolution—seems literally interminable.[9] This standoff is repeated in a variety of legal contexts involving issues of personal, economic, religious, and sexual liberty.[10] When the judge reaches an epistemological impasse and of necessity bases decision, whether reflectively or unreflectively, on some ethical or political principle, or public opinion, or whatever, he is unlikely to have escaped indeterminacy. The interesting question will then be what accident of psychology or personal history or social circumstances moved him to adopt one social or political principle rather than another. The nation's legal heterogeneity mirrors its moral heterogeneity.

7. See Clifford Geertz, *Local Knowledge: Further Essays in Interpretive Anthropology* 16 (1983). On the rise in skepticism concerning professionalism, see Thomas L. Haskell, "Introduction," in *The Authority of Experts: Studies in History and Theory* xiii–xviii (Haskell ed. 1984). Admittedly, the pattern is more complicated than I have sketched in the text. There was a burst of conformism in the 1950s; perhaps we are about to see another. Disorder and dissensus are most visible in university faculties, which increasingly are unrepresentative of American society as a whole.

8. Or at least is *revealed* to be more heterogeneous. In a hierarchical society the moral distance between persons may be great; we should not think of the antebellum South or Periclean Athens, each with large slave populations, or India with its caste system, or class-ridden England, as "homogeneous" societies *tout court*. But the official norms, prescribed as they are by the top of the hierarchy, will tend to be monolithic in such societies. And it is the official norms that the courts enforce.

9. See Alasdair MacIntyre, *After Virtue: A Study in Moral Theory* 6–10 (2d ed. 1984).

10. Judge Learned Hand once remarked: "Values are incommensurable. You can get a solution only by a compromise, or call it what you will. It must be one that people won't complain of too much; but you cannot expect any more objective measure." "A Personal Confession," in Hand, *The Spirit of Liberty: Papers and Addresses of Learned Hand* 302, 307 (3d ed. 1960). This is too sweeping, if my analysis in the previous chapters is correct; but the domain in which Hand's observation is accurate is large and, I think, growing. Hand's moral skepticism (on which see also Michael Moore, "More Reality," 1982 *Wisconsin Law*

Policy versus Pedigree as Warrants for Judicial Action

Reasonableness as the Judicial Lodestar. Where does all this leave the judge? I can think of no better approach than for judges to conceive of their task, in every case, as that of striving to reach the most reasonable result in the circumstances—which include though are not limited to the facts of the case, legal doctrines, precedents, and such rule-of-law virtues as stare decisis.[11] Bland as this recommendation may seem,[12] it differs from both the orthodox legal view of the judge's task and the various natural law approaches by substituting the humble, fact-bound, policy-soaked, instrumental concept of "reasonableness" for both legal and moral rightness. Yet it also differs from Holmes's conception of the judge as interstitial legislator,[13] or, equivalently, from Article I(2) of the Swiss Code of 1807, which provides that "if no rule can be derived from the statute, the judge shall decide in accordance with the rule which he would promulgate if he were the legislator."[14] The picture of the judge as an interstitial legislator is both unedifying and, on a realistic view of the legislative process, misleading. It suggests that the only difference

---

Review 1061, 1066, and references cited there) was more than a parlor pose. It played a large role in a series of opinions he wrote upholding the refusal to grant U.S. citizenship to resident aliens guilty of moral lapses. See, for example, Johnson v. United States, 186 F.2d 588, 589–590 (2d Cir. 1951) ("people differ as much about moral conduct as they do about beauty . . . So it seems to us that we are confined to the best guess we can make of how such a poll [a poll of citizens regarding the conduct in question—desertion and adultery] would result"); Repouille v. United States, 165 F.2d 152, 153 (2d Cir. 1947) ("only a minority of virtuous persons would deem the practice [euthanasia] morally justifiable, while it remains in private hands, even when the provocation is as overwhelming as it was in this instance"). Incidentally, if it is correct that society is becoming morally more diverse, this is a blow to moral realism, just as an increase in disagreement among scientists would be a blow to scientific realism.

11. The suggested approach is close to that proposed by Kent Greenawalt, "Discretion and Judicial Decision: The Elusive Quest for the Fetters That Bind Judges," 75 *Columbia Law Review* 359, 377 (1975). See also Aharon Barak, *Judicial Discretion* 25–27 and ch. 4 (1989); cf. Wade L. Robison, "The Functions and Limits of Legal Authority," in *Authority: A Philosophical Analysis* 112, 119 (R. Baine Harris ed. 1976); Steven J. Burton, "Judicial Duty and Discretion: The Good Faith Thesis" (unpublished article, University of Iowa Law School, April 25, 1989).

12. And vulnerable as it is to mockery: Ambrose Bierce in *The Devil's Dictionary* defined "reasonable" as "Accessible to the infection of our own opinions. Hospitable to persuasion, dissuasion, and evasion." *The Collected Writings of Ambrose Bierce* 187, 339 (1946).

13. See Southern Pacific Co. v. Jensen, 244 U.S. 205, 221 (1917) (dissenting opinion). See also Benjamin N. Cardozo, *The Nature of the Judicial Process* 113–115 (1921); John Bell, *Policy Arguments in Judicial Decisions* 17–20, 226–246 (1983).

14. I am indebted to Gerhard Casper for the translation. Notice Article I(2)'s departure from the formalism characteristic of Continental law, mentioned in the Introduction.

between a judge and a real legislator is that the former fills the gaps left by the latter. If the comparison is taken literally—as no doubt the framers of the Swiss Code did *not* intend—the judge should feel free to engage in poll taking, vote trading, naked interest-group politics, and other common practices of legislators. In fact there are important institutional and procedural differences between courts and legislators, and they impose bounds on the domain of the reasonable in judging that are not found in legislating. They differentiate the judicial product from that of a legislature but do not dictate the outcome of difficult cases—they may rule out some outcomes, but not all except one. The judge in the difficult case is more a policy maker than a conventional lawyer and within his domain of freedom or discretion may be as free-wheeling as a legislator. But neither is unconstrained, and, more to the point, the constraints are different.

Nor is the judge an arbitrator or ombudsman or village wise man—which is to say, a type of dispute settler entitled to ignore "the law." In one sense this is the opposite extreme from thinking of the judge as a legislator and in another sense the same thing—both the arbitrator and the legislator being "above" the law in the sense of not being bound by preexisting legal norms. But at both extremes, if that is what they are, what is distinctive about law and adjudication drops right out of the picture. The circumstances that determine the reasonableness of judicial decisions include statutory language, precedents, and all the other conventional materials of judicial decision making, including such prudential virtues familiar to lawyers as sensitivity to the limits of judicial knowledge and to the desirability of stability in law. These conventional resources and constraints of judicial decision making are foreign to both the legislator and the arbitrator. In many cases the conventional materials will lean so strongly in one direction that it would be unreasonable for the judge to go in any other. But in some they will merely narrow the range of permissible decision, leaving an open area within which the judge must perforce attempt to decide the case in accordance with sound policy—in those grand symbolic cases that well out of the generalities and ambiguities of the Constitution, in accordance with a vision of the good society—while paying due heed to the imprudence of trying to foist an idiosyncratic policy conception or social vision on a recalcitrant citizenry. To repeat a previous point, the open area is not always smaller for judges than it is for legislators. Judges are not as subject to interest-group pressures and popular sentiment as legislators are, and in particular areas these forces may constrain legislators more tightly than judges are constrained by the constraints on the judicial process. Federal judges, for example, have as a practical matter more freedom in bringing about changes in the conditions of state prisons than state legislators do. But at the same time the lack of a popular mandate, the lack of fiscal authority, and the requirement of providing a reasoned, written justification for decisions impose constraints on judges that legislators do not face. It is not possible to say, in general, which official—judge or legislator— is less constrained, and therefore more powerful.

A judge who conceives of his role in difficult cases as that of policy maker rather than that of conduit for policy decisions made elsewhere in the political system need not on that account be a judicial activist. Judicial self-restraint in the sense of hesitation to overturn the decisions of other branches of government may be part of the judge's vision of the good society. But judicial self-restraint is a political theory rather than the outcome of legal reasoning; it cannot be deduced from legal materials or otherwise rigorously (or even very convincingly) derived from them. Those materials may determine how broad the area of judicial discretion is, but they will not determine how bold or timid the judge should be within that area in making decisions that pinch another branch of government.

I shall illustrate my conception of sound judicial decision making with the example of antitrust law. Step 1 in deciding a tough antitrust case, a case not controlled by precedent or otherwise susceptible of confident judgment at a first pass, is to extract (not—it goes without saying—by a deductive process), from the relevant legislative texts and history, from the institutional characteristics of courts and legislature, and, lacking definitive guidance from these sources, from a social vision as well, an overall concept of antitrust law to guide decision. A popular candidate for such a concept today is that of wealth maximization, but it is, needless to say, a contestable choice. Having made this choice (the current Supreme Court has almost but not quite made it for him),[15] the judge will then want to canvass the relevant precedents and other sources for information that might help in deciding the case at hand. This is step 2. Step 3 is a policy judgment—in some cases, though, it might approximate a logical deduction—resolving the case in accordance with the tenets of wealth maximization. Step 4 returns to the precedents, but they are now viewed as authorities rather than merely

15. See, for example, Broadcast Music, Inc. v. Columbia Broadcasting System, 441 U.S. 1, 19–20 (1979); Reiter v. Sonotone Corp., 442 U.S. 330, 343 (1979); Matsushita Electric Industrial Co. v. Zenith Radio Co., 475 U.S. 574 (1986).

as data, the judge will want to make sure that the policy judgment made in step 3 is not ruled out by authoritative precedent. Actually this is the third rather than the second time the judge will have consulted precedents. They must be consulted at the outset to determine whether the case is indeed in the open area; if not, the four-step analysis that I have described is pretermitted.

The suggested approach describes the actual, though often implicit, reasoning process that most judges use in tough cases. It also recasts legal analysis in those cases as a form of policy analysis. The judge has to make a policy choice, and the choice is dictated by the results of surveying and evaluating the consequences of alternative choices: consequences for the rule of law, for the parties, for the economy, for public order, for civilization, for the future—in short, for society. In noncommercial settings one might prefer to describe the analysis as ethical analysis rather than as policy analysis. But that would not alter the basic point: strictly legal materials are used only for help in setting an initial orientation and in providing specific data, and later as sources of possible constraints.

Antitrust happens to be a field in which there is a large body of nonlegal—specifically, economic—learning upon which judges can draw for policy guidance. In many fields there is not much extralegal learning to draw on. In resolving novel issues of free speech, for example, a judge is likely to be forced back on his personal notions of the proper balance between liberty and order, and on public values crystallized in earlier judicial opinions. But this does not affect my basic point, which is that the decision of difficult legal cases is very often a form of policy analysis rather than the product of a distinctive methodology of legal reasoning.

The policy-soaked reasoning process that I have described with the aid of the antitrust example is reasoned, not arbitrary, but it is more likely to foreclose some outcomes than to generate a unique one, and not too much should be made of being able to rule out some points on a distribution. We would not think much of a weather forecaster who assured us that the temperature tomorrow would be between 120° Fahrenheit and −40° Fahrenheit but was unable to exclude any intermediate possibilities. Within the feasible range of legal outcomes (corresponding to the feasible range of temperatures for the climate and time of year), the observer, depending on his own values, policy preferences, temperament, social vision, life experiences, and so forth, will find one outcome more congenial, attractive, or persuasive than another but will not be able to demonstrate its correctness. In short, decisions in difficult cases often are not "bivalent" (that is, either true or false).[16]

Elsewhere I have suggested two principles for stabilizing judicial decisions against the problem of indeterminacy.[17] One is the avoidance of contradiction by the judge, not only within an individual opinion but across his opinions; the judge must employ his powers of critical logic unflinchingly. This precept may seem so obviously correct as to be trivial; yet if adhered to rigidly it would prevent the judge from changing his mind. Foolish consistency is not an oxymoron. This is another example of how limited the domain of logic is; it is not illogical to change one's mind on the basis of new information. The second principle, the "publicity principle" as I called it, is that the judge avow the true grounds of decision. Adherence to this principle will prevent the judge from rejecting consensus views; but since on many important political and social questions there is no consensus, the principle has a weak bite. It is also unenforceable; there is no mechanism for inducing judges to be candid.

Other ways of attempting to stabilize legal doctrine include the principle of judicial self-restraint, rules limiting the circumstances in which judges consider themselves free to overrule previous cases (that is, stare decisis), and the conversion of multifactored tests to formulas or algorithms.[18] None of these devices will close the open area all the way, and all rest on policy judgments that can be and are contested. Among still other auxiliary principles—as one might call them by analogy to the auxiliary hypotheses of science—that might be used, for good or ill, to stabilize legal doctrine are strict construction, rigid adherence to precedent, favoring the underdog, trying to promote private ordering, and insistence on definite, "bright-line" rules. None of these principles can be derived by the methods of legal reasoning. Some are inconsistent with others. All depend on judgments of political theory. They are methods not of closing the open area but of helping us learn to live with it. They impart to judicial decision making not objectivity but pseudo-

---

16. Cf. Catherine Z. Elgin, "The Relativity of Fact and the Objectivity of Value," in *Relativism: Interpretation and Confrontation* 86 (Michael Krausz ed. 1989); Gordon C. F. Bearn, "The Horizon of Reason," in id. at 205; Joseph Margolis, "The Truth about Relativism," in id. at 232. For an example from quantum theory see Elgin, above, at 92.

17. See *The Federal Courts*, note 6 above, at 205–206.

18. On self-restraint, see id. at 198–222; on overruling, see my article "The Constitution as an Economic Document," 56 *George Washington Law Review* 4, 36–37 (1987); and on the conversion of multifactored tests to algorithms see American Hospital Supply Corp. v. Hospital Products Ltd., 780 F.2d 589, 593–594 (7th Cir. 1986).

objectivity, unless we are content to equate the objective with the reasonable.

Emphasizing as it does the importance of policy in judicial decision making, my discussion in this section may seem to imply that it would make sense to draw some judges from the ranks of nonlawyers—especially appellate judges, since a substantial fraction of appellate cases will be underdetermined by legal reasoning.[19] But there are compelling objections to this idea. First, many of the cases that come up to an appellate court *are* determinate (as I noted in Chapter 2), and lawyers can deal with them more proficiently than nonlawyers can. Second and related, law is among other things a language. The nonlawyer will be at a loss to figure out what the lawyers are talking about in their briefs and arguments, and is likely to fall under the sway of his professional colleagues. The third and most interesting point is that even if the nonlawyer has an epistemic contribution to make to appellate judging, a well-functioning legal system involves a trade-off between truth and stability. The uniformity of the legal profession reduces the vigor of legal inquiry but helps to stabilize legal obligation.

The Pedigree Approach. The concept of judicial decision making implicit in the preceding chapters and here made explicit raises a question of judicial legitimacy: who has licensed judges to decide cases in accordance with social vision? But to state the question this way is to appeal covertly to a particular political theory, one that regards the judge as an agent of legislators, of constitutional framers, or of earlier judges and thus insists that every judicial decision be fairly referable to a command by a principal—in other words, that decisions be pedigreed.[20] "The Constitution demands that all power be authorized . . . Judges applying the Constitution . . . must take their guidance and authority

19. The argument is made in Frederick Schauer, "Judging in a Corner of the Law," 61 *Southern California Law Review* 1717, 1732 (1988), and criticized in Lawrence B. Solum, "The Virtues and Vices of a Judge: An Aristotelian Guide to Judicial Selection," in id. at 1735. Cf. Doris Marie Provine, *Judging Credentials: Nonlawyer Judges and the Politics of Professionalism* (1986).

20. The analogy is to the way in which we learn such things as our name and birthplace, or that France once had an emperor named Napoleon Bonaparte; we build a chain between ourselves and the original eyewitnesses. But that is a method of establishing epistemic authority rather than political authority. The most powerful contemporary advocacy of what I am calling the "pedigree" theory of judicial legitimacy is by Frank Easterbrook. See, for example, "Method, Result, and Authority: A Reply," 98 *Harvard Law Review* 622 (1985); "The Influence of Judicial Review on Constitutional Theory," in *A Workable Government? The Constitution after 200 Years* 170 (Burke Marshall ed. 1987); "The Role of Original Intent in Statutory Construction," 11 *Harvard Journal of Law and Public Policy* 59 (1988).

from decisions made elsewhere. Otherwise they speak with the same authority they . . . and I possess when we fill the law reviews with our speculations and desires: none. And the other branches owe no obedience to those who speak without authority . . . Judges can legitimately demand to be obeyed only when their decisions stem from fair interpretations of commands laid down in the texts."[21]

The pedigree approach rests on a questionable notion of why judicial decisions are and should be obeyed (that is, because they are pedigreed). The main reason they *are* obeyed is that the consequences of disobedience are unpleasant; there are heavy sanctions for flouting court orders. Although these consequences depend ultimately on the willingness of the executive branch to enforce judicial decrees and of the legislative branch to pay for these enforcement efforts—indeed, to pay for the courts themselves—it would be naive to suppose that the willingness of the other branches to cooperate with the judicial branch depends on the courts' confining themselves to "fair interpretations of commands laid down in the texts." That willingness may be related to public confidence in the courts.[22] But there is no evidence that such confidence depends on the scrupulousness with which courts confine themselves to fair interpretations of commands laid down in the texts—about which the public knows little—as distinct from notions of justice or fairness that are independent of fidelity to texts.[23]

21. "Method, Result, and Authority," note 20 above, at 628–629.

22. Cf. Tom R. Tyler, Kenneth A. Rasinski, and Kathleen M. McGraw, "The Influence of Perceived Injustice on the Endorsement of Political Leaders," 15 *Journal of Applied Social Psychology* 700 (1985).

23. One straw in the wind is the public reaction to Robert Bork's nomination to the Supreme Court: Bork's positivism seems to have counted against him in the public eye. Another (if slightly inconsistent) straw is the quite astonishing lack of public awareness of courts, including the Supreme Court. See Alan Hyde, "The Concept of Legitimation in the Sociology of Law," 1983 *Wisconsin Law Review* 379, 408; Austin Sarat, "Studying American Legal Culture: An Assessment of Survey Evidence," 11 *Law and Society Review* 427, 438–439 (1977). For direct evidence that public confidence in the courts, such as it is, is independent of judicial adherence to craft values—a matter about which the public knows nothing—see Richard Lehne and John Reynolds, "The Impact of Judicial Activism on Public Opinion," 22 *American Journal of Political Science* 896 (1978); Gregory Casey, "The Supreme Court and Myth: An Empirical Investigation," 8 *Law and Society Review* 385 (1974); Roger Handberg and William S. Maddox, "Public Support for the Supreme Court in the 1970s," 10 *American Politics Quarterly* 333 (1982). "The people see the Supreme Court as an institution in the normal context of American politics. They view the Court as Republicans and Democrats, and they judge it in the same offhand way as they do their acknowledged politicians during elections." Kenneth M. Dolbeare and Phillip E. Hammond, "The Political Party Basis of Attitudes toward the Supreme Court," 32 *Public Opinion Quarterly* 16, 30 (1968). The sheer *unreality* of the legal profession's professed conception of the polit-

If we switch gears and ask why people, official and otherwise, have a *duty* to obey judicial decisions, the natural answer (which happens also to be the answer given by the natural lawyer) is that they should obey them because they are just.[24] But what does "just" mean in this context? Is a decision just by virtue of having a good pedigree? If a statute, or a provision of the Constitution, is unjust, is a decision enforcing that statute or constitutional provision nevertheless just by virtue of its fidelity to its unjust source? An affirmative answer would be para- doxical, and would imply the further paradox that the unjust decision provides the acid test of judicial legitimacy; it makes the very strongest claim to be obeyed by the other branches of government, because it shows that the judges are indeed faithful agents—only such fidelity could explain the unlovely outcome. One is put in mind of Angelo in *Measure for Measure*. "It is the law, not I, condemn your brother. / Were he my kinsman, brother, or my son, / It should be thus with him" (Act II, sc. 2, ll. 84–86).

We are entitled to ask *why* the "faithful agent" conception of the judge is the right one. To set a good example to other people in agency roles? To restore a needed sense of discipline in public life? To promote cer- tainty? To reduce judicial workloads? To spare the courts from political controversy? To allocate governmental functions in accordance with comparative institutional competence? (Maybe legislators are better at making policy than judges are.) Because the virtues of the rule of law— and they are genuine and important virtues—cannot, either as a practical or as a theoretical matter, be otherwise attained? Some or all of these may be good answers—maintaining public confidence in the courts is not a good answer—but this needs to be demonstrated, not merely asserted. Another bad answer, offered by Hamilton in *Federalist No. 78*, is that judges who hew close to the original meaning of the Constitution are the authentic oracles of popular sovereignty, since the Constitution was adopted by the people of the United States. This is artificial even apart from the framers' well-known distrust of popular government (remember that in the original Constitution, only the House of Repre- sentatives was to be elected directly). Everyone who voted for the Con-

---

ical setting in which courts operate is powerfully argued in Stephen M. Griffin, "What Is Constitutional Theory? The Newer Theory and the Decline of the Learned Tradition," 62 *Southern California Law Review* 493, 506–529 (1989).

24. The theme of Philip Soper, *A Theory of Law* (1984). This assumes that there is a moral duty to obey law. I am not sure; see Chapter 7.

stitution is long dead, and to be ruled by the dead hand of the past is not self-government in any clear sense.

It is true that all judges are required to take an oath "to support the Constitution" and all federal judges another oath to decide cases "agreeably to the Constitution."[25] So the lawful judge is constrained by the Constitution. But the question is the nature of the constraint in cases where the Constitution does not provide clear guidance, and it is not a question that the oaths illuminate. It may not be supportive of or agreeable to the Constitution if the judges fold their hands when the text, history, or structure fails to yield an answer to a question of interpretation or application.

The inadequacy of the "faithful agent" approach is exhibited in Learned Hand's argument against judicial adventurism. "For myself it would be most irksome to be ruled by a bevy of Platonic Guardians . . . I should miss the stimulus of living in a society where I have, at least theoretically, some part in the direction of public affairs."[26] This is an argument not for faithful agency but against constitutional law. The faithful agent will sometimes be enforcing restrictions that irk. If with regard to such restrictions modern judges allow modern views to influence their decisions, then living people have at least an indirect role in the area of public affairs that is within the scope of the judiciary. But if modern judges are faithful expositors of decisions made by the framers of the Constitution centuries ago and ignore contemporary public opinion, today's citizens are deprived of an opportunity to shape their own destiny in areas within the prohibitory scope of the old enactments, except through the cumbersome process of constitutional amendment.

The issue of the proper freedom for judges is intractable at the theoretical level; it ought to be recast in empirical, pragmatic terms. Do we want judges to play a bigger or a smaller role in the direction and implementation of governmental policy? (And who are "we" in this question?) What are the trade-offs? Which choice would have the better consequences (insofar as we can discern them), all things considered? The question whether judges should be passive rather than active, modest rather than aggressive, ought to be confronted head-on rather than obscured by endless talk about legitimacy. In fact, consequentialist arguments are often made in support of formalist positions. The formalist will point out for example that judges risk their prestige, their perceived disinterest, perhaps their long-term effectiveness, if they become

25. U.S. Const., art. IV; 28 U.S.C. §453.
26. *The Bill of Rights: The Oliver Wendell Holmes Lectures, 1958* 73 (1958).

dragged into politically controversial areas. This is true, but one must ask what the judges are hoarding their prestige, their power to do good, for, and what the costs of this hoarding are.

The judge who believes that he cannot speak authoritatively except as the agent or mouthpiece of the sovereign is likely to be a "strong" legal positivist, that is, one who believes that ethical considerations (broadly construed to include considerations of public policy often thought too mundane to count as ethical) are not proper sources of legal obligation unless they are embodied in a statute or constitution. And inside the strong legal positivist lurks the moral and epistemic skeptic. A recent essay, noting that Holmes was such a one, argues that his "assertion that there is no viewpoint that can claim precedence on the basis of its presumed objectivity" led him to conceive "of his role as judge not as that of an umpire who must determine the merits of each case, but as that of a conductor who must in each case determine which voice shall be heard . . . The duty of the judge is to consider what person or institution is most entitled to have its viewpoint count in adjudicating the case."[27] The choice of metaphors is a bit jarring, since we are apt to think of a musical conductor as a more "activist" figure than an umpire. However that may be, "conducting" is undoubtedly an important part of the judge's task. And the more skeptical the judge is about his access to the wellsprings of objectivity, the more willing he will be to allow a multitude of voices to be raised. Or will he? If he is denied that access, so are the legislative and executive-branch officials to whom he is asked to defer. It seems a standoff. In any event, if the issue is the proper amount of deference by judges to other officials, why not say so straight out rather than cast it as one of legitimacy?

The "strong" positivist is not a skeptic about one moral value: that of deferring to higher authority. But is it not a warped moral stance to be skeptical about all values except obedience? Is it not rather too Prussian for an American judge? It is one thing to announce that the heavens will fall if judges abandon the myth (or perhaps the actuality) of being

27. Catharine Wells Hantzis, "Legal Innovation within the Wider Intellectual Tradition: The Pragmatism of Oliver Wendell Holmes, Jr.," 82 *Northwestern University Law Review* 541, 590–591 (1988). Notice that the skeptical judge may want to delegate as much judicial authority as possible to nonjudges (administrators, jurors, etc.), recognizing that the exercise of such authority involves an inescapable amount of sheer will and sensing the inconsistency between this characteristic of the judicial process and conventional expectations about the process. Holmes, however, perhaps because of his admiration for the will as a human faculty (see Chapter 7), was not bashful about basing judicial decisions on what he liked to call the sovereign prerogative of choice.

faithful agents of the people and of the people's representatives; this is merely incorrect. It is another thing to say that the heavens *should* fall. Obedience to rules is just one virtue among many,[28] and it cannot be given its proper weight without considering the content of the rules and other pertinent social and moral values. It is surprising that a nation which has embraced an ideology of hostility to bureaucrats contains so many judges who apotheosize the bureaucratic virtues.

I have said that the pedigree approach needs to be justified, not just asserted. But maybe not too much effort should be devoted to that task. The approach may have little content or thrust. For it need not preclude a role, even a large one, for the judicial exercise of social vision. If framers of statutory and constitutional provisions know, as they must, that there is an open area in judging that judges can close only by bringing in policy preferences, ethical values, and the like, maybe they can be taken to have authorized this type of decision in advance. Another possibility of course is that they accept it as the unavoidable price of an independent judiciary but do not desire it. This is conjecture too. They may want to give their agents a long tether so that statutes, and especially the Constitution, whose framers made it difficult to amend, would not obsolesce too fast.

Legal scholars who believe that judges should be faithful agents tend also to believe that legislators are—and above all, that framers of the Constitution were—wise and far-sighted people whose commands deserve a conscientious effort at obedience. This belief shades into framer idolatry—the view that the framers of the Constitution knew more about governing twentieth-century America than the Justices of the Supreme Court do today. The framers may have been an abler group than any Supreme Court in our history, but they were not clairvoyant. This is not to suggest that the general principles embodied in the Constitution are obsolete, let alone that a contemporary effort to rewrite the Constitution would produce a superior document (some observers believe that this is what the Supreme Court has attempted to do, and with the predicted result). The economic principles expounded by Adam Smith may well be as apt for twentieth-century America as for eighteenth-century England. The problem both in law and in economics is that the difficult cases are at the level not of principle but of application. Almost everyone can agree with the general principles embodied in the Constitution, precisely insofar as they are general, or with the specifics that do not matter (for example, how many days the

---

28. See Judith N. Shklar, *Legalism: Law, Morals, and Political Trials* 109 (1964).

President has to veto a bill); it is the application of those principles to situations that the framers did not foresee and provide for that causes controversy. The framers gave us a compass, not a blueprint.

In any event, the wiser and more far-sighted the framers are assumed to have been, the less rather than more plausible it becomes to impute to them the view that judges should not exercise independent judgment. If the framers were *that* wise, they knew how the judges of the unprecedentedly powerful judiciary they were authorizing would behave. Do not people intend (in a meaningful sense of the word "intend") the natural and probable consequences of their acts? Moreover, the most influential framers were lawyers, and it is unlikely that they greatly feared an "imperial" judiciary. Such fear was not entirely absent from their deliberations: the Seventh Amendment's guaranty of trial by jury in federal civil cases attests to anxiety about the power of federal judges. But this was a concession to popular feeling—for when have members of the legal establishment complained about courts' being too powerful? The legal realists of the 1920s and 1930s, who did complain, and today's conservatives, who do complain, were (are) a distinct minority in the profession. Furthermore, the rights included in the Bill of Rights were for the most part rights that had been created by the English judiciary, on which the provision for a federal judiciary in Article III of the Constitution is modeled. Article III envisaged a judiciary even more independent than the English royal courts. The framers' distrust was of legislatures. True, Article III was enacted before the Bill of Rights, which the framers accepted grudgingly; and without the Bill of Rights the role of the federal courts would have been smaller than it has been—although it would still have been large, for consider the constitutional decisions of John Marshall's Supreme Court, which were based not on the Bill of Rights but on the original Constitution. One of the difficulties of extracting coherent policy from the Constitution is that it is not a single document but a palimpsest reflecting confusingly superimposed values of different political factions and of different stages in American political history.

A final point is that the framers were revolutionaries, that they exceeded their terms of reference in submitting the Constitution for ratification by the people, and that the southern states were forced to ratify the Civil War amendments at gunpoint. The "title deeds" of constitutional law are written in blood; the "pedigree" begins in usurpation. Cardozo's suggestion (see Introduction) that the judicial decision which makes good sense displays on its face the title deed that matters has much to recommend it.

Yet despite its vulnerabilities the pedigree theory can lay claim to being the official theory of statutory and constitutional interpretation, by which I mean the theory that a plurality of judges subscribe to publicly. This may be due in part to the hold of formalist thinking on the legal mind, in part to the desire of public officials to duck responsibility—and shoving off the responsibility on long-dead framers is a convenient dodge—and in part to the vagueness of the pedigree theory. The last two points are related; what could be more attractive to judges than a theory of judicial legitimacy that allowed them to do anything they wanted provided they employed a rhetoric determinedly self-abnegating?

Not all official theories are correct. Our government might not function if the people running it took seriously every bromide about democracy and popular sovereignty. Among alternatives to the pedigree theory, two resonate particularly well with the themes of this chapter. One, the conservative (in the attitudinal, not political, sense), points out that American judges seem always and everywhere to have followed something like the four-step approach that I described with the aid of the antitrust example, and infers that it would probably be futile and maybe risky to make them stop. ("Better the devil you know . . .") The other approach, which is pragmatic, argues that if this sort of judicial decision making "works" we should not lose sleep over the fact that it cannot be fitted into a neat table of organization constructed from the Constitution and democratic theory. But how do we know it works, and how far should we extend it? Who knows? Maybe the burden of persuasion should rest on whoever is urging a change in settled practices, in either direction—toward a more aggressive judiciary or toward a less aggressive one. Or is this to succumb too readily to the tyranny of the status quo?

These two theories of judicial legitimacy are not impressive, I admit. Also they are not so remote from the pedigree approach as they may seem, and not only because of the latter's sponginess. The four-step approach that I proposed as an example of pragmatic or "realistic" adjudication does not deny that an independent judiciary creates a potentially serious agency problem or recommend that judges reconceive their role as that of principals rather than agents. It assigns them a creative role but within a framework in which the judge is in some sense subordinate to the framers of constitutional statutes and, of course, of the Constitution itself. The issue is in what sense and how best to fulfill this role.

The strongest argument for the pedigree approach and against a pragmatic or "realistic" one may itself be pragmatic: judges just are not smart enough to make wise policy decisions, balancing a myriad of conflicting considerations that include the rule-of-law arguments against balancing. I agree; and rules do reduce the burdens of thought. But the choice is not between unwise policy decisions and wise decisions applying rules. Wisdom in applying rules requires a sense of when the rules run out and (what is not necessarily a different question) when it would be a serious mistake to apply a particular rule "as written." The decision to, and how to, apply a rule is a policy decision. More fundamentally, how do we know that legislators really are better policy makers than judges? No doubt they *could* be—if only they could throw off the yoke of interest-group pressures, reform the procedures of the legislature, and extend their own policy horizons beyond the next election. If they cannot do these things, their comparative institutional advantages may be fantasy. To compare real judges with ideal legislators is to commit the Nirvana fallacy.

To sum up: If the pedigree approach were somehow compelled—perhaps because it was latent in the definition of adjudication—then we would have to accept it, as we accept that the square root of 9 is 3. But since it is not compelled, it has to be justified; it has to be shown to be a good thing, or at least a better thing than the alternatives. This the proponents have yet to show.

Examples. I begin with an example of "formalist anxiety," the judicial dread of appearing to be making policy choices. Often statutes are passed without a provision limiting the time within which suit under the statute must be brought, that is, without a statute of limitations. When this happens, courts cast about for a similar statute that has a statute of limitations and "borrow" that statute of limitations for use with the defective enactment (in equity cases, they may invoke the judge-made principle of "laches," which bars a suit unless brought within a "reasonable" time). Why do judges do this, rather than pick a term of years suitable to that enactment? The standard answer is that the selection of a statute of limitations is a matter peculiarly within legislative rather than judicial competence. This response cannot be right, however. If it were, it would be a conclusive argument against borrowing. Actually the considerations bearing on the selection of a statute of limitations are better known to judges than to legislators, for those considerations are the effect of passage of time on the accuracy of adjudication, the effect of old claims on the court queue for new claims, and the desirability of enabling potential defendants after a known period of time to go about their business without worrying about the possibility of being sued. The reason courts will not select a period of limitations is that it is impossible even to appear to *reason* to a number. A judge can give reasons why one statute is like another, but he cannot give reasons for selecting 3 years rather than 4 years, or 10 years rather than 8 years, or 180 days rather than 240 days, as the outer limit of bringing a suit. The element of free choice, of discretion, cannot be concealed. Judges want to conceal the fact that many of their choices are free (including the choice of which statute of limitations to borrow!) in the sense that a different choice could be defended just as strongly. Yet the borrowing method, viewed as a form of reasoning by analogy, seems thoroughly spurious, quite apart from the general weaknesses of that methodology. Statutes are frequently the product of deals with interest groups (see Chapter 9), so there is no presumption that the statutory limitations period is a bona-fide stab at the optimal period. By borrowing it for use in a statute that contains no limitations period, the court may be capriciously projecting an interest-group deal into an area remote from the contemplation of the deal makers and thereby gratuitously disserving the public interest.

My next example of adjudication as policy making is *Bolling v. Sharpe*,[29] decided the same day as *Brown v. Board of Education*. The issue was whether racial segregation of the District of Columbia's public schools was unconstitutional, and the Supreme Court held that it was, finding in the due process clause of the Fifth Amendment a guaranty of equal protection. This was a strained interpretation. The Fourteenth Amendment contains an equal protection clause as well as a due process clause but is inapplicable to the federal government. The Fifth Amendment, which is applicable to (and only to) the federal government, has no equal protection clause; so far as pertains to the *Bolling* case, it has only a due process clause, nothing in the language of which hints at any prohibition of racial discrimination. Although the term "due process" has vague antecedents that even before the Civil War had led some judges to suppose it might contain principles of natural law,[30] the Supreme Court in modern times has generally though not consistently forsworn this interpretation in an attempt to set some bounds to con-

---

29. 347 U.S. 497 (1954).

30. The most famous, although an ambiguous, example is the discussion of "law of the land" in Murray's Lessee v. Hoboken Land & Improvement Co., 59 U.S. (18 How.) 272, 276 (1855); for criticism, see David P. Currie, *The Constitution in the Supreme Court: The First Hundred Years: 1789–1888* 272, 276 n. 304 (1985). Other antecedents are discussed in Daniel A. Farber, "Legal Pragmatism and the Constitution," 72 *Minnesota Law Review* 1331, 1350–1353 (1988), and in Suzanna Sherry, "The Framers' Unwritten Constitution," 54 *University of Chicago Law Review* 1127 (1987).

stitutional law. And there is the problem of identifying the "liberty" or "property" of which the plaintiffs in *Bolling* had been deprived. (The due process clause is limited to deprivations of life, liberty, or property.) Furthermore, if the due process clause of the Fifth Amendment does forbid racial discrimination, it is hard to see why the framers of the Fourteenth Amendment, having decided to impose the due process clause on the states, bothered to add an equal protection clause. If by doing so they were merely trying to make assurance doubly sure, why didn't they make the equal protection clause applicable to the federal government, to avoid a negative implication?

The framers of the Fourteenth Amendment may well have confined the equal protection clause to the states deliberately. The Fourteenth Amendment was an assertion of federal power. States, not the federal government, were oppressing black people wholesale. Deliberate or not, it is hard to get around the language of the clause, which forbids only *states* to deny persons the equal protection of the laws. Any orthodox theory of law implies that the equal protection clause was inapplicable to the District of Columbia schools and the due process clause unavailable to fill the gap. The Supreme Court must have felt, however, that there would be an intolerable anomaly, in a political rather than a conventionally "legal" sense, in allowing the public schools of the nation's capital to remain segregrated when the Supreme Court, sitting in that capital, had just outlawed segregation by states. It would have looked as though the Court wanted to make sure that the inconveniences of desegregation would not be visited on its own venue. Such a decision not only would have seemed hypocritical but also would have blurred the message of *Brown v. Board of Education* and undermined that decision's moral and political force.

Bolling tests the limits of what a court can properly do in the teeth of conventional legal materials. There is something profoundly amiss in a legal system in which judges regularly say to themselves or to each other, "The law requires outcome A, but B makes better political sense so we'll go with B." (They would never say so publicly.) Yet at some point the outcome that lacks political sense, that represents bad policy, that has distinctly untoward anticipated consequences, may *by virtue of that fact* not be the outcome required (permitted?) by law.

Hans Linde has attacked *Bolling* as the epitome of "realistic" judicial decision making, a style he deprecates.[31] Yet he devotes half his attack

---

31. See Hans A. Linde, "Judges, Critics, and the Realist Tradition," 82 *Yale Law Journal* 227, 233–234 (1972).

to conjecturing that the practical consequences of a decision in favor of segregation would not have been untoward—that such a decision might actually have galvanized Congress into dealing responsibly with the segregation problem in general and by doing so might even have headed off the South's massive resistance to *Brown v. Board of Education*. The reader comes away with an impression, perhaps unintended, that consequences, including what would normally be considered political consequences, are relevant to the judicial task after all. Linde has no confidence in the ability of judges to evaluate the consequences correctly, and he has a point there. But what is the alternative? He proposes "construing the living meaning of past political decisions,"[32] but what does that mean?

Ray v. Blair[33] provides another illustration of judicial *Realpolitik*. The Alabama legislature had enacted a statute that required presidential electors, who under Alabama law were chosen in a statewide primary, to pledge to vote in the Electoral College for the nominees of their party's national convention. That statute was challenged on the plausible ground that it took away the electors' independence. The framers of the Constitution unquestionably intended the Electoral College to be an independent, deliberative body rather than a rubber stamp of the state's voters.[34] It was one of several democracy-diluting measures that the framers built into the governmental system they were creating. Nevertheless the Supreme Court upheld the Alabama statute. The American people have come to believe that the President is elected by *them,* not by a cabal of "independent" electors most of whom are unknown to the people. The Alabama statute had been passed in the wake of a revolt by "Dixiecrat" electors against Truman's election in 1948. The prospect of runaway electors is a deeply unsettling one, containing the seeds of a genuine constitutional crisis; the Court displayed political wisdom in declining to provide a nurturing soil.

The fact that Justice Jackson dissented in *Ray* is a bit of a surprise, since he had been the author a decade earlier of one of the greatest pragmatic opinions in the history of the Supreme Court. I refer to the second flag-salute case, *West Virginia State Board of Education v. Barnette*.[35] Three

---

32. Id. at 255. By "past political decisions," he means those made by the Constitution's framers.
33. 343 U.S. 214 (1952).
34. See id. at 228–229 nn. 15–16, and *Federalist No. 68* (Hamilton).
35. 319 U.S. 624 (1943). Subsequent page references to this opinion are in the text.

years earlier, in *Minersville School District v. Gobitis,*[36] the Court had held that the Constitution did not require public school authorities to excuse the children of Jehovah's Witnesses from having to salute and pledge allegiance to the American flag, even though these acts violated the Witnesses' conscience. In *Barnette,* in what may be the most eloquent majority opinion in the history of the Supreme Court, the Court reached a contrary conclusion and overruled *Gobitis.*[37] Justice Frankfurter, the author of *Gobitis,* wrote a fiery dissent.

Jackson acknowledges that his decision is not compelled by the text or history of the Constitution (let alone by precedent):

> the task of translating the majestic generalities of the Bill of Rights, conceived as part of the pattern of liberal government in the eighteenth century, into concrete restraints on officials dealing with the problems of the twentieth century, is one to disturb self-confidence. These principles grew in soil which also produced a philosophy that the individual was the center of society, that his liberty was attainable through mere absence of governmental restraints, and that government should be entrusted with few controls and only the mildest supervision over men's affairs. We must transplant these rights to a soil in which the *laissez-faire* concept or principle of non-interference has withered at least as to economic affairs, and social advancements are increasingly sought through closer integration of society and through expanded and strengthened governmental controls. These changed conditions often deprive precedents of reliability and cast us more than we would choose upon our own judgment. (pp. 639–640)

The offensiveness of the flag salute and pledge to the Jehovah's Witnesses was plain enough; the tough question was whether it was overbalanced by the needs of national unity. The *Gobitis* opinion had remarked, "National unity is the basis of national security."[38] Describing this remark as "the very heart of the *Gobitis* opinion" (p. 640), Jackson makes his own opinion pivot on the question—a question factual rather than legal—whether a compulsory flag salute and pledge are effective in

36. 310 U.S. 586 (1940).

37. "We think the action of the local authorities in compelling the flag salute and pledge transcends constitutional limitations on their power and invades the sphere of intellect and spirit which it is the purpose of the First Amendment to our Constitution to reserve from all official control." P. 642. Actually Justice Jackson's opinion is a plurality opinion, for only three other Justices joined it in its entirety; but the verdict of time has awarded it majority status. For a sad commentary on the decline of judicial eloquence, compare the opinions in *Barnette* with those in Texas v. Johnson, 109 S. Ct. 2533 (1989)—the *Barnette* of the eighties, invalidating a state statute that forbade desecrating the American flag.

38. 310 U.S. at 595.

promoting national unity. The lesson of history, he concludes, including modern history, is no:

> Ultimate futility of such attempts to compel coherence is the lesson of every such effort from the roman drive to stamp out Christianity as a disturber of its pagan unity, the Inquisition, as a means to religious and dynastic unity, the Siberian exiles as a means to Russian unity, down to the fast failing efforts of our present totalitarian enemies. Those who begin coercive elimination of dissent soon find themselves exterminating dissenters. Compulsory unification of opinion achieves only the unanimity of the graveyard . . . The First Amendment . . . was designed to avoid these ends by avoiding these beginnings . . . The case is made difficult not because the principles of its decision are obscure but because the flag involved is our own. (p. 641)

The reference to "the fast failing efforts of our present totalitarian enemies" is particularly significant. *Gobitis* had been decided in June 1940, when the Germans were riding high—partly, it seemed, because of their impressive national unity *("Ein Volk, Ein Reich, Ein Führer!")*. By June 1943, when *Barnette* was decided, the Germans were on the run. Their national unity didn't look so impressive any more, nor did democratic disorder seem as reckless as it had three years earlier. Experience seemed to have falsified the premise of *Gobitis*. Jackson goes on to make a quintessentially pragmatic observation about the benefits of diversity: "We can have intellectual individualism and the rich cultural diversities that we owe to exceptional minds only at the price of occasional eccentricity and abnormal attitudes" (pp. 641–642). Throughout the opinion the emphasis is not on the dogmatics of constitutional law but on the consequence of the compulsory flag salute and pledge, both for the Jehovah's Witnesses and for the rest of the community.

How Are Judges' Visions Changed?

I have suggested that political factors, and sometimes social vision, are decisive in the most difficult cases. The point can be put more strongly: consequences are never irrelevant in law. If they are sufficiently grave they can sway decision, whatever the balance of conventional legal arguments, which for example strongly favored Justice Jackson's dissent in *Ray v. Blair*. But just *how* are consequences or politics decisive? If two social visions clash, which prevails? Equivalently, how does a judge choose between competing social visions? Often the choice will be made on the basis of deeply held personal values, and often these values will be impervious to argument. Persuasion will figure in some cases but it will be persuasion by rhetoric rather than by the coolest forms of reasoned exposition. By definition the latter will not arbitrate between competing social visions—a point strikingly illustrated by Hilary Putnam's suggestion that "respectful contempt" is the honest and natural attitude toward a person with whom one has profound disagreements over political philosophy.[39] The judge who wants to "sell" his social vision to colleagues or future judges does so by presenting it— often, by presenting himself (the tactic that rhetoricians call the "ethical appeal")—in an appealing, a winning, light, in the hope of converting the reader to his views. So the liberal might present himself as hard-headed, the conservative present himself as compassionate, in order to combat the stereotypes attached to the "liberal" and "conservative" labels and attract followers from the other camp or at least cool the ardor of their opposition. Or the contenders might seek to "evoke . . . the core values of [the] audience in a powerful and plausible way" and argue that those values require a particular resolution to the dispute in question.[40] Justice Jackson makes much use of this technique in *Barnette*.

I mentioned conversion in the last paragraph advisedly, having in mind the following passage in Wittgenstein:

> May someone have telling grounds for believing that the earth has only existed for a short time, say since his own birth?—Suppose he had always been told that,—would he have any good reason to doubt it? Men have believed that they could make rain; why should not a king be brought up in the belief that the world began with him? And if Moore [G.E. Moore, whose views on skepticism Wittgenstein is criticizing] and the king were to meet and discuss, could Moore really prove his belief to be the right one? I do not say that Moore could not convert the king to his view, but it would be a conversion of a special kind; the king would be brought to look at the world in a different way.
>
> Remember that one is sometimes convinced of the *correctness* of a view by its *simplicity* or *symmetry*, that is, these are what induce one to go over

39. *Reason, Truth and History* 166 (1981). Putnam is describing his attitude toward his colleague Robert Nozick.

40. Michael Walzer, *Interpretation and Social Criticism* 88–89 (1987). On the rhetoric of judicial opinions, see my book *Law and Literature: A Misunderstood Relation*, ch. 6 (1988); Peter Goodrich, *Reading the Law: A Critical Introduction to Legal Method and Techniques*, ch. 6 (1986); Goodrich, *Legal Discourse: Studies in Linguistics, Rhetoric and Legal Analysis*, pt. 2 (1987); cf. Robert A. Ferguson, "Holmes and the Judicial Figure," 55 *University of Chicago Law Review* 506 (1988). The increase in recent years in the number of difficult cases has been accompanied by a decline in the quality of judicial rhetoric. Remarkably little first-rate judicial prose has been written since the 1950s.

to this point of view. One then simply says something like: "*That's* how
it must be."[41]

Transposed to the legal setting, conversion has unsettling overtones. We
tend to think of it as a sudden, deeply emotional switch from one non-
rational cluster of beliefs to another that is no more (often less) rational,
although Wittgenstein's example is of the opposite, and we tend not to
think of the fact of conversion as a significant point in favor of the winning faith. Although most lawyers think of themselves as engaged in
rational inquiry rather than religious affirmation, the religious impulse
is well-nigh universal; it is particularly strong in the United States;[42] and
in many secular Americans trained in law the impulse gets channeled
into veneration of the Constitution as a sacred text and a decision to
attend one of the churches at which it is worshiped. It is not only on
points of constitutional law that lawyers, judges, and law professors
defend positions with a zeal that approaches the religious. Central to the
women's movement, which has become influential in several areas of
law, is the conversion, or gestalt switch, that consists of taking the traditional woman's role (housewife, mother, "better half," etc.) and looking at in a different light—not as division of labor, recognition of essential differences, quietly heroic self-abnegation, or service to the species
but as brainwashing, oppression, and slavery. Many women and some
men have been brought in recent years to think of the traditional role of
women in this way—not by being shown evidence that this is the way
things "really" are but by being offered a fresh perspective that, once
glimpsed, strikes many with a shock of recognition.

Metaphor, narrative, simile, and analogy in its figurative or metaphoric sense are important terms here. Think of the efforts to defend
the abortion decision by comparing the pregnant woman forbidden to
abort her fetus to a bystander forced against his will to render nine
months of life support to a stranger. (We shall glance at these efforts in
Chapter 11.) The comparison does not change any of the facts about
abortion or even bring new facts to light. Its purpose is to jar people
out of their accustomed ways of thinking about pregnancy and abor-

41. Ludwig Wittgenstein, *On Certainty* 14e (G. E. M. Anscombe and G. H. von Wright
eds. 1969) (¶92). See also id. at 81e (¶612), and William James, *The Varieties of Religious
Experience* 162 (Frederick H. Burkhardt gen'l ed. 1985).
42. See *Gallup Report No. 236: Religion in America 50 Years, 1935–1985* 1, 53 (1985).

tion.[43] Swift put it neatly: "You cannot reason a person out of something he has not been reasoned into."

These points are pragmatic. Persuasion and reason tend to merge in a pragmatist view of truth. If what is good or useful to believe or what one just can't help believing is, for all practical purposes, truth, then persuasion as well as proof can establish truth, since persuasion can be a source of tenacious beliefs. But the fusion of reason and persuasion makes the concept of "truth" problematic, as we have already seen, and by doing so it undermines the law's rational pretensions. Yet, like it or not, something like the process described by Wittgenstein does seem to explain—along with changes in judicial personnel (but that is really the same thing)—many of the seismic shifts that have occurred in our law, such as the great expansion of liability on virtually all fronts since the 1950s, the expansion in the rights of criminal defendants and of prisoners, the increased recognition of women's rights, the explosive growth of constitutional law.

Consider reapportionment. Until the late 1950s the idea that malapportionment of state legislatures might violate the equal protection clause was virtually unthinkable; twenty years later the idea that it might not had become virtually unthinkable. What changed in the interim? New information had not exposed an error in the old ways. There had been no new discoveries about the "real" meaning of the equal protection clause. And there was very little evidence in the 1950s and 1960s, and there is very little today, that legislative malapportionment has significant consequences for public policy.[44] For reasons that are unclear, judges and lawyers started looking at the equal protection clause and the

---

43. Cf. "What Metaphors Mean," in Donald Davidson, *Inquiries into Truth and Interpretation* 245, 261–264 (1984). On the centrality of metaphor in law, see Steven L. Winter, "Transcendental Nonsense, Metaphoric Reasoning, and the Cognitive Stakes for Law," 137 *University of Pennsylvania Law Review* 1105 (1989); also references in Chapter 13 of this book.

44. See, for example, William H. Riker, "Democracy and Representation: Reconciliation of *Ball V. James* and *Reynolds V. Sims*," 1 *Supreme Court Economic Review* 39, 41–55 (1982); Larry M. Schwab, *The Impact of Congressional Reapportionment and Redistricting* 196–200 (1988); Timothy G. O'Rourke, *The Impact of Reapportionment* 159 (1980). A few studies have found a potentially significant effect of reapportionment on policy. See in particular Roger A. Hanson and Robert E. Crew, Jr., "The Policy Impact of Reapportionment," 8 *Law and Society Review* 69 (1973); Douglas G. Feig, "Expenditures in the American States: The Impact of Court-Ordered Legislative Reapportionment," 6 *American Politics Quarterly* 309 (1978). No study that I am aware of, however, finds that the strict "one man one vote" approach taken by the Supreme Court has policy significance.

federal judicial role in a new way.[45] We exaggerate the efficacy of appeals to objective truths in altering legal doctrine, and in doing so we exaggerate the importance of such truths in law.

I do not mean to suggest that everything is contingent, "up for grabs," so that the gifted poet or rhetorician can by skill in generating new metaphors or new perspectives alter society. I do not believe in the infinite plasticity of human nature or social arrangements. Gifted poets and others can awaken people to facts but cannot create facts. In Chapter 13 I offer a "material" explanation for the women's movement. The inconsistency of legislative malapportionment with democratic theory was not something that the Supreme Court created in *Baker v. Carr*. It just had not seemed the sort of abuse that federal courts should attempt to correct, in part because the attempt might (it was feared) precipitate a confrontation with state legislatures. In the event, the fear proved to be unfounded; after several decades of federal judicial activism we now know that states are for the most part delighted and relieved to cede power and responsibility to the federal government in general and to the federal courts in particular. Had they not been, *Baker* might have become as controversial a venture in judicial activism as *Roe v. Wade* has become. My point is that the about-face that was *Baker v. Carr*, like the other great turning points in twentieth-century American law (and in law, period), was not the product of deep reflection on the meaning of the Constitution and the common law. Often such turning points are not even the product of newly obtained information (and these— meaning and data—are not clearly different things), but instead reflect changing outlooks. We shall consider a dramatic example in Chapter 10: the overruling in *Brown v. Board of Education* of *Plessy v. Ferguson*.

The flag-salute cases are still another example. Frankfurter too had appealed to consequences, in particular the consequences for a proper balance between courts and legislatures if the Court took too aggressive a role in striking down illiberal statutes. Somehow those consequences looked less impressive in 1943 than they had in 1940. Today we can see that *Barnette* was the first step toward a larger and more powerful federal judiciary than some believe to be good for the country; and perhaps, too, a greater individualism than is healthy. I suggest not that the step should not have been taken but that its best explanation lies in a change of outlook rather than in an acquisition of new information, although

45. Cf. Jan G. Deutsch, "Neutrality, Legitimacy, and the Supreme Court: Some Intersections between Law and Political Science," 20 *Stanford Law Review* 169, 224 (1968).

the course of the war had provided some new, if oblique, information regarding the consequences of the compulsory flag salute.[46]

Critical Legal Studies

I have concentrated in Part I on challenging exaggerated beliefs in the autonomy and cogency of legal reasoning rather than on challenging the opposite exaggeration, the exaggeration of law's indeterminacy and subjectivity. My emphasis reflects the fact that the beliefs on which I have been focusing not only are more ingrained, being common to both the liberal and the conservative segments of the legal-political spectrum, but also are more plausible than the opposite view, espoused by some legal realists in previous generations and by many members of the critical legal studies movement in this one, that all law is politics in a narrow and disreputable sense and right-wing politics at that. This view is difficult to evaluate because it is stated in a nonfalsifiable form. Whenever a judge is found acting contrary to his presumed political interests, his behavior is explained as throwing sand in the public's eye—forging even tighter ideological bonds by appearing to be evenhanded. Maybe the judge *is* doing this. A rule-of-law ideology would not be a persuasive method of mystification and cooptation were it not occasionally employed against the rich and powerful.[47] But this makes it exceedingly difficult to distinguish empirically between a genuinely evenhanded administration of the law and an administration permeated by class bias, or even to choose between them normatively. Since judges are human, we cannot expect a perfectly evenhanded administration of justice; and if tilt is therefore inevitable, why should an administration of justice subtly tilted in favor of the upper class be thought more disreputable than one subtly tilted in favor of the lower class?

This discussion shows, moreover, that the critical legal studies movement is prey to the genetic fallacy. Even if the motives for judges' adherence to rules are sometimes basely political, to the extent the judges do adhere to them law *is* different from politics. A Peirce-style pragmatist

46. A consequence I have not mentioned is the wave of private violence against Jehovah's Witnesses that followed the *Gobitis* decision. Yet the wave was concentrated in the month after the decision and had abated by the time *Barnette* was decided. See David R. Manwaring, *Render unto Caesar: The Flag-Salute Controversy* 164–165, 169 (fig. 1), 172 (1962). The proposition that experience falsified *Gobitis* is argued in Richard Danzig, "Justice Frankfurter's Opinions in the Flag Salute Cases: Blending Logic and Psychologic in Constitutional Decisionmaking," 36 *Stanford Law Review* 675, 722–723 (1984).

47. See E. P. Thompson, *Whigs and Hunters: The Origin of the Black Act* 258–269 (1975).

(see Chapter 5) would be inclined to put this more strongly: the proposition that judges adhere to the rule of law because they are sly politicos and the proposition that they do so because they are good judges have the same consequences and therefore the same meaning.

The "law is politics" school also ignores the existence of easy cases and exaggerates the significance of the indeterminate ones (of which there are indeed plenty) by insisting that law is not law unless it lives up to its most extravagant formalist billings. Yet between the formalist model, at one extreme, and "conversion," at the other, there are not only the variety of methods of practical reason discussed in previous chapters but also

> discourse in which "agreed-upon criteria for reaching agreement" are not the axis upon which communication turns and the evaluation of disparate views in terms of some accepted framework within which they can be objectively assessed and commensurated with one another is not the organizing aim. Hope for agreement is not abandoned. People occasionally do change their minds or halve their differences as a result of intelligence concerning what individuals or groups of individuals whose minds run on other tracks believe. But "exciting and fruitful disagreement"—how do I know what I think until I see what you say—is recognized as a no less rational process . . . It can also be, less dramatically, a practicable method for living in a situation where dissensus is chronic, probably worsening, and not soon to be removed.[48]

Disagreement can be rational and creative, or at least cathartic, even if it does not lead to consensus or demonstrable truths; and the positions of the contending parties need not be vulgarly political in character or motivation. It can be cathartic simply by virtue of being a substitute for physical violence. It can elicit information that may reduce the intensity of disagreements that are based in part on misunderstandings, and it can further reduce that intensity simply by revealing the contestants to each other as serious and rational. But it can also intensify disagreements by revealing the true depth of the chasms between persons who have different values on fundamental questions.

Mark Kelman's analysis of *Regina v. Cunningham*[49] illustrates critical legal studies in action. In the course of breaking open a gas meter in the cellar of a house and stealing the eight shillings that were in the meter, Cunningham ripped the meter off the wall, with the consequence—

48. Geertz, note 7 above, at 223–224.
49. 41 Crim. App. 155 (1957); see Mark G. Kelman, "Assume Nothing!" 22 *Stanford Lawyer,* Spring 1988, at 18.

unintended by and unknown to him—that the gas main fractured, causing gas to seep through the cellar wall to the house next door; the gas
seriously injured a woman who lived there. Cunningham was convicted
of larceny and sentenced to six months in prison. He was also convicted
of "unlawfully and maliciously causing a noxious thing to be taken so
as thereby to endanger life," and he was sentenced to five years in prison
for that crime. On appeal he argued that the judge should not have
instructed the jury that "maliciously" meant simply that the defendant
knew he had no business taking the meter. The appellate court reversed,
holding that the jury should have been told to determine whether the
defendant "foresaw that the removal of the gas meter might cause injury
to someone but nevertheless removed it." In Kelman's view, the appro-
priateness of punishing Cunningham for "poisoning" (as Kelman calls
malicious endangering) depends on the arbitrary choice between treating him "as being in the situation of someone dealing with gas meters
or someone stealing from gas meters."[50] If the former, he is guilty
regardless of how careful he was; theft is an unreasonable mode of dealing with a gas meter and any risk created thereby is undue. If the latter,
Cunningham should get off if he was as careful as the average meter
thief.

Why the care of the average thief should be thought an appropriate
benchmark for criminal liability, other than in a society of thieves,
escapes me. It implies that if Cunningham had been a clumsy repairman
rather than a thief, he might have been punished more heavily than
Cunningham the thief, because the average meter repairman is more
careful than the average meter thief. The point of *Regina v. Cunningham*
is that a thief who is careless of the consequences of his theft for human
safety is more dangerous to the community than a careful thief and
should therefore be punished more severely. This much seems unexcep-
tionable; and asking whether the thief foresaw those consequences is an
indirect way of asking how dangerous a person he is. The difficult question, not so much about the case as about the situation depicted in it—
but a question that Kelman's analysis does not touch—is whether Cunningham should have been punished because the method of stealing
from the gas meter endangered human safety, even if he was too dumb
to realize this. In other words, should mere negligence be criminally
actionable, either generally or in the particular case of a careless thief?
This question can be answered by comparing the civil and criminal sanctions for negligence. The civil sanction is damages, and since most

50. Id. at 46–47.

thieves are indigent the threat of a civil sanction for negligent injuries inflicted in the course of a theft is unlikely to deter. We need a criminal sanction to do that, which means we need a criminal sanction on top of the sanction for (careful) theft so that the thief will have an incentive to be careful.

Readers who find this approach to *Regina v. Cunningham* persuasive may nevertheless be inclined to question whether the approach is, at bottom, distinguishable from that of critical legal studies. I have offered an economic explanation for the decision, and thereby denied the specialness of law. Have I then, all unknowingly, signed on to Duncan Kennedy's attempted exposé of the bankruptcy of conventional legal thought?

> Teachers teach nonsense when they persuade students that legal reasoning is distinct, *as a method for reaching correct results,* from ethical and political discourse in general (*that is,* from policy analysis). It is true that there is a distinctive lawyers' body of knowledge of the rules in force. It is true that there are distinctive lawyers' argumentative techniques for spotting gaps, conflicts, and ambiguities in the rules, for arguing broad and narrow holdings of cases, and for generating pro and con policy arguments. But these are *only* argumentative techniques. There is never a "correct legal solution" that is other than the correct ethical and political solution to that legal problem. Put another way, everything taught, except the formal rules themselves and the argumentative techniques for manipulating them, is policy and nothing more. It follows that the classroom distinction between the unproblematic, legal case and the policy-oriented case is a mere artifact: each could as well be taught in the opposite way.[51]

Until the last sentence, my only criticism is that Kennedy seems to be saying more than he is. Yes, everything in law is ultimately a "what to do" problem, and so in a sense an ethical problem. And therefore it can indeed be said that there is never a correct legal solution that is other than the correct ethical or, if you please, political solution (for ethical questions are themselves political in a society that is ethically diverse). But the impression conveyed by stating this as a naked proposition is that the correct solution to every legal problem is the solution that would be arrived at by a careful student of ethics who knew nothing about law. And that is wrong. The ethicist and the judge are subject to different ethical principles. The latter is, and the former is not, a decision maker in a system of government, and such a decision maker must be

---

51. "Legal Education as Training for Hierarchy," in *The Politics of Law: A Progressive Critique* 40, 47 (David Kairys ed. 1982).

concerned not only with doing substantive justice in the case at hand but also with maintaining a legal fabric that includes considerations of precedent, of legislative authority, of the framing of issues by counsel, of the facts of record, and so forth. All this Kennedy ignores, and the oversight leads him to an erroneous conclusion. For there *are* unproblematic legal cases; they are so precisely by virtue of the considerations that he ignores. If such cases were taught as policy cases the teacher would not be teaching law, and if the real policy cases—the cases in the open area, where the conventional springs of legal decision making dry up—were taught as unproblematic legal cases the teacher would not be teaching policy where it ought to be taught.

PART II ❧

THE ONTOLOGY
OF LAW

5 ∽

Ontology, the Mind, and Behaviorism

Ontological Skepticism

Part I treated the question of law's objectivity primarily as one of epistemology, the branch of philosophy concerned with establishing (or disestablishing) foundations or warrants for knowledge. Epistemology is closely related to ontology, which deals with questions of existence (less provocatively, with what is). The relation lies in the fact that positing entities of debatable ontology is a frequent device for attempting to solve epistemological problems. If we agreed with Plato that there is a Form of Justice accessible to persons having certain aptitudes and experiences, then we might believe that the soundness of a legal decision could be gauged simply by comparing the decision with the Form; and likewise if we thought God had inscribed the principles of justice in the book of nature in a form accessible to human reason. Without going so far, we might think we could guarantee the ability of good judges to decide even difficult cases[1] correctly by showing that for every question about law there exists a right answer, even if there is continuing, perhaps interminable, controversy over which answer is the right one. Conversely, the skeptical position will be strengthened if it can be shown that lawyers and judges encounter serious difficulties in trying to latch on to useful entities.

Philosophers have long puzzled over immaterial "things," although their enthusiasm for such debates is beginning to wane. Chicago and

---

1. I am deliberately avoiding the more common, but misleading, expression "hard cases." The term originally meant cases that tug at the heartstrings; that is its meaning in the old saw "hard cases make bad law." By semantic drift it has come to mean difficult cases, which makes nonsense of the old saw. Only difficult cases make law, good or bad. Cases that are easy to decide are so by virtue of being controlled by existing law.

New York, we may agree tentatively, are things, or assemblages of things. But what about the "fact" that Chicago is west of New York—is that a thing, too? What about another relation, the Pythagorean theorem? Is that a thing, despite its apparent lack of a spatio-temporal locus, and, if so, would it still be one if no one had ever discovered it? Numbers and other mathematical entities are objective, in a way that pains and colors are not. Yet they are not actual, in a way that pains and colors are. So which are "real"? The words printed on this page are things, but are the propositions they express? A horse is a thing; what about Pegasus, in the sentence (which happens to be true) "Pegasus is a mythical horse"? Might not the assertion that something does not exist be thought to imply that it is a "thing" of some kind? Heating water to a certain temperature causes it to boil; does this make causation a thing? What about the *capacity* of water to boil? More generally, are dispositions—color, the speed of an ocelot at rest, the weight of a massive boulder firmly perched, the temper of a choleric person—things? Are intentions things? Do we have a material part (the body) and an immaterial part (the mind, or if you prefer, the soul)? A rabbit is a thing; is law a thing? And what about moral "entities"? Is "goodness" real? "Justice"?

It is easy to become dizzy thinking about such questions. But they are only the beginning. On reflection, even the distinction between material and immaterial things blurs. A "solid object"—a table, for instance—is a material thing that consists mostly of empty space (the space within and between its atoms), and a flock of pigeons is a material thing with visible spaces between its constituents. "America's cities" is another discontinuous, more-or-less material thing. But "a pigeon in New York and a sparrow in Chicago" is not a thing; not all sets of noncontiguous objects count as things. Exposure to these puzzles makes it difficult to retain a robust faith in a clear-cut ontology, one that contains rabbits, minds, the law, fictional characters, numbers, and so forth in happy coexistence. Our use of words and ideas seems driven by expediency rather than by a striving for correspondence with things "as they are."

The baffling character of questions of existence gives Charles Peirce's pragmatic approach to meaning—the meaning of a proposition is its consequences, so that propositions that have no consequences are meaningless—a strong appeal even though as a definition of meaning it is forced and polemical. The proposition that God created the universe but then withdrew, and has never intervened in its operations and never will, is not meaningless, even though it has no consequences in the sense either that experiments or observation could falsify or confirm the proposition or that we might behave differently if the proposition were true than we would if it were false. It would be more accurate, if less dramatic, to say not that the proposition is meaningless but that it is not worth bothering one's head about. Nevertheless that is an important statement too, and it will give us a handle on dealing with questions of ontology. We can ask, for example, what the consequences are of believing that people do or do not have minds. Maybe there are no consequences. Maybe the heavy talk in law about such mental entities as intent and premeditation, or such metaphysical entities as causation and justice, is bogus.

The reader familiar with philosophical debates may smell a whiff of logical positivism, the view that all propositions can be sorted into one of three bins: the tautological, the empirically verifiable, and the nonsensical. And a whiff of the antimetaphysicality of the later Wittgenstein and of J. L. Austin. Or the antirealism or conventionalism, already alluded to, that teaches either that our grammar (broadly defined) and perceptual structure divide up the world into convenient slices that need not correspond to the actual structure of things—the view neatly summarized by William Blake in "The Mental Traveller" as "the Eye altering alters all"—or, alternatively, that things, material and immaterial, are the joint creation of nature and the human frame of reference, which is itself a product of nature.[2]

The details, variants, and pedigree of what I am calling with some license the pragmatic approach to meaning, and, by extension, to questions of ontology, need not concern us. All that is important is that the approach be able to improve our understanding of law. Its implications are skeptical, and thus complement the implications of the epistemological approach of Part I. But they are not, or at least need not be, radically skeptical, and again this is in tune with the earlier chapters. Indeed the approach can be used to deflect (although how effectively is an open question) the skeptical ploy of asking you to prove that you are not just a brain in a vat, receiving impressions of an external world from a mad scientist who controls your access to the sensory world. (This is the

---

2. The literature on these issues is vast; places to start include Hilary Putnam, *The Many Faces of Realism: The Paul Carus Lectures,* lectures 1 and 3 (1987); Willard Van Orman Quine, "On What There Is," in Quine, *From a Logical Point of View: Nine Logico-Philosophical Esasys* 1 (2d ed. 1980); Quine, *Theories and Things* (1981); Nelson Goodman, *Of Mind and Other Matters,* chs. 2–3 (1984); Bertrand Russell, *The Problems of Philosophy* (1912). Of incomparable vividness is William James's discussion of ontology in *The Principles of Psychology,* vol. 1, pp. 285–286, and vol. 2, pp. 291–293 (1890). The mind's construction of objects is explored from a biological perspective in J. Z. Young, *Philosophy and the Brain* 80–82 (1987).

modern, technocratic version of the age-old puzzle: How do we know there is a real world out there, when all we have is sensations?) Most efforts to defend against the brain-in-a-vat attack founder on the absence of an external reference point with which to compare the experience of being a brain in a vat with the experience of inhabiting the "real" world. The conundrum is cleverly designed to eliminate any such point. If you are a brain in a vat, unlike a person dreaming, who also has (or believes he has!) a waking state, you have by assumption the identical sensations you would have if you were not a brain in a vat—so how do you know whether you are one or not?

The pragmatic answer to this is that believing oneself to be a brain in a vat can have no consequences for one's behavior, unless one is crazy. One carries on just as before. The belief has no consequences and therefore makes no serious claim to assent.[3] You may be tempted to reply that someone who was convinced he was a brain in a vat would realize that his life was meaningless, and that this realization would affect his behavior—he would not exert himself as much as he otherwise would. But how could you be *convinced* you were a brain in a vat? You might entertain this as a possibility but, by hypothesis, there is no way of proving it or even of showing it to be more probably true than false. In fact it is more probably false than true; so it would not be rational to act on it. In further fact we seem incapable of entertaining such a belief except when playing philosophy.

The qualifications implicit in such language as "rational" and "unless one is crazy" may seem to give the game away, however. If attempting to act on the belief that one is a brain in a vat is taken to demonstrate insanity, and the irrelevance of the belief to action is demonstrated by the fact that only an insane person would act on it, one is arguing in a circle. But the circle can be broken by considering the other beliefs and actions of the insane. A person who really believes he is a brain in a vat is bound to have other crazy beliefs. We know they are crazy by watching him act on them. We observe that he is a poor guide to acting rationally in the sense of adapting means to ends. His behavior displays a high

---

3. An alternative approach, also pragmatic, is to treat the existence of the external world as simply the most plausible hypothesis about "reality"; Bertrand Russell's discussion of the ontology of the cat, quoted in Chapter 2, illustrates this approach. Another argument (from the standpoint of evolutionary epistemology, mentioned in a note in Chapter 3) is that a belief in an external world is so much more conducive to survival and reproduction than disbelief in it that the belief is "hard-wired" into our brains; we simply are incapable of *really* believing, in the sense of being prepared to act on, the proposition that there is no external world.

degree of contradiction and futility, and these are reasons for not counting his "vote" on the question whether people are brains in vats.[4]

This discussion of rationality casts a sidelight on the test of time.
Chapter 3 suggested a voting analogy, noting that time broadens the
franchise. Since there are eligibility requirements for voting, the analogy
implies that maybe some potential voters in the temporal election
should be disfranchised. Yet to use rationality as a criterion for judging
the test of time undermines the claim that the test is the (or an) ultimate
foundation of or warrant for our knowledge.

A question related to whether there is an external world, but more
pertinent to the problems of jurisprudence, is whether other people, or
animals, really have minds; for one can never observe another creature's
mind. On one level this is an absurd question—we simply cannot help
thinking that there are other minds.[5] But on another level it is a fruitful
question, or at least a spur to fruitful speculation. There is after all something deeply puzzling about "the mind."[6] It is not only unobservable but
immaterial, yet despite its immateriality it seems to be in control of a
material object, the body. Even the concept of mind is unclear. Mind
seems related to consciousness (the set of one's conscious thoughts is a
typical dictionary definition of mind), yet it would be odd to say that

4. Cf. David Pears, *The False Prison: A Study of the Development of Wittgenstein's Philos*
ophy, vol. 1, pp 32–33 (1987); and recall the distinction made in Chapter 3, with specific
reference to commitment for insanity, between coercive and competitive objectivity. Rorty
takes a more skeptical view: "the limits of sanity are set by what *we* can take seriously.
This, in turn, is determined by our upbringing, our historical situation." "The Priority of
Democracy to Philosophy," in *The Virginia Statute for Religious Freedom: Its Evolution and*
Consequences in American History 257, 267 (Merrill D. Peterson and Robert C. Vaughan eds.
1988).

5. In Wittgenstein's characteristic formulation, "just try to keep hold of this idea [that
the people around me are automata, lack consciousness, even though they behave the same
way as usual] in the midst of your ordinary intercourse with others, in the street, say! Say
to yourself, for example: 'The children over there are mere automata; all their liveliness is
mere automatism.' And you will either find these words becoming quite meaningless; or
you will produce in yourself some kind of uncanny feeling." Ludwig Wittgenstein, *Philo-*
sophical Investigations 126e (3d ed., G. E. M. Anscombe trans , 1968) (¶420). Compare
Hume's view of skepticism: "that all his [Bishop Berkeley's] arguments, though otherwise
intended, are, in reality, merely sceptical, appears from this, *that they admit of no answer and*
produce no conviction. Their only effect is to cause that momentary amazement and irreso-
lution and confusion, which is the result of scepticism." *An Enquiry Concerning Human*
Understanding 155 n. 1 (3d ed., P. H. Nidditch ed., 1975), (§12, pt. 1).

6. As demonstrated in Gilbert Ryle's classic, *The Concept of Mind* (1949). For a serviceable recent discussion of the mind-body problem, see Myles Brand, *Intending and Acting:*
Toward a Naturalized Action Theory (1984). Another recent discussion, one that is both fascinating and very much in the spirit of Ryle's work in doubting the explanatory value of
the idea of the mind, is Arthur W. Collins, *The Nature of Mental Things* (1987).

people have no minds while they are sleeping or that all the things people do without conscious thinking—which might include writing an inspired passage of music or poetry[7]—are mindless. Much, perhaps most, thought is unconscious; recall the discussion of tacit knowing in Chapter 3. Maybe, therefore, the idea of the mind has no consequences, at least no interesting or pertinent ones.

I am not a philosophical skeptic and will not pretend to be agnostic about whether I am the only person in the world with a mental life. Obviously most adults and older children can and do speak without vocalization (that is, can "conceal their thoughts") and form mental images. But this barebones concept of mind, which essentially equates mind to consciousness, is different from the idea that there is a something, the "mind," which is the locus of intentions, the invisible puppeteer, the inner man or woman. It is that idea which may have no consequences for law and should perhaps be discarded, despite the law's emphatic (but, I shall argue, shallow) commitment to it.

An alternative approach, also broadly pragmatic, is to ask *why* we cannot help thinking that other people have minds. I suggest that we often use the word "mind" (either in the weak sense of consciousness or in the strong sense of intentionality and control) not to name a thing, not to make an ontological assertion, but to cover our ignorance of certain causal relationships.[8] Dispel the ignorance, and the concept of mind ceases to have consequences and can be—and what is more interesting, is—discarded. For example, we are more likely to impute a mind to a cat than to the most powerful computer, even though the computer will beat the world's smartest cat at chess every time.[9] We think we know more about the causality of a computer's operations than about the causality of a cat's behavior. We are not sure why a cat jumps onto one

7. On the importance of the unconscious in creativity, see, for example, *The Creative Process: A Symposium* (Brewster Ghiselin ed. 1952).

8. Compare Wittgenstein's "beetle" example: "Suppose everyone had a box with something in it: we call it a 'beetle'. No one can look into anyone else's box, and everyone says he knows what a beetle is only by looking at *his* beetle.—Here it would be quite possible for everyone to have something different in his box . . . But suppose the word 'beetle' had a use in these people's language?—If so it would be used as the name of a thing." Wittgenstein, note 5 above, at 100e (¶293). But we do not say that we know what the mind is *only* by looking at our own mind; we draw inferences in the manner suggested in Chapter 2.

9. Actually, a cat is much more intelligent than any computer—indeed, the world's most powerful computer probably has no more computational power than a cockroach. (This will change.) Computers are special-purpose calculators, unlike animals, and through specialization can "beat" animals (including people) at certain specific, well-defined, "routinizable" tasks. See Philip Elmer-DeWitt, "Fast and Smart: Designers Race to Build the Supercomputers of the Future," *Time Magazine,* March 28, 1988, at 54.

person's lap rather than another's, why it meows in a certain way, why sometimes it purrs and at other times it flattens its ears; we are not sure that all this is just instinctual, programmed. (Maybe zoologists are sure; if they are, I would expect them to attribute less mental activity to a cat than does the man in the street.) We impute a mind to a cat in the hope that we can predict and therefore influence the cat's behavior in the same way that we try to anticipate and adjust to people's behavior by assuming they think the way we do. This would not be a plausible strategy for dealing with computers, at least as they are currently designed.

This analysis suggests that as human beings learn more about the world, the number of posited mental entities or states diminishes—and so we observe. Ancient and primitive peoples often impute minds to "inanimate" objects, such as the sea. This is notable in Homer; and it is unlikely that he or his audience regarded Poseidon as merely a fictional construct.[10] Ignorance about nature made the imputation of mind to "inanimate" objects plausible. The sea behaves in a tempestuous and unpredictable fashion, a little like a person; maybe it *is* a person, and therefore can be placated the way a wrathful, powerful person sometimes can be. Once we learn that the causality of a tempest is different from that of a human temper tantrum, we cease imputing mental activity to the sea. If we understood the stock market better, we would cease personifying it. Aristotle's physics treats objects in nature much as if they were animate beings, with goals; today we are more likely to treat animate beings on the model of objects.

Mental and Other Metaphysical Entities in Law

I am about to cross the line from general ontology to legal ontology, and it may be useful to indicate at the outset what we shall be encountering on the other side. I shall begin with the question of mental entities in law—intent, premeditation, "free will" (as in the principle that a defendant's confession, to be admissible in a criminal trial, must be the product of the defendant's free will). I shall argue, in the spirit of the preceding section, that these are entities of distinctly dubious ontology (along with such other well-worn courtroom entities as "causation" and "reputation"), and that the law recognizes that at some level and is much less mentalistic than legal semantics implies. I propose that we can do without the concept of mind in the strong sense even when analyzing

10. I grant that this is a difficult question. See Paul Veyne, *Did the Greeks Believe in Their Myths? An Essay on the Constitutive Imagination* (1988).

judicial behavior. The next chapter asks whether there exist "right answers" either to controversial legal questions or to the difficult factual questions that arise in litigation; to overstate slightly, my answer is no. Chapter 7 gives the same answer to the question whether law itself is an entity. I propose instead that it is an activity, though I recognize the incompleteness of the activity theory.

Mens Rea. Oliver Wendell Holmes believed, much in the spirit of the first section of this chapter, that the role of mental states in law diminishes as law becomes more sophisticated, reflecting the progress of scientific knowledge; this is a major theme of his classic, *The Common Law* (1881). Recall that in early law a deodand—it might be the wheel of a cart that had run over and killed someone—was often punished as a criminal, on the theory that it had an evil will, which had caused it to kill. From these and other examples Holmes argued that as law matures, liability—even criminal liability—becomes progressively more "external," that is, more a matter of conduct than of intent. There is plainly some merit to the idea. For example, if we had a complete model of the criminal act, so that we could predict a crime with one hundred percent accuracy from information about a person's genes and upbringing, we probably would not require proof that the act had been "intended," in order to punish the actor. Maybe we would talk about people being programmed to kill rather than deciding to kill, and maybe we would no longer use the word "punishment." We would deal with criminals as we deal with unreasonably dangerous machines, which implies that, where feasible, we would intervene before the crime was committed. Holmes foretold such a development.[11] In doing so he was standing the concept of deodand on its head: instead of treating dangerous objects as people, he was proposing to treat dangerous people as objects.

One could argue that as law becomes more sophisticated, states of mind should play an ever larger role in liability. Our understanding of the mind may improve—maybe we will learn to read minds. But maybe there is nothing to read, or maybe we are not interested in what the murderer was thinking when he pulled the trigger. If we take seriously the actor's adage that no man is a villain in his own eyes, we can expect to find, if we ever succeed in peering into the murderer's mind, an elaborate, perhaps quite plausible, rationalization for his deed. But so what? We would punish him all the same.[12] The social concern is with the deed

11. In his essay "The Path of the Law," 10 *Harvard Law Review* 457, 470–471 (1897).

12. Compare A. D. Nuttall, "Did Meursault Mean to Kill the Arab?—The Intentional Fallacy Fallacy," 10 *Critical Quarterly* 95 (1968).

(whether impending or already committed) rather than with the mental state that accompanies it.

The one mental element presupposed by this view of law is the capacity of the potential lawbreaker to understand the legal threat and the other relevant circumstances in which he is operating, including any threat posed by the victim. This may seem a significant qualification of my antimentalist stance, because it opens up the possibility of excuses based on mistake or insanity. In fact the only sort of mistake likely to exculpate an offender is the reasonable mistake, which is simply the inference from average behavior; and the only type of insanity that is likely to exculpate is the insanity that manifests itself in behavior—in "acting crazy"—apart from behavior during the crime itself. We can use formal or informal methods of statistical inference to draw inferences from observed behavior, but we cannot discover private thoughts, at least not without torture and probably not with it, for the intentional component of human action may not be conscious.

So while it is true that even a behaviorist (or determinist—I use the terms interchangeably) view of law assumes that the persons whose behavior we want to constrain know what the law requires in the situation in which they find themselves, as well as what that situation is factually (what choices the actor has, and so forth), the ability to comprehend does not require a mind that harbors intentions and directs muscles. Many animals can understand orders. The distinction between comprehension and volition is the distinction suggested earlier between a weak and a strong sense of "mind." A parallel distinction is between rational and mental activity—equivalently, between a rational decision and thinking. The laboratory rat that, faced with a choice between a larger and a smaller quantity of food, chooses the larger is being rational, but this characterization does not commit us to the idea that the rat has a "mind." The person who refrains from committing a crime because, when the threat of punishment is added to the other disutilities of such conduct, the net expected utility from the deed is negative is being rational too. And unlike the rat, he must possess language, to understand the threat and choose in light of it (but so, in a sense, must a dog taught to heel—it must understand commands). But whether and how he thinks the choice through and "makes up his mind" is of no concern in a behaviorist conception of law, the conception Holmes bequeathed us.

That conception is prominent in the economic analysis of law. William Landes and I have proposed an analysis of intentional torts that dispenses with the notion of "intent" other than as a proxy for certain characteristics of the tortious act, notably a large gap between the cost of the act to the victim and the small or even negative cost to the injurer of not committing the act.[13] The difference between negligence and deliberate wrongdoing, on this view, is that the negligent person is one who does not devote enough resources (care, or whatever) to avoiding inflicting injury, whereas the deliberate wrongdoer is one who expends resources on inflicting it. It is the difference between the person who takes another's umbrella by foolish mistake and the person who is "careful" to take an umbrella that is not his. In the word "deliberate," however, is concealed a notion of purposive activity—and can a non-mentalist account of purpose be given? It can. "Purpose" describes the fitting of means to ends. You do A because that is the least costly way of bringing about state B, the state that confers the greatest net benefits on you. What we were doing, then, was substituting what is rational for a person to do for what the person intends to do,[14] and this substitution was a natural one because the process by which hypostasized mental states give way to behavioral hypotheses is central to economic analysis. The "utility function" in economics is a concept parallel to "intent" in law. It summarizes the tastes, values, preferences, and objectives of the individual characterized by the function. A goal of economic research is to change as many of the elements of the utility function—mysterious mental entities—as possible into parameters, which can be measured.[15] So one might begin by suggesting that some people have a "taste" for obtaining a college education but then show that this taste is instrumental to a more general goal; call it income maximizing. The propensity to attend college will now be seen as a function of the cost of college and of the effect of college in raising one's lifetime income.[16]

13. William M. Landes and Richard A. Posner, *The Economic Structure of Tort Law* 149–189 (1987).

14. For similar approaches from a philosophical angle, see Nuttall, note 12 above; Anthony Kenny, "Intention and Purpose in Law," in *Essays in Legal Philosophy* 146, 159–161 (Robert S. Summers ed. 1968); Daniel C. Dennett, *The Intentional Stance*, ch. 2 (1987).

15. A particularly bold example of this approach is George J. Stigler and Gary S. Becker, "De Gustibus Non Est Disputandum," 67 *American Economic Review* 76 (1977).

16. See Gary S. Becker, *Human Capital: A Theoretical and Empirical Analysis, with Special Reference to Education* (2d ed. 1975). There is extensive empirical support for the economic model of higher education; for a small sample of the literature, see W. W. McMahon, "Expected Rates of Return to Education," in *Economics of Education: Research and Studies* 187 (George Psacharopoulos ed. 1987); Christopher A. Pissarides, "From School to University: The Demand for Post-Compulsory Education in Britain," 92 *Economic Journal* 654 (1982); Alex Maurizi, "Rates of Return to Dentistry and the Decision to Enter Dental School," 10 *Journal of Human Resources* 521 (1975); Frank A. Sloan, "The Demand for Higher Education: The Case of Medical School Applicants," 6 *Journal of Human Resources* 466 (1971); Mark C.

Ideally, one could predict whether people would go to college even if one knew nothing about their thoughts on the subject; and then one might stop talking, in analytical work at least, about people "wanting" to go to college or "thinking about" going to college. People would still have desires and thoughts, but these would be strictly epiphenomenal.[17]

I have not mentioned free will, and this may seem a serious omission. That many of the economists who plump most strongly for a determinist approach to human behavior are libertarians may seem to demonstrate a deep fissure in the economic model; and how can a behaviorist approach handle such classic intrusions of "free will" thinking into law as the principle that a criminal's "involuntary" confessions cannot be used against him at his trial? It may be that in fastening on the measurable dimensions of human behavior, the economists are overlooking its most important dimension.

In trying to answer these questions I begin by setting to one side the brand of determinism that asserts or, more commonly, implies that everything in history, including my writing this sentence, was determined at the moment of the big bang—that not only did everything that is or will be come from that explosion but that the whole course of history was somehow programmed into it, so that a sufficiently powerful mind observing the event could have foretold everything to come. But merely to suppose that there is randomness in the universe—even to suppose that in some sense not everything that happens is caused[18]— does not make plausible the idea of free will in its strong sense of self-caused human action. A random action is not free; a person who made every decision in his life by flipping a coin would be a practicing deter-

Berger, "Predicted Future Earnings and Choice of College Major," 41 *Industrial and Labor Relations Review* 418 (1988); Yoshi-fumi Nakata and Carl Mosk, "The Demand for College Education in Postwar Japan," 22 *Journal of Human Resources* 377 (1987).

17. Young, note 2, above, at 73–74, presents fascinating biological evidence that conscious intentions are indeed epiphenomenal—that they follow rather than precede the brain's "decision" to initiate "voluntary" action. The more basic point, well argued in Collins, note 6 above, ch. 6, is that our ability to give a *reason* for an action in terms of a goal does not make the goal the *cause* of the action. In like vein, Catherine Fitzmaurice and Ken Pease, in *The Psychology of Judicial Sentencing* 39 (1986), note that people may infer their reasons for behaving as they do from observing that very behavior; this is deliberation as rationalization.

18. The apparent implication, strongly resisted by Einstein, of quantum theory. The story is well told in Arthur Fine, *The Shaky Game: Einstein, Realism, and the Quantum Theory* (1986). For an ingenious pragmatist construal of quantum theory, illustrating the utility of pragmatism in dealing with—or eliding—difficult ontological questions, see Dugald Murdoch, *Niels Bohr's Philosophy of Physics* 224–235 (1987).

minist rather than a free man, because he would have submitted himself to an external force. This implies, and one observes, that a person who acts in accordance with compelling reasons is normally thought to be acting freely;[19] somehow, removing the random element—reducing uncertainty about the consequences of action—enhances freedom. We think of "deliberation" as the characteristic behavior of a free person, but, as Hobbes argued, the "de" of "deliberation" is like the "de" of "deemphasize"; by deliberating we narrow our choices, ideally to one. If through deliberation or cognate analytical methods all uncertainty about the consequences of alternative courses of action can be removed, the choice is likely to be "predetermined"; for uncertainty is what principally makes a choice difficult rather than easy. If you ask a mathematician what the second derivative of $x^2 + 1$ is, you *know* he'll say 2.

The significance of consciousness may be not as a mechanism of choice but as a mechanism for enabling a person to "see" more clearly the pros and cons of alternative actions. He makes representations of those actions, and this enables him to estimate the benefits and costs of alternative actions without actually performing those actions. In many circumstances this is a more efficient procedure than trial and error. But it is possible that once consciousness or imagination has enabled the person to form a clear idea of the advantages and disadvantages of alternative courses of action, his choice among them is determined; he goes where the balance of advantages leans. Consciousness, in this account, is a means of acquiring information rather than the agency of free choice;[20] indecision is the state in which a person has not obtained the optimal amount of information; and a free person is one who does not decide what to do until he has obtained the optimal amount of information bearing on his choices, and who then acts rationally. Stated dif-

---

19. See Thomas Nagel, *The View from Nowhere*, ch. 7 (1986); and on the dilemmas of "free will" generally, see Daniel C. Dennett, *Elbow Room: The Varieties of Free Will Worth Wanting* (1984); Anthony Kenny, *Will, Freedom, and Power* (1975) (especially ch. 8); P. F. Strawson, "Freedom and Resentment," in Strawson, *Freedom and Resentment, and Other Essays* 1 (1974); Benson Mates, *Skeptical Essays,* ch. 2 (1981); Peter van Inwagen, *An Essay on Free Will* (1983); Gary Watson, "Free Action and Free Will," 96 *Mind* 145 (1987); Ted Honderich, "One Determinism," in *Essays on Freedom of Action* 187 (Honderich ed. 1973); Ryle, note 6 above, ch. 3; *Responsibility, Character, the Emotions: New Essays in Moral Psychology* (Ferdinand Schoeman ed. 1987); Ernest Nagel, *The Structure of Science: Problems in the Logic of Scientific Explanation* 592–606 (1961).

20. It is not inconsistent with this view that if you "know" what a person is about to do and tell him, he may do something else; for the information you have imparted alters his environment. If you knew how he would react to your telling him what he was going to do, you could predict his behavior, as parents of small children learn to do.

ferently, we have desires, and we have beliefs—formed with the help of consciousness—about how to fulfill those desires; and the conjunction of the desires and beliefs determines, without need to posit a faculty of free will, our volitional behavior.[21]

The concept of choice that I am expounding resembles the economist's idea of decision under uncertainty,[22] or what I have been calling "rational decision." It also resembles Quine's view that an act is "free insofar as the agent's motives or drives are a link in its causal chain. Those motives or drives may themselves be as rigidly determined as you please."[23] On either approach there is no *entity* that can properly be called "free will." Adjectival rather than substantive, the term describes certain behavior, being in this respect like the word "luck." "Luck" is not a thing that people possess; it no more has a locus in space and time than the speed of a jaguar at rest has. It is a way of characterizing people's experiences after the fact. Similarly, "free will" is not a thing but a description of behavior not wholly constrained by forces external to the motives and drives of the actor. If I am thrown onto my neighbor's land, I do not act of my own free will; if I am not thrown but step onto his land, I do so act.

Admittedly this solution to the problem of free will leads to paradoxes: a drug addict is free and, for that matter, so is a sparrow. Yet this is not so odd as it sounds. We may simply understand the motives or drives of creatures whose motives or drives are relatively simple (sparrows) or who are in the iron grip of a single overmastering drive (addicts) better than we understand the motives and drives of the average man or woman. And it is important to distinguish prediction from control. If the causality of the sparrow's behavior is simple enough, we may be able to predict that behavior with great accuracy. But the sparrow is free—from us. (And so with the addict.) It is not free from its instincts and circumstances, however, and maybe we are no more free from our instincts and circumstances, vastly complicated though they are.

Just as one can be free without consciousness of freedom (I am assuming the sparrow does not have consciousness), one can be unfree yet think one is free. Knowing the addict's weakness, I may be able to

---

21. See Donald Davidson, "Actions, Reasons, and Causes," in Davidson, *Essays on Actions and Events* 3 (1980).

22. See Donald Davidson, "Replies to Essays I–IX," in *Essays on Davidson: Actions and Events* 195, 199–201 (Bruce Vermazen and Merrill B. Hintikka eds. 1985).

23. W. V. Quine, "Things and Their Place in Theories," in *Theories and Things*, note 2 above, at 1, 11. See also Hume, note 5 above, at 95 (§8, pt. 1, ¶73).

control his behavior as effectively as I could if my brain rather than his gave directions to his muscles. One can be free in the Hume-Quine sense yet determined in an equally good sense. Even if we had "true" free will—a faculty of unfettered choice—it would not guarantee our freedom, for it might lack causal efficacy, as when I "choose" to stay in a room not knowing that it is locked from the outside. A final paradox, closely related to my earlier remark on random choice, is that an unpredictable choice may be less free than a predictable one. A person who chooses irrationally—who given a choice between what he likes and what he dislikes chooses the latter—is not a free person, but rather a person who is incapable of exercising free will.

Whether the conception of free will that I am defending—one that essentially equates free will with rational choice in the sense of fitting means to ends, however those ends be chosen and whether or not the "fitting" involves conscious mental activity—is right or wrong, complete or incomplete, edifying or unedifying, it has the merit of summarizing what is unquestionably an influential, perhaps dominant, strain in the law's actual as opposed to ostensible approach to controlling human behavior. What progress the law has made in controlling behavior, particularly in the criminal area, has come from the replacement of mentalist with behavioral explanations—not only in dealing with deodands but also, to take a less exotic example, in determining how severely to punish particular offenders and offenses. Criminologists have developed models of recidivism that enable them to predict, on the basis of characteristics such as drug addiction, lack of education, youth, and criminal record that have nothing directly to do with the criminal's thoughts or conscious choices, which criminals are likely to commit crimes after being released from prison.[24] The behavioral model works better than any mental model of criminal propensities.

---

24. The accuracy of these models is the subject of a vast literature, mostly finding that their accuracy is only fair. See, for a small sample of the literature, Peter Schmidt and Ann Dryden Witte, *Predicting Recidivism Using Survival Models* 157–160 (1988); Stephen P. Klein and Michael N. Caggiano, *The Prevalence, Predictability, and Policy Implications of Recidivism* 37–38 (1986); Stephen L. Bieber et al., "Predicting Criminal Recidivism of Insanity Acquittees," 11 *International Journal of Law and Psychiatry* 105 (1988); Peter B. Hoffman and James L. Beck, "Recidivism among Released Federal Prisoners: Salient Factor Score and Five-Year Follow-Up," 12 *Criminal Justice and Behavior* 501 (1985); Andrew von Hirsch and Don M. Gottfredson, "Selective Incapacitation: Some Queries about Research Design and Equity," 12 *Review of Law and Social Change* 11, 44–45 (1983–84); Kevin N. Wright, Todd R. Clear, and Paul Dickson, "Universal Applicability of Probation Risk-Assessment Instruments: A Critique," 22 *Criminology* 113 (1984); F. J. Spellacy and W. G. Brown, "Prediction of Recidivism in Young Offenders after Brief Institutionalization," 40 *Journal of Clinical*

Even when the criminal law seems most mentalist, as in punishing premeditated crimes more severely than impulsive ones, the underlying policy and even the mode of implementation may be nonmentalist. The criminal who premeditates is more likely to succeed in his criminal aim (and thus do more harm) than is the impulsive criminal, and the premeditator is also harder to apprehend and punish and therefore less likely to be punished. On both counts effective deterrence requires a heavier punishment if he is caught.[25] A further point is that the would-be criminal who plans his crime—that is, who projects in his imagination the alternative courses of action of committing and refraining from committing the crime—may be more responsive than the impulsive criminal to the threat of punishment, because he sees in his mind's eye the full array of costs and benefits, including punishment, before deciding which course to follow. Punishing him may therefore be socially more productive than punishing the impulsive criminal.

Not only do we punish the premeditating criminal more severely for reasons having nothing to do with free will, but in deciding whether a crime is premeditated we employ—oxymoron though it may seem—a behaviorist account of deliberation.[26] We examine the circumstances of the crime: Was it concealed? Had the criminal made arrangements for a getaway? Had he obtained the means of committing the crime in advance? Were those means suitable to the end (suitably lethal, in the case of a murder)? Did the criminal have much to gain from the crime? From these circumstances a model of a deliberating criminal could be constructed—an "objective" reconstruction of the criminal's motivational experience, created by attributing to him a certain type of rationality. But the step is unnecessary, or perhaps merely heuristic. "Conscious" choice can be redescribed in nondeliberative terms as cost-benefit analysis, utility maximization, or means-end rationality; even some philosophical accounts of deliberation do this.[27] It thus is possible, if paradoxical, to understand premeditation in behavioral terms, as a

---

Psychology 1070 (1984); Terrill R. Holland et al., Comparison and Combination of Clinical and Statistical Predictions of Recidivism among Adult Offenders," 68 *Journal of Applied Psychology* 203 (1983); Howard Wainer and Anne M. B. Morgan, "Robust Estimation of Parole Outcome," 19 *Journal of Research in Crime and Delinquency* 84 (1982).

25. See my article "An Economic Theory of the Criminal Law," 85 *Columbia Law Review* 1193, 1222–1223 (1985).

26. See the fascinating discussion in Nuttall, note 12 above.

27. See, for example, D. S. Clarke, Jr., *Practical Inferences* 15–69, 109–126 (1985); Davidson, note 21 above.

roundabout way of describing the criminals who are most likely to succeed. The persistence of mentalist language in law may merely bespeak the cultural conservatism of the legal enterprise.

The approach that I am suggesting does not eliminate the mental element entirely. Planning is mental—an affair of consciousness. I deny not the existence of mental phenomena but the utility for law of the concept of mind in which intentions and free will figure. "The division of acts into some for which a man is regarded as responsible, and others for which he is not, is part of the social apparatus of reward and punishment: responsibility is allocated where rewards and punishments have tended to work as incentives and deterrents."[28] And being social rather than philosophical in purpose, the allocation of responsibility need not follow the division between free and coerced acts. A person who freely, indeed eagerly, kills in self-defense is excused from criminal liability, but not the killer who would not have killed had he not been raised in a poor home by harsh parents. Punishment would be counterproductive in the first case, but not in the second. Society has no desire to license people who have had a bad upbringing to kill, and it believes that the threat of punishment (which to be credible must be carried out when it fails to deter) will deter most such people from killing. Both cases involve the exercise of free will in Quine's sense. In contrast, one who kills another in *unreasonable* fear for his own safety, or who has sexual intercourse with an underage female whom he reasonably believes to be of age, is guilty of a crime, even though in neither case does the criminal know he is committing a criminal act. These are examples of the strict-liability component in criminal law. There are also explicit strict-liability crimes, mainly involving the sale of adulterated or unsafe foods or drugs. If my analysis is correct, there is no anomaly in sometimes imposing criminal liability on the pure of heart or the empty of mind. The criminal law is an instrument of social control, and—I am contending—treats people as objects, not as Kantian subjects.

The "cold and calculating" killer is not punished more severely than the impulsive killer because his will was freer. He may have been acting under a heavier compulsion from his past, his genes, his psyche, or his upbringing. To decide would require a type of investigation that is not

28. Quine, "Smart's Philosophy and Scientific Realism," in *Theories and Things,* note 2 above, at 92, 94–95. (Ryle, note 6 above, at 69, makes a similar point.) The proof of this particular pudding (that legal responsibility and free will can be and are divorced) is the fact that when experts on free will discuss practical questions of responsibility, such as criminal responsibility, they offer analyses no different from those of lawyers ignorant of philosophy. See, for example, Dennett, note 19 above, at 158–165.

conducted in criminal trials, and that a determinist would consider a snipe hunt. Either the courts are deeply deceived, or the point is simply that the criminal who plans his crime in advance is on average more dangerous than the impulsive criminal because he is more likely to do harm and more difficult to apprehend, and dangerousness is a reason for punishing one criminal more severely than another. He is punished, in Nietzsche's term, as "an irresponsible piece of fate."

It is true that people who commit crimes under an irrational compulsion are not punished. They are not deterrable by the threat of punishment, because they cannot bring the expected cost of punishment to bear in "deciding" whether to commit the crime. They should be and are taken out of circulation, because they are highly dangerous, but there is nothing to be gained by going through the rigmarole of punishment. In contrast, there is a gain from punishing strict-liability crimes such as statutory rape; the threat of such punishment encourages the would-be offender to steer well clear of the protected class, and thereby protects the class more securely. The most difficult case to explain is that of punishing the person who acts out of an unreasonable fear—how is he different from the person who acts from an irrational compulsion? Evidentiary problems aside, it may be that we think the threat of punishment will induce sane people to act with greater care in circumstances of apparent danger, but not insane people. The benefits of punishment are therefore greater in the first case.

Deterrence presupposes a capacity to make decisions and act on them—presupposes, in a word, rationality, though no stronger sense of free will—and evidently our modern conception of criminal punishment is linked to deterrability and through it to rationality. Purely incapacitative or even retributive theories of punishment might sever that link.

Behaviorist approaches to criminal responsibility disturb thoughtful students of law and morals. (In contrast, the "reasonable man" standard of tort law and the "objective" theory of contracts raise few hackles.) We are not comfortable thinking of people on the model of animals or automata, or in supposing that the criminal justice system "thinks" of them in those terms, although that is largely what the system does, and it does so for two excellent reasons: we cannot peer into people's minds, at least not with the clumsy tools of legal procedure, and if we could we are not at all sure that we would find the intentions, malice, premeditation, or other entities that the mentalist language of law invites us to expect. The behaviorist approach seems to leave no room for appeals to conscience, for a sense of guilt, of remorse; it seems to strip the moral as well as the distinctively human content from the criminal law. The pragmatic reply is, So what? There are no realistic grounds for fearing that speculations in the philosophy of mind are likely to affect respect for, let alone observance of, law. A behaviorist metalanguage will not sap people of their sense of moral responsibility—and not only because most people will remain unaware of the metalanguage and its implications. Philosophers who believe in determinism behave in their personal lives just like other people. If freedom is an illusion, it is one of those illusions (like the illusion of three-dimensional perception after we have learned that the retina is two-dimensional) that we cannot shake off no matter what our beliefs or opinions are.[29] And there is no mystery about the survival value of the illusion (if that is what it is) of freedom, and thus no mystery about why it may be hard-wired into our brains. The feeling of freedom forces us to act deliberately, in the sense of gathering as much relevant information as possible concerning the pros and cons of alternative courses of action before we act.

Admittedly I am defending behaviorism (or determinism) merely against the charge that it will have bad effects, whereas the main charge is that it reflects an impoverished conception of human nature. It lies at the farthest possible remove from Kant's influential view that human beings should not treat each other just as objects.[30] But the question is not what is good for us to believe on the score of freedom and determinism but what premise is good for the law to proceed on. Behaviorism is the only practical working assumption for law, and its dangers have been exaggerated. Moreover, even if behaviorist approaches to criminal law pose serious dangers, so do mentalist ones. The heavy reliance on confessions in medieval and early modern law helps explain the surprising frequency of nonexistent criminal acts, such as acts of witchcraft and sorcery. Perhaps we should neither mentalize nor moralize criminal law.

Although behaviorism is a modern idea, it makes a smooth if precarious fit with Enlightenment ideas of personal freedom and autonomy—which seems doubly paradoxical: because freedom is the antithesis of determinism and because in treating people as objects behaviorism is the antithesis of Kant's insistence on the autonomy of the human subject. The paradox diminishes when we descend from the theoretical to the practical plane. Confining governmental regulation to external behavior

---

29. For a striking example, see Howard Margolis, *Patterns, Thinking, and Cognition: A Theory of Judgment* 38 (1987) (fig. 2.1) (the "Lincoln grid"). And compare Meir Dan-Cohen, "Decision Rules and Conduct Rules: On Acoustic Separation in Criminal Law," 97 *Harvard Law Review* 625 (1984).

30. For an eloquent statement, see "Freedom and Resentment," note 19 above, at 9.

leaves the realm of thought and feeling as one of personal autonomy. The separation is precarious, however, because nothing in behaviorism bars the way to using Pavlovian conditioning to prevent antisocial behavior—and that is "messing with minds" in a dramatic way.

Coerced Confessions. Mention of confessions brings to mind a particularly difficult question relating to the question of free will: the distinction between "voluntary" and "involuntary" confessions, the former being admissible in the criminal trial of the person who confessed, the latter not.[31] Even if criminal behavior is not "mentalist" in a strong sense, there is no denying that most criminals are aware of what they have done (even if, to repeat, they were not "free" to avoid doing it) and can be induced to confess it. And many crimes could not be solved except at exorbitant, and sometimes at infinite, cost unless the criminal confessed. If the means used to coerce a confession are so painful or threatening ("confess or I'll kill you on the spot") that the person being interrogated would find it less costly to confess even to a crime that he had not committed than to undergo the interrogation, we would almost certainly want to disallow the confession, and this regardless of considerations of free will. The costs of obtaining evidence of such dubious reliability would in all but the rarest cases exceed the value of the evidence, given that there usually are other means of establishing guilt. But the modern law goes further. It excludes reliable confessions induced by threats, promises, or misrepresentations when the pressure exerted by these methods is deemed unreasonable even though not necessarily so extreme as to be likely to induce an innocent person to confess. For example, the police might promise a murderer that he would be let off with a light sentence if he confessed. The promise would if believed sway a murderer, but probably not an innocent person (of sound mind—a potentially significant qualification) who had been falsely suspected. Nevertheless such a promise, if false, would make the confession induced by it inadmissible, on the ground that it was "involuntary."

In a society as depressingly rife with crime as that of modern America,

31. On the legal position, see, for example, Beckwith v. United States, 425 U.S. 341 (1976); Schneckloth v. Bustamonte, 412 U.S. 218, 223–227 (1973) (not a confession case, but a particularly good summary of coerced-confession doctrine); Spano v. New York, 360 U.S. 315 (1959); Frazier v. Cupp, 394 U.S. 731 (1969); Haynes v. Washington, 373 U.S. 503 (1963); Jurek v. Estelle, 623 F.2d 929 (5th Cir. 1980); other cases succinctly summarized by Judge Friendly in United States ex rel. Hughes v. McMann, 405 F.2d 773, 776 (2d Cir. 1968); Fred E. Inbau, John E. Reid, and Joseph P. Buckley, *Criminal Interrogation and Confessions* 308–326 (3d ed. 1986); Joseph D. Grano, "Voluntariness, Free Will, and the Law of Confessions," 65 *Virginia Law Review* 859 (1979); Stephen J. Schulhofer, "Confessions and the Court," 79 *Michigan Law Review* 865 (1981).

the rule against involuntary confessions may seem a luxury we can't afford. I will not address that issue. The point of philosophical interest lies in the connection between the legal idea of voluntariness and the philosophical idea of free will. That there is a connection is nothing new; but I shall argue that the connection is with the Hume-Quine concept of free will, a concept determinist in spirit.

Recall that a random choice is not free. By definition it is one made under radical ignorance of its consequences. If the police use threats, lies, false promises, or the like to alter the environment in which the criminal suspect must decide whether or not to confess, this is like forcing the suspect to roll the dice; for a false sense of the consequences of choice is no better than no sense. The point is not that the promises, threats, or misrepresentations *cause* the suspect to confess and by doing so negate his free will. A free choice is not an uncaused one. Otherwise courts would have to exclude most statements obtained in interrogations, because the interrogation is a cause of the confession elicited by it— clearly so when the suspect is in custody and is being interrogated by armed police officers skilled at overcoming objections, playing on the suspect's anxieties, exploiting slips, and otherwise taking advantage of a favorable setting.[32] Yet although interrogation in these circumstances may make confession far more likely, it does not confront the suspect with a false environment that prevents a reasoned choice—a weighing of the actual (psychic as well as practical, of course) consequences of alternative courses of action free at least from manufactured uncertainty. Despite the mentalist language in which the law of coerced confessions comes wrapped,[33] the theory as I have articulated it is consistent with

32. The fascinatig Inbau treatise, note 31 above, pt. 1 and appendix, is a "how to" handbook on extracting a confession by raising the suspect's anxiety level to the point where it exceeds his perception of the adverse consequences of confessing (and the interrogator is taught to minimize those consequences). See also Edwin D. Driver, "Confessions and the Social Psychology of Coercion," 82 *Harvard Law Review* 42 (1968). The cases recognize the inherently coercive character of police interrogation but are correct from a philosophical as well as practical standpoint in refusing to jump to the conclusion that no confession obtained by such interrogation should be admissible. See, for example, Oregon v. Mathiason, 429 U.S. 492, 495 (1977) (per curiam).

33. "Confronted with the express threat of continued incommunicado detention and induced by the promise of communication with and access to family, Haynes understandably chose to make and sign the damning written statement; given the unfair and inherently coercive context in which made, that choice cannot be said to be the voluntary product of a free and unconstrained will." Haynes v. Washington, 373 U.S. 503, 514 (1963). Maybe the past tense would be more appropriate for the statement in text; the Supreme Court's affection for the "free and unconstrained will" approach to confession law is rapidly waning. See next footnote.

the overall behaviorist approach of the criminal law.[34] Remember that rational choice is not the same as free will in the strong sense. A rational choice is objectively right; no assumptions are made about the chooser's freedom or subjectivity.

A behaviorist approach to the law of confessions may appear to do better with misrepresentation than with the creation of psychic distress (for example, holding the suspect incommunicado). The latter form of pressure or coercion is more accurately described as placing a price on refusing to confess than as preventing a rational, informed decision on whether or not to confess, although if the price is high enough it may elicit an unreliable confession. There is, however, a third alternative. The pressure may interfere with clear thinking (in the nonmentalist sense in which a pigeon might be said to be "thinking" of which bit of food to eat next), may distract and confuse, undermining the power of reasoned choice even if the pressure is not so severe that it would be likely to elicit a false confession.[35]

The law's commitment to preventing the obtaining of confessions by misrepresentation is not absolute; a certain amount of trickery is permitted in interrogations. In particular, exaggeration of the other evidence that the police have gathered against the suspect, a tactic designed to make him feel that he has nothing to lose by confessing, is permitted. The main reason, I conjecture, is that ordinarily the police will exagger-

---

34. The Court has said that a criminal defendant has no "right . . . to confess to his crime only when totally rational and properly motivated." Colorado v. Connelly, 479 U.S. 157, 166 (1986). "We have never read the Constitution to require that the police supply a suspect with a flow of information to help him calibrate his self-interest in deciding whether to speak or stand by his rights." Moran v. Burbine, 475 U.S. 412, 422 (1986). Judicial tolerance of psychological pressure to extract a confession is well illustrated by Miller v. Fenton, 796 F.2d 598 (3d Cir. 1986). As this and many other cases make clear, the statement in Bram v. United States, 168 U.S. 532, 542–543 (1897), that to be voluntary a confession must not have been "extracted by any sort of threats or violence, nor obtained by any direct or implied promises, however slight," is no longer authoritative.

35. The possibility of eliciting false confessions by relatively mild forms of psychological pressure should not be underrated, however. See William Sargent, *Battle for the Mind: A Physiology of Conversion and Brain-Washing,* ch. 9 (1957). The interrogator's object is to raise the suspect's anxiety level, and an innocent person may suffer from anxiety, and his anxiety is likely to be exacerbated by police questioning. This might seem to imply that innocent people would be *more* likely to confess than guilty ones. Not so, at least in a system such as ours where (see next chapter) few innocent people are convicted. Knowledge of this fact will tend to allay the innocent person's anxiety. In addition, he has more to lose from confessing than the guilty person, for there is more likely to be other evidence of guilt, besides a confession, against a guilty person than against an innocent one. But all this assumes that the innocent person is rational and reasonably well informed, even if anxious, and the assumption is not always warranted.

ate the strength of the other evidence only if that evidence is indeed weak—why exaggerate otherwise? But this implies that they really *need* the confession. And the trickery allowed is not the sort that is likely to elicit a false confession. The careful reader will discern the rudiments of cost-benefit analysis here. When the desire for effective law enforcement outweighs the aversion to the use of a confession obtained by trickery to convict, the judges call the confession "voluntary." Law follows philosophy only so far as it is expedient to do so.

There may be a further point. In *Julius Caesar,* Caesar's decision to go to the Capitol on the fatal day is procured by the flattery and misrepresentations of the conspirators, whose skillful playing on Caesar's vanity overcomes his wife's fears. Yet we would not be inclined to deny that the decision was an act of free will by Caesar. The decision was in character—profoundly so—and that seems enough. It may likewise be the case that when police interrogators procure a confession by playing to the weaknesses of a suspect's character, we nevertheless are inclined to think of the confession as authentically the suspect's, and we therefore allow it to be admitted against him at his trial.

It might be argued that the decision to confess can never be rational, because invariably the criminal thinks better of the decision later and tries to withdraw his confession. But the impression of uniform retraction is just another illustration of how sample bias complicates legal analysis. The only *litigated* confession cases are those in which the defendant had second thoughts about his decision to confess, true; but only a small percentage of criminal cases are litigated, most being disposed of on the basis of a guilty plea. Nor need regret show that the regretted decision was not rational. The confession may have been impelled by stings of remorse that fade with time. The balance of costs and benefits that determines decision in a behaviorist model of human action changes over time; so opposite decisions made at different times may be consistent.

The person who (whether innocent or guilty) confesses under a credible threat to kill him on the spot unless he confesses is striking a rational balance between the costs and benefits of confession; should his confession therefore be admissible? It should not be; but the reason is that the rational choice under such a threat is to confess *regardless of guilt,* rather than that the threat prevents a rational choice from being made. The choice induced by the threat is perfectly rational but the confession that results from the choice is unreliable and therefore inadmissible. A similar case would be one in which the police promised a ne'er-do-well suspected of a minor crime $100,000 to confess and fully intended to fulfill their promise. There would be no misrepresentation and no other inter-ference with rational choice, but there would be a serious danger of eliciting a false—although entirely voluntary—confession. Like the threat in the previous case, the promise in this one would make the confession inadmissible. In both cases the confession is voluntary, yet unreliable and therefore properly excluded.

What if in either case the confession is corroborated? Two situations must be distinguished. In the first there is merely other evidence of the confessor's guilt. This evidence may make it more likely than not that the confession is true, but it does not make the confession itself a reliable piece of evidence, any more than "corroborative" evidence would enhance the reliability of a confession known to have been forged. In the second and more interesting situation, the confession produces leads that validate its truthfulness; for example, it may disclose facts that only the perpetrator of the crime could have known. The exclusion of such a confession from the defendant's trial—a confession both voluntary in the Hume-Quine sense and reliable—is, like the exclusion of the leads themselves, justifiable only on a deterrence rationale. We want to dis-courage a class of confessions that we believe to be unreliable on aver-age, so we forbid the police to derive any benefit from obtaining a confession in that class, even a confession whose reliability is demon-strable. This strategy makes sense from a behaviorist standpoint only if the reliable confessions are a small fraction of the total class, but perhaps that is the case.

Let us compare my explanation of the legal principles governing the admissibility of confessions with the alternative explanations. The alter-native already examined and found wanting is that the legal system has subscribed to a strong sense of free will. Another possibility is that involuntary confessions (involuntary in the Hume-Quine sense, that is) are inadmissible because they are likely to be unreliable. This explana-tion fails on two counts. First, many involuntary confessions are so well corroborated by physical or other evidence that their reliability is not open to serious question, although the qualification *well* corroborated is important. Corroboration may show no more than that the defendant knew something about the crime, perhaps because he participated peripherally in it. (So corroboration shares the infirmities of induction—is perhaps the same thing.)

Second, if reliability were the underlying concern in these cases, we would expect the standard for admissibility to be—reliability, period, for that is a simpler and more familiar criterion for admission of evi-dence than voluntariness is. We could not explain a case like *Townsend*

v. Sain,[36] where the Supreme Court held involuntary a confession procured by a truth serum. If a truth serum works, the confession procured
by it will be reliable. But the truth serum will deprive the person interrogated of his power of choice by preventing him from weighing the
pros and cons of confessing and going where the balance inclines. This
is a good illustration of the difference between an involuntary and an
unreliable confession.

Still another explanation for the exclusion of involuntary confessions
is that we are horrified by brutal police methods. But a truth serum is
not brutal, and few misrepresentations are brutal; yet confessions
obtained by a truth serum or misrepresentations (especially promises of
lenient treatment) are deemed involuntary and are inadmissible. The
proponent of the police-methods theory may retreat to the argument
that it is not the brutality but merely the felt inappropriateness of particular interrogative methods that condemns them. That begs the
question.

The pattern of the confession cases is more perspicuous once the mentalist, nondeterministic concept of free will is discarded. This is a pragmatic reason for seeking to go beyond the mentalist language in which
the judges articulate their reasons. To the complaint that the Hume-
Quine view is unedifying—that what is gained in clarity is lost in sym-
bology and resonance—my reply is as before: show me what practical
harm will ensue from greater realism about law in general and confession law in particular.

Other Applications. If the above analysis is correct, the defense of
duress in contract law also has nothing to do with free will. A promise
to pay, extracted at the point of a gun, is a product of free choice, just
as with the parallel case of confessing in the face of a mortal threat. We
refuse to enforce the promise because we don't want to encourage such
threats, not because they deprive people of free will.

Another entity the law could do without is "reputation." When it is
viewed as a thing, the tendency is to think of it as an asset of the person
"whose" reputation it is. From there it is but a small step to thinking
that someone who reveals a true but unflattering fact about a person is
taking something away from him and should be liable for the resulting
harm. But why should people have a legal right to deceive others about
their true qualities? What is actually involved is not taking something
from the person who is harmed by disclosures about his character or
past conduct; it is facilitating informed transactions with the person by

36. 372 U.S. 293, 307–308 (1963).

dispelling misconceptions that actual or potential transacting parties may have. And notice how recognition of a right to deceive would undermine the policy behind the rule on coerced confessions.

Denying the "thingness" of reputation is the key step in demystifying the legal concept of privacy.[37] It enables one to see that, insofar as privacy is more than just the desire not to have one's peace and quiet disturbed by loud music or by telephone solicitors and other pests, it is a desire to be able to deceive the persons with whom one transacts in economic, marital, and other markets. Yet the favorable connotations of the term are doubtless what induced the Supreme Court to appropriate it for a line of decisions (involving mainly contraception and abortion) that involve the interest neither in solitude nor in deception, but in sexual liberty.

All this is not to deny that privacy and sexual liberty are genuine goods. Most people, myself included, would prefer the burden of unmasking the self-aggrandizing deceptions of the persons with whom they deal to being forced to forego such deceptions themselves—to parade as it were naked before the world. I am objecting merely to the reification of the concept of privacy.

Continuing the struggle against metaphysical entities in law, Landes and I have argued that causation in tort law is a dispensable category, because, as Quine might say, the question whether to impose liability on conduct belongs to the social apparatus of blame and punishment.[38] We related our approach to the

> strain in the modern philosophical literature on causation [that] regards the cause of an occurrence as whatever antecedent condition, necessary or sufficient, is most significant in relation to the reasons for which causal ascription is being made. A chemist might ascribe fire to the presence of oxygen in the atmosphere; the fire marshal, to a failure to comply with some fire regulation. Thus, one must know the purpose of causal ascription in tort law before one can say what causation in that law means. If the purpose of tort law is to promote economic efficiency, a defendant's conduct will be deemed the cause of an injury when making him liable for the consequences of the injury will promote an efficient allocation of resources. When it would not promote efficiency for the defendant to behave differ-

---

37. As I attempt to do in my book *The Economics of Justice*, pt. 3 (1981).

38. See Landes and Posner, note 13 above, ch. 8; also Steven Shavell, *Economic Analysis of Accident Law*, ch. 5 (1987). This is not to deny causality: it is to deny that the law requires a concept, definition, or doctrine of causation.

ently, the cause of the accident will be ascribed to an "act of God" or some other force on which liability cannot rest.[39]

There are striking examples of the dispensability of causation in criminal law as well—in particular, the punishment of attempts and conspiracies that cause no harm at all but demonstrate the dangerousness of the perpetrator with sufficient reliability to warrant taking him out of circulation for a while.

The debunking of metaphysical entities in law is not new. It was a pastime of the legal realists.[40] Their favorite target was the corporation. The corporation, being not a thing or person but the name for a pattern of contractual relationships, indeed has a dubious ontology. The realists' lesson has not been learned. Most lawyers and judges still think that one can speak meaningfully of powerful or wealthy corporations, or of placing taxes on corporations rather than on persons. But a corporation is not a rich person, natural or artificial; it is a network of relationships among people (shareholders, workers, customers, suppliers, executives), some wealthy, some not. The difference between the individual income tax and the corporate income tax is not that people pay the former and institutions the latter, but that different people pay, and often at different rates, under the two taxes. After the dust settles, it may turn out that a tax on corporate income operates as a regressive tax on consumers. The realists' emphasis was different: not on the social costs of corporate liability but on the injustice of corporate privileges. This was just the leftist streak in legal realism; it was nothing organic to a skeptical, antimetaphysical, pragmatic conception of law.

Behaviorism and the Judicial Perspective

In commending a behaviorist approach to law I may seem to be assuming a stance not only radically inconsistent with my own profession as a judge, which requires me to make decisions, implying mental activity and the exercise of free will, but, more important, inconsistent with any plausible theory of the judicial process. The behaviorist perspective is

39. Landes and Posner, note 13 above, at 229. For good discussions of this sort of "contextual causation," see Charles M. Yablon, "The Indeterminacy of the Law: Critical Legal Studies and the Problem of Legal Explanation," 6 *Cardozo Law Review* 917, 925–929 (1985); Ernest Nagel, note 19 above, at 582–587; cf. John Borgo, "Causal Paradigms in Tort Law," 8 *Journal of Legal Studies* 419 (1979).

40. See, for example, Felix S. Cohen, "Transcendental Nonsense and the Functional Approach," 35 *Columbia Law Review* 809 (1935).

external rather than internal. How can it be adequate to the self-conscious activity of a judge?

There is no inconsistency. Parents, economists, psychologists, marriage counselors, and probation officers all have the experience of being able to predict correctly what another person will do even when the person himself is undecided. This is just the sparrow and addict examples writ large. "We may imagine we feel a liberty within ourselves; but a spectator can commonly infer our actions from our motives and character."[41] An ambiguity lurks here. We have genuine "liberty" in the sense that most of our actions are free from gross coercion of the sort found in duress ("your money or your life") cases. That liberty is Hume-Quine free will. The spurious liberty of which Hume is speaking here is the sense we sometimes have in making choices of being free from the constraints of instinct, culture, character, and other immutable or relatively immutable features of our person and environment. In fact the interaction of those features may, without our realizing it, determine all our choices.

To return to my examples, the point is not that the expert or the grown-up knows the contents of another's mind better than the other does—an irrelevant, perhaps even meaningless, suggestion—but that the expert or parent has a method of prediction that the person whose actions are being predicted either does not command, for want of the necessary training or experience, or cannot use on himself because of his emotional involvement; it is easier to be analytical about other people than about oneself. And there is something deeper. People systematically misrepresent their motivations to themselves. Almost everyone pretends to himself that he is less concerned with money and status, less selfish, more courageous, more ethical, than he actually is. What Regan said of Lear applies to everyone: "He hath ever but slenderly known himself." Judges are no exception. Their self-image of stern self-discipline and self-denial, of rigorous impartiality—a self-image fostered by psychological factors discussed below—may not be consonant with reality. The internal perspective on judging may not provide the best explanation for what judges do. A simple behaviorist model may have greater explanative force. Most judges may be quite predictable even though no judge thinks himself predictable.

Yet it must be admitted that only limited progress has been made in predicting judges' votes on the basis of ideology, personality, social

---

41. David Hume, *A Treatise of Human Nature* 408 (L. A. Selby-Bigge ed. 1888) (Bk. II, pt. 3, §2).

class, party affiliation, or other characteristics, and this mainly (as one
would expect) in areas where judges have the most discretion, that is,
are least cabined by rules—such areas as Supreme Court decision making and criminal sentencing.[42] And courts, as distinct from individual
judges, really are unpredictable in an important sense. The difference is
again due to sample bias. If parties to a dispute converge in their predictions of how the court will decide their case, they will almost certainly settle rather than litigate. The sample of litigated cases is drawn
from those disputes in which the court's resolution is difficult to predict—as well it may be even if most judges are quite predictable. For
example, in a court with seven members, if three always vote a stereotyped "conservative" line and three a stereotyped "liberal" line, the
unpredictability of the remaining judge will make the court as a whole
unpredictable. One needs only a fraction of unpredictable judges in a
fraction of cases to make courts unpredictable. This may seem to imply
that the problem of unpredictability is less acute at the trial level, where
the judges (in all but a trivial fraction of cases) sit alone rather than in
panels. But in jury trials there are in effect many judges. And the possibility of appeal may render the ultimate outcome of the litigation
uncertain even if there is no jury and the trial judge is predictable. Also,

42. The recent literature of judicial behaviorism is illustrated by *Judicial Conflict and
Consensus: Behavioral Studies of American Appellate Courts* (Sheldon Goldman and Charles
M. Lamb eds. 1986); Robert A. Carp and C. K. Rowland, *Policymaking and Politics in the
Federal District Courts* (1983); Glendon Schubert, *Political Culture and Judicial Behavior* (1985);
Philip E. Tetlock, Jane Bernzweig, and Jack L. Gallant, "Supreme Court Decision Making:
Cognitive Style as a Predictor of Ideological Consistency of Voting," 48 *Journal of Person-
ality and Social Psychology* 1227 (1985); Michael J. Saks and Reid Hastie, "Social Psychology
in Court: The Judge," in *Judgment and Decision Making: An Interdisciplinary Reader* 255 (Hal
R. Arkes and Kenneth R. Hammond eds. 1986); Martha A. Myers, "Social Background
and the Sentencing Behavior of Judges," 26 *Criminology* 649 (1988); Anthony Champagne
and Stuart Nagel, "The Psychology of Judging," in *The Psychology of the Courtroom* 257
(Norbert L. Kerr and Robert M. Bray eds. 1982); James L. Gibson, "Judges' Role Orien-
tations, Attitudes, and Decisions: An Interactive Model," 72 *American Political Science
Review* 911 (1978); Harold J. Spaeth and Stuart H. Teger, "Activism and Restraint: A Cloak
for the Justices' Policy Preferences," in *Supreme Court Activism and Restraint* 277 (Stephen
C. Halpern and Charles M. Lamb eds. 1982); Jeffrey A. Segal, "Predicting Supreme Court
Cases Probabilistically: The Search and Seizure Cases, 1962–1981," 78 *American Political
Science Review* 891 (1984); S. Sidney Ulmer, "Social Background as an Indicator to the
Votes of Supreme Court Justices in Criminal Cases: 1947–1956 Terms," 17 *American Journal
of Political Science* 622 (1973); Vladimir J. Konecni and Ebbe B. Ebbesen, "The Mythology
of Legal Decision Making," 7 *International Journal of Law and Psychiatry* 5 (1984). One implication of these studies, I note self-servingly—for like most judges I feel the tug of the
"faithful agent" conception—is that intermediate appellate judges are more disciplined and
restrained than either trial judges or supreme court justices because they have the least
discretionary power.

trial judges have a lot of avowedly discretionary authority—over scheduling, admission of evidence, and other matters.

I am not denying that judges exercise free will in the sense of making choices that are voluntary rather than the product of misrepresentation or disorientation. I am denying that judicial introspection, and *a fortiori* judges' avowals concerning the nature of judicial decision making, are good explanations for judicial action. It is a mistake to take at face value descriptions of judges as engaged always in a search for "the" correct answer, rather than as exercising discretion under the influence of personal values and preferences determined by temperament and selective life experiences rather than by a considered, somehow self-chosen judicial philosophy.[43] A teenager may honestly feel that he is deliberating over a choice of colleges that his parents know is foreordained by factors of which the teenager himself is unaware. Adults deceive themselves as well. We should distrust not only the self-serving descriptions of the judicial mind by the judges themselves but also the descriptions of that mind by academics who, when they are not merely advocating a powerful judiciary,[44] or inferring the judicial mentality from the rhetoric of judicial opinions—an illustration of the difficulty of obtaining knowledge of other minds—are projecting onto persons who generally lack the background, temperament, tastes, and aptitudes of academics the academic's vision of what it would feel like to be a judge.

Here is a typical account, by a distinguished student of jurisprudence: "What judges do say and write in justification of their decisions rather appears as an attempt to show that these decisions are dictated by authoritative legal standards; since they are just as well able to follow jurisprudential discussions as anyone else, it would seem that if the prevailing view that judges are legislators is correct, we must conclude that they are either stupid, ignorant of the jurisprudential issues involved, or hypocritical. None of these conclusions is very appealing."[45] Not "appealing" maybe, but implausible? Judges are not well versed in jurisprudential controversies, are not always intelligent, and are not free from that form of hypocrisy (if that is the right word) which consists of

43. For empirical evidence that the reasons judges give for their decisions are often rationalizations of actions caused by psychological factors of which they are unaware, see Fitzmaurice and Pease, note 17 above, ch. 3.

44. That is, government by lawyers. The next best thing to governing is to be governed by people like oneself; so it is natural, quite apart from financial incentives, that many academic and other lawyers favor the aggrandizement of the judiciary at the expense of the other branches of government.

45. Rolf Sartorius, "Social Policy and Judicial Legislation," 8 *American Philosophical Quarterly* 151, 158 (1971).

adopting a public face not altogether consistent with one's innermost feelings.

Indeed much of what judges say about their jobs in speeches and opinions partakes of the same falsity that characterizes other political discourse. Just as elected officials believe that their effectiveness depends on the public's thinking they serve the public interest rather than their personal interests or those of the most powerful special interests, so most judges believe, without evidence (indeed in the face of the evidence of public ignorance about courts noted in Chapter 4), that the judiciary's effectiveness depends on a belief by the public that judges are finders rather than makers of law. Although judges will occasionally lift the veil a bit, as I am doing in this chapter, they rarely level with the public—and not always with themselves—concerning the seamier side of the judicial process. This is the side that includes the unprincipled compromises and petty jealousies and rivalries that accompany collegial decision making,[46] the indolence and apathy that life tenure can induce, the flickers of ambition for different or higher office (judicial or otherwise), the boredom and burnout that heavy caseloads over a long period of years can induce, the pervasive reliance of modern American judges on ghostwriters (most judicial opinions nowadays are drafted by law clerks), the isolation from normal human concerns that is experienced by people

46. Holmes is said to have described the Justices of the Supreme Court as "nine scorpions in a bottle." An alternative metaphor is an arranged marriage by indifferent parents in a system with no divorce. Judges do not pick their colleagues; most of those colleagues serve until retirement; and the appointing authorities give little weight to the interest in judicial collegiality in deciding whom to appoint. Regarding problems of collegiality I am speaking of appellate rather than trial courts, since trial judges very rarely sit in panels. For a vivid case study of one of many famous feuds between colleagues on an appellate court, see Melvin I. Urofsky, "Conflict among the Brethren: Felix Frankfurter, William O. Douglas, and the Clash of Personalities and Philosophies on the United States Supreme Court," 1988 *Duke Law Journal* 71.

On the psychology of judging, see Andrew S. Watson, "Some Psychological Aspects of the Trial Judge's Decision-Making," 39 *Mercer Law Review* 937 (1988). Efforts to relate judicial decisions to the personal psychological makeup of the judge have generally foundered. For a review of such efforts—which may be said to have begun with Jerome Frank, *Law and the Modern Mind* (1930), a book that attributes legal formalism to authoritarian personality and recommends that all judges undergo psychoanalysis—see Champagne and Nagel, note 42 above, at 262–264; Leon Shaskolsky Sheleff, "The Illusions of Law—Psychoanalysis and Jurisprudence in Historical Perspective," 9 *International Journal of Law and Psychiatry* 143 (1986). But the study by Tetlock, Bernzweig, and Gallant, cited in note 42 above, presents, at last, persuasive evidence that personality systematically affects judicial decision making. And there is a good deal of suggestive evidence, regarding the importance of leadership ability, personality, and socialization, in the studies collected in *Judicial Conflict and Consensus: Behavioral Studies of American Appellate Courts*, note 42 above; for a summary of the summaries, see "Epilogue," in id. at 275–291.

who spend all day, day after day, observing the world through the prism of law's "artificial reason," and the desire, conscious or not, to shape the law to one's personal values.[47] These are the occupational hazards of judging, and they resemble those of bureaucracy. Not all judges succumb to them; none succumbs to all of them (at least at the same time), if only because some of the temptations are inconsistent with others. But it is a mistake to credit the Olympian depictions of judges by the judges themselves or by academics and other lawyers who believe in a powerful judiciary and want the public to be comfortable with the concept. From the fact that judges and their defenders in the profession emit a continuous stream of disclaimers that judges exercise power or (in other words) behave like other public officials, we should not infer that judges are *that* special.

This conclusion is reinforced by a number of additional points. First, a judge may *feel* constrained—may feel ruled rather than ruling—yet this feeling may be due to principles such as self-restraint and stare decisis that are (1) chosen by judges on (2) contestable grounds—two facts that judges often forget. Second, because policy and ethical considerations are permissible elements of judicial decision in our legal culture, a judge may lack a sharp sense of where legal reasoning leaves off and policy judgment or social vision (essential tools for resolving the indeterminate case) begins. Indeed, the judge is likely to lack a sharp sense of the line between the pure judicial hunch and a well-founded proposition of law.

Third, neither the conditions of judging nor the methods of selecting judges—including self-selection—would lead one to expect the deep introspection and moral insight that academic literature often attributes to judges. Being a judge, like being a military commander, is an "ensemble" job. To be done well it requires a combination of qualities, of which reflective intellect is only one, and moral insight only another. One would not expect a judge or a commander to be as intellectually able, on average, as a person pursuing a parallel activity on a purely intellectual plane, such as legal scholarship or military science, even if the selection of judges were nonpolitical—which in this country it is not.

47. A desire impeded, however, by the random order in which cases come before judges and by the great variety of cases. These things make it difficult for a judge to set an agenda for altering public policy. Hence a discretionary jurisdiction, such as that possessed by the Supreme Court, makes it easier for a court to set an agenda. Specialized courts, too, have an easier time than generalist courts in targeting particular policies for change. On the other hand, on a generalist court a judge with specialized knowledge in a particular field may overawe his colleagues in a way that would be impossible on a specialized court. The tendency is held in check by the practice, common in state supreme courts, of assigning opinions to individual judges in rotation, making it more difficult for a judge to become (or remain) a specialist.

Nor should we overlook the narrowing effect on the lawyer's and judge's mind of a professional lifetime spent reading judicial opinions.

The judge's essential activity, moreover, is the making of a large number of decisions in rapid succession, with little feedback concerning their soundness or consequences. People who are uncomfortable in such a role—and perhaps they are the most introspective, sensitive, and scrupulous people—do not become judges, do not stay judges, or are unhappy judges. The judge who is comfortable in his role makes the best decision he can and does not look back.[48] Denied the luxury of being able to withhold decision until persuaded by objectively convincing arguments that the decision will be correct, he no more wants to wallow in uncertainty and regrets than a law student wants to retake an exam in his mind after having taken it in the examination room. The starting point of Peirce's pragmatism is the idea that people hate being in a state of doubt and will do whatever is necessary to move from doubt to belief, and this is as true of judges as of anyone else.[49]

A closely related point is that since no one likes to think he is making a lot of mistakes, the psychology of judging is characterized by a belief that one is almost always (some judges think always) right. This point is an illustration of the theory of cognitive dissonance—the theory that people (and ostriches) will do almost anything to relieve the mental distress caused by an incongruity between their deepest beliefs, assumptions, and aspirations on the one hand and reality on the other.[50] Most means of avoiding or resolving cognitive dissonance (of which the most common is a simple denial of the disturbing reality) are "irrational," so persons who resort to them normally pay a price—but not judges. There is no penalty for judicial complacency—for ignoring Holmes's dictum that "certitude is not the test of certainty."[51] Like other people, moreover, judges want to diffuse responsibility for their unpopular, controversial, or simply most consequential actions. (This is also related to the desire to wield power effectively.) They do this by persuading them-

48. For a notable exception, see David Pannick, *Judges* 2 (1987), reporting that a judge left money in his will to a litigant whom he decided he had ruled against erroneously.

49. See "The Fixation of Belief," in *Collected Papers of Charles Sanders Peirce* 223, 231–233 (Charles Hartshorne and Paul Weiss eds. 1934). See also William James's essay, "The Sentiment of Rationality," in *William James: The Essential Writings* 25, 32 (Bruce W. Wilshire ed. 1984).

50. See, for example, Elliot Aronson, "The Theory of Cognitive Dissonance: A Current Perspective," in *Cognitive Theories in Social Psychology* 181 (Leonard Berkowitz ed. 1978); George A. Akerlof and William T. Dickens, "The Economic Consequences of Cognitive Dissonance," 72 *American Economic Review* 307, 308–310 (1982).

51. "Natural Law," 32 *Harvard Law Review* 311, 312 (1918).

selves and others that their decisions are dictated by law rather than the result of choice. The false sense of constraint parallels the false sense of liberty noted by Hume.

If we are realistic about judges, we shall refuse to take seriously the suggestion that Supreme Court Justices should think of themselves as the secular counterparts of the Old Testament prophets, and act accordingly.[52] Yet to the extent that judges are not constrained by positive law, a role of moral leadership will on occasion be thrust on them, whether to be played well (as by Justice Jackson in *Barnette*) or badly. Which is not to say that even in those cases judges are "free" in an ultimate sense—a proposition that would be contrary to the entire thrust of this chapter. They are constrained, all right, but by their genes and upbringing, their temperament, fears, and ambitions, rather than by rules. The decision to obey a rule is compelled not by the rule itself but by the consequences of disobeying it. Nor is it the case that most judges actually feel constrained all of the time. Judges feel a mixture of freedom and constraint in proportions that vary with the nature and rank of the court, the nature of the particular decision to be made, the nature of the case, and the judge's temperament.

In summary, judges decide cases with greater confidence than the realities of judicial decision making permit, and speak and write with more confidence than they feel. This situation is unlikely to change without profound, *and not necessarily desirable,* changes in the political system. I emphasize this qualification in order to make clear that in urging a "naturalistic" view of the judge I am not engaged in criticism. I am describing the conditions of adjudication that make it unrealistic to believe that our judges can render objective decisions in difficult cases, if "objective" is to mean more than muddling through in the conduct of an all-too-human enterprise.

As always it is essential not to go overboard and ignore the elements that keep the judicial process from running off the rails into utter subjectivity, "pure politics." In emphasizing the gap between what judges do and what they say they do I have been skating perilously close to the fallacy, itself mentalist in character, of reducing knowledge to conscious knowledge. The judge whose conscious thoughts are banal might still be a great judge, just as a person can be a great billiards player without

---

52. See Michael J. Perry, *The Constitution, the Courts, and Human Rights: An Inquiry into the Legitimacy of Constitutional Policymaking by the Judiciary* 97–110 (1982). I note in passing that this suggestion may misconceive the social role of the prophets. They were social critics—see Michael Walzer, *Interpretation and Social Criticism,* ch. 3 (1987)—a strange role in which to cast a society's most powerful judicial officials.

knowing Newton's laws of motion. But the parallel is not exact. We know the billiards player is great by observing him play, and win, in competition with other players; we do not have as objective a method of evaluating judicial performance.

A related point is the difference between the internal and the external perspective of a job. From the internal perspective most jobs—private and public, glamorous and mundane, dangerous and safe, powerful and powerless—are pretty much the same, the job holder being concerned at the conscious level mainly with the mundane incidents (income, taxes, touchy co-workers and subordinates, difficult suppliers or customers, the physical conditions of work, and so on) that are common to all jobs.[53] The letters and diaries of great writers and artists are illuminating in this regard. The fact that a person's conscious preoccupations are trivial does not make the person or the person's work product trivial.

We must also be wary of confusing cause and justification. The motives driving a great scientist to succeed might be envy, greed, or thirst for glory. That would not undermine the validity of his scientific discoveries. The same is true, in principle, of law. But because we rightly mistrust our ability to verify the soundness of legal decisions, we are concerned that candidates for judicial office have the moral and temperamental qualities that conduce to good judging. Yet we are not sure what those qualities are. Moreover, they are difficult to screen for. And, once appointed, the judge is subject to the psychological tugs—which operate to a greater or lesser extent on all persons thrust into a judicial role—noted earlier.

Finally, the effect of professional norms and criticisms must be considered. The belief that judges are constrained by law, that there is more to law than the will to power, is a deeply ingrained feature of the legal culture. And this makes the expectation that judges will behave in accordance with that belief to an extent self-validating. A judge who flouts this expectation is likely both to feel uncomfortable and to attract professional criticism, which will make him more uncomfortable (although judges' ability to shrug off criticism as being motivated by politics, envy, ignorance, or sour grapes should not be underestimated). Feeble retribution, perhaps? But here the institution of judicial indepen-

---

53. Notice that I am inverting the usual argument—that a prediction theory of judicial behavior (on which further see Chapter 7), or other behaviorist explanation, is unfaithful to the internal perspective of the judge. Few people who write about that perspective have been judges.

dence is important and, paradoxically, may have the effect of constraining judges more effectively than if they were dependent on the good will of the legislative or executive branches. By removing the most powerful incentives to action, judicial independence brings to the fore incentives that might otherwise hold little sway. Certainly one who is skeptical about free will will tend to regard institutions such as judicial independence or academic tenure as altering rather than eliminating incentives. The designers of those institutions seem, consistent with the analysis in this chapter, to have acted on an implicitly behaviorist conception of the judicial process.

The desires to be comfortable with oneself and to avoid academic criticism from professors are, I suspect, powerful motives only when money is not a major factor. But that is the situation of judges. It is not unique. We notice that people seem to behave morally in situations in which the costs of behaving morally are small, but to respond to incentives in situations in which those costs are large. One way to encourage moral behavior, therefore, is to reduce its costs, which is done in the judicial arena by trying to make judicial decisions independent of the judges' incentives.

Another paradox is that judges in a system of political appointment may be *less* political than judges in a civil service type of judiciary, such as we find on the Continent. Judges who are appointed because of friendship with legislators or other politicians, because of political services that they have rendered, or because of their own political influence have more power than ordinary civil servants would have to ward off political interference with the judiciary. The combination in our federal courts of (1) political appointment to judgeships carrying (2) life tenure may maximize the independence of these courts and hence their ability to act as bulwarks of liberty, although not their "professional" quality, their craft skills. In this example we can see the line between law and politics fraying badly.

Judicial independence, with or without political criteria of appointment, has of course a negative aspect. The careful circumscription of judicial temptations and ambitions reduces the judge's drive to get things right; tenure is an anodyne. The joys of power and fame are a factor in the balance, too; and as the legal culture becomes even more diverse, the possibility grows that virtually any judicial posture—if consistent, but perhaps even more so if inconsistent!—will attract praise. The fracturing of the legal culture has removed a check on judicial willfulness. Yet this is not necessarily an argument against such fracturing, against diversity. Although the more uniform the legal culture—the more like-minded the judges—the easier it will be to fix the premises for decision and therefore to identify and criticize incorrect decisions, the agreement of the like-minded is not a powerful warrant for truth. The dilemma is fundamental. Legal objectivity, it seems, can be purchased only with a uniformity that can be deadly for intellectual inquiry. Yet a diverse judiciary makes painfully apparent the weakness of the law's methodology for resolving difficult issues.

6 ✍

Are There Right Answers to Legal Questions?

Questions of Law

Ronald Dworkin has flung down the gauntlet to legal skepticism by arguing that there are right answers to even the most difficult and controversial legal questions. In a well-known essay he asks whether the persistence of controversy over the correct outcome of a difficult case demonstrates that there are no right answers to the legal questions posed by such cases, and he answers no.[1] Controversy continues over whether Richard III ordered the little princes killed. Nevertheless, he either did or did not,[2] so there is a right answer to the question notwithstanding the controversy over it, and we would arrive at that answer if only we knew more of the facts; so it is with the law (p. 120).[3]

---

1. Ronald Dworkin, "Is There Really No Right Answer in Hard Cases?" in Dworkin, *A Matter of Principle* 119 (1985). Subsequent page references to this essay are in the text.

2. Well, not really; there are intermediate states, such as encouragement, ratification, and condonation, and there is also the possibility that the little princes died of natural causes, or in an accident, rather than being killed pursuant to an order (whether or not such an order was given). Here is a better example of a question that has a right answer (provided "blades of grass" and "boundary" have exact denotations) that is unlikely ever to be discovered: "It is either true or false that there was an odd number of blades of grass in Harvard Yard at the dawn of Commencement Day, 1903." "What Price Bivalence?" in W. V. Quine, *Theories and Things* 31, 32 (1981). I have already questioned (see Chapter 4) whether bivalence is a property of decisions in difficult cases.

3. The argument is offered in passing, and I may be making too much of it, especially since Dworkin later retracted the metaphysical implications of the "Right Answer" paper, although not the right-answer thesis itself. See Ronald Dworkin, *Law's Empire* viii–ix (1986). For additional criticisms of the thesis, see Jacob Paul Janzen, "Some Formal Aspects of Ronald Dworkin's Right Answer Thesis," 11 *Manitoba Law Journal* 191 (1981); Michael S. Moore, "Metaphysics, Epistemology, and Legal Theory," 60 *Southern California Law Review* 453 (1987); Kent Greenawalt, "Discretion and Judicial Decision: The Elusive Quest for the Fetters That Bind Judges," 75 *Columbia Law Review* 359 (1975).

But "the law" does not have the same ontological status that Richard III and the little princes have. Although what exactly it means to have knowledge of the past is a nice philosophical question, there is no reasonable doubt that Richard III and the little princes were real people and that the princes were killed by someone. That the question "by whom?" is a question about the past no more makes it unanswerable than the fact that the theory of evolution is a theory about the past makes that theory unscientific. But if we ask, for example, whether the Fourteenth Amendment forbids racial segregation of public schools, we are not asking a question about, or only about, historical events. We might be asking such a question if we thought the only basis for an affirmative answer would be that the draftsmen and ratifiers of the Fourteenth Amendment had meant to order the courts to forbid public school segregation. The question whether they issued such an order would be like the question whether Richard III ordered the little princes killed. But it is not Dworkin's theory of constitutional interpretation that we should ask whether a challenged practice was in the conscious thoughts of the framers. He wants courts to consider the level of generality of the provision, the values that inform it, the course of events unforeseen by the framers, the judicial decisions that have interpreted it. Ascertaining "the law," for Dworkin as for most other legal thinkers, is not a simple matter of asking whether the framers issued an order long ago to modern judges to do this or that. The law is not the same kind of entity as the events of Richard III's reign. (Maybe it is no kind of entity, as we shall see.) Even to ask whether "it is true" that the Fourteenth Amendment means this or that has an odd ring.

I am not arguing that controversy is proof per se of indeterminacy. Often—this is a central insight of pragmatism—it is stimulus and precursor to solution. But that observation yields little comfort once we distinguish between determinacy in principle and determinacy in practice. Even if there must be a right answer to the question about Richard III and the little princes, if the answer is inaccessible it is as if there were no right answer, or as if (as a pragmatist might believe) the question were meaningless. The situation is even worse in law. We can wait patiently—if need be forever—for the historians to discover the truth about Richard; but a legal case must be decided when it arises, and the decision may engender reliance that precludes reconsideration when the "right answer" is finally discovered.

Dworkin moves quickly off the Richard III example and tries two other tacks. The first is to contend that a question of law is not indeterminate so long as no observer would describe the question as a "tie" (p. 144). Here metaphor impedes understanding. The arguments in difficult cases cannot be "weighed," so it is indeed awkward to describe them as being in equipoise. Yet a dispute in which it is impossible to tell which side has the stronger argument is indeterminate.[4] Second, and at much greater length, Dworkin argues that correctness in law is similar to correctness in literary interpretation (pp. 138–143). A literary interpretation succeeds to the extent that it accounts for the relevant data— the incidents, language, and other aspects of the work. Likewise, suggests Dworkin, a legal interpretation succeeds to the extent that it accounts for the relevant ethical and political data that inform legal decision making. In both domains, then, the literary and the legal, there are right and wrong answers. But this argument overlooks the fact that, despite the scientific form of the inquiry into "fit"—an interpretation is proposed as a hypothesis, and verified or falsified by its success in explaining the data furnished by the text—a literary interpretation is not verifiable by the methods of exact inquiry, because the data do not lend themselves to experimental, statistical, or otherwise exact observation. No more does a legal interpretation, which is why in Chapter 3 I classified interpretation as a problem in practical reason.

The literary example is particularly inapt because of the peculiar ontology of fictional characters. In investigating the question whether Richard III ordered the little princes killed we can bring to bear our normal understanding of how people respond to various stimuli as well as our knowledge of English political history. But no law of literary composition requires that fictional characters behave "realistically" or have coherent life stories.[5] If, to borrow an example of Wittgenstein's, there is a picture of a teakettle with steam coming out of the spout, does this mean that the kettle in the picture contains boiling water?

4. See John Mackie, "The Third Theory of Law," in Mackie, *Persons and Values: Selected Papers,* vol. 2, pp. 132, 137–138 (Joan Mackie and Penelope Mackie eds. 1985).
5. This is the irony and the pathos of Keats's speculation, in "Ode on a Grecian Urn," about the town from which the people portrayed on the urn had come to attend the ceremony depicted on it:

> What little town by river or sea shore,
>   Or mountain-built with peaceful citadel,
>   Is emptied of this folk, this pious morn?
> And, little town, thy streets for evermore
>   Will silent be; and not a soul to tell
>   Why thou art desolate, can e'er return.

Consider the famous question, Do the Macbeths in Shakespeare's play have children?[6] There are ambiguous hints going both ways, but no direct evidence. Macbeth's obsessive concern with founding a dynasty is incomprehensible unless he and his wife have or are planning to have children, yet if they do have children, it is such an important fact that it would be bound to be discussed in the play. And they do not seem young enough to be planning a family. Anyway, it is quite impossible to visualize the Macbeths as parents, actual or prospective. So in one sense they must have children and in another and equally powerful sense they must not. This would be unsatisfactory in history but causes no distress to the audience of *Macbeth,* for whom the rules of logic, of psychological realism, of history, are happily suspended. This carefree ontology will not do for law.

If there is no demonstrably right answer, does this mean there is also no demonstrably wrong one? It does if there are only two possible answers (yes and no), but not otherwise. If there is neither a demonstrably right nor a demonstrably wrong answer, does this mean there is no answer worth giving? Not necessarily. There is a difference between saying "kale tastes bad" and saying "I don't think Richard III killed the little princes," or "I don't think the audience for *Macbeth* should think the Macbeths childless," or "I don't think the due process clause forbids racial segregation in the District of Columbia's public schools." It is possible, indeed obligatory, to give reasons for the last three statements although not for the first. The difference may reflect a belief that reasoning about these issues somehow advances the ball. But this may not be saying a great deal. The belief may be wrong. Or "reasoning" here may carry the persuasive or rhetorical sense noted in the discussion in Chapter 4 of competition among social visions (which is not to say that rhetorical "conversation" between advocates of opposed social visions is worthless). So far as giving reasons for legal judgments is concerned, we may simply feel qualms about doing things that hurt other people unless we give a reason—*some* reason, perhaps not very reasoned—for our action. Yet we allow juries to deliver verdicts without any statement of reasons. This is some evidence that the felt obligation to reason to a judgment is more fundamental than the obligation to give reasons for the judgment; for it has been considered unethical since the trial of Justice Bridlegoose in *Gargantua and Pantagruel* for a judge to flip a coin in order to determine the winner of a case that the judge considers a toss-

6. See the compact discussion in William Empson, *Essays on Shakespeare* 142–143 (1986).

up.[7] Is this just judicial public relations? Or is the fear that the judge will give up thinking too soon? A further point, which may explain why judges (but not jurors) normally are required to state reasons for their rulings, is that even made-up reasons might contribute to the policy debate. After all, the reasons lawyers give in advocating a client's cause often are made up rather than sincere, yet judges find them helpful anyway.

However these matters be sorted out, there is a gulf between saying that discussion of moral, historical, political—and difficult legal—questions is interesting or even socially productive and saying that there are in principle correct answers to all or most such questions. The idea that there are correct answers to all or most *moral* questions is called "moral realism,"[8] and in a heterogeneous society this is likely to seem even less plausible than a belief that there are right answers to even the most difficult legal questions. Dworkin is a moral realist.[9] Or so at least it seems when his belief that there are right answers to legal questions is juxtaposed with his belief that judges should "identify legal rights and duties, so far as possible, on the assumption that they were all created by a single author—the community personified—expressing a coherent conception of justice and fairness."[10] For these are moral terms.

I want to suggest three more respects in which Dworkin's comparison of statutory (and constitutional) interpretation to literary interpretation actually undermines the quest for right answers in law:

First, it is easy to find literary examples of utterly indeterminate questions: not perhaps whether the Macbeths had children but whether they had fair or swarthy complexions, blue or brown eyes, or were born in

---

7. Maybe the law has been too hasty in rejecting "aleatory" decision making in all cases. For an interesting discussion, see Robert H. Mnookin, "Child-Custody Adjudication: Judicial Functions in the Face of Indeterminacy," 39 *Law and Contemporary Problems* 226, 289–291 (Summer 1975).

8. A position vigorously defended in Michael Moore, "Moral Reality," 1982 *Wisconsin Law Review* 1061. See also Note, "Relativistic Jurisprudence: Skepticism Founded on Confusion," 61 *Southern California Law Review* 1417 (1988). Notice once again the potential confusion caused by the fact that philosophy and law use different terminologies. The legal counterpart to moral realism is not legal realism but legal formalism. For this reason, and also because the opposite of moral realism is moral relativism, it might be better to call moral realism "moral absolutism." See Gilbert Harman, "Is There a Single True Morality?" in *Relativism: Interpretation and Confrontation* 363 (Michael Krausz ed. 1989).

9. See Larry Alexander, "Striking Back at the Empire: A Brief Survey of Problems in Dworkin's Theory of Law," 6 *Law and Philosophy* 419, 425 n. 14 (1987).

10. *Law's Empire,* note 3 above, at 225.

leap years. There is an infinite number of questions like these.[11] They are ignored because nowadays no serious person is interested in them. (I recognize that this explanation is circular.) But suppose a law were passed entitling anyone with such a question to compel the Modern Language Association to answer it.[12] Then we would see "litigation" over indeterminate questions with a vengeance. Many legal questions are indeterminate in a similar sense. The authors of the relevant texts have not provided the reader with enough information to enable an answer. But it would be extraordinary if the judges said, "We won't decide your case because we don't have enough information to figure out what the right answer is." They may resolve the indeterminate case by placing the burden of persuasion on one party, but that just regresses the debate to who should be assigned the burden—that is, who should lose.

Imaginative writers might seem to have greater license than legislators to omit essential clues or to decide what may count as a relevant question about the text. Shakespeare was writing for a theater audience, which would not have time to ponder every implication in the text; so he could leave gaps, as he did with the question of the Macbeths' children. Legislators do not have that luxury. Yet often, as the price of obtaining majority agreement, they deliberately leave a question unanswered. Even more often do they do this inadvertently. The result in either case is a gap that our conventions of adjudication require the judges to fill rather than allow them to ignore, as their literary counterparts can do.

Second, people with similar educational backgrounds, politics, religious beliefs, and so forth will tend to interpret a work of literature convergently, while people with different backgrounds will tend to interpret it divergently; and it is much the same with law. A legal profession whose members have the same social and educational background, politics, religion, professional experience, and the like will tend to agree on the premises for decision; and, to repeat a chord struck frequently in this book, the more agreement there is on premises, the more legal reasoning can follow the syllogistic model. Then law will appear—will, in

---

11. See the interesting discussion in Simon Blackburn, *Spreading the Word: Groundings in the Philosophy of Language* 203–210 (1984).

12. Cf. Frank H. Easterbrook, "The Influence of Judicial Review on Constitutional Theory," in *A Workable Government? The Constitution after 200 Years* 170, 174 (Burke Marshall ed. 1987).

a sense, *be*—objective, impersonal.[13] In just the same way, objective interpretation presupposes an interpretive community that is homogeneous. These conditions for objectivity do not exist in the American legal community today any more than they exist in its literary community. Reflecting larger fissures in society, the legal community is politically and culturally divided. Its heterogeneity, interacting with the predominance of forms of law that give judges great discretion—common law, constitutional law, and statutes enacted by legislatures in which party discipline is so weak that many statutes are the product of complex, hard-fought, often unprincipled compromises—has created a legal terrain in which the consensus that might fix the premises for decision and allow law to proceed on logical tracks is unattainable.

Third, the closest analogy of literary to statutory interpretation is the occasional attempt to predict from a writer's life and works how he would have responded to some contemporary issue. If George Orwell had lived longer (he died in 1950), would he have sided with the United States in Vietnam? Would he be a neoconservative today? A Green? A fan of Gorbachev?[14] Such questions, whose fatuity should be self-evident, resemble questions such as whether the framers of the Constitution would be opposed to wiretapping, or "dial-a-porn," or malapportionment, or flag burning, or abortion, if they were living today. Experience with literature suggests that texts and biographical insights cannot be reliably projected into the remote or even, as the case of Orwell shows, the near future, and it therefore provides no support for defenders of law's objectivity.

Questions of Fact

The ontology of legal fact-finding, at least, may seem unproblematic. Something happened, and it is the job of the court to find out what. Reconstructing the past can be difficult, of course, as the question about Richard III and the little princes shows, but can there be anything spe-

---

13. This is the abiding lesson of studies of the English common law, illustrated by Brian Simpson, "The Common Law and Legal Theory," in *Legal Theory and Common Law* 8 (William Twining ed. 1986), and of comparisons of English and American law. See, for example, P. S. Atiyah and Robert S. Summers, *Form and Substance in Anglo-American Law: A Comparative Study of Legal Reasoning, Legal Theory, and Legal Institutions* (1987).

14. See John Rodden, *The Politics of Literary Reputation: The Making and Claiming of "St. George" Orwell* (1989).

cially troublesome about that? I think there can be, though I do not accept the crude "fact skepticism" of some of the legal realists.[15]

The past cannot be recovered, and this makes it difficult to verify or falsify hypotheses about it.[16] Not in every case, to be sure; if the murder suspect tells the police that he buried the victim's body at a certain place, and the police go there and, lo and behold, there it is, this is confirmation that he was telling the truth. It is an example of successful prediction—about the past; but much scientific prediction, too, is really postdiction; many of the events "predicted" by astronomers occurred billions of years ago. There are nevertheless a large number of legal cases in which the question of what happened is indeterminate, and must be resolved by a decision on who shall bear the burden of producing evidence or of persuading the trier of fact; bluntly, who shall lose in cases of doubt. It might appear that the problem of factual indeterminacy would be greatly exacerbated by the importance that so many legal doctrines seem to place on state of mind as an element of liability; but we saw in the last chapter how the legal system elides this difficulty by adopting a behavioral approach to mental phenomena. Yet in a sense these are dodges rather than solutions. Even the burial case is less straightforward than it appears to be. We must ask what exactly is being predicted when the murder suspect tells the police where he buried the victim's body: only that the body will be found at the indicated place. The fulfillment of the prediction is consistent with the hypothesis that the suspect is indeed the murderer, but like scientific confirmation in general it is also consistent with other hypotheses, such as that the true murderer told the suspect where the body was buried.

A distinct problem arises from the heavy but largely unremarked reliance that the law places on being able to determine counterfactuals. Counterfactual conditionals[17] pervade our thinking about causes and

15. See William Twining, "Some Scepticism about Some Scepticisms," 11 *Journal of Law and Society* 137 (1984). In distinguishing factual from legal questions I do not mean to suggest that there is a bulkhead between them. To a convinced materialist, legal questions are at bottom questions of fact. For an interesting discussion, see Peter Tillers, "The Value of Evidence in Law," 39 *Northern Ireland Legal Quarterly* 167 (1988).

16. A point stressed, in the legal setting, in Paul Bator, "Finality in Criminal Law and Federal Habeas Corpus for State Prisoners," 76 *Harvard Law Review* 441 (1963). On the philosophical issues involved in knowledge of the past, see, for example, Arthur C. Danto, *Narration and Knowledge* (1985). And on the reliability of historical testimony, see Stephen M. Stigler, "John Craig and the Probability of History: From the Death of Christ to the Birth of Laplace," 81 *Journal of the American Statistical Association* 879 (1986).

17. On which see, for example, Richard Otte, "Indeterminism, Counterfactuals, and Causation," 54 *Philosophy of Science* 45 (1987); *Causation and Conditionals* (Ernest Sosa ed. 1975); David Lewis, *Philosophical Papers,* vol. 2, pt. 6 (1986).

consequences. Often they are unproblematic. When we say that X shot Y, we mean that if X had not pulled the trigger Y would not have been shot. But suppose instead the question is whether X discharged Y because Y is a woman. That is, suppose we have to answer a "why" question rather than just a "what" question—the "what" question in this case, Was she discharged? being trivial. Maybe Y admits she did things that would have been grounds for discharge but claims she would not have been discharged were she a man. The task for the trier of fact is to determine what would have happened in the imaginary, the counterfactual world that is just like our world (if one can get over the fact that it does not exist) except that in it Y is a man rather than a woman. Does this mean the trier of fact must ascribe to the counterfactual Y every characteristic of a man except for a man's primary and secondary sexual characteristics? If so, however, would she still be Y in anything but name? Indeed, would she still be a woman? For women may differ systematically from men in other ways besides the obvious physical differences (see Chapter 13).

Putting these questions aside, one can determine whether Y would have been fired if she were a man only by comparing her treatment with that of men employed by X. But all people are different. Even if men and women do not differ systematically with respect to attributes relevant to performing the job in question, none of the men will be identical to a Y shorn of her female identity, and the job-discrimination laws do not forbid arbitrary decisions—only decisions traceable to the sex (or race, or other protected characteristic) of the employee. If the work were so routinized, so uniform, that from the employer's standpoint the employees really were interchangeable, provided only that they satisfied readily observable minimum performance criteria, the determination of the elusive counterfactual question about Y would be answerable with some confidence. Or if there were a great number of male and female workers, statistical evidence could be used to generate a more or less reliable probabilistic judgment. But in cases where neither condition is satisfied, the outcome is likely to depend on the burden of proof, or on the court's biases and prejudices, rather than on "the truth."

Thus far I have assumed that the court is seeking truth and only truth, but this is an unrealistic assumption, especially in the American legal system.[18] To pick a humble example, evidence of repairs made by the defendant to his premises after an accident in which the plaintiff was

---

18. See Atiyah and Summers, note 13 above, ch. 6; Mirjan R. Damaška, *The Faces of Justice and State Authority: A Comparative Approach to the Legal Process* 119–125 (1986).

injured is not admissible to show that the condition of the premises before the accident was hazardous. The evidence is relevant, but if it were admissible injurers would be discouraged from making repairs after an accident. The fact finder's concern with other values besides factual accuracy parallels the judicial rule maker's concern, stressed in previous chapters, with other values besides a rule's truth value.

I do not mean that the American system is uninterested in factual truth, but only that the goal of truth is in competition with other goals, such as economy, preserving certain confidences, fostering certain activities, protecting constitutional norms. A goal that receives less attention than it should is to provide catharsis for people with grievances, real or imagined. People who think their rights have been violated are indignant, and they want a forum to vent their indignation. It has been the observation of many trial judges—and I have observed the same thing in the occasional trials that I have conducted—that even when a plaintiff loses his case he feels better than if he had never been able to air his grievance in a public forum in which the grievance was, if not vindicated, at least taken seriously and the defendant, his oppressor, put to the bother and anxiety of defending himself. This cathartic or therapeutic function of litigation is related to the roots of law in revenge and to the corrective-justice theory of law, both discussed in Chapter 11.

Succinctly, the procedural system seeks the optimal trade-off between accuracy and cost, the latter broadly conceived. A cost weighted heavily in the English and American legal traditions is that of a judicial bureaucracy, and as a result great effort has been made to minimize the size of that bureaucracy. In contrast to the Continental legal systems, primary responsibility for developing the facts of the case is hived off on private lawyers; truth seeking is made competitive. This is not necessarily a bad idea, apart from the intensely practical point that Americans have little aptitude for organizing and staffing high-quality civil services. We recall that Popper's theory of scientific progress emphasizes competition; and there is a connection between competition in developing facts and the classical liberal tradition that exalts competitive markets generally. One strain in liberal thought is skepticism about claims to possess the ultimate truth about anything. To such skepticism a marketplace notion of truth in the courts—adjudication as a struggle between competing hypotheses presented and supported by private lawyers—is congenial.

But the analogy between science and the adversary system has limited force. As David Luban emphasizes, scientists do not compete—not routinely at any rate—by moving to suppress probative evidence or by trying to rattle fellow inquirers by cross-examination.[19] The adversary system does not much resemble the concept of unforced inquiry that is the pragmatists' ideal and the scientists' ethic. Furthermore, the competitors in our privatized, competitive system of justice often have markedly and irremediably unequal resources. Most criminal defendants lack the resources to hire counsel equal in skill and experience to the public prosecutor, and public subvention of the cost of counsel for indigent criminal defendants has not been sufficiently generous to close the gap.[20] Not all scientific research centers have the same resources, of course. But they compete for resources, whereas a criminal defendant cannot, just by virtue of having a good case, procure high-priced legal talent to defend him.

Rather than equalize the resources of prosecutors and defendants, the legal system has erected formidable procedural obstacles to conviction. These have succeeded in reducing the probability of convicting innocent persons to an extremely low level, but the price is that many guilty persons are acquitted (especially those who can afford to hire top-quality lawyers), or are never charged, or are allowed to plead guilty to crimes much less serious than those they actually committed. Even in civil as distinct from criminal law, the privatization of fact gathering and proof is problematic, because of a dearth of reliable information in the market for legal services. Lawyers' performance is difficult to evaluate, making competition among lawyers highly imperfect. But problems of information can also plague a system in which the responsibility for gathering the facts is, as in Continental legal systems, vested in investigative magistrates and other public officials; both their superiors and the public may have difficulty monitoring their performance.[21] The only practical way to solve such problems is to make only simple facts legally relevant, but this "reform" would require a wholesale redefinition of legal rights and wrongs.

19. See "The Adversary System Excuse," in *The Good Lawyer: Lawyers' Roles and Lawyers' Ethics* 83, 93–94 (David Luban ed. 1984). This is not to deny the existence of some pretty rough competition among scientists, as emphasized in David L. Hull, *Science as a Process: An Evolutionary Account of the Social and Conceptual Development of Science* (1988).

20. See, for example, Stephen J. Schulhofer, "Criminal Justice Discretion as a Regulatory System," 17 *Journal of Legal Studies* 43, 53–56 (1988).

21. For a debate over the relative merits of the Anglo-American and Continental methods of determining facts, see Ronald J. Allen et al., "The German Advantage in Civil Procedure: A Plea for More Details and Fewer Generalities in Comparative Scholarship," 82 *Northwestern University Law Review* 705 (1988); John H. Langbein, "Trashing *The German Advantage*," in id. at 763; Ronald J. Allen, "Idealization and Caricature in Comparative Scholarship," in id. at 785.

The United States is alone among the civilized nations in continuing to use juries routinely in civil trials, and our rules of evidence are shaped by the perceived (more precisely, the conjectured) limitations of jurors' understanding. In part we preserve the civil jury merely because we distrust the judges, sometimes justifiably. In part, perhaps we preserve it in order to make the judicial role seem more objective than it is, by consigning difficult questions to laypersons and thereby reducing the number of cases in which judges have to decide indeterminate questions. And it is precisely the factually difficult questions that the jury decides. If the question is easy—if a rational jury could not fail to answer it a particular way—the judge will take the case away from the jury by granting a motion for a directed verdict or for judgment notwithstanding the verdict. (Compare the pardon power, which provides an escape hatch from legal judgments that is located outside the formal legal system.) On this analysis, the survival of the civil jury is due not to the populist streak in American culture, as is generally believed, but to formalist anxieties.

The combination of juries and poor judges may not be a happy one, epistemologically speaking. The high regard in which the civil jury is held in some quarters is suspect. Its most influential supporters, besides lawyers for tort plaintiffs, are trial judges, and their support is largely unrelated to the accuracy of fact-finding by juries. They like the jury system because, to begin with, the burden of decision is shared: the jury assumes the primary responsibility for the decision—and judges like to deflect responsibility from themselves; and when the judge is not the decider, he is not required to write out his findings of fact and conclusions of law, which is a bother. Also jury trials are more dramatic and exciting than bench trials, and provide the judge with a larger audience as well as with a larger field for the exercise of his people skills and his dramaturgical and managerial aptitudes. And judges have a natural tendency to think that "their" juries—the juries they have instructed, in the trials they have managed—get things right, since if they did not it might reflect poorly on the judge's conduct of the trial. This tendency (a nice example of resolving cognitive dissonance) is reinforced by the fact that many trial judges do not pay close attention to the evidence in a jury trial, because they are not the triers of fact in such trials; the judge's natural tendency therefore is to agree with the jury, which (whatever the other failings of trial by jury) does play close attention.

Confidence in the civil jury should be undermined by the fact that when people are free to design their own methods of determining facts, including the same type of historical facts that are at issue in civil trials, they never "invent" the jury. For example, there are no juries in arbitration, the private counterpart to public adjudication. And the "judges"—that is, the arbitrators—are often specialists, which is a count against our heavy reliance on generalist judges and randomly chosen jurors. The rules that frame the jury's inquiry, moreover, are inexplicable except on the hypothesis that we are dealing with a fact-finding body that is as gullible as it is inexperienced. One may not be willing to go as far as Ambrose Bierce, who said that "most momentous actions, military, political, commercial and of every other kind, are daily undertaken on hearsay evidence. There is no religion in the world that has any other basis than hearsay evidence."[22] But one could hardly deny that the hearsay rule—like the best-evidence rule, the rules of direct examination and of cross-examination, the rules on expert witnesses, the rules governing the selection and deliberations of juries, the rule that excludes evidence of a criminal defendant's criminal record unless he takes the stand (in which event his record can be used to attack the credibility of his testimony), and the other characteristic rules of American legal procedure that are intended to protect the simplest jurors from being confused—is a second-best solution to the problem of factual uncertainty. The solution is dictated by our reliance on inexpert triers of fact facing competitive producers of evidence. These are not the rules we would expect to find in an inquiry unconstrained by the extrinsic considerations that have shaped our legal procedure. They are remote from scientific procedure. The fact that juries, unlike judges, do not give any justification for their decisions is a dead giveaway; a requirement that jurors explain their votes would be a source of profound embarrassment to the legal system.

Another reason for questioning the capacity of our—perhaps of any—legal system to discover "truth" is the tendency of the litigation process

---

22. *The Devil's Dictionary,* in *The Collected Writings of Ambrose Bierce* 270 (1946) (entry for "Inadmissible"). He added: "Nothing in any existing court was ever more thoroughly proved than the charges of witchcraft and sorcery for which so many suffered death." Id. at 271. This is a reminder, if any is needed, of the fallibility of legal fact-finding. On forensic proof of witchcraft, see, for example, Barbara J. Shapiro, *Probability and Certainty in Seventeenth-Century England: A Study of the Relationships between Natural Science, Religion, History, Law, and Literature,* ch. 5 (1983); Sanford J. Fox, *Science and Justice: The Massachusetts Witchcraft Trials* (1968). The legal system continues to be credulous with regard to certain types of evidence. See, for example, D. Michael Risinger, Mark P. Denbeaux, and Michael J. Saks, "Exorcism of Ignorance as a Proxy for Rational Knowledge: The Lessons of Handwriting Identification 'Expertise,'" 137 *University of Pennsylvania Law Review* 731 (1989).

to select for trial precisely those cases in which the facts are uncertain.[23] I discussed a parallel tendency with regard to legal issues earlier in this book, noting that it exaggerates the degree to which law is uncertain. But just as that tendency ensures a high degree of legal uncertainty in the appellate process, so the tendency to select for trial those cases in which the facts are in doubt ensures a high degree of factual uncertainty in the trial process. The cases that go to trial because the parties are unable to predict how the judge or jury will resolve the key factual disagreements are also the cases that the judge or jury will have the greatest difficulty deciding correctly.

This may not matter *too* much. As long as the courts can decide the easy cases correctly, and litigants and potential litigants know this, at least the system will be resolving, albeit indirectly, a large fraction of all relevant factual questions correctly. Nevertheless, the tendency of litigated cases to turn on difficult factual questions, when combined with the difficulties that fact finders, especially in the American legal system, have in answering such questions, may make judicial opinions a mine of misinformation. If factual uncertainty is disproportionately characteristic of litigated cases (from which the reported cases are drawn), then, given the difficulty of dispelling such uncertainty by the methods of litigation, we can expect the factual recitals in published judicial opinions to be wrong much of the time. In addition, the facts cited in an opinion are often merely those contained in the plaintiff's complaint, which, having been dismissed on some legal ground, will be taken for purposes of appeal to be truthful, even if fanciful. Further, the appellate process tends to bleach out the facts of the dispute. By the time the case reaches the appellate court many of the facts of the dispute may have become irrelevant; as a result, the appellate opinion may paint a highly truncated and even misleading picture of what actually happened.

And especially in cases where there is no published dissent, judicial opinions exemplify "winners' history." The appellate court will usually state the facts as favorably to its conclusions as the record allows, and

23. There is an extensive literature on the determinants of the decision to go to trial rather than settle, emphasizing uncertainty, whether legal or factual, as a necessary although not sufficient condition. See, for example, William M. Landes, "An Economic Analysis of the Courts," 14 *Journal of Law and Economics* 61 (1971); Patricia Munch Danzon and Lee A. Lillard, "Settlement Out of Court: The Disposition of Medical Malpractice Claims," 12 *Journal of Legal Studies* 345 (1983); Richard A. Posner, *Economic Analysis of Law* §21.5 (3d ed. 1986); George L. Priest and Benjamin Klein, "The Selection of Disputes for Litigation," 13 *Journal of Legal Studies* 1 (1984); Steven Shavell, "Suit, Settlement, and Trial: A Theoretical Analysis under Alternative Methods for the Allocation of Legal Costs," 11 *Journal of Legal Studies* 55 (1982).

often more favorably. This unedifying practice reflects both the psychology of judging (having persuaded himself that a particular outcome is correct, the judge or judge's law clerk will tend unconsciously to screen out facts that support a contrary outcome) and the formalist style. An opinion would not look as powerful, as confident, as certainly right if it acknowledged the strength of opposing views. The tendency I have described is abetted by the reluctance of academic commentators to expand their study of cases beyond judicial opinions. Rarely will the commentator get hold of the briefs and record to check the accuracy of the factual recitals in the opinion.

All this would be of relatively little importance were it not that lawyers' and particularly judges' knowledge of the world, or at least of the slice of the world relevant to legal decision making, derives to a significant degree from judicial opinions. One of the distinctive features of judges as policy makers—and it should be clear by now that judges in our system *are,* to a significant degree, policy-making officials—is that they obtain much of their knowledge of how the world works from materials that are systematically unreliable sources of information.[24]

Since certainty is unattainable in most trials, should the question of legal proof be explicitly characterized as one of probabilistic determination? If so, what theory of probability should be adopted?[25] Probability is a mysterious entity, like number, but we can skip most of the mysteries[26] and merely sketch two of the rival concepts. One is frequen-

---

24. For an illustration of the significance of this point in the law of privacy, see my book *Law and Literature: A Misunderstood Relation* 4–5 (1988), discussing Melvin v. Reid, 112 Cal. App. 285, 297 Pac. 91 (1931), a famous privacy case whose "facts," drawn entirely from the plaintiff's implausible complaint, have shaped the thinking of generations of privacy scholars. I discuss a parallel example, *Tuttle v. Buck,* in Chapter 8 of the present book.

25. The issue is thoroughly canvased in "Boston University School of Law Symposium on Probability and Inference in the Law of Evidence," 66 *Boston University Law Review* 377 (1986). (Most of the papers in the symposium appear in *Probability and Inference in the Law of Evidence: The Uses and Limits of Bayesianism* [Peter Tillers and Eric D. Green eds. 1988].) See also Richard Eggleston, *Evidence, Proof and Probability* (2d ed. 1983); Joseph L. Gastwirth, *Statistical Reasoning in Law and Public Policy* (2 vols. 1988); *The Evolving Role of Statistical Assessments as Evidence in the Courts* (Stephen E. Fienberg ed. 1989). The problems of judicial evidence are discussed from a philosophical standpoint in L. Jonathan Cohen, *The Probable and the Provable,* pt. 2 and ch. 18 (1977). See also Ferdinand Schoeman, "Cohen on Inductive Probability and the Law of Evidence," 54 *Philosophy of Science* 76 (1987); L. Jonathan Cohen, "On Analyzing the Standards of Forensic Evidence: Reply to Schoeman," 54 id. at 92 (1987).

26. For an uncommonly lucid discussion, see L. Jonathan Cohen, *An Introduction to the Philosophy of Induction and Probability* (1989). Other good discussions include J. L. Mackie, *Truth Probability and Paradox: Studies in Philosophical Logic,* ch. 3 (1973); Terrence L. Fine, *Theories of Probability: An Examination of Foundations,* ch. 9 (1973); Clark Glymour, *Theory and Evidence,* ch. 3 (1980).

cy. To say that the probability that a randomly selected lightbulb is defective is .001 means, to a "frequentist," that if a sequence of randomly selected lightbulbs, produced under identical conditions, is tested, the relative frequency of defective lightbulbs will, in accordance with the law of large numbers, tend toward .001 as the number tested increases without limit. The frequentist approach is of limited utility to the law because its conditions (random selection, identical conditions, many tests) are difficult to satisfy in a trial setting; one exception is where guilt or liability turns on fingerprint evidence or some other form of evidence the accuracy of which has been determined by statistical studies of large samples.

The second approach, the Bayesian, views probability in subjective terms. If a bookmaker lays odds of 9 to 1 against a particular horse's winning, then as far as the bookmaker is concerned the probability of that horse's winning is .1. (Of course, the decision to place a bet depends on more than the odds—it depends, for example, on the bettor's attitude toward risk. But I ignore this complication and thus forgo discussion of risk preference or risk aversion.) Subjective probability unquestionably plays an important role in litigation. For example, each litigant must decide whether to settle or to go to trial, and in making that decision he will calculate, consciously or unconsciously, the odds of winning if he goes to trial. But does Bayesianism provide a good model of the decisional process of a judge or jury?[27] For example, does (should) a jury convict a criminal defendant provided its members would lay odds of at least 9 to 1 or perhaps 19 to 1 against the innocence of the defendant? This seems unlikely, not only because the jury, unlike the litigant or the gambler, is not wagering anything on its assessment of the chances of guessing right, but also because it is not instructed by judge or counsel about odds. Many judges do not try to give the jury even a verbal explanation of the standard of proof in criminal cases, "beyond a reasonable doubt"; that is left to the jury's imagination.[28] The jury is making a decision under uncertainty, of course, but it is not invited to

27. See Lea Brilmayer and Lewis Kornhauser, "Quantitative Methods and Legal Decisions," 45 *University of Chicago Law Review* 116, 135–148 (1978), for a helpful discussion.

28. On the oddity of refusing to instruct the jury on the meaning of what might appear to be the master concept for their deliberations, see the majority and concurring opinions in United States v. Hall, 854 F.2d 1036 (7th Cir. 1988); also Eggleston, note 25 above, ch. 9. The entire issue of effective communication with juries is deeply problematic. Jury instructions usually are couched in legal jargon; it is uncertain how well the average juror understands them. See Walter W. Steele, Jr., and Elizabeth G. Thornburg, "Jury Instructions: A Persistent Failure to Communicate," 67 *North Carolina Law Review* 77 (1988).

consider the decision in that light; and perhaps that is for the best. In so saying, I am speaking of how these questions should be presented *to a jury;* I am not opining on the ultimate merits of Bayesian versus frequentist (or other) theories of probability. Most criticisms of Bayesian probability theory may well be either ill informed or incomplete.[29] Nor am I contending that only betting cultures understand decision under uncertainty, and then only in explicit betting situations. People make decisions under uncertainty in their own lives every day. But jurors are making decisions that affect other people's lives.

Essentially the jury is told in criminal cases not to convict unless it is certain of the defendant's guilt, with the proviso that it is not to insist on a degree of certainty unreasonable in the circumstances (that is, it is to put aside unreasonable doubts): the kind of certainty that attends propositions such as that $2 + 2 = 4$ or that cats do not grow on trees or that no person born before 1800 is still alive. Obviously this approach, which used to be called "moral certainty" and meant "the kind of certainty that is adequate for practical life"[30]—and is thus an important example of the use of practical reason in law—is at bottom probabilistic. Nevertheless it may be better than telling jurors about probabilities, betting odds, confidence intervals, and the like, at least until we either have a populace with some education in statistical inference or alter our criteria for selecting jurors.

I am not, however, arguing that law's "expressive" function would be undermined[31] if we faced up to the fact that the determination of facts in criminal cases is probabilistic rather than certain and brought the best scientific tools to bear on the question. My only concern is that juries might be confused. I am not sure law *has* an expressive function—that is, a function of creating or reinforcing a set of social norms or an ideology. That law affects behavior not only directly, by creating rewards and sanctions, but indirectly, by altering attitudes and through them behavior is an article of faith for most legal professionals, especially judges and professors. But consistent with the lack of scientific curiosity that is so marked a characteristic of legal thought, the legal profession

29. As argued in the comments by Stephen E. Fienberg and David H. Kaye in the Boston University symposium, note 25 above, at 651, 657, 693, 701.

30. Glenn Shafer, "Moral Certainty," 5 *Encyclopedia of Statistical Sciences* 623 (1985).

31. As argued recently in Charles Nesson, "The Evidence or the Events? On Judicial Proof and the Acceptability of Verdicts," 98 *Harvard Law Review* 1357 (1985), and attacked in Michael J. Saks and Robert F. Kidd, "Human Information Processing and Adjudication: Trial by Heuristics," in *Judgment and Decision Making: An Interdisciplinary Reader* 213 (Hal R. Arkes and Kenneth R. Hammond eds. 1986).

has for the most part neither participated in conducting nor even paid any attention to (even to the extent of criticizing) studies designed to confirm or refute the existence of such consequences.[32] The lack of evidence that these consequences exist—even the evidence that they do *not* exist[33]—has failed to shake the profession's faith.

The stubbornness of that faith is surprising because so much legal discourse tacitly assumes the opposite—that law is a social follower rather than a social leader. A police search infringes the Fourth Amendment if it violates the "reasonable expectations of privacy" of the person searched. This criterion would be circular if people were assumed to take from the law itself their cues on how much privacy to expect. The criterion for applying the doctrine of promissory estoppel (whereby a promise may be legally enforceable even if not supported by consideration) is whether the promisee reasonably relied on the promise. It would be circular if people relied on precisely those promises they knew the law would enforce. In general, the commercial law of this country,

32. Sociologists and psychologists have conducted a number of such studies. See, for example, Gary B. Melton and Michael J. Saks, "The Law as an Instrument of Socialization and Social Structure," in *The Law as a Behavioral Institution* 235, 255–263 (Gary B. Melton ed. 1986); Richard D. Schwartz, "Law and Normative Order," in *Law and the Social Sciences* 63 (Leon Lipson and Stanton Wheeler eds. 1986); *The Impact of Supreme Court Decisions: Empirical Studies* (2d ed., Theodore L. Becker and Malcolm M. Feeley eds., 1973); Adam Podgorecki et al., *Knowledge and Opinion about Law* (1973); Robert L. Kidder, *Connecting Law and Society: An Introduction to Research and Theory,* ch. 6 (1983). The expressive or educative function of law is discussed from a philosophical standpoint in Joel Feinberg, *Harmless Wrongdoing* 294–300 (1988) (vol. 4 of his treatise *The Moral Limits of the Criminal Law*).

33. For example, Berl Kutchinsky, "'The Legal Consciousness': A Survey of Research on Knowledge and Opinion about Law," in Podgorecki et al., note 32 above, at 101, 112–120, points out that many studies have found that criminals have approximately the same knowledge of and beliefs about the legal system as law-abiding persons do. This is some evidence that having the "right" attitude toward law does not strengthen social norms. A study by Kirk R. Williams, Jack P. Gibbs, and Maynard L. Erickson, "Public Knowledge of Statutory Penalties: The Extent and Basis of Accurate Perception," 23 *Pacific Sociological Review* 105 (1980), finds that although people have a pretty good knowledge of statutory penalties for crime, their perceptions reflect their preferences as to appropriate sanctions, and those preferences in turn are reflected in the statutes. So it is public opinion that determines the penalties, rather than the penalties that determine public opinion. A study by Sally Engle Merry, "Everyday Understandings of the Law in Working-Class America," 13 *American Ethnologist* 253 (1986), finds that even when people obtain first-hand knowledge of the operations of our undignified local courts, they retain their faith in the rule of law. These and other studies (some cited in Chapter 4) undermine the view that preserving myths about the legal system is necessary to secure the maximum feasible compliance with law. Another type of attitudinal impact is illustrated by the effect of the *Gobitis* decision (Chapter 4 again) in stirring up violence against Jehovah's Witnesses. But the impact was short-lived.

codified in the Uniform Commercial Code, follows commercial custom, rather than custom following law. All this is not to say that law never alters attitudes, but it does underscore the uncertainty about the question.

However this larger question be answered, there seems no reason to believe either that the legal profession's efforts to exaggerate the certainty of legal determinations (both legal and factual) fool the public or that such deception if successful would serve a worthwhile social purpose. It is strange that an important part of American government should seek to rule by mystery, in the manner of Dostoevsky's Grand Inquisitor, rather than by informed consent.[34] Strange or not, it hardly seems necessary in this instance.

Even in a civil case, where the jury is told to render judgment for the plaintiff if the plaintiff has proved his case by a "preponderance of the evidence," it seems that what the jury is being asked to do is not to lay a bet but to decide whether it believes the plaintiff's side of the case. It cannot be sure, of course, and it need not be as confident as in a criminal case, but it is not simply deciding whom it would bet on—plaintiff or defendant—if it were placing an even bet. That may be why the plaintiff who presents no or very little evidence will lose even though in the absence of any evidence the jury might think it slightly more likely than not that the plaintiff had a good case.[35] Stated differently, the jury wants to understand what happened—wants to be able to build a causal chain from the defendant's acts to the plaintiff's harm—rather than to estimate probabilities, because people are more comfortable with causal than with statistical explanations.[36] An alternative explanation, however, is consistent with the probabilistic approach: in the absence of special circumstances, the plaintiff's inability to come up with evidence suggests that he has no case—that the defendant's case is the more persuasive, the case to "bet on." If the plaintiff puts in some evidence, the defendant's failure to put in evidence of his own may, in turn, tell against him. Of course, in either case, the inference may be unwarranted; the missing evidence may simply be unavailable.

34. The legal profession has known for centuries that legal fact-finding is probabilistic. See Shapiro, note 22 above, at 178–182, 187. But it is reluctant to share the knowledge with the lay public.

35. For an interesting discussion, see Mary Dant, "Gambling on the Truth: The Use of Purely Statistical Evidence as a Basis for Civil Liability," 22 *Columbia Journal of Law and Social Problems* 31 (1988).

36. Cf. L. Jonathan Cohen, *The Dialogue of Reason: An Analysis of Analytical Philosophy* 157–187 (1986).

How pervasive is the problem of factual error in law? For starters, there is the well-known fact that many guilty people are acquitted, because of the heavy burden that the prosecution bears. Whether many innocent persons are convicted is likely to depend on the extent and care with which prosecutors screen their cases.[37] If prosecutors never prosecuted people who were not in fact guilty, the standard of proof could be as low as one wanted and still no innocent people would be convicted. Conversely, if prosecutors engaged in no screening but instead prosecuted anyone against whom a complaint was lodged, the percentage of innocent persons convicted might be significant, since the jury need only be reasonably certain of the defendant's guilt to convict.

How much screening is done by prosecutors probably depends to a large extent on their resources relative to the amount of crime. The lower this ratio the more carefully prosecutors will screen, and the ratio is extremely low in this country today. The implication, which is counterintuitive, is that fewer innocent people will be convicted in a society with a high (and, especially, a rising) crime rate than in one with a low crime rate. Prosecutorial screening leaves untouched, however—indeed exacerbates—the problem of acquittal of the guilty. The more screening there is, the fewer guilty people are convicted; the screening gives them an additional chance to beat the rap. In general, unless the resources devoted to determining guilt and innocence are increased, the only way to reduce the probability of convicting the innocent is to reduce the probability of convicting the guilty as well.

In attempting an overall evaluation of the accuracy of our legal system, one must bear in mind the distinction between formal and substantive accuracy. Formal accuracy is easily achieved by delegation—of the fact-finding function, for example—to a body viewed as somewhat apart from the legal system itself; by assignment of burdens of proof; and by choice of the standard of appellate review.[38]

Delegation is illustrated by the jury—jurors are not legal professionals and judges will not assume responsibility for their mistakes—and by the pardon power.

The function of burden of proof in achieving formal accuracy is to

---

37. Cf. Glanville Williams, "Letting Off the Guilty and Prosecuting the Innocent," 1985 *Criminal Law Review* 115.

38. These and other techniques for reducing the appearance of judicial indeterminacy are discussed in Rachel F. Moran, "Review Essay: Reflections on the Engima of Indeterminacy in Child-Advocacy Cases," 74 *California Law Review* 603, 629–638 (1986), and Michael A. Rebell and Arthur R. Block, *Educational Policy-Making and the Courts: An Empirical Study of Judicial Activism* 50–54 (1982).

allow a court to reach a definitive result in a case where it may not have the faintest idea whether the defendant wronged the plaintiff, and if so how seriously. One might think it a reproach to a legal system that it so often has no clue to the merits of the legal disputes brought before it for resolution, but the reproach is deflected by using burden of proof as a placeholder for the missing knowledge.

When a reviewing court uses a deferential standard of review (the rationality standard used to review jury verdicts, or the abuse of discretion standard used to review most trial rulings and many administrative-agency decisions), again the court is able to render definitive judgments even if it hasn't the foggiest notion whether the rulings that it is reviewing are correct.

The avoidance of difficult causal issues in criminal cases (not always to the criminal defendant's advantage) is still another of the legal system's techniques for avoiding the implications of its inability to resolve difficult issues of fact; a person can be convicted of attempt without a determination whether, if the attempt had not been interrupted, the crime that was attempted would actually have been committed. And so with aborted conspiracies, which are punishable even though they cause no harm. The behaviorist character of our criminal law (see Chapter 5) may reflect above all the legal system's limited ability to resolve difficult factual questions, as may the law's reluctance, despite appearances, to decide questions about intention. The celebration by lawyers and judges of the "fairness" of a system in which it is thought better to acquit ten guilty defendants than to convict one innocent defendant is an attempt to put a good face on what is actually a confession of systemic ineptitude in deciding questions of guilt and innocence. Finally, in determining whether a trial error was harmless and therefore not reversible, we ask not whether the jury would in fact have found the way it did but for the error, but whether a *rational* jury would have so found. So again we skirt a difficult counterfactual question, and incidentally reduce the discretionary power of juries. These legal adaptations to factual uncertainty may be intelligent, or at least inescapable, but they may also fool the legal profession into thinking it knows more than it does.

The impossibility of recovering the past with complete confidence by the methods of litigation should remind us of the pragmatists' insistence that scientific inquiry must proceed without assurance that objective truth is attainable. The pragmatists' insight, in turn, may make us properly cautious about (for example) adding layers of postconviction review to the criminal justice system in the hope of finding out *for certain* whether the rights of the criminal defendant have been violated. The need is to balance what may be slight gains in reducing one type of error (violating the defendant's rights) against the costs in increasing another type of error (mistaken acceptance of the defendant's claim of right), in undermining the finality of the criminal process, and in burdening the courts to the detriment of defendants with valid claims that get lost in the shuffle.

The problem of the law's weak sense of fact is not confined to facts about particular disputes, but extends to facts on which legal rules are based. For example, under the chief justiceship of Earl Warren the Supreme Court interpreted the Bill of Rights' criminal-procedure provisions, the federal habeas corpus statute, and the due process clause of the Fourteenth Amendment expansively; as a result the rights of criminal defendants were multiplied. The trend abated in the 1970s, and in recent years some rights of criminal defendants have been curtailed, mainly although not solely by generous interpretation of the concept of harmless error and by narrow interpretation of the Fourth Amendment's protection against unreasonable searches and seizures. (On other fronts the expansion of defendants' rights has continued—but I am painting with a broad brush.) Neither the decisions expanding the rights of criminal defendants nor the decisions cutting back were compelled by the text or history of the relevant provisions.[39] Nor had they (outside the area of capital punishment) a powerful moral impetus. They were primarily policy judgments, founded on or at least defended by reference to factual assessments. Liberal judges believe that expanding the rights of criminal defendants neither increases the crime rate significantly nor diverts substantial resources from other social programs to the criminal justice system, and that curtailing those rights exposes the poorest people in our society, many of them innocent, to discrimination and oppression. Conservative judges believe that the expanded rights of criminal defendants have been a factor in rising crime rates and impose heavy costs on the criminal justice system, and doubt that curtailing those rights somewhat will result in the conviction of the innocent or in other social harms.

No one knows who is right in this debate. This is a shocking acknowledgment when one reflects that it has been going on for at least half a century. The factual issues are difficult, of course, and judges cannot wait for the issues to be resolved before they make their decisions. What is remarkable is how little urgency legal professionals feel about resolving these issues. Lawyers and judges are usually conscientious

---

39. Compare this discussion to the treatment of reapportionment in Chapter 4.

about the facts of particular disputes, but they are for the most part uninterested in investigating, or encouraging the academy to investigate, the social facts upon which the soundness of legal doctrine depends. They are content with their intuitions and priors. There is no more striking testament to the absence from law of the scientific attitude.

7 ⁓

What Is Law, and Why Ask?

Is It a Body of Rules or Principles, an Activity, or Both?

We are now prepared to deal with the largest, although not necessarily the juiciest, ontological question in jurisprudence: the question of what law is. Stated so baldly, the question is virtually meaningless. "Law" is a word like "religion," "time," "politics," "democracy," and "beauty" that can be used without creating serious problems of comprehension but cannot be defined unless the purpose of the definition is understood. If you ask what "law" means in the statement that international law should be taught in law school, you will get a different answer than if you ask whether Judge X knows more "law" than Judge Y, or whether the Supreme Court under Chief Justice Warren was "lawless," or whether *Roe v. Wade* is "the law." But at least you will get answers. If you ask simply, What is law? you will touch off a jurisprudential debate. The specific questions I have put either address particular issues in pedagogy, judicial behavior, or legal practice, or invite specific comparisons, as in the question, Is primitive law "really" law?—which means, How strong is the family resemblance between primitive law and modern law? But the general question What is law? seems to assume—what is most debatable—that "law" is some kind of thing (or collection of things), like "New York" or "Dom Perignon" or "salamanders," or perhaps a set of propositions, as in the expression "the law of contracts."

It will help to distinguish three senses of the word "law."[1] The first is law as a distinctive social institution; that is the sense invoked when we ask whether primitive law is really law. The second is law as a collection

1. See Ronald M. Dworkin, "Introduction," in *The Philosophy of Law* 1 (Dworkin ed. 1977).

of sets of propositions—the sets we refer to as antitrust law, the law of torts, the Statute of Frauds, and so on. The third is law as a source of rights, duties, and powers, as in the sentence "The law forbids the murdering heir to inherit." The third sense is the focus of this chapter. The fact that "the law" seems to command and empower, to channel and forbid, makes it intuitive to suppose that it is indeed a thing of some sort or perhaps a set of things, specifically rules—for rules command, forbid, empower—or, if not rules (or not just rules), norms and principles. I shall argue against this conception. Holmes was on the right track when he proposed that law is a prediction of what judges will do when faced with a specific case.[2] Widely considered self-contradictory, passé, and thoroughly discredited, the "prediction theory" has been written off too soon.

The Prediction Theory. In denying that law consists of objective, external, impersonal norms, the theory bespeaks a skeptical view of law — not in the metaphysical sense of skepticism about the existence of an external world or other minds, but in the commonsensical sense, which is the skepticism of the scientist and the pragmatist. Holmes's jurisprudence was pervasively skeptical in this sense. His hostility to the syllogism, that symbol of legal formalism, is one token[3] and his fondness for external standards of liability another, this one related to his skepticism about peering into people's minds. Holmes's metaphor for freedom of speech—the marketplace of ideas[4]—rests on skepticism about the possibility of settling intellectual disputes by reason, which could then be embodied in law. This is the same conjectural view of knowledge that is found in Popper and the pragmatists and that underlies the test of time

2. See Oliver Wendell Holmes, "The Path of the Law," 10 *Harvard Law Review* 457, 461 (1897) ("The prophecies of what the courts will do in fact, and nothing more pretentious, are what I mean by the law"). On the provenance of Holmes's prediction theory, see M. H. Fisch, "Justice Holmes, the Prediction Theory of Law, and Pragmatism," 39 *Journal of Philosophy* 85 (1942). And for analysis pro and con (mostly con), see Henry M. Hart, Jr., "Holmes' Positivism—An Addendum," 64 *Harvard Law Review* 929, 932–934 (1951); H. L. A. Hart, "Scandinavian Realism," 1959 *Cambridge Law Journal* 233, David H. Moskowitz, "The Prediction Theory of Law," 39 *Temple Law Quarterly* 413 (1966); Robert Samuel Summers, *Instrumentalism and American Legal Theory,* ch. 5 (1982); George C. Christie, "The Universal Audience and Predictive Theories of Law," 5 *Law and Philosophy* 343 (1986); Thomas C. Grey, "Holmes and Legal Pragmatism," 41 *Stanford Law Review* 787 (1989).

3. He liked to say the syllogism couldn't wag its tail (that is, was inorganic, dead). See, for example, letter to John C. H. Wu, of April 1, 1923, in *The Mind and Faith of Justice Holmes: His Speeches, Essays, Letters, and Judicial Opinions* 419 (Max Lerner ed. 1943).

4. See Abrams v. United States, 250 U.S. 616, 630 (1919) (dissenting opinion) ("The best test of truth is the power of the thought to get itself accepted in the competition of the market").

as a method of settling disputed questions.[5] The characteristically abrupt, incompletely reasoned nature of many of Holmes's most famous opinions[6] is relevant here, as is his view of the judge as an interstitial legislator, since legislators are acknowledged makers of law. Other tokens of Holmes's skepticism about legal reasoning, truth, and goodness are his quintessentially positivistic statement that if the people of the United States wanted to go to hell it was his job as a judge to help them get there as quickly as possible;[7] the hands-off stance that he adopt-

5. Compare the statement in "Natural Law," 32 *Harvard Law Review* 40 (1918), that "our test of truth is a reference to either a present or an imagined future majority in favor of our view," with Peirce's definition of truth (see Chapter 3): "The opinion which is fated to be ultimately agreed to by all who investigate, is what we mean by the truth." (Notice, though, the more optimistic, even idealistic, flavor of Peirce's formulation as compared with Holmes's.) Parts of the *Abrams* dissent (see note 4 above) seem almost a paraphrase of Peirce's great essay "The Fixation of Belief," in *Collected Papers of Charles Sanders Peirce*, vol. 5, p. 223 (Charles Hartshorne and Paul Weiss eds. 1934). Corresponding to Holmes's view that the only foundation of belief was what Holmes called his "can't helps" ("When I say that a thing is true, I mean that I cannot help believing it," "Ideals and Doubts," in Oliver Wendell Holmes, *Collected Legal Papers* 303, 304 [1920]) is Peirce's statement that "what you cannot in the least help believing is not, justly speaking, wrong belief . . . For you it is the absolute truth." "What Pragmatism Is," 15 *Monist* 161, 169 (1905). (For the revival of this view by a pragmatist of the present day, see Richard Rorty, *Contingency, Irony, and Solidarity* 46–47 [1989]; and recall my implicit reliance on it in Chapter 2 to rebut Arthur Leff's extreme moral skepticism.) The possibility that Holmes derived his theory of external standards of liability from Peirce is explored in Note, "Holmes, Peirce, and Legal Pragmatism," 84 *Yale Law Journal* 1123 (1975); see also the extensive discussion of Holmes's possible intellectual debts to Peirce in Roberta Kevelson, *The Law as a System of Signs* (1988). Having noted the affinity between Holmes and Popper, let me complete the circle by noting the affinity between Peirce and Popper. Here is Popper in a nutshell: "The scientific man is above all things desirous of learning the truth and, in order to do so, ardently desires to have his present provisional beliefs (and all his beliefs are merely provisional) swept away, and will work hard to accomplish that object." "Preface to Scientific Metaphysics," in *Collected Writings of Charles Sanders Peirce*, above, vol. 6, pp. 1, 3. Both Peirce and Popper believe that only doubt powers progress—that there is no inclination to move off a position of nondoubt.

6. See G. Edward White, "The Integrity of Holmes' Jurisprudence," 10 *Hofstra Law Review* 633, 650–652, 664, 668–671 (1982); David P. Currie, "The Constitution in the Supreme Court: Full Faith and the Bill of Rights, 1889–1910," 52 *University of Chicago Law Review* 867, 900 (1985); Currie, "The Constitution in the Supreme Court: 1910–1921," 1985 *Duke Law Journal* 1111, 1145–1155, 1161; and my book *Law and Literature: A Misunderstood Relation* 281–289 (1988).

7. "I hope and believe that I am not influenced by my opinion that it is a foolish law [the Sherman Act]. I have little doubt that the country likes it and I always say, as you know, that if my fellow citizens want to go to Hell I will help them. It's my job." Letter to Harold Laski of March 4, 1920, in *Holmes-Laski Letters: The Correspondence of Mr. Justice Holmes and Harold J. Laski, 1916–1935*, vol. 1, pp. 248–249 (Mark DeWolfe Howe ed. 1953). Of similar character is Holmes's pronouncement, "I hate justice," reported in Learned Hand, "A Personal Confession," in Hand, *The Spirit of Liberty* 302, 306 (3d ed. 1960).

ed toward state and federal legislation (other than that restricting freedom of speech) that he personally thought foolish or worse; the reduction of law to consequences, as in his claim that a contract is merely a promise to pay unless a stated contingency (either performance or some excusing condition) comes to pass,[8] and above all his conception of law as merely a prediction of judges' rulings.

Although unlikely to posit the existence of so abstract an entity as "the law," Holmes realized that since law affected behavior it was "real" in some sense. The solution to the dilemma was to ask *how* law affects behavior. The state has coercive power, and people want to know how to keep out of the way of that power. So they go to lawyers for advice. All they want to know is whether the power of the state will come down on them if they engage in a particular course of action. To advise them the lawyer must predict how the judges, who decide when the state's coercive power may be applied to a person, will act if his client engages in the proposed course of action and is sued. Law is thus simply a prediction of how state power will be deployed in particular circumstances. Law, an abstract entity, is dissolved into physical force, also an abstract entity but one that has a more solid ring and, more important, can be interpreted in behavioral terms: if I do X, the sheriff will eventually seize and sell property of mine worth $Y. The prediction theory conceives the law as disposition rather than as object. To say of an act that it is unlawful is to predict certain consequences if the act is performed, just as to say that an object is heavy is to predict certain consequences if it is dropped or thrown.

This conception overlooks the people who obey the law *because* it is the law, and so it has come to be called the "bad man" theory of law. But the oversight may not be critical. There may not be many "good men" in the specific sense of people who comply with laws merely out of respect for law, a felt moral obligation to obey it. The low saliency of courts to Americans (see Chapter 4) and the evidence cited in Chapter 6 against law's having expressive effects are suggestive in this regard. This is not to say that sanctions are the only cause of compliance with law. Many people obey the law because they would not profit from breaking it even if there were no formal sanctions—they are restrained by habit, conscience (insofar as law tracks morals, as it frequently does), concern with reputation or other considerations of reciprocity, lack of net expected gain when risks and opportunity costs are taken into

8. See Holmes, note 2 above, at 462; see also Oliver Wendell Holmes, Jr., *The Common Law* 300–301 (1881).

account, or sympathy or affection for the potential victims of their wrongdoing. Analytically these people are part of the first group, Holmes's "bad men," who obey the law as far as it pays them to do so but no farther (with "pay" understood broadly, however). Whether there is an independent moral obligation to obey law may thus be an issue of supreme practical unimportance.

The most frequently encountered objection to the prediction theory is that though it may work for the lawyer who is advising a client about the legal consequences of a course of action, it will not work for the judge—he cannot predict his own behavior. The objection is formidable only with respect to the judges of the highest court of the jurisdiction. The judge of a lower court can predict how a higher court would decide his case in exactly the same way that the lawyers in the case can predict how that judge (or the higher judges) will decide it. In cases in which federal jurisdiction is based on the diversity of citizenship of the parties, and in other cases in which the court is applying the substantive doctrines of another jurisdiction, the judge has a feasible task in predicting how other judges at the same level would decide his case. If a case is novel, the judge can decide it by predicting how a majority of other judges probably would decide it. Even a judge of the highest court could try to decide a case predictively, by predicting how his predecessors, the authors of the precedents cited to him by counsel in the case, would have decided it.

It is easy to understand the lawyer's incentive to conceive of law in predictive terms; that is how he will best serve his client's interests. But why should judges conceive of their function in similar terms, even if it is feasible for them to do so? Not all judges do conceive their function thus. Some decide cases in accordance with their own view of the law and, by doing so, court reversal. Reversal is after all not *so* painful. Yet most judges are highly sensitive to being reversed, and for them the prediction theory makes good sense to follow. Weak sanctions can operate powerfully on judges. One is criticism, and reversal is a form of criticism (an exception will be noted in a moment). Most judges try to avoid being reversed, and this commits them to the prediction theory. But this analysis has no application to judges of the highest court of the jurisdiction.

The theory has greater explanatory force than its critics allow, but it is unusable in areas of profound legal uncertainty. There judges and lawyers can do no better than to predict that the highest judges will decide the case (if it is appealed to them) in accordance with the law or the best view of the law. We have not escaped the ontological question; for what is this entity, the law, that the judge is going to steer by?

We can save Holmes's account by noting that if the law is ultimately a prediction of what the highest judges will *do,* it is meaningless to ask how *they* can use prediction to discover the law. The law is not a thing they discover; it is the name of their activity.[9] They do not act in accordance with something called "law"—they just act as best they can. They decide the case, and as a by-product throw out clues to how they might decide the next case. The law is the set of hypotheses that lawyers and lower-court judges propose concerning the regularities in the higher courts' behavior.

We can if we like say that the judges, in acting—that is, in deciding cases—"make law," and so the law is what judges do as well as predictions of what they will do. There is no contradiction once the prediction theory is subsumed under a broader activity theory of law. The important thing is that law is something that licensed persons, mainly judges, lawyers, and legislators, do, rather than a box they pull off the shelf when a legal question appears, in the hope of finding the answer in it— thus inviting debate over whether the box includes only rules, or rules plus principles, or rules, principles, and policies, or perhaps the whole of political morality. The common law, although judge-created, is law and so is equity jurisprudence, with its open-ended maxims (the core of what Dworkin calls "principles"); so are freewheeling interpretations of statutes and the Constitution; so, too, are exercises of avowedly discretionary powers by judges, such as the power to determine what sentence to impose in a criminal case within the range fixed by the legislature, a discretion curtailed for federal judges, but not eliminated, by the new federal sentencing guidelines. Even a decision to make law more political, by giving greater power to the jury or selecting judges in partisan elections or enlarging the pardon power, is a decision within law—a decision about the kind of law the dominant groups in society want— rather than a decision to shrink law's domain.

If the activity theory is right (I think it is mostly, but not entirely, right), the question whether the law consists just of rules or also includes the considerations to which judges turn when the rules run out or when a brand-new rule is created, is a pseudo-question—a gambit, really, in a

---

9. I am indebted to Robin West for this point. A different "activity" conception of law is proposed in Thomas D. Eisele, "The Activity of Being a Lawyer: The Imaginative Pursuit of Implications and Possibilities," 54 *Tennessee Law Review* 345 (1987).

political and ideological game. Because the word "lawless" is a pejorative, and aggressive judges want to conceal the exercise of judicial discretion in order to give their decisions a more "objective," less political, and therefore more authoritative ring, commentators who approve of an aggressive judiciary define "law" as broadly as possible, while those desiring greater judicial restraint define it more narrowly. It is just a semantic game (the game of "persuasive definition"), and it may not be an important game. Indeed, it may just be shadow boxing, because the public to whom the contestants are appealing may be indifferent to anything but the outcomes of decisions.

Even the ideological stakes are small. However interesting and important, the question whether judicial decision making should be more or less freestyle is a question neither about the nature of the law nor about the future of liberalism. The law has no nature, no essence; and liberalism is both vague enough and resilient enough to accommodate active and passive styles in constitutional interpretation and greater and lesser ratios of rule to discretion.

In denying the law's "thingness," I am not saying that it is nothing. It is a practice, easily recognizable in most of its manifestations. But a practice or activity is different from a set of concepts. The distinction can help us see that the question whether the law consists just of rules laid down by public authorities (traditional legal positivism) or also includes some "higher law" that can be used to change the rules, adjust them to new circumstances, or—what amounts to the same thing—fill gaps between them is misspecified. The question assumes that we are exploring the boundaries of a set of concepts, whereas we should be asking about a practice. Specifically, we should be asking whether judges can decide cases by modifying old rules or creating new ones (and applying their inventions to the case at hand, that is, retroactively) without being assailed by indignant charges of lawlessness. They can, in our system anyway, within broad limits that cannot be determined in advance. Evidently one can still be doing law even if one is not just applying rules. And this need not mean appealing to a metaphysical or moral entity—"natural law" in an ontological sense.

I offer several more observations about the prediction theory. First, it cannot be a complete theory, because it implies a slavish subordination of the judgment of lower-court judges to the will of higher-court judges. The first task that the theory assigns to the lower-court judges is to predict how their superiors would decide the case, and only if they cannot predict are they allowed to exercise an independent judgment. But as noted in Chapter 2, we want lower-court judges to exercise *some* independent judgment. This may be why it would be considered inappropriate for a judge of a lower court to predict the decision of his judicial superiors from knowledge of an impending change in the membership of the higher court. The lower-court judges are supposed to be subordinates, but not courtiers.

Second—and in tension with the first point—the prediction theory implies a more creative scope for the lower-court judge confronted by a seemingly dispositive precedent of a higher court than the theory that law is a set of concepts. The latter theory might be taken to imply that the precedent *is* the law—it is a part of the contents of the box labeled "law." The prediction theory, when viewed normatively, implies that the function of the lower-court judge is to predict how the higher court would decide his case. Precedents are essential inputs into the predictive process but they are not "the law" itself, so the lower-court judge who has a strong reason to believe that the higher court would not follow its own precedent if the case arose today is not being lawless in declining to follow that precedent.

Third, and closely related, the prediction theory avoids a paradox created by the notion of law as a set of concepts. Suppose that two lower courts, A and B, have before them cases identical both to each other and to a case decided by the higher court many years ago but never overruled or even substantially undermined by later decisions. Nevertheless it is evident to A and B that if the same case arose today the higher court would abandon the precedent because experience has shown that it was a mistake. A, which adheres to the prediction theory, disregards the precedent—and is affirmed.[10] B, which adheres to the theory of law as a set of concepts, follows the precedent—and is reversed. On the prediction theory A is right and B is wrong, and therefore the affirmance of A and reversal of B are just what one would expect in a system in which error is corrected by higher courts. But on the theory of law as a set of concepts A is wrong and B is right, producing the paradox that the court that decided the case in accordance with law was reversed as though it had committed an error, while the court that flouted the law was affirmed. The fact that a court is permitted to overrule its own precedents is thus an argument in favor of the prediction theory, which expresses a forward-looking view of law.

---

10. This is what the lower court did in the second flag-salute case, discussed in Chapter 4. It disregarded *Gobitis,* correctly foreseeing that the Supreme Court would overrule that decision, and invalidated the state's compulsory flag-salute law. See *Barnette v. West Virginia State Board of Education,* 47 F. Supp. 251 (S.D. W. Va. 1942).

But, fourth, the idea that *every* accurate prediction of an overruling identifies a change in "law" is difficult to swallow. Suppose that because of the retirement of one judge and his replacement by another it is predictable that a particular precedent will be overruled the next time a case presenting the issue comes before the court. Would it be correct to say that the change in court membership had changed the law? The prediction theory implies an affirmative answer, but such an answer is at variance with normal usage. We think of law not only as what judges do but also as the criterion for evaluating what they do. The activity theory is incomplete. Its critics are right that it is an impoverished theory of law. But it is only mildly impoverished. When slightly enriched with a weak sense of natural law, it becomes the best positive theory of law that we have.

Fifth, the prediction theory really can (despite my second point) be normative for lower-court judges, especially if the judicial system values stability highly. The effect of scrupulous adherence to the theory by such judges is to concentrate judicial discretion in the judges of the highest court. There are fewer of them, they are more carefully selected than the lower-court judges, they have a broader perspective, and their decisions are subjected to greater scrutiny; for all these reasons they can be expected to exercise discretion more responsibly.

Nuremberg and the Limits of Positivism. The foregoing analysis bears on the much-debated question, which has long seemed central to the controversy over what law is, whether the Nuremberg Trial of the Major War Criminals was legitimate.[11] The laws applied by the Allied tribunal were invented for the occasion and thus had not existed (other than as ethical principles) when the defendants had violated them; and the defendants had been acting in conformity with Nazi laws or decrees that were valid according to the rules of recognition of the Third Reich. It is not enough to say that because the Nuremberg Tribunal was a court, its judgments were law. Whether and in what sense it was a court are difficult, perhaps unanswerable, questions. We cannot, as we can in dealing with national courts (even Nazi courts), treat its judgments as the activity of licensed individuals and therefore lawful; for we are not sure who had the authority to issue such supranational licenses. If the theory of law as a set of concepts is rejected, as I have argued it should be, and the activity approach is inapplicable by its own terms, the question

---

11. For an excellent recent discussion, see David Luban, "The Legacies of Nuremberg," 54 *Social Research* 779 (1987). A notable earlier treatment is Judith N. Shklar, *Legalism: Law, Morals, and Political Trials* 154–178 (1964).

whether the Nuremberg judgments were lawful is meaningless. Rather than beat our heads against the wall we should consider the pragmatic question whether punishing the Nazi leaders using the *forms* of law was a sensible way to proceed. I think it was. It was unthinkable to let those monsters go free, so the question can be recast as whether they should have been killed summarily or after a trial. The value of the trial, deficient as it was in the elements of due process (adequate warning of criminal liability, an unbiased tribunal) was that it enabled a public record to be compiled and gave the defendants a chance to say what they could in their behalf, which for most of them was very little. As a result their moral guilt was established more convincingly in the eyes of the world than if they had been liquidated hugger-mugger.[12]

Reading from a distance of thirty years the debate between H. L. A. Hart and Lon Fuller over the legality of Nazi laws,[13] I am struck by how little was at stake. Hart is fearful that if law and morals are run together, the moral condemnation of the Nazi laws will be diluted. He does not want the moral issue obscured by switching attention from it to the legalistic-sounding question of whether the laws were really laws; he does not want people to think they have a moral duty to obey any law whose legal validity is unassailable. So he proposes to make the word "law" synonymous with positive law, which the Nazi laws were but the legal principles enforced by the Nuremberg Tribunal were not. Fuller is concerned that if law is defined so broadly—broadly in the sense of including all positive laws, however evil, although narrowly in the sense of excluding natural law viewed either as an independent source of legal obligation or as a filter to screen out evil positive laws—the legitimacy of the Supreme Court's broad interpretations of the Constitution may be called into question. He also argues that if the Nazi laws were law, then in evaluating the wickedness of the Nazis we shall be forced to give them at least a few points for fidelity to law—but how, he says, can a thoroughly immoral law give rise to even the most qualified moral claim to obedience? Yet, oddly, Fuller's emphasis is not on the immorality of the Nazi laws but on their procedural irregularity, in particular their secrecy. The emphasis is curious if only because most Nazi laws, including the Nuremberg racial laws, were public and regular. It shows

12. Shklar, note 11 above, stresses additional, no less pragmatic considerations: the educative effect of the Nuremberg Trial on the German public, and the social advantages of regularized retribution over spontaneous vengeance.

13. See H. L. A. Hart, "Positivism and the Separation of Law and Morals," 71 *Harvard Law Review* 593, 615–621 (1958); Lon L. Fuller, "Positivism and Fidelity to Law—A Reply to Professor Hart," 71 *Harvard Law Review* 630, 632–633, 648–657 (1958).

the lawyer's faith in process[14] (although this is rather a side issue in the debate) and in persuasive definition; Fuller wants to "condemn [unjust decisions] to grammatical death through definitional execution."[15]

In Fuller's emphasis on the U.S. Constitution we have a clue that the debate between him and Hart—between an American and an Englishman—was as much cultural as intellectual. Since the United States has a judicially enforceable constitution that contains both open-ended provisions such as those guaranteeing equal protection and due process and a number of specific prohibitions and guarantees as well, while England has neither a written constitution nor a practice of judicial review of the validity of legislation, profoundly immoral laws are apt to be illegal in the United States and merely profoundly immoral in the United Kingdom. The overlap between law and morality is different in the two countries.

In any event, I disagree with both Hart and Fuller. The word "law" is frequently, and harmlessly, used to denote both positive law, however wicked, and natural law[16] (which is to say, approximately, basic political morality). Murder is deliberate *unlawful* killing, yet we say without

14. Recall the Frankfurter quotation in Chapter 2. The peculiar twist that Fuller gives to this faith is to suppose that scrupulous adherence to the forms of law not only minimizes error in the application of law but also conduces to *good* law. Yet Shklar, note 11 above, at 17, is correct that "procedurally 'correct' repression is perfectly compatible with legalism." See also id. at 209. The experience with the enforcement of the fugitive slave acts and other slave laws in the United States before the Civil War shows this. As to whether legal positivism can keep judges in line, Shklar notes that Germany's "official classes, especially its judiciary, were not induced by positivism to accept and apply the law of the Weimar Republic. In fact, they sabotaged it with no legalistic compunctions. Positivism was only invoked to rationalize their far greater readiness to comply with Hitler's New Order." Id. at 72. However, I shall argue in later chapters that one aspect of traditional legalism does seem likely to promote liberty and protect minorities: the principle of governance by general rules, as distinct from personal, discretionary justice.

15. Shklar, note 11 above, at 107.

16. This needs qualification; natural law cannot be substituted for positive law in all discussions of law. For example, between two judges, one of whom knew slightly more positive law but much less about the sources, tradition, and content of natural law than the other, it would be exceedingly peculiar to describe the second as knowing more law than the first, or to deny that the first knew more law than the second. We might say that the second judge was a better judge even though he didn't know as much law as the first, but that would be quite different. Questions about legal knowledge are questions about positive law, perhaps because the lawyer's and judge's *distinctive* knowledge is knowledge of positive law rather than knowledge of political or other morality. Moreover, we would be more likely to describe a judge as *sensitive* to the moral dimensions of his decisions than as *knowing* a lot about morality. Morality is on most accounts an affair of practical reason in its action-oriented rather than cognitive sense (see Chapter 2), although Plato famously disagreed, and I shall note an exception to the modern view in Chapter 12.

semantic strain that the Nazis "murdered" the Jews even though the killings were authorized by the positive law of the Nazi state.[17] There is no contradiction in saying that the Nazis were obeying positive law yet violating natural law—many natural lawyers acknowledge, contrary to Fuller, that even hideously unjust laws are "law" in a meaningful sense[18]—or that the Constitution has been interpreted as authorizing the courts to use natural law principles to invalidate positive law. One does not feel obliged to give the Nazis points for their contribution to upholding the rule of law. If a constitutional amendment were passed re-enslaving black people or ordering them deported to Africa, a federal judge asked to enforce the amendment could gain no moral absolution by pointing out that he was obeying valid positive law.[19] Inflexible adherence to positive law is less likely to ennoble the adherents than to undermine the rule of law by making the rule-of-law virtues—regularity, predictability, impersonality, self-abnegation—seem grotesque, parodic, or inhuman. The only dangers in using legal terminology to analyze the moral issues raised by Nazi decrees and adjudications lie in supposing that either Nazi laws *or* the principles administered by the Nuremberg Tribunal are typical of what we mean when we speak of "law," or in imagining that the question whether either body of "law" was *really* law can be answered.

The latitudinarian usage of the words "law" and "lawful"—the usage that embraces at one end wicked positive laws and at the other end natural law—is not only harmless but useful. Abandoning it might be thought to imply, wrongly, that if a judge thought the legal arguments on both sides of a case evenly balanced he should dismiss the case, on the ground that it could not be decided by law. Or that at some point in the argument of the really difficult case, counsel should say to the judge, "Judge, we've finished our legal arguments; now let's talk about the nonlegal considerations that ought to influence your decision," or "Judge, we've done a lot of research, and there's no law to apply to this

17. The ultimate order to destroy the Jews was apparently an oral command by Hitler, but his oral commands were positive law under the Third Reich's "rule of recognition." Cf. Luban, note 11 above, at 795–796.

18. See, for example, John Finnis, *Natural Law and Natural Rights* 363–366, 367 n. xii.4 (1980).

19. The idea of the judge as an independent moral agent, accountable for his decisions and not permitted to hide behind a legislature's—or even behind "the people's"—skirts, is emphasized in Robert M. Cover, "Violence and the Word," 95 *Yale Law Journal* 1601 (1986), and in Robin L. West, "Adjudication Is Not Interpretation: Some Reservations about the Law-as-Literature Movement," 54 *Tennessee Law Review* 203 (1987).

case, so let's all go home."[20] The established approach in this country requires judges (rightly, as we are about to see) to decide even the most difficult cases as best they can, provided the cases are real cases and within the judges' jurisdiction. This implies that any consideration relevant to deciding the case, whether drawn from positive law or natural law sources, is a legitimate input in the manufacture of "law," and that the judge's decision—though of course not immune to criticism—will have to be pretty crazy before it can fairly be called "lawless."

One could argue that if the legal issue is so uncertain that no resolution of it would be demonstrably correct, the defendant should not be made to pay damages or incur other costs. But why should there be this strong asymmetry in the rights of plaintiffs and defendants? Even if there should be, it would not follow that the judge who went ahead and decided the close case against the defendant was being lawless. A questionable decision, even a wrong decision, is not lawless. To call it so is to attempt to resolve by persuasive definition what is properly a question of political theory. Equally, to call the judge's decision lawful is not to commit oneself to belief in strongly objective legal norms outside of those expressed in positive law.

There is a deeper objection to refusing to decide borderline cases: it will change the borderline. A case that used to be well within the frontier will become the frontier. The law will tend to unravel—for every judge-made doctrine, common law or interpretive, was once an extension beyond "existing law."

We tend in thinking about law to put it temporally before the resolution of legal disputes, but by doing so we make the mistake (derived from the fallacy of conceiving law as concept rather than activity) of thinking that law exists apart from the process by which legal duties and sanctions are imposed on the persons subject to it. The reverse sequence is more illuminating. A human society seethes with conflict and dispute, and for certain types of dispute finds it expedient to have a permanent cadre of officials who resolve disputes in accordance with official norms. These are the judges, and their business is to resolve disputes in a way that will vindicate those norms and, more fundamentally, satisfy social needs. To lend a necessary regularity and predictability to the process,

---

20. I am indebted for these examples to an unpublished review by A. W. Brian Simpson of Ronald Dworkin's book *Law's Empire*.

The Administrative Procedure Act does refer to a category of cases where there is no law to apply, see 5 U.S.C. §701(a)(2)—meaning not that the administrative agency is acting lawlessly but that the agency's exercise of discretion is not judicially reviewable (the matter has been confided to the *agency's* discretion).

legislatures make rules for the judges to apply, and the judges make their own rules to fill the gaps (which are sometimes enormous) in the legislative product; if there is no legislature they make all the rules. (Yet in neither case, for reasons stressed in Chapter 4, are the judges legislators *tout court*.) But usually the most important thing is to resolve the dispute. Not always; sometimes the best resolution, especially when the rules are unclear, is to let the dispute simmer awhile. Many disputes, however, have to be resolved at once, even if the rules are unclear or have to be made up on the spot; and then the judges do the best they can, using whatever information and insight that the lawyers give them or that they can dredge up out of their own reading and experiences. This untidy, unrigorous process we call "law." It may influence, though perhaps only slightly, the development of the "moral law," while, in turn, moralistic criticisms of judicial decisions may cause the judges to change legal doctrine; so there is a complex interweaving of positive and natural law or, if one prefers of law and morality.[21]

Judges who are especially protective of the judiciary's prestige would prefer not to have to decide difficult, uncertain cases. Such judges are like generals who do not want to give battle unless they have a one hundred percent chance of victory. It is precisely to resolve the most difficult, the most uncertain, disputes that we have judges. Compelled to decide such cases, many judges pretend—sometimes to themselves as well as to the world—that what they have done is added two and two and gotten four, so that anyone who disagrees with their decision is crazy, or that what they have done is chosen Right over Wrong, so that anyone who disagrees with the decision is morally obtuse. In fact they are more likely to have engaged in the same kind of inconclusive practical reasoning, heavily influenced by personal experiences and by temperament, that jurors and politicians and civil servants use to make judgments. The distinctive things about the judges are that their incentives are a bit "purer" than those of most other officials, that their experiences are those of a lawyer, that their reading is dominated by legal materials largely unknown and incomprehensible to the lay public, and that convention requires of them (as it does not of most other government officials) a written justification of their important rulings. This last requirement imparts a certain thoughtfulness to what they do, as do the other procedural constraints of judicial decision making as well as the conditions of judicial employment.

21. The similarity between legal and moral thinking is stressed by Shklar, note 11 above, at 60–62.

The conception of the judicial function that I am advancing is low-keyed—so low-keyed perhaps as to make one wonder why anyone would feel a moral obligation to obey judicial decrees,[22] or would even respect the courts. One response is that as long as the judges are honest and decorous and do not get too far out ahead of dominant public opinion, the public can be expected to respect courts as an integral part of a system of government that seems on the whole to serve us well, or at least better than would the alternatives. We may disagree with particular decisions, but if we value the concept of an independent judiciary we must take the bitter with the sweet. Another response is that, as far as anyone knows, it is just a lawyers' fancy that public respect for courts is a significant influence on the extent to which a society is law-abiding. Most people are uninformed and incurious about courts, especially those courts lawyers most dither over—appellate courts. Compliance with law is more a matter of incentives than of deference or respect.

Still, it is an interesting analytical question whether there can be a moral obligation to obey positive laws that are not somehow underwritten by natural law. The argument against such a moral obligation is straightforward: moral obligations are obligations either to obey moral norms or to complete certain voluntary undertakings (for example, promises) to which moral obligation attaches; but positive law, on the positivist view, has no necessary foundation in morals and is not in a realistic sense consented to by those who are subject to it. The positivist's argument for a moral duty to obey law is necessarily of the implied-contractual form: we would all be better off adhering to all the laws voluntarily (thus economizing on enforcement costs) rather than picking and choosing among them; so, ex ante—at the constitutional stage or in the original position—we would agree to be law-abiding. But the words "picking and choosing" load the dice. The question rather is whether to suspend moral judgment regarding a body of laws that, according to the positivist hypothesis, bears only a contingent relation to morality. If a particular law happens to be immoral, as well it may be, it is hard to see how a duty to obey it can be derived from the fact that voluntary compliance with law economizes on transaction costs, unless we place overriding value on public order. And, subject to the same qualification, it is not obvious why we should discourage people from making moral judgments about the laws they live under and from acting on those judgments. Under pressure from these points, the moral obligation to obey law, an obligation based on considerations of mutual

22. For a good discussion of this question, see Kent Greenawalt, *Conflicts of Law and Morality,* pt. 2 (1987).

advantage and the social contract, dwindles to a weak, easily defeasible obligation to obey laws that are not morally offensive.

Implicitly, however, I have been discussing cases in which disobeying the law does not benefit the violator at the expense of others. Even if the law you disobey is silly or vicious, if you are disobeying it in order to take advantage of the law-abiding your conduct invites moral disapproval. You are displaying the disposition that Aristotle called *pleonexia*—wanting more than your fair share—and that a system of corrective justice seeks to hold in check (see Chapter 11).

Since the lawless judge ordinarily is not acting for private gain, on what basis can we say that judges have a moral duty to obey the law by enforcing the rules within the judges' jurisdiction? By raising this question I draw attention to a neglected function of the judicial oath. A solemn promise to administer law without fear or favor, it reinforces whatever general moral duty there is to obey law with the somewhat clearer moral duty to obey one's promises. But what exactly is the promise? Is it a promise to enforce positive law to the hilt, or a promise to do justice? Perhaps a promise to do "justice under law"? But this formula may allow positive law to yield sometimes to natural law.

A further point is that promises are rarely absolute, are usually defeasible. And we make many promises, and they may conflict, forcing us to choose.

Whether or not the argument for a moral duty to obey positive law persuades, and whatever the precise scope of such a duty, the enterprise, now several thousand years old, of establishing the existence and content of a natural law that underwrites positive law[23] is hopeless under the conditions of modern American society. If the result of this failure is a diminished sense of moral obligation to obey laws, so it will have to be. Even the term "natural law" is an anachronism. The majority of educated Americans believe that nature is the amoral scene of Darwinian struggle. Occasional attempts are made to derive social norms from nature so conceived,[24] but they are not likely to succeed. It is true that a variety of widely accepted norms, including the keeping of certain

23. Modern theories of natural law are thoroughly and sympathetically discussed in Deryck Beyleveld and Roger Brownsword, *Law as a Moral Judgment* (1986).

24. For recent attempts, see Richard A. Epstein, "The Utilitarian Foundations of Natural Law" 12 *Harvard Journal of Law and Public Policy* 713 (1989); Peter Railton, "Moral Realism," 95 *Philosophical Review* 163 (1986). The best-known attempt remains that of Herbert Spencer, whose Social Darwinism influenced American law in the late nineteenth and early twentieth centuries. See Arthur L. Harding, "The Ghost of Herbert Spencer: A Darwinian Concept of Law," in *Origins of the Natural Law Tradition* 69 (Harding ed. 1954). On Social Darwinism generally, see the interesting discussion in Michael Ruse, *Taking Darwin Seriously: A Naturalistic Approach to Philosophy* 73–82 (1986).

promises, the abhorrence of unjustified killing of human beings, and perhaps even the sanctity of property rights, promote the adaptation of the human species to its environment. But so does genocide. Within limits, the destruction of nonhuman species spreads human genes, and likewise a race that exterminates other races spreads its members' genes. If the Nazis' geopolitical ambitions had been fulfilled, Hitler would have been entitled to kudos from those who believe that Darwinism is a source of moral norms. We do not admire human behavior merely because it conforms to genetic programs. There are, of course, alternative conceptions of nature to the Darwinian, a pertinent example being Plato's, in which moral norms are part of the furniture of the universe. But the modern secular intellect finds Plato's, and the successor Christian, notion of a "good" nature unbelievable.

The underlying problem of moral objectivity is that there are neither facts to which moral principles correspond (as scientific principles, for example, appear to correspond to things in nature) nor a strong tendency for moral principles to converge. A tiny handful of moral principles—for example, that unrestricted killing of members of one's own society is bad—seem essential to social existence, but the rest are conventional and culture-bound to a far greater extent than scientific principles are.[25]

If we put aside nature or other possible sources of ontologically objective moral principles—principles that are "out there" in some sense—the precondition of strong "natural law" (now a misnomer) is that the members of society, whether because they share the same religious beliefs or because they are otherwise culturally homogeneous or in thrall to a powerful ideology, agree on moral principles to a level of detail that enables a legal code to be derived from those principles. Most Americans agree on many things—that unrestricted killing is bad, that Nazis are bad, that incest is bad, that certain forms of discrimination are bad—but not on enough things to prescribe anything like a comprehensive system of legal rights and obligations. In such a society, natural law theorists are exposed to devastating criticisms.[26]

25. Cf. R. M. Hare, "Ontology in Ethics," in *Morality and Objectivity: A Tribute to J. L. Mackie* 39 (Ted Honderich ed. 1985). For a strong argument (contrary to the position I am taking) for scientific *and* moral realism, see Richard N. Boyd, "How to Be a Moral Realist," in *Essays on Moral Realism* 181 (Geoffrey Sayre-McCord ed. 1988). On the general question of moral realism (absolutism, objectivism) versus moral (or ethical) relativism, see, besides the collection of essays just cited, the following collections: *Relativism: Interpretation and Confrontation* (Michael Krausz ed. 1989); *Rationality and Relativism* (Martin Hollis and Steven Lukes eds. 1982); *Ethical Relativism* (John Ladd ed. 1973).

26. See, for example, Lloyd L. Weinreb, *Natural Law and Justice*, chs. 4–8 (1987).

It hardly matters in this regard whether one is a moral realist, a conventionalist, an anything. If the community is morally heterogeneous, moral principles function as arguments rather than as criteria, and it is then better to speak of natural law considerations than of natural law *simpliciter*. This is not "anything goes" relativism, but merely recognition that many moral disputes cannot be resolved by peaceful means in a heterogeneous community. Legal means are not necessarily peaceful means in this sense. If a legal decision has no roots in moral consensus, it may rise no higher than the armed force that stands behind it.

In a setting of moral "dissensus," the invocation of the emotionally charged term "natural law" answers primarily to the rhetorical aim of calling our personal opinions law and the laws we dislike personal opinions. To the extent that our language invites us to frame many of our policy considerations in moral language, we may say that natural law, viewed as the sum of those policy considerations that can be so described, influences positive law. "It is the stuff out of which human or positive law is to be woven, when other sources fail."[27] But as a repository of frequently warring principles, natural law in this sense cannot resolve difficult cases.

I am not saying that none of our moral beliefs is more than a personal opinion. Many of those beliefs are as firmly rooted as our epistemic certitudes, as I remarked in discussing Arthur Leff's moral skepticism. That is why I have not thought it necessary to pause to explain why I called the Nazis "monsters"; indeed the explanation would have added nothing interesting to the bare statement. The moral beliefs that we hold with great conviction gain no analytic strength from having the label "natural law" affixed to them; the reasons for using the forms of law against the Nazis must be sought elsewhere. And contested moral beliefs gain no analytic strength by being advanced as propositions of natural law.

In suggesting that there was little at stake in the Hart-Fuller debate, I mean precisely that the *analytic* stakes were small. Debates over entities of doubtful ontology or, what is here and usually the same thing, over

---

Michael Moore, in "Moral Reality," 1982 *Wisconsin Law Review* 1061, does a wonderful job of summarizing all the objections to the existence of objective moral norms, but his effort to refute those objections is weak, almost perfunctory. It amounts to the reiterated observation that some moral propositions are as solidly established as some factual propositions—which is true but unhelpful, because those are not the moral propositions that might answer controversial legal questions. Saying that the Holocaust was a crime against humanity (which, by the way, is *not* a proposition that commands a worldwide consensus) will not determine the answer to the question whether abortion is morally wrong.

27. Benjamin N. Cardozo, *The Nature of the Judicial Process* 132 (1921).

the meaning of undefinable words can have profound effects in the "real" world—can cause religious wars, for example. One can understand how people who believe that natural law exists as a set of consistent, definite, and knowable commands are no more willing to allow constitutional text or history or precedent to stand in their way than the positive law of the Nazi regime was allowed to stand in the way of justice at Nuremberg. The curiosity about the Hart–Fuller debate is that the debaters seem not to have disagreed on any substantive point. Their disagreement was over the rhetoric in which to express their shared values. The debate was at bottom pragmatic, the debaters' ultimate concern being about which vocabulary—that of positive law or that of natural law—is more conducive to the realization of those values. It is an unnecessary choice. Our dominantly positivistic discourse has enough natural law play in its joints to give us all the rhetorical flexibility we need.

Reflection on the Hart-Fuller debate points up two flaws in the activity theory of law. First, if as I have argued the use of the term "natural law" is admissible both to describe those (few) ethical or political principles that command a consensus and seem therefore as imperative as positive law or even more so and, more modestly, to summarize the ethical considerations that bear on the decision of close cases, then we have a concept of law that is something other than an activity. For whose activity is it to produce natural law? There are no licensed professionals to point to. The relevant concept of law in such a setting is one of law as custom or tradition rather than as a professional activity, or more precisely as a professional activity bounded and shaped by custom, tradition, community feeling, and so on.

Second and closely related, the debate raises the question how one determines when the professional who is licensed to make positive law is acting within the scope of his license. If we say that the Nazis "murdered" the Jews, is this not tantamount to saying that Nazi judges, prosecutors, executioners, and so forth exceeded the bounds of their licensed activities? If so, this means that the criteria for when a person is licensed to do law are supplied from outside the activity itself. I hinted at this problem earlier when I said that a judge's decision would have to be pretty crazy to be pronounced lawless. If it is so crazy that it is lawless, what does this imply about the criteria for deciding what is law? What does "crazy" mean in this context? Apparently some considerations that a judge might use to decide a difficult case are out of bounds—but who fixes the bounds? The significance of natural law may lie not in its capacity for resolving the normal issues that arise in a civilized legal system but in the assistance it provides in determining what a civilized legal system is.

If this is correct, have not the categories "positive law" and "natural law" outlived their usefulness? As a source of duties, rights, and powers, the law seems best regarded as an activity of licensed professionals (judges and lawyers), cabined by vague but powerful notions of professional propriety rooted ultimately in social convenience or, equivalently, durable public opinion. Positive law and natural law materials are inputs into the activity we call law.

At this level of generality, Ronald Dworkin's concept of law converges with mine. While rejecting legal positivism and emphasizing elements in legal reasoning that are emphasized by natural lawyers as well, such as rights and moral principles, Dworkin is careful not to describe himself as a natural lawyer. He evidently wants to avoid what is indeed a jejune dichotomy. His argument at its most general is that the judge is trying to fashion the best outcome out of the diverse materials that are at hand, materials that include not only precedents and statutory language and other distinctively "legal" materials but also the elements of political morality. This is an accurate portrayal of the American judge, and I agree with Dworkin that the judge so portrayed is not a lawless judge. But I disagree that the judge becomes lawless when he allows "rights" based on "principles" to be overcome by "policies," where "policy" is defined by Dworkin as a collective goal. Many collective goals, ranging from national survival and public order to prosperity and social insurance, are no less deeply woven into the fabric of our political morality than such principles as that equals should be treated equally or that no person should be allowed to profit from his wrongdoing. To distinguish between policies and principles and to link rights with the latter but not the former is arbitrary. There is no basis for excluding collective goals in determining the scope of legal rights.

Holmes, Nietzsche, and Pragmatism

Holmes wrote *The Common Law* just a few years before Nietzsche's great work *On the Genealogy of Morals,* and both employ an effective method of skeptical analysis: the genealogical. In the *Genealogy* and other works Nietzsche tried to undermine the ontological status of Christian morality by arguing that moral beliefs reflect the needs and circumstances of the dominant groups in the communities that happen to hold them. Morality, in other words, is relative rather than absolute; in fact, morality is public opinion. *The Common Law* does the same thing with law. By tracing legal doctrines to their origins and thus relating each doctrine to a particular constellation of social circumstances, Holmes showed the absurdity of supposing, as did the nineteenth-century formalists against whom he was writing, that legal doctrines were unchangeable formal concepts like the Pythagorean theorem. He enforced the lesson of ethical relativism, thereby turning law into dominant public opinion in much the same way that Nietzsche turned morality into public opinion.[28]

The genealogical technique continues to be an effective one in law. Often one traces a line of precedents to its source and finds that the first of the line is a mere assertion and that the next merely cited the first, and so on to the latest decision. The genealogical technique can thus show that a rule that seems firmly grounded in precedent actually rests on sand. Or it can show, as Holmes memorably did in discussing the evolution of proceedings to condemn deodands into actions *in rem* in admiralty, how—in Nietzsche's words—"the cause of the origin of a thing and its eventual utility, its actual employment and place in a system of purposes, lie worlds apart; whatever exists, having somehow come into being, is again and again reinterpreted to new ends."[29]

Nietzsche was not the only nineteenth-century genealogist, of course. Higher criticism of the Bible (that is, the critical study of its authorship), the tracing of man's descent of man from the lower animals, and Marx's theory of history are other notable examples of the nineteenth century's penchant for using history to challenge essentialist or transcendental notions. But Nietzsche's exposé of the origins of Christianity may be the closest parallel to what Holmes did to law, even though their attitude toward their subject matter was different (and the two were even more different of course, in tone, Nietzsche being a most irresponsible writer).

More than genealogical method connects these two great nineteenth-century skeptics. They both are sub- or antimentalists. Nietzsche's will to power animates not just man and animals but the rocks and the

---

28. See, for example, Lochner v. New York, 198 U.S. 45, 75 (1905) (dissenting opinion); Holmes, "Herbert Spencer: Legislation and Empiricism," in *Justice Oliver Wendell Holmes: His Book Notices and Uncollected Letters and Papers* 104 (Harry C. Shriver ed. 1936). Robert W. Gordon, "Holmes' *Common Law* as Legal and Social Science," 10 *Hofstra Law Review* 719, 746 (1982), notes—unfortunately without elaboration—Holmes's "Nietzschean insight into the power relations underlying systems of rights and morals."

29. *On the Genealogy of Morals and Ecce Homo* 77 (Walter Kaufmann ed. 1967) (Second Essay, §12, of *On the Genealogy of Morals*).

stars,[30] and Holmes reduces law to force and makes the will the preferred mode of resolving the close case. The aphoristic style of both writers may reflect a shared skepticism about the power of rational thought. The illiberal aspects of Holmes's thought, notably his fondness for war, struggle, and eugenic breeding of human beings (that is, man as animal), have close parallels in Nietzsche;[31] and it is perhaps natural that people who are skeptical about reason should celebrate its antithesis.

I do not want to go overboard in comparing Homes to Nietzsche. Holmes's free-speech and habeas corpus opinions embody a humane and democratic perspective that is remote from anything in Nietzsche. And Holmes's militant skepticism and relativism coexist with a tame utilitarianism that would have nauseated Nietzsche. Within the space of a few pages in "The Path of the Law," Holmes both suggests that it would be a good thing "if every word of moral significance could be banished from the law altogether, and other words adopted which should convey legal ideas uncolored by anything outside law," *and* advises lawyers to

---

30. See the excellent discussion in Alexander Nehamas, *Nietzsche: Life as Literature* (1985), and note this typical remark of Nietzsche's: "He who possesses strength divests himself of mind." Friedrich Nietzsche, *Twilight of the Idols* and *The Anti-Christ* 76 (R. J. Hollingdale trans. 1968) ("Expeditions of an Untimely Man," §14, in *Twilight of the Idols*). Yet the line between the antimental and the pan-psychic is an uncertain one. The extremes of subjectivity and objectivity, of idealism and realism, tend to merge. This is also shown by the following illustration of Holmes's antimentalism, his famous adage, "We must think things not words." Oliver Wendell Holmes, "Law in Science and Science in Law," 12 *Harvard Law Review* 443, 460 (1899). The idea that words stand in a one-to-one correspondence to things is a form of naive realism that may seem remote from the picture I am drawing of Holmes; it is certainly remote from anything in Nietzsche. But a highly referential theory of language is compatible with a disdain for abstraction (as in Bentham); what is not a thing, is nothing.

31. On Nietzsche, see J. P. Stern, *Nietzsche* (1979); *Law and Literature: A Misunderstood Relation*, note 6 above, ch. 3. On Holmes, see, for example, Edmund Wilson, "Justice Oliver Wendell Holmes," in Wilson, *Patriotic Gore: Studies in the Literature of the American Civil War* 743 (1962); Buck v. Bell, 274 U.S. 200 (1927). Typical is this statement in Holmes's opinion in Missouri v. Holland, 252 U.S. 416, 433 (1920): "It was enough for them [the framers of the Constitution] to realize or to hope that they had created an organism; it has taken a century and has cost their successors much sweat and blood to prove that they created a nation." Another link between Holmes and Nietzsche is that both admired and were influenced by Ralph Waldo Emerson. On Holmes and Emerson, see Sanford Victor Levinson, "Skepticism, Democracy, and Judicial Restraint: An Essay on the Thought of Oliver Wendell Holmes and Felix Frankfurter" (Ph.D. diss., Dept. of Govt., Harvard University, April 1969). On Nietzsche and Emerson, see "Translator's Introduction," in Friedrich Nietzsche, *The Gay Science* 3, 7–13 (Walter Kaufmann trans. 1974); Charles Andler, *Nietzsche: Sa vie et sa pensée*, ch. 2 (1958).

study economics, where "we learn that for everything [we want] we have to give up something else, and we are taught to set the advantage we gain against the other advantage we lose, and to know what we are doing when we elect."[32] The idea that law ought to be a tool for promoting social welfare understood in economic terms is a moral principle; Homes in the two passages I have quoted is both rejecting morality and proposing a morality to shape law's future.

Holmes is not a nihilist after all, at least not a consistent one; is he a pragmatist? Beware the tyranny of lables—Nietzsche, greatest of nihilists, denounced nihilism. There are significant pragmatist strands in Holmes's thought, and given the salutary vagueness and breadth of the term "pragmatist," no more is needed to label him one.[33] But it would be wrong to suppose that every aspect of his thought, even of his philosophical thought, is pragmatist. Holmes's Social Darwinism is not; and a skepticism that teaches that a legal decision has only two components, logic and will, or that advocates a simple referential theory of language, or that is hostile to factual inquiry is foreign to most versions of pragmatism—and these are all positions that Holmes (at times, anyway)

---

32. Holmes, note 2 above, at 464, 474.

33. The Fisch and Grey articles cited in note 2 emphasize the parallels between Holmes and John Dewey, thus linking Holmes to the broader pragmatist school which Peirce may be said to have been a part of (indeed, to have founded), despite the many differences among him, Dewey, and James, some noted in Yosal Rogat, "The Judge as Spectator," 31 *University of Chicago Law Review* 213, 251 n. 194 (1964); as noted in Morton White, "The Revolt against Formalism in American Social Thought of the Twentieth Century," in White, *Pragmatism and the American Mind: Essays and Reviews in Philosophy and Intellectual History* 41, 52–53 (1973), Dewey was a great admirer of Holmes—see, for example, John Dewey, *Experience and Nature* 417–419 (1929); Dewey even wrote a very Holmesian paper on legal inquiry: "Logical Method and Law," 10 *Cornell Law Quarterly* 17 (1924). I noted the affinities between Holmes and Peirce in note 5 above. On Holmes and pragmatism generally, Grey's article, note 2 above, is especially good; see also Catharine Wells Hantzis, "Legal Innovation within the Wider Intellectual Tradition: The Pragmatism of Oliver Wendell Holmes, Jr.," 82 *Northwestern University Law Review* 541 (1988); Frederic Rogers Kellogg, *The Formative Essays of Justice Holmes: The Making of an American Legal Philosophy,* ch. 3 and bibliographical essay (1984); Marcia J. Speziale, "By Their Fruits You Shall Know Them: Pragmaticism and the Prediction Theory of Law," 9 *Manitoba Law Journal* 29 (1978); Edward J. Bloustein, "Holmes: His First Amendment Theory and His Pragmatist Bent," 40 *Rutgers Law Review* 283 (1988). Holmes's debt to pragmatism is questioned in H. L. Pohlman, *Justice Oliver Wendell Holmes and Utilitarian Jurisprudence* (1984), but primarily on the basis of dismissive remarks Holmes made about Peirce and James. See also Sheldon M. Novick, *Honorable Justice: The Life of Oliver Wendell Holmes* 426–427 (1989) (n.4). These remarks show merely that Holmes, like many people of genius, tended to exaggerate his own originality.

embraced.[34] Pragmatism is a house of many rooms, as we shall see, and a pragmatist jurisprudence is no more committed to the thought of Oliver Wendell Holmes than to that of Richard Rorty (see Chapter 12).

Of all Holmes's "heresies" against the pragmatic faith, the most pertinent to this chapter is his "strong" legal positivism, his belief—erratically maintained, to be sure, but emphatically stated in the passage I quoted about the desirability of banishing all moral terms from law—that law and morals should have as little to do with each other as possible (perhaps nothing). The belief is false. Law cannot be reduced to rules clearly stated in statutes or constitutions, or to rules plus arbitrary assertions of will. Much of the law applied by judges, not to mention the "law" that tells us whether the rules or for that matter the judges themselves are lawful, consists of moral and political considerations. How could legal ideas be "uncolored by anything outside the law," when, as Holmes himself emphasized, the law is—and should be—shaped by social needs and interests? The same essay states that the premise of a common law doctrine "can do no more than embody the preference of a given body in a given time and place."[35] This is not right either. It denies the possibility that a law might reflect a sufficiently wide and durable interest to be fairly described as moral, as something more than a local and transient preference. Moreover, although the preferences of the dominant groups in society both constrain and give broad direction to law, law is more than simply the embodiment in coercive decrees of the results of the latest public opinion poll or canvass of special interest groups. Holmes seems in these passages in the grip of an overmastering conception of what law must be to count as law. This essentialism is foreign to the pragmatic approach—to which, however, he returned later in the essay, when he suggested that lawyers need a good dose of economics to be able to guide the law in the path of the general social advantage. A similar tension is found in his judicial oeuvre, where candid acknowledgment of the judge's need to make choices based on policy preferences coexists with powerful formalist

34. On partitioning the decisional process into logic and will, see next chapter; on Holmes's referential theory of language, see note 30 above; on his dislike of factual inquiry, see, for example, letter to Harold Laski of March 18, 1919, in *Holmes-Laski Letters,* note 7 above, vol. 1, p. 205 ("I hate facts").

35. Holmes, note 2 above, at 466. And in the same vein, "The law can ask no better justification than the deepest instincts of man." Id. at 477. Why no *better?* "Good" and "instinctual" are on different axes.

disclaimers of the relevance of consequences to judicial decision making.[36] Although Holmes may be the founder and greatest exemplar of pragmatic jurisprudence, a commitment to pragmatism neither requires nor even permits a wholesale embrace of his jurisprudential views.

36. For illustrations, compare Tyson & Brother v. Banton, 273 U.S. 418, 446–448 (1927), and Olmsted v. United States, 277 U.S. 438, 469 (1928), with Adkins v. Children's Hospital, 261 U.S. 525, 570–571 (1923); Schlesinger v. Wisconsin, 270 U.S. 230, 241 (1926), and Louis K. Liggett Co. v. Baldridge, 278 U.S. 105, 115 (1928). These are all dissenting opinions.

PART III ∾

INTERPRETATION REVISITED

8 ✑

Common Law versus Statute Law

A number of scholars (notably Ronald Dworkin, whose interpretive approach we first met in Chapter 6) believe that interpretation is the path to saving the law's objectivity. Others—notably practitioners of critical legal studies—believe that the path leads nowhere, because interpretation is indeterminate. An initial question is whether interpretation is relevant throughout law, and specifically whether it has anything to do with common law, a term I use broadly to mean any body of law created primarily by judges through their decisions rather than by the framers of statutes or constitutions. Common law thus includes not only tort and contract and other fields originally created by the English common law courts but also admiralty law, the law of equitable remedies, family law, and other bodies of law made primarily by judges, even if not by common law judges in the strict sense lawyers employ.

There seem to be profound differences between common law and statute law, the fundamental difference being precisely that between a conceptual system on the one hand and a textual system on the other. This difference would appear to make interpretation central to the latter but peripheral, even irrelevant, to the former. The appearance may be deceptive. A word of broad, even indefinite, meaning, interpretation can mean as little as working within a tradition, as opposed to taking a God's-eye view of things.[1] It can signify even less: it can function merely as a reminder that our understanding of "the world" is mediated, perhaps even constituted, by language. It is the latest in a long, long list of words abused by lawyers. Nevertheless the difference between a conceptual and a textual system is an interesting one.

A field of common law, such as tort law, and a field of statute law,

---

1. This is the sense it bears, for example, in Michael Walzer, *Interpretation and Social Criticism* (1987).

such as labor law, will resemble each other in that each will consist of a body of rules and standards resting in turn on a body of concepts. The rule that makes people prima facie liable for injuries caused by their negligence rests on the concept of negligence, that is, of failing to take due care. Concepts, like propositions but unlike, say, metaphors, are not tied to particular verbal formulations. There are many equivalent ways to state the concept of negligence, or consideration, or reliance, or assumption of risk, or constructive possession, or the myriad other common law concepts, and though some of these statements are more influential than others none is authoritative in the sense that it controls decisions applying the doctrine; the concept controls. Because of its conceptual character, common law is unwritten law in a profound sense. Indeed, a common law doctrine is no more textual than Newton's universal law of gravitation is. The doctrine is inferred from a judicial opinion, or more commonly from a series of judicial opinions, but the doctrine is not those opinions or the particular verbal formulas in them just as Newton's law, although first learned from the words in which Newton published it, is not those words. We prefer to state Newton's law in our own language rather than in seventeenth-century English, and likewise we prefer to state the doctrines of the common law, some of which are as old as Newton's *Principia,* in our own language. Translation may be imperfect and alter the meaning of the original doctrine; nevertheless many common law doctrines have a stable meaning, though expressed in a variety of different ways. We are not afraid that we would lose the meaning of negligence if we put it in different words from those used by Learned Hand, or William Prosser, or some other authoritative expositor of the concept.

Statutory law differs in that the statutory text—the starting point for decision, and in that respect (but only that respect) corresponding to judicial opinions in common law decision making—is in some important sense not to be revised by the judges, not to be put into their own words. They cannot treat the statute as a stab at formulating a concept.[2] They have first to extract the concept from the statute—that is, interpret the statute. (There is a sense in which common law judges "interpret" common law, but it is the sense in which "interpretation" means "understanding.") Antitrust law is as rich in difficult concepts as tort law is, but in determining whether an antitrust case has been decided correctly the observer must consider not only whether the judge prop-

2. See, for example, Edward H. Levi, *An Introduction to Legal Reasoning* 6–7, 28–30 (1949); A. W. B. Simpson, "The *Ratio Decidendi* of a Case and the Doctrine of Binding Precedent," in *Oxford Essays in Jurisprudence* 148, 165–167 (A. G. Guest ed. 1961).

erly understood and applied the relevant concepts but also whether those concepts are justifiable interpretations of the antitrust statutes. This point is independent of the generality of the statutory language. Statutes often enact standards—such as "unfair methods of competition," "equal protection of the laws," "good faith"—that are as general as those of common law; indeed, many statutes obtained their terminology from the common law ("good faith," "restraint of trade," and so on). But the formula is never quite so malleable when it is statutory as when it is part of the common law, because it is always necessary to consider the meaning of the statutory formula in a text that is normative for the judges.

This is not to say that deciding statutory cases is inherently more problematic than deciding common law cases. Just as statutory concepts must be justified by demonstrating their provenance in statutory texts, so common law concepts must be justified by demonstrating their provenance in sound public policy. Given two concepts, one statutory and one common law, with an equal weight of precedent behind them, it is proper to ask whether the statutory concept is anchored in the statute itself, but it is equally proper to ask whether the common law concept is anchored in whatever principles, policies, or goals the particular area of common law is thought to serve. If we can agree that the goal of the common law of negligence is to maximize society's wealth in the sense to be explored in Chapter 12, then by comparing the concept of negligence to that goal we can evaluate the soundness of the concept. Similarly, if we can agree on the meaning of the Sherman Act we can evaluate an antitrust concept such as the "rule of reason" by comparing it to that meaning. In the common law case we will be making a political or ethical judgment, a type of judgment discussed in Part IV. In the statutory case we will be making an interpretive judgment, the type of judgment examined in this part. It is not clear which is more difficult; it is not even clear how different they are in practice. And, in either case, once we are satisfied that the concept has been properly derived, we can proceed to use logical reasoning to apply it to specific facts. So there is a domain for formalistic reasoning (in the neutral sense that equates it to logical reasoning) in both common law and statutory fields; and conceivably it is the same size, which may not be a large size, in both.[3]

---

3. I hope this discussion corrects the misleading implications of my statement in "Legal Formalism, Legal Realism, and the Interpretation of Statutes and the Constitution," 37 *Case Western Reserve Law Review* 179, 187 (1986–87), that formalism has no application to statutory law. What I should have said is that deduction (the central formalist technique) will not get one from the statute to the concept, because interpretation is not a branch of logic. But the process of generating common law concepts from "sound" policy is not deductive either.

The failure to recognize that a political or ethical judgment is necessary in order to get common law reasoning going is the hallmark of the nineteenth-century American school of formalism attacked by Holmes. As he explained, "law schools pursue an inspirational combined with a logical method, that is, the postulates are taken for granted upon authority without inquiry into their worth, and then logic is used as the only tool to develop the results."[4] Since the correct choice of premises on grounds of policy or ethics is less certain than the correct deduction of the conclusion of a syllogism from its premises, formalists like to give the impression that the premises of common law decision making are self-evident—and meanwhile they pack as much into the major premises as possible, to shorten the chain of deductions.

For example, Langdell said that someone who returns a lost article for which the owner has offered a reward has no contractual right to the reward if he did not know about the offer, because then his returning it could not have been a conscious acceptance of the offer, and without such acceptance there is no contract.[5] We can sense here the "notion, which has ruled philosophy since the time of the Greeks, that the office of knowledge is to uncover the antecedently real, rather than, as in the case with our practical judgments, to gain the kind of understanding which is necessary to deal with problems as they arise."[6] Langdell was treating the concept of contract as if it were a thing that could not be altered without becoming something different. If you take the legs off a table (permanently—not just for storage or moving), it is no longer a table. But it does not follow that without an acceptance there is no contract. "Contract" is not a preexisting entity of fixed dimensions; it is not a Platonic Form; it is the name given to a promise that courts will enforce. If there is a good reason, they can decide to enforce a promise

---

4. "Law in Science and Science in Law," 12 *Harvard Law Review* 443, 460 (1899). Common law formalism coexisted with an almost nakedly political approach to the interpretation of the Constitution, a point Holmes hinted at in "The Path of the Law," 10 *Harvard Law Review* 457, 467–468 (1897). See Herbert Hovenkamp, "The Political Economy of Substantive Due Process," 40 *Stanford Law Review* 379 (1988). This combination is consistent with the false and manipulative character of so much legal formalism.

5. See Christopher C. Langdell, *A Summary of the Law of Contracts* 2–3 (2d ed. 1880), and the excellent discussion of Langdell's brand of formalism in Thomas C. Grey, "Langdell's Orthodoxy," 45 *University of Pittsburgh Law Review* 1 (1983).

6. John Dewey, *The Quest for Certainty: A Study of the Relation of Knowledge and Action* 17 (1929). Here is another respect, besides those discussed in Chapter 2, in which the name "Socratic method" is aptly applied to the case method of instruction pioneered by Langdell. See Josef Redlich, *The Common Law and the Case Method in American University Law Schools: A Report to the Carnegie Foundation for the Advancement of Teaching* 12–13 (1914).

that was made in the form of an offer but not consciously accepted, and call it a contract, just as the criminal courts can punish a drug dealer for his underling's possession of illegal drugs by saying that the dealer has "constructive" possession. (But must they say it? Must they use fictions?) The answer to the question whether the return of the lost article is the acceptance of a contract offer should depend on whether, if so, more lost articles will be returned—a difficult question, as it happens,[7] and one unrelated to logic.

We might try to show that common law reasoning is strongly objective by the following argument. When we say that a decision applying a statute is correct, we generally take for granted the policy choice embodied in the statute. It might be a foolish statute, but (provided it is constitutional—that is, not too foolish, not vicious, and not contrary to one of the specific prohibitions in the Constitution) if it is correctly interpreted and applied, the judges have done their job and no more can be asked. Since common law is law made by judges, they are the legislators, so maybe we should take for granted the concepts that underlie common law doctrines and ask merely whether the doctrines follow from the concepts and the decisions from the doctrines. But this move gives the game away. It admits that judges wear two hats, a judicial and a legislative, and that when they are wearing their legislative hat they are no more rationally accountable than an acknowledged legislator would be; *naturally* they are voting either their values or those of some constituency—what else would you expect a legislator to do? Holmes at times came close to this position, and not only in his concept of the judge as "interstitial legislator." Consider the following statement: "Where there is doubt the simple tool of logic does not suffice, and even if it is disguised and unconscious the judges are called on to exercise the sovereign prerogative of choice."[8] This attempt to partition the domain of legal decision into just two parts, logic and will, overlooks the possibility of using science or practical reason to select premises for legal reasoning. The very theme of Holmes's essay from which I have just quoted contradicts his dictum. ("The Path of the Law" contains the identical contradiction, as we saw in the last chapter.) The theme is that science can make law more rational by enabling the weight of competing considerations to be measured more precisely than the existing methods of legal inquiry permit. If we knew the effect on the return of lost articles of allowing the finder to claim the reward that (un-

7. See my book *Economic Analysis of Law* 89–90 (3d ed. 1986).
8. "Law in Science and Science in Law," note 4 above, at 461.

beknownst to him) the owner had offered, it would be easy to decide whether the owner should be contractually bound, yet the decision would be neither a logical deduction nor mere whimsy. Holmes believed in policy analysis but lacked the patience to do it.

The common law contains many examples of an approach intermediate between the formalism of a Langdell and the irrationalism of Holmes (in some moods)—an approach that, like the one I just suggested for the lost-article case, can fairly be called pragmatic. Consider *Farwell v. Boston & Worcester R. R.,*[9] which established the fellow-servant rule in American common law. The rule (now superseded by workers' compensation statutes) is that an employee injured by the negligence of a fellow employee is not entitled to impute the fellow worker's negligence to their common employer and therefore cannot obtain damages from the employer for the injury. Chief Justice Lemuel Shaw of the Massachusetts Supreme Judicial Court begins the opinion with an acknowledgment that "this is an action of new impression in our courts, and involves a principle of great importance" (p. 55). Earlier cases had held that the employer was responsible for negligent conduct of his employees that injured nonworkers; this is the principle of respondeat superior. But the situation of the worker victim is different. He has a contract, express or implied, with his employer. Liability, Shaw argues, should depend on its terms. After noting that "as there is no express contract between the parties, applicable to this point, it [the plaintiff's claim] is placed on the footing of an implied contract of indemnity, arising out of the relation of master and servant" (p. 56), Shaw remarks:

> The general rule, resulting from considerations as well of justice as of policy, is, that he who engages in the employment of another for the performance of specified duties and services, for compensation, takes upon himself the natural and ordinary risks and perils incident to the performance of such services, and in legal presumption, the compensation is adjusted accordingly. And we are not aware of any principle which should except the perils arising from the carelessness and negligence of those who are in the same employment. These are perils which the servant is as likely to know, and against which he can as effectually guard, as the master. They are perils incident to the service, and which can be as distinctly foreseen and provided for in the rate of compensation as any others. (p. 57)

There is a nod to formalism in the words "in legal presumption"; it

9. 45 Mass. (4 Met.) 49 (1842). Subsequent page references to this opinion appear in the text.

should be a question of fact whether workers' pay adjusts to compensate them for the hazards of the workplace. But otherwise the analysis is practical. Provided that workers are aware of the dangers posed by careless fellow workers, self-interest will lead them to demand a higher wage and, if the employer refuses, to seek safer work elsewhere. Shaw notes later in his opinion that the plaintiff had received a raise when he took the job in which he was injured.

Shaw realized that there are cases in which an employer is liable for the negligence of his employees toward persons with whom he has a contract, even though in such cases the contract price, analogous to the wage of the worker exposed to danger from his fellow workers, would (one might think) adjust to compensate for the hazards posed by such negligence. For example, a common carrier is liable for negligence of its employees that results in damage to baggage or in injury to passengers. Significantly prefacing his discussion of these cases (and of the related case of the innkeeper's liability to his guests) with the statement, "In considering the rights and obligations arising out of particular relations, it is competent for courts of justice to regard considerations of policy and general convenience, and to draw from them such rules as will, in their practical application, best promote the safety and security of all parties concerned" (p. 58), Shaw argues that the shipper or passenger, unlike a fellow worker, has no ability either to prevent the carrier's employees from behaving negligently or (especially in the case of lost baggage) even to prove negligence in a suit against the employee. Shaw drives home the distinction by noting that when in a common undertaking "the safety of each depends on the care and skill with which each other shall perform his appropriate duty, each is an observer of the conduct of the others, can give notice of any misconduct, incapacity or neglect of duty, and leave the service, if the common employer will not take such precautions and employ such agents as the safety of the whole party may require" (p. 59).

There is other noteworthy analysis in the opinion: a discussion of why the fellow-servant rule should not be limited to workers in the same department, and a suggestion that there may be some implied warranties of the employer to his employee after all, although not against the negligence of fellow employees—for example, implied warranties that the employer will furnish the employee with safe equipment and that the employer will exercise due care in selecting the employee's fellow workers. These discussions, too, are practical rather than legalistic. But I have said enough to indicate the character of the analysis. That the analysis may be all wet[10] is a strength rather than a weakness. The analysis depends on empirical assertions—principally that workers know the hazards of the workplace and that wages adjust to compensate them for the hazards—that can be tested. It does not depend on the "essence" of the employment relation, yet neither is it a matter of the sheer will of the judges. It is policy analysis. The difference between the rejection of the fellow-servant rule and the rejection of the rule of capture is that the latter was refuted empirically—was shown not to conduce to any goal that property law might be thought to serve—whereas to this day it is unclear whether the common law of industrial accidents was more or less efficacious or equitable than the workers' compensation statutes that replaced it.

Without my going any further it should be plain that the traditional view that analogizes common law reasoning to induction and statutory interpretation to deduction is misleading. Interpretation is not deduction, although once a concept is extracted from a statute by interpretation the judge may be able to proceed in deductive fashion (for example, the Sherman Act—by interpretation—forbids cartels, X is a cartel, therefore X is forbidden). And obtaining the premises from which common law reasoning proceeds need not be an induction from previous cases; it was not in *Farwell*. Moreover, once the premises are selected the common law judge can use deduction to the same degree—which is not to say, to a high degree—as can the statutory judge once interpretation yields a concept for him to apply. Sometimes, it is true, the premises for common law reasoning are obtained by a process that can fairly be described as induction from a line of cases. One observes that promises are enforced if supported by consideration but not otherwise (with certain exceptions, of course, but we can ignore these), and one extracts from these observations the rule that, to be enforceable, promises must be supported by consideration. To move from observed regularity to rule (the expectation that the regularity will continue) is induction in a legitimate sense, although it would be a mistake to make too much of this, for the reasons explained in Part I.

Although formalism cannot make common law decision making determinate, the conclusion does not follow, as some members of the critical legal studies movement believe (with support in Holmes, as we have just seen), that common law decision making is indeterminate,

---

10. The usual view; for references and a dissent from that view, see William M. Landes and Richard A. Posner, *The Economic Structure of Tort Law* 309–310 (1987); also my article "A Theory of Negligence," 1 *Journal of Legal Studies* 29, 44–45, 67–71 (1972).

random—"all politics." Such a conclusion overlooks the possibility that the tools of practical reason can resolve many common law issues with tolerable definiteness, so that the judge does not have to fall back on personal values or raw politics. The counterargument, forcefully advanced by James Boyle among others, is that for every reason one might offer in support of a particular outcome an equally powerful reason against could, with just a bit of imagination, be found.[11] Boyle presents a checklist of techniques for arguing in favor of plaintiff or defendant. He claims that each technique can be used equally well by either party and hence that legal reasoning is indeterminate.

The first technique is that of "formalistic" argument: "explain the meaning of the word [the key word in a rule] by taking it out of context, and without considering the purpose behind the rule" (p. 1052). That is not a defensible way to read any document. Examples of it can be found, goodness knows, in plenty of lawyers' briefs and judges' opinions, but Boyle is arguing not for the prevalence of sloppy thinking in law but for the indeterminacy of legal reasoning, even by masters. The second technique, "purposive interpretation," requires the advocate to "'imagine' the purpose which lies behind the rule and define the word in light of this purpose" (pp. 1052–1053). The scare quotes imply that the interpreter must be imputing rather than finding purpose. Yet the purposes behind rules can usually, although not always, be discovered, and once discovered they provide reliable guidance in applying the rule to a new situation.

The next technique is that of narrowing a rule to the particular facts of the case in which it was stated or, if one prefers, broadening the rule, by analogy, to cover a case factually remote from the one that stated the rule. Boyle illustrates this technique with *Vosburg v. Putney*.[12] One schoolboy kicked another. Although the kick was deliberate, there was no intent to injure. Unbeknownst to the kicker, however, the victim had a preexisting injury at the site of the kick and as a result sustained a severe injury. The court held the injurer liable for the full, even though unforeseeable, extent of the injury. Boyle offers a broad reading of the case—that all people, including children, lunatics, and others not generally thought to be fully responsible are liable for the full even if unfore-

11. See "Appendix: First Year Mystification and Legal Argument: How to Avoid the Former and Master the Latter," in Boyle, "The Anatomy of a Torts Class," 34 *American University Law Review* 1003, 1051 (1985). Boyle states that the appendix is based on published and unpublished writings by Duncan Kennedy, a leading figure in the critical legal studies movement. Subsequent page references to Boyle's article are in the text.

12. 80 Wis. 523, 50 N.W. 403 (1891).

seen consequences of their intentional acts—and a narrow reading: if one child hits another after class has been called to order, the presumption that his action is intentional is strengthened. These readings are off the mark, the first because it is an overgeneralization, the second because the intentionality of the kick was not in dispute. Boyle overlooks the rule that has actually emerged from *Vosburg* and has been confirmed in hundreds of cases: the tortfeasor (whether or not an intentional one) takes his victim as he finds him, and is therefore not excused from paying damages merely because, had it not been for some preexisting weakness of the victim, the tort would not have caused so severe an injury. This "thin-skull" rule makes good sense; without it tortious injuries would be undercompensated and underdeterred. It is a more natural and sensible interpretation of *Vosburg v. Putney* than the alternatives suggested by Boyle.

Boyle next discusses five types of policy or ethical argument, each double-edged. The first is administrability, which involves arguing that the case should be decided either by a rule (to maximize certainty of legal obligation) or by a standard (to do equity and close loopholes). This is indeed an important and often a difficult choice, but it is not an arbitrary one. A scholarly literature not cited by Boyle identifies the trade-offs between rule and standard.[13] Making these trade-offs is often difficult, but they nevertheless involve a process of reasoning and not, as Boyle appears to believe, a merely whimsical or ideological choice.

The second type of policy argument concerns the relative institutional competence of courts and legislatures. If a court is asked to recognize a new common law right, the defendant can argue that the invitation should be declined because the legislature, as a more representative body and also as one with greater access (at least in principle) to "legislative" facts, is in a better position to decide whether to create a new right. The counterargument is that legislatures are not really that representative (being buffeted by interest-group pressures), that their fact-finding capabilities are in truth rudimentary and rarely employed, and that courts should not disrupt the legislature's inherently limited agenda by dumping problems in its lap. The counterargument is more consistent with what we know about the legislative process than is the argument. And since by definition we are in a common law area—an area the legislature has left to the courts—it would take extraordinary circumstances to justify the court's batting the shuttlecock back to the legislature.

Boyle contends that "moral arguments," just like policy arguments,

13. See note 8 in Chapter 1 of this book.

are readily deployable in pairs of opposites, such as "people should keep their bargains" versus "why should this large corporation be able to enforce this document against a person who did not have equal bargaining power and who did not read the small print?" (p. 1058). This is a poor example. The long list of excuses recognized in law for not performing contracts shows that there is no general legal principle that "people should keep their bargains."[14] The "large corporation" is a fiction (see Chapter 5) and the concept of unequal bargaining power vacuous and also distinct from the problem of fine-print terms. If the material terms of the contract were written in print too fine to be easily read, in what sense did the promisor actually strike the bargain that the large corporation is seeking to enforce? The pair of opposed arguments collapses to a point.

The last two categories of argument in the list of five—arguments from deterrence and economic arguments—are actually one, as Boyle implicitly acknowledges in discussing the same problem of information costs under both headings. (One of the "moral arguments"—the fine-print argument—also involved information costs and could have been cast in economic terms.) The economic analyst of law may neglect how incentives get communicated to the people whose behavior society wants to alter, may assume that a change in the average sentence for a particular crime will operate just as a change in price does in a conventional market, although he has not investigated whether prospective criminals actually learn about such changes. Such changes are not advertised, as price changes in explicit markets are. Arguments from deterrence are a subset of economic arguments—the subset that consists of arguments about the response of behavior to changes in incentives.

Boyle considers economic arguments to be indeterminate, hence equally available to both sides in every case, but the particular example he gives is a poor one. Citing *Tuttle v. Buck*,[15] he asks whether someone who starts a business with the aim of ruining another businessman, yet with no (other) ulterior purpose such as obtaining a monopoly, should be liable for the losses that his actions inflict on the intended victim. Boyle thinks that one can argue as an economist against liability on the ground that consumers are made better off by additional competition, whatever the competitor's motive, and equally for liability on the ground that "economic science demands that we exclude from the market place all motives other than the desire for profit" (p. 1062). These

14. He means, of course, keep their *promises*.
15. 107 Minn. 145, 119 N.W. 946 (1909).

are not good economic arguments. The issue for the economist is not motive but likely consequence. The economist is uninterested in motive (the province of psychology and ethics), and nothing in economic science requires excluding from markets motives other than the profit motive.

How should the case be analyzed? It may seem that since the defendant has no desire to serve the market (his costs may be too high to permit him to earn a profit even if he has no competition) and therefore probably will leave it as soon as his victim is ruined, consumers are likely to be worse off on balance; they will have low prices for a time, but afterward no source of supply. This depends, however, on whether the plaintiff really will be ruined or will just bide his time on the sidelines, waiting for the defendant to withdraw, and on whether other potential sellers, as efficient as the defendant, are in the wings waiting to enter the market if and when he leaves. Yet even if the existence of potential competition prevents effective monopolizing, so that consumers do not face a threat of monopoly pricing, the defendant's conduct is objectionable from an economic standpoint. For like the resources consumed in the murder of a hated enemy, the defendant's investment in ruining the plaintiff has no net expected social product. It transfers utility from plaintiff to defendant without increasing the social pie.

The defendant in *Tuttle v. Buck* won, and the court gave reasons consistent with the analysis just sketched. *Tuttle* was one of those cases in which the only "facts" before the court are those alleged in the plaintiff's complaint, for the trial judge had thrown out the case on the ground that even if the facts alleged were true they did not state a claim. The complaint presents an implausible case of motiveless malignity—something out of a Dürrenmatt novel—but the court was stuck with it. The court first observes, much in the spirit of the economic analysis sketched above, that "when a man starts an opposition place of business, not for the sake of profit to himself, but regardless of loss to himself, and for the sole purpose of driving his competitor out of business, *and with the intention of himself retiring upon the accomplishment of his malevolent purpose,* he is guilty of a wanton wrong and an actionable tort."[16] But after combing the complaint and finding "no allegation that the defendant was intentionally running the business at a financial loss to himself, or that after driving the plaintiff out of business the defendant closed up or

16. 107 Minn. at 151, 119 N.W. at 948 (emphasis added).

intended to close up his shop,"[17] the court affirms the dismissal of the complaint. For all that appears, the plaintiff was driven out of business simply because he was less efficient than the defendant, and the defendant means to stay, in which event consumers clearly will be better off in the long run as well as in the short run. The decision for the defendant, although it cannot be proved correct (for *Tuttle* is not an easy case), is reasonable and illustrates the power of practical reason to yield weakly objective results in many (not all) difficult cases. The qualification "weakly objective" is important. It is just one step above arbitrary. But Boyle wants to say more than that difficult cases permit only weakly objective decisions. He wants to say that all legal arguments cancel out, so that legal reasoning is phony.

He may have been misled by the fact that legal discourse is dialectic, antinomian.[18] If the plaintiff argues that the case should be governed by a particular rule and tries to strengthen his position by reference to the advantages of rules over standards, the defendant will have an incentive to parry the thrust by pointing out the advantages of standards over rules. The adversary process generates opposing positions on the policy issues that are pertinent to the resolution of new and difficult cases. But this is just to say that a competitive process is at work (albeit imperfectly) in the legal system—an observation more likely to gratify the philosopher of science, at least if he is a fallibilist in the tradition of Peirce and Popper, than to persuade him that legal inquiry must be indeterminate.

Could we do better by thinking of the common law in interpretive rather than conceptual terms? To show that we can, Ronald Dworkin has offered the analogy of a "chain novel."[19] The first case in a line of precedent is like chapter 1 of a chain novel; it does not determine the next decision (corresponding to chapter 2), but it constrains it, since the judge who decides the next case, like the author of chapter 2 of the chain novel, must strive to make a smooth fit with the previous decision. But

17. Id.

18. See J. L. Balkin, "The Crystalline Structure of Legal Thought," 39 *Rutgers Law Review* 1 (1986).

19. See, for example, *Law's Empire* 228–250 (1986). (A chain novel is a novel in which each chapter is written by a different author.) Dworkin does not limit the analogy to common law, but it is particularly unconvincing with regard to constitutional and statutory law. See my book *Law and Literature: A Misunderstood Relation* 258–259 (1988). For other criticisms, see Jessica Lane, "The Poetics of Legal Interpretation," 87 *Columbia Law Review* 197 (1987); John Stick, "Literary Imperialism: Assessing the Results of Dworkin's Interpretive Turn in *Law's Empire*," 34 *UCLA Law Review* 371 (1986).

why must he? A precedent is either an authority—that is, a reason apart from its soundness for deciding the next case a particular way—or a source of relevant information to the decider of the next case. There is no social interest in continuity or a smooth fit, as such, between successive cases. Stability and predictability are merely two of the considerations that will determine whether the next case follows or departs from the previous one—maybe the two most important, but that would not affect the argument. The goal of the subsequent judge is not interpretive; it is to make the best decision he can, bearing in mind that one thing that makes a decision good, although not the only and often not the most important thing, is that it leaves expectations created by earlier decisions undisturbed. Decisions are not the only source of expectations—far from it. Changing the law to bring it into closer harmony with lay intuitions of justice and fair dealing may protect rather than defeat the parties' expectations.[20] After weighing this and other relevant considerations the judge may decide to cast out the earlier "chapters" and make a new start. The second and subsequent authors of a chain novel cannot do that—or if they do, they are no longer playing the game.

The chain-novel analogy might be thought to echo T. S. Eliot's conception of a literary tradition:

> What happens when a new work of art is created is something that happens simultaneously to all the works of art which preceded it. The existing monuments form an ideal order among themselves, which is modified by the introduction of the new (the really new) work of art among them. The existing order is complete before the new work arrives; for order to persist after the supervention of novelty, the *whole* existing order must be, if ever so slightly, altered; and so the relations, proportions, values of each work of art toward the whole are readjusted; and this is conformity between the old and the new.[21]

This is a richer conception than Dworkin's of a traditionary or, if one prefers, an "interpretive" approach to meaning. The previous chapters of the chain novel are unaltered by subsequent chapters, whose authors have, therefore, progressively less freedom, whereas those who contribute to a tradition alter it with their contributions; the meaning of Marlowe is different after Shakespeare, as is that of Blake after Yeats, for we

---

20. See Benjamin N. Cardozo, *The Nature of the Judicial Process* 142–143 (1921); Paul H. Rubin, *Business Firms and the Common Law: The Evolution of Efficient Rules* 162–165 (1983).

21. "Tradition and the Individual Talent," in Eliot, *Selected Essays* 3, 5 (new ed. 1950).

read the earlier writers in light of our knowledge of the later ones.[22] It is much the same in law. The later judges use their interpretive freedom to alter, even when they do not explicitly overrule (and they do that, too, of course), earlier holdings. But there is a major difference. The "order" in art is indeed one of "monuments," and respectful attention to them is enforced by their quality. The order in law is of decisions by the lawyers' committees that we call appellate courts, and these decisions frequently are ill informed, outmoded, or ignoble. The obeisance that judges owe them depends on the intrinsic merit of the previous decisions, which is variable, and on the balance between the claims of stability and of substantive justice. To call this obeisance traditionary or interpretive is to conceal what is and should be a pragmatic analysis.

We do not need, and can I think make little use of, the concept of interpretation in order to understand and evaluate the common law. For one like myself who believes that interpretation is not a generally dependable method of achieving certainty or even confidence about how to decide difficult cases (see the next two chapters), it is a relief not to have to worry about interpretation when dealing with common law cases. But to repeat an earlier point, it does not follow that common law decision making is more objective than statutory or constitutional decision making is. For just as statutory and constitutional decisions are frequently based on highly contestable interpretations, so common law decisions are frequently based on highly contestable, although not necessarily arbitrary, policy analyses or ethical judgments.

22. Gadamer's interpretive theory is similar. See Hans-Georg Gadamer, *Truth and Method* (1975); William N. Eskridge, Jr., "Gadamer/Statutory Interpretation" (unpublished paper, Georgetown University Law School, May 1989).

9 ⚬

Objectivity in Statutory Interpretation

The Plain-Meaning Fallacy

Interpreting a text is not deduction, as we saw in Chapter 3, but maybe it is something almost as straightforward—a matter of reading carefully and letting the plain meaning of the words dictate the interpretation of the text. Holmes offered an influential version of the plain-meaning approach: "We ask, not what [the author] meant, but what those words would mean in the mouth of a normal speaker of English, using them in the circumstances in which they were used."[1] Adherent to a referential theory of language that he was, Holmes did not consider interpretation of the written word problematic. And, antimentalist that he was, he did not want judges to waste their time trying to peer into people's minds. Apart from the philosophical and evidentiary problems of doing so, there is the distinct possibility that the effort will be fruitless simply because the author meant nothing so far as the case at hand is concerned.[2] A question of interpretation that arose and was addressed in the legislative proceedings may be readily answerable, provided the proceedings are recorded and the question was not divisive. But since there will be no mental state to recover if the question did not arise, a Pentothal theory of statutory interpretation will have at best a limited domain.

Holmes's theory is not much better, however. If, as the quoted passage seems to imply, the meaning of words depends on what the text's

---

1. "The Theory of Legal Interpretation," 12 *Harvard Law Review* 417–418 (1899). He is talking about contract interpretation but later makes clear that he thinks statutes should be interpreted the same way. See id. at 419–420.

2. For an illustration, see Zechariah Chafee, Jr., "The Disorderly Conduct of Words," 41 *Columbia Law Review* 381, 400 (1941).

authors understood by them, weird discontinuities in reference arise, akin to the suggestion that Democritus and Bohr were not referring to the same thing when they said "atom." The Fourth Amendment on this view could not reach wiretapping or other electronic eavesdropping, because no user of the English language in 1789 could have understood the words "searches and seizures" to refer to wiretapping. The "press" to which the First Amendment refers could not mean a television network. If the government subsidized religious broadcasters, this could not be an establishment of religion. Congress's power to create an army and a navy would not authorize the creation of an air force.

Holmes's "normal English speaker" test designates one of several possible linguistic communities (America 1789, in the case of the Bill of Rights) as authoritative and forbids translation between it and any other such community, including America 1989. Whether the authors' linguistic community is the right one to use to fix statutory meaning is not, as Holmes seems to have thought, self-evident. A statute imposes a duty on imported vegetables but not on imported fruits, and the question arises whether the duty applies to tomatoes.[3] To the botanist, a tomato is a fruit, but so are peas and beans, and to ordinary folk these are all vegetables because they are not eaten for dessert. Which is the relevant interpretive community? Suppose it were known somehow that all the legislators who voted for the statute had thought it exempted tomatoes; what weight if any should their understanding have? Or suppose that although in 1883, when the statute was passed, everyone classified tomatoes as fruits, today everyone classifies them as vegetables, and the statute has not been repealed. Should today's meaning govern here, as most lawyers would think it should govern in the constitutional examples I gave in the preceding paragraph, or should the original meaning? Whatever the answers, Holmes's formulation begs the questions.

The inadequacy of that formulation can be further shown by distinguishing between internal (or semantic) ambiguity and external ambiguity, a distinction corresponding to the contract lawyer's distinction between intrinsic and extrinsic ambiguity. Internal ambiguity is present when a person who reads a sentence and knows the language that it is written in, but nothing about the circumstances in which it was written, finds it unclear. Either there is an internal contradiction, or the grammar and syntax of the sentence fail to disambiguate a word or phrase that has more than one meaning, for example, "due process" in the Fifth and

---

3. The issue in Nix v. Hedden, 149 U.S. 304 (1893). The court answered "yes."

Fourteenth Amendments or "equal" in the equal protection clause of the Fourteenth Amendment. External ambiguity is present, and with the same consequence, when the sentence, though clear to a normal English speaker ignorant of its background, is unclear, garbled, or means something different from what the normal English speaker thinks to someone who *does* know the background. An example is the word "press" in the First Amendment, which to the normal English speaker refers to print media only but, so limited, seems incongruous in light of modern methods of disseminating news and opinion. Another example is the inheritance statute in *Riggs v. Palmer,* the murdering-heir case discussed in Chapter 3. The statute said that a bequest in a will complying with specified formalities was enforceable. There was no ambiguity until one brought in from outside the fact that the person named in the bequest had murdered the author of the will. Holmes's plain-meaning approach rules out arguments of external ambiguity, and by doing so artificially truncates the interpretive process. One can understand the appeal of such an approach to a formalist, because it treats meaning as an affair purely of words, unaffected by the things to which the words might be taken to refer. But Holmes was not a formalist, and his approach looks good only in comparison with a plain-meaning approach that by completely ignoring the author's linguistic community puts itself at the mercy of semantic drift.

We can begin to sense the *variety* of interpretive methods that compete for the law's attention. But more important to the quest for interpretive objectivity than flexing our taxonomic muscles is developing a sense of what kind of text a statute is. If we think it is like a work of literature, we might as well throw up our hands, because the prospects for finding agreed-upon meaning in such works are at present dim; the interpretive community in literature has become so fragmented that the meanings of the great literary texts cannot be fixed. The differences between legal and literary texts are so great that the lawyer should not be troubled by the disarray in the literary community, but at the same time he cannot expect much help from the methods of literary interpretation.[4] I think a statute is better understood not as a literary work but as a command, so that Holmes was on the right track when he suggested (but not when he promptly retracted the suggestion, without explanation, in favor of

---

4. See my book *Law and Literature: A Misunderstood Relation,* ch. 5 (1988). I do think there are some fruitful analogies—I suggested several in Chapter 6. I also think that the interpretive disarray in the two fields may have common causes. See id. at 265–266. But no specific techniques of literary interpretation seem usable in the statutory arena.

the plain-meaning approach) that "in the case of a statute . . . it would be possible to say that as we are dealing with the commands of the sovereign the only thing to do is to find out what the sovereign wants."[5]

This may not be *quite* right, even if we put aside the question of exactly who is the sovereign in the American constitutional system. If what the sovereign wants is unjust or unreasonable, the judges may have some lawful power to blunt the statute's thrust even if the statute is constitutional. Although this notion of a power to make civilizing interpretations whereby "unjust and partial laws" are mitigated by "the scruples of the court" is prominent in *Federalist No. 78* (Hamilton),[6] and although the basic idea is as old as Aristotle's notion of the equity of a statute (see *Rhetoric,* Bk. I, §13), the legitimating source of such a power is obscure, and the power is further troublesome because of its shapelessness. Holmes dramatically rejected the existence of such a power when he said that if the people of the United States wanted to go to hell it was his duty as a judge to help them get there. This attitude is irresponsible; it is not the raison d'être of the judicial system to give lessons in mindless obedience. But the attitude is not, as one might think, inconsistent with Holmes's rejection of formalism. Enforcing an utterly unjust law is attractive to the formalist because it enables him to prove that the law is different from the judge's desire, but it is also attractive to the positivist because it decisively illustrates the separation of law and morals. This double whammy helps explain the appeal of formalism to the legal profession.

If we set aside the question of "civilizing interpretations," the idea of a statute's being a command issued by a superior body (the legislature) to a subordinate body (the judiciary) provides a helpful way of framing inquiry into the principles of statutory interpretation. Helpful because it enables us to shift our attention from the nebulous idea of "interpretation" to the somewhat more concrete idea of communication, an idea that is obscure in the plain-meaning approach. We all understand in a rough way what a communication is; we know that there is such a thing as successful communication; and a command is a type of communication. So in the command theory of legislation we have an intelligible starting point for the analysis of statutory interpretation.

A starting point—not an algorithm. The problem is correctly posed, but it is not solved. The Constitution provides (Art. II, §1, cl. 5) that no person younger than thirty-five may be President. X presents himself

5. "The Theory of Legal Interpretation," note 1 above, at 419.
6. *The Federalist Papers* 226, 231–232 (2d ed., Roy P. Fairfield ed., 1981).

as a candidate. He is thirty-three, but argues that he is more mature than most thirty-five-year-olds or even most sixty-five-year-olds, that people mature earlier today than they did in the eighteenth century, that the provision should be construed liberally lest the field of presidential selection be unduly curtailed, and that the people can be trusted to give proper weight to a candidate's age. These arguments will fail to convince a court. Yet the constitutional command, considered without regard to its social context, is too cryptic to be clear,[7] even though all the words are clear and the grammar and syntax are straightforward. We are apt to overlook the importance of social context in this example because the context happens to be so familiar. But if age in this country were measured from conception (as it is in India) rather than from birth, or if birth dates were not recorded, or if the length of a year were highly variable, or if we changed the calendar, or if we used numbers qualitatively (as in Homer—where "ten years" means a long time rather than a fixed interval) rather than quantitatively, the provision on age of eligibility might mean only that a candidate for President has to be a mature person. (A standard too vague to enforce, perhaps? But the courts could take the position that it was enforceable by the force of public opinion only—always a possible stance in dealing with a vague constitutional provision.)

None of the posited conditions obtains. Instead the age thirty-five provision recognizably belongs to a family of rules that establish arbitrary dates of eligibility in preference to authorizing officials to make qualitative judgments. Legislatures fix eighteen or twenty-one, rather than attainment of maturity, as the age of majority; and so with eligibility for marriage, for a driving license, for a senior citizen's discount, for the order of layoffs in a unionized plant, and so forth. The electoral process would be enormously complicated if the eligibility of candidates depended on a qualitative assessment that often could not be completed until after the election—which would be too late. All this was clear in 1787 and is clear today. Thanks to the coherence and continuity of the relevant interpretive community (that is, the community consisting of lawyers, judges, and politicians from 1787 to the present), we have no difficulty interpreting the command of the Constitution's framers; we can see what they were driving at.

7. Cf. Francis Lieber, *Legal and Political Hermeneutics* 28–29 (enlarged ed. 1839), and Bo Hanson, *Application of Rules in New Situations: A Hermeneutical Study* 88–89 (1977), both emphasizing the importance of implied conditions in communication. This is also one of the points of MacCallum's ashtray example, discussed in Chapter 3, and is dramatically illustrated by the statute in *Riggs v. Palmer.*

Yet to make this straightforward interpretation we had to range far beyond the text of the provision being interpreted. It is true that in this case Holmes's suggested test—the understanding of the normal English speaker—would yield the same interpretation. But that is because, as luck would have it, the key words in the age thirty-five provision (age, thirty-five, years, President, eligible) have the same dictionary meanings they had two centuries ago. This is an accident, as I shall argue with the help of two cases in which the statutory language was clear in Holmes's sense but the correct interpretation was not. The first is an opinion that Holmes himself wrote, when he was Chief Justice of the Massachusetts Supreme Judicial Court.[8] The Massachusetts constitution provided that members of the state's house of representatives "shall be chosen by written vote." Many years later the legislature decided to use voting machines in place of written votes, and asked the court for an advisory opinion on the constitutionality of such a substitution. Apparently some of the machines used no paper at all, and all dispensed with the use of a separate piece of paper to record each vote. Nevertheless the substitution was held to be constitutional. Holmes thought the important thing was not the mental picture that the framers of the constitution had had in mind, but the benefits they had sought to secure or the evils they had sought to prevent. He explained that they had intended to prevent oral or hand voting, and as the voting machine did this it was constitutional. This is purposive rather than literal interpretation.

My second example does not have so happy an outcome. In *United States v. Locke,*[9] a federal statute required firms having unpatented mining claims on federal lands to reregister their claims annually "prior to December 31." Claims not registered in time were forfeited. The plaintiffs filed on December 31, and the Supreme Court held that this was too late. Although the statute was only nine years old and no semantic drift had occurred that might have made the referents of "December 30," "prior to," or "December 31" unclear, it seems highly likely that when Congress said "prior to December 31" it meant "by December 31." The end of the year is a common deadline, and no explanation of why Congress might have wanted to set the deadline in this statute a day earlier, thereby creating a trap for valuable property rights, has ever been suggested. Legislative confusion is further suggested by the distinction in the same section of the statute between claims "located prior to October

8. In re House Bill No. 1,291, 178 Mass. 605, 60 N.E. 129 (1901).
9. 471 U.S. 84 (1985), interpreting section 314(a) of the Federal Land Policy and Management Act of 1976, 43 U.S.C. §1744(a).

21, 1976," and claims "located after October 21, 1976," thus leaving a gap for claims located on October 21, 1976—if "prior to" is read literally. Notice that if this provision is considered part of the statutory text that is being interpreted, the statute has an internal ambiguity; otherwise the ambiguity is external.

Reading "prior to December 31" literally was a wooden, unimaginative response to the legislative command, like that of the assistant in MacCallum's example who, when told to fetch all the ashtrays he could find, ripped some off the walls. That was a case where the command was (to the outsider to the culture in which it was given) incomplete. *Locke* is a case where the command was garbled. We encounter such cases frequently in everyday life. Suppose I ask my secretary to call Z and tell him I must cancel our lunch date today—I have been called out of town suddenly. The secretary notices that on my calendar I have marked lunch with Y, not Z, but it is too late to check back with me, because I have left the office and cannot be reached. Is it not plain that the secretary should call Y, even though there was no semantic or internal ambiguity in my instruction? And is not *Locke* a similar case? Well, you may say, statutes are not casual commands; surely if Congress had meant *by* December 31 it would have said so. But it is not unusual for statutes to contain inexplicable typographical or logical errors. Statutory drafting is often a rushed and careless process.[10]

These cases expose an ambiguity in Holmes's suggestion that a statute means what a normal English speaker would understand its words to mean. A normal English speaker does not interpret a message merely by consulting the dictionary definitions of each word (assume these definitions are stored in his brain) and the relevant grammatical and syntactical principles. He does not ignore what I have called external ambi-

10. For examples, see United States v. Colon-Ortiz, 866 F.2d 6 (1st Cir. 1989); Shine v. Shine, 802 F.2d 583 (1st Cir. 1986); In re Adamo, 619 F.2d 216 (2d Cir. 1980); United States v. Babcock, 530 F.2d 1051 (D.C. Cir. 1976); Stock v. Department of the Air Force, 186 F.2d 968 (4th Cir. 1950); Pressman v. State Tax Commission, 204 Md. 78, 102 A.2d 821 (1954); Johnson v. United States Gypsum Co., 217 Ark. 264, 229 S.W.2d 671 (1950); State ex rel. Attorney General v. Chicago Mill & Lumber Corp., 184 Ark. 1011, 45 S.W.2d 26 (1931); Ronson Patents Corp. v. Sparklets Devices, Inc., 102 F. Supp. 123 (E.D. Mo. 1951). The dissent in Sorenson v. Secretary of the Treasury, 475 U.S. 851, 867 n. 2 (1986), quotes a newspaper report of the enactment of a bill "with parts of it photocopied from memorandums, other parts handwritten at the last minute . . . some final sections hastily crossed out in whorls of pencil marks [and] such cryptic and accidental entries in the bill as a name and phone number—'Ruth Seymour, 225–4844'—standing alone as if it were a special appropriation item." On the frequent inadvertent use of "or" to mean "and," see, for example, De Sylva v. Ballentine, 351 U.S. 570 (1956); Unification Church v. Immigration & Naturalization Service, 762 F.2d 1077 (D.C. Cir. 1985).

guity. He consults the totality of his relevant experience, which in my example of the direction to cancel a lunch date includes what is written on my calendar; in the voting machine case includes the march of science; in *Locke* includes other passages in the statute, social practices with regard to deadlines, and arguably a background norm against setting traps for the unwary; in *Riggs* includes an even more powerful background norm that people should not be allowed to benefit from murder;[11] in the ashtray example includes notions of property rights; and in the age thirty-five provision includes (among other things) the system of recording birth dates, the conduct of elections, and the use of numbers. Meaning depends on context as well as on the semantic and other formal properties of sentences. The effort to avoid grappling with the things of the world in ascertaining meaning is a formalist dodge surprising in Holmes.

The Quest for Interpretive Theory

Characterizing a statute as a command makes it natural to think of interpretation in terms of ascertaining the drafters' wants, to which their words are only a clue. A lieutenant, commanding the lead platoon in an attack, finds his way blocked by an unexpected enemy pillbox. He has two choices (other than to break off the attack): to go straight ahead at the pillbox or to try to bypass it on the left. He radios his company commander for instructions. The commander replies "Go—" but before he can say anything more the radio goes dead. If the platoon commander decides that, not having received an intelligible command, he should do nothing until communications are restored, his decision will be wrong. The part of the message that was received indicates that his commander wanted him to continue with the attack, and almost certainly the commander would have preferred the lieutenant, as the man on the spot, to make his own decision on how to do this than to do nothing and let the attack fail. For the lieutenant to take the position that he should do nothing because he lacks a clear order would be an irresponsible "interpretation" of his captain's command.

Notice the forward-looking character of the interpretive method illustrated by my military example, compared with the backward-looking

11. Yet it is generally assumed that express statutory authorization is needed in order to confiscate the murderer's profits from writing a book about the murder. There is a difference, though, in the strength of the background norms: people occasionally murder in order to inherit, but no one murders in order to make money from writing about the murder.

character of the truth-serum, or mental-excavation, and plain-meaning approaches. There is a difference, if only in tone or attitude—but such differences can be important—between an interpretive approach that emphasizes fidelity to the past and one that emphasizes adaptation to the future (what is to be *done*?).[12] It is the difference between a traditionalist and a pragmatic approach to law. The pragmatist will recognize the aptness to statutory interpretation of W. H. Auden's description (in his poem "In Memory of W. B. Yeats") of the interpretation of a poem: "The words of a dead man / Are modified in the guts of the living." The plain-meaning approach to statutory interpretation excludes consideration of present-day conditions; the pragmatic approach views a statute as a resource for coping with the problems of the present, which is to say the statute's future. It makes no difference on the pragmatic account whether the text is superficially clear (that is, clear without regard to the world); unclear; or, as in the military example, patently incomplete (a particularly transparent form of unclarity).

American judges are frequently in the position of the platoon commander in my example. The legislature's commands are unclear and the judges cannot ask the legislators for clarification.[13] In that situation the judges should not think of themselves as failed archaeologists or antiquarians. They are part of a living enterprise—the enterprise of governing the United States—and when the orders of their superiors are unclear this does not absolve them from responsibility for helping to make the enterprise succeed. The responsible platoon commander will ask himself what his captain would have wanted him to do if communications should fail, and similarly judges should ask themselves, when the message imparted by a statute is unclear, what the legislature would have wanted them to do in such a case of failed communication. The answer may be "nothing"; or there may be no answer; but the question ought to be asked.

The military analogy, and the command theory of statutory interpretation that it supports, may seem to cast the legal process in too militaristic a light and thereby exalt obedience too far above other values—a

---

12. See T. Alexander Aleinikoff, "Updating Statutory Interpretation," 87 *Michigan Law Review* 20, 21–22 (1988).

13. In California, legislators can be called as witnesses to testify regarding the intended meaning of a statute. See Comment, "Statutory Interpretation in California: Individual Testimony as an Extrinsic Aid," 15 *University of San Francisco Law Review* 241 (1980). The danger is that a legislator may try to alter the statute by offering an interpretation that was or would have been rejected by a majority of the legislators when the statute was passed; the interpretation may not correspond to the legislature's current preferences either.

danger I warned against in Chapter 4. Actually the point of the analogy is virtually the reverse. *Even* in a system that is a model of deference, obedience, and hierarchy—the military—orders must at times be *interpreted,* which imposes on subordinates a duty of creativity and imagination.[14] But is "interpretation" a helpful term to describe what is going on here? The activity seems more like completion than translation; more like the division of labor between a remote superior and the man on the spot than the parsing of texts. The deeper point is that "interpretation" is a chameleon. When a performing musician "interprets" a work of music, is he expressing the composer's, or even the composition's, "meaning," or is he not rather expressing *himself* within the interstices of the score? Is the cy pres doctrine, whereby a charitable trust may because of changed conditions be diverted to a different purpose from that ordained by its creator (for example, a grant for research on tuberculosis converted into a grant for research on emphysema), rather than terminated and the trust corpus distributed to the testator's residuary legatees, interpretive in a fruitful sense?

The more one thinks about interpretation in general, the farther away one is carried from the important question concerning statutory interpretation, which is political rather than epistemic: how free *should* judges feel themselves to be from the fetters of text and legislative intent in applying statutes and the Constitution? From the fact that interpretation is a vague, encompassing, even boundless concept, it does not follow that judges should consider themselves to have carte blanche in interpreting statutory and constitutional provisions. Some "interpretivists" think that by insisting on the interpretive character of statutory and constitutional decision making they are arguing for judicial restraint. Not at all; the boundaries of interpretation are too elastic. Holmes's plain-meaning approach, like the truth-serum approach, truncates rather than defines the interpretive process, and can be justified if at all only on political and institutional, not on semantic or epistemic, grounds.

It might be better to discard the word "interpretation" altogether and speak instead in pragmatist fashion of the consequences of competing

14. So the subordinate should not be punished if it turns out that his interpretation did not coincide with his superior's intention. There may be a lesson for law: maybe government officials should not be held liable for the consequences of adopting one of several plausible interpretations of the statutes they are charged with administering. To some extent the lesson has been learned—witness the doctrines giving officials immunity from damages liability for good-faith interpretations of existing laws and requiring courts to defer to administrative interpretations of statutes, and the practice of indemnifying officials for their nonwillful statutory violations.

approaches to the judicial function in statutory and constitutional cases—the approach that stresses the judge's freedom versus the approach that stresses the judge's responsibility as a subordinate official in the scheme of government. I shall return to this suggestion in the next chapter.

A military organization is more homogeneous than a government, and this difference may seem to cut against the analogy I am exploring. Legislators and judges, unlike superior and subordinate military officers, may not share the same values—indeed, a statute may reflect nothing more exalted than the political muscle of an interest group that was able to obtain a legislative redistribution of wealth from a less well organized group. The common enterprise that judges are pledged to advance, however, is not a set of specific substantive values but the peaceable and orderly governance of the United States—a value too, of course, but one both widely shared and compatible with disagreement over specific policies. One element of the enterprise is the separation of powers, and its corollary—that judges must make a good-faith effort to effectuate legislation regardless of their agreement or disagreement with its means or ends. The position of the judges thus resembles that of military subordinates, who may or may not fully share the tactical or political goals of their superiors.

I am not arguing that the shared values of the judges and legislators can be used to decide difficult cases in a way that can be said to carry out the wishes of the legislators; my point is rather that the existence of shared values is a partial answer to criticisms that judicial creativity is inherently usurpative. Nor am I retracting my criticisms of the "pedigree" theory of interpretation (see Chapter 4). That is a theory for deciding cases in which the judges, having made a good-faith effort to interpret the statute or constitutional provision in question, come up empty. Few will question the judges' obligation to make that effort and, if it is fruitful, to abide by the result, save possibly for what I have described as a limited room to make civilizing interpretations. But if the effort does not bear fruit, the judge is on his own.

It can be argued that if the platoon commander cannot decode his superior's order he will just do what he thinks best, which a judge should not do. However, the platoon commander is a subordinate officer, and one of the things he is subordinate to is a body of doctrine. It is not for a lieutenant to decide what shall be the offensive doctrine of the United States Army. No more should a judge interpreting an unclear legislative text attempt to shape public policy to his personal conception of right and wrong—provided the policy of the statute is discernible.

But it may not be, or even if it is, it may not provide guidance to answering the specific interpretive question that has arisen. In law as in war, doctrine carries only so far.

A related objection to the military analogy is that the platoon commander has no time to consult his superiors. But it is much the same with judicial interpretation of statutes. The judges cannot consult the legislators, and lack the time, temperament, and training to conduct a full-fledged investigation of legislative background and purpose—the sort of investigation a professional historian or political scientist might conduct. A better criticism of the analogy is that the order to the judge, unlike the order to the lieutenant, is apt to be remote in time, making it more difficult for the judge to reconstruct the intention behind the order.[15]

The basic point of the military analogy survives all these criticisms. It is that even in a system more hierarchical and homogeneous than the judicial, interpretation is creative rather than mechanical. It is an effort to make sense of a situation (compare the interpretation of dreams), not just of a text or other communication. When confronting unclear statutes, judges, like junior officers confronting unclear commands, have to summon all their powers of imagination and empathy, in an effort—doomed to frequent failure—to place themselves in the position of the legislators who enacted the statute that they are being asked to interpret. They cannot only study plain meanings; they must try to understand the problem that the legislators faced.

This is the method of "imaginative reconstruction" introduced in Chapter 3.[16] It works splendidly with the statute in *Riggs;* how fitting that the majority opinion cited Aristotle, the inventor (or first expositor) of the method. The risk is that of making a statute appear to say what

15. See William N. Eskridge, Jr., "Spinning Legislative Supremacy" (unpublished paper, Georgetown University Law School).

16. Besides the references cited there, see Bedrich Baumann, *Imaginative Participation: The Career of an Organizing Concept in a Multidisciplinary Context,* ch. 7 (1975); and on the difficulties of the method, see, for example, David Boucher, "Conversation and Political Thought," 18 *New Literary History* 59 (1986); Hans-Georg Gadamer, *Truth and Method* (1975); E. D. Hirsch, Jr., "Meaning and Significance Reinterpreted," 11 *Critical Inquiry* 202 (1984). Notice that to the extent imaginative reconstruction works, it provides a practical antidote to the "other minds" skepticism discussed in Chapter 2 and also requires qualification of the anti-intentionality stance that I adopted in Chapter 5 in discussing criminal law. But only a modest qualification. For instead of asking what the legislators wanted or intended, we can ask what answer to the interpretive question would rationally promote the enterprise set on foot by the statute's enactment. Practically this is the same question, but it is in nonmentalist terms. (Recall in that chapter my nonmentalist construal of "purpose.")

the judges think it ought to say. Recall the age thirty-five provision, and suppose the judges were utterly convinced that it was an archaic, arbitrary, pernicious limitation on people's freedom to vote for the presidential candidates of their choice and that if the framers could be brought back to life and confronted with all the changes that have occurred since 1787— changes that include an expansion of the democratic principle (we now have direct election of the President and of Senators rather than indirect election of these officials, as in the original Constitution), a decline in reverence for authority based on age, and a more educated though perhaps not better informed electorate—they would agree that the age thirty-five provision ought to be interpreted flexibly. Bold as this interpretation would be, could it not be defended as consistent with the method of imaginative reconstruction and with my view of how *Locke* should have been decided? I think not. But my reasons are practical rather than semantic or historical or (in a narrow sense) "interpretive"—not only the need for certainty about the eligibility of candidates but, an even more practical and up-to-date consideration, the greater harm that the President can do in the nuclear age as opposed to the eighteenth century, which makes maturity a more important qualification for the office now than then, yet no easier to measure.

The danger that the line between interpretation and policy making will disappear altogether and that statutory interpretation will dissolve into common law is illustrated by the version of imaginative reconstruction proposed by Hart and Sacks (see Chapter 3). They want judges in interpreting a statute to assume that the legislators were reasonable persons intending reasonable results in the public interest. There are two ways to take this. One is that courts should refuse to enforce unreasonable enactments; this is the idea of the "civilizing" office of interpretation, but is almost certainly not what Hart and Sacks had in mind. The other is that the judge should do what he thinks best, confident that the legislators, being reasonable people like himself, would have wanted him to proceed thus. Particularly in the case of an old statute—as reasonable legislators would understand—the courts have the advantage of a body of experience that the legislators could not have taken into account in drafting the statute, because of the limitations of human foresight. Statutes in this view are more like precedents than like commands—tentative formulations of legal concepts that courts are free to revise on the basis of experience since enactment.

Something like this view was in fact urged by James Landis, a predecessor of Hart and Sacks in what might be called the school of "pro-

gressive formalism," and has been revived recently by Guido Calabresi.[17] One might say that Landis and Calabresi (especially the latter, for
Landis's emphasis is on the possible use of statutes as precedents in common law areas) want judges to be allowed to treat statutes as disrespect-
fully as they already treat previous cases. The view is latent in Aristotle,
in whom equitable interpretation and imaginative reconstruction
merge—a merger perhaps inevitable in anyone who, like Aristotle, Hart
and Sacks, Landis, and Calabresi, holds a public interest rather than
interest-group theory of legislation (see note 20).

Imaginative reconstruction so conceived sometimes works, especially
when the judge is dealing with public interest legislation such as the
wills statute in *Riggs*. Its abiding weakness is its patness. There is no
trick to putting yourself in Homer's shoes in an effort to understand the
Iliad (one of Vico's examples of imaginative reconstruction), *if* Homer
was just another reasonable guy, like you and me. It is no great trick to
put yourself in the shoes of the framers of the Constitution if the framers
differ from us only in that we know more, having the benefit of an
additional two centuries of history and a knowledge of today that they
of course lacked. But suppose we are realistic and acknowledge that the
framers were different from us, had different training, upbringing, and
experiences and therefore different values. Then we have the impossible
task of imagining how they would decide a question arising today if
they knew what we know. It is impossible not only in practice but in
theory. People are what they are, have the values they have, and so forth
not only because of temperament but also because of what they know
through experience and study; they are historically situated. If the framers had known what we know, they might have had different values
from those they in fact had. Clones of Hamilton, Madison, and the
other framers, if living today, might think better or worse of federalism,
fundamental rights, religion, and sexual license than their originals did.

Here is a homely illustration of the limitations of imaginative reconstruction. I have invited a friend for dinner at 7:30, and I want to know
whether he will be on time. It's unlikely that I will try, or would succeed
if I did try, to imagine myself him; instead I will use induction from his
record of promptness or tardiness on other occasions to estimate
whether he will be early or late (and if so by how much) this time.[18]
Induction is full of pitfalls, but imaginative reconstruction has even

17. See James M. Landis, "Statutes and the Sources of Law," in *Harvard Legal Essays* 213
(Roscoe Pound ed. 1934); Guido Calabresi, *A Common Law for the Age of Statutes* (1982).
18. Cf. Gilbert Ryle, *The Concept of Mind* 92 (1949).

more. The situation is much the same when statutory interpretation is viewed as a problem in predicting how the legislators would have responded to the interpretive question presented by the case at hand. Usually it will be infeasible for the judge to imagine himself the legislator (in part, of course, because he would have to imagine himself the whole legislature), and he will be remitted to induction. But this will be induction from the past behavior not of friends but of legislators—people the judge probably does not know personally or even know much about—and will be a daunting task.

Statutes passed at a time when women were not eligible to vote often provided that jurors were to be selected from lists of persons eligible to vote. When women get the vote, do they become eligible for jury duty?[19] The legislators who voted for these statutes probably did not think that women should serve on juries. If we say that were they living today they would have a different view, we are changing them into different people—ourselves—and this is always a danger with imaginative reconstruction. We could take the following tack: the apparent *purpose* of the statutes was to tie juror eligibility to voter eligibility, thus ensuring minimum qualifications without the bother of establishing and enforcing separate criteria for jurors. As criteria for voting eligibility change, the criteria for jury eligibility change automatically. The legislators' streamlined approach to determining eligibility for jury duty would be thwarted if every change in the criteria for voting eligibility drove a wedge between those criteria and the criteria for jury eligibility. But if we are to be faithful to legislative purpose, we would have to consider how strongly the legislators opposed the idea of women's serving on juries. Did they feel so strongly on this subject—in enacting a statute not directed at the issue of women on juries at all—as to want to project their feelings into a future era in which the social role of women had changed? That seems unlikely. But perhaps this sort of counterfactual speculation is bootless, and should be avoided altogether.

Against purposive interpretation it can be further argued that statutes are often the result of a compromise between contending factions or interest groups,[20] and purposive interpretation can easily undo a com-

19. Compare Commonwealth v. Maxwell, 271 Pa. 378, 114 Atl. 825 (1921), holding that they do, with People ex rel. Fyfe v. Barnett, 319 Ill. 403, 150 N.E. 290 (1926), and Commonwealth v. Welosky, 276 Mass. 398, 177 N.E. 656 (1931), holding that they do not.

20. The interest-group theory of legislation, and its bearing on statutory interpretation, are the subject of a vast scholarly literature in law, economics, and political science. See,

promise. Suppose the legislature has enacted a statute forbidding some form of securities fraud but has failed to authorize persons injured by a violation of the statute to bring damages suits against violators; and suppose it is demonstrable that there would be greater compliance with the statute if such suits were possible. Should we say that the purpose of the statute would be served by interpreting the statute to authorize them? The omission of any statutory reference to damages suits may have been the price the statute's supporters had to pay in order to assemble a majority in the face of doubts about the statute's wisdom, pressures from securities firms, or whatever. If so, the purposive interpretation would give one of the contending factions a benefit it had been unable to win in the legislative arena. We must also consider what the legislators knew about how courts treat statutes that do not mention damages actions. Suppose they had no idea, maybe because courts were not consistent in their treatment. This would imply that rather than striking a compromise on whether damages actions would be allowed, the legislators had left the question to the courts.

The alternative to purposive interpretation is to attempt to ascertain the deal embodied in the statute and enforce that deal. But since the deal is likely to be under the table, how is the court to determine its terms? Contracts are deals, too, but they set on foot a cooperative activity, and often it is apparent what interpretation is necessary to protect or promote that activity. A legislative deal may simply be a wealth transfer to an interest group, and it may be impossible to discover by the methods available to judges whether the transfer seems incomplete because that was as far as the deal went or because the legislators merely failed, through lack of foresight, to provide for the contingency that has arisen. It does not seem that *all* legislation is of this character, but it is exceptionally difficult for courts to determine whether they are dealing with an unprincipled deal that has no spirit to guide interpretation, with a statute that was passed in the public interest and ought to receive a generous, a purposive, interpretation, or finally with a statute that was

---

for example, Arthur F. Bentley, *The Process of Government: A Study of Social Pressures* (1908); David B. Truman, *The Governmental Process: Political and Public Opinion* (1951); James M. Buchanan and Gordon Tullock, *The Calculus of Consent: Logical Foundations of Constitutional Democracy* (1962); George J. Stigler, *The Citizen and the State: Essays on Regulation* (1975); Gary S. Becker, "Pressure Groups and Political Behavior," in *Capitalism and Democracy: Schumpeter Revisited* 120 (Richard D. Coe and Charles K. Wilbur eds. 1985); "Symposium on the Theory of Public Choice," 74 *Virginia Law Review* 167 (1988).

passed in the public interest but contains limitations included at the behest of powerful interest groups—limitations that were the price of getting the statute passed.[21] Judges are tempted to ignore such limitations, but if they do, this may make it difficult for such statutes to get passed in the future. And judges would cause an uproar if they refused to enforce a statute whose purpose was clearly discernible on the ground that the statute, though constitutional, reflected an unprincipled deal with some special-interest group and therefore was unworthy of being enforced.

The "deals" approach can be tucked into the purposive approach by noting that the relevant purpose is not that of the faction that was pushing the legislation but that of the enactment itself with any compromises that may have been built into it. But this is one of these semantic reconciliations that gives no satisfaction to the practically minded. Purposive interpretation is useless if the purposes cannot be discerned, and the presence of compromise makes the discernment of purpose difficult and often impossible. Notice, finally, the attraction of the deals approach to the legal positivist: brisk and confident judicial enforcement of the nakedly, amorally redistributive statute exemplifies the separation of law and morals.

Indeterminate Statutory Cases

When imaginative reconstruction fails, when purposive interpretation fails, or when these techniques reveal simply that the matter in question has been left to the courts to decide according to their own lights, statutory interpretation is transformed into judicial policy making, and the usual problems of judicial objectivity arise. This helps explain the enduring appeal of the plain-meaning approach; it avoids the uncertainties of interpretation. But it does so at a high price: that of refusing to take seriously the communicative intent, and broader purposes alike, of the legislators in the many cases in which that intent can be discerned, and of refusing to play a constructive role in the development of sound public policies in the remaining cases.

---

21. The general point has been well stated by the Supreme Court: "No legislation pursues its purposes at all costs. Deciding what competing values will or will not be sacrificed to the achievement of a particular objective is the very essence of legislative choice—and it frustrates rather than effectuates legislative intent simplistically to assume that *whatever* furthers the statute's primary objective must be the law." Rodriguez v. United States, 480 U.S. 522 (1987) (per curiam). Unfortunately, the Court rather spoils things by relying heavily in the same opinion on canons of construction whose artificiality is in stark contrast to the realism of the passage just quoted.

In the first two eventualities with which I began this section (cases of interpretive failure, one might call them), we have no clue to what the legislature wanted, and in the third one we know or think we know that it wanted the judges to make up their own minds. So the last is a matter of delegation and might be thought to vest the courts with common law rule-making powers, while the first two raise questions of legitimacy—who has authorized the courts to decide statutory cases when the meaning of the statute is unknown? But practically the three cases are the same. The fact that a legislature is unable to resolve a policy issue, such as whether a particular statute should be enforceable by suits for damages, does not warrant an inference that it *wanted* the courts to resolve it or that the courts should accept the role of supplementary legislature. The legislature may have had neither desire nor opinion as to whether the courts should try to close the gaps and dispel the ambiguities in its handiwork. Whether a gap in legislation arises because the legislators lacked foresight or because they were unable to agree on how to close the gap or because they lacked the time to deal with the question or because they just did not care does not dictate what attitude the courts should take toward the gap. Cases where legislatures explicitly delegate policy-making tasks to courts are rare, so the difference between the accidental and the deliberate gap has little practical significance. In either case the court must decide whether to fill it. If it does fill it, the court will be exercising the kind of discretion that a common law court uses to decide a question not ruled by precedent.

Efforts have been under way for centuries to resist this conclusion and establish that meaningful interpretation is possible in every statutory or constitutional case; the efforts have failed and the problem remains. The plain-meaning rule and the other "canons of construction" are the subject of a large and, on the whole, negative literature.[22] The soundest criticism is not that the canons are wrong, although some are, including some of the most innocuous-seeming.[23] It is that they are just a list of relevant considerations, at best of modest utility. They are things to bear

---

22. See references and discussion in William N. Eskridge, Jr., and Philip P. Frickey, *Cases and Materials on Legislation: Statutes and the Creation of Public Policy,* ch. 7 (1988).

23. For example, that the court should start with the words of the statute. See, for example, International Brotherhood of Teamsters v. Daniel, 439 U.S. 551, 558 (1979). Before one can make sense out of the words of a text one needs not only a basic linguistic competence (the canon can be understood to assume that much) but an extensive cultural competence, illustrated by the discussion of the latent ambiguities of the age thirty-five provision. This point is well recognized in the literature on literacy training. See, for example, George A. Miller, "The Challenge of Universal Literacy," 241 *Science,* Sept. 9, 1988, at 1293.

in mind: don't invalidate a statute if a saving construction is possible, don't lightly assume that by passing a new statute the legislature inadvertently repealed a previous one, don't ignore surrounding provisions, don't (the valid core of the plain-meaning rule) be too quick to override the apparent meaning, and so on. There are a vast number of canons,[24] corresponding to the vast number of considerations that come into play (often unconsciously) when one is reading. Cautionary rather than directive, often pulling in opposite directions[25] like their counterparts, the maxims of ordinary life ("haste makes waste," but "he who hesitates is lost"), the canons are the collective folk wisdom of statutory interpretation and they no more enable difficult questions of interpretation to be answered than the maxims of everyday life enable the difficult problems of everyday living to be solved.

Many of the canons are not interpretive at all, in the sense of helping a court figure out what the legislature meant. Instead they establish presumptions, based on substantive policy, for resolving indeterminate statutory cases. Examples are the canon that statutes waiving sovereign immunity are to be narrowly construed and the canon that statutes regulating Indian affairs are to be construed in favor of the Indians. Such canons[26] cannot be defended by reference to concepts of interpretation. Substantive political principles used to decide cases when interpretation fails, they are an acknowledgment of the impossibility of resolving all statutory questions interpretively. The substantive canons are less powerful than constitutional principles because they can be overridden by a clear statute. But their provenance is more suspect than that of constitutional principles because there is no text in the picture. They are a federal common law of statutes, and the federal judiciary has traditionally been hesitant to assert common law powers. The pedigree of these substantive canons is therefore deficient, but this means only that their justification, if any, is political and pragmatic—that they conduce to better results than would an uncanonized approach.

A pair of examples will indicate the depth of the problem of indeterminate statutory interpretation. The first also illustrates the limitations of canons of construction.

In 1862 Congress made a land grant to the Union Pacific Railroad to induce the railroad to build a transcontinental line. The land was divided

---

24. F. A. R. Bennion, *Statutory Interpretation: Codified, with a Critical Commentary* (1984), lists 396 principles of statutory interpretation.

25. See Karl N. Llewellyn, *The Common Law Tradition: Deciding Appeals* 521–535 (1960).

26. As emphasized in Cass R. Sunstein, *After the Rights Revolution: Constitutional Government and the Regulatory State* (1990).

into checkerboard sections, each a square mile in size, and the odd–numbered sections were given to the railroad and the even-numbered ones retained by the government. The construction of the line was expected to increase the value of the adjacent lands, and the railroad and the government would divide the increment evenly. *Leo Sheep Co. v. United States*[27] arose more than a century after the grant. Successors in interest to the Union Pacific owned land that blocked access to a reservoir owned by the government. The government wanted to build an access road to the reservoir and argued that Congress had implicitly reserved an easement of access when it granted the land to the Union Pacific back in 1862. The Supreme Court disagreed, which is fine, but pretended that it was doing so on interpretive grounds, which in the circumstances was disingenuous.

The opinion notes that the grant contains several specific reservations to the government, such as a reservation of mineral rights, and "given the existence of such explicit exceptions, this Court has in the past refused to add to this list by divining some 'implicit' congressional intent" (p. 679). Although the Court does not explain why the existence of explicit exceptions should negate an implicit one, it must be alluding to the well-known canon of construction that *expressio unius est exclusio alterius*—the expression of one thing is the exclusion of another. Level of detail can be a clue to meaning, so the canon is not completely sense less. However, a legislature might create an exception to a general grant without thereby wanting to prevent the courts from recognizing additional exceptions, unforeseen at the time of enactment, that would be consistent with the grant's purposes. So, like most canons of construction, *expressio unius* has a weak bite.

Next the Court addresses the argument that all the government wants is an easement of necessity, and since such an easement would be implied in any private conveyance of real estate (if you sell the land that surrounds your house but retain the house, you retain by implication a right of access to the house), it should also be implied in a public one. The Court's first reply is that "whatever right of passage a private landowner might have, it is not at all clear that it would include a right to construct a road for public access to a recreational area" (id.). To say a proposition is not at all clear is not to say it is false, yet without attempting to demonstrate its falsity the Court changes the subject and observes that "the easement is not actually a matter of necessity in this case because the Government has the power of eminent domain" (pp. 679–

27. 440 U.S. 668 (1979). Subsequent page references to the opinion appear in the text.

680), which a private landowner (unless a railroad or utility) would not have. Unremarked is the difference between having a right of free access and having to pay the fair market value of the land required for the access.

The Court points out that some states do not recognize easements of necessity in favor of the government and that others have abolished the doctrine in favor of giving all owners of surrounded lands the power of eminent domain. The Court makes no effort to connect these recent developments with either the Congress or the common law of 1862, but instead veers off and remarks that "we do not find the tenuous relevance of the common-law doctrine of ways of necessity sufficient to overcome the inference prompted by the omission of any reference to the reserved right asserted by the Government in this case" (p. 681). The inference appears to be derived solely from the *expressio unius* canon. Next the Court says, "It is possible that Congress gave the problem of access little thought; but it is at least as likely that the thought which was given focused on negotiation, reciprocity considerations, and the power of eminent domain as obvious devices for ameliorating disputes" (p. 681, footnote omitted). So it's a standoff. The Court hasn't a clue regarding what if anything Congress thought about the problem of access.

The Court confronts an objection based on "the familiar canon of construction that, when grants to federal lands are at issue, any doubts are 'resolved for the Government, not against it'" (p. 682). This objection illustrates one of the standard problems with the canons of construction—there are so many of them that often one finds canons tugging both ways in the same case, and they are very difficult to weigh against each other.[28] The Court rejects the public-land-grants canon on the ground that "this Court long ago declined to apply this canon in its full vigor to grants under the Railroad Acts" (p. 682). No reason is given for this rejection except the authority of two very old decisions (pp. 682–683); the Court neglects to mention that the canon had recently been applied to the very grant at issue in *Leo Sheep*.[29]

---

28. The canons' tendency to trip over each other is illustrated by this passage from United States v. Hurt, 795 F.2d 765, 770 (9th Cir. 1986): "In construing a statute, we must first look to the plain language used by Congress. If the language of the statute is unambiguous, it is conclusive unless there is a 'clearly expressed legislative intention to the contrary . . .' Although we are aware of the rule of strict construction for criminal statutes, that rule does not allow us to ignore a statute's evident purpose."

29. In United States v. Union Pacific R. R., 353 U.S. 112 (1957). The old cases are United States v. Denver & Rio Grande R. Co., 150 U.S. 1 (1893) (see id. at 14), and Winona & St. Peter R. v. Barney, 113 U.S. 618 (1885).

Apart from repeated allusions to the *expressio unius* canon, the Court spends all its time batting down the government's arguments rather than making a case for its own interpretation until, at the very end of the opinion, it says that "we are unwilling to upset settled expectations to accommodate some ill-defined power to construct public thoroughfares without compensation" (pp. 687–688, footnote omitted). This is whistling in the dark. The opinion has discussed no evidence of settled expectations. There is no reason to think the power claimed by the government would be any more "ill defined" than the common law easement of necessity. The suggestion that the government wants to build its access road without compensating the owners of the underlying land begs the question, since if the government is correct the owners never obtained the property right that they are demanding compensation for surrendering.

I am just carping, in a sense, because I have no idea how the case should have been decided. It is true that the government does not need an easement as much as a landlocked private owner would need one, because the power of eminent domain protects the government against being "held up" for more than the market value of the land it wants. Yet it seems doubtful that the Congress of 1862 would have countenanced a situation in which government land might be blockaded by the recipients of congressional largesse, albeit the blockade could always be lifted by paying the market value of the necessary easement. Still, it was a time when legislatures handed out all sorts of goodies to railroads. It was also during the Civil War, when the government may have been especially eager to enlist the aid of railroads in projects of national unification and may have been willing to pay a high price. When in irremediable doubt about the meaning of a statute, maybe the court should rule against the party invoking the statute—but who was that here, the landowners relying on the congressional grant or the government, which contended that the grant contains an implied exception?

Here is a better-known example of an indeterminate statutory case. Kaiser Aluminum and Chemical Corporation owned a plant in Louisiana at which fewer than 2 percent of the skilled craftworkers were black, even though the work force in the area was almost 40 percent black. Kaiser agreed with the union representing the plant's skilled craftworkers to reserve for blacks half the places in a training program for filling craft openings. Weber, a white worker excluded from the program because the quota for blacks left no room for him, brought suit under Title VII of the Civil Rights Act of 1964, claiming that he had been discriminated against on account of his race. He lost.[30] Yet his argument was a powerful one. The statute forbids employers and unions "controlling apprenticeship or other training or retraining, including on-the-job training programs[,] to discriminate against any individual because of his race"—whatever that race might be, for the Court had held in an earlier case that discrimination against whites was covered. Although Kaiser had not been acting out of hostility to the white race, the statutory term "discriminate . . . because of his race" apparently just means "treat unfavorably because of his race"—not treat unfavorably because of his race in order to hurt him rather than merely to help someone else. For elsewhere the statute makes it an unlawful practice "to fail or refuse to hire or to discharge any individual, or *otherwise* to discriminate against" him (emphasis added), and this implies that "discriminate" means treat adversely, not adversely *and* invidiously. This is further suggested by the statutory defense for cases where religion, sex, or national origin "is a bona fide occupational qualification reasonably necessary to the normal operation of" the employer; this defense would be unnecessary if the discrimination, to be actionable, had to be invidious. (But statutes are frequently redundant.) Another provision states that nothing in the statute "shall be interpreted to require any employer . . . to grant preferential treatment to any individual or to any group because of the race . . . of such individual or group on account of an imbalance which may exist with respect to the total number or percentage of persons of any race . . . employed by any employer . . . in comparison with the total number or percentage of persons of such race . . . in the available work force." The statute's supporters had assured opponents and fence sitters that it would not empower courts or enforcement agencies to impose racial quotas; the purpose of the statute was to create equality of opportunity rather than of results.

The problem with all this evidence in favor of Weber is that it can be sidestepped by observing that Congress in 1964 never considered the possible application of the statute to voluntary private efforts by white employers (or employers controlled by white people, as Kaiser surely was and is) to promote employment of blacks. The problem at that time was discrimination against blacks, not in favor of them. The legislature did foresee the possibility that impatient courts or enforcement agencies would use racial quotas to advance the goals of the statute, and made clear that it did not want them to do this merely on grounds of racial

30. United Steelworkers of America v. Weber, 443 U.S. 193 (1979). The statute is 42 U.S.C. §2000e.

imbalance, as distinct from doing so as a remedy for violations of the statute. But apparently it did not foresee the possibility that an employer would adopt such quotas voluntarily.

Since textual arguments can be traps, the fact that the affirmative action practiced by Kaiser and the union is embraced by the semantics of Title VII does not compel a conclusion that the statute prohibits the practice. Anyway, the textual arguments in *Weber* are not as one-sided as I have implied. The statutory proviso against a court's compelling affirmative action except as a remedy for discrimination would be unnecessary if, but for the proviso, the statute prohibited nonremedial affirmative action. "Otherwise to discriminate" could refer to the form (that is, other than to fire or fail to hire) rather than to the purpose (that is, whether individuous or benign) of the discrimination. And the exception for the use of sex, religion, or national origin when it is a bona-fide occupational qualification could be thought to support a distinction between deliberate and incidental discrimination: between wanting to exclude blacks—or whites—or women, or whomever, and excluding them as the incidental consequence of favoring another group on non-invidious grounds. It could be argued that only the first type of discrimination requires the discriminator to establish a bona-fide occupational qualification, and that the second is not even a prima facie violation of the statute.

In the absence of Title VII, an employer could discriminate in favor of blacks all he wanted. It seems odd to use a statute whose primary purpose was to benefit blacks as a weapon against them, although it can be argued that they must take the bitter with the sweet, and the argument is supported by the generality of the statutory definition of discrimination. A further point, however, is that the imbalance between the percentage of black craftworkers at Kaiser's plant and the percentage of black workers in the area's skilled work force, coupled with the long history of discrimination against blacks by craft unions, made Kaiser and the union likely targets for investigation and complaint on grounds of discriminating against blacks. In this light the affirmative action plan becomes a prudent measure of anticipatory compliance. Did Congress mean to forbid *this* back in 1964, and thereby place employers on a razor's edge?

10 ☙

How to Decide Statutory
and Constitutional Cases

So finely balanced are the competing interpretive arguments in *United Steelworkers v. Weber* that one's judgment on whether the case was decided correctly is bound to turn on whether one thinks affirmative action good (for blacks, for the nation) or bad. Recognition of this point seems implicit in Bernard Meltzer's powerful attack on the decision, for he criticizes the Supreme Court not only for misreading the statute but also (as implied by the title of his essay) for failing to appreciate that affirmative action may undermine rather than assist the civil rights movement.[1] A case like *Weber* cannot be decided by some neutral method of interpretation; it cries out for a political or ethical judgment. Ronald Dworkin for one has answered the cry; he argues that affirmative action can be justified by the concept of equality.[2] His argument both illustrates the difficulty of resolving—"circumventing" might be the better word—questions of interpretation on substantive (that is, policy) grounds and affords a glimpse of the sorts of question examined below in Part IV. Dworkin's approach attempts to do at retail what the substantive canons of construction mentioned in the last chapter attempt to do at wholesale: shift the plane of analysis from how to extract the meaning that the legislators may be said to have put into the statute to how to impart the politically or ethically best meaning.

Dworkin begins by imagining a disappointed white law-school appli-

1. See Bernard D. Meltzer, "The *Weber* Case: The Judicial Abrogation of the Antidiscrimination Standard in Employment," 47 *University of Chicago Law Review* 423, 457–458 (1980).

2. See *Taking Rights Seriously*, ch. 9 (1977). Although Dworkin later wrote an essay on the *Weber* case itself, see Ronald Dworkin, *A Matter of Principle*, ch. 16 (1985), that essay is not about the pros and cons of affirmative action. It is concerned with establishing, through a close examination of the majority and dissenting opinions in *Weber*, the indeterminacy of

cant who charges that the school "violated his individual right of equality for the sake of a policy of greater equality overall" and thereby raises the question "what rights to equality do citizens have as individuals which might defeat programs aimed at important economic and social policies, including the social policy of improving equality overall?"[3] One might have thought that whether affirmative action, even if it does increase the average income or social status of blacks, thereby increases "equality overall" would depend on the meaning of equality. But Dworkin does not attempt to define the word. He *assumes* that the "social policy of improving equality overall" has and should have reference to equality of results across races rather than to other concepts of equality, such as equality of opportunity, which was Kant's sense of equality,[4] or distribution according to merit, which as we shall see in Chapter 11 was Aristotle's.

Dworkin distinguishes two "rights to equality" that the disappointed white applicant might assert in opposition to the "social policy of improving equality overall." One is the right to equal treatment. But there is no "right to equal treatment in the assignment of law school places . . . Legal education is not so vital that everyone has an equal right to it" (p. 227). Dworkin believes there are equal rights only to *really* important things, such as voting, and not to professional or employment opportunities as well, although if this is so it undermines the case for affirmative action. The second right to equality that the white applicant might invoke is "the right to *treatment as an equal*": "If I have two children, and one is dying from a disease that is making the other uncomfortable, I do not show equal concern if I flip a coin to decide which should have the remaining dose of a drug" (id.). So the right to treatment as an equal is just a right not to be treated callously or arbitrarily, and again the white applicant loses.

By defining rights to equality narrowly, Dworkin has knocked out the white applicant but at the same time has gravely weakened the argument against discriminating *in favor of* whites. Although he says that

---

that case as a matter of ordinary interpretation, leading him to propose the following decision procedure: "One justification for a statute is better than another, and provides the better direction for coherent development of the statute, if it provides a more accurate or more sensitive or sounder analysis of the underlying moral principles." Id. at 328–329. Dworkin's analysis of *Weber* thus sets the stage for applying to Title VII the moral analysis of affirmative action that he had presented in *Taking Rights Seriously*.

3. *Taking Rights Seriously,* note 2 above, at 226–227. Subsequent page references are in the text.

4. See Bruce Aune, *Kant's Theory of Morals* 160 (1979).

"any form of segregation that disadvantages blacks is, in the United States, an automatic insult to them, and . . . offends their right to be treated as equals" (p. 238), this confident assertion is belied by his example of what treatment as an equal requires. If the dying child could not be helped by the remaining dose while the less seriously ill child could be, then giving the drug to the latter would not violate the former's right to treatment as an equal. If all the right to equal treatment means is that individuals should not be subjected to heartless and capricious impositions, the right of a black person to treatment as an equal depends on whether proponents of segregation are able to give plausible reasons for the practice, a question Dworkin does not examine (possibly because he assumes that his readers will agree that there are no such reasons). His concept of equality is equivocal, undeveloped, and surprisingly narrow.[5]

Dworkin also tries to distinguish between discrimination against and in favor of blacks by distinguishing "personal preferences" from "external preferences" (pp. 234–235, 275). An individual's personal preference is a preference to have something, his external preference a preference that others have or not have something. If I want a higher income, that is a personal preference, but if I think blacks should be kept out of public schools because they are inferior to whites, that is an external preference and government action pursuant to it would violate the right to treatment as an equal. But this gambit is unsuccessful, because most external preferences are at bottom internal. If I want to keep blacks out of the public schools because I think my children will get a better education or be safer or happier in an all-white school, I am expressing an internal preference. Not all those people who move to lily-white suburbs are racists in Dworkin's sense.

If this example is representative, it is doubtful that political or moral philosophy will resolve the statutory and constitutional cases that interpretation cannot resolve. That makes the search for some overarching principle for dealing with the interpretively indeterminate statutory or constitutional case an urgent one, but so far it has turned up nothing satisfactory. One of the most interesting suggestions is that of Frank Easterbrook, whose "pedigree" theory of judicial legitimacy we encountered in Chapter 4; his theory of statutory and constitutional interpretation is an application of the pedigree theory. He proposes to classify all statutes in two categories: those that tell the courts to create common

5. See Jules L. Coleman, Book Review (of *Taking Rights Seriously*), 66 *California Law Review* 885, 915–918 (1978).

law doctrine (he instances the Sherman Act, which in his view is a directive to the courts to create a common law of antitrust), and those that contain no such delegation. The latter are to be strictly construed against the party to a lawsuit who seeks an advantage from them. The proposal, in short, is to declare "legislation inapplicable unless it either expressly addresses the matter or commits the matter to the common law."[6] Often, however, it is unclear which party is the one seeking an advantage from the statute (a problem in *Leo Sheep* but also in *Weber*—for Weber was relying on one part of the statute, and Kaiser and the union on other parts). And few statutes contain a delegation of common law authority to courts. The Sherman Act is not one of them. The Act makes it a crime to agree, conspire, or combine to restrain trade or to monopolize, attempt to monopolize, or conspire to monopolize. The term "restraint of trade" has a common law meaning, but it does not follow that Congress meant the term to become a judicial plaything; indeed, by making "*every* contract, combination in the form of trust or otherwise, or conspiracy, in restraint of trade or commerce . . . illegal,"[7] Congress may have been trying to limit rather than to confer judicial discretion.[8] At all events, deciding that the Sherman Act is on the common law side of the divide does not guarantee objectivity of results.

6. Frank H. Easterbrook, "Statutes' Domains," 50 *University of Chicago Law Review* 533, 552 (1983).

7. Sherman Act, §1, 15 U.S.C. §1 (emphasis added). "The Sherman Act passed by the 1890 Congress was a statute containing real policy choices rather than the open-ended delegation to the courts ascribed by the conventional wisdom." Thomas C. Arthur, "Workable Antitrust Law: The Statutory Approach to Antitrust," 62 *Tulane Law Review* 1163, 1171–1172 (1988). Nevertheless, as noted in Chapter 1, the Sherman Act deals with problems—monopolization and cartelization—about which we have learned a great deal in the century since the Act was passed. Maybe Congress should be understood to have wanted the courts to use evolving knowledge to make the statute work better. This is no more than plausible, but a pragmatist judge will feel free to adopt the socially preferable interpretation of a statute when the choice is open.

8. This is a good example of the limitations of Holmes's "normal English speaker" approach. In the common law, "restraint of trade" had a clear meaning: it was a covenant not to compete, a type of contract routinely made as an incident to the sale of a business or the formation of a partnership. By making "every" contract in restraint of trade illegal, the Sherman Act seemed to be forbidding all such covenants. That would have been absurd, however; so, as Justice Stevens has explained with unusual candor for a judge, the courts interpreted the Act as if the word "unreasonable" appeared before "restraint of trade." *National Society of Professional Engineers v. United States*, 435 U.S. 679, 687–688 (1978). This was a bolder form of interpretation than if the dissent in *Locke* had prevailed. Yet Easterbrook both believes that *Locke* was decided correctly and accepts Holmes's plain-meaning view of interpretation. See Frank H. Easterbrook, "The Role of Original Intent in Statutory Construction," 11 *Harvard Journal of Law and Public Policy* 59, 62, 65 (1988).

The heart of Easterbrook's proposal is that courts are to give statutes that do not delegate rule-making power to the courts no effect outside of those factual situations "expressly addressed" by the legislature. There are three (not entirely mutually exclusive) ways to take this. The first is as a variant of Holmes's "normal English speaker" approach: the factual situation must be encompassed by the words of the statute as understood when the statute was passed. Weber might win his case; so too the women jurors; but wiretapping would not be within the scope of the Fourth Amendment. The second way to take the suggestion is that the situation must be encompassed by the words as they are understood today, regardless of what the legislators may have meant by them. But this approach, by ignoring the problem of external ambiguity, can create weird semantic traps, equivalent to supposing that "the gay nineties" refers to a period of homosexual ascendancy or the Nonintercourse Act to celibacy.

The third possibility, which seems to be the one Easterbrook intends, is that unless the judges can say (by a plain-meaning analysis?) that the legislature answered the interpretive question, the statute will be deemed inapplicable to the case. In other words, statutes other than those that delegate rule-making or policy-making powers to courts should be narrowly construed. But why? The answer can have nothing to do with interpretation viewed as a prepolitical practice—cannot be implicit in the meaning of "interpretation," given the breadth and ambiguity of the word—but must instead be political in character. This is further demonstrated by the arguments that Easterbrook makes in defense of his suggested approach. He refers to the constitutionally built-in limitations of the legislative process (for example, the President's veto power, bicameralism, the committee system, the requirement of majority vote), which are circumvented if judges allow themselves to interpret the spirit (when it has a spirit) as well as the letter of a statute.[9] There is something to this; for courts would not enforce an unenacted measure, no matter how convincing the evidence that a majority of the legislators had supported it and, if only time had permitted, would have voted for it. Yet the framers of the Constitution, although concerned with legislative excesses, did not seek to curb them by making legislation expire with the enacting Congress, as much legislation would if its domain of application were limited to the definitions understood by, or the mental pictures held by, the legislators who voted for it. Moreover, Easterbrook would allow the limitations on the leg-

9. See "Statutes' Domains," note 6 above, at 548–549.

islative power to be got round by the delegation, explicit and even implicit (usually, indeed, implicit), to the courts of the power to make common law—and "implicit delegation" is a euphemism for no legislative guidance, since all it means is that by drafting a statute in general terms the legislators have perforce given it a broad *potential* scope, thereby expanding the range of judicial choice.[10] At this point the chain of title that connects the judicial decision to the legislative decision is seriously corroded.

If a court is reasonably sure what the legislators were driving at (though often it will not be—in *Weber,* for example), a refusal to give effect to their purposes because they did not dot every *i* and cross every *t* is defensible only if one has some principled objection to legislation in general.[11] So one is not surprised to find that Easterbrook also defends his suggested approach by reference to the political principle of limited government. "There is *still* at least a presumption that people's arrangements prevail unless expressly displaced by legal doctrine."[12] Some of us may wish there were still such a presumption, but to say there is one, in the closing years of the twentieth century, is wishful thinking. Anyway, the point is not whether Easterbrook's political theory is right or wrong; it is that like everyone else he is forced to defend an interpretive theory on noninterpretive grounds.

The point is general. The interpretation of statutes is highly sensitive to theories of the legislative process,[13] and these are controversial political theories and hence do not provide sure footing for judicial decisions. Those who believe that legislatures embody the popular will and who venerate popular democracy are likely to attach great weight to any indications of how a majority of the legislature might have answered the

10. See Charles P. Curtis, "A Better Theory of Legal Interpretation," 3 *Vanderbilt Law Review* 407, 425–426 (1950).

11. "The major premise of the conclusion expressed in a statute, the change of policy that induces the enactment, may not be set out in terms, but it is not an adequate discharge of duty for courts to say: We see what you are driving at, but you have not said it, and therefore we shall go on as before." Johnson v. United States, 163 Fed. 30, 32 (1st Cir. 1908) (Holmes, J.). This statement by Holmes is both inconsistent with, and more persuasive than, his "normal English speaker" approach.

12. "Statutes' Domains," note 6 above, at 549. I have italicized the word "still" to indicate that Easterbrook apparently considers the political concepts of today pertinent to interpretation. And properly so. The framers themselves may well have believed in a presumption in favor of private ordering and minimum government, but it is unclear to what extent they wanted the presumption to govern the remote future.

13. See, for a persuasive demonstration, Michael Froomkin, "The Sound of One House Clapping: Courts, Legislative Acquiescence, and Democratic Theory" (unpublished paper, July 21, 1988).

interpretive question that has arisen. Those who regard the impediments to the legislative process as salutary checks on the excesses of democracy are likely to be distrustful of any expressions of legislative preference that have not run the gauntlet. There is no basis in law—maybe no basis, period, in current political theory—for choosing between these positions. "Interpretation" is not foundational; it sits uneasily on shifting political foundations.

As a further illustration consider Cass Sunstein's proposal, alluded to in Chapter 9 (note 26), for using frankly substantive canons of construction, such as the principle that statutes should be construed in favor of American Indians and other minorities, to decide close cases. These canons would operate as presumptions merely and therefore could be overridden not only by evidence of legislative purpose but also by the legislature itself, which could both reject any canons it did not like and amend any statute to change an interpretation it did not like. Commendable both for its acknowledgment that ordinary interpretation will not resolve all cases and its quest for publicly stated, neutrally applied principles to resolve them in lieu of leaving resolution to ad hoc decision on undisclosed, perhaps idiosyncratic or even invidious grounds, Sunstein's proposal is in effect that judges create in common law fashion substantive rules, standards, or presumptions for answering questions that are raised by statutes but that legislatures have failed to supply adequate materials for answering. There is no pretense that judges and legislators have the same values.

The difference between "real" common law and statutory common law à la Sunstein is that the former is rooted in policies that command a broad if incomplete social consensus, such as corrective justice and efficiency (see Chapters 11 and 12), while the latter is bound to draw on a more contested and problematic set of values, as does legislation itself. The idea that statutes should be interpreted to favor a particular minority or to promote a host of other values that Sunstein deems public and relates to his own ideology of civic republicanism (see Chapter 13) is political in a fairly narrow sense; his canons would therefore give a definite political tilt to the decision of close statutory cases. This politicizing of the interpretive process is troublesome—which is not to deny that the alternative approaches are at root political too, but rather to underscore the inescapability of politics in the decision of difficult statutory cases.

The concrete question raised by Sunstein's proposal is whether it is better on the one hand to have an overarching political orientation, such as the promotion of civic republicanism through use of substantive canons of construction or the promotion of private ordering through strict construction, or on the other hand to have a decentralized, ad hoc approach. The advantage of the latter is that it tends to diffuse political power. The judges are not subjected to rules having a uniform political thrust nor invited to pronounce statutes uninterpretable in order to get on with the interesting business of implementing the judiciary's political program for a better America. Under Sunstein's approach, the result in *Weber* could be defended by reference to a federal common law principle favoring affirmative action and that in *Leo Sheep* by reference to a federal common law principle favoring private ownership. Both decisions would then be "principled," but when the principles of judicial action are so patently political the gains over ad hoc adjudication are questionable, and we have not the substance but the shadow of formalism and the rule of law.

The proposal is only for a default rule. The legislature would retain the whip hand. But that is true in all areas of law other than constitutional law. The truth is that legislatures have severely impacted agendas, making it infeasible in most cases to overrule judicial initiatives legislatively.

Is Communication Ever Possible?

By stressing the negative I risk leaving the impression that I think *all* statutory and constitutional interpretations are policy decisions by judges. That would amount to a denial of the possibility of written communication. Some people do deny this possibility—though in the same spirit, which is to say purely speculative, in which some people deny the existence of an external world. The communication skeptics think, or rather say, that the possibility of communication depends on the outmoded epistemology in which I have a mental picture (say, of the tree in front of my house) that I want to convey to you, I therefore encode it in a sign that you will recognize (the spoken words "tree in front of my house"—assuming we are both normal English speakers), you use the sign to create the identical picture in your head, and in that way an idea is conveyed intact from one mind to another. If this theory were correct, it would indeed make communication "objective" in a strong sense; communication would be a method of conveying an object from sender to recipient. Although properly emphasizing the importance of symbols in communication, the theory is not correct, or at least is radically incomplete.[14] It fails to recognize that most communication is conducted without any mental images; that simple, easily visualizable physical objects are an infrequent subject of communication—yet successful communication is not infrequent; that successful communication depends on a host of unspoken understandings; that (illustrating the last point) to insist on the sharing of mental images leads to the absurdity of the assistant in MacCallum's example who failed to bring back any ashtrays because he was not sure which of the ones he had seen were the ones his boss had "in mind"; and that, as the same example also shows, communication is possible even when the communicants have different mental images of the objects being discussed.

We know that spoken communication works not because we can peer into the minds of the speaker and the listener and observe "intersubjectivity" but because we observe that the listener does what the speaker wanted him to do (the assistant fetched the ashtrays, and without tearing any off the walls, either). Written communication works too,[15] even though the recipient of a written communication will not have the cues provided by inflection and facial expression and may have no opportunity to ask the writer to repeat or explain the message.[16] We can show this by the same type of evidence by which we show that oral communication works. Consider the assembly of a piece of equipment from

14. As emphasized by the modern hermeneutic school of Gadamer and others. For useful discussions, see Joseph Rouse, *Knowledge and Power: Toward a Political Philosophy of Science,* ch. 3 (1987) (esp. pp. 42–47); Peter Goodrich, *Reading the Law: A Critical Introduction to Legal Method and Techniques,* ch. 4 (1986). Cf. Hilary Putnam, *Representation and Reality* 6–7, 24–25 (1988).

15. "The possibility of filling mail orders correctly depends on a critically innocent use of language." Peter Caws, "Critical Innocence and Straight Reading," 17 *New Literary History* 165, 167 (1985).

16. Yet life might be simpler if legislation were spoken! For then we might know whether there is indeed such a thing as the "negative" or "dormant" commerce clause—that is, whether the commerce clause not only empowers Congress to regulate interstate and foreign commerce but also forbids the states to interfere with such commerce without Congress's authorization. Article I, §8, cl. 3 of the Constitution provides so far as pertinent here that "The Congress shall have Power . . . to regulate Commerce with foreign Nations, and among the several States." If the emphasis is placed on "Commerce," this is just a grant of power. If it is placed on "Congress," maybe the clause can be understood to be also allocating power between the states and Congress (an alternative, however, is that it is allocating power between Congress and the executive branch). Another way to look at this particular interpretive puzzle is with the aid of Collingwood's dictum that "every statement that anybody ever makes is made in answer to a question." R. G. Collingwood, *An Essay on Metaphysics* 23 (1940). The meaning of the commerce clause may depend on whether it is an answer to the question Who can regulate interstate commerce? or to the question Can Congress regulate interstate commerce? or to both questions.

a set of written directions. With patience, common sense, and some understanding of the purpose of the equipment, the reader of the directions can construct the equipment without conferring with the author, and the successful construction verifies the hypothesis that written as well as oral communication is possible—sometimes, anyway. Although it cannot be proved that written communication can also work when the writer is dead, or is a committee (all of whose members may be dead), or wrote in a language different from that of the reader,[17] none of these conditions, or even all taken together, is inconsistent with the possibility of effective communication. Once we get away from the idea that communication requires being able to peek into the sender's mind, we need no longer fear that the fact that there are no group minds, and hence no "legislative intent" in a literal sense, makes the communication of statutory commands impossible.

Extreme communication skeptics are, without exception, academics. This is curious. They more than most people depend on, and daily experience, successful communication. Their careers depend on their ability to communicate with other people (often many other people) in writing. When their books and articles are misunderstood they are indignant. When they write an examination they expect their students to understand it; if the examination contains an ambiguity the teacher is embarrassed—he does not say to the students, "Well, what did you expect?" A leading text skeptic was not amused when, his article submitted to the *University of Chicago Law Review* having been turned down after a letter from the editors that he interpreted as a promise to publish the piece, he was told by the editors that they interpreted the letter differently. If there are correct and incorrect interpretations, it must be more than an "essentialist piety" to believe that texts constrain, albeit they constrain only readers having the linguistic and cultural competence presupposed by the author. Text skepticism, like philosophical skepticism generally, is a pose rather than a practice.

There probably are many correct statutory interpretations, but no stronger statement seems possible and it would be wrong for orthodox lawyers to take too much comfort from the weak one. As so often in law, the lack of a feedback mechanism makes it impossible to test claims

17. But anyone who thinks deconstruction has *disproved* these things does not understand deconstruction, on which see my discussion in *Law and Literature: A Misunderstood Relation,* ch. 5 (1988), and references there; also Reed Way Dasenbrock, "Accounting for the Changing Certainties of Interpretive Communities," 101 *Modern Language Notes* 1022 (1985); Alexander Nehamas, "Truth and Consequences: How to Understand Jacques Derrida," *New Republic,* Oct. 5, 1987, at 31.

about the success of statutory and constitutional interpretation (or about its failure—a point the skeptics sometimes lose sight of). We cannot ring up the framers and ask them whether we are reading their words aright. Even when a legislature overrules a judicial decision interpreting a statute, this does not show that the decision was wrong; the composition of the legislature is bound to have changed (and the balance of political forces may have changed) between the time the statute was passed and the time it was amended to overrule the judicial interpretation. With every passing year, moreover, the Constitution becomes more remote; and we live in a period when the interpretive community that fixes the meaning of statutes and the Constitution is fragmented. Not since the Civil War have the legal profession, the judiciary, and the legislatures all been so diverse, politically and culturally. To repeat the central objection to the plain-meaning rule: meaning does not reside simply in the words of a text, for the words are always pointing to something outside.[18] Meaning is what emerges when linguistic and cultural understandings and experiences are brought to bear on the text. The diversity of modern legal culture makes it inevitable that there will be a large area of interpretive indeterminacy, as part of the broader phenomenon of legal indeterminacy that I discussed earlier without specific reference to legislation. Again we notice the curious fact that epistemic confidence in law is heavily dependent on political consensus. Agreement on the meaning of legal texts may in many cases depend ultimately on force—law's ultimate backing.

Mention of the broader phenomenon of legal indeterminacy yields a clue to a tension within formalism. A judge who believes that constitutional and statutory texts usually yield a determinate meaning on careful reading will be reluctant to bow to precedent in statutory and constitutional law; he will want to get down to bedrock. A judge who believes that such texts rarely yield a determinate meaning may be inclined to defer to the precedents interpreting them, believing that he is unlikely to do better by a fresh reading of the text. The first judge, the plain-meaning formalist, the "originalist," will thus be inclined to

---

18. Hence I am skeptical about the interesting argument of Dasenbrock, note 17 above, at 1034–1036, that persuasive interpretation consists of drawing the reader's attention to overlooked aspects of the text. It often is unclear to what extent something new is being discovered in the text and to what extent new generations of readers are bringing new experiences, values, and so forth to it. To put this differently, a text has a slippery ontology; it is difficult, perhaps impossible, to determine what is "in" the text and what is "out." See Joseph Margolis, *Pragmatism without Foundations: Reconciling Realism and Relativism* 25–26 (1986) (vol. 1 of his treatise *The Persistence of Reality*).

kick away one of the main struts of traditional legal reasoning—decision according to precedent.

I have made scattered references to hermeneutics, and the reader may be wondering whether this term is the key to developing a methodology of legal interpretation, or perhaps dashes any hope of such a development. The fact that both possibilities are conceivable is a clue that neither is probable. The term refers to the efforts by nineteenth- and twentieth-century German scholars from Schleiermacher to Gadamer, including the German-American Francis Lieber, to develop a reliable methodology of interpretation.[19] The emphasis is on the interpretation of history, the Bible, and works of literature and art; lately there has been attention to law, primarily by American and English scholars.[20] The hermeneuticists make a variety of sensible points: Imagination is important in interpreting the works of the past. You must try to put yourself in the place of the author you are trying to interpret and understand the problems that he was trying to solve. Documents must be read as a whole. Much communication is tacit—a matter of shared practices—so you must understand an entire culture in order to be able to understand its writings. You cannot understand the parts of a statement without understanding the whole and you cannot understand the whole without understanding the parts; to break this circle you will want to begin by giving the whole statement a quick once-over before proceeding to a detailed examination of the parts (the individual sentences, or whatever). Interpretation across time or cultures, like translation from a foreign language, is a form of collaboration in which the horizons or perspectives of two cultures fuse; meaning is the common ground between writer and reader.

All this is sound advice, though not always easy to apply. But it neither adds up to a distinctive methodology nor demonstrates the impos-

---

19. For an excellent although dated history, see Wilhelm Dilthey, "The Development of Hermeneutics," in W. Dilthey, *Selected Writings* 247 (H. P. Rickman trans. 1976). Also good are Josef Bleicher, *Contemporary Hermeneutics: Hermeneutics as Method, Philosophy, and Critique* (1980); David Couzens Hoy, *The Critical Circle: Literature, History, and Philosophical Hermeneutics* (1978); Richard E. Palmer, *Hermeneutics: Interpretation Theory in Schleiermacher, Dilthey, Heidegger, and Gadamer* (1969); Georgia Warnke, *Gadamer: Hermeneutics, Tradition, and Reason* (1987).

20. See, for example, Goodrich, note 14 above; Brad Sherman, "Review Article: Hermeneutics in Law," 51 *Modern Law Review* 386 (1988), and references cited there; William N. Eskridge, Jr., "Gadamer/Statutory Interpretation" (Georgetown University Law School, May 1989, unpublished paper). Lieber was a nineteenth-century pioneer in legal hermeneutics, however; and Gadamer discusses legal hermeneutics briefly in *Truth and Method*.

sibility of objective interpretation. The problem of interpretation, after all, is not that people don't know how to read carefully and with due allowance for cultural distance; the problem is that there are no techniques for generating objective interpretations of difficult texts. Hermeneutics poses the problem; it does not offer a solution. It is neither the salvation of legal interpretation nor the annunciator of its doom. Hermeneutics will not teach you how to interpret the Eighth Amendment or the Sherman Act. It will not even tell you whether to construe legal texts broadly or to hew close to the surface meaning. That is a political judgment; and given how little we know about the consequences of the choice, it may well be that for a long time to come the choice between strict and flexible, narrow and broad interpretation will depend not on analytical considerations but on judges' temperaments. Some people are more sensitive to the costs of instability and others to the costs of stagnation. Some are more conscious of their obligations to the past and have firmly fixed in their minds Santayana's adage that those who forget the past are condemned to repeat it, and others are fearful of imitating the Bourbon kings, who learned nothing and forgot nothing. This is just the indeterminacy of the canons of construction, writ large.

Consider in this connection Francis Lieber's argument for the flexible interpretation of old laws:

> The benefit of the community is the supreme law, and however frequently this may have been abused, and is daily abusing, it is nevertheless true. Whether we rejoice in it or not, the world moves on, and no man can run against the movement of his time. Laws must be understood to mean something for the advantage of society; and if obsolete laws are not abolished by the proper authority, practical life itself, that is, the people, will and must abolish them, or alter them in their application; even a Mansfield was obliged to charge the jury, in some cases, to find the value of stolen articles under forty shillings, when the real and evident value was far higher.
>
> Great evil has arisen at various epochs from insisting on established laws in times of great crisis; as if the human mind could be permanently fettered by laws of by-gone generations . . . Previous to almost every revolution, there exists a party whose characteristic trait is this mistake.[21]

---

21. *Legal and Political Hermeneutics* 135 (enlarged ed. 1839). And see id. at 33 for a precocious anticipation of the "picture" theory of meaning propounded in Wittgenstein's *Tractatus Logico-Philosophicus*.

This is great stuff, but it owes little to a distinctive hermeneutical methodology—there is no such thing—and it will not convince the Santayanans.

Beyond Interpretation

Despite my brave words in the previous section in defense of interpretation against attacks by extreme text skeptics, I readily acknowledge that the concept may be too various and loose to guide the application of statutes and the Constitution, and that we might be better off without it. Interpretation can be decoding of communications (and there it is least problematic), understanding, translation, extension, completion, transformation, even inversion. All that the term means concretely is that there is a text in the picture, the text is authoritative, and the decision must be related in some way to the text. Although this formulation may be slightly more directive than a definition of interpretation as the mediation of reality by language, it is not a formula for distinguishing sound interpretations from unsound ones. Maybe there is no formula, no methodology. Correctness in interpretation depends on the goal of the particular kind of interpretation, which may be why, for example, musical interpretation is not a useful analogy to statutory interpretation. But there is no agreement on what the goal of statutory or constitutional interpretation is. Maybe there are plural goals—fidelity to framers' intent, certainty, coherence, pragmatically good results. These are related, but different interpreters will give them different weights.

We could translate interpretive questions into questions about consequences. I come to a street crossing and the traffic light says "Walk." What does this mean? It certainly is not a command. It is not permission, either, for that would imply that "Wait" is a prohibition, which it is not in a realistic sense. If I cross the street when the light says "Wait," I am not going to be punished unless I am in one of the very few cities in the world in which jaywalking laws are enforced. "Wait" is a warning against the danger of crossing when vehicles have the right of way. What "Walk" means, as a practical matter, is that vehicles are unlikely to enter the crossing (other than by turning into it), because if they do they will be running a red light, a type of conduct that, unlike jaywalking, *is* punished. Thus the meaning of a green or a red light is discerned by imagining the consequences of alternative interpretations (for example, interpreting "Wait" to mean "Walk"). "I'll eat my hat," an example from Chapter 3, is a sentence that is interpreted ironically because of the consequences of interpreting it literally. Gerald MacCallum's ashtray examples are of the same character. Maybe the best thing to do when a statute is invoked is to examine the consequences of giving the invoker what he wants and then estimate whether those consequences will on the whole be good ones.[22]

This approach, which is pragmatic, does not justify, much less entail, ignoring the text. Not only is the text a source of information about the consequences of alternative "interpretations," but among the consequences to be considered is the impact that unpredictable statutory applications will have on communication between legislature and court. Normally, indeed, if communicative intent or legislative purpose can be discerned—in other words, if imaginative reconstruction works—that will be the end of the case.

Everything that now gets discussed in terms of interpretation would still get discussed but a term that seems no longer to have a useful meaning would be avoided, a fig leaf removed. The activist judge could not deny personal responsibility for his decisions by saying that all he was doing was interpretation, albeit loose rather than strict; neither could the restrained judge deny personal responsibility for his decisions by saying that all *he* was doing was interpretation, albeit strict rather than loose.

The approach is no cure-all. All too often, pragmatism without science is mush. The consequences foreseeable to a judge equipped only with legal training and experience, life experiences, and some common sense will be heavily influenced by the judge's personal values. The more diverse the judiciary is, the more difficult it will be to predict the outcome of statutory and constitutional cases if outcome depends on a projection and comparison of consequences. But since the American judiciary is and will remain diverse, would renewed dedication to "interpretation" be a better solution—or an evasion?

Guido Calabresi's approach of treating statutes like precedents (see Chapter 9) is pragmatic too, but its implications are too radical for my taste. He wants courts to be able to overrule obsolete statutes, just as they can overrule obsolete cases—that is, without having to declare the statute unconstitutional. Since courts overrule recent as well as remote precedents, the logic of Calabresi's proposal would allow courts to do the same thing with regard to statutes. If I am right that the common law method is not interpretive in a useful sense, then Calabresi is pro-

---

22. See Max Radin, "Statutory Interpretation," 43 *Harvard Law Review* 863, 884 (1930), for a similar formulation.

posing to abolish statutory interpretation in favor of an approach that treats statutes as inputs into a decisional process presumably dominated by considerations of policy. This is fine if legislators can be equated to judges, so that the relationship between a court and a legislature is the same as that between the current and former members of the court; then the common law analogy is close indeed. But the equation is proper only if the belief that Calabresi shares with Hart and Sacks, the belief in a legislature composed of reasonable persons pursuing reasonable ends reasonably, is realistic. Since it is not, Calabresi is proposing not only to enlarge the effective legislative power by enlisting the judges in the legislative process (with unexamined, but probably highly adverse, consequences for already heavy judicial workloads), but also to change the character and therefore consequences of the process. It is true that under his proposal the legislature can in principle restore an overruled statute, just as it can overrule a common law decision that it does not like; one of Calabresi's goals, indeed, is a mode of judicial review of statutes that will be less apocalyptic than constitutional review—that will preserve the possibility of dialogue between the branches of government. But the practice is bound to differ from the principle. Legislative agendas are crowded, the procedural barriers to enactment formidable, and as a result legislatures usually can't undo judicial decisions they don't like. In effect, Calabresi's proposal is to give primary legislative power to persons who are not legislators, and he has not justified so far-reaching a change in our basic political arrangements. Dworkin's chain-novel analogy, when applied to statutes and constitutions, likewise trips on the fact that the authors of chapter 1—that is, legislators or constitution framers—are not the same kind of official as the authors of the subsequent chapters, the judges.

It may seem paradoxical that Calabresi and Dworkin, the political liberals, favor an approach that would maximize the freedom that courts have with statutes, and that Easterbrook, the political conservative, favors an approach that would minimize that freedom; by and large liberals favor a more active legislature and conservatives a less active one. But the paradox is superficial. The approaches taken by Calabresi and Dworkin reduce the costs of statutory enactment—by enlarging the power of courts to repair the legislative product—at the same time that they put the judges in the driver's seat; the approach taken by Easterbrook curtails judicial power to make legislation effective in changed circumstances. These consequences are a further illustration of the political significance of interpretive theories and the impossibility of politically neutral interpretations.

One more proposal for eliding the difficulties of interpretation should be noted: a shift of focus from the interpretive process itself to the power of statutory and constitutional amendment.[23] The interpretive process is frequently indeterminate. So what? The legislature can always reject an interpretation it does not like, and a constitutional interpretation can be corrected by a constitutional amendment. In the interim between decision and amendment there are losers, of course, but there is no permanent damage; the amendment power ensures that judicial interpretation will never stray far from authorial intentions. We can even see in the interplay between court and legislature a Darwinian process, in which judicial innovations compete for legislative favor and only those that are agreeable to the legislators' desires survive.

The objections are at the level of practice, and most have been mentioned already. Legislative agendas are impacted, the process of constitutional amendment is excruciatingly difficult and protracted,[24] legislative majorities are volatile, judicial decisions may bring into being special-interest groups that can thwart efforts at legislative overruling. As a result, courts enjoy enormous discretion with regard to statutes and the Constitution; they are the primary makers of statutory and constitutional law.

A Case Study of Politics and Pragmatism

One of the most famous "interpretive" decisions in our history is the decision outlawing public school segregation. Fixed star in our judicial firmament that it is, *Brown v. Board of Education*[25] cannot be shown to be correct as a matter of interpretation.[26] As is so often true of legal decisions, its correctness is political rather than epistemic, pragmatic rather than apodictic.

The proposition that racial segregation in public schools denies black schoolchildren the "equal protection of the laws" guaranteed by section

23. See Akhil Reed Amar, "Civil Religion and Its Discontents," 67 *Texas Law Review* 1153, 1162–1167 (1989).

24. Resulting in imaginative, if to most lawyers overbold, proposals to recognize methods of informal constitutional amendment uncabined by Article V. See Bruce Ackerman, "Discovering the Constitution," 93 *Yale Law Journal* 1013, 1051–1070 (1984); Akhil Reed Amar, "Philadelphia Revisited: Amending the Constitution outside Article V," 55 *University of Chicago Law Review* 1043 (1988).

25. 347 U.S. 483 (1954).

26. Do not forget the contemporary criticisms of the result by distinguished jurists. See Learned Hand, *The Bill of Rights: The Oliver Wendell Holmes Lectures, 1958* 54–55 (1958); Herbert Wechsler, "Toward Neutral Principles of Constitutional Law," 73 *Harvard Law Review* 1, 31–34 (1959).

1 of the Fourteenth Amendment does not have the inevitability of inter-preting the age thirty-five provision to "mean what it says." The words "equal protection" are not obviously incompatible with a system of seg-regated schools, provided that the black schools are as good as the white ones. If they are not as good, the natural remedy, one might think, would be to order them improved. Since the motive for segregated schools was to keep blacks from mixing with whites, segregation stamped blacks with a mark of inferiority that common sense suggests could be very damaging to their self-esteem. But there is little evidence on this point, perhaps because the real damage was (and continues to be) done by the discriminatory attitudes that underlie racial discrimi-nation rather than by the fact of segregation, which is an expression of those attitudes. Notice, by the way, that if this is right, it is further evidence against the view that law changes the attitudes of Americans as well as their behavior.

There is of course much more to be said about the issue of public school segregation. Apart from the psychological damage segregation may have caused blacks, it denied them the opportunity for valuable associations with whites—associations actually more valuable for blacks than for whites[27]—and probably produced more racial segregation than a free market in education would have done. Segregation had costly spillover effects in the northern states to which many blacks migrated in order to get away from it. And no doubt a white majority that insist-ed on segregation would have been unwilling to support truly equal public schools for blacks, yet the disparity would have been difficult to remedy by judicial decree. A goal of "separate but equal" might as a practical matter have been unattainable.

Against this powerful case for interpreting the equal protection clause to forbid public school segregation, however, it can be and was argued that the framers of the Fourteenth Amendment did not intend to bring about true equality between whites and blacks, but merely wanted to give the blacks certain fundamental political rights, not including the right to attend public schools on a footing of equality with whites.[28]

27. See my book *The Economics of Justice* 355 (1981), criticizing the argument by Wechs-ler, note 26 above, that the costs which segregation imposed on blacks by preventing them from associating with whites were symmetrical with the costs that integration imposed on whites of unwanted association with blacks.

28. On the framers' intent, see Alexander M. Bickel, "The Original Understanding and the Segregation Decision," 69 *Harvard Law Review* 1, 56–59 (1955); Raoul Berger, *Govern-ment by Judiciary: The Transformation of the Fourteenth Amendment,* ch. 7 (1977); Aviam Soifer, "Protecting Civil Rights: A Critique of Raoul Berger's History," 54 *New York University Law Review* 651, 705–706 (1979).

Many white Northerners, as well as almost all white Southerners, would have thought it right and natural in 1868 that black people should attend segregated and inferior schools. Moreover, in 1896 the Supreme Court held that racial segregation in public facilities was constitutional,[29] and the public institutions of the South were built on that ruling. Any change, one could argue, should come from Congress, with its broad powers under the commerce clause and under section 5 of the Fourteenth Amendment (which empowers Congress to enforce the substantive provisions of the amendment).[30] It is true that congressional action was out of the question; southern Democrats controlled the key committees by virtue of their seniority. They owed their seniority to their safe seats, the consequence of the South's one-party system—which in turn was the consequence in part of discrimination against blacks and in part of the South's continued resentment of Reconstruction. But a formalist would argue that a court should not consider such things; the opinion in *Brown* does not allude to them.

The "on the one hand, on the other hand" character of this analysis suggests that the ultimate justification for the *Brown* decision must be sought not in technical legal materials but in such political and ethical desiderata as improving the position of blacks; adopting a principle of racial (and implicitly also religious and ethnic) equality to vindicate the ideals for which World War II had recently been fought; raising public consciousness about racial injustice; promoting social peace through racial harmony; eradicating an institution that was an embarrassment to America's foreign policy;[31] reducing the social and political autonomy of the South ("completing the work of the Civil War"); finding a new institutional role for the Supreme Court to replace the discredited one of protecting economic liberty; breathing new life into the equal protection clause. If such considerations are not admissible, as on certain formalist accounts they are not, the decision in *Brown* is questionable.

I am not a formalist and do not regard the considerations I have mentioned as being out of bounds; nor do I think it was improper for the

---

29 See Plessy v. Ferguson, 163 U.S. 537 (1896).

30. It is questionable whether Congress could lawfully use section 5 to overrule a Supreme Court decision; that would not be *enforcing* the amendment, at least if the Court is considered the authoritative interpreter of the Constitution's meaning. See Oregon v. Mitchell, 400 U.S. 112, 128–129 (1970) (opinion of Justice Black). But this problem would disappear if Congress based legislation outlawing segregation on the commerce clause as well as on section 5 of the Fourteenth Amendment, as it did in the Civil Rights Act of 1964.

31. This point is emphasized in Mary L. Dudziak, "Desegregation as a Cold War Imperative," 41 *Stanford Law Review* 61 (1988).

Court to consider the infeasibility of congressional action in the matter. Far from criticizing the decision in *Brown,* I believe that in retrospect the moral norm that it vindicates is powerful enough to illustrate my earlier point that some ethical principles are almost as firmly grounded as our epistemic certitudes are. "In retrospect" may, to be sure, conceal an important qualification. Suppose the *Brown* decision itself, by the encouragement it gave to the civil rights movement, which in turn made black people politically more assertive and, eventually, politically effective, contributed to the present ethical consensus on the immorality of segregation. Then it would be bootstrapping to try to justify the decision by reference to that consensus. I myself doubt that judicial decisions have much effect on attitudes,[32] but those who disagree should consider carefully the possible implications of their view for the legitimacy of the *Brown* decision. Their view of law's esemplastic power may make attempted justifications of *Brown* circular.

Brown has another, if again equivocal, significance for earlier themes in this book. Anyone who thinks that law is just force or (what may not be sharply different) dominant public opinion must be given pause by a decision that vindicated the rights of a minority at a time when that minority was politically weak. We have just seen that the decision cannot be regarded as a mere emanation of the undoubted force—the arbitrament of arms that was the Civil War—which lies behind the enactment of the Fourteenth Amendment. But I have noted practical reasons why the majority may have wanted to end official segregation, and to these it must be added that the decision did not pit a minority against a national majority, but a national minority (the blacks) against a regional majority that was also a national minority (white Southerners).

My central point is that *Brown* is not correct by virtue of being a demonstrably correct *interpretation* of the Constitution, and I take issue with Robert Bork's interesting attempt to show that it is. His premise is that "where constitutional materials do not clearly specify the value to be preferred, there is no principled way to prefer any claimed human value to any other. The judge must stick close to the text and the history, and their fair implications, and not construct new rights."[33] (If this is

---

32. Although it is tempting to suppose that *Brown* was a causal factor in the growth of racial tolerance in this country, there is no evidence it was, and the contrary is powerfully argued in a forthcoming study by Professor Gerald Rosenberg of the Department of Political Science at the University of Chicago.

33. "Neutral Principles and Some First Amendment Problems," 47 *Indiana Law Journal* 1, 8 (1971). Subsequent page references to this article are in the text.

right, *Brown* was wrong.) Bork says that all that can be got out of the equal protection clause and its history is that the clause "was intended to enforce a core idea of black equality against governmental discrimination" (p. 14). Judges, Bork continues, must avoid injecting their own values; instead they must "choose a general principle of equality that applies to all cases. For the same reason, the Court cannot decide that physical equality is important but psychological equality is not. Thus, the no-state-enforced-discrimination rule of *Brown* must overturn and replace the separate-but-equal doctrine of *Plessy v. Ferguson*"(pp. 14–15).

Bork uses a conception of the institutional limitations of courts (they must not interject their own values) to precipitate out of the equal protection clause a concept from which the result in *Brown* can be deduced. But the appearance of analytical rigor is misleading. Bork assumes rather than argues that the only way the Supreme Court could have stayed within the bounds of its institutional competence while enforcing the "core idea of black equality" was to define the core to include psychological as well as physical equality. The Court could just as well have said: "We do not know how large the core was supposed to be, so we will enforce only physical equality, which is easier to determine and avoids our getting mired in psychological conjectures." (Actually, physical equality might, as I said, be difficult to monitor and enforce, but Bork does not discuss that intensely pragmatic aspect of the question.) This would not be a value judgment about the relative importance of physical and psychological equality. It would be a drawing in of the judicial horns, consistent with Bork's conception of a modest and highly positivistic judicial role, one that avoids the making of value judgments.

Bork's second tacit premise is that achieving a better approximation to the intent of the framers of the equal protection clause—an intent that, as Bork stresses, is largely unknown—was worth the sacrifice of the values of stare decisis that was entailed by overruling *Plessy v. Ferguson*. Comparing fidelity to original intent with fidelity to precedent, or the value of getting the law right with the value of legal stability, is not interpretation in a helpful sense (is there a helpful sense?). Bork's third implicit premise is that courts should read "equal protection of the laws" more broadly than the words themselves might be thought to imply when taken in conjunction with the breakdown in law and order in the South after the Civil War. The words and their background imply merely that a state cannot discriminate in the provision of police, fire, and other protective services—cannot make black people (or members of some other unpopular group) outlaws, thereby exposing them to the tender mercies of private terrorist groups such as the Ku Klux Klan.

Bork might reply that the words "equal protection of the laws" were deliberately chosen as a vague formula to give the courts maximum flexibility. But are they so vague? And if the framers' intent was to delegate a discretionary, common law authority to the courts, how can *Brown* be defended as an *interpretation* of the Constitution? One might as well call every state common law decision an exercise in statutory interpretation on the ground that the state legislature had implicitly authorized the state's courts to exercise a common law jurisdiction by not forbidding them to do so. We can see the idea of interpretation being stretched to the breaking point in a desperate effort to preserve the appearance of law's objectivity.

The interpretive problem cannot be solved by hermeneutics. It has been argued that in moving from *Plessy* to *Brown*, "in effect the Court slowly came to see what the Constitution meant. From this example, we may infer that the power of the text to alienate the reader from his situation is superior to the rooted sense of belonging that the reader brings to the hermeneutical experience."[34] But a text as vague as section 1 of the Fourteenth Amendment has no power to compel the reexamination of a settled and plausible interpretation. The problem with the decision in *Plessy* was not that it had distorted the text of the equal protection clause but that it had come to seem, in the fullness of time, bad ethics and bad politics. It was not the "pull of the text"[35] that compelled reexamination of *Plessy* but the vagueness of the text that *permitted* reexamination of the decision in light of half a century of social and political change. It was not brooding over the words "equal protection of the laws" but a change in the nation's ethical and political climate that resulted in the decision in *Brown*.

This is not to say that Justice Harlan's famous dissent in *Plessy* was wrong—that he was a premature integrationist. Although the difficulty that the federal courts had in enforcing *Brown* makes me doubt whether a different outcome in *Plessy* would actually have resulted in the desegregation of public facilities in the South, who knows? Maybe the political situation was more fluid in 1896 than in 1954. Maybe a reverse *Plessy* would at least have made a difference outside the South—the public schools of Indiana, for example, were by statute racially segregated until the late 1940s, and the defendant in *Brown* was the Board of Education

34. Francis J. Mootz III, "The Ontological Basis of Legal Hermeneutics: A Proposed Model of Inquiry Based on the Work of Gadamer, Habermas, and Ricoeur," 68 *Boston University Law Review* 523, 606 (1988).

35. Id. at 606.

of Topeka, Kansas. As an interpretation of the equal protection clause *Plessy* could have gone either way, but so could *Brown,* and not only because *Plessy* was a precedent to which the Court in *Brown* could have deferred.

Nor am I saying that the only possible dispositions toward *Brown* are interpretive certainty and utter agnosticism. In addition to (but related to) the natural law justification offered earlier (*Brown* as vindication of a moral norm that was influential then and that now commands a consensus), consider what we would think of a decision by the Supreme Court overruling *Brown* tomorrow on the ground that the decision was an incorrect interpretation of the Fourteenth Amendment. We would pronounce such a decision wrong even if we agreed that it rested on a defensible theory of constitutional interpretation. The decision would be an enormous provocation, stirring racial fears and hostilities in a nation more rather than less racially heterogeneous than when *Brown* was decided; it would be promptly overruled by Congress in the exercise of its powers under section 5 or the commerce clause; it would unsettle all of constitutional law, most of which rests on interpretive grounds no more powerful (and often much less so) than those of *Brown*; and whatever its actual motivations it would be thought to bespeak the politicization of the Court. It would in short be socially, politically, and legally destabilizing.

The example suggests that our legal certitudes are pragmatically rather than analytically grounded. The strongest defense of *Brown* is that the consequences of overruling it would be untoward. To borrow William James's formula, we believe that *Brown* is correct because that is a good, a useful, thing to believe. This may be true of most judicial decisions whose authority we are not disposed to question, whether they are ostensibly interpretive decisions or are leading cases in common law fields.

Hans Linde would reject a pragmatic approach to *Brown*. A vigorous critic of legal realism (which he appears to equate to pragmatism, by which the legal realists were indeed influenced), he has offered as an example of its failures the attempt by the Supreme Court in *Brown* to justify the conclusion that school segregation is unconstitutional by reference to psychological studies of black children's self-image and self-esteem.[36] The studies were indeed inconclusive—at best.[37] One of the

36. See Hans A. Linde, "Judges, Critics, and the Realist Tradition," 82 *Yale Law Journal* 227, 239–240 (1972).

37. See Richard Kluger, *Simple Justice: The History of "Brown v. Board of Education" and Black America's Struggle for Equality* 497–504 (1976); Mark A. Chesler, Joseph Sanders, and

best known, the "two-doll" study, gave black children a choice between a black doll and a white doll. Most chose the white doll, implying (to the investigator) impaired self-esteem—but the percentage was actually higher among black children in the unsegregated North than among those in the segregated South. Moreover, the two-doll study has been repeated a number of times since *Brown*—most recently in 1987—and the results have remained virtually unchanged.[38] Linde argues that courts should base their decisions on firmer grounds than the shifting sands of social science research. Of course courts should try not to be gulled by shoddy research, of which there is no shortage. And there are firmer grounds for the *Brown* decision than studies of the psychology of black children. But those grounds are matters of fact and consequence too,[39] not matters of legal theory or distinctive legal materials. They are not grounds that hit one between the eyes after a careful reading of the equal protection clause and the debates that preceded its enactment and ratification. They are grounds based on political history, common sense and common knowledge, and ethical insight. They are interpretive in a legitimate but not a limiting, and perhaps not even a useful, sense.

Debra S. Kalmuss, *Social Science in Court: Mobilizing Experts in the School Desegregation Cases* 23–24 (1988).

38 See Darlene Powell-Hopson and Derek S. Hopson, "Implications of Black Doll Preferences among Black Preschool Children and White Preschool Children," 14 *Journal of Black Psychology* 57 (1988), and references cited there.

39. As emphasized in Charles Black's defense of *Brown*: "I was raised in the South, in a Texas city where the pattern of segregation was firmly fixed. I am sure it never occurred to anyone, white or colored, to question its meaning." Charles L. Black, Jr., "The Lawfulness of the Segregation Decisions," 69 *Yale Law Journal* 421, 424 (1960). "The case seems so onesided that it is hard to make out what is being protested against when it is asked, rhetorically, how the Court can possibly advise itself of the real character of the segregation system. It seems that what is being said is that, while no actual doubt exists as to what segregation is for and what kind of societal pattern it supports and implements, there is no ritually sanctioned way in which the Court, as a Court, can permissibly learn what is obvious to everybody else and to the Justices as individuals . . . The fact that the Court has assumed as true a matter of common knowledge in regard to broad societal patterns, is (to say the very least) pretty far down the list of things to protest against." Id. at 427–428.

PART IV ∽

SUBSTANTIVE JUSTICE

11 ❧

Corrective, Retributive, Procedural, and Distributive Justice

The quest for objectivity in law that has consumed so much of our attention thus far has yet to reveal the Holy Grail that will enable judges to decide the most difficult cases on grounds more impressive, "professional," and imperative, and less subjective, "political," and (often) idiosyncratic, than their personal values and their ethical and policy preferences. Yet we just saw, in considering *Brown v. Board of Education,* that when a strong ethical or political consensus has formed on an issue, the observer (at least looking back) may be able to pronounce confident judgment on the soundness of the legal decision resolving the issue. Maybe, therefore, rather than seeking in legal materials incisive methods—compendiously, "legal reasoning"—for answers to specific legal questions, we should be looking for an overarching principle of justice, a political-ethical norm that could be used to ground legal obligations. The three chapters of Part IV examine the possibility of finding such a principle or principles, and Chapter 14 completes the circle by asking whether the answer to the question of objectivity in law doesn't lie right at home after all, in the humble conventions of legal practitioners.

Corrective Justice and the Rule of Law

The idea of corrective justice comes down to us from Aristotle, and it has seemed to many legal scholars an attractive principle for orienting legal inquiry, particularly in such common law fields as torts and contracts. Book V, chapter 2 of the *Nicomachean Ethics* mentions the concept briefly; chapter 4 develops it. We learn in chapter 3 that distributive justice—justice in the distribution by the state of money, honors, and other things of value—requires distribution according to merit (*kat' axian*). Corrective ("rectificatory," "commutative") justice is different. The corrective principle (*diorthotikos*—literally, "making straight") applies not to awards but to transactions (*sunallagamata*) both voluntary and involuntary, the distinction corresponding roughly to that in our law between contracts and torts.[1] From the standpoint of corrective justice "it makes no difference whether a good man has defrauded a bad man or a bad man a good one, nor whether it is a good or a bad man that has committed adultery; the law looks only to the distinctive character of the injury, and treats the parties as equal, if one is in the wrong and the other is being wronged, and if one inflicted injury and the other has received it."[2] As far as the actual correction (remedy) is concerned, Aristotle says that "the judge tries to equalize things by means of the penalty, taking away from the gain of the assailant. For the term 'gain' is applied generally to such cases, even if it be not a term appropriate to certain cases, e.g. to the person who inflicts a wound—and 'loss' to the sufferer . . . The judge restores equality . . . It is for this reason also that it is called just [*dikaion*], because it is a division into two parts [*dika*] . . . and the judge [*dikastes*] is one who bisects [*dichastes*] . . . Therefore the just . . . consists in having an equal amount before and after the transaction."[3]

There is more, but chapter 4 is brief and the passages I have quoted are its gist; and though the *Nicomachean Ethics* is notoriously obscure (consisting as it does of classroom notes of Aristotle's lectures), there is little disagreement over the basic features of corrective justice. In Joachim's paraphrase, "If, for example, the thief was a gentleman and the injured party a beggar—a member of an inferior class in the State—this difference of rank is nothing to the law . . . All that the law is concerned with is that, of two parties before it, one has got an unfair advantage

---

1. As instances of voluntary transactions, Aristotle mentions sale, purchase, lending, pledging, and so on, and as instances of involuntary ones, theft, murder, and the like. See *Nicomachean Ethics*, Bk. V, §2, in *The Complete Works of Aristotle*, vol. 2, pp. 1784–1785 (Jonathan Barnes ed. 1984) (p. 1131, col. a, ll. 1–9, in the standard Greek edition of Aristotle's works).

2. Id., vol. 2, at 1786 (p. 1132, col. a, ll. 2–6). Literally: "for it makes no difference whether a fair [moderate, upper-class, good, reasonable] man robs [bereaves, defrauds] a man of low [bad, inferior] station or a man of low station robs a fair man, or whether a fair man commits adultery [against a man of low station] or a man of low station [commits adultery against a fair man]; the law looks to the distinction alone of the injury, and treats as equals, if one acts unjustly and the other is wronged, and if one injures and the other is injured." The literal translation (my own) brings out the relation between the concept of corrective justice and differences in the litigants' social status.

3. Id., vol. 2, at 1786–1787 (p. 1132, col. a, ll. 9–12, 25–32; col. b, ll. 19–21).

and the other has suffered an unfair disadvantage. There is, therefore, a wrong which needs redress—an inequality which has to be equalized."[4]

Three points should be noted at the outset about Aristotle's concept of corrective justice. First, the duty to rectify is based not on the fact of injury alone but on the conjunction of injury and wrongdoing. The injurer must do wrong (*adikei*) as well as do harm (*eblapsen*) and the victim must be wronged (*adiketei*) as well as harmed (*beblaptei*). What is wrongful or unjust—*adikos*—is not defined in chapter 4, but is assumed; chapter 8, however, implies that only intentional wrongs are acts of injustice.[5]

Second, the exclusion of distributive considerations ("it makes no difference whether a good man has defrauded a bad man or a bad man a good one") is a procedural rather than an ethical principle. It does not imply that such considerations should not affect the definition of rights or the determination of what sorts of act are unjust or wrongful. The point is that the *judge* is interested only in the character—whether it is wrongful—of the injury, and not in the character or deserts of the parties; "the moral worth of persons . . . is ignored."[6] So, to take a modern example, corrective justice would imply that in deciding whether an injurer has been negligent within the meaning of the Hand formula (B < PL), facts such as that the injurer has a high income and therefore high opportunity costs of care (thus increasing B) or that the harm to potential victims, a group of poor people, is limited by their lack of earning potential (thus reducing L) must be allowed their full weight in the formula, without regard to the possible injustice of a distribution of income that produced these consequences.

Third, Aristotle was writing against the background of the Athenian legal system of his day, where not only torts and breaches of contract but also crimes were prosecuted by private individuals, normally the victim or a member of his family, rather than by the state. It was therefore natural for him to assume that correcting wrongs would be a matter of private rather than public law. But nothing in his concept of correc-

4. H. H. Joachim, Aristotle: *The Nicomachean Ethics: A Commentary* 144 (D. A. Rees ed. 1951). See also W. F. R. Hardie, *Aristotle's Ethical Theory* 192–195 (1968); J. A. Stewart, *Notes on the Nicomachean Ethics of Aristotle,* vol. 1, pp. 430–431 (1973); Ernest J. Weinrib, "Aristotle's Forms of Justice," in *Justice, Law, and Method in Plato and Aristotle* 133 (Spiro Panagiotou ed. 1987).

5. See Max Hamburger, *Morals and Law: The Growth of Aristotle's Legal Theory* 70 (1951); Edgar Bodenheimer, *Treatise on Justice* 210–213 (1967).

6. *Ethics of Aristotle,* vol. 2, p. 113 n. 3 (4th rev. ed., Alexander Grant ed., 1885).

tive justice implies that *only* private suits—tort suits or suits for breach of contract—satisfy the remedial demands of corrective justice.

Aristotle's notion of corrective justice thus is narrow and formal, the essential elements being just two (I will discuss an arguable third element later): (1) people injured by wrongful conduct should have the right to activate a corrective machinery administered by judges who (?) give no weight to the character or social status of the victim and the injurer. Since the wrong and the injury are assumed, Aristotle seems to be saying little more than that there should be an impartial governmental machinery for redressing redressable wrongs.

To understand how so spare and seemingly platitudinous a concept of justice could be thought an advance and could echo down through the centuries, we must recall the historical discussion of jurisprudence in the Introduction. The notion that if A wrongs B, B should be able to get a remedy from a judge who will consider only the character of the act and not that of the actors is not, as it might seem to us to be, self-evident. It belongs to a relatively advanced stage of civilization and even today is contested in some quarters. In the earliest stage of law (one might prefer to call this stage prelaw), B might be left to his own devices. This is law as revenge, and one way to think of corrective justice is as a close substitute. It preserves the idea that the wronging of B by A is primarily a matter between A and B, and like revenge itself (especially when civilized into the notion of exact retribution—an eye for an eye) conveys an emotionally satisfying impression of an equilibrium. This impression, which Aristotle's emphasis on the restoration of equality reinforces, is prominent in early literature. A takes X from B; the judge takes X from A and gives it back to B—at least so far as this can be done. For as shown by his discussion of the remedy for violations of corrective justice, Aristotle is well aware that X may be the kind of loss that does not show up as an equivalent gain to the injurer. That was the case in *Oedipus Tyrannus*. Another example is when A kills B in order to steal something of slight value. Adultery is another example.

The idea that the wrong plus its redress constitute a strictly bilateral transaction between victim and injurer may be worth preserving but is certainly not inevitable in the sense that the alternatives are unthinkable. One might take the position that A's act was a social harm (because B is a member of the society), to which the response should be guided by notions of what is best from a social standpoint rather than by the idea that B has some entitlement by virtue of having been wronged. Society might give B a right to sue but do so strictly as an instrument to an end conceived of as social rather than as private, or might withhold the right in favor of a purely public, noncompensatory remedy. The contrast between the social approach and corrective justice enables us to see the latter as simultaneously an advance over the concept of justice as revenge[7] and an outgrowth of the earlier concept rather than a clean break with it.

The second feature of corrective justice—also not self-evident, though it may appear so to us—is the idea of administering justice "without respect to persons," as the oath taken by federal judges puts it. This is a further illustration that corrective justice is a step beyond revenge, for one of the big problems of a revenge system is that the revenger is in effect a judge in his own cause. And in the judge's "abstracting" from the personal characteristics of the litigants we can see a model for, or at least a parallel to, the use of abstraction in scientific inquiry and in market relations.

Let me say, speaking as a judge, that it is not *natural* to judge without respect to persons. It is a learned, and eventually a habitual, mode of proceeding rather than second nature. The natural way of proceeding is, precisely, to judge the persons and to take account of the act only insofar as it affects that judgment. It might be that A has defrauded B, but did so in order to support A's starving family; and B is a miser, childless, ugly, and cruel, and moreover had mocked A for his poverty. Or perhaps A is a scientific genius who committed fraud to obtain funds for his research, and B is a pimp or a con man. Maybe A is the head of state—and a good head of state, despite his dishonesty—and if his fraud is exposed in a court of law he will fall from power, and the state will be the worse for his fall. Maybe he is a war hero, forced to eke out a living in his declining years on a meager pension and driven to crime by an understandable sense of having been ill used by his country. In all of these cases, as in judging wrongs committed by members of our own families, our instinct is to judge the person and not (or not just) the deed: the opposite of what Aristotle recommends.

Mention of family members exposes an ambiguity in the idea of personal justice conceived as the antithesis of legal justice in Aristotle's sense. Personal justice could refer to any or all of three distinct styles of dispute resolution. The first is resolving the dispute in accordance with the judge's personal stake in the case as parent, investor, or other interested party—which, by the way, is a feature of justice as revenge. The second is resolving the dispute in accordance with the character, status,

---

7. The manifold deficiencies of which I discuss in *The Economics of Justice*, ch. 8 (1981), and in *Law and Literature: A Misunderstood Relation*, ch. 1 (1988).

appearance, or other personal characteristics of the disputants rather than the (impersonal) merits of their claims. The third is rendering substantive rather than formal justice; that is, resolving the dispute in the way that seems best in light of the particulars of the case, rather than by the application of a general rule. The first style of dispute resolution has long been thought corrupt, and the third involves an issue that Aristotle did not touch on in discussing corrective justice: the optimal trade-off between rule and standard. The second is personal justice in the sense that Aristotle rejects.

Natural as personal justice in this sense (as well as in the first sense) is, Aristotle was right to reject it. By greatly expanding the boundaries of the relevant, personal justice makes the process of decision enormously cumbersome and legal obligations unpredictable. It also magnifies the effects of disparities in social and economic status between litigants, even if the disparities are due to chance or oppression rather than to differences in skill or industry. It promotes judicial corruption by increasing the benefit to litigants of seeking to curry favor with the judges, and it encourages socially wasteful expenditures on obtaining or simulating the social graces or other characteristics that appeal to judges—though not all expenditures on improving one's character should be regarded as wasteful! It discourages trade, and transactions with strangers in general, because in a system of personal justice a foreigner or other outsider will be at a great disadvantage in litigation with a local person and will therefore feel that he lacks legal protection in his business dealings with such persons. (Shylock makes this point in *The Merchant of Venice* in arguing why it is in Venice's interest to enforce his bond with Antonio.) It stifles individuality; as Socrates discovered, the unpopular man cannot obtain justice in a system of popular, "whole man" justice. It is inconsistent with the idea of an independent judiciary, because it implies that the judges can be overawed by grandees, and hence it retards the emergence of a competent professional judiciary. Corrective justice is thus an intermediate stage in the progression from revenge to a full-fledged rule-of-law ideology, although Aristotle does not take the last step in the *Nicomachean Ethics* (for that one must consult the *Politics,* Bk. III, §§15–16).

Personal justice in Aristotle's sense is different from decision according to standards rather than rules, but there is a relation. A totally personal system of justice would have no rules, since liability would depend not on the relationship between conduct and norms but on the characteristics of the litigants. And governance by standards, because it enlarges the judges' discretion, makes it easier for personal justice to enter through the back door even if barred from the front.[8] A shift from a personal to an impartial system of justice may therefore be correlated with a shift from standards to rules. But it is not identical; a standard, like a rule, concerns conduct rather than character. Even the empirical correlations on the one hand between rules and impartial justice and on the other hand between standards and personalized justice are weak. Because the administration of standards requires more information than the administration of rules, we observe greater reliance on rules relative to standards in less advanced societies than in more advanced ones. Yet we do not find the rule of law more securely established in the less advanced societies. This is because the principle of impartial justice—of justice that does not respect persons—is likely to be on a far weaker footing in those societies. The combination of precise and voluminous rules with judges who are overawed by powerful litigants is a common one in societies struggling to achieve modernity. Heavy reliance on rules, indeed, may reflect a desperate effort to stem the tides of personal justice, and a shift toward standards may reflect growing confidence in the judges' ability to transcend personal justice.

This discussion shows how the rule of law can promote justice even if the rules themselves simply reflect dominant public opinion. (A moral relativist would question any higher aspiration for the content of rules of law.) The evenhanded administration of law reduces the likelihood that the law will be used to exploit vulnerable groups. It enables members of those groups to take advantage of whatever benefits the rules as formulated happen to confer on them; and by visiting the costs of a rule on all persons who happen to be within its scope, it forges a potential alliance between the vulnerable and others who are hit by the rule. To put the second point slightly differently, the generality of rules compared with orders or decrees directed at particular persons, a generality that is another dimension of the traditional conception of the rule of law, protects the vulnerable by putting others who are less vulnerable in the same legal boat with them. This is the root meaning of equal protection of the laws—a commitment to rules *general* in scope and *evenhanded* in application, which are characteristics of law that benefit weak and iso-

---

8. Francis Lieber, *Legal and Political Hermeneutics* 164 (enlarged ed. 1839), illustrates with a provision of a Chinese penal code that stated (according to an English translation), "Whoever is guilty of improper conduct, and such as is contrary to the spirit of the laws, though not a breach of any specific article, shall be punished at the least with forty blows; and when the impropriety is of a serious nature, with eighty blows." On the administration of discretionary justice by the Islamic *qadi*, see Lawrence Rosen, *The Anthropology of Justice: Law as Culture in Islamic Society* 56–78 (1989).

lated members of a society independently of any doctrines designed specifically for their benefit.

The generality of law has a temporal dimension as well as the "spatial" dimension just discussed. The rule of law implies that cases will be decided in accordance with "principles established in cases decided in more tranquil periods."[9] Quite apart from any constitutional protection against the actions of temporary, inflamed majorities, the practice of judges in deciding cases on the basis of previously established principles provides some insulation against the passions of the day. But how much insulation may be doubted. It is ironic that Justice Frankfurter made the statement I have just quoted in an opinion concurring in the judgment upholding the conviction of the Communist leaders under the Smith Act—a conviction now thought by many to have reflected the anticommunist hysteria of the McCarthy period. And yet, although in retrospect Americans' fear of the Communist Party U.S.A. seems to have been greatly exaggerated, this was not so clear in 1951; and principles made in more tranquil times may be inapt for less tranquil times.

In law, particulars are forever tugging against generalities. Rules not only are modified to take account of changing circumstances, such as a decline in domestic tranquillity, but also are subject to exception. The practical consequence is to blur the line between rules and standards; and we must consider whether the rule of law may be said to exist in a legal system permeated by standards or standardlike rules. I think so. A standard is general in terms, like a rule (indeed more general), and there is nothing contradictory in the idea of evenhanded application of a standard, although in practice a standard may not be administered as evenhandedly as a rule is because of the scope the standard allows for the exercise of discretion. It would be absurd to say that a jurisdiction that resolved accident cases in accordance with the negligence standard rather than strict liability lacked the rule of law. The relevant contrast is between, on the one hand, a rule or standard that is general in terms and applied without regard to persons, and, on the other hand, a system in which one's rights and obligations depend on who one is.

The contrast begins to blur, however, when we consider proposals, as in feminist jurisprudence, for both greater emphasis on standards relative to rules and greater sensitivity to the particular needs, interests, and experiences of members of groups that have been discriminated

9. Dennis v. United States, 341 U.S. 494, 528 (1951) (Justice Frankfurter, concurring).

against in the past or otherwise pushed to the social margin.[10] One can, of course, imagine a legal system deliberately biased in favor of women, minorities, or other groups, but then it would be difficult to regard the members of the favored groups as marginal or oppressed. Virtually by definition, a group powerful enough or sympathetic enough to win favored legal treatment is not a group of pariahs. The genuine pariah may fare better under a system of impartial justice reliant on general rules than under a system that makes status pertinent to legal rights or that emphasizes the particulars of the case rather than the generality of the rules.

The first feature of Aristotle's concept of corrective justice—the bilateral nature of legal redress—is less modern than the idea of judging without respect to persons; in a modern setting more problematic; and, worst of all, possibly empty. Obviously there ought to be remedies for wrongs. Otherwise, there will be no check on wrongdoing, which is by definition conduct that society wants to prevent if it can. But the decision on whether the remedy should take the form of a private suit (presumably although not inevitably by the victim), a public prosecution, or measures designed to make corrective justice moot by preventing the wrongful injury (as by punishing drunk drivers whether or not they have an accident) so that no occasion for corrective justice arises, is a judgment of expediency rather than an entailment of justice. Suppose the social costs of accidents would be reduced if tort liability for automobile accidents due to negligence were discarded in favor of a combination of no-fault insurance and stepped-up criminal prosecutions of dangerous drivers. Then victims of merely negligent drivers would have no legal remedy; but if despite this consequence we were convinced that the system produced fuller compensation, fewer accidents, and lower insurance premiums, which of us would oppose it on the ground that it failed to do corrective justice, and why?

Could we even say that it *did* fail to do corrective justice? It would be doing it at the wholesale level, and Aristotle might think this good enough in the circumstances. More important, the abolition of a particular remedy can always be reconceived as a change in the underlying right. If the expedient factors mentioned above induced the legislature to reclassify careless driving so that it was no longer a legal wrong, what purchase could one find in Aristotle for regarding such a decision as a

10. See Chapter 13 of this book, and also discussion and references in *Law and Literature*, note 7 above, at 108–113.

denial of corrective justice? The definition of wrongs is prior to the duty of corrective justice. Once conduct is classified as wrongful, the failure to provide any form of redress may indeed be shocking. But society is always free, at least as a matter of corrective justice, to alter the definition of wrongful conduct.

The idea that wrongs that cause injury should be corrected may be perilously close to being a tautology. Wrongful conduct in Aristotle's sense appears to be conduct that society wants to prevent because it causes injuries that are not justified. This impression is reinforced by the fact that his word for wrongful, *adikos,* means both wrongful in a moral sense and unlawful. Aristotle did not distinguish between these senses, and the fact that, as indicated by the passage quoted at note 3, he appears to be discussing real judges and judging suggests that he is talking about the legal system that he knew and not about some abstract ideal of justice. (This is an illustration of Judith Shklar's point, noted in Chapter 7, that legal thinking and moral thinking frequently run on parallel tracks.) Unlawful conduct virtually *means* conduct that is subject to legal sanctions. If no machinery is provided for actually imposing sanctions, something is amiss. The need for correction is built into the definition of the wrong. We should not be surprised that the failure to redress injuries that ought to be redressed is considered a failure to do justice.

There may be more to the remedial aspect of Aristotle's idea of corrective justice than I have let on thus far: an idea, natural in light of the evolution of law from vengeance, that if measures to prevent wrongdoing fail and the wrong occurs and causes injury, some correction must be attempted after the fact—in the form either of a tort suit to compensate the victim or, if that is infeasible (the injurer may be insolvent), of criminal punishment of the wrongdoer. It is not enough to let bygones be bygones. If there is something in Aristotle's idea of corrective justice that is different from either the notion of impartiality, of doing justice without regard to persons—a sound and important idea, but for functional reasons—or the notion that the state should provide a machinery for redressing those wrongs that ought to be redressed—which is little more than a tautology—it seems to be this idea that the provision of *some* remedy for a wrongful injury *after* the injury occurs is a duty independent of functional reasons for sanctions against wrongful conduct. The idea may explain Aristotle's otherwise puzzling emphasis on the bilateral character of legal redress.

Although Aristotle but hints at the idea, its psychological and historical roots seem evident; they are the same roots as those of revenge. People react with instinctive indignation to invasions of their rights, and demand justice; it is this demand, I suggest, that underlies a notion of corrective justice that is distinct from broader rule-of-law notions. Corrective justice is therefore a natural law concept in a literal sense. Constituted as we are, we demand that the state provide a machinery for correcting wrongful injuries after they occur. But the details of the machinery are unimportant. Compensation may not be essential. Punishment that imposes on the wrongdoer injury commensurate with that which he inflicted on the victim of the wrong may be good enough— may restore equality in Aristotle's sense, albeit at a level where both parties are worse off than before the wrongful act. Only there has to be something.

If, even when elaborated, the content of Aristotle's concept of corrective justice seems a bit meager, still one might have supposed that more than two millennia of exegesis and elaboration of Aristotle's moral and political philosophy would have given the concept a richer meaning. In fact there has been little discussion of corrective justice by philosophers, and the concept remains essentially where Aristotle left it.[11] In recent years, it is true, a number of scholars have tried to milk the concept for its specific implications for legal doctrine, but with little success and less development of the concept, as a brief discussion of a few of these attempts will show.

In a series of articles written in the 1970s, Richard Epstein advocated an expanded role of strict liability in tort law. In support of this position he appealed to "the principles of corrective justice," that is, of "rendering to each person whatever redress is required because of the violation of his rights by another."[12] This is a perfectly good paraphrase of Aristotle, but reading on one discovers that Epstein is stretching Aristotle to make his point. He speaks of "the distribution of vested rights demanded by a corrective justice theory" and says that "corrective justice principles . . . help us to decide who is a wrongdoer and who is an innocent driver" and again that "corrective justice arguments identify

---

11. Aquinas's concept of commutative justice appears to be identical to Aristotle's concept of corrective justice. See Thomas Aquinas, *On Law, Morality, and Politics* 164–170 (William P. Baumgarth and Richard J. Regan eds. 1988). Kant's concept of retributive justice, as we shall see in the next section, is closely related to the aspect of corrective justice that requires redress ex post for wrongful injury whether or not that redress makes sense from a present or forward-looking perspective. See Jeffrie G. Murphy, "Does Kant Have a Theory of Punishment?" 87 *Columbia Law Review* 509 (1987). This relation underlines the continuity between vengeance (to which retribution is closely linked) and corrective justice.

12. Richard A. Epstein, "Nuisance Law: Corrective Justice and Its Utilitarian Constraints," 8 *Journal of Legal Studies* 49, 50 (1979); see also Epstein, "Defenses and Subsequent Pleas in a System of Strict Liability," 3 *Journal of Legal Studies* 165 (1974).

the wrongdoer."[13] In fact corrective justice will not reveal who is a wrongdoer or who has vested rights.

Epstein associates two ideas with corrective justice: that the victim of a wrong is entitled to compensation from the wrongdoer and that the fact of injury "permits the plaintiff to show that the initial balance between the two parties is in need of redress because of the defendant's conduct."[14] The first idea, that of a right to compensation, is indeed part of Aristotle's discussion of corrective justice, as we have seen, but apparently as background; the system of private damages actions was the one he knew. The second idea, that injury creates a duty of compensation, is not part of the Aristotelian conception of corrective justice; for Aristotle, it is only *wrongful* injury that creates a duty to compensate. There is no support in Aristotle for a notion of strict liability (liability based on cause rather than on fault), but in any event such notions belong to the sphere of distributive justice, which determines what entitlements— for example, to be free from injury even if it is not due to fault on the part of the injurer—a person has.

John Borgo accepts from Epstein that corrective justice is "the notion that when one man harms another the victim has a moral right to demand, and the injurer a moral duty to pay him, compensation for the harm," and asks what idea of causation (the only thing besides injury that the plaintiff must prove in a system of strict liability) could carry the moral freight that Borgo associates with corrective justice so conceived.[15] Many injuries, even when inflicted knowingly, seem not to call for legal redress. If A opens a shop in competition with B, he is quite likely, and he knows he is quite likely, to injure B—indeed he probably will *have* to injure him, in the sense of taking sales away from him, in order to make a go of his own shop. Yet we do not conclude that competition should be a tort; remember *Tuttle v. Buck* in Chapter 8.

Epstein had tried to overcome this problem with an idiosyncratic account of causation, whereby the only causes that count for law are those that resemble the account of causing physical injury implicit in the example "A hit B."[16] Borgo does not accept this and instead suggests

---

13. "Nuisance Law," note 12 above, at 77, 101.

14. "Defenses and Subsequent Pleas," note 12 above, at 167–168, 198–199, and n. 87.

15. Borgo, "Causal Paradigms in Tort Law," 8 *Journal of Legal Studies* 419–420, 454 (1979). "The linchpin of a system of corrective justice is a nonorthodox doctrine of causation. Such a doctrine makes it possible to focus analysis on the causal relation between the defendant's conduct and the plaintiff's harm. That relation in turn provides the basis for ascribing moral, and therefore legal, responsibility for harm." Id. at 454.

16. See, for example, Epstein, "Intentional Harms," 4 *Journal of Legal Studies* 391, 431–432 (1975).

that, for purposes of tort law, causation should be equated to moral or legal responsibility for consequences.[17] He is right to the extent that conclusions about causation are frequently influenced by normative considerations. We may single out a sufficient condition as the cause of something because we want to bring the something about; creating a sufficient condition will, by definition, bring it about—that is what a sufficient condition is. Or we may single out a necessary condition as the cause of something because we want to prevent the something from occurring, which (again by definition) we can do by preventing one of its necessary conditions from occurring. So we might pick the cheapest of these conditions to prevent and call it the cause. Causation has an opportunistic, functional, pragmatic, or, if one prefers, ethical charge on it.[18] But causation and responsibility are not synonyms. The competition example shows this: the successful competitor really has caused his rival's losses, but no opprobrium attaches. The madman who kills is the cause of his victim's death, even if not culpable. If A gives C a slow poison, and B administers a lethal wound to C a moment before the poison would have killed C, both A and B would be liable in tort to C's survivors; likewise if A and B each set fires that joined and rushed down on C's house and consumed it. In neither case is either A's or B's act a necessary condition of C's loss (although each act is a sufficient condition), yet the law does not hesitate to hold both A and B liable.

Even if, in the teeth of such examples, causation could be equated to responsibility, this would be a proposition not of corrective justice but of distributive justice. We would be talking about the scope of the entitlement to be free from injury rather than about what corrective measures are due when that entitlement is violated.

Others besides Epstein and Borgo have made the equation of injury to wrongful injury,[19] but I will skip over these to discuss Jules Coleman's

17. See Borgo, note 15 above, at 444.

18. See, for example, R. G. Collingwood, *An Essay on Metaphysics,* ch. 31 (1940); Thomas Nagel, *Mortal Questions* 24, 28–31 (1979); "Proximate and Remote Cause," in Nicholas St. John Green, *Essays and Notes on the Law of Tort and Crime* 1, 11–13 (1933) (article first published in 1870). The fullest discussion of issues of legal causation from a philosophical standpoint is H. L. A. Hart and Tony Honoré, *Causation in the Law* (2d ed. 1985), the first part of which contains a good discussion of philosophical theories of causation.

19. See George P. Fletcher, "Fairness and Utility in Tort Theory," 85 *Harvard Law Review* 537 (1972); Frederick L. Sharp, "Aristotle, Justice, and Enterprise Liability in the Law of Torts," 34 *University of Toronto Faculty Law Review* 84 (1976)—both discussed in my article "The Concept of Corrective Justice in Recent Theories of Tort Law," 10 *Journal of Legal Studies* 187, 191–193, 199–201 (1981); see also Alan Schwartz, "Responsibility and Tort Liability," 97 *Ethics* 270 (1986).

extensive efforts to extract substantive implications for tort law from the concept of corrective justice.[20] He has been concerned among other things with the question whether a system of no-fault liability is consistent with corrective justice (which he sometimes calls compensatory or rectificatory justice). He thinks it is. If an injury is wrongful, the victim is entitled to be compensated, but not necessarily by the injurer; in particular, if the injurer did not gain from the wrongful act, corrective justice does not require that he be the source of the victim's compensation. There are two problems. The first is that the victim is not compensated in any sense relevant to corrective justice when he merely collects the proceeds of an insurance policy for which he has paid (has been *forced* to pay—that is what a no-fault system is: compulsory accident insurance). The second is that the injurer *does* gain something from his wrongful act. If he was driving negligently when the accident occurred, and thereby economized on resources devoted to safe driving (time and concentration, or possibly regular maintenance of his car), but thanks to the no-fault system does not have to pay the victim anything, then he is gaining at his victim's expense in the same sense as the murderer who steals a trifle. The gain is not commensurate with the loss in either case, but Aristotle was explicit that this asymmetry does not diminish the duty to do corrective justice.

Although I am not persuaded by Coleman's defense of the no-fault principle against a charge of denying corrective justice, neither do I believe that no-fault liability raises a problem of corrective justice. No fault involves a redefinition of rights, such that what used to be a wrongful injury (negligently running down someone) is no longer wrongful. If it is not wrongful, there is no duty of corrective justice.

Might this conclusion be altered if we shifted the emphasis from injury to taking, or in other words from corrective to restitutionary justice? The driver who runs me down while he is driving to (let us say) an appointment with a valued customer has in effect made my body an input into his productive activities. He has taken something from me;

20. See the following articles by Coleman: "The Structure of Tort Law," 97 *Yale Law Journal* 1233, 1240–1253 (1988); "Corrective Justice and Wrongful Gain," in Coleman, *Markets, Morals, and the Law* 184 (1988); "Moral Theories of Torts: Their Scope and Limits: Part II," 2 *Law and Philosophy* 5 (1983); "Mental Abnormality, Personal Responsibility, and Tort Liability," in *Mental Illness: Law and Public Policy* 107 (Baruch A. Brody and H. Tristram Engelhardt, Jr., eds. 1980); "Reply to Pilon," 59 *Personalist* 307, 312–313 (1978); "The Morality of Strict Tort Liability," 18 *William and Mary Law Review* 259 (1976); "Justice and the Argument for No-Fault," 3 *Social Theory and Practice* 161 (1974). Coleman acknowledges a debt to James W. Nickel, whose views may be found in "Justice in Compensation," 18 *William and Mary Law Review* 379 (1976).

shouldn't he have to pay? Yes, if he was driving carelessly, for then there is a wrong, and Aristotle's notion of corrective justice requires recitification. But if there is no negligence or other ground for finding wrongful conduct, the driver's use of my body is a lawful form of exploitation akin to using a valuable invention that has fallen into the public domain upon the expiration of the inventor's patent.

The restitutionary perspective may seem more apt when a manufacturer sells a product that injures some of his customers. Under a regime of strict products liability, he must compensate the injured even if the injury could not have been prevented by the exercise of due care. In effect, all those who buy the product contribute to the compensation fund by paying the slightly higher price that the manufacturer will charge in order to defray the cost of the occasional tort judgment. Hence those who benefit from the product pay for the costs that it imposes on the unlucky consumer who is injured by it; if they did not have to pay, it would be as if they had stolen something of value (life, limb, money) from that consumer. But again it must be emphasized that the decision whether to treat a particular taking as a wrong is prior to any judgment about corrective justice. And actually the taking in this example is equivocal. The injured consumer who is not compensated was a beneficiary of the lower price, along with the uninjured customers, because he paid less than he would have had to pay if the manufacturer had had a duty to compensate injured customers. He would actually be a net beneficiary, ex ante, if the price discount was greater than the cost of buying full insurance against personal injury caused by a dangerous or defective product and if the accident was truly unavoidable, meaning that it would have occurred even under a regime of strict liability. It would be weird to say there had been a taking, a wrong, in a case where by hypothesis the victim would have voted against strict liability before the accident occurred.

In addition, and in tension with defending no fault, Coleman argues that the tort system as we know it is better understood as a system of corrective justice than as a system of minimizing social losses. "The reason the victim brings to court his injurer, rather than bringing the world of potentially cheaper cost-avoiders [by which Coleman means other persons or institutions that might have prevented the accident at a cost lower than the cost to the injurer], is that his claim to compensation as a matter of justice is *analytically* connected to some facts he seeks to establish about the injurer's conduct."[21] Coleman is emphasizing here the

---

ʾ 21. "The Structure of Tort Law," note 20 above, at 1249.

bilateral character of corrective justice—the idea of corrective justice as a rectificatory transaction between the injurer and the injured—but is overlooking the opportunistic or functional idea of causation, and hence the possibility that deciding *who* the injurer is may depend on finding out who the cheapest cost-avoider is. It is true that in a tort system the victim has a remedy only against the person who caused his injury, but in deciding who that person is the courts are not indifferent to the various ways in which accidents can be prevented and to the various "candidates" that there are, therefore, for the role of injurer. Suppose that A, while driving a truck, injures B. B may decide to sue A—but he may also (or instead) decide to sue the manufacturer of the truck; A's employer; the driver of a car that swerved into A's path; the designer of the road; the public agency that failed to maintain it properly; the state that licensed A to drive; the manufacturer of the traffic light that failed to operate properly; the tavern that served A liquor before he started on the trip. All are necessary conditions; the question which will be deemed the cause of the accident will be decided on expedient grounds and the answer will determine who is to compensate B. Cause and responsibility are not identical but do overlap. Plural causes and joint liability are of course possible in the example.

To all this carping it may be replied that if modern scholars depart from Aristotle's concept of corrective justice, so much the worse for Aristotle. This riposte would be crushing—since it would be absurd to suppose that Aristotle had said the last word on legal justice or on any other subject—if these scholars had articulated and defended a new concept of corrective justice. But most of them think that they are using Aristotle's concept,[22] and they are not. They are arguing from authority, and they have got the authority wrong. Their error is to disregard the narrow, formal character of Aristotle's concept. It is a useful concept; it has significant content; but it is too limited to underwrite legal-doctrinal analysis.

Ernest Weinrib, like Coleman, wants to develop an account of tort law that will be independent of economic analysis. He realizes that while reflection on corrective justice may show that economic analysis of tort law is incomplete—the idea of an unshakable duty to make correction ex post for a wrongful injury is not an economic idea—it will not answer any specific questions about tort liability, but he thinks Kant supplies the missing link, so that a combination of Aristotle and Kant will pro-

22. The exception is Coleman. See "Corrective Justice and Wrongful Gain," note 20 above, at 197.

vide a complete ethical foundation for tort law.[23] The ethics of Kant are too abstract, however, to guide the design of legal doctrines. Weinrib's only example of the application of Kant's thought to a legal question concerns whether negligence should be an "objective" concept (that is, should mean the failure to exercise the care that the average person would have exercised) or a "subjective" one (failure to exercise the care that this particular injurer, who may have been below average in his ability to avoid accidents, could have exercised). In arguing for the former position, which happens also to be the position that tort law has taken, Weinrib invokes Kant for the proposition that the subjective approach would amount to "a claim that the boundary between the defendant's right to act and the plaintiff's right to freedom from the effects of that action is marked by the defendant's subjective powers of evaluation," making the plaintiff's right "dependent on the defendant's subjectivity"; this "contradicts the very conception of a right," since "a right is something which a person has . . . by virtue of his being an end in himself" and it therefore "cannot be dependent on someone else's subjectivity."[24] The word "subjectivity" is equivocal, however. The law uses it to denote a standard that varies with the capabilities of the individual defendant; Weinrib uses it to denote an attempt by one person to subject another to his will. The person who injures another because he is incapable of taking the care of an average person (maybe he is retarded or has a nervous disorder) is not trying to subject the other to his will; he can't help what he's done. In his situation, negligence becomes a form of strict liability[25]—which makes Weinrib's rejection of strict liability, as being incompatible with a Kantian conception of tort liability,[26] inconsistent.

More could be done with Aristotle's concept of corrective justice to explain features of our legal system. Deterrence, for example, depends both on the probability that the perpetrator of an offense will be apprehended and punished and on the severity of the punishment; and these are reciprocals. So for a given crime, a 10 percent probability of punishment combined with a ten-year average sentence might produce the same deterrence as a 50 percent probability of punishment combined with a two-year sentence. The second combination might well be more

<hr />

23. Weinrib, "Toward a Moral Theory of Negligence Law," 2 *Law and Philosophy* 37 (1983).

24. Id. at 51–52.

25. See William M. Landes and Richard A. Posner, *The Economic Structure of Tort Law* 123–128 (1987).

26. See Weinrib, note 23 above, at 57–62.

costly, because it would require a greater deployment of police and pro-secutorial resources to maintain the higher probability of punishment. This is clear in the example, where the aggregate number of prisoners is the same each year under either approach (as can be seen by multiply-ing each probability of imprisonment by the number of years in prison associated with that probability), so that the only difference in cost is that the second combination requires more police and more prosecutors. Although this is an artifact of the example, the general principle—that one can economize on police and prosecutors by making punishment more terrifying, and come out ahead from a deterrent standpoint even though a lower percentage of criminals are caught—is plausible. Yet society might prefer the less economical approach because it does cor-rective justice better—fewer crimes go unpunished. This explanation for people's uneasiness at a criminal justice system in which chance plays a very large role is different from the usual explanation, which is that the inequality of ex post outcomes under a lottery-style criminal justice sys-tem offends the sense of distributive justice.

A Note on Retributive Justice—and on Rights

Corrective justice rests on two foundations: the inadequacy of personal justice; and the indignation and demand for satisfaction that are the nat-ural—I mean this literally—reactions to an invasion of one's rights. From this perspective we can think of the tort system as a civilized sub-stitute for vengeance; and we can see that the system rests ultimately therefore on notions of retributive justice.[27] I would love to know whether the scholars who plump for making corrective justice the foun-dation of tort law would, as I think consistency requires, endorse a retri-butivist theory of criminal law. The alternative is to view both fields in

27. On which see, besides Murphy's article cited in note 11 above, C. L. Ten, *Crime, Guilt, and Punishment: A Philosophical Introduction,* ch. 3 (1987); Michael S. Moore, "The Moral Worth of Retribution," in *Responsibility, Character, the Emotions: New Essays in Moral Psychology* 179 (Ferdinand Shoeman ed. 1987); John Mackie, "Morality and the Retributive Emotions," in Mackie, *Persons and Values: Selected Papers,* vol. 2, p. 206 (Joan Mackie and Penelope Mackie eds. 1985); Jeffrie G. Murphy and Jean Hampton, *Forgiveness and Mercy* (1988); Robert Nozick, *Philosophical Explanations* 363–397 (1981); Elizabeth H. Wolgast, "Intolerable Wrong and Punishment," 60 *Philosophy* 161 (1985); Herbert Fingarette, "Pun-ishment and Suffering," 50 *Proceedings of the American Philosophical Association* 499 (1977). A distinction should be noted between retribution as *ground* and as *limitation* of punishment. The proposition that retribution is a duty is obviously not the same as the proposition that a wrongdoer should not be punished more severely than is required for retribution. The first proposition is the one relevant to the discussion in text.

instrumental terms. We want to accomplish certain goals—deterrence or compensation or whatever—and tort suits and criminal prosecutions are among the instruments available for attaining these goals. The most highly developed instrumental approach to tort and criminal law is the economic approach, discussed in Chapter 12.

Stressing the primitive character of corrective and retributive justice—the roots of these concepts in behavior having plausible sociobiological interpretations—is a necessary corrective to the common belief that Aristotelian and Kantian ideas of justice are more "moral" than pragmatic and instrumental views. Although Aristotle and Kant obviously had no opportunity to read *The Origin of Species,* their ideas about remedial justice—the justice of sanctions for transgression—are rooted in a view of human nature, as quintessentially vengeful, that is highly compatible with a Darwinian view. This is fine, but makes no great claim to ethical superiority over ideas derived from more social or civic conceptions of human nature.

A parallel point is that "rights" is a primitive rather than a sophisticated concept. I am thinking now not of the legal and economic distinction between cases in which a person cannot be forced to surrender something without his consent ("property right") and cases in which he can merely demand compensation for injury ("liability rule"),[28] but of the usage more common in moral and political philosophy, in which a right is an important interest presumptively protected against interference by others. The sense we all have of having certain rights it would be wrong to deprive us of is a primitive feature of our psychological make up—one as well developed in children and in the inhabitants of primitive societies as it is in modern American adults, and found in animals as well. Survival in a competitive environment requires some minimum sense of the essential things that are one's own to keep or dispose of as one will, and of a readiness to fight for this control—this readiness *is* the sense of entitlement. The creature that does not feel a sense of moralistic indignation when another creature seeks to take from it the things that are essential to its survival is not likely to survive and reproduce, so there will be a selection in favor of creatures genetically endowed with such a sense.[29] The content of rights will change with a changing social environment but the sense of having rights will be a

28. See Guido Calabresi and A. Douglas Melamed, "Property Rights, Liability Rules, and Inalienability: One View of the Cathedral," 85 *Harvard Law Review* 1089 (1972); Landes and Posner, note 25 above, ch. 2.

29. See Robert L. Trivers, "The Evolution of Reciprocal Altruism," 46 *Quarterly Review of Biology* 35, 49 (1971); Posner, *The Economics of Justice,* note 7 above, at 211–212.

constant, and this helps to explain the persistence into twentieth-century American law of notions of vengeance, retributive justice, and corrective justice.

Sociobiology—the theory that characteristic dispositions toward other people, such as altruism, envy, aggressiveness, and vengefulness, are strongly influenced by the genes—is highly controversial, in part of because of its perceived political implications. But it would be wrong to reject sociobiology on political grounds, and its scientific character is attested by sober philosophers of science.[30] At the very least, naturalistic rights theory is a healthy antidote to the inflated rhetoric of rights that is so marked a characteristic of contemporary jurisprudential discourse.

Formal Justice

Aristotle's concept of corrective justice is a member of a class of formal principles that might be thought to narrow the range of discretion of judges and other makers and appliers of law and thereby make law more "lawlike," regular, impersonal. Others include:[31] (1) A legal command must be capable of being complied with by those to whom it is addressed; (2) it must treat equally those who are similarly situated in all respects relevant to the command; (3) it must be public; and (4) there must be a procedure for establishing the facts necessary to the application of the command. This grouping, which is sometimes taken as constitutive of a distinctively legal sense of justice, or as defining the rule of law or the inner morality of the law, or as offering an answer to the question of what law is, is a thin gruel.

Point 3 is part of point 1; together they are intended to rule out the enormity of imposing sanctions on people who lack a fair opportunity to avoid their imposition by complying with the law. But do they succeed in ruling this out? Recurring to the *locus classicus* of retroactive lawmaking, the judgment of the Nuremberg Tribunal, we may note that even if the Nazi leaders could not, when they committed their crimes

30. See Michael Ruse, *Sociobiology: Sense or Nonsense?* (2d ed. 1985); Florian von Schilcher and Neil Tennant, *Philosophy, Evolution, and Human Nature,* ch. 2 (1984). The most ambitious proposals for applying sociobiological insights to law are those of John H. Beckstrom. See his books *Sociobiology and the Law: The Biology of Altruism in the Courtroom of the Future* (1985); *Evolutionary Jurisprudence: Prospects and Limitations on the Use of Modern Darwinism throughout the Legal Process* (1989).

31. See John Rawls, *A Theory of Justice* 237–239 (1971), and references there; Tom Campbell, *Justice* 23–35 (1988). And recall the discussion in Chapter 7 of Lon Fuller's views. Rawls's criteria owe much to Kant's theory of law, ably summarized in Ernest J. Weinrib, "Law as a Kantian Idea of Reason," 87 *Columbia Law Review* 472 (1987).

against humanity, have foreseen the precise content of the norms applied at Nuremberg, they should have known—most of them did know— that their conduct was so contrary to basic civilized norms that if Germany lost the war a terrible retribution would be visited on them. This example suggests both that pure retroactivity is rare and that impure retroactivity is tolerated. Further evidence for the latter half of this proposition is that judges invariably apply a new principle to the case in which the principle is announced, without troubling themselves over whether the losing party should have foreseen those principles. (Probably he would not have litigated the case, if he had.) The judges do this for reasons of expediency. Unless the winning party had the benefit of a new principle, he would have no incentive to press for one, and the process of legal change would be impeded. And even though legislation normally is prospective in form, in effect it often is retroactive, as when by a change in tax rates or in regulation or in public spending the legislature brings about substantial changes in the capital value of the assets affected by the new legislation. The avoidance of retroactivity is just one other consideration to weigh in the social balance; it is not an indispensable condition of justice under law. This is not to say that it is an unimportant consideration, but its importance will vary with the circumstances, and with the weight the observer attaches to stability relative to other social values.

Point 1 is also overbroad. Taken literally, it implies that strict liability is unjust. Strict criminal liability often is attacked as unjust (perhaps superficially, as noted in Chapter 5); strict tort liability rarely, though we saw an example of such an attack in discussing Weinrib's views. If point 1 is interpreted flexibly, as merely an injunction against law's expecting the impossible of the people subject to it, it becomes trivial.

The proposition that equals should be treated equally (point 2) is at one level a platitude, at another a falsehood. A rational system for making judgments will avoid arbitrary in the sense of illogical (that is, contradictory) distinctions; this is the only "inequality" that can be condemned at the formal level, that is, without getting into the merits of particular substantive issues, such as racial discrimination. Formal equality will rule out certain outcomes but leave a vast open area. Moreover, no real-world legal system can—or, what is more interesting, should—avoid *all* arbitrary distinctions. Judges must be allowed to change their minds, even though the consequence will be an "arbitrary" distinction between litigants in period one and those in period two. And since the costs of operating a legal system free from errors would be prohibitive, the best of real-world systems will exhibit a copious inequality of legal outcomes. Point 4, finally, seems at once correct and uninteresting.

A bit more can be done with notions of formal justice. We can say, without too much fear of contradiction, that a law is unjust if it is so contrary to dominant public opinion that virtually no one will either obey or enforce it, or if it is so incomprehensible that no one *can* obey it, or if it is enforced so rarely that people forget about it and it becomes a trap for the unwary. All these are aspects of points 1 and 3; in general, if not in every case, the purposes of a law are defeated if compliance is impossible, and this futility is felt as injustice when the violation of the law carries with it heavy sanctions; for then law seems all costs and no benefits. The apparent exception for strict liability, whether in tort law or in criminal law, is misleading; strict liability may induce—and may be intended to induce—potential injurers to avoid injury by curtailing their activity or steering clear of dangerous activity, or it may be a device for making injurers insure their victims against unavoidable accidents. In either case it only appears to compel the impossible.

Coupled with Aristotle's twofold conception of corrective justice, the discussion in the preceding paragraph yields a rule-of-law ideology that places sensible constraints on legal discretion, but not tight ones; the quest for those will carry us into the tenebrous realm of distributive justice.

Distributive Justice

If the existing structure of legal rights is taken for granted, the problem of supplying objective answers to legal questions is simplified, because one is then merely trying to find the best means to agreed ends; a question of value becomes one of fact. Suppose it is accepted that everyone has a right not to be injured by a careless driver, but that, conversely, no driver who exercises due care is liable for the injuries he inflicts. With this as our starting point we might assess proposals to substitute strict liability for negligence by asking whether potential injurers and potential victims would agree to such a change. Presumably they would if (reversing our previous example) the sum of accident and liability insurance premiums under strict liability were lower than under negligence, as they might be if strict liability were cheaper to administer and more effective in deterring dangerous behavior as well as in providing fuller compensation when an accident occurred. But now suppose that someone argues that people ought to have a right not to be injured by *any* driver, even one driving carefully; how do we assess such a proposal?

No longer is it a question of finding the cheapest and most efficacious means to an agreed end, that of maximizing the value of a given distribution of rights; it is a matter of deciding what people's initial entitlements shall be.

Not much guidance on this question can be found within the enterprise of law. The lawyer can point out that certain initial entitlements might be cumbersome or impracticable, and he might point to statutes of limitations and to certain provisions of the Constitution (notably the impairment-of-contracts clause, the takings clause, and the ex post facto clause) as evincing recognition of the inexpediency of continually reshuffling rights in an effort to achieve a perfectly just distribution. He might also point out that people feel profound resentment at being deprived of what they have come to believe are their rights. The lawyer will not get far in attempting to formulate a theory of distributive justice, however, and will soon have to turn to the political or moral philosopher, but in doing so he will be seeking to dispel obscurity by plunging into deeper obscurity.

We find, to begin with, that if Aristotle's account of corrective justice is spare, his account of distributive justice is sparer.[32] Book V, chapter 3 of the *Nicomachean Ethics* explains that the principle that should guide the state in the allocation of money or honors is the relative merit of the potential recipients. The standard of merit depends in turn on the values of the society. If the society is aristocratic (Aristotle's conception of the just society), the principle of distribution will be according to virtue or excellence: the more virtuous citizen will be entitled to a proportionately larger share of the distribution than the less virtuous one. This is fine as far as it goes, but it does not go far, especially since Aristotle did not conceive of the state as initially owning all of society's resources and then parceling them out among the citizens. He assumed that in the private sphere people would be free to trade and amass what wealth they could (starting with whatever assets they happened to possess—an inheritance, raw talent, an iron will, or whatever), subject to a duty of avoiding unjust acts such as theft and fraud (see Book V, chapters 4 and 5). His principle of distributive justice did not operate over the whole wealth of society.

In its lack of particularity Aristotle's account of distributive justice is representative of later philosophical accounts of distributive justice as well. We have had a glimpse of this point in Kant; we could make the

---

32. On the relation between corrective and distributive justice in Aristotle, see John Finnis, *Natural Law and Natural Rights* 178–184 (1980).

same point about Rawls. We must turn to philosophizing lawyers for concrete conceptions of distributive justice. Consider Bruce Ackerman's conception.[33] He imagines a highly simplified social setting consisting of the passengers of a spaceship about to land on a virgin planet that has a fixed stock of resources. He imposes ground rules for debating claims to be allowed to possess or to do things (to have rights and exercise powers, in other words). A claim is defeated when its spokesman is reduced to silence—that is, when he can no longer defend his claim without violating one of the ground rules. By this method, in which the influence of the contemporary German philosopher Jürgen Habermas is visible, Ackerman derives both the basic principle that all persons should start their (adult) lives with equal wealth, and certain secondary principles relating to education, abortion, democracy, and other political-ethical topics. Only one of the ground rules, however, actually figures importantly in his analysis. That one is neutrality, meaning that "no reason is a good reason if it requires the power holder [that is, the claimant] to assert (a) that his conception of the good is better than that asserted by any of his fellow citizens, *or* (b) that, regardless of his conception of the good, he is intrinsically superior to one or more of his fellow citizens" (p. 11).

Most of the time, Ackerman could go directly from his premise of neutrality to his conclusions about distributive justice and other policy and ethical matters without the intermediate step of a debate among the passengers of a spaceship, a step that complicates and retards the development of his argument. But his insistence that debate itself, rather than just the reasons offered in a debate, is the basis for legitimizing state action does make a difference in one area: that of defining the rights of people (or creatures) who lack "dialogic competence" (p. 75) and of nonhuman beings who have it. Citizenship and the rights flowing from it derive in Ackerman's view from participation in rational discourse about political legitimacy. This makes the status of idiots and children—even of adults who are not sufficiently intelligent or well educated to be able to debate issues of political legitimacy—problematic: "The rights of the talking ape are more secure than those of the human vegetable" (p. 80).

Ackerman's concept of neutrality is neither clear nor well defended.

33. *Social Justice in the Liberal State* (1980). Page references to this book are in the text. For criticisms of the book distinct from but overlapping my own, see J. L. Mackie, "Competitors in Conversation," *Times Literary Supplement,* April 17, 1981, at 443. For defense of Ackerman's "dialogic" procedure, see Bruce Ackerman, "Why Dialogue?" 86 *Journal of Philosophy* 5 (1989).

But since part (a) seems simply to rule out bare assertions, and part (b) to exclude appeals to lineage, caste, or race as grounds for preferential treatment, these constraints are too modest to get one far without the aid of Ackerman's trick of renaming wealth "power," so that every claim on material goods is recast as a political claim and becomes an invitation to public intervention. The beggar's rags are the gift of the state, and the beggar must justify his possession of them by stating a valid political claim. Since the grounds on which political claims can be upheld in Ackerman's world are limited by the neutrality concept, with its strong if vague egalitarian overtones (Ackerman deduces from it that "everybody is at least as good as everybody else," p. 249), it is only a small step to an equal initial distribution of wealth; such a distribution becomes as natural as an equal distribution of votes.

Ackerman might reply that in a work of political philosophy, devoted to investigating the legitimacy of the political arrangements that both allow and protect the ownership of private property, such ownership cannot be assumed—cannot be considered natural, prepolitical—but must be justified. But it is as arbitrary to start with the assumption of common ownership—to regard this as the default position if the advocate of privatization fails to persuade—as it is to start with the assumption of private property. Ackerman's assumption rapidly hardens into an irrebuttable presumption in favor of an equal initial distribution.

The dice are further loaded by Ackerman's choice of the allocation of "manna" (the one good in his spaceship world) to be the model of the power struggle among individuals for private goods. Because manna is found rather than produced, the struggle over it is a zero-sum game; one person's gain is another's loss. This is indeed the character of the power struggle among political candidates and interest groups—it is one of the things that make so much political competition unedifying—but it is not the character of the struggle for material possessions. In a well-functioning market economy one can increase one's wealth only by offering other people attractive trades, which means that in the process of amassing wealth one will increase the prosperity of one's trading partners as well. These mutual benefits are the "gains of trade."

Granted, Ackerman is talking about the *initial* distribution, presumably of things that already exist (such as land) rather than things that are created, since created items would come later and thus would not be part of the original distribution. He would allow the creation of new goods and services through markets. This alleviates the static quality of his analysis but opens a hole in his egalitarian scheme. People have different propensities for dealing in markets, as well as different tastes, talents, and luck, and these differences are likely to dominate the lingering effects through time of differences in the initial distribution. It is unclear that the distribution of wealth in the United States would be more equal today if land and other natural resources had been distributed with perfect equality when the nation was founded.

I said that if you give Ackerman his assumptions there is only a small distance to an egalitarian conception of distributive justice. But he is not able to cover that distance, and not only for the reason I have just given, which is that the effects of the initial distribution (equal or unequal) are likely to dissipate after a few generations and make the issue of the initial distribution uninteresting from a practical standpoint. More fundamentally, he is unable to justify an equal initial distribution of wealth. To anyone who would claim more than a pro rata share of society's initial stock of wealth, Ackerman offers the following reply, intended to be decisive: "Since I'm at least as good as you are, I should get at least as much of the stuff we both desire" (p. 58), that is, the manna. But the claimant could easily rejoin, "Your unsupported assertion of relative goodness in an unspecified sense is not a rational basis for giving you an equal share of the wealth." This rejoinder would not violate the concept of neutrality—a point that demonstrates the arbitrariness of Ackerman's assumption that the "default" solution (when everyone is reduced to silence) is equal shares. Ackerman offers, it is true, a slightly fuller statement of the claim to an equal share: "I am a person with a conception of the good . . . Simply by virtue of being such a person, I'm at least as good as you are" (p. 66). But to have a conception of the good is not to be good, to be deserving. Hitler had a conception of the good, and could talk as well as Ackerman. The dialogic method is less constraining than Ackerman believes.

Michael Walzer has made a similar point, discussing Habermas. "There is a dilemma here: if the circumstances of what Habermas calls ideal speech or undistorted communication are specified in detail, then only a limited number of things can be said, and these things could probably be said by the philosopher himself, representing all the rest of us . . . If, however, the circumstances are only roughly specified, so that ideal speech resembles democratic debate, then the participants can say almost anything, and there is no reason why the results should not (sometimes) turn out to be 'very strange and even contrary to good morals.' "[34]

Ackerman modifies his egalitarian concept of distributive justice to

34. Michael Walzer, *Interpretation and Social Criticism* 11 n. 9 (1987).

allow for compensating inequalities—affirmative action in a broad, and also in its conventional narrow, sense. But he does this by manipulating the words "dominate" and "exploit." A blind or otherwise seriously handicapped person is said by Ackerman to be "suffer[ing] from irremediable domination" (p. 247). Such a person is therefore entitled to a more expensive education than his fellows; and since, even after he is as well educated as they (the extra expense being necessary to overcome the handicap to the extent possible), he will be less well off (still "dominated"), society in Ackerman's view must give him even more education, wealth, or whatever is necessary to bring about net equality and so end domination. However strongly such a result may appeal to our humane and altruistic instincts (or pretensions), it not only is remote from traditional conceptions of liberalism but envisages a scale of redistribution that would require crushing levels of taxation, with all the coercive machinery that extremely high levels of taxation entail. Such a program would be more attractive if the targets were domination and exploitation in meaningful senses, but as Ackerman uses the words they are synonyms for inequality. He justifies measures to redress inequalities in welfare by pointing out that there are inequalities and calling them names.

People who try to construct comprehensive social systems from the ground up often feel themselves becoming trapped by logical but crazy implications of the system, and unless they are Plato (in the *Republic*) or Bentham,[35] they struggle to escape. So Ackerman, having questioned the rights of the "human vegetable" and having endorsed a right of abortion because the "fetus fails the dialogic test—more plainly than do grown-up dolphins" (p. 127), gingerly approaches the question of infanticide.[36] Although "a day-old infant is no more a citizen than a nine-month fetus," Ackerman says that the state can forbid infanticide by invoking the "principle against wanton cruelty": the "'natural' parents have it within their power simply to pass the child on to another, yet they prefer to kill it instead. What other reason can they give for their

---

35. See my discussion of Bentham in *The Economics of Justice* 31–47 (1981).

36. The question had also troubled Kant and had evoked the following extraordinary answer. He is discussing the killing of an illegitimate child by its mother: "A child born into the world outside marriage is outside the law . . . and consequently it is also outside the protection of the law. The child has crept surreptitiously into the commonwealth (much like prohibited wares), so that its existence as well as its destruction can be ignored (because by right it ought not to have come into existence in this way); and the mother's disgrace if the illegitimate birth becomes known cannot be wiped out by any official decree." *The Metaphysical Elements of Justice* 106 (John Ladd trans. 1965).

action but their desire to impose pain upon mute creation?" (p. 129). To begin with, it is unclear *why* they must give another reason, any more than people who wanted to destroy rather than to eat their manna would have to give a reason. It would violate the neutrality conception to treat the conception of the good held by the parents—wanton cruelty—as inferior to competing conceptions; this is the Hitler problem again. And since the infant has no standing in the community, he cannot counter his parents' conception of the good by saying that he is as good as they are. Ackerman also ignores the possibility that no one else wants the child, in which event the parents can easily give a reason for killing it other than a desire to inflict pain: they may simply have changed their mind about having the child after they saw it. And they may not want to inflict pain, and may in fact kill painlessly. They may even fear the child; remember why Oedipus's parents tried to kill him.

Part of Ackerman's problem is the acontextual, ahistorical character of his inquiry. Like Plato and Bentham, not to mention Hobbes and Rawls and Nozick, he wants to start from scratch, from a master principle. That is why he has such difficulty understanding the humanity of a retarded child. Judges do not start from scratch in deciding cases. So while the sheer strangeness of Ackerman's book need not detract from its academic merits, it should give pause to anyone who thinks that judges should steer by the lights of political or moral philosophy.[37] Philosophers are sometimes driven to conclusions at variance with the moral values of their society; in our present state of moral and intellectual diversity, at variance too with the conclusions of most other philosophers. If there is a mechanism for arbitrating between moral philosophies, it is not possessed by judges. It may not be possessed by philosophers either. At bottom we test our theories by reference to our intuitions, the things we cannot help believing. In today's United States, people's moral intuitions are diverse—so much so that different segments of the community seem to inhabit different moral universes. The

---

37. Cf. Michael Walzer, "Philosophy and Democracy," 9 *Political Theory* 379 (1981). On the inadequacies of egalitarian theories in general, see the superb discussion in Harry G. Frankfurt, "Equality as a Moral Ideal," in his book *The Importance of What We Care About: Philosophical Essays* 134 (1988); also this pithy observation by John W. Chapman: "The equality and cooperative solidarity characteristic of prehistoric bands or good families does not translate into a workable social idea, although this psychic heritage may well help to account for our endemic discontent with modern society." "Justice, Freedom, and Property," in *Nomos XXII: Property* 289, 311 (J. Roland Pennock and John W. Chapman eds. 1980).

moral theories that convince one community will not convince the others, no matter how brilliant the theorists' argumentation.

The intellectual odyssey of Richard Epstein, another brilliant law professor (but this time a conservative one) fascinated by issues of distributive justice, will further illustrate the difficulty of these issues and the unlikelihood that appeals to distributive justice can generate objective allocations of legal rights or duties. In his early tort articles, which I mentioned in discussing corrective justice, Epstein thought he had found in the categories and usages of ordinary, nonlegal language an important repository of moral ideas. One was that people are morally responsible for the harms they cause and should be made, prima facie, legally responsible as well; therefore, subject to certain defenses, strict liability should be the ruling principle of tort law. As a corollary Epstein argued that it would be improper to impose liability on a person who had not caused another's injury but had merely failed to help the other—the bystander who sees a flower pot about to drop on a person's head and says nothing, or a strong swimmer who refuses to go to the aid of a person who is drowning before his eyes.

The distinction between harming and not helping, corresponding to the distinction in the ethics of Kant between respect for other people and concern for other people, or in radical and feminist jurisprudence between individualistic and communitarian notions of obligation, is an important one. But to defend it by appeal to ordinary language fails on a number of grounds, and this regardless of whether ordinary language is regarded as a fount of wisdom or of error (it is both). As we saw in discussing whether competition should be a tort, it is not true that ordinary language equates causation and moral responsibility; the successful competitor causes his rival's discomfiture and perhaps (commercial) demise, but we are apt to hold the rival himself responsible for those losses. And although we can pick out some causal interactions in which it seems natural to regard the injurer as responsible for the injury—for example when A strikes B intentionally and offers no excuse for doing so—they provide no reason for confining legal responsibility to such cases. Indeed, the more narrowly the causal interactions that give rise to legal responsibility are circumscribed, the less plausible it becomes to regard causality as a prerequisite to such responsibility. But my basic point is a simple logical one: from the fact that if A hits B, A should be liable to B, it does not follow that if A fails to help B, A should not be liable to B.

Epstein allows that if A does help B, A may be entitled to recover his expenses from B on a theory of implied contract, since if the parties could have negotiated in advance of the emergency that placed B in peril, B would surely have agreed to compensate A for the expense of the rescue. (Recall the discussion of this example in Chapter 2.) But once implied-contractual thinking is allowed, it becomes permissible to speculate that A and B (and everyone else) might have agreed, if negotiations over the matter had been feasible, to form a mutual-protection society—the state—in which each member would be obligated, on pain of tort liability if he defaulted, to come to the aid of any other member who found himself in peril, provided the rescue could be effected at a reasonable cost. Moreover, as we saw in examining Coleman's theory of corrective justice, the concept of an implied contract might be used to show that strict liability was not the right system after all.

Epstein soon realized that he could get nowhere in his project of recasting tort law in strict liability terms and rejecting "good Samaritan" liability unless he made the identification of rights the first step in his inquiry into legal responsibility. A would be liable for hitting B, because B had a property right in his body. A would not be liable for failing to help B, because B had no property right in A's labor. But how do we know who has what rights? If we accept the existing legal position, we have no leverage for reform; under existing law, B does not have a property right in his body, for, provided A is not careless, B has no legal recourse when A runs him down. If we reject the present legal position we must explain why, and our reasons need have nothing to do with causation, since causation and responsibility are not synonyms. There is another problem: why must tort liability always be tied to property rights? Suppose commercial fishermen incur business losses because an oil spill ruins the fishing grounds where they fish. The fishermen's property rights have not been invaded, because fishing grounds are not owned and there is no property right in a wild animal until it is caught. On this ground Epstein argued that the fishermen should have no right to sue the oil company, even if the company had been negligent in allowing the spill.[38] Yet the ruin of the fishing grounds is a genuine and, by the assumption that the oil company was acting negligently, readily avoidable social loss and one that is concentrated on the commercial fishermen. Why should they not be allowed to recover their loss?

Epstein's "rights" theory, like his earlier "responsibility" theory, needed foundations, and in subsequent work Epstein has tried to find them first in the libertarian or individualistic ideals of classical liberalism

---

38. See "Nuisance Law," note 12 above, at 51–52, criticizing *Union Oil Co. v. Oppen,* 501 F.2d 558 (9th Cir. 1974).

exemplified in the work of John Locke, later in utilitarianism, and most recently in a combination of nature and utility.[39]

Locke's conception, as sketched by Epstein, is simple. People come together in a society in order to protect their life, liberty, and property—the rights they enjoy in the state of nature, before there is society. These rights are inviolate. The government is not entitled to take away one person's right and give it to another; therefore, anyone who loses a right because of governmental intervention is entitled to compensation. Indeed, government's main function is to prevent people from invading other people's rights. But not its only function. Transaction costs may prevent people from exchanging rights to their mutual advantage, and when this is a problem the government can properly intervene and try to bring about results similar to what the market would bring about if the market could be made to work. This is just another way of securing the full enjoyment of property rights.

Epstein finds in the Fifth Amendment's just-compensation clause the legal embodiment of Locke's system of libertarian justice. If government can use taxation to redistribute wealth, then, Epstein argues, it is in effect taking property from A and giving it to B without compensating A. Epstein therefore confines the legitimate domain of governmental regulatory, taxing, and spending authority to preventing people from harming others, defending the state from external enemies, minimizing transaction costs (as by providing courts to enforce contracts),[40] and financing these activities by taxes proportioned to the benefits received by the taxpayer. Wealthy people have more property to protect, so it is right that they should pay higher taxes, but this implies proportional rather than progressive taxation. Progressive taxation is redistributive and hence confiscatory, as is any welfare program that does not return to the taxpayers who defray its costs a benefit proportional to those taxes.

As the Constitution was drafted and ratified long before there were income taxes and costly welfare programs, it may be overbold to infer

39. See the following works by Epstein: "Possession at the Root of Title," 13 *Georgia Law Review* 1221 (1979); *Takings: Private Property and the Power of Eminent Domain* (1985); "The Public Trust Doctrine," 7 *Cato Journal* 411 (1987); "The Utilitarian Foundations of Natural Law," 12 *Harvard Journal of Law & Public Policy* 713 (1989); also his contributions to "Proceedings of the Conference on Takings of Property and the Constitution," 41 *University of Miami Law Review* 49 (1986).

40. Actually, *all* governmental functions in the minimal, night watchman state can be viewed as efforts to overcome transaction costs—even national defense, since a voluntary system of national defense would be unworkable; expenditures by A on deterrence would benefit B even if B contributed nothing.

that the framers, by forbidding (in a single clause buried deep in the Fifth Amendment) confiscation in the narrow sense of physical takings that was current at the time, erected an absolute barrier to the creation of the welfare state almost two centuries later. Among reasons for doubting this is that taxes and regulations, unlike piecemeal takings (for example, of someone's land for a military base), hit a lot of people and therefore are subject to some political checks, which piecemeal takings are not.[41] So the distinction is not as arbitrary as Epstein supposes, although opponents of taxes and regulations are not always able to form effective interest groups to lobby against the measures.

But a more pertinent criticism of Epstein's constitutional philosophy is that the line between regulation that is permissible because efficient (overcoming transaction-cost problems and the like—broadly, protecting property rights) and regulation that is purely redistributive and therefore forbidden is too uncertain to support the structure of permissions and prohibitions that Epstein erects on it. Suppose that because of malice or envy poor people find rich people deeply offensive. Could we not say that the rich people are hurting the poor people? Then redistributive measures would be a method of correcting negative externalities. We might not think this the sort of hurt that ought to give rise to government intervention, but to justify this view we would have to go beyond Epstein's libertarian reading of Locke.

The libertarian also has no good reply to the argument that redistribution may be the cost-justified way of heading off revolution or, less dramatically, violence, by the have-nots—and hence may be the way that the owners of property would themselves choose. Even if the envy and restlessness of the poor have no ethical status, they are brute facts that may put much redistribution into the same legal-ethical category as laws against trespass: the category of laws that protect property. If this is correct then the rich should finance redistribution, through progressive income taxes if necessary, since the rich have the most property to protect. Once redistribution is admitted into the armory of the "night watchman" state on these expedient grounds, that state begins to bear an uncanny resemblance to the modern welfare state.

So the libertarian approach is porous; but if this problem could be overcome the approach would encounter the objection that it is anti-democratic, because it greatly curtails the scope of democratic decision

---

41. See William A. Fischel and Perry Shapiro, "Takings, Insurance, and Michelman: Comments on Economic Interpretations of 'Just Compensation' Law," 17 *Journal of Legal Studies* 269 (1988).

making. The people get to choose the administrators, but not, for the most part, the policies; those are prescribed by libertarian theory. I do not wish to seem misty-eyed about democracy. Although no one who has read Pericles' funeral oration or followed recent events in the Communist world can doubt that democracy is a faith worth fighting for, and no student of history will be inclined to deny that democratic government, with all its grievous faults, is superior to the alternatives in point of stability and resilience as well as freedom and prosperity, the precise extent to which the democratic principle should be allowed to prevail over competing political principles is highly contestable. At the same time the Prussian idea of a limited state, which is closer to the libertarian ideal than modern democracy is, implies a significant curtailment of the democratic principle, and a pragmatist will demand that the libertarian demonstrate that the risks entailed by such a curtailment are acceptable.

A deeper, or at least more "philosophical," objection to the libertarian approach focuses on its benchmark, the concept of the "natural." In a state of nature people would not have much in the way of life, liberty, or property to protect. The long life, spacious liberties, and extensive property of the average American citizen are the creation not of that American alone but of society—a vast aggregation of individuals, living and dead—and of geographical luck (size, topography, location, natural resources, climate).[42] Assuming two equally able and hard-working people, one living in a wealthy society and the other in a poor one, the former will almost certainly have more income and wealth than the latter, and the difference will be due to the efforts of other members, living and dead, of the wealthier society, as well as to the accidents of geography. Human nature being what it is, the employment of the government's taxing and spending powers to redistribute the "social" component (as one might call it) of a person's income will adversely affect the incentives of both the taxpayer and the welfare recipient. But there is no necessary breach of the social contract. The taxed person is still much better off than he would be in the state of nature. Maybe he could be made even better off in a system that had no redistribution, but he could not argue for such a system on grounds of "nature." It might nevertheless be terribly unjust for the state to reduce him to the standard of living of the average inhabitant of Bangladesh or even to forbid recognition of

---

42. See, for example, Russell Hardin, *Morality within the Limits of Reason* 131–132 (1988), and references cited there.

his productivity if it is above the average for the state's citizens. But such a conclusion could not be derived from reflection on natural rights.

The point can be made in slightly different terms, with the help of the Hegelian insight that the idea of individual rights—indeed of individuality—is socially constructed rather than presocial. Men's natural state is not one of equality and sturdy independence; it is one of dependence on more powerful men. Economic freedom in the classic liberal sense is one of the luxuries made possible by social organization. The individual's "right" to property is not "natural." His possessions are a product of social interactions rather than of his skills and efforts alone. Moreover, those skills may be, at least in part, a social product too. American workers are paid more than South Korean workers; are they better workers? Better people?

These sallies, and many more that could be made (such as, at the most basic level, asking *why* conditions in a state of nature, whatever precisely they might be, should determine rights in society), suggest that libertarianism cannot be the foundation for a philosophy of law, but must be derived from some other principle. Rather than attempt this derivation—a task that may well be impossible—Epstein, responding to critics who stressed the "ungroundedness" of the libertarian premises of his book on the just-compensation clause, has embraced utilitarianism as the foundational principle of his libertarian conception of law.[43] The rules that constitute the minimal state provide in this view the framework necessary and perhaps sufficient to achieve rule utilitarianism. But the marriage of utilitarianism and libertarianism is an uneasy one, because the relationship between utilitarianism—the principle that the goal of persons and society should be to maximize the sum of human happiness (in some versions the qualification "human" is dropped)—and individualism is so equivocal. On the one hand, in the notion, which is basic to the greatest-happiness principle, that everyone's wants are as good as everyone else's (pushpin is as good as poetry, in Bentham's expression), utilitarianism is individualistic; it allows each person to choose his own conception of the good. On the other hand, in treating society as in effect a single person whose happiness we want to maximize—because one person's misery can in principle offset another's happiness, which indicates that it is the aggregate that counts rather than its distribution across persons—utilitarianism is radically collectivist. In this it resembles a number of other questionable "isms"—nationalism, racialism,

---

43. See "A Last Word on Eminent Domain," 41 *University of Miami Law Review* 253, 256–258 (1986); "The Utilitarian Foundations of Natural Law," note 39 above.

statism, communism—all of which also treat the individual as a cell of a larger organism. It may happen to be the case, as Epstein believes, that the institutions necessary and appropriate to maximizing the greatest happiness of the greatest number are precisely those of the night watchman state that is implied by libertarian political philosophy.[44] But this would depend on a variety of contingent factors about preferences, aversions, markets, and the like, and it would still leave us floating in air, with libertarianism supported tenuously by a philosophy the premises of which are largely antithetical to the ideals of libertarianism and which in any event is open to serious objections. We shall consider in Chapter 12 whether it is possible to kick away all foundations and defend a libertarian regime on pragmatic grounds.

In an even more recent paper, "The Utilitarian Foundations of Natural Law," Epstein seeks to connect utilitarianism to natural-rights philosophy through sociobiology. His idea is that, given human nature (strongly self-interested, weakly altruistic), a laissez-faire organization of society is the one that is in fact most likely to promote the general welfare.[45] This may well be true, but it is an issue, once again, concerning optimal utilitarian institutions, not the ethical merits of utilitarianism. Epstein's point establishes at best an accidental connection between individual rights and social justice.

The attempt to root law in biology has a checkered history,[46] yet Epstein may be on the right track after all, as I have already suggested in discussing rights and retribution. Many of our moral notions appear to be generalizations or rationalizations of the instinctive emotions that enabled our earliest ancestors to survive and flourish as social beings. The main "reason" why the "philosophical" idea that robots or talking

44. Some utilitarians disagree, of course. See, for example, Hardin, note 42 above, chs. 3–4. "Frightened by the strangeness of their own arguments, most utilitarian philosophers fiddle with the felicific calculus so that it yields results closer to what we all think." Walzer, note 34 above, at 7.

45. See note 39 above. In equating laissez-faire with natural law, Epstein resembles nineteenth-century Supreme Court Justice Stephen Field. See, for example, Butchers' Union Slaughter-house v. Crescent City Livestock Landing, 111 U.S. 746, 756–758 (1884) (concurring opinion); C. M. A. McCauliff, "Constitutional Jurisprudence of History and Natural Law: Complementary or Rival Modes of Discourse?" 24 *California Western Law Review* 287, 303–311 (1988).

46. An example is the legal status of women in England and America before this century. As shown in Nicholas St. John Green's notable essay on the question, "Married Women" in *Essays and Notes on the Law of Tort and Crime,* note 18 above, at 31 (an essay first published in 1871), "the law of the status of women," which Green describes as "the last vestige of slavery" (id. at 48), was defended on the basis of the "natural" differences between the sexes.

apes might have more rights than newborn or profoundly retarded children seems outlandish and repulsive may simply be that our genes force us to distinguish between our own and other species and that in this instance disembodied rational reflection will not overcome feelings rooted in our biology. But viewed as a guide to right conduct, moral philosophy is a selection from among our emotions rather than merely an uncritical celebration of them: a selection in favor of moralistic indignation, say, but against genocide and envy. Nature itself cannot be the criterion of selection.

What Has Moral Philosophy to Offer Law?

As should be clear by now, I am skeptical that moral philosophy has much to offer law in the way of answers to specific legal questions or even in the way of general bearings. The primary value of moral philosophy to law is critical. It helps us spot the weaknesses in ambitious social theories that might be used to generate or validate or overthrow legal obligations, and thus it reinforces the lesson of skepticism, a leitmotif of this book. But when it comes to specific cases, it lets us down.[47] The reason is that moral philosophy is largely a metadiscourse. It is less about supplying an answer to the question of how we shall live a good life than about whether such questions *have* answers and how moral questions differ from scientific ones. When the moral philosopher gets down into the trenches and wrestles with specific moral questions, or when the lawyer turns moral philosopher in an effort to resolve difficult legal questions, it becomes apparent that moral philosophy does not hold the keys to solving—rather, it mirrors—the moral dilemmas that make so many legal questions difficult to answer.

The reasons for the failure of moral philosophy at the practical level are twofold. First, knowledge is tested ultimately by our intuitions, and moral intuitions tend to be at once more stubborn and more divergent than intuitions about the physical world. Some moralists, such as Ackerman, work from the top down, starting with a master principle from which they then try to deduce answers to specific moral questions. But when the deduction—for example, that a talking ape or a chess-playing computer should have more rights than a retarded child—collides with our intuitions, we reject the principle rather than reexamine our intuitions. Other moralists work from the bottom up. Each such

---

47. A point distinguished philosophers have made. See Gilbert Harman, *The Nature of Morality: An Introduction to Ethics* viii–ix (1977); Bernard Williams, *Moral Luck: Philosophical Papers 1973–1980* ix–x (1981).

moralist argues from his own intuitions, his own absolutes or "can't helps," and when, as frequently happens, these differ greatly among different moralists, argument will not bridge the gap. Second, the resolution of moral dilemmas requires immersion in the particulars of each dilemma, and philosophers do not have the time or the training to specialize in the details of capital punishment, slavery, genocide, abortion, or other moral issues upon which oceans of ink have been spilled.

We have seen a number of examples of the failure of moral philosophy at the practical level, including Dworkin's attempt to give a moral grounding to affirmative action in law-school admissions, Ackerman's to justify abortion and redistribution, and Epstein's to defend the refusal of the common law to require people to act as good Samaritans. Dworkin's failure is exemplary. He never considers what the consequences of affirmative action in law-school admissions might be. If an elite law school gives black applicants preference in admissions, the first-order effect is that a black who would otherwise have gone to a lower-ranked law school will go to the elite school, and a white who would have gone to the elite school will take the black's place in the lower-ranking school. Only if the schools at the bottom of the pecking order give blacks preferential treatment will the total number of black law students increase. Hence the gains for blacks are probably modest, especially because many whites resent affirmative action, and affirmative action stigmatizes members of the favored minorities.[48] Yet it can be argued that accepting the most promising blacks in elite law schools may help to create a more responsible black leadership and to direct the aspirations of young blacks into socially productive channels. All these are matters that bear more directly on the proper legal response to affirmative action than speculation about what it means abstractly to treat people with equal concern and respect.

Judith Jarvis Thomson's famous article on abortion is a further illustration of the indeterminacy of moral philosophy when applied to specific issues.[49] In defense of a right of abortion she offers—this is the heart of the article—the analogy of a person whom society forces, for the sake

48. Cf. Stephen L. Carter, "Loving the Messenger," 1 *Yale Journal of Law & Humanities* 317, 331–334 (1989).

49. "A Defense of Abortion," 1 *Philosophy and Public Affairs* 47 (1971), reprinted along with a number of her other papers on jurisprudence in Thomson, *Rights, Restitution, and Risk: Essays in Moral Theory* (William Parent ed. 1986). The article is much discussed in the philosophical literature on abortion. See, for example, Michael Davis, "Foetuses, Famous Violinists, and the Right to Continued Aid," 33 *Philosophical Quarterly* 259 (1983); Davis, "Strasser on Dependence, Reliance, and Need," 36 *Philosophical Quarterly* 384 (1986). And, for an elaboration of her argument, see Donald H. Regan, "Rewriting *Roe v. Wade*," 77 *Michigan Law Review* 1569 (1979).

of a complete stranger who happens to be a famous violinist with potentially fatal kidney disease, to spend nine months in bed connected to the violinist by a network of tubes. Thomson points out correctly that it would offend our moral sense to impose this duty, however exigent the need and merit of the sick person, and she suggests that it is equally offensive to force a pregnant woman to carry the child to term.

What she is offering is not an argument but a metaphor designed to change the way in which we think about abortion—to make us see it in a new light. This is a valid technique of persuasion, as we have seen, but it owes nothing to what might be thought the discipline of moral philosophy. She might as well have written a short story. And as far as illuminating the issue of abortion is concerned the "story" casts only a dim light. Thomson is right that we don't force people to donate kidneys to strangers, or even to family members. But normally the potential donor is not responsible for the condition that he is asked to alleviate, in the way that a woman (unless she has been raped) is responsible, although only in part, for the fact that she is pregnant. The difference in evidentiary difficulty between asking who hit X and asking who failed to save X is a strong practical reason against liability for failing to be a good Samaritan. So although bystanders are not required to rescue persons in distress, someone who creates the danger, even if nontortiously, may be required to attempt rescue,[50] and perhaps that is the proper analogy to the pregnant woman who wants to terminate her pregnancy.

Moreover, since tort law may require someone who begins a rescue, even if under no legal duty to make the attempt, to see it through to completion with all due care,[51] abortion could be compared to the case where, having agreed to donate a kidney, you change your mind on the operating table and if you are permitted to withdraw at that late date the intended recipient will die. Of course the woman does not, by virtue of agreeing to intercourse, agree to become pregnant. But perhaps we should ask whether she took reasonable measures to minimize the risk of pregnancy—whether, in other words, she was careless in permitting herself to become pregnant; for someone who tortiously endangers another has a clear legal duty to aid the endangered person. One of the

50. See, for example, Montgomery v. National Convoy & Trucking Co., 186 S.C. 167, 195 S.E. 247 (1938); Zylka v. Leikvoll, 274 Minn. 435, 144 N.W.2d 358 (1966); Scatena v. Pittsburgh & New England Trucking, 2 Mass. App. 683, 319 N.E.2d 730 (1974); South v. National Railroad Passenger Corp., 290 N.W.2d 819 (N. Dak. 1980); Maldonado v. Southern Pacific Transportation Co., 129 Ariz. 165, 629 P.2d 1001 (Ariz. App. 1981).

51. See, e.g., Farwell v. Keaton, 396 Mich. 281, 240 N.W.2d 217 (1976).

undiscussed issues in the abortion debate is, indeed, promiscuity (indiscriminate or extramarital sex), although it cuts both ways. Insofar as an unwanted pregnancy is the by-product of promiscuous intercourse, the pregnant woman is not in a strong moral position to object to assuming responsibility for the fetus; at least the common law analogies are against her. Yet the average child of a promiscuous woman may not have good prospects of growing up to be a productive and responsible member of society, so the case for saving the fetus is weakened. But this is chilly. And perhaps we need also consider the social pressures that lead to what I am calling promiscuity, and the male's responsibility in conception.

All this is a great muddle, but it should at least be clear that I am not criticizing Thomson's *strategy*. There is no rational method of resolving the moral dilemma of abortion in a society as morally diverse as ours,[52] so a literary technique may be the best way to advance the ball. But it does not provide a sure footing for judicial decisions. This is especially so because, though legal and moral thinking run on parallel tracks, legal questions implicate prudential considerations that the pure moralist may not feel obliged to confront: in the abortion context, such questions as whether an issue should be resolved at the national level (the effect of *Roe v. Wade*) or locally, whether laws against abortion are enforceable at tolerable cost, whether judges interpreting the Constitution ought to take sides on burning moral issues, whether changes in women's lives are altering the cost-benefit analysis in favor of allowing abortion (working women tend to marry and have children later, and the likelihood of deformed offspring—prime candidates for abortion—soars with the age at pregnancy),[53] to what extent a ban on abortion would aggravate poverty, especially among black teenage women, and endanger women's health, and whether overruling *Roe v. Wade* would be politically or socially destabilizing, or at least distracting.

In criticizing efforts to derive legal rights from moral principles in a society as diverse in moral opinions as ours is, I hope I will not be thought to be exaggerating the difference between facts and values. If we had sufficient knowledge, many of our moral dilemmas would disappear. If we knew that God exists and anathematizes abortion, the abortion debate would be over. Perhaps if we knew that the number of abortions was invariant, or largely so, to the legality of abortion, this

52. As persuasively argued in Alasdair MacIntyre, *After Virtue: A Study in Moral Theory* 6–11 (2d ed. 1984).

53. A further point is that advances in medical technology are making it possible to keep more, and more seriously, deformed infants alive, but at great expense, borne largely by the taxpayer.

would also end the debate; it would surely reduce its intensity. The pornography debate might be ended if the effects of pornography were known. The sheer empirical *failure* of Prohibition and of fascism, to name two passionate "moral" crusades of our century, may be the most important reason for the waning of debate over their morality; communism may go the same way and for the same reason. Moral debate rages most fiercely in an atmosphere of factual ignorance; it is when people lack objectively replicable knowledge that they fall back on intuitions rooted in individual psychology and upbringing, and personal experiences. But this is of small comfort to law, given its weak sense of fact and its resistance to the scientific ethos.

I am also not an adherent to the extreme skepticism that asserts that no "ought" proposition can ever be derived from an "is" proposition. If a watch is not working, it ought to be fixed. In this example the "ought" is derived from two "is's": that the watch is not working, and that the function of a watch is to tell time.[54] The problem in moral discourse is that the second "is" often is highly contestable. Not always: there will not be much disagreement with the proposition that a police officer should not sleep on duty. But with difficult questions of legal justice, such as whether abortion should be forbidden or (what may or may not be a parallel case) bystanders required to aid people in distress, the premises that correspond to the propositions that a watch is for telling time and that policemen should keep awake while on duty are controversial. Thomson thinks it intuitive that we have a right to do what we want with our bodies; one of her critics, John Finnis, has the opposite intuition: "Considered as a fully deliberate choice (which it doubtless only rather rarely is), suicide is a paradigm case of an action that is always wrong."[55] Commenting on this unbridgeable gap between Thomson and Finnis, R. M. Hare argues that it is impossible for people, including philosophers, to "discuss abortion without making up their minds about the fundamental problems of moral philosophy."[56] No doubt Thomson and Finnis *had* made up their minds. The methods of political and moral philosophy are not powerful enough to resolve moral debates about which people feel strongly and by resolving them provide solid grounds for legal judgments. Indeed, weak as the methods of legal reasoning are, they are no weaker than the methods of moral reasoning.

54. Actually there are a lot of buried assumptions as well—concerning our need for the watch, the cost of fixing it, and so on. It is the multitude of such assumptions in moral and legal discourse that makes deductive logic of such limited utility in these fields.

55. "The Rights and Wrongs of Abortion: A Reply to Judith Thomson," 2 *Philosophy and Public Affairs* 117, 129 (1973).

56. "Abortion and the Golden Rule," 4 *Philosophy and Public Affairs* 201, 222 (1975).

12 ∽

The Economic Approach to Law

The most ambitious and probably the most influential effort in recent years to elaborate an overarching concept of justice that will both explain judicial decision making and place it on an objective basis is that of scholars working in the interdisciplinary field of "law and economics," as economic analysis of law is usually called.[1] I am first going to describe the most ambitious version of this ambitious effort and then use philosophy to chip away at it and see what if anything is left standing.

The Approach

The basic assumption of economics that guides the version of economic analysis of law that I shall be presenting is that people are rational maximizers of their satisfactions—*all* people (with the exception of small children and the profoundly retarded) in *all* of their activities (except when under the influence of psychosis or similarly deranged through drug or alcohol abuse) that involve choice. Because this definition embraces the criminal deciding whether to commit another crime, the litigant deciding whether to settle or litigate a case, the legislator deciding whether to vote for or against a bill, the judge deciding how to cast his vote in a case, the party to a contract deciding whether to break it, the driver deciding how fast to drive, and the pedestrian deciding how bold-

---

1. The literature is vast; for diverse viewpoints, see *The Economic Approach to Law* (Paul Burrows and Cento G. Veljanovski eds. 1981); Robert Cooter and Thomas Ulen, *Law and Economics* (1988); Mark Kelman, *A Guide to Critical Legal Studies,* chs. 4–5 (1987); A. Mitchell Polinsky, *An Introduction to Law and Economics* (2d ed. 1989); Steven Shavell, *Economic Analysis of Accident Law* (1987); "Symposium: The Place of Economics in Legal Education," 33 *Journal of Legal Education* 183 (1983); and my book *Economic Analysis of Law* (3d ed. 1986).

ly to cross the street, as well as the usual economic actors, such as businessmen and consumers, it is apparent that most activities either regulated by or occurring within the legal system are grist for the economic analyst's mill. It should go without saying that nonmonetary as well as monetary satisfactions enter into the individual's calculus of maximizing (indeed, money for most people is a means rather than an end) and that decisions, to be rational, need not be well thought out at the conscious level—indeed, need not be conscious at all. Recall that "rational" denotes suiting means to ends, rather than mulling things over, and that much of our knowledge is tacit.

Since my interest is in legal doctrines and institutions, it will be best to begin at the legislative (including the constitutional) level. I assume that legislators are rational maximizers of their satisfactions just like everyone else. Thus nothing they do is motivated by the public interest as such. But they want to be elected and reelected, and they need money to wage an effective campaign. This money is more likely to be forthcoming from well-organized groups than from unorganized individuals. The rational individual knows that his contribution is unlikely to make a difference; for this reason and also because voters in most elections are voting for candidates rather than policies, which further weakens the link between casting one's vote and obtaining one's preferred policy, the rational individual will have little incentive to invest time and effort in deciding whom to vote for. Only an organized group of individuals (or firms or other organizations—but these are just conduits for individuals) will be able to overcome the informational and free-rider problems that plague collective action.[2] But such a group will not organize and act effectively unless its members have much to gain or much to lose from specific policies, as tobacco farmers, for example, have much to gain from federal subsidies for growing tobacco and much to lose from the withdrawal of those subsidies. The basic tactic of an interest group is to trade the votes of its members and its financial support to candidates in exchange for an implied promise of favorable legislation. Such legislation will normally take the form of a statute transferring wealth from unorganized taxpayers (for example, consumers) to the interest group. If the target were another interest group, the legislative transfer might

---

2. A free rider is someone who derives a benefit without contributing to the cost of creating the benefit. For example, even if A and B both favor the enactment of a statute, X, each will prefer the other to invest what is necessary in getting X enacted, since the benefit of X to A or to B will be the same whether or not he contributes to the cost of obtaining it. In Chapter 11 I gave national defense as an example of an activity that would encounter severe free-rider problems if provided privately.

be effectively opposed. The unorganized are unlikely to mount effective opposition, and it is their wealth, therefore, that typically is transferred to interest groups.

On this view, a statute is a deal (recall the "deals" theory of legislation in Chapter 9). But because of the costs of transactions within a multi-headed legislative body, and the costs of effective communication through time, legislation does not spring full-grown from the head of the legislature; it needs interpretation and application, and this is the role of the courts. They are agents of the legislature. But to impart credibility and durability to the deals the legislature strikes with interest groups, courts must be able to resist the wishes of current legislators who want to undo their predecessors' deals yet cannot do so through repeal because the costs of passing legislation (whether original or amended) are so high, and who might therefore look to the courts for a repealing "interpretation." The impediments to legislation actually facilitate rather than retard the striking of deals, by giving interest groups some assurance that a deal struck with the legislature will not promptly be undone by repeal. An independent judiciary is one of the impediments.

Judicial independence makes the judges imperfect agents of the legislature. This is tolerable not only for the reason just mentioned but also because an independent judiciary is necessary for the resolution of ordinary disputes in a way that will encourage trade, travel, freedom of action, and other highly valued activities or conditions and will minimize the expenditure of resources on influencing governmental action. Legislators might appear to have little to gain from these widely diffused rule-of-law virtues. But if the aggregate benefits from a particular social policy are very large and no interest group's ox is gored, legislators may find it in their own interest to support the policy. Voters understand in a rough way the benefits to them of national defense, crime control, dispute settlement, and the other elements of the night watchman state, and they will not vote for legislators who refuse to provide these basic public services. It is only when those services are in place, and when (usually later) effective means of taxation and redistribution develop, that the formation of narrow interest groups and the extraction by them of transfers from unorganized groups become feasible.

The judges thus have a dual role: to interpret the interest-group deals embodied in legislation and to provide the basic public service of authoritative dispute resolution. They perform the latter function not only by deciding cases in accordance with preexisting norms, but also—especially in the Anglo-American legal system—by elaborating those norms. They fashioned the common law out of customary practices, out of ideas borrowed from statutes and from other legal systems (for example, Roman law), and out of their own conceptions of public policy. The law they created exhibits, according to the economic theory that I am expounding, a remarkable (although not total—remember the extension of the rule of capture to oil and gas) substantive consistency. It is as if the judges *wanted* to adopt the rules, procedures, and case outcomes that would maximize society's wealth.

I must pause to define "wealth maximization," a term often misunderstood. The "wealth" in "wealth maximization" refers to the sum of all tangible and intangible goods and services, weighted by prices of two sorts: offer prices (what people are willing to pay for goods they do not already own); and asking prices (what people demand to sell what they do own). If A would be willing to pay up to $100 for B's stamp collection, it is worth $100 to A. If B would be willing to sell the stamp collection for any price above $90, it is worth $90 to B. So if B sells the stamp collection to A (say for $100, but the analysis is qualitatively unaffected at any price between $90 and $100—and it is only in that range that a transaction will occur), the wealth of society will rise by $10. Before the transaction A had $100 in cash and B had a stamp collection worth $90 (a total of $190); after the transaction A has a stamp collection worth $100 and B has $100 in cash (a total of $200). The transaction will not raise measured wealth—gross national product, national income, or whatever—by $10; it will not raise it at all unless the transaction is recorded, and if it is recorded it is likely to raise measured wealth by the full $100 purchase price. But the real addition to social wealth consists of the $10 increment in *nonpecuniary* satisfaction that A derives from the purchase, compared with that of B. This shows that "wealth" in the economist's sense is not a simple monetary measure, and explains why it is a fallacy (the Earl of Lauderdale's fallacy) to think that wealth would be maximized by encouraging the charging of monopoly prices. The wealth of producers would increase but that of consumers would diminish—and actually by a greater amount, since monopoly pricing will induce some consumers to switch to goods that cost society more to produce but, being priced at a competitive rather than a monopoly price, appear to the consumer to be cheaper. The fallacy thus lies in equating business income to social wealth.[3]

Similarly, if I am given a choice between remaining in a job in which I work forty hours a week for $1,000 and switching to a job in which I

3. On these and other technical details of wealth maximization, see my article "Wealth Maximization Revisited," 2 *Notre Dame Journal of Law, Ethics, and Public Policy* 85 (1985).

would work thirty hours for $500, and I decide to make the switch, the extra ten hours of leisure must be worth at least $500 to me, yet GNP will fall when I reduce my hours of work. Suppose the extra hours of leisure are worth $600 to me, so that my full income rises from $1,000 to $1,100 when I reduce my hours. My former employer presumably is made worse off by my leaving (else why did he employ me?), but not more than $100 worse off; for if he were, he would offer to pay me a shade over $1,100 a week to stay—and I would stay. (The example abstracts from income tax.)

Wealth is *related* to money, in that a desire not backed by ability to pay has no standing—such a desire is neither an offer price nor an asking price. I may desperately desire a BMW, but if I am unwilling or unable to pay its purchase price, society's wealth would not be increased by transferring the BMW from its present owner to me. Abandon this essential constraint (an important distinction, also, between wealth maximization and utilitarianism—for I might derive greater utility from the BMW than its present owner or anyone else to whom he might sell the car), and the way is open to tolerating the crimes committed by the passionate and the avaricious against the cold and the frugal.

The common law facilitates wealth-maximizing transactions in a variety of ways. It recognizes property rights, and these facilitate exchange. It also protects property rights, through tort and criminal law. (Although today criminal law is almost entirely statutory, the basic criminal protections—for example, those against murder, assault, rape, and theft—have, as one might expect, common law origins.) Through contract law it protects the process of exchange. And it establishes procedural rules for resolving disputes in these various fields as efficiently as possible.

The illustrations given thus far of wealth-maximizing transactions have been of transactions that are voluntary in the strict sense of making everyone affected by them better off, or at least no worse off. Every transaction has been assumed to affect just two parties, each of whom has been made better off by it. Such a transaction is said to be Pareto superior, but Pareto superiority is not a necessary condition for a transaction to be wealth maximizing. Consider an accident that inflicts a cost of $100 with a probability of .01 and that would have cost $3 to avoid. The accident is a wealth-maximizing "transaction" (recall Aristotle's distinction between voluntary and involuntary transactions) because the expected accident cost ($1) is less than the cost of avoidance. (I am assuming risk neutrality. Risk aversion would complicate the analysis but not change it fundamentally.) It is wealth maximizing even if the victim is not compensated. The result is consistent with Learned Hand's formula, which defines negligence as the failure to take cost-justified precautions. If the only precaution that would have averted the accident is not cost-justified, the failure to take it is not negligent and the injurer will not have to compensate the victim for the costs of the accident.

If it seems artificial to speak of the accident as the transaction, consider instead the potential transaction that consists of purchasing the safety measure that would have avoided the accident. Since a potential victim would not pay $3 to avoid an expected accident cost of $1, his offer price will be less than the potential injurer's asking price and the transaction will not be wealth maximizing. But if these figures were reversed—if an expected accident cost of $3 could be averted at a cost of $1—the transaction would be wealth maximizing, and a liability rule administered in accordance with the Hand formula would give potential injurers an incentive to take the measures that potential victims would pay them to take if voluntary transactions were feasible. The law would be overcoming transaction-cost obstacles to wealth-maximizing transactions—a frequent office of liability rules.

The wealth-maximizing properties of common law rules have been elucidated at considerable length in the literature of the economic analysis of law.[4] Such doctrines as conspiracy, general average (admiralty), contributory negligence, equitable servitudes, employment at will, the standard for granting preliminary injunctions, entrapment, the contract defense of impossibility, the collateral-benefits rule, the expectation measure of damages, assumption of risk, attempt, invasion of privacy, wrongful interference with contract rights, the availability of punitive damages in some cases but not others, privilege in the law of evidence, official immunity, and the doctrine of moral consideration have been found—at least by some contributors to this literature—to conform to the dictates of wealth maximization. (And recall the discussion of the fellow-servant rule, and of competition as a tort, in Chapter 8.) It has even been argued that the system of precedent itself has an economic equilibrium. Precedents are created as a by-product of litigation. The greater the number of recent precedents in an area, the lower the rate of litigation will be. In particular, cases involving disputes over legal as distinct from purely factual issues will be settled. The existence of abundant, highly informative (in part because recent) precedents will enable the parties to legal disputes to form more convergent estimates of the

---

4. See *Economic Analysis of Law,* note 1 above, pt. 2 and ch. 21; William M. Landes and Richard A. Posner, *The Economic Structure of Tort Law* (1987).

likely outcome of a trial, and as noted in previous chapters, if both parties agree on the outcome of trial they will settle beforehand because a trial is more costly than a settlement. But with less litigation, fewer new precedents will be produced, and the existing precedents will obsolesce as changing circumstances render them less apt and informative. So the rate of litigation will rise, producing more precedents and thereby causing the rate of litigation again to fall.

This analysis does not explain what drives judges to decide common law cases in accordance with the dictates of wealth maximization. Prosperity, however, which wealth maximization measures more sensitively than purely monetary measures such as GNP, is a relatively uncontroversial policy, and most judges try to steer clear of controversy: their age, method of compensation, and relative weakness vis-à-vis the other branches of government make the avoidance of controversy attractive. It probably is no accident, therefore, that many common law doctrines assumed their modern form in the nineteenth century, when laissez-faire ideology, which resembles wealth maximization, had a strong hold on the Anglo-American judicial imagination; Shaw's opinion in the *Farwell* case (Chapter 8) is a good example.

It may be objected that in assigning ideology as a cause of judicial behavior, the economist strays outside the boundaries of his discipline; but he need not rest on ideology. The economic analysis of legislation implies that fields of law left to the judges to elaborate, such as the common law fields, must be the ones in which interest-group pressures are too weak to deflect the legislature from pursuing goals that are in the general interest. Prosperity is one of these goals, and one that judges are especially well equipped to promote. The rules of the common law that they promulgate attach prices to socially undesirable conduct, whether free riding or imposing social costs without corresponding benefits.[5] By doing this the rules create incentives to avoid such conduct, and these incentives foster prosperity. In contrast, judges can, despite appearances, do little to redistribute wealth. A rule that makes it easy for poor tenants to break leases with rich landlords, for example, will induce landlords to raise rents in order to offset the costs that such a rule imposes, and tenants will bear the brunt of these higher costs. Indeed, the principal redistribution accomplished by such a rule may be from

5. Such imposition is well illustrated by acquisitive crimes: the time and money spent by the thief in trying to commit thefts and the property owner in trying to prevent them have no social product, for they are expended merely in order to bring about, or to prevent, a redistribution of wealth. Overall wealth decreases, as in the case of monopoly, discussed earlier.

the prudent, responsible tenant, who may derive little or no benefit from having additional legal rights to use against landlords—rights that enable a tenant to avoid or postpone eviction for nonpayment of rental—to the feckless tenant. That is a capricious redistribution. Legislatures, however, have by virtue of their taxing and spending powers powerful tools for redistributing wealth. So an efficient division of labor between the legislative and judicial branches has the legislative branch concentrate on catering to interest-group demands for wealth distribution and the judicial branch on meeting the broad-based social demand for efficient rules governing safety, property, and transactions. Although there are other possible goals of judicial action besides efficiency and redistribution, many of these (various conceptions of "fairness" and "justice") are labels for wealth maximization,[6] or for redistribution in favor of powerful interest groups; or else they are too controversial in a heterogeneous society, too ad hoc, or insufficiently developed to provide judges who desire a reputation for objectivity and disinterest with adequate grounds for their decisions.

Finally, even if judges have little commitment to efficiency, their inefficient decisions will, by definition, impose greater social costs than their efficient ones will. As a result, losers of cases decided mistakenly from an economic standpoint will have a greater incentive, on average, to press for correction through appeal, new litigation, or legislative action than losers of cases decided soundly from an economic standpoint—so there will be a steady pressure for efficient results. Moreover, cases litigated under inefficient rules tend to involve larger stakes than cases litigated under efficient rules (for the inefficient rules, by definition, generate social waste), and the larger the stakes in a dispute the likelier it is to be litigated rather than settled; so judges will have a chance to reconsider the inefficient rule.

Thus we should not be surprised to see the common law tending to become efficient, although since the incentives of judges to perform well along any dimension are weak (this is a by-product of judicial independence), we cannot expect the law ever to achieve perfect efficiency. Since wealth maximization is not only a guide in fact to common law judging but also a genuine social value and the only one judges are in a good position to promote, it provides not only the key to an accurate description of what the judges are up to but also the right benchmark for crit-

---

6. For example, it is unclear whether Weinrib's Kantian theory of tort law (see Chapter 11) has different substantive implications from the economic theory; the differences may be in vocabulary only.

icism and reform. If judges are failing to maximize wealth, the economic analyst of law will urge them to alter practice or doctrine accordingly. In addition, the analyst will urge—on any legislator sufficiently free of interest-group pressures to be able to legislate in the public interest—a program of enacting only legislation that conforms to the dictates of wealth maximization.

Besides generating both predictions and prescriptions, the economic approach enables the common law to be reconceived in simple, coherent terms and to be applied more objectively than traditional lawyers would think possible. From the premise that the common law does and should seek to maximize society's wealth, the economic analyst can deduce in logical—if you will, formalist—fashion (economic theory is formulated nowadays largely in mathematical terms) the set of legal doctrines that will express and perfect the inner nature of the common law, and can compare these doctrines with the actual doctrines of common law. After translating from the economic vocabulary back into the legal one, the analyst will find that most of the actual doctrines are tolerable approximations to the implications of economic theory and so are formalistically valid. Where there are discrepancies, the path to reform is clear— yet the judge who takes the path cannot be accused of making rather than finding law, for he is merely contributing to the program of realizing the essential nature of the common law.

The project of reducing the common law—with its many separate fields, its thousands of separate doctrines, its hundreds of thousands of reported decisions—to a handful of mathematical formulas may seem quixotic, but the economic analyst can give reasons for doubting this assessment. Much of the doctrinal luxuriance of common law is seen to be superficial once the essentially economic nature of the common law is understood. A few principles, such as cost-benefit analysis, the prevention of free riding, decision under uncertainty, risk aversion, and the promotion of mutually beneficial exchanges, can explain most doctrines and decisions. Tort cases can be translated into contract cases by recharacterizing the tort issue as finding the implied pre accident contract that the parties would have chosen had transaction costs not been prohibitive, and contract cases can be translated into tort cases by asking what remedy if any would maximize the expected benefits of the contractual undertaking considered ex ante. The criminal's decision whether to commit a crime is no different in principle from the prosecutor's decision whether to prosecute; a plea bargain is a contract; crimes are in effect torts by insolvent defendants because if all criminals could pay the full social costs of their crimes, the task of deterring antisocial behavior could be left to tort law. Such examples suggest not only that the logic of the common law really is economics but also that the teaching of law could be simplified by exposing students to the clean and simple economic structure beneath the particolored garb of legal doctrine.

If all this seems reminiscent of Langdell, it differs fundamentally in being empirically verifiable. The ultimate test of a rule derived from economic theory is not the elegance or logicality of the derivation but the rule's effect on social wealth. The extension of the rule of capture to oil and gas was subjected to such a test, flunked, and was replaced (albeit through legislative rather than judicial action) by efficient rules. The other rules of the common law can and should be tested likewise.

Criticisms of the Positive Theory

Stated as boldly, as provocatively, as I have stated it, the economic thesis invites attack from a variety of quarters. The discussion in earlier chapters will turn out to be helpful in evaluating some of these attacks. It will be convenient to divide the attackers into two camps: those who attack the positive aspect of the economic theory of law (law can best be understood in wealth-maximizing and rent-seeking terms, the former being the domain of common law, the latter of statute law), and those who attack the normative aspect (law should be made to conform as closely as possible to the dictates of wealth maximization). Of course often the same people attack on both fronts.

Two criticisms of the positive theory are fundamental. The first is that the economic model of human behavior is wrong, and economic science phony. The second is that the proper study of economics is markets rather than nonmarket activity, the latter being the category that includes crime, adjudication, and other characteristic concerns of the legal system.

Economists pride themselves on being engaged in a scientific endeavor.[7] From the basic premise that people are rational maximizers of their

---

7. There is a rich literature on the methodology of positive economics. The place to start is Daniel M. Hausman's superb review essay, "Economic Methodology in a Nutshell," 3 *Journal of Economic Perspectives,* Spring 1989, at 115. For illustrative longer works reflecting a variety of points of view, see *The Boundaries of Economics* (Gordon C. Winston and Richard F. Teichgraeber III eds. 1988); *Rational Choice: The Contrast between Economics and Psychology* (Robin M. Hogarth and Melvin W. Reder eds. 1987); Lawrence A. Boland, *The Foundations of Economic Method* (1982); Bruce J. Caldwell, *Beyond Positivism: Economic Methodology in the Twentieth Century* (1982); Martin Hollis and Edward J. Nell, *Rational Economic Man: A Philosophical Critique of Neo-Classical Economics* (1975); Homa Katouzian, *Ideology*

satisfactions the economist deduces a variety of hypotheses, of which the best known is the "law of demand"—a rise in the relative price of a product will, other things held constant, cause a reduction in the quantity of the product demanded. These hypotheses are confirmed or refuted by studies of actual economic behavior. Usually the studies are statistical in nature, though much of the evidence that actually persuades people that there is "something to" economics is of a more casual sort—for example, observing that nonprice rationing leads to queuing. Although many positive economists are followers of Karl Popper and therefore believe that falsifiability is the defining characteristic of a scientific theory, empirical economists in practice place far greater emphasis on confirmation than on falsification.[8] In part this is because economic theory has become so rich, so complex, that almost any hypothesis,

---

and Method in Economics (1980); Alexander Rosenberg, *Microeconomic Laws: A Philosophical Analysis* (1976), and *Sociology and the Preemption of Social Science* 53–91 (1980) (modifying the argument of *Microeconomic Laws*). Among works that address the methodology of social science as part of a larger concern with scientific method, Ernest Nagel, *The Structure of Science: Problems in the Logic of Scientific Explanation,* chs. 13 and 14 (1961), is particularly good, although dated.

8. Popper's influence on economic methodology has been great, but this fact is not well known because the principal vehicle by which he was introduced into economics—Milton Friedman's famous article "The Methodology of Positive Economics," in Friedman, *Essays in Positive Economics* 3 (1953)—does not cite Popper. The article also blurs its Popperite message by its exaggeratedly positivist suggestion that the only purpose of economic theories is to generate verifiable predictions and by its related emphasis, at once unnecessary and misleading, on the supposed desirability of making the assumptions of economics *unrealistic*. What Friedman means, I believe, is not that lack of realism is a plus in a scientific theory but that a theory is not a description. The theorist abstracts from the inessential features of the behavior that he is interested in studying. To this it can be added that a theory need not be intuitive to be correct—the heliocentric example once again. Further, commitment to the assumptions of economics need only be methodological; it need not induce political action (fear that it will is one of the causes of academic hostility to economics). Just because the analyst believes that economic theory, perhaps drastically simplified, is the most powerful tool for *studying* social behavior, it does not follow that he must be guided in his personal life or political preferences by the theory. Here is an example of the difference between pure reason and practical reason in its first sense mentioned in Chapter 2.

Withal, economics does have a decidedly positivist flavor, as shown by the fondness of economists for "as if" hypotheses: for example, the hypothesis that the best explanation of the common law of torts is that it is "as if" the judges were trying to maximize wealth. See Landes and Posner, note 4 above, at 1. This type of hypothesis leaves unexplored the underlying "reality" that causes judges to behave in this way. It invites the observation that theories with good predictive power may be false: Ptolemaic astronomy is false even though it generates accurate predictions concerning the apparent location of the stars and can therefore be used to guide navigation.

even one that appeared to deny a fundamental implication of the theory such as the law of demand, could be made to conform to the theory. For example, a finding that the demand for a product had risen in response to an increase in its price could be rationalized by arguing either that the product was a Giffen good[9] or that consumers had been fooled by the price increase into thinking that the quality of the product had improved; consumers often take prices as an index of quality and often are warranted in doing so. In fact, the law of demand seems robust; but it is distressingly easy to explain away empirical findings that appear to conflict with the basic theoretical assumptions and propositions of economics.

Falsifiability is placed still farther beyond the economist's reach by the infeasibility in most areas of economic inquiry of performing controlled experiments. The normal method of seeking to confirm or falsify an economic hypothesis is by conducting a "natural" experiment: an economic model is used to predict a relationship between statistical variables (for example, between price data and quantity data) and the reliability of the prediction is evaluated by applying tests of statistical significance. The problems with this methodology include the tedium, expense, and sometimes impossibility of obtaining the data that the model implies are relevant, and as a result of these obstacles the low ratio of empirical to theoretical work; the absence of professional rewards for negative findings, or, what amounts to the same thing, career pressures to come up with positive results by hook or by crook; the large, sometimes indefinite number of omitted independent vari-

---

9. This is a special type of what economists call an "inferior good," which is a good the demand for which rises when people's incomes fall. Potatoes in Ireland are the conventional example of an inferior good. If a large fraction of a person's income is consumed in buying an inferior good and the price of that good rises, the person may be so impoverished as a result that he consumes even more of the good (for example, he buys even more potatoes—and much less meat). A good with this property is known as a Giffen good. It is not clear that such a good has ever existed. See, for example, George J. Stigler, "Notes on the History of the Giffen Paradox," 55 *Journal of Political Economy* 152 (1947); Rogert Koenker, "Was Bread Giffen? The Demand for Food in England circa 1790," 59 *Review of Economics and Statistics* 225 (1977); L. A. Boland, "Giffen Goods, Market Prices, and Testability," 16 *Australian Economic Papers* 72 (1977); Gerald P. Dwyer and Cotton M. Lindsay, "Robert Giffen and the Irish Potato," 74 *American Economic Review* 188 (1984); Morten Berg, "Giffen's Paradox Revisited," 39 *Bulletin of Economic Research* 79 (1987). Certainly there have not been many of them, so the possibility that not all demand curves are downward-sloping because some of them may describe Giffen goods is not a serious embarrassment for economic theory. Nor is it economic theory alone that requires auxiliary principles (in this instance, the empirical unlikelihood of Giffen goods) in order to give the theory predictive power. This is a general feature of science. See, for example, Hilary Putnam, *Representation and Reality* 9 (1988).

ables that may be correlated with the independent variables the researcher is trying to test for; the typically very low percentage of the variance in the observations that is explained by the model, suggesting either that the data are poor or that the economic model is able to capture only a small part of the social phenomenon being investigated; the ease of explaining away poor results as being due to problems with data; and the fact that the results being predicted are known in advance, which creates both pressure and opportunity to tinker with the model in order to make it conform better to the data—and the complexity of economic theory makes such tinkering easy to do. The last two points may explain why negative findings are likely to be ascribed to lack of imagination on the part of the researcher.

A theory that is not effectively falsifiable, but only confirmable, is tenuously grounded. One can never be certain whether observations that confirm (that is, are consistent with) theory A are not really confirming theory B instead, which overlaps with or includes A. The low percentage of variance explained by most econometric studies makes this a lively possibility. This is a less serious problem for sciences that do not only generate insights into natural phenomena, such as the origin of the universe or of species, but also enable dramatic interventions. The atomic bomb is proof (not conclusive, but then no proof is) that modern atomic theory is more than just another clever speculation about invisible entities; and so with biotechnology and genetic theory. Although economics, too, has its technological side as well as its academic side— economic theory can take credit for some new trading strategies in securities markets, some new methods of pricing, and some new public policies, such as the deregulation of transportation and banking—these interventions are less dramatic, and more ambiguous in their results and interpretation, than the interventions of natural science in such areas as weaponry and medicine.

There is a further problem. The basic assumption of economics—that people are rational maximizers—seems not only counterintuitive (a common feature of scientific theory, however, well illustrated by the heliocentric theory of the solar system and by evolution, not to mention by quantum theory) but also seriously incomplete. People have difficulty in dealing with low-probability events, which are important in many areas of behavior studied by economists; and much human behavior appears to be impulsive, emotional, superstitious—in a word, irrational. These are reasons for concern that observations which confirm theory A (economics) may in fact be confirming a more inclusive, more realistic, theory B.

These points suggest that economics is weak in comparison with the natural sciences, although it is the strongest of the human sciences. But the discussion has not shown, and it would be a mistake to believe, that it is a false science, like astrology, or an ideology, like Marxism.[10] On the contrary, it seems to capture an important part, though possibly only a small part, of the phenomena it seeks to explain. In this respect as well as in its heavy reliance on calculus for the formulation of its models, economics resembles Newtonian physics. This resemblance points up the confusion in the common criticism of economics as "reductionist" in seeking to use mathematical models to describe human social behavior. All science involves abstraction. Newton's law of falling bodies abstracts from many of the particulars of such bodies (for example, was the apple red?) in an effort to discover a law of nature—specifically, a law to describe the behavior of a variety of bodies, from apples to tides to cannonballs to stars, that differ in many of their particulars. "All scientific theorizing proceeds by abstraction. It concerns itself with spatial relations, with number, with motion, with the evolution of biological species, and so on. If a theory attempted to concern itself instead with, say, the concrete aggregate of actual animals, which not only have shapes and numbers and the ability to move and breed but also an indefinite variety of other characteristics, the theoretical enterprise would inevitably choke on a superfluity of detail."[11] We do not describe this process as reductionism; we reserve, or should reserve, that word for unsuccessful efforts to explain one thing in terms of another, for example, ideas in terms of molecular changes in the brain.

We should not forget that an important branch of physics, astrophysics, is for the most part not an experimental science; that there are other nonexperimental natural sciences as well, including geology and paleontology; that some of the most important theories in science, notably theories of evolution in biology and geology, cannot as a practical matter be falsified;[12] that experiments are highly fallible, since an excluded

---

10. On the characteristics of a pseudo-science, see the interesting discussion in Raimo Tuomela, *Science, Action, and Reality,* ch. 10 (1985), esp. p. 229. For some economists, of course, economics is an ideology as well as a method of analysis.

11. L. Jonathan Cohen, *The Dialogue of Reason: An Analysis of Analytical Philosophy* 123 (1986). To which it could be added that if a theory is too rich, it may not be falsifiable—a looming danger for economics, as I have noted. Maybe economics isn't reductionist enough!

12. The methodological problems of the theory of evolution, indeed of biology generally, are very similar to those of economic theory. Cf. Michael Ruse, *Philosophy of Biology Today,* ch. 1 (1988); Alexander Rosenberg, *The Structure of Biological Science* (1985). And

variable may be the real cause that the experiment is trying to test for, and the variable that the experimenter finds to be the cause merely a correlate of the real cause; that much of science is breathtakingly counterintuitive—an offense to common sense (quantum theory, for example, or the evolution of the human eye); that scientists often make arbitrary, unprovable assumptions (such as that the laws of physics as we know them hold throughout the universe); and that because of the impossibility of ever really "confirming" a scientific hypothesis it might be best to view all scientific knowledge as conjectural. In short, some of the most salient methodological weaknesses, real or apparent, of economic science are shared with natural science—to which it should be added that economists and other social scientists do on occasion conduct controlled experiments.[13]

Should the weaknesses of economics discourage attempts to apply economics to nonmarket behavior? Surely not. Although much nonmarket behavior is indeed baffling, this is so whether one approaches it from the standpoint of economics, which assumes that human beings behave rationally, or from the standpoint of other human sciences, which do not make that assumption but have nothing to put in its place. The economics of law may well be a weak field, partaking of the general weakness of economics and of additional weaknesses specific to itself. But is the psychology of law strong? The sociology of law? Legal anthropology? Jurisprudence as a positive theory of law? These fields of interdisciplinary legal studies, and others that could be named, are older than economic analysis of law yet are weaker candidates for a leading role in fashioning a positive theory of law.

Some arguments against applying economics to nonmarket behavior are particularly interesting from the perspective of this book because they are based on stubborn philosophical fallacies, in particular that of essentialism, the idea that everything has a property that defines it and is, indeed, its metaphysical essence, so that if this property is missing, the thing to which it is supposed to be attached is a different thing from what we thought it was. (Langdell was an essentialist.) Thus it is argued

---

David L. Hull, *Science as a Process: An Evolutionary Account of the Social and Conceptual Development of Science* 495 (1988), points out that actual falsification in the natural sciences is a rare event and that contrary to Popper's theory scientists will often accept a theory that has not been subjected to serious attempts at falsification. Popper himself long ago moved away from the strict falsificationism of his early writings.

13. See Alvin E. Roth, "Laboratory Experimentation in Economics," 2 *Economics and Philosophy* 245 (1986).

that economics *means* the study of markets, so the study of nonmarket behavior is simply outside its scope, is not—cannot be—economics. In fact, "economics," like "law" (or "philosophy," or "democracy," or "religion"), has neither a fixed intension nor a fixed extension; that is, it cannot be defined or the complete set of things to which it applies enumerated. It is not like "rabbit," a word that can be defined and then "attached" unambiguously to each member of a finite set of real-world objects that satisfy the definition. (Well, not quite, because the word is not misused when it is applied to Harvey or the Easter Bunny, or to a timid human being.) Definitions of economics are hopeless. One cannot say that economics is what economists do, because many noneconomists do economics—or do they become economists by doing so? One cannot, at least when attempting to speak precisely, call economics the science of rational choice. There are theories of rational choice that do not resemble economics, either because they assume unstable preferences, which alters many of the predictions of economics, or because they assume a plurality of rational actors within each human being—for example, an impulsive self and a future-regarding self. And there are theories of economics that are nonrational or not consistently rational. These include survival theories in industrial organization (firms that happen to hit on more efficient methods of doing business will grow relative to less efficient firms) and the many macroeconomic theories in which people are assumed to have propensities (to save, to consume, to hold a fixed fraction of their assets in cash) that are not derived from the rational model of human behavior. One cannot call economics the study of markets, because other disciplines study markets—for example, sociology and anthropology—and because it begs the question of the proper domain of economics to define economics as the study of markets and refuse to defend the definition.

What is true is that historically the emphasis of economics has been on studying markets. This is partly because data of the sort useful for economic analysis have been abundant, partly because (unlike such areas of human behavior as law, religion, education, statecraft, love, and madness) the study of markets has been of only marginal interest to practitioners of other human sciences, partly because economic theory has many applications to the understanding of markets, partly (related to the last point) because rational behavior seems more pervasive in markets than in most other arenas of social interaction, and partly because money offers a measuring rod for the study of markets comparable to the role of mass and velocity in physics. But the history of a field—even the character of its greatest triumphs—does not determine its future or delimit its scope.

Nor is it a good argument that the extension of economics to non-market behavior must wait upon the solution of the main problems of market economics. It is indeed tempting to ask how economists can hope to explain the divorce rate when they cannot even explain behavior under oligopoly. But this question reflects the fallacy that economics has a fixed domain. The methods of economics may be no good for answering a number of important questions about behavior in markets; that is no reason to keep hitting one's head against the wall. Economics does not have a predestined mission to dispel all the mysteries of the market. Maybe it will do better with some types of nonmarket behavior than with some types of market behavior, even if it can answer more questions about market behavior than about any other type.

Nor is it a good argument that the economist cannot possibly compete on the lawyer's turf because the economist lacks formal initiation into the mysteries of legal thinking. Not only are those mysteries exaggerated, but it is just another form of essentialism to assume that law is what is done by a person with a law degree and by no one else. Or, for that matter, that economics is what is done by a person who has a Ph.D. in economics and by no one else. An economist is someone who does economics, and if he does economics without the degree (maybe because he is a lawyer, and is tired of graduate education) or in collaboration with someone who has one, it is still economics: maybe less fancy, less polished, less sophisticated, less rigorous, less mathematical, but not necessarily less capable of enlarging our knowledge of law or other nonmarket activity.

It is an empirical question whether economics has much to contribute to human knowledge outside the domain of explicit markets,[14] but the answer seems to be yes, judging from the extensive economic literature dealing with such nonmarket fields as education, economic history, anthropology, the causes of regulation, the behavior of nonprofit institutions, racial and other forms of discrimination, the family, and pri-

---

14. For a skeptical view, see Ronald H. Coase, "Economics and Contiguous Disciplines," 7 *Journal of Legal Studies* 201 (1978). But it would be more accurate to say that Professor Coase believes not that economics has little to contribute outside this domain but that *economists* have little to contribute. Coase thinks lawyers, sociologists, psychologists, and so on will borrow the parts of economic theory that are useful in their own fields and, thus equipped, will have a decisive advantage over economists in doing research in their own fields because they know more about them.

vacy.[15] This in turn suggests that the economic theory of law ought to be evaluated on its merits—always bearing in mind that the weaknesses of economics as a science require caution in assessing claims made in any area of economics—rather than dismissed on the basis of an a priori conception of the scope of economics.

A number of specific objections are made to the positive side of the economic theory of law.[16] The first is that the theory cannot really be tested (and is therefore pseudo-scientific), because the data required to form a judgment on whether a particular legal doctrine is wealth maximizing are, as a practical matter, unobtainable. This criticism, which is frequently and inconsistently joined to the criticism that particular doctrines believed by economic analysts of law to be efficient can be shown to be inefficient, is overstated. The data required to test the positive theory—in the case of tort doctrines, data on number of accidents, number and cost of lawsuits, levels of liability insurance and accident insurance premiums, and variations in legal doctrine, both statutory and

15. See, for example, Jack Hirshleifer, "The Expanding Domain of Economics," 75 *American Economic Review* 53 (special anniversary issue, Dec. 1985); *Discrimination in Labor Markets* (Orley Ashenfelter and Albert Rees eds. 1973); *Education, Income, and Human Behavior* (F. Thomas Juster ed. 1976); *Household Production and Consumption* (Nestor E. Terleckyj ed. 1975); *Economics of the Family: Marriage, Children, and Human Capital* (Theodore W. Schultz ed. 1974); *The Reinterpretation of American Economic History* (Robert William Fogel and Stanley L. Engerman eds. 1971); Gary S. Becker, *The Economic Approach to Human Behavior* (1976); Becker, *A Treatise on the Family* (1981); Victor R. Fuchs, *Women's Quest for Economic Equality* (1988); James M. Buchanan and Gordon Tullock, *The Calculus of Consent* (1962); Michael Grossman, *The Demand for Health* (National Bureau of Economic Research 1972); George J. Stigler, *The Citizen and the State: Essays on Regulation* (1975); and my book *The Economics of Justice* (1981). For efforts to extend the domain of economics even into psychology, see, for example, Thomas C. Schelling, "Self-Command in Practice, in Policy, and in a Theory of Rational Choice," 74 *American Economic Review Papers and Proceedings* 1 (May 1984); Richard H. Thaler and H. M. Shefrin, "An Economic Theory of Self-Control," 89 *Journal of Political Economy* 392 (1981); George A. Akerlof and William T. Dickens, "The Economic Consequences of Cognitive Dissonance," 72 *American Economic Review* 307 (1982). The careful reader of the present book will have noted that in various places I imply that economics may have a foundational role to play in dealing with a number of philosophical issues in the areas of epistemology and ontology—but to develop this suggestion would require another book.

16. Most of these will be found in articles in "Symposium on Efficiency as a Legal Concern," 8 *Hofstra Law Review* 485, 811 (1980); see also Cento Veljanovski, "Legal Theory, Economic Analysis, and the Law of Torts," in *Legal Theory and Common Law* 215 (William Twining ed. 1986); Peter Carstensen, Book Review (of Landes and Posner, *The Economic Structure of Tort Law*), 86 *Michigan Law Review* 1161 (1988); Tom Campbell, *Justice*, ch. 5 (1988); Frank I. Michelman, "Norms and Normativity in the Economic Theory of Law," 62 *Minnesota Law Review* 1015 (1978). For a defense of the positive approach, see Landes and Posner, note 4 above, ch. 1.

common law—are obtainable, and are no more scanty or refractory than the data that are required for testing many other economic theories. What is true, however, is that few statistical tests have been performed on the positive economic theory of law and that instead analysts have been largely content to make a qualitative assessment of the wealth-maximizing properties of the legal rules, doctrines, and decisions being studied. It would be error to think that rules cannot be data for science; several branches of linguistics that study language rules are scientific.[17] But characterizing legal rules as efficient or inefficient, in circumstances where the measurement of costs and benefits is infeasible or simply not attempted, is fraught with subjectivity and makes it difficult to evaluate claims that the theory has been confirmed or falsified by being confronted with the actual rules of law or outcomes of cases. The looseness of economic theory does not help.

This is a substantial criticism, but one easily exaggerated. A number of common law doctrines, including Hand's negligence formula, verge on being explicitly economic. In others the implicit economic logic lies just beneath the surface. And in still others a comparison between counterpart doctrines in different jurisdictions (for example, England and America) reveals differences suggestively correlated with differences in economic conditions—density of habitation, amount of land in cultivation, and so forth.[18]

A related criticism of the positive theory is that either it has been acknowledged by its proponents to be false or it is too ill defined to be falsifiable. As no one believes either that every common law rule is wealth maximizing or that every statute merely redistributes wealth in favor of some interest group, the strongest form of the theory—that it accurately describes the total behavior of the legal system, as Newtonian physics was once thought to describe the motion of every object in the universe—is totally untenable. What then is the weak form to which proponents retreat? Either that the positive theory describes most legal rules or merely that it has identified one influence, perhaps one of a great many, on the formation of legal rules. In either form the theory is unsatisfactory because it leaves unexplained many, possibly most, of the phe-

---

17. See Frederick J. Newmeyer, *The Politics of Linguistics* (1986); *Historical Linguistics* (B. Brainerd ed. 1983); Theodora Bynon, *Historical Linguistics* (1977); William Labov, *Sociolinguistic Patterns* (1972); John T. Waterman, *Perspectives in Linguistics* (2d ed. 1970). For a skeptical view on whether any part of linguistics has yet achieved scientific status, see Victor H. Yngve, *Linguistics as a Science* (1986).

18. For examples, see Landes and Posner, note 4 above.

nomena it set out to explain, without providing any suggestions for how this large residuum of ignorance might be shrunk.

Next is the objection that no adequate explanation has been offered for *why* judges would shape common law doctrine in the direction indicated by the norm of wealth maximization.[19] The evolutionary explanations sketched earlier are unsatisfactory. The intervals over which the common law has "evolved" are too short for a random process to have generated efficient rules, and the particular random process posited (the greater propensity to litigate cases in which the stakes are large than cases in which they are small) is likely to be dominated by other determinants of legal rules—in particular by the judges' policy goals. Explanations that focus on judges' incentives trip over the fact, exasperating to an economist, that the judicial process is designed to remove the principal incentives that economists use for predicting behavior. The conditions of judicial employment are intended to make the judge indifferent, from the standpoint of his pecuniary self-interest, to how he decides. Pecuniary self-interest does not exhaust the economic concept of self-interest. But the other dimensions can be difficult to identify, let alone measure. Although judges are as self-interested as other people, it is the exceptional case in which a particular decision will promote a judge's self-interest other than by giving him the satisfaction of having performed his duty (which may involve the promotion of an ideology, even one he is not aware of) to the best of his ability—and this particular maximand does not seem readily amenable to economic analysis.

Yet, poorly understood as judicial incentives are, it is at least plausible that they push judges toward common law rule making that promotes the diffuse but powerful social policy of making markets work. For this may be the only social policy that the tools of the judicial process enable judges to promote in a consistent and reasonably uncontroversial fashion; if so, wealth maximization offers judges a comfortable as well as socially useful guidepost. Against this it can be argued that the articulation of legal rules in judicial opinions is a self-conscious, expressive activity, unlike a consumer's response to a change in relative prices; so that if wealth maximization were really the life blood of the common law we could expect to find the judges using the vocabulary of economics—especially now that economic analysts have extended that vocabulary to embrace legal doctrine. The vocabulary of economics, however, is designed for the use of specialists in economics. We should

19. For a helpful discussion, see Paul H. Rubin, "The Objectives of Private and Public Judges: A Comment," 41 *Public Choice* 133 (1983).

be no more surprised that judges talk in different terms while doing economics than that businessmen equate marginal cost to marginal revenue without using the terms and often without knowing what they mean. And we should bear in mind that *any* "structure possessed by judicial opinions will be a deep structure, not one that is at once apparent on the face of the text," because the common law system (and Anglo-American adjudication generally) does not have "a crisply defined form of legal opinion, or a closed canon of justificatory material, or a convention that effectively depersonalizes the court's opinion."[20]

The last important criticism of the positive economic theory of law, and the bridge to the criticisms of the normative theory, is that wealth maximization is so incoherent and repulsive a social norm that it is inconceivable that judges would embrace it. Let me defer consideration of this criticism for a moment and ask the reader to accept provisionally the conclusion of the next section: that as a universal social norm wealth maximization is indeed unsatisfactory, but that it is attractive or at least defensible when confined to the common law arena. With this stipulation, let us see where the positive theory stands. Plainly it has many weaknesses; legal theory has not yet had its Isaac Newton or its Adam Smith. Nor can these weaknesses be waved away with the observation that one can beat a theory only with a better theory. This observation is true—what else could one *beat* a theory with?—but trivial. If the only theoretical explanation that has been offered for a phenomenon is unconvincing despite the absence of a competing explanation, one is entitled to regard the phenomenon as unexplained. Maybe *compelled* to do so: an absence of competing explanations is one reason for believing an explanation, and if nevertheless you do not believe it the proponent cannot force you to do so merely by pointing out that there are no competing explanations. There is much about society (as about nature) that we do not yet understand.

But this would be the wrong note on which to end discussion of the positive economic theory of law. Apart from its pedagogical merit in enabling the jumble of common law rules and doctrines to be arranged in a coherent system, the theory has alerted legal scholars to the possibilities of scientific theorizing about law and has challenged them to seek competing theories, although so far the search has been pretty barren. Moreover, in its weakest form the positive economic theory can claim some empirical support. It seems that intuitions about wealth maximi-

20. A W. B. Simpson, "Legal Reasoning Anatomized: On Steiner's *Moral Argument and Social Vision in the Courts,*" 13 *Law and Social Inquiry* 637, 638 (1988).

zation *have* shaped to a significant degree the doctrines of the common law and that statute law *does* reflect to a much greater degree the pressure of interest groups. Although it would be a gross overstatement to conclude from the evidence gathered to date that the logic of the common law has been wealth maximization and the logic of statute law wealth redistribution, the statement contains some truth—and, to return to one of the abiding concerns of this book, undermines suggestions that law is an autonomous field of social thought and action.

An extreme Popperian might respond that as long as there is a *single* anomalous observation—in the present setting, a single rule or doctrine or decision of the common law that is inefficient, or a single legislative rule that is efficient—the positive economic theory of law has been refuted. But such a response would reflect a misunderstanding of scientific method.[21] The natural law that water boils at 212° Fahrenheit is not refuted by the observation that it boils at a lower temperature at high altitudes, but qualified; we subsume the law under a broader theory of the effects of heat. Some day what I have been calling the positive economic theory of law will be subsumed under a broader theory— perhaps, although not necessarily, an economic theory—of the social behavior we call law. Meanwhile, like the principle that water boils at 212°F, the economic theory of law is a default rule, or presumption— the right place to start, although not necessarily to end, in analyzing law from a positive standpoint.

Criticisms of the Normative Theory

The question whether wealth maximization *should* guide legal policy, either in general or just in common law fields (plus those statutory fields where the legislative intent is to promote efficiency—antitrust law being a possible example), is ordinarily treated as separate from the question whether it *has* guided legal policy, except insofar as the positive theory may be undermined by the inadequacies of the normative theory. Actually the two theories are not as separable as this,[22] illustrating again the lack of a clear boundary between "is" and "ought" propositions. One of the things judges ought to do is follow precedent, although not inflexibly; so if efficiency is the animating principle of much common

---

21. Cf. William C. Wimsatt, "False Models as Means to Truer Theories," in *Neutral Models in Biology* 23 (Matthew H. Nitecki and Antoni Hoffman eds. 1987). Popper himself, as I noted, would no longer accept it.

22. I am indebted to Steven Hetcher for this point.

law doctrine, judges have some obligation to make decisions that will be consistent with efficiency. This is one reason why the positive economic theory of the common law is so contentious.

The normative theory has been highly contentious in its own right. Most contributors to the debate over it conclude that it is a bad theory, and although many of the criticisms can be answered, several cannot be, and it is those I shall focus on.[23]

The first is that wealth maximization is inherently incomplete as a guide to social action because it has nothing to say about the distribution of rights—or at least nothing we want to hear. Given the distribution of rights (whatever it is), wealth maximization can be used to derive the policies that will maximize the value of those rights. But this does not go far enough, because naturally we are curious about whether it would be just to start off with a society in which, say, one member owned all the others. If wealth maximization is indifferent to the initial distribution of rights, it is a truncated concept of justice.

Since the initial distribution may dissipate rapidly,[24] this point may have little practical significance. Nor is wealth maximization completely silent on the initial distribution. If we could compare two otherwise identical nascent societies, in one of which one person owned all the others and in the other of which slavery was forbidden, and could repeat the comparison a century later, almost certainly we would find that the second society was wealthier and the first had abolished slavery (if so, this would further illustrate the limited effect of the initial distribution on the current distribution). Although it has not always and everywhere been true, under modern conditions of production slavery is an inefficient method of organizing production. The extensive use of slave labor

23. For the major criticisms, see Jules L. Coleman, "Economics and the Law: A Critical Review of the Foundations of the Economic Approach to Law," 94 *Ethics* 649 (1984); Coleman, *Markets, Morals, and the Law*, pt. 2 (1988); Ronald M. Dworkin, "Is Wealth a Value?" 9 *Journal of Legal Studies* 191 (1980), reprinted in Dworkin, *A Matter of Principle*, ch. 12 (1985); Anthony T. Kronman, "Wealth Maximization as a Normative Principle," 9 *Journal of Legal Studies* 227 (1980); Nicholas Mercuro and Timothy P. Ryan, *Law, Economics, and Public Policy* 130–137 (1984); Joseph M. Steiner, "Economics, Morality, and the Law of Torts," 26 *University of Toronto Law Journal* 227 (1976); Ernest J. Weinrib, "Utilitarianism, Economics, and Legal Theory," 30 id. at 307 (1980). For answers to some of the criticisms, see "Wealth Maximization Revisited," note 3 above; Lloyd Cohen, "A Justification of Social Wealth Maximization as a Rights-Based Ethical Theory," 10 *Harvard Journal of Law and Public Policy* 411 (1987); D. Bruce Johnsen, "Wealth *Is* Value," 15 *Journal of Legal Studies* 263 (1986).

24. "Almost all earnings advantages and disadvantages of ancestors are wiped out in three generations." Gary S. Becker and Nigel Tomes, "Human Capital and the Rise and Fall of Families," 4 *Journal of Labor Economics* S1, S32 (1986).

by the Nazis during World War II may seem an exception—but only if we disregard the welfare of the slave laborers.

This response to the demand that wealth maximization tell us something about the justice of the initial distribution of rights is incomplete. Suppose it were the case—it almost surely *is* the case—that some people in modern American society would be more productive as slaves than as free persons. These are not antisocial people whom we want to punish by imprisoning (a form of slavery that is tolerated); they are not psychotic or profoundly retarded; they just are lazy, feckless, poorly organized, undisciplined people—people incompetent to manage their own lives in a way that will maximize their output, even though the relevant output is not market output alone but also leisure, family associations, and any other sources of satisfaction to these people as well as to others. Wealth would be maximized by enslaving these people, provided the costs of supervision were not too high—but the assumption that they would not be too high is built into the proposition that their output would be greater as slaves than as free persons, for it is net output that we are interested in. Yet no one thinks it would be right to enslave such people, even if there were no evidentiary problems in identifying them, the slave masters could be trusted to be benign, and so on; and these conditions, too, may be implicit in the proposition that the net social output of some people would be greater if they were slaves.

It is no answer that it would be inefficient to enslave such people unless they consented to be enslaved, that is, unless the would-be slave-master met the asking price for their freedom. The term "*their* freedom" assumes they have the property right in their persons, and the assumption is arbitrary. We can imagine assigning the property rights in persons (perhaps only persons who appeared likely to be unproductive) to the state to auction them to the highest bidder. The putative slave could bid against the putative master, but would lose. His expected earnings, net of consumption, would be smaller than the expected profits to the master; otherwise enslavement would not be efficient. Therefore he could not borrow enough—even if capital markets worked without any friction (in the present setting, even if the lender could enslave the borrower if the latter defaulted!)—to outbid his master-to-be.

This example points to a deeper criticism of wealth maximization as a norm or value: like utilitarianism, which it closely resembles, or nationalism, or Social Darwinism, or racialism, or organic theories of the state, it treats people as if they were the cells of a single organism; the welfare of the cell is important only insofar as it promotes the welfare of the organism. Wealth maximization implies that if the prosperity of the society can be promoted by enslaving its least productive citizens, the sacrifice of their freedom is worthwhile. But this implication is contrary to the unshakable moral intuitions of Americans, and as I stressed in the last chapter, conformity to intuition is the ultimate test of a moral (indeed of any) theory.

Earlier chapters provide illustrations of collisions between, on the one hand, moral intuitions that have been influential in law and, on the other hand, wealth maximization. Recall, first, that the idea of corrective justice may well include the proposition that people who are wronged are entitled to some form of redress, even in cases when from an aggregate social standpoint it might be best to let bygones be bygones. Such an idea has no standing in a system powered by wealth maximization. Second, the prohibition of involuntary confessions rests on a notion of free will that has no standing in a system of wealth maximization, even though the particular notion of free will that the law uses equates free will with capacity for rational choice, and rational choice is fundamental to economics. The lawfulness of confessions in a system single-mindedly devoted to wealth maximization would depend entirely on the costs and benefits of the various forms of coercion, which range from outright torture to the relatively mild psychological pressures that our legal system tolerates. Cost-benefit analysis might show that torture was rarely cost-effective under modern conditions, being a costly method of interrogation (especially for the victim, but perhaps also for the torturer) that is apt to produce a lot of false leads and unreliable confessions. Nevertheless, even the most degrading forms of torture would not *necessarily* be ruled out, even in the investigation of ordinary crimes. I suggested in Chapter 5 that cost-benefit thinking has made inroads into coerced-confession law, but at some point these inroads would collide with, and be stopped by, strong moral intuitions that seem incompatible with economic thinking.

Or suppose it were the case—it may be the case—that some religious faiths are particularly effective in producing law-abiding, productive, healthy citizens. Mormonism is a plausible example. Would it not make sense on purely secular grounds, indeed on purely wealth-maximizing grounds, for government to subsidize these faiths? Practitioners of other religious faiths would be greatly offended, but from the standpoint of wealth maximization the only question would be whether the cost to them was greater than the benefits to the country as a whole.

Consider now a faith that both has few adherents in the United States and is feared or despised by the rest of the population. (The Rastafarian

faith is a plausible example.)[25] Such a faith will by assumption be imposing costs on the rest of the community, and given the fewness of its
adherents, the benefits conferred by the faith may, even when aggregat-
ed across all its adherents, be smaller than the costs. It could then be
argued that wealth maximization warranted or even required the
suppression of the faith. This example suggests another objection to
wealth maximization, one alluded to in the discussion of slavery: its
results are sensitive to assumptions about the initial distribution of
rights—a distribution that is distinct from the initial distribution of
wealth (which is unlikely to remain stable over time), but about which
wealth maximization may again have relatively little to say. If Rastafarians are conceived to have a property right in their religion, so that the
state or anyone else who wants to acquire that right and suppress the
religion must meet their asking price, probably the right will not be
sold. Asking prices can be very high—in principle, infinite: how much
would the average person sell his life for, if the sale had to be completed
immediately?[26] But if rights over religious practices are given to the part
of the populace that is not Rastafarian, the Rastafarians may find it
impossible to buy the right back; their offer price will be limited to their
net wealth, which may be slight.

No doubt in this country, in this day and age, religious liberty is the
cost-justified policy. The broader point is that a system of rights—
perhaps the system we have—may well be required by a *realistic* conception of utilitarianism, that is, one that understands that given the realities
of human nature a society dedicated to utilitarianism requires rules and
institutions that place checks on utility-maximizing behavior in particular cases. For example, although one can imagine specific cases in
which deliberately punishing an innocent person as a criminal would
increase aggregate utility, one has trouble imagining a system in which
government officials could be trusted to make such decisions.[27] "Wealth
maximizing" can be substituted for "utilitarian" without affecting the
analysis. Religious liberty may well be both utility maximizing and
wealth maximizing, and this may even be why we have it. And if it
became *too* costly, probably it would be abandoned; and so with the

25. See Reed v. Faulkner, 842 F.2d 960 (7th Cir. 1988); Note, "Soul Rebels: The
Rastafarians and the Free Exercise Clause," 72 *Georgetown Law Journal* 1605 (1984).

26. We of course "sell" years of expected life by living in an unhealthy fashion, engaging
in dangerous sports, driving too fast, and so on.

27. See Russell Hardin, "The Utilitarian Logic of Liberalism," 97 *Ethics* 47, 62–67
(1986); Hardin, *Morality within the Limits of Reason* 101–105 (1988); John Rawls, "Two Concepts of Rules," 64 *Philosophical Review* 3, 10–11 (1955).

prohibition of torture, and the other civilized political amenities of a wealthy society. If our crime rate were much lower than it is, we probably would not have capital punishment—and if it gets much higher, we surely will have fewer civil liberties.

But at least in the present relatively comfortable conditions of our society, the regard for individual freedom appears to transcend instrumental considerations; freedom appears to be valued for itself rather than just for its contribution to prosperity—or at least to be valued for reasons that escape the economic calculus. Is society really better off in a utilitarian or wealth-maximizing sense as a result of the extraordinarily elaborate procedural safeguards that the Bill of Rights gives criminal defendants? This is by no means clear. Are minority rights welfare maximizing—when the minority in question is a small one? That is not clear either, as the Rastafarian example showed. The main reasons these institutions are valued seem not to be utilitarian or even instrumental in character. *What* those reasons are is far from clear; indeed, "noninstrumental reason" is almost an oxymoron. And as I have suggested, we surely are not willing to pay an infinite price, perhaps not even a very high price, for freedom. While reprobating slavery we condone similar (but more efficient) practices under different names—imprisonment as punishment for crime, preventive detention, the authority of parents and school authorities over children, conscription, the institutionalization of the insane and the retarded. The Thirteenth Amendment has been read narrowly. Although the only stated exception is for punishment for crime ("neither slavery nor involuntary servitude, except as a punishment for crime whereof the party shall have been duly convicted, shall exist within the United States, or any place subject to their jurisdiction"), laws requiring jury service, military service, and even working on the public roads have been upheld.[28] We reprobate the infliction of physical pain as a method of extracting confessions or imposing punishment but, perhaps in unconscious tribute to the outmoded dualism of mind and body, condone the infliction of mental pain for the same purposes.

Still, hypocritical and incoherent as our political ethics may frequently be, we do not permit degrading invasions of individual autonomy merely on a judgment that, on balance, the invasion would make a net addi-

28. See Hurtado v. United States, 410 U.S. 578, 589 n. 11 (1973); Selective Draft Law Cases, 245 U.S. 366, 390 (1918); Butler v. Perry, 240 U.S. 328 (1916); cf. Robertson v. Baldwin, 165 U.S. 275, 288 (1897). No *expressio unius est exclusio alterius* here!

tion to the social wealth. And whatever the philosophical grounding of this sentiment,[29] it is too deeply entrenched in our society at present for wealth maximization to be given a free rein. The same may be true of the residue of corrective-justice sentiment.

I have said nothing about the conflict between wealth maximization and equality of wealth, because I am less sure of the extent of egalitarian sentiment in our society than that of individualistic sentiment (by "individualism" I mean simply the rivals to aggregative philosophies, such as utilitarianism and wealth maximization). Conflict there is, however, and it points to another important criticism of wealth maximization even if the critic is not an egalitarian. Imagine that a limited supply of growth hormone, privately manufactured and sold, must be allocated. A wealthy parent wants the hormone so that his child of average height will grow tall; a poor parent wants the hormone so that his child of dwarfish height can grow to normal height. In a system of wealth maximization the wealthy parent might outbid the poor parent and get the hormone. This is not certain. Amount of wealth is only one factor in willingness to pay. The poor parent might offer his entire wealth for the hormone, and that wealth, although meager, might exceed the amount of money the wealthy parent was willing to pay, given alternative uses to which he could put his money. Also, altruists might help the poor parent bid more than he could with only his own resources. The poor might actually be better off in a system in which the distribution of the hormone were left to the private market, even if there were no altruism. Such a system would create incentives to produce and sell the hormone sooner, and perhaps at a lower price, than if the government controlled its distribution; for the costs of production would probably be lower under private rather than public production, and even a monopolist will charge less when his costs fall.

But what seems impossible to maintain convincingly in the present ethical climate is that the wealthy parent has the *right* to the hormone by virtue of being willing to pay the supplier more than the poor parent can; more broadly, that consumers have a right to purchase in free markets. These propositions cannot be derived from wealth maximization. Indeed, they look like propositions about transactional freedom rather than about distribution only because I have assumed that the growth hormone is produced and distributed exclusively through the free mar-

---

29. Perhaps it is the Kantian sense that we should not treat one another merely as objects (as, I argued in Chapter 5, the criminal law does and should). See P. F. Strawson, "Freedom and Resentment," in Strawson, *Freedom and Resentment, and Other Essays* 1, 9 (1974).

ket. An alternative possibility would be for the state to own the property right in the hormone and to allocate it on the basis of need rather than willingness to pay. To argue against this alternative (socialist medicine writ small) would require an appeal either to the deeply controversial idea of a natural right to private property, or to purely instrumental considerations, such as the possibility that in the long run the poor will be better off with a free market in growth hormone—but to put the question *this* way is to assume that the poor have some sort of social claim by virtue of being poor, and thus to admit the relevance of egalitarian considerations and thereby break out of the limits of wealth maximization.

A stronger-seeming argument for the free-enterprise solution is that the inventor of the hormone should have a right to use it as he wishes, which includes the right to sell it to the highest bidder. But this argument seems stronger only because we are inclined to suppose that what has happened is that *after* the inventor invented it the government decided to rob him of the reward for which he had labored. If instead we assume that Congress passes a law in 1989 which provides that after the year 2000 the right to patent new drugs will be conditioned on the patentee's agreeing to limit the price he charges, we shall have difficulty objecting to the law on ethical, as distinct from practical, grounds. It would be just one more restriction on free markets.

We saw in Chapter 11 why a quest for a natural-rights theory of justice is unlikely to succeed. Although the advocate of wealth maximization can argue that to the productive should belong the fruits of their labor, the argument can be countered along the lines suggested in that chapter—production is really a social rather than individual effort—to which it can be added that wealth may often be due more to luck (and not the luck of the genetic lottery, either) than to skill or effort. Furthermore, if altruism is so greatly admired, as it is by conservatives as well as by liberals, why should not its spirit inform legislation? Why should government protect only our selfish instincts? To this it can be replied that the spirit of altruism is voluntary giving. But the reply is weak. The biggest reason we value altruism is that we *desire* some redistribution—we may admire the altruist for his self-sacrifice but we would not admire him as much if he destroyed his wealth rather than giving it to others—and we think that voluntary redistribution is less costly than involuntary. If redistribution is desirable, some involuntary redistribution may be justifiable, depending on the costs, of course, but not on the principle of the thing.

There is a still deeper problem with founding wealth maximization on a notion of natural rights. The economic perspective is thoroughly (and fruitfully) behaviorist. "Economic man" is not, as vulgarly supposed, a person driven by purely pecuniary incentives, but he is a person whose behavior is completely determined by incentives; his rationality is no different from that of a pigeon or a rat. The economic task from the perspective of wealth maximization is to influence his incentives so as to maximize his output. How a person so conceived could be thought to have a *moral* entitlement to a particular distribution of the world's goods—an entitlement, say, to the share proportional to his contribution to the world's wealth—is unclear. Have marmots moral entitlements? Two levels of discourse are being mixed.

By questioning anti-egalitarian arguments I do not mean to be endorsing egalitarian ones. We glimpsed some of their weaknesses in Chapter 11, and here is another. The egalitarian is apt to say that differences in intelligence, which often translate into differences in productivity, are the result of a natural lottery and therefore ought not guide entitlements. But if differences in intelligence are indeed genetic, as the argument assumes, then liberal and radical arguments about the exploitiveness of capitalist society are undermined. A genetic basis for intellectual differences and resulting differences in productivity implies that inequality in the distribution of income and wealth is to a substantial degree natural (which is not to say that it is morally good), rather than a product of unjust social and political institutions. It also implies that such inequality is apt to be strongly resistant to social and political efforts to change it.

The strongest argument for wealth maximization is not moral, but pragmatic. Such classic defenses of the free market as chapter 4 of Mill's *On Liberty* can easily be given a pragmatic reading.[30] We look around the world and see that in general people who live in societies in which markets are allowed to function more or less freely not only are wealthier than people in other societies but have more political rights, more liberty and dignity, are more content (as evidenced, for example, by their being less prone to emigrate)—so that wealth maximization may be the most direct route to a variety of moral ends. The recent history of England, France, and Turkey, of Japan and Southeast Asia, of East versus West Germany and North versus South Korea, of China and Tai-

30. For another fine pragmatic defense of economic liberalism, see Arnold C. Harberger, "Three Basic Postulates for Applied Welfare Economics: An Interpretive Essay," in his book *Taxation and Welfare* 5 (1974). See generally C. L. Ten, *Mill on Liberty* (1980); Norman P. Barry, *On Classical Liberalism and Libertarianism* (1987).

wan, of Chile, of the Soviet Union, Poland, and Hungary, and of Cuba and Argentina provides striking support for this thesis.[31]

Writing in the early 1970s, the English political philosopher Brian Barry doubted the importance of incentives. "My own guess," he said, "is that enough people with professional and managerial jobs really like them (and enough others who would enjoy them and have sufficient ability to do them are waiting to replace those who do not) to enable the pay of these jobs to be brought down considerably . . . I would suggest that the pay levels in Britain of schoolteachers and social workers seem to offer net rewards which recruit and maintain just enough people, and that this provides a guideline to the pay levels that could be sustained generally among professionals and managers."[32] He rejected the "assumption that a sufficient supply of highly educated people will be forthcoming only if lured by the anticipation of a higher income afterwards as a result," adding that "it would also be rash to assume that it would be an economic loss if fewer sought higher education" (p. 160 and n. 3). He discussed with approval the Swedish experiment at redistributing income and wealth but thought it hampered by the fact that "Sweden still has a privately owned economy" (p. 161). He worried about "brain drain" but concluded that it was a serious problem only with regard to airline pilots and physicians; and a nation can do without airlines and may be able to replace general practitioners "with people having a lower (and less marketable) qualification" (p. 162). (Yet Barry himself was soon to join the brain drain, and he is neither a physician nor an airline pilot.) He proposed "to spread the nastiest jobs around by

31. See, for example, Samuel Brittan, *The Role and Limits of Government: Essays in Political Economy,* ch. 10 (1983) (discussing the "British sickness"); Alan Ryan, *Property and Political Theory,* ch. 7 (1984) ("Why There are So Few Socialists"); Nick Eberstadt, *The Poverty of Communism* (1988); John McMillan, John Whalley, and Lijing Zhu, "The Impact of China's Economic Reforms on Agricultural Productivity Growth," 97 *Journal of Political Economy* 781 (1989); Paul Wiedemann, "Comparing the Process of Socio-Economic Development in Market and Non-Market Economies: The EEC and CMEA," 8 *Cambridge Journal of Economics* 311 (1984); Janos Horvath, "Economic Reform in Hungary: Role of Plan and Market," 4 *Cato Journal* 511 (1984); Francis G. Castles, "Whatever Happened to the Communist Welfare State?" 19 *Studies in Comparative Communism* 213 (1986); Jerry Z. Muller, "Capitalism: The Wave of the Future," 86 *Commentary,* Dec. 1988, at 21. Comparing the recent trend toward free markets with the long history of depictions of capitalism as being in its "late" (and last) phase, Muller comments mordantly: "After late capitalism comes more capitalism." Id. at 23.

32. *The Liberal Theory of Justice: A Critical Examination of the Principal Doctrines in "A Theory of Justice" by John Rawls* 159 (1973). Subsequent page references to this book are in the text. The book was written while Barry was teaching at Oxford. He later moved to the United States and has now returned to (Margaret Thatcher's) England.

requiring everyone, before entering higher education or entering a profession, to do, say, three years of work wherever he or she was directed. (This would also have educational advantages.) To supplement this there could be a call-up of say a month every year, as with the Swiss and Israeli armed forces but directed towards peaceful occupations" (p. 164).

At least with the benefit of hindsight we can see that Barry wrote a prescription for economic disaster. It may be impossible to lay solid philosophical foundations under wealth maximization, just as it may be impossible to lay solid philosophical foundations under the natural sciences, but this would be a poor reason for abandoning wealth maximization, just as the existence of intractable problems in the philosophy of science would be a poor reason for abandoning science. We have reason to believe that markets work—that capitalism delivers the goods, if not the Good—and it would be a mistake to allow philosophy to deflect us from the implications, just as it would be a mistake to allow philosophy to alter our views of infanticide (see Chapter 11).

A sensible pragmatism does not ignore theory. The mounting evidence that capitalism is more efficient than socialism gives us an additional reason for believing economic theory (not every application of it, to be sure). The theory in turn gives us greater confidence in the evidence. Theory and evidence are mutually supporting. From the perspective of economic theory, brain drain is not the mysterious disease that Barry supposes it to be; it is the rational response to leveling policies by those whose incomes are being leveled downward.

I said that Mill's defense of free markets in *On Liberty* is most persuasive when viewed in pragmatic terms. This suggestion will jar some readers, for whom pragmatism is associated with socialism. Many leading pragmatists have been socialists, such as Dewey, Habermas, and Wittgenstein. But Holmes was a pragmatist, and he was not a socialist; ditto with Sidney Hook. If there is a correlation between pragmatism and socialism, it tells us more about academic fashions than about the nature of pragmatism. I will illustrate with an article by Richard Rorty that outdoes Brian Barry in political and economic naïveté, and with less excuse, because it was published in 1988 rather than in 1973.[33] Dis-

---

33. Rorty, "Unger, Castoriadis, and the Romance of a National Future," 82 *Northwestern University Law Review* 335 (1988). Barry appears, however, to be unregenerate. See Brian Barry, "Does Democracy Cause Inflation? Political Ideas of Some Economists," in *The Politics of Inflation and Economic Stagnation: Theoretical Approaches and International Case Studies* 280, 317 (Leon N. Lindberg and Charles S. Maier eds. 1985).

cussing Roberto Unger's socialist revolutionary treatise, *Politics,* Rorty expresses the hope that some Third World nation may be inspired by Unger's work to experiment with a radical restructuring of society—for example, by decreeing an absolute equality of incomes. The fact that one can offer no good arguments for such an experiment ought not count as a significant objection, Rorty argues; our inability to offer good arguments may reflect simply the poverty of our imagination and (in William Blake's phrase) the "mind-forged manacles" of our culture.

> Suppose that somewhere, someday, the newly-elected government of a large industrialized society decreed that everybody would get the same income, regardless of occupation or disability. Simultaneously, it instituted vastly increased inheritance taxes and froze large bank transfers. Suppose that, after the initial turmoil, it worked: that is, suppose that the country did not collapse, that people still took pride in their work (as streetcleaners, pilots, doctors, canecutters, Cabinet ministers, or whatever), and so on. Suppose that the next generation in that country was brought up to realize that, whatever else they might work for, it made no sense to work for wealth. But they worked anyway (for, among other things, national glory). That country would become an irresistible example for a lot of other countries, "capitalist," "Marxist," and in-between. The electorates of these countries would not take time to ask what "factors" had made the success of the experiment possible. Social theorists would not be allowed time to explain how something had happened that they had pooh-poohed as utopian, nor to bring this new sort of society under familiar categories. All the attention would be focused on the actual details of how things were working in the pioneering nation. Sooner or later, the world would be changed.[34]

34. Rorty, note 33 above, at 349–350. Yet Rorty believes that capitalism (in its welfare-state rather than laissez-faire version) is best for the United States, although irrelevant for most of the rest of the world. See *Consequences of Pragmatism (Essays 1972–1980)* 207, 210 (1982); *Contingency, Irony, and Solidarity* 53, 63 (1989); "Thugs and Theorists: A Reply to Bernstein," 15 *Political Theory* 564, 565–567 (1987); "On Ethnocentrism: A Reply to Clifford Geertz," 25 *Michigan Quarterly Review* 525 (1986). This belief has earned him the fierce enmity of the far Left. See, for example, Rebecca Comay, "Interrupting the Conversation: Notes on Rorty," in *Anti-Foundationalism and Practical Reasoning: Conversations between Hermeneutics and Analysis* 83 (Evan Simpson ed. 1987); Robert Burch, "Conloquium Interruptum: Stopping to Think," in id. at 99; Richard J. Bernstein, "One Step Forward, Two Steps Backward: Richard Rorty on Liberal Democracy and Philosophy," 15 *Political Theory* 538 (1987). Rorty's belief that capitalism is best for us seems inconsistent with his belief that you can't know whether you would prefer a different social system until you have tried it.

Rorty realizes that no Western country is likely to embark on such an experiment, but he hopes that a Third World country might be desperate enough to try.[35]

The pragmatist character of Rorty's analysis is unmistakable. Reason and argument are not everything; the big changes are gestalt switches; life is an experiment;[36] trial and error is the method of science; people are historically situated, and their situation must change before they will. We recall that John Dewey founded the Laboratory School at the University of Chicago, and with it progressive education. But there is something big missing from Rorty's analysis—learning from experience. The experiment he describes—eliminating or radically curtailing the use of material incentives to guide economic production—has been tried many times, in the Third World as elsewhere, with catastrophic consequences to the experimental subjects. A pragmatist might be expected to have concluded by this time that other forms of social experimentation are likely to be more fruitful than radical egalitarianism. Rorty, however, believes in the infinite plasticity of human nature and social institutions. His position is compatible with pragmatist philosophy, but not compelled by it. Neither Barry nor Rorty, it should be added, attempts to evaluate his utopian proposals from the standpoint of history or economics.[37]

In implying that Barry and Rorty would change their minds and agree with *my* pragmatic judgment—that capitalist wealth maximization offers the Third World (and the First and the Second) a lot more than socialism—if they knew more about economics and modern history, I

35. "If there is hope, it lies in the Third World." Rorty, note 33 above, at 340. "No single change could do more to expose the contingency, poverty, and insignificance of some of the central signifiers of the national neuroses of both superpowers than some third country's success at equalizing incomes." Id. at 351.

36. See John Dewey, "The Need for a Recovery of Philosophy," in Dewey, *Creative Intelligence: Essays in the Pragmatic Attitude,* 3, 7–8 (1917); Abrams v. United States, 250 U.S. 616, 630 (1919) (Holmes, J., dissenting).

37. Rorty has a weak sense of fact. This is evident in his political musings (writing in 1987, he denounced as a "gang of thugs" "the shadowy millionaires [unnamed] manipulating Reagan" and predicted the "gradual absorption of the Third World by the Second" because "time seems to be on the Soviet side," "Thugs and Theorists," note 34 above, at 566–567), and is perhaps connected to his coolness toward science, both natural and social, and resulting indifference to empirical investigation, the systematic study of social fact, and learning from past experiments. In this respect he is very different from his hero, Dewey. For criticism of Rorty's view of science, and in particular his airy dismissal of the differences between scientific and theological reasoning as revealed in the debate between Galileo and Cardinal Bellarmine over the moons of Jupiter, see Richard W. Miller, *Fact and Method: Explanation, Confirmation, and Reality in the Natural and the Social Sciences* 488–493 (1987).

may seem to be flirting with moral realism à la Plato. I am indeed saying that what appears to be an ethical disagreement is a disagreement over facts; that with knowledge will come ethical convergence. But my proposition is not that all value questions are reducible to questions of fact, but that the fact-value distinction shifts as knowledge grows. There happens to be substantial consensus in our society concerning ends (including ends for other societies). The disagreement is over means, and it will lessen as more of us learn more about how economic systems work.

My pragmatic judgment is, moreover, a qualified one. All modern societies depart from the precepts of wealth maximization. The unanswered question is how the conditions in these societies would change if the public sector could somehow be cut all the way down to the modest dimensions of the night watchman state that the precepts of wealth maximization seem to imply. That is a difficult counterfactual question (it seems that no society's leadership has both the will and the power to play the guinea pig in an experiment with full-fledged wealth maximization), though one untouched by Barry's musings on economics or by Rorty's romantic experimentalism. Until it is answered, we should be cautious in pushing wealth maximization; incrementalism should be our watchword.

The fact that wealth maximization, pragmatically construed, is instrumental rather than foundational is not an objection to its use in guiding law and public policy. It may be the right principle for that purpose even though it is right only in virtue of ends that are not solely economic. At least it may be the right default principle, placing on the proponent of departures from wealth maximization the burden of demonstrating their desirability.

Even if my observations on comparative economic performance in the Third World and elsewhere are correct, do such matters belong in a book on jurisprudence? They do. The object of pragmatic analysis is to lead discussion away from issues semantic and metaphysical and toward issues factual and empirical. Jurisprudence is greatly in need of such a shift in direction. Jurisprudence needs to become more pragmatic.

Common Law Revisited

The case for using wealth maximization as a guiding principle in common law adjudication is particularly strong. The common law judge operates within a framework established by the Constitution, which, by virtue of a number of the amendments, not only rules out of bounds the ethically most questionable applications of wealth maximization but largely eliminates the problems of incompleteness and indeterminacy that result from the uncertain relationship between wealth maximization and the initial distribution of rights. That initial distribution is more or less a given for the common law judge. A related point is that such a judge operates in a domain where distributive or egalitarian considerations can play at best only a small role. The judge whose business is enforcing tort, contract, and property law lacks effective tools for bringing about an equitable distribution of wealth, even if he thinks he knows what such a distribution would be. He would be further handicapped in such an endeavor by the absence of consensus in our society on the nature of a just distribution, an absence that undermines the social acceptability of attempts to use the judicial office to achieve distributive goals. A sensible division of labor has the judge making rules and deciding cases in the areas regulated by the common law in such a way as to maximize the size of the social pie, and the legislature attending to the sizes of the slices.

The case is strongest in those common law areas where the relevant policies are admitted to be economic. Suppose the idea of an implied warranty of habitability—which entitles a tenant to sue his landlord if the premises fall below the standards of safety and comfort specified in the local housing code—is defended, as normally it is defended, on the ground that it is needed to protect tenants from deception and overreaching by landlords and will not lead to a reduction in the stock of housing available to poor people or to higher rentals than the poor are willing and able to pay. If research demonstrates that these assumptions are incorrect, the proponent, if fair-minded, will have to withdraw the proposal. In this example, in principle (for the necessary research is difficult to conduct), legal questions can be made determinate by the translation of a legal question into a social-scientific one in a setting of common ends, and therefore the valid Benthamite project of placing law on a more scientific basis can be advanced without injury to competing values.

If it could be shown or if it is conceded that common law decision making is indeed not an apt field for efforts to redistribute wealth, then it may be possible to ground wealth maximization (as used to guide such decision making) in a more powerful normative principle of economics, the Pareto principle. A transaction is Pareto superior when it makes at least one person better off and no one worse off. A simple contract approximates a Pareto-superior transaction. Neither party would sign the contract unless he thought he would be better off as a result. So, assuming adequate information (which does not mean assuming omniscience) and no adverse effects on third parties, the contract will be Pareto superior. At least this will be so on an ex ante basis, for as things turn out one of the parties (perhaps both) may be made worse off by the contract. This possibility is inevitable if there is uncertainty, and uncertainty is inevitable.

The ethical appeal of the Pareto principle is similar to that of unanimity. If everyone affected by a transaction is better off, how can the transaction be socially or ethically bad? There are answers to this question,[38] yet a Pareto-superior transaction makes a powerful claim for ethical respect because it draws on intuitions that are fundamental to both utilitarianism and Kantian individualism—respect for preferences, and for persons, respectively. It may seem paradoxical to derive a norm of wealth maximization from the principle of Pareto superiority, when the hallmark of the latter is compensation of all potential losers (for remember that no one must be made worse off by the transaction if it is to be Pareto superior), while wealth maximization requires only that the winners' gains exceed the losers' losses. But if, as in the contract example, compensation is permitted to be ex ante, the paradox disappears.

The difference between the ex ante and ex post perspectives is fundamental, and failure to attend to it underlies much confused thinking about markets and transactional competence. Because many choices are made, unavoidably, under conditions of uncertainty, a fair number *must* turn out badly. Ex post, they are regarded as mistaken and engender regret, yet ex ante they may have been perfectly sensible. Suppose I have a choice between two jobs. One would pay me $50,000 every year with certainty, the other either $500,000 a year (with a 90 percent probability) or nothing (with a 10 percent probability). The expected income in the first job is $50,000 and in the second $450,000. (Notice the use of Bayesian probability, mentioned in Chapter 6.) The second, however, involves uncertainty. If I am risk averse—and let us assume I am—I will value an uncertain expectation at less than its actuarial equivalent. Hence the second job will not really be worth $450,000 to me, and let us suppose it will be worth only one-third as much—$150,000. Still, that is more than $50,000, so I will take the second job. But I am unlucky, the 10 percent chance materializes, and my income is zero. I would be less (or more) than human if I did not regret my choice, rail against my fate,

---

38. As argued, for example, in Robin West, "Authority, Autonomy, and Choice: The Role of Consent in the Moral and Political Visions of Franz Kafka and Richard Posner," 99 *Harvard Law Review* 384 (1985), to which I respond in *Law and Literature: A Misunderstood Relation,* ch. 4 (1988). I consider the authenticity of preferences in Chapter 13.

berate myself for having chosen stupidly. But in fact I made the right choice—and would make it again, given the same uncertainty as before.

Consider now the case where negligence is the more efficient principle, in a wealth-maximizing sense, than strict liability because when all the costs and benefits are toted up the negligence regime turns out to produce the greater excess of benefits over costs. If so, the sum of liability and accident insurance premiums will be lower in the negligence regime and all drivers will be better off ex ante, although ex post, of course, some may do better in a regime of strict liability. Actually, not *all* will be better off even ex ante. Some people who are more prone to be injured than to injure will be worse off, since negligence favors injurers relative to strict liability, and some who are more prone to injure than to be injured will be better off. The "losers" will lose little, though—a matter of slightly higher insurance premiums. And both the "winners" and the vast majority of drivers who are neither disproportionately likely to injure than to be injured nor vice versa will be better off. Complete unanimity will be unattainable, but near unanimity can be presumed and the few losers will hardly be degraded, their autonomy wrecked, or their rights destroyed by having to pay a few dollars a month more in automobile insurance premiums.

I am painting with slightly too rosy a palette. Some people will lack the knowledge, intelligence, and foresight to buy insurance (I am putting to one side the deliberate risk takers); some may not be able to afford adequate insurance; and insurance that pays off as generously as common law damages may not be available in the market. When a person becomes a victim of a serious accident in which the injurer is not at fault, it may spell a financial disaster not attributable to the choices or the deserts of the victim—a disaster that strict liability could have avoided. An alternative, of course, is social insurance—the famous safety net. If cases of catastrophic uninsured nonnegligent accidental injury are rare, social insurance may be a better solution than a strict liability system that would require compensation through the tort system in all accident cases.

The essential point is that the availability of insurance, private or social, is necessary to back wealth maximization with the ethical weight of the Pareto principle. Once it is so backed, however, wealth maximization provides an ethically adequate guide to common law decision making—indeed a superior guide to any other that has been suggested. And the adequacy of private and public insurance markets, on which this conclusion depends, is an empirical, a studiable, issue.

No doubt most judges (and lawyers) think that the guiding light for common law decision making should be either an intuitive sense of justice or reasonableness, or a casual utilitarianism.[39] But these may all be the same thing,[40] and if pressed such a judge would probably have to admit that what he called utilitarianism was what I am calling wealth maximization. Consider whether a thief should be permitted to defend himself at trial on the ground that he derived greater pleasure from the stolen item than the pain suffered by the owner. The answer obviously is no, but it is offered more confidently by the wealth maximizer than by the pure utilitarian. The former can point out that the thief is bypassing the market system of exchange and that the pleasure he derives from the good he has stolen has no social standing because his desire for the good is not backed by willingess to pay. These are separate points. The thief might be willing to pay if he had to—that is, he might value the good more than its owner—yet prefer theft because it is a cheaper way for him to acquire the good. So theft might be utility maximizing, although this is unlikely because a *practice* of theft would result in enormous, utility-reducing expenditures on protection of property.

Since utility is more difficult to estimate than wealth, a system of wealth maximization may seem a proxy for a utilitarian system, but it is more; its spirit is different. Wealth maximization is an ethic of productivity and social cooperation—to have a claim on society's goods and services you must be able to offer something that other people value—while utilitarianism is a hedonistic, unsocial ethic, as the last example showed. And an ethic of productivity and cooperation is more congruent with the values of the dominant groups in our society than the pure utilitarian ethic would be. Unfortunately, wealth maximization is not a pure ethic of productivity and cooperation, not only because even lawful efforts at maximizing wealth often make some other people

---

39. See, for example, James Barr Ames, "Law and Morals," 22 *Harvard Law Review* 97 (1908); Henry T. Terry, "Negligence," 29 *Harvard Law Review* 40 (1915); Lon L. Fuller, "Consideration and Form," 41 *Columbia Law Review* 799 (1941), Benjamin Kaplan, "Encounters with O. W. Holmes, Jr.," 96 *Harvard Law Review* 1828, 1849 (1983). "The law is utilitarian. It exists for the realization of the reasonable needs of the community. If the interest of an individual runs counter to this chief object of the law, it must be sacrificed." Ames, above, at 110. Recall the utilitarian flavor of Chief Justice Shaw's analysis in the *Farwell* case (Chapter 8); and see next footnote.

40. *Farwell* is again a good example; Shaw's analysis of the fellow-servant rule in terms of justice, policy, and the convenience of the public is isomorphic with an analysis of the rule in terms of wealth maximization. Or consider a representative utilitarian analysis of criminal law, R. B. Brandt, "The Insanity Defense and the Theory of Motivation," 7 *Law and Philosophy* 123 (1988)—it reads very much like an analysis in terms of wealth maximization, except that the vocabulary is philosophical rather than economic.

worse off, but more fundamentally because luck plays a big role in the returns to market activities. What is worse, it is always possible to argue that the distribution of productivity among a population is itself the luck of the genetic draw, or of upbringing, or of where one happens to have been born, and that these forms of luck have no ethical charge. There are counterarguments, of course, but they are not decisive. So, once again, the foundations of an overarching principle for resolving legal disputes are rotten, and one is driven back to the pragmatic ramparts.

13 ⚬◦⟆

Literary, Feminist, and Communitarian Perspectives on Jurisprudence

The suggestions implicit in this chapter's title that literature might have a bearing on jurisprudence, that jurisprudence might have genders, and that these two suggestions might be related may startle many readers. Yet the first and third suggestion are plainly true, and the second possibly so, although I am dubious. As with the perspectives on jurisprudence already considered, we shall discover that the literary and feminist perspectives, and other communitarian approaches briefly considered in the final section, do not support the project of making law a determinate and autonomous field of social thought and action. Indeed, they point in the opposite direction. This may be one reason why they are rather off-putting to conventional legal thinkers.

Law and Literature

The growing body of scholarly writings on the relationship between law and literature[1] identifies several areas in which literature—not only the works of literature themselves but also works of literary theory and of literary criticism—may help solve the problems of jurisprudence. The most obvious area, but the least fruitful, is that of interpretive method. Works of literature resemble statutes and the Constitution in being difficult texts, and the difficulties of interpreting them have brought into being a vast literature of literary theory and criticism. This literature is more sophisticated than the corresponding literature in law. Yet so different are literary and legal texts that the interpretive methods useful for the one kind are not useful for the other. The interpretive analogies

---

1. See the Introduction to my book *Law and Literature: A Misunderstood Relation* (1988), for a brief survey.

between the two fields ventured in Chapter 6 may exhaust the potential for a fruitful illumination of interpretive practice or theory in one field by interpretive practice or theory in the other.

Statutes and constitutional provisions are commands, a type of communication that requires the recipient to make a good-faith effort to carry out the sender's wishes. Literature—especially great literature, the focus of literary scholarship—is the body of texts that survive the immediate occasion of their creation to live on in cultures and times remote from that creation. They can do this only if they have a considerable generality, ambiguity, or adaptability—an "omnisignificance" that enables them to survive vicissitudes of culture and taste. Texts of such character are the opposite of commands. There is also no felt need to make literary interpretation uniform or predictable because of the social, economic, or political consequences of alternative interpretations of the same text. And interpretations of literature that stray far from the intentions or understandings of the original authors do not raise issues of political legitimacy. The command analogy, of course, will not resolve every question of statutory interpretation. But literary scholars have not discovered universal laws of textual interpretation or pointed the way to definitive interpretations of legal texts. They offer no answers to the baffling questions of legal interpretation pondered in Part III.[2]

The study of literature can, however, aid in understanding the intensely rhetorical character of judicial opinions.[3] This help should be welcomed by anyone who accepts the argument in Chapter 4 that change in law—especially when it is big, rapid change—is often the consequence not of arguments addressed to the rational intellect but of rhetorical thrusts ("warm" argument, addressed to emotion and empathy rather than to intellect) that may trigger a "conversion" or gestalt switch. Holmes's most famous and possibly most influential opinion, the dissent in *Lochner v. New York,* is not well reasoned; its power is due to its masterful employment of metaphor and other literary devices.[4] Although the dissent would not have been influential had it not struck a responsive chord among lawyers and judges predisposed to reject the

2. For a fuller discussion of the inapplicability to law of the interpretive methods used in literature, see id., ch. 5.

3. See id., ch. 6.

4. See id. at 282–287. And the use of history and the evaluation of consequences in *West Virginia State Board of Education v. Barnette* are less impressive than the rhetorical skill with which Justice Jackson marshaled such evidence as he was able to find for his conclusion. On the rhetoric of *Barnette,* see Robert A. Ferguson, "The Judicial Opinion as Literary Genre" (unpublished paper, Columbia University Department of English).

constitutional jurisprudence of the *Lochner* majority, it took literary power to strike that chord.

Recall the discussion of affirmative action, one of a cluster of legal-ethical issues (abortion, capital punishment, sex discrimination, homosexuality, and obscenity are others) that seem not to yield to conventional methods of legal analysis and around which no ethical or political consensus has formed. James Boyd White, a leading figure in the law and literature movement, has tried to break the logjam by asking us to compare the white victims of affirmative action to the Union soldiers in the Civil War, who made greater sacrifices on behalf of oppressed blacks than the sacrifices demanded of any white person today by affirmative action.[5] There are objections to the comparison: most Union soldiers were fighting to save the union, not to free the slaves; and although the sacrifice demanded of white victims of affirmative action is indeed less, so is the urgency and justice of the cause. But the comparison has rhetorical power, and rhetorical power counts for a lot in law. Science, not to mention everyday thought, is influenced by metaphors.[6] Why shouldn't law be?

Literature can also illuminate the perennial issues of jurisprudence that arise from the tension between law and equity (and more broadly between formal and substantive justice), and it can shed light on the critical stages in the growth of law, the subject of historical jurisprudence.[7]

In Euripides' *Hecuba,* the Greek fleet, carrying Hecuba and the other Trojan women as slaves, has stopped in Thrace on its way back from

---

5. See "A Response to 'The Rhetoric of Powell's *Bakke,*'" 38 *Washington and Lee Law Review* 73, 75 (1981).

6. Besides references cited in Chapter 2, see Alvin I. Goldman, *Epistemology and Cognition* 239–241 (1986); *Philosophical Perspectives on Metaphor* (Mark Johnson ed. 1981); George Lakoff and Mark Johnson, *Metaphors We Live By* (1980). And recall the example from Chapter 1 of "proving" the validity of the syllogism by means of a metaphor. Of course, reasoning by metaphor is full of pitfalls, as emphasized, with specific reference to law, in Michael Boudin, "Antitrust Doctrine and the Sway of Metaphor," 75 *Georgetown Law Journal* 395 (1986), and Haig Bosmajian, "The Metaphoric Marketplace of Ideas and the Pig in the Parlor," 26 *Midwest Quarterly* 44 (1984). See also C. K. Ogden, *Bentham's Theory of Fictions* (1932). And do not suppose from my use of White's example that metaphor is always on the liberal side of issues. Consider William Paley's metaphoric defense of capital punishment: "He who falls by a mistaken sentence, may be considered as falling for his country." "Moral and Political Philosophy," in *The Works of William Paley,* vol. 3, pp. 1, 315 (new ed., 1838).

7. For pertinent discussions, see Martha C. Nussbaum, *The Fragility of Goodness: Luck and Ethics in Greek Tragedy and Philosophy* 409–418 (1986); *Law and Literature: A Misunderstood Relation,* note 1 above, at 38–40.

the Trojan War. During the stopover, Hecuba discovers that the king of Thrace, Polymestor, has killed her only surviving son, Polydorus, whom Priam had entrusted along with a large quantity of gold to Polymestor's charge in the hope of preserving the boy and the gold from the perils of war. Polymestor does not deny killing Polydorus, but argues that he did it to protect the Greeks from the danger that Polydorus might have rebuilt Troy and sought revenge for his father's death and for the other disasters that had befallen his family. This if true would not be a negligible argument. It would not acquit Polymestor of a serious charge of breach of trust; but this is war. Certain that Polymestor killed Polydorus merely for the gold, however, Hecuba implores Agamemnon (the commander of the Greek forces), in the first of two informal "trial" scenes in the play, to punish Polymestor.

Here is the heart of her plea (ll. 790–805):[8]

> give me my revenge on that treacherous friend
> who flouted every god in heaven and in hell
> to do this brutal murder.
>   At our table
> he was our frequent guest; was counted first
> among our friends, respected, honored by me,
> receiving every kindness that a man could meet—
> and then, in cold deliberation, killed
> my son.
>   Murder may have its reasons, its motives,
> but this—to refuse my son a grave, to throw him
> to the sea, unburied!
>   I am a slave, I know,
> and slaves are weak. But the gods are strong, and over them
> there stands some absolute, some moral order
> or principle of law more final still.
> Upon this moral law the world depends;
> through it the gods exist; by it we live,
> defining good and evil.
>   Apply that law
> to me. For if you flout it now, and those
> who murder in cold blood or defy the gods
> go unpunished, then human justice withers,
> corrupted at its source.

A slave, Hecuba has none of the rights of a citizen. It is therefore natural for her to appeal to the law of nature rather than to the positive law of

---

8. My quotations are from William Arrowsmith's translation in *The Complete Greek Tragedies*, vol. 3 (Euripides) (David Grene and Richmond Lattimore eds. 1955).

a specific political community; and natural too for her to speak of revenge, which has roots in instinct, rather than of criminal punishment, which is part of positive law. In any case there are no formal institutions of justice in the martial society depicted in the play, and their absence supports Hecuba's invocation of natural law. We are made to understand that the fundamental social norms that condemn unwarranted killing precede the institutions of positive law and set bounds to a purely positivistic conception of law. Euripides' audience knew, moreover, that Agamemnon would feel the lash of natural law—that he would be killed for having (en route to Troy) sacrificed his daughter Iphigenia in violation of natural law. Natural law had more bite in Greek thought than it has in ours.

Agamemnon is sympathetic to Hecuba's plea but unwilling to take action against Polymestor. In part this is because Cassandra, Hecuba's surviving daughter, is Agamemnon's mistress, so he would be suspected of partiality in taking the Trojan side of the dispute between Hecuba and Polymestor, an ally of the Greeks. As Agamemnon explains (ll. 852–861):

> So far as justice is concerned, god knows,
> nothing would please me more than to bring
> this murderer to book.
>   But my position
> here is delicate. If I give you your revenge,
> the army is sure to charge that I connived
> at the death of the king of Thrace because of my love
> for Cassandra. This is my dilemma. The army
> thinks of Polymestor as its friend,
> this boy as its enemy. You love your son,
> but what do your affections matter to the Greeks?
> Put yourself in my position.

Two aspects of Agamemnon's reply are noteworthy. The first is his setting entirely expedient considerations against the precepts of natural law; evidently he believes that law should reflect or at least flatter dominant public opinion, here that of the Greek forces. The style of his reply is not entirely remote from that of the modern judge. A standard judicial flourish is to concede the natural justice of a litigant's case yet decide against him on the ground that positive law, which is on one view simply organized public opinion, entitles his opponent to judgment. And one characteristic of modern American positive law, as of ancient Greek positive law, is that citizens have greater rights than aliens.

The second noteworthy aspect of Agamemnon's "ruling" is the difficulty of doing justice when the judicial function is commingled with the executive. Agamemnon cannot confine himself to issues of right and duty on the ground that the political implications of rendering judgment for an enemy national are the business of another branch of government; he *is* that other branch. Justice under law is facilitated when judges are able credibly to deny that the politics of the case are their business, and when the political branches of government are able to say with equal credibility that they are forbidden to interfere in judicial decision making. By that Alphonse-Gaston shuffle legal justice is protected.

Although he refuses to help Hecuba directly, Agamemnon places no obstacles in the way of her attempting private revenge on Polymestor—and with the aid of her female attendants she succeeds in blinding him and in killing all of his children. Now it is Polymestor's turn to appeal to Agamemnon for justice, in the second informal trial scene in the play. With the damage done, Agamemnon can assume a more judicial stance: "No more of this inhuman savagery now. / Each of you will give his version of the case / and I shall try to judge you both impartially" (ll. 1129–1131). They give their competing versions of why Polymestor killed Polydorus. Persuaded by Hecuba, Agamemnon finds Polymestor guilty of murder and tells him he must bear the consequences that Hecuba has visited on him.

In the course of delivering this judgment Agamemnon makes two revealing remarks. The first is that "I should cut a sorry figure in the world / if I allowed this case to come to court / and then refused or failed to give a verdict." The second is that since "We Greeks call [killing a guest] murder . . . [how] could I acquit you now / without losing face among men?" (ll. 1242–1249). One's first reaction is that this just proves that Agamemnon is playing a political game. He is interested in the ultimate justice of Hecuba's case only insofar as it might move public opinion against him if he acquits Polymestor. By standing aloof from the actual punishment of Polymestor he has managed to avoid the appearance of siding with a Trojan against a Greek ally, while at the same time enabling justice to be done—although with the great violence and excess that typify revenge as a method of doing justice; Polymestor's children had not been complicit in their father's crime.

But this evaluation of Agamemnon's position is incomplete. In appealing to what "we Greeks" believe on the subject of killing a guest, he is invoking a concept of law different both from natural law and from law as public opinion. This is the concept of law as a deep-rooted custom fulfilling powerful social needs. Although the reasons for regarding the murder of guests with special abhorrence are not spelled out in the play, they are plain enough. In a society where trade is both valuable and, because there are no public institutions of law enforcement, exceedingly dangerous and precarious, the duty of hosts to protect guests, especially guests from afar bearing precious commodities (such as the gold that Polydorus—whose name means "Richly Endowed"—had brought with him to Thrace), is a potent customary norm. It is a norm more plausibly justified by practical social need than by supernatural edict, although it may be given supernatural backing in order to make it more impressive and therefore more likely to be obeyed. And it is local—"we Greeks," not necessarily "we Greeks and you Trojans too," especially since a Trojan abuse of hospitality had touched off the Trojan War. In both these respects the norm is different from a concept of natural law that, being based on the existence of a normative order in nature, can be said to be universal. And although (or perhaps because) a customary norm has deep public support, it is not subject to the same rapid shifts in public opinion as ordinary legislation. In this it resembles a constitutional norm.

This analysis of the concepts of law in *Hecuba* leaves unexplained, however, Agamemnon's change of heart between the first and second "trials." In suggesting that since Hecuba in effect had done Agamemnon's dirty work for him he could switch sides without causing an uproar among the Greeks, I was giving an explanation that placed Agamemnon's motives in a disreputably "political" light, consistent with his reiterated concern with "face." Yet alternatively we might see in Agamemnon's performance of the judicial function legality tempered by prudence. He is the leader, but not the tyrant, of the Greek forces. It behooves him, just as it would a democratic leader, to heed public opinion. He must balance Hecuba's claims against the larger public interest that he is charged with protecting. The effectiveness of his leadership, and hence his ability to protect the larger public interest, depends on his prestige ("face"); so he must be protective of that too. We catch here a glimpse of the jurisprudence of prudence, of which more in the next chapter.

The point of particular interest for historical jurisprudence is the vividness with which *Hecuba* portrays the transition from a system of private vengeance—which bloodily enforces a handful of norms that not only seem to be a part of nature but in a sense are a part of it because they are innate in human social existence rather than legislated by formal institutions—to a system of public enforcement of laws shaped by public opinion and administered by persons burdened with civic and political obligations. The same transition is visible in a better-known Greek tragedy, *Antigone,* in which Antigone corresponds to Hecuba and Creon to

Agamemnon.[9] With governmental institutions so undifferentiated, we should not expect, and do not find, that the judicial function is performed well. The dominant impression conveyed by both Agamemnon and Creon is of political trimmers deaf to the claims of natural law. They are the first legal positivists, and it is not surprising that in its earliest stage positivism should appear in an unimpressive light, as it also does in Plato's depiction of Thrasymachus in the *Republic*. To work well, positivism requires institutions that take much time to evolve, although even in its earliest and crudest stage it marks a great advance over a system of private vengeance.

Alessandro Manzoni's great novel, *I Promessi Sposi* (The Betrothed), depicts a distinct but parallel problem of positive law struggling to establish itself.[10] The novel is set in northern Italy (mainly the Duchy of Milan, owned by Spain) in the early seventeenth century, a time and place of great political turmoil. Powerful nobles, deploying armed bands of *bravi*, flout the laws and terrorize the countryside. The governor issues edict after edict outlawing the *bravi* and making them subject to impressively harsh punishments, but the edicts are ignored and the *bravi* and their patrons flourish. Renzo, a young peasant, is engaged to Lucia, whom one of the riotous nobles, Don Rodrigo, covets. Don Rodrigo sends his *bravi* to intimidate the village curate so that he will refuse to marry the couple. The attempt at intimidation succeeds. Naively believing that law is law and innocently carrying the latest edict against *bravi* with him, Renzo goes for help to the local lawyer, who is nicknamed Dr. Quibbler (*Azzeccagarugli*—literally, "fastener of tangled threads"). Quibbler assumes that Renzo is a *bravo*, who wants him to find a loophole in the edict, and sets about this task with the lawyer's enthusiasm for technicalities. (Most laypeople believe this is the lawyer's *only* enthusiasm.) When Quibbler discovers that Renzo wants help in enforcing the edict against Don Rodrigo and his gang, he is horrified and ejects Renzo from his office. The lawless nobles, including Don Rodrigo, have hired the lawyers to defeat the governor's pathetic edicts; Quibbler will not turn against a patron.

The picture is thus of a legal system entirely ineffectual despite its good intentions, in part because the legal profession is craven. But vengeance is not an option for Renzo, as it was for Hecuba. So how, if at all, is mankind's powerful impulse for justice to be expressed? An

9. See *Law and Literature: A Misunderstood Relation*, note 1 above, at 111–112; and on the transition from vengeance to law generally, see id., ch. 1.

10. For background, see Gian Piero Barricelli, *Alessandro Manzoni* 111–163 (1976).

implied answer is offered by the change in emphasis in the novel from the failures of law at the beginning to the triumphs of religion in the middle and end.[11] Driven from his village when his attempt to trick the curate into performing a marriage ceremony fails, Renzo eventually finds himself in Milan during a gruesome outbreak of plague. He survives (as does Lucia, who had escaped to Milan after being kidnapped by Don Rodrigo) and returns home, to find Don Rodrigo dying of plague. The curate's fear lifts; Renzo and Lucia are finally married and live happily ever after. The key figures who ward off disaster to the young couple and engineer the happy ending are two heroic clerics, Father Cristoforo and Cardinal Borromeo. The latter (a real historical figure, by the way) is also instrumental in mitigating the horrors of the plague. The sense conveyed is that religious faith enables dreadful conditions—plague and anarchy—to be, if not actually overcome, at least ameliorated and coped with. The positive law may be quite hopeless, but a divinely sponsored natural law remains in the picture—at the very least as a criterion for evaluating positive law. And sometimes natural law is vindicated, against all odds.

With another great literary meditation on natural law—*King Lear*—the transition from historical jurisprudence, where the meaning of natural law tends to be taken for granted (because the focus of historical jurisprudence is on the evolution of law rather than on substantive issues in jurisprudence), to literary reflections on that meaning is complete. There are three trial scenes in *King Lear*.[12] The first is the mock trial of Lear's evil daughters by Lear and his disheveled entourage on the heath. The second, which is almost simultaneous with the first, is the trial of Gloucester on false charges of treason ginned up by his bastard son Edmund. That trial ends in a verdict of guilt and Gloucester's punishment by blinding. The third trial is the trial by battle in which Edgar, Gloucester's legitimate son, slays Edmund. The second trial is the only one that complies with the forms of law in a modern sense (modern to Shakespeare as well as to us)—and it is a sinister farce. The first, an ostensible farce, renders true though ineffective justice by denouncing the evil daughters.

---

11. The same contrast is presented in another great "legal" novel, *The Brothers Karamazov*, where in addition the failures of law are presented as failures of human reason in general. See *Law and Literature: A Misunderstood Relation*, note 1 above, at 166–171.

12. For pertinent discussions, see John F. Danby, *Shakespeare's Doctrine of Nature: A Study of "King Lear"* (1949); Dorothy C. Hockey, "The Trial Pattern in *King Lear*," 10 *Shakespeare Quarterly* 389 (1959); Note, "Shakespeare and the Legal Process: Four Essays," 61 *Virginia Law Review* 390, 429–432 (1975).

The third trial harks back to medieval English law, when God was believed to decide legal disputes by awarding victory to the combatant whose cause was just.[13] But to conclude from Edgar's victory that natural law is vindicated in *Lear* and positive law once again painted in repulsive colors would be to oversimplify the play's implied attitude toward "nature." By setting the play in the period before England became Christian, Shakespeare is able to give free rein to speculations that in a Christian setting would be blasphemous. He takes full advantage of the opportunity. The picture of nature that the play conveys is not that of a normative order, but (with an exception about to be noted) of very nearly the opposite. Edmund sets the tone in his first soliloquy (Act I, sc. 2, ll. 1–22), which begins "Thou, nature, art my goddess; to thy law / My services are bound." As Edmund explains, from the standpoint of nature he is not only as legitimate as his brother Edgar but more so, because his conception "in the lusty stealth of nature" partook more of nature's vital essence than conception "within a dull, stale, tired bed" of married persons; so he resolves to supplant Edgar, and later their father, by whatever means lie to hand. And if Regan and Goneril are unnatural in their lack of filial piety, they are only too natural—in the sense in which animals are natural—in their greed, selfishness, cruelty, and promiscuity. Although both are married women, they compete shamelessly for Edmund's bed, and Goneril has an affair with her servant Oswald. Finally, if Lear is unnatural in his initial rejection of Cordelia, he is all too natural in his senile (= childish) desire to be loved without any limits and to enjoy the pleasures of life with none of the responsibilities.

The depiction of nature in *King Lear* is remarkably modern (which does not surprise us in Shakespeare); it is the nature red in tooth and claw that Darwinism later teaches us to expect. The sense of justice to which Lear (when the scales fall from his eyes) and Gloucester appeal is not—or not only, for after all Edgar *does* prevail in his trial by combat with Edmund—a normative order in nature. It is a complex of civilized values built on property, piety, and hierarchy: the complex that fixes—against the riotous claims of nature—the lawful and proper positions of Lear, Edmund, Edgar, Oswald, and the rest.

This is not to deny the important sense in which an Elizabethan audience would consider the behavior of Edmund, Regan, and Goneril (like

13. For a splendid discussion of medieval trial by combat, see R. Howard Bloch, *Medieval French Literature and Law* 46–53 (1977).

that of Lear in initially rejecting Cordelia) "unnatural" and Edmund's defeat by Edgar, therefore, a vindication of natural law. Such an audience, heavily imbued with the values of medieval thought, which were the orthodox values of Renaissance England as well, would think that these three were behaving like animals and that to behave so is to act contrary to our human "nature."[14] This is not an absurd distinction. Even if man is an animal, not every animal has the same nature. It is in the nature of a bear to hibernate, but a man who hibernates is not acting naturally. We can go a step further and agree with Aquinas (from whom the orthodox Renaissance conception of nature derives) that human nature is distinguished by the presence of a capacity for reason not found in animals. But the capacity to reason does not dictate its use for good ends. Edmund, Iago, and the other Shakespearean villains use their reason to commit their villainies, so if we are to call them unnatural it seems that there is no escape from dividing human nature into a good nature and a bad nature. But this makes naturalistic morality impossible, because "nature" will no longer tell us where to make the cut. The "good" human nature is what God implanted in us and is therefore normative because it is divinely underwritten—because it is an *idealized* concept of nature—rather than because it is an accurate description of human beings. When we abandon nature as a source of norms, we are forced back on social conventions.[15] Much is lost by this retreat. It is always possible to criticize law, but the concept of natural law had offered the possibility of objective criticism. In *Lear* we see the "object" beginning to disappear (I say "beginning" because Edmund's defeat by Edgar can be taken as a sign of divine justice). We learn that social life offers the vantage point from which to perceive nature as amoral, instead of nature's offering the vantage point from which to judge human law; and social life lacks fixity.

14. This point is emphasized by Danby, note 12 above; see also George C. Herndl, *The High Design: English Renaissance Tragedy and the Natural Law* 44–48 (1970). Paul Delany, in "*King Lear* and the Decline of Feudalism," 92 *Publications of the Modern Language Association* 429 (1977), argues that Edmund represents the values of nascent capitalism, and Lear and his party the vanishing feudal values. Certainly natural law is one of the institutions that secular individualism challenges.

15. See, with specific reference to *Lear,* Robert J. Bauer, "Despite of Mine Own Nature: Edmund and the Orders, Cosmic and Moral," 10 *Texas Studies in Literature and Language* 359 (1968). And recall a point made in Chapter 7—that any form of moral realism is problematic without an ontology that makes moral principles part of the furniture of the universe.

Natural Law and Feminist Jurisprudence

In both *Hecuba* and *Antigone* a woman is seen appealing to natural law against a male embodiment of legal positivism. This is a recurrent pattern in literature. One thinks of Portia appealing to Shylock's (nonexistent) sense of mercy in *The Merchant of Venice,* of Isabel appealing to Angelo's sense of mercy in *Measure for Measure,* of Captain Vere instructing the court-martial in *Billy Budd* to disregard "the feminine in man," of the rebellion of the women in Susan Glaspell's story "A Jury of Her Peers" against male justice.[16] The most curious example is the discussion of legal cases in the Cyclops episode of Joyce's *Ulysses,* where "the law," and the people who delight in its technical twists and turns, are described in male imagery, while Bloom, sympathizer with those unable to negotiate the shoals of technical law, is described in female imagery.[17]

The sense that emerges from these works is that there is a distinctive masculine outlook on law—an outlook that revels in legalisms, technicalities, rules, strict construction, "hard" cases (in the sense explained in note 1 of Chapter 5)—and an equally distinctive feminine outlook, which emphasizes equity, broad standards, substantial justice, discretion. The masculine outlook abstracts from the rich particulars of a dispute a few salient facts and makes them legally determinative. That is law by rules—that is what rules *do*. The feminine outlook prefers to base judgment on the total circumstances of a case, unhampered by rules that require a blinkered vision, untroubled by a felt need to conform decision to general, "neutral" principles.[18] The emphasis on particulars establishes another link between the feminist and literary approaches to law. Literary expression is characteristically concrete, and many feminists are critical of abstraction, regarding it as a distinctively masculine method of apprehending reality. Feminist legal scholars have both contributed to the law and literature movement and used literary examples in their other writing.

In the view I am expounding, the masculine outlook is that of legal

16. See *Law and Literature: A Misunderstood Relation,* note 1 above, at 112–113. And on the Furies in *Eumenides,* see Paul Gewirtz, "Aeschylus' Law," 101 *Harvard Law Review* 1043 (1988).

17. See Jon Bunge, "Bloom's Attack on Law in the 'Cyclops' Episode of Joyce's *Ulysses*" (seminar paper, University of Chicago Law School, March 27, 1988).

18. For a fuller list of the dichotomies that enable a legal thinker to be placed along a spectrum at one end of which is justice at its most legalistic and at the other end is justice at its most discretionary and personalistic, see *Law and Literature: A Misunderstood Relation,* note 1 above, at 108 ("Table of Opposed Conceptions of Law").

positivism, the feminine that of natural law. At the "masculine" end of the spectrum of legal conceptions, law is monstrous, inhuman; this is a common layperson's conception of law and one well represented in imaginative literature.[19] At the "feminine" end, law turns into the anarchy of "popular justice," symbolized by the trial of Socrates and by the kangaroo courts of totalitarian regimes, such as Mao's "people's courts." A mature legal system rejects both extremes in favor of a mixture of rules and discretion, law and equity, rule and standard, positive laws and ethical principles (corresponding to natural law), logic and practical reason, professional judges and lay judges, objectivity and subjectivity. The "feminine" pole may be the very last thing any member of an oppressed group—if that is how the modern American woman should be regarded—should desire in a legal system. As Shylock rightly feared, in arguing for a literal interpretation of his bond with Antonio, discretion is apt to be exercised against the pariah.[20]

Is the mixed system I am recommending really a mixture of masculine and feminine characteristics, or does this suggestion rest on a stereotypical association of men with logic, abstraction, and severity and of women with intuition and softness? If the former, this would imply that as women come to play a larger role in the legal profession generally and the judiciary in particular, the character of our law will change; we shall see fewer rules and more standards, less talk about logic and more about practical reason, less anxiety with maintaining law's determinacy, objectivity, and impersonality.

The suggestion that there is more than an adventitious connection between genders on the one hand and styles in law and justice on the other owes much to Carol Gilligan, who is not a lawyer but in an influential book distinguishes between an "ethic of rights" that she deems distinctively masculine and an "ethic of care" that she deems distinc-

---

19. See id., ch. 3. A particularly horrifying depiction of law and the legal profession as "antilife" is *The Death of Ivan Ilych,* Tolstoy's great tale of a judge's gruesome death from cancer. It should be one of the sacred texts of critical legal studies.

20. This point has been made recently by minority legal scholars in criticism of the antirights rhetoric of the critical legal studies movement. See "Minority Critiques of the Critical Legal Studies Movement," 22 *Harvard Civil Rights–Civil Liberties Law Review* 297 (1987). In an area of highly discretionary law, such as divorce law, lawyers distinguish themselves not by knowing the rules but by knowing the ropes. See Austin Sarat and William L. F. Felstiner, "Lawyers and Legal Consciousness: Law Talk in the Divorce Lawyer's Office," 98 *Yale Law Journal* 1663 (1989). The insider, the socially connected, is more likely to know the ropes than the pariah.

tively feminine.[21] Her principal evidence is the different attitudes of boys and of girls toward the "enforcement" of rules in games. Boys are quick to "adjudicate" alleged violations and condemn the violator. Girls, being more empathetic than boys, tend to stop playing when an infraction is charged, for fear that an attempt to determine the right and wrong of the charge would result in hurt feelings. Boys tend to judge infractions according to hard and fast rules. Girls tend to evaluate the alleged infraction in its full human context, with particular attention to the importance of preventing a disruption of relationships. Gilligan does not speculate on whether these differences in behavior, which she finds not only in games but also in the responses that boys and girls offer to hypothetical moral situations, are due to biology or to upbringing, and if the latter whether they may not be an indirect result of discrimination against women.

It would be a mistake to reduce Gilligan's position to a claim that women are less principled than men. Rather, the principles are different.[22] Women are more conscious of the costs of strict adherence to rules (a cost particularly emphasized is the impact on a relationship of insisting that one party is in the wrong, the other in the right), men more conscious of the benefits. This difference, Gilligan believes, leads the sexes to different views of the appropriate principles to govern conflict situations.

The ethic of rights sketched by Gilligan corresponds to the formalistic style of law ("rules") and the ethic of care to the more contextual, personal, and discretionary style ("substantive justice"). Gilligan's suggestion therefore contains the potential for a full-fledged feminist juris-

---

21. See *In a Different Voice: Psychological Theory and Women's Development* (1982); also *Mapping the Moral Domain* (Carol Gilligan, Janie Victoria Ward, and Jill McLean Taylor eds. 1988). In like vein, see Nel Noddings, *Caring: A Feminine Approach to Ethics and Moral Education* (1984); Mary Field Belenky et al., *Women's Ways of Knowing: The Development of Self, Voice, and Mind,* ch. 6 (1986). Gilligan's findings have been questioned. See, for example, Catherine G. Greeno and Eleanor E. Maccoby, "How Different Is the 'Different Voice'?" 11 *Signs* 310 (1986); William J. Friedman, Amy B. Robinson, and Britt L. Friedman, "Sex Differences in Moral Judgments? A Test of Gilligan's Theory," 11 *Psychology of Women Quarterly* 37 (1987), and references cited there; Lawrence Kohlberg, *Essays on Moral Development,* vol. 2, *The Psychology of Moral Development* 338–370 (1984). Empirical support for Gilligan's position may be found in Maureen Rose Ford and Carol Rotter Lowery, "Gender Differences in Moral Reasoning: A Comparison of the Use of Justice and Care Orientations," 50 *Journal of Personality and Social Psychology* 777 (1986); Mary K. Rothbart, Dean Hanley, and Marc Albert, "Gender Differences in Moral Reasoning," 15 *Sex Roles* 645 (1986). On feminist theory generally, see Alison M. Jaggar, *Feminist Politics and Human Nature* (1983); Jean Grimshaw, *Philosophy and Feminist Thinking* (1986), esp. ch. 7.

22. See id. at 209–211.

prudence—a jurisprudence that is not limited to women's legal issues such as comparable worth, rape, pornography, and sexual harassment in the workplace, but seeks to remake all law so that it will be less masculine (formalist, rule-bound). Most feminist jurisprudence is addressed to women's issues, which are not the concern here. But is there a distinctive feminine outlook on law in general, as distinct from a superior feminine sensitivity to issues that particularly concern women?

I think not. Whatever may be the attitudes of male and female children toward rule infractions in games, the "ethic of care" of which Gilligan speaks is not a female preserve. Men have controlled the legal system from the beginning, yet that system has never been as dominated by formalism, strict rules, relish for hard cases, and the like as the legal establishment has claimed. For every Blackstone there has been a Bentham (and is there not a sense in which utilitarianism is the most empathetic, the most caring of philosophies?), for every Langdell a Cardozo, for every Frankfurter a Murphy, for every Rehnquist a Brennan. The emphasis in this book on a pragmatic, "realistic" jurisprudence no more makes it a work of feminist jurisprudence than the pragmatists' rejection of Cartesian dualism, scientific realism, and other "isms" that feminists believe characteristic of masculine thinking makes pragmatist philosophers feminists. And if we want to emphasize not the epistemological virtues of case-specific legal reasoning but instead sympathy for the underdog (one aspect of the ethic of care), then we have only to list the many male judges who have worn that sympathy on their sleeve. Even the emphasis on maintaining ongoing relationships is not special to feminism; it is the stock in trade of those legal scholars, most of them male, who emphasize the "relational" aspects of long-term contracts. Maybe more women than men have the characteristics that feminists regard as distinctively feminine, but this need imply no more than a shift along a known spectrum as opposed to a new way of looking at jurisprudence.

I therefore disagree with Suzanna Sherry's suggestion that "a feminine jurisprudence, evident, for example, in the decisions of Justice O'Connor, might thus be quite unlike any other contemporary jurisprudence."[23] What Sherry finds in O'Connor's opinions are a dislike of

23. "Civic Virtue and the Feminine Voice in Constitutional Adjudication," 72 *Virginia Law Review* 543 (1986). Among other writing in this vein, see, for example, Judith Resnik, "On the Bias: Feminist Reconsiderations of the Aspirations for Our Judges," 61 *Southern California Law Review* 1877 (1988); Marjorie E. Kornhauser, "The Rhetoric of the Anti-Progressive Income Tax Movement: A Typical Male Reaction," 86 *Michigan Law Review* 465 (1987). With each year's batch of O'Connor opinions, the feminist interpretation of her judicial philosophy becomes less and less plausible.

"bright-line" rules and a sensitivity to community interests (that is how Sherry explains the fact that O'Connor is a "law and order" conservative in criminal cases). She would have found the same things in the opinions of Justice Tom Clark or any number of other conservative jurists.

From one opinion by O'Connor, Frank Michelman has similarly inferred that her use of a balancing test may reflect a distinctively feminine outlook.[24] But many is the male jurist who has been attracted to balancing tests; indeed, such attraction is one of the defining characteristics of the pragmatic, instrumental, "realist" style of judging. Granted, there are balancing tests and balancing tests; but I doubt that anyone could pick out O'Connor's opinions in a blindfold test.

Both Sherry and Michelman relate what they consider the distinctive features of O'Connor's judicial style not only to feminism but to "republicanism," a version of the Madisonian conception of the American republic.[25] Sherry suggests that there is a deep affinity between republicanism in this sense and the distinctive outlook that comes from being a woman. I am skeptical. To the extent there is a distinctive republican jurisprudence not exhausted in the structure of the governmental system bequeathed us by Madison and the other framers of the Constitution, it emphasizes civic and political virtues that are distinct from—in some respects inconsistent with[26]—the ethic of care.

Leslie Bender suggests that feminist tort law would replace the reasonable man with the caring neighbor.[27] Again I am skeptical. The "reasonable man" rule in tort law serves to prevent both the injurer and the victim from arguing that although the average person could have avoided the accident, the actual party in the case could not have done so, because he had a below-average capacity to take care. I do not understand Bender to be quarreling with this result. Her point rather is that in deciding how much care is optimal, we should suppose that potential injurers are not complete strangers to their potential victims but are mildly altruistic toward them (a caring neighbor is more altruistic than

24. See "The Supreme Court, 1985 Term: Foreword, Traces of Self-Government," 100 *Harvard Law Review* 4, 17 n. 68, 33–36 (1986). Michelman advances the suggestion with great tentativeness, however.

25. See "Symposium: The Republican Civic Tradition," 97 *Yale Law Journal* 1493 (1988); also references cited in Richard H. Fallon, Jr., "What Is Republicanism, and Is It Worth Reviving?" 102 *Harvard Law Review* 1695 (1989).

26. Cf. Grimshaw, note 21 above, at 196.

27. See "A Lawyer's Primer on Feminist Theory and Tort," 38 *Journal of Legal Education* 3, 30–32 (1988).

a stranger but less so than a close relative). However, people are what they are; most neighbors are not caring, and most accident victims are not neighbors. Human nature will not be altered by holding injurers liable for having failed to take as much care as a caring neighbor would have taken. The only effect of adopting Bender's proposal would be to change negligence liability in the direction of strict liability. Suppose an accident having an expected cost of $100 could be prevented only by an expenditure of $110 on care. Then the failure to prevent the accident would not be negligent, and under normal principles of tort liability the injurer would not be liable to the victim. *Maybe* a caring neighbor would go the extra step to prevent the accident, though this is by no means clear, since the Hand negligence formula requires the potential injurer to take as much care as if he were the potential victim, and few altruists would take *more* care for others than for themselves. But forget this, and assume the caring neighbor is presumed to be more careful than the average person; then under Bender's proposal the injurer would be liable if he failed to prevent the accident. However, liability would not induce him to take the extra care. By definition it would cost more than the expected accident cost, so unless he *was* a caring neighbor or some other kind of strong altruist he would prefer to pay the occasional judgment rather than take the extra care. In effect he would be strictly liable, for strict liability entails that the injurer must compensate the victim even when the injury is unavoidable at reasonable cost. The merits of Bender's proposal are therefore those of strict liability.

Strict liability is sometimes defended on the ground that it compensates more accident victims; and maybe a feminine outlook of law could be expected to stress compensation—obviously Bender associates altruism with women. On the other hand, strict liability is more rulelike, less standardlike, less contextualist, less sensitive to the particulars of the individual accident, than negligence is; in that respect it is the more masculine regime. Bender's feminism may not be coherent.

Robin West has articulated a different version of feminist jurisprudence, although again one whose debt to Gilligan is apparent.[28] West begins by describing a formalistic conception of law that she calls "legal liberalism." (Critics of liberalism like to assume that it depends on a formalistic approach to law; as pointed out in Chapter 1, it does not.) West stresses the importance that the legal liberal ascribes to autonomy (individual liberty) as a value served by law and the legal liberal's dread of having his individuality submerged in the community. The radical

28. See West, "Jurisprudence and Gender," 55 *University of Chicago Law Review* 1 (1988).

males of the critical legal studies movement relabel autonomy as alienation and turn it from an object of longing to one of dread; and relabel-
ing annihilation as connection, they perform a similar inversion of the
liberal's dread. Women differ fundamentally from men in that their basic
experience is of connection (because of pregnancy and breast-feeding
and because women are penetrated, rather than penetrating, in sexual
intercourse) rather than of individuality. The liberal feminist, who is
basically satisfied with this order of things, replaces the liberal legalist's
value of autonomy with the value of intimacy and the liberal legalist's
dread of annihilation with a dread of separation. The radical feminist,
however, unlike the radical male, longs for autonomy and dreads not
alienation but invasion, intrusion.[29]

Here we may pause to consider whether any of this is true. This is a
large question to which I cannot do justice here. My tentative view is
that there are two (possibly three) fundamental, and probably innate,
differences between men and women, besides the obvious differences in
primary and secondary sexual characteristics (including height and
physical strength): women are less aggressive than men, more devoted
to their children, and perhaps more caring, more nurturant, generally.
These are differences only *on average*. The male and female distributions
of attributes intersect. Many women are more aggressive and less nurturant than many men, just as many women are taller than many men,
although the average man is taller than the average women. (Hence the
existence of "real" differences between the sexes is not a good argument
for excluding all women from jobs for which the average man may be
better qualified than the average woman.)

What I have called the average differences between men and women
are related, and could well be a product of natural selection. Biological
or not, they do not appear to be mere artifacts of discrimination. As
Gilligan remarks in a recent article, "stereotypes of males as aggressive
and females as nurturant, however distorting and however limited, have
some empirical claim. The overwhelmingly male composition of the
prison population and the extent to which women take care of young
children cannot readily be dismissed as irrelevant to theories of morality
or excluded from accounts of moral development. If there are no sex
differences in empathy or moral reasoning, why are there sex differences
in moral and immoral behavior?"[30]

29. These relationships are summarized in a table in id. at 37. That table, by the way—
and the tables in id. at 36, 63, and 68—lend an ironically self-referential air to West's article.
The article is taxonomic, abstract, "reductionist." Its feminist fist wears a masculine glove.

30. Carol Gilligan and Grant Wiggins, "The Origins of Morality in Early Childhood
Relationships," in *The Emergence of Morality in Young Children* 278, 278–279 (Jerome Kagan

But what, if any, implications these differences have for law—beyond the trivial conjecture that women are less likely to be excessively combative in litigation or to be willing to work the absurd hours demanded of partners and associates at some law firms—are obscure. Nor are these the differences that interest West. But her idea that "connectedness" is the defining characteristic of the female experience, and her attribution of this characteristic to the female role in reproduction, are neither well supported by empirical evidence nor, on the whole, highly plausible. Women may be on average less selfish than men, but it does not follow that most women lack a sense of themselves as individuals or that this sense is diminished by pregnancy and breast-feeding. The point about penetration is unconvincing; one could as well describe the female as ingesting as the male as penetrating. The fact that girls are raised primarily by the parent of the same sex, and boys primarily by the parent of the opposite sex, provides a more plausible, but speculative, ground for thinking that boys may grow up to be more individualistic in their orientation than girls.[31]

Supposing West's analysis to be correct, the implications for feminist jurisprudence would still be modest. They would not include making law feminine, either in Gilligan's (or Sherry's or Bender's or Michelman's) sense or in West's version of Gilligan's thesis. West's analysis implies that the law should become more protective of women's interests, by recognizing the vulnerabilities that the woman's sense of connectedness creates;[32] the legal profession, the judiciary, and legislatures should at least *try* to understand women's distinctive experience, just as

and Sharon Lamb eds. 1987). For supporting evidence, see June Machover Reinisch and Stephanie A. Sanders, "A Test of Sex Differences in Aggressive Response to Hypothetical Conflict Situations," 50 *Journal of Personality and Social Psychology* 1045 (1986); Alice H. Eagly and Valerie J. Steffen, "Gender and Aggressive Behavior: A Meta-Analytic Review of the Social Psychological Literature," 100 *Psychological Bulletin* 309 (1986); Alice H. Eagly and Maureen Crowley, "Gender and Helping Behavior: A Meta-Analytic Review of the Social Psychological Literature," 100 id. at 283 (1986). The possibility that the differences described in the passage may be at least partly genetic is discussed in Alice S. Rossi, "Gender and Parenthood," 49 *American Sociological Review* 1 (1984). The possibility that they may have nothing to do with genes or even with sex is suggested by evidence that the epistemology of Western women is similar to that of Africans of both sexes. See Sandra Harding, *The Science Question in Feminism,* ch. 7 (1986). For a powerful argument against the proposition that there is a distinctive feminine epistemology, whether genetically or culturally based, see Mary E. Hawkesworth, "Knowers, Knowing, Known: Feminist Theory and Claims of Truth," 14 *Signs* 533 (1989).

31. For debate over this question, see Judith Lorber et al., "On *The Reproduction of Mothering:* A Methodological Debate," 6 *Signs* 482 (1981).

32. See West, note 28 above, at 58–72; see also West, "The Differences in Women's Hedonic Lives: A Phenomenological Critique of Feminist Legal Theory," 3 *Wisconsin Women's Law Journal* 80 (1987).

they should try to understand the distinctive experiences of blacks or Jews, Asians or Mormons.[33] One cannot quarrel with these aspirations, provided that West has identified what is indeed distinctive in women's experience. But the implications for jurisprudence are limited. And even those who urge a distinctive feminist outlook on law as a whole (as distinguished from the parts of law that affect women particularly) may simply be mixing familiar colors from what, as I have emphasized throughout this book, is a more variegated legal palette than formalists are wont to acknowledge. Some of the mixtures resemble familiar positions along the legal spectrum, including the "conservative realism" that Suzanna Sherry associates with Justice O'Connor but that she could equally have associated with any number of male jurists.

Lately Robin West has urged a more radical reorientation of judicial thinking. Judges should abandon the pretense (or actuality, as the case may be) of detachment.[34] Their guiding light should be empathy with the litigants and with the other persons affected by judicial decisions. One objection to this proposal is severely practical: judges lack the time and emotional energy to enter deeply into the feelings of the litigants, let alone others who might be affected by the judges' rulings. Another objection is the inherent unpredictability of a jurisprudence of empathy, and another is the undesirability of encouraging judges to give free rein to their emotions—not all of which will be benign. There is negative as well as positive empathy—the revulsion of contemplating a style of living alien to the judges' own experiences.

Worst is the *inherent* bias of empathy. As Adam Smith pointed out in *The Theory of Moral Sentiments,* empathy in the sense of altruistic sympathy (which appears to be West's sense) diminishes rapidly with the social distance between the persons involved. An American will feel the death of one friend more deeply than the deaths of tens of thousands of Armenians in an earthquake or a million Ethiopians in a famine. Litigation commonly involves persons at different social distances from the judge, and the more proximate will garner the more sympathetic response regardless of actual desert. It is easier for the judge to sympa-

33. The case for judicial awareness of the multiple perspectives in which it is possible to examine legal claims is urged in Martha Minow, "The Supreme Court, 1986 Term: Foreword, Justice Engendered," 101 *Harvard Law Review* 10 (1987). The case, if accepted, supplies an argument for a diverse judiciary. See also Richard Danzig, "Justice Frankfurter's Opinions in the Flag Salute Cases: Blending Logic and Psychologic in Constitutional Decisionmaking," 36 *Stanford Law Review* 675, 719–721 (1984).

34. See "Taking Preferences Seriously" (unpublished paper, Maryland Law School, 1988).

thize with a tenant pleading for an injunction against eviction than with the unknown persons who will experience difficulty renting apartments where they want and at the price they want because landlords' costs have risen as a consequence of judges' favoritism toward tenants. Suppose that a decision in favor of some utterly pathetic plaintiff would (by virtue of its precedential effect) impose costs totaling $1 million, distributed evenly over 10,000 people, each of whom would, therefore, lose $100. Unbiased empathizing would require the judge to imagine the impact of a loss of $100 on each of these 10,000 people, or to imagine the impact of that loss on the representative member of the affected class and multiply that impact by 10,000. Neither procedure is feasible. West is inviting judges to render short-sighted substantive justice and forgetting that one of the greatest challenges judges face is that of looking beyond the pathetic plaintiff or pathetic defendant to the unknown others who may be affected by a judicial decision.

Whatever its merits, the jurisprudence of empathy is a natural culmination of West's contributions to the law and literature movement,[35] and underlines the continuity between the literary and feminist perspectives on jurisprudence. A notable characteristic of great works of literature is their authors' empathetic relationship to human types that the audience for the works, and the authors themselves, probably found revolting. As I have written elsewhere, concerning Shakespeare's portrayal of Shylock in *The Merchant of Venice,* "to visualize a Jew as fully if wickedly human was something few Elizabethans could have done; Shakespeare's great contemporary, Christopher Marlowe, could not do it. To portray Satan as a heroic figure, Milton was bordering on blasphemy. And the *Iliad* is the oldest surviving expression of awareness that foreigners who are your mortal enemies might nevertheless have the same feelings as you."[36] I went on to urge, much in the spirit of West, that judges and lawyers ought to cultivate their empathetic faculties.[37] But this is a far cry from urging judges to discard the conventional principles of legality, as I understand West to be doing. Her advice confuses the judicial and literary roles.

35. See "Jurisprudence as Narrative: An Aesthetic Analysis of Modern Legal Theory," 60 *New York University Law Review* 145 (1985); "Authority, Autonomy, and Choice: The Role of Consent in the Moral and Political Visions of Franz Kafka and Richard Posner," 99 *Harvard Law Review* 384 (1985); "Adjudication Is Not Interpretation: Some Reservations about the Law-as-Literature Movement," 54 *Tennessee Law Review* 203 (1987); "Communities, Texts, and Law: Reflections of the Law and Literature Movement," 1 *Yale Journal of Law and the Humanities* 129 (1988).

36. *Law and Literature: A Misunderstood Relation,* note 1 above, at 304.

37. See id. at 304–305.

Communitarianism

Feminism is one of several communitarian ideologies that are influential in current jurisprudential thinking. Another is civic republicanism. And another is the constructive (as distinct from skeptical) side of the critical legal studies movement; Roberto Unger is the representative figure here, although all practitioners of critical legal studies pay at least lip service to communitarianism, and there are thematic and methodological links between them and communitarian political philosophers of diverse ideological hue, such as Alasdair MacIntyre, Michael Walzer, and Michael Sandel.[38] A Catholic strain, for example, is perceptible in Unger and in MacIntyre. And Aristotle is a tutelary figure. Nevertheless, except among some of the republicans, the mood is romanticist. The forms of modern society are disparaged; the urge to transcend the apparent limits that human nature places on aspiration is overmastering. "Because there is nothing timeless about [the deepest values of a society], we might simply decide to abandon them."[39]

What principally unites the various strands is hostility to liberalism, conceived as the ideology of capitalism, individualism, and the limited state. The communitarians want an activist state that will promote social solidarity, whether directly or by inculcating qualities (of altruism, civic virtue, or whatever) conducive to people's pulling together rather than pursuing selfish or narrowly familial goals. The ethical and political questions raised by the communitarian movement (if so politically heterogeneous a body of thought can be called a movement) are beyond the scope of this book,[40] but I shall say a few words about the jurisprudential problems that the movement raises.

The basic problems concern objectivity and feasibility. It is hard enough to get agreement on premises within a group of persons committed to liberal norms; it seems quite impossible to get agreement on premises once those norms are rejected. The irony of critical legal studies is that having demonstrated to its own satisfaction that American law is totally devoid of objectivity, is totally manipulable and politicized, it asks that the law be reoriented in accordance with the utterly

38. See Stephen Holmes, "The Community Trap," *New Republic*, Nov. 28, 1988, at 24.

39. Mark Tushnet, "Critical Legal Studies: An Introduction to Its Origins and Underpinnings," 36 *Journal of Legal Education* 505, 509 (1986). Notice the resemblance to Richard Rorty's belief in the infinite plasticity of human behavior (Chapter 12), and see generally Lawrence Lessig, "Plastics: Unger and Ackerman on Transformation," 98 *Yale Law Journal* 1173 (1989).

40. For good discussions, see Holmes, note 38 above, and Nancy L. Rosenblum, *Another Liberalism: Romanticism and the Reconstruction of Liberal Thought,* ch. 7 (1987).

plastic tenets of communitarianism. Plasticity is a two-edged sword. The critical legal studies movement is reluctant to acknowledge that communitarianism comes in conservative and reactionary as well as liberal and radical forms, that there are no simple ways of choosing between them, and that the rejection of liberal values in the hope of replacing them with something—as yet unknown—better is reckless.[41] Even a single facet of the communitarian tradition, such as civil republicanism, covers the political-ideological spectrum.[42] Some modern republicans are welfare-state liberals with a strong commitment to eradicating discrimination against minorities and women. Others are social conservatives who think that from a republican perspective *Gobitis* makes more sense than *Barnette,* and *Bowers v. Hardwick* than *Roe v. Wade.* Republicanism originated in ancient Rome as an ideology of austerity, militarism, and political expansion. The republicanism of the founders of this nation is midway between the Roman and modern models. How are we to choose among the different versions of republicanism? How are we to choose between the Catholic version of community and the Castroite version? And how are we to trade off the benefits of community, whatever exactly they are, against what Chapter 12 suggested may be its large economic costs?[43] The communitarians have chosen community before investigating what that choice entails.

To all this communitarians can reply that if community is an unstable ground for public policy, so is individuality. Apart from the socially constituted nature of individuality, there is a question of the authenticity of individual preferences. Cass Sunstein has repeatedly invoked the psychologists' concept of cognitive dissonance as a basis for questioning preferences. Faced with a conflict between deep-seated beliefs on the one hand and harsh reality on the other, the individual, in order to alleviate his mental distress, may deny the reality rather than abandon his beliefs. So a black who has been taught that America is the land of equal opportunity and then encounters racial discrimination may decide to blame himself rather than admit that his basic political beliefs are flawed; or a blue-collar worker whose self-esteem is bound up with his job may

41. I vividly recall an Iranian friend, hostile to the Shah, who when the Shah abdicated remarked that, whatever doubts one might have about the Ayatollah Khomeini, things *couldn't* get worse than they had been under the Shah.

42. This point is stressed in Cass R. Sunstein, "Beyond the Republican Revival," 97 *Yale Law Journal* 1539 (1988), in discussing criticisms of modern republicanism.

43. For additional evidence of those costs, see Dan Usher, Book Review (of Samuel Bowles and Herbert Gintis, *Democracy and Capitalism: Property, Community, and the Contradictions of Modern Social Thought* [1986]), 27 *Journal of Economic Literature* 75 (1989).

refuse to believe evidence that the job is unsafe or unhealthful.[44] Such persons are acting unrealistically, and shouldn't the law try to protect them from the consequences?

I have my doubts. First, one person's cognitive dissonance is another's epistemic conservatism. It is not rational to abandon deep-seated beliefs on the basis of isolated evidence that they may be false. Instead one tries to adjust to the new evidence with minimal disturbance to one's core beliefs. Provisional denial is one method of adjustment, is rational, yet is difficult to distinguish empirically from cognitive dissonance.

Second, even if one could be confident about the government's ability to diagnose cognitive dissonance, it would be perilous to base public policy on its diagnoses—and this apart from the killjoy quality of a doctrine that teaches that people should not be permitted to be happy but instead should be made to realize they are living in a fool's paradise. The assumption underlying government intervention on grounds of cognitive dissonance would be that a large part of the population was suffering from a profound cognitive disorder. Like its Marxist cousin "false consciousness," this assumption would legitimize extraordinarily far-reaching interferences with personal autonomy.

Third, also like false consciousness, cognitive dissonance invites a disregard for democratic preferences. Anything the people like that the analyst does not like can be ascribed to cognitive dissonance and disregarded. When used as a ground for policy formation and legal interpretation, cognitive dissonance invites judges and legislators to coerce the rest of society to adopt their personal policy preferences.

Fourth, the magnitude of the phenomenon is unknown.

The other big problem of communitarianism is that of feasibility (it is a more serious problem, the more radical the communitarian vision). The communitarians advocate in effect a "supermorality," that is, a code of individual behavior that is substantially more demanding than the code followed by most members of contemporary society. Experience suggests that communitarian ethics are unworkable except in small, isolated communities, and then only temporarily; world history is littered with the ruins of communitarian experiments. But reliance on experience is open to Richard Rorty's objection that such reliance keeps us in our accustomed groove, preventing us from discovering entirely new ways of looking at things. Moreover, like all inductive learning it is

---

44. See, for example, Melvin J. Lerner and Dale T. Miller, "Just World Research and the Attribution Process: Looking Back and Ahead," 85 *Psychological Bulletin* 1030 (1978). See generally Elliot Aronson, *The Social Animal*, ch. 4 (5th ed. 1988).

open to the further objection that without a causal theory we have no reason to think that tomorrow will be like today.

John Mackie, however, has offered three reasons why a code of communitarian supermorality is unlikely to work,[45] and these provide strong grounds for believing that the failures of communitarian experiments are not accidental. First, communitarian supermorality cuts deeply against the genetic grain; we are selfish, individualistic animals—not completely, of course, for then social and even family existence would be impossible. But our altruism is limited; few of us are capable of prolonged heavy altruism toward strangers. People vary in their mixture of selfish and altruistic qualities, and perhaps the mixture can be influenced to some extent. But (this is Mackie's second point, and is partially explanatory of the first) as more and more people behave better and better—more altruistic, more honest—the gains from cheating rise. The selfish and dishonest flourish, and the altruistic and the upright begin to feel like fools. Supermorality thus is not a social equilibrium, and high levels of coercion would therefore be required to maintain it—and would be an acknowledgment of failure to achieve a true super*morality*. And any society that did succeed in maintaining a code of supermorality by these means would be vulnerable to international competition—brain drain, even conquest.

With these first two points we see nature brought back into the ethical picture, though as a source not of norms but of constraints that define the feasible scope of ethical aspiration. It is true that nature can often be overcome; but the communitarians have been unable to design feasible, civilized, noncoercive methods of overcoming human selfishness and strategic behavior. And, to repeat, the more altruistic some people become, the more the gains to selfishness increase for the rest.

Mackie's third point concerns the radical indeterminacy of the goal of supermoral behavior. Communitarians are unable to explain what they hope to achieve by it. It is easy to see how if everyone were honest and peaceable the level of social welfare would rise, but the critical legal studies movement—the best-known jurisprudential school of communitarianism—seems to want more than a society of bourgeois virtue. What is that more? This is never explained. The movement seems at

45. "Co-Operation, Competition, and Moral Philosophy," in Mackie, *Persons and Values: Selected Papers,* vol. 2, pp. 152, 164–165 (Joan Mackie and Penelope Mackie eds. 1985). To similar effect see B. Douglas Bernheim and Oded Stark, "Altruism within the Family Reconsidered: Do Nice Guys Finish Last?" 78 *American Economic Review* 1034 (1988); Richard A. Epstein, "The Utilitarian Foundations of Natural Law," 12 *Harvard Journal of Law & Public Policy* 713 (1989).

once too skeptical about legal reasoning and too credulous about the possibilities of social improvement: at once too critical and too utopian. It proposes no concrete goals of social reform and offers no indication of what would count as concrete progress toward those goals.

The republican versions of communitariansim are not as vulnerable to these criticisms, in part because they tend to be rich in concrete proposals. But the proposals are for the most part a selection from the current smorgasbord of left-liberal proposals, and the selection does not display a coherence that is illuminated by being described as republican. Here is a recent summary: "The most powerful versions of republicanism . . . borrow from a significant strand of the liberal tradition, emphasizing political equality, the need to provide outlets for self-determination by the citizenry, the impossibility of maintaining democracy without a degree of citizen mobilization, the value of institutional and rights-based constraints on factionalism and self-interested representation, and the deliberative function of politics. Above all, republican theories stress the importance of dialogue and disagreement in the governmental process; they are designed to ensure, not that political actors are disembodied, but that to the extent possible they look through the eyes of all those affected."[46] I read this as a cautious endorsement of a modestly *dirigiste* state in place of our looser, still rather (classically) liberal, welfare state. It is a stance at once more concrete and more responsible than that of the other communitarian movements. But I question what it gains from being described in republican terms, and I worry that its aspirations are inconsistent with what we know about human social behavior as distinct from what we hope.

The republican movement seems too optimistic in an additional sense. It has unwarranted confidence in law's power to change attitudes, and specifically to inculcate civic virtue. No doubt if we had no legal system at all people would have a concept of civic responsibility different from what they have today. But the interesting choice is not between a legal system and anarchy; it is between a legal system that pretty much confines itself to altering incentives and one that, in addition, seeks to mold character and shape attitudes. As noted in Chapter 6, there is little evidence that Americans take their civic cues from law, so perhaps it would be a waste of resources to enlist law in the effort to revive or for that matter transcend the founding fathers' republicanism.

The feminist and communitarian movements are related at a deeper level than what I contend is an unrealistic aspiration for universal altru-

---

46. Sunstein, note 42 above, at 1589 (footnote omitted).

ism. The change in the view of the woman's role in society is a dramatic recent example that profound social gestalt switches are possible. The example keeps alive the communitarian dream that theories of human nature and social interaction that seem confirmed by thousands of years of experience may nevertheless be contingent and reversible. The particular example is not a persuasive one, however. The idea of women's equality is not new.[47] What is new is its wide acceptance, and the causes of that acceptance are economic and sociological: the reduction in child mortality (no longer need a woman be continually pregnant in order to have a reasonable assurance that one or two of her children will live to adulthood); improved methods of contraception; the development of labor-saving devices for the home; and the decline in the fraction of jobs in the labor force that are dirty, dangerous, or physically strenuous. The interaction of these trends has increased both the supply of and the demand for women in the labor force, and the result has been a dramatic increase in female participation in that force and a corresponding change in the conception of the woman's proper role in society.[48] No similar forces are on the horizon that might make capitalism go the way of patriarchy. On the contrary, socialism seems less feasible the more complex a society becomes. The women's movement is not a testament to the plasticity of human nature after all. Radical communitarians chip away at legal concepts thought to supply the underpinnings of the liberal state, in the hope that Utopia will rise from the ashes. Increasingly the hope seems a forlorn one.

47. See, for example, Mary Wollstonecraft, *Vindication of the Rights of Woman* (1792).

48. For supporting data and references, see my paper "An Economic Analysis of Sex Discrimination Law," 56 *University of Chicago Law Review* 1311 (1989).

PART V

JURISPRUDENCE WITHOUT FOUNDATIONS

14 ✺

Neotraditionalism

A major thread in the argument of this book has been skepticism about whether and to what extent law is an autonomous department of social thought. It would be such if even the most difficult legal issues could be resolved definitively, or at least satisfactorily, without straying outside the conventional boundaries of the legal culture—in other words, without using any tools of argument or proof besides those that lawyers acquire by virtue of their legal training and experience. A second thread has been that collateral subjects like philosophy and economics, despite their richness, cannot make up the deficit in legal thought. A third thread is pragmatic; such fixity as legal doctrines have derives from their having socially desirable consequences. When interwoven these threads create what is from the standpoint of many legal professionals a meager and disappointing tapestry. Lawyers and judges are seen to be muddling through, struggling with questions that often cannot be resolved other than by the lights of the decision maker's personal values and preferences, constituting a social vision that may be in irreconcilable conflict with other people's equally plausible social visions. The implications of the book are therefore skeptical in the commonsense meaning of the word, although its skepticism is tempered by recognition that most legal disputes *can* be resolved readily enough, by the manifold tools of practical reasoning, and that in any case much of law's social value lies not in resolving disputes but in preventing them from arising by laying down the rules that people live by (speed limits, rules governing the requirements for making a valid will, the prohibitions of criminal acts, and so on). This picture of law is not lofty enough to satisfy many in the legal profession, so one is not surprised at the continuing efforts to demonstrate the autonomy and objectivity of legal reasoning, futile as the enterprise may seem.

The legal theorists whom I shall call "neotraditionalists" insist that law contains within itself all the resources necessary for the correct resolution of legal disputes, no matter how momentous the dispute (it might be over racial or sexual justice, abortion, economic liberty, capital punishment—whatever). In previous writings I called these theorists "the new conventionalists," but the term is not felicitous. It is confusing to philosophers, to whom "conventionalism" means something different (that the principles of logic, mathematics, science, and morals are true by convention or agreement), although it is related in its antimetaphysicality to legal theorists' use of "conventionism," in much the same way that philosophical positivism is related to legal positivism. Also, the term seems rather belittling, and it is vaguer than it need be. An alternative formulation might be "traditional legalism"[1]—*redivivus*. What makes this "back to basics" movement especially pertinent here is that it uses philosophy to try to demonstrate philosophy's irrelevance to law. It shares with pragmatism a distaste for foundations.

The Decline of Law as an Autonomous Discipline

To understand neotraditionalism (whose affinities with "neoconservatism" I shall not attempt to explore), one must understand the dramatic change in academic thinking about law that has taken place since the early 1960s. I am particularly conscious of this change because, graduating from law school in 1962, I was educated at the tail end of the era in which—the attack of the legal realists having been blunted—law was confidently regarded as an autonomous discipline, and at the law school that epitomized this conception. The self-sufficiency of legal thought was until the 1960s the relatively secure, though periodically contested, premise of legal education and scholarship. We have inspected its political roots and seen that almost a century earlier Langdell had made the autonomy of law an academic idea—indeed an academic faith[2]—and that Holmes had challenged this faith. Holmes went so far as to say that the future of legal studies belonged to the economist and the statistician rather than to the "black letter" lawyer.[3] But because the economist and the statistician—not to mention the philosopher, the sociologist, the political scientist, the historian, the psychologist, the linguist, and the

1. Dennis M. Patterson, "An Introduction to Conventionalism," 10 *Western New England Law Review* 43, 58 (1988).

2. In an anonymous review of Langdell's treatise on contract law, Holmes called him "the greatest living legal theologian." 14 *American Law Review* 233, 234 (1880).

3. "The Path of the Law," 10 *Harvard Law Review* 457, 469 (1897).

anthropologist—were not much interested in law, Holmes's assault on Langdell did not undermine the autonomy of the law as a discipline. Holmes himself was steeped in the philosophical thought, both ethical and epistemological, of the late nineteenth century. But few lawyers realized how fundamental his philosophical outlook was not only to his legal thought but also to his greatness as a judge. The lesson drawn from his career and from the careers of the other notable legal thinkers in the period from the publication of *The Common Law* in 1881 to the publication of H. L. A. Hart's *The Concept of Law* in 1961 (a period of such luminaries in the American legal firmament as Benjamin Cardozo, Louis Brandeis, Roscoe Pound, John Wigmore, Felix Frankfurter, Robert Jackson, Karl Llewellyn, Learned Hand, Jerome Frank, Henry Hart, and Lon Fuller) was that a legal thinker should be broadly educated and abreast of the intellectual currents of his times—not that any of the keys to understanding law might be held by disciplines other than law And only Holmes in this group thought (at times anyway) that there were no keys.

Against this background it is not surprising that law professors of the period, with only a few exceptions, believed that the only thing law students needed to study was authoritative legal texts—judicial opinions mainly, but also administrative opinions, statutes, the Constitution, and judicial and administrative rules—because the only essential preparation for a legal scholar, beyond what he could be expected to bring to his work from his college education and his general reading, was knowledge of what was in those texts and in the pertinent commentary on them, plus the power of logical discrimination and argumentation that came from the study of legal texts through close reading and vigorous discussion, rather than from the application of any formal or systematic methodology. The only change from Langdell's day—a change that was the legacy of Holmes and the legal realists—was that law was increasingly recognized to be a purposive instrument of social control, so that one had to know something about society to be able to understand, criticize, and improve law. But that "something" was what any intelligent person with a good general education and common sense knew or could pick up from the legal texts themselves (viewed as windows on social custom) or, failing these sources of insight, would acquire naturally in a few years of practicing law. It was a set of basic ethical and political values, some knowledge of institutions, and some acquaintance with the workings of the economy.

This faith in law's autonomy as a discipline was not a complacent faith; it was justified by the then recent history of the profession. In a period of only twenty-five years, from the mid-1930s to the late 1950s, lawyers had with little help from other disciplines reformed (through the Federal Rules of Civil Procedure) the procedural system of the federal courts and by force of example were well on the way to reforming the procedural systems of the state courts as well; had corrected the profound epistemological error that had led the Supreme Court to claim the authority to create a general federal common law in cases based on diversity of citizenship;[4] had brought commercial law into harmony with modern commercial practices through the Uniform Commercial Code; had saved (under considerable political pressure, to be sure) the independence of the Supreme Court by abandoning "liberty of contract" as a substantive constitutional right; had brought much nearer to completion the work of the Civil War by outlawing racial segregation in public schools and in other government institutions, both state and federal; had resurrected, in the second flag-salute case and other decisions, the Constitution as a charter of civil liberties; had in the Administrative Procedure Act systematized and regularized the administrative process, itself the foundation for imaginative new systems of legal regulation of labor relations and securities markets; had taken substantial steps to civilize state criminal procedure; had overcome the traditional judicial hostility to statutes; had tidied up the common law by means of the Restatements of Law promulgated by the American Law Institute; had rethought criminal law in the ALI's Model Penal Code; had eliminated many arbitrary barriers to legal liability, such as the privity limitation in products liability; and had come to terms with the New Deal. In addition, they were well on their way to dismantling the remaining archaic, vestigial, formalistic, illiberal, or dysfunctional rules of the common law, such as the intricate rules governing the liability of landowners to persons injured as a result of dangerous conditions on the

---

4. I refer to the error of believing that the common law was something that existed apart from the judicial decisions of each state, and hence was not covered by the Rules of Decision Act (now 28 U.S.C. §1652), which directed the federal courts to apply "the laws of the several states" in cases in which those laws were applicable; this would certainly include diversity of citizenship cases. See Erie R. Co. v. Tompkins, 304 U.S. 64 (1938), overruling Swift v. Tyson, 41 U.S. (16 Pet.) 1 (1842). *Swift* was more than an epistemological error, however; it was also an effort, ultimately seen as misguided, to bring about a greater national uniformity of commercial law. See Grant Gilmore, *The Ages of American Law* 30-35 (1977).

Readers who want documentation for the assertions made in this chapter concerning the course and consequences of legal reform in the modern era should consult my article "The Decline of Law as an Autonomous Discipline: 1962-1987," 100 *Harvard Law Review* 761 (1987).

land. In hindsight some of these achievements can be questioned, and there were always some doubters, but on the whole the lawyer's traditional faith in the autonomy of his discipline seemed well founded.

Buttressing this faith was the failure of other disciplines to generate significant insights about law. Until the publication in 1961 of articles by Ronald Coase and Guido Calabresi,[5] economics seemed to have little to say about law outside the antitrust field. Even within antitrust there were grounds for skepticism, for antitrust was then the domain of a particularly soft area of economics—"industrial organization" in the era of "workable competition" theory. Ethical and political philosophy was in a slump, and analytic philosophy seemed, as far as jurisprudence was concerned, relevant only to the question What is law? A nonphilosophical work such as Hart and Sacks's *The Legal Process* (1958) seemed more pertinent to jurisprudence than did explicitly philosophical works.

But perhaps the main reason for the prevailing faith in the autonomy of law was the political consensus in the United States in the post–World War II period—the return to normalcy after the turbulence of the New Deal and the war. Since 1940 there had been little ideological difference between the major political parties. The radical Right had been discredited first by its isolationism and then by its racism, and the radical Left had been squashed by the Cold War. Secular, humanistic, patriotic, and centrist, the American intellectual scene in the 1950s and the early 1960s was remarkably free of ideological strife. It was natural in such a period to think of law not in political but in technical terms. Just as society had left the design of bridges to civil engineers, it could leave the design of legal institutions to lawyers. If civil engineers disagreed fundamentally about wind resistance, society could not safely leave the design of bridges entirely to them; similarly, if lawyers disagreed about the aims, functions, and consequences of law, society could not leave the design of legal institutions to them. But in the period I am writing about there was little such disagreement and therefore little opposition to the lawyers' claim to have an autonomous discipline. And although ultimately law, unlike most applications of civil engineering, *is* political, this fact is unlikely to be noticed when the entire respectable band of the professional spectrum agrees on the basic political issues that bear on law (maybe in such a case they cease to *be* political). With political conten-

5. See Ronald H. Coase, "The Problem of Social Cost," 3 *Journal of Law and Economics* 1 (1960) (actually published in 1961); Guido Calabresi, "Some Thoughts on Risk Distribution and the Law of Torts," 70 *Yale Law Journal* 499 (1961).

tion not infecting legal analysis, law appeared to be—in a sense was—a technical and objective discipline.

Of course, it had not always been thus. As recently as the 1930s the legal realists had argued that much of law was the emanation of a politicized judiciary. But by the 1950s, when many of the reforms advocated by the legal realists had been adopted and many of the leading realists had been co-opted into the judiciary, the drafting of uniform laws, and other mainstream professional roles, law seemed to have achieved political neutrality.

The supports for the faith in law's autonomy have now been kicked away. First, the political consensus associated with the "end of ideology"[6] has shattered. The spectrum of political opinion in law schools, which in 1960 (except in Catholic law schools) occupied a narrow band between mild liberalism and mild conservatism, today runs from Marxism, radical feminism, and nihilism on the left to economic and political libertarianism and Christian fundamentalism on the right. Even if we lop off the extremes, a broad middle area remains, running from, say, Ronald Dworkin and William Brennan on the left to Robert Bork and Antonin Scalia on the right—two pairs of entirely respectable, "establishment" figures but so distant from each other ideologically that there is little common ground of discourse.[7] We now know that if we give a difficult legal question to two equally distinguished legal thinkers chosen at random, we may well get opposite answers.

The shattering of political consensus would not matter if American law dealt only with nonpolitical issues; chemistry has not ceased to be an autonomous discipline because of the greater political diversity among chemists today than in the 1950s. But law has become ever more entangled in political issues.[8] This is due partly to the aggressiveness with which the Supreme Court in the 1960s and 1970s created constitutional rights in politically controversial areas, such as abortion (and other matters involving sex), reapportionment, political patronage, and school and prison conditions, and partly to the expansion of govern-

6. See Daniel Bell, *The End of Ideology: On the Exhaustion of Political Ideas in the Fifties* (1960).

7. See Ronald Dworkin, "Reagan's Justice," *New York Review of Books,* Nov. 8, 1984, at 27.

8. For empirical evidence, see Robert A. Carp and C. K. Rowland, *Policymaking and Politics in the Federal District Courts* 50 (1983), finding that political party affiliation of federal district judges has increasing power as an explanatory variable of the judges' decisions. I don't of course deny that there are political issues in science. Genetics, weapons technology, organ transplants, evolution, and other areas of scientific and technological research have generated intense political controversy.

ment generally, which has brought more and more politically touchy subjects into the courts, such as campaign financing, environmental protection, and the plight of disabled people. Moreover, the Supreme Court's aggressive judicial activism inspired state courts and lower federal courts to make controversial extensions of rights in such common law fields as tort and contract law—resulting in the extraordinary travails, dramatic changes in judicial personnel, and consequent ideological *volte-face,* of the supreme court of California. And, especially when Earl Warren was Chief Justice of the United States—an era that continues to set the tone for much legal debate—a majority of the U.S. Supreme Court disdained the principles of conventional legal reasoning symbolized by the Harvard Law School in its heyday.

Many lawyers have difficulty understanding the contingency of legal doctrines that is the outstanding lesson of recent legal history, because they take the Warren era as the baseline and regard the Supreme Court's subsequent retrenchment as a political challenge to the rule of law. (This outlook, which pervades "liberal" criticism of decisions by the Supreme Court under the Burger and Rehnquist chief justiceships,[9] was evident during the hearings on Robert Bork's nomination to the Supreme Court.) But this is the same light in which the decisions of the Warren period were regarded by orthodox lawyers then: as a political challenge to the rule of law embodied in the decisions of the previous period.

Accompanying the decline in political consensus since the early 1960s has been a boom in those disciplines, such as economics and philosophy (and game theory, statistics, public choice theory, and literary theory), that can be brought to bear—and, it seems, with increasing power—on legal topics. As if all this were not enough, confidence in the ability of lawyers on their own to put right the problems of the legal system has been undermined. Not only have some of the triumphs of the 1930s through 1950s been revalued downward (examples are the idea of notice pleading that informs the Federal Rules of Civil Procedure and the judicialization of administrative proceedings by the Administrative Procedure Act), but since the early 1960s all sorts of legal reforms have miscarried. These include a bankruptcy code that has produced a vast increase in the number of bankruptcy filings; a runaway expansion of tort liability that is endangering the insurance system and has not been slowed by the movement (itself disappointing, and rich in untoward and

---

9. See, for example, Laurence H. Tribe, *Constitutional Choices* (1985), reviewed in Richard A. Posner, "The Constitution as Mirror: Tribe's Constitutional Choices," 84 *Michigan Law Review* 551 (1985).

unintended side effects) to no-fault automobile compensation; a no-fault divorce movement that has boomeranged against the women's movement that had supported its adoption; the creation of a system of environmental regulation at once fearfully complex and either perverse or ineffective in much of its operation; the destruction of certainty in the field of conflict of laws as a result of the replacement of the mechanical common law rules by "interest analysis"; the hapless blundering of the federal courts into immensely contentious, analytically intractable ethical-political questions in such areas as capital punishment, prison conditions, sex and the family, political patronage, the role of religion in public life, and affirmative action; the accidental growth of the class action, through what had seemed a minor amendment to the Federal Rules of Civil Procedure, into an engine for coercing the settlement of cases that have no merit yet expose defendants to astronomical potential liabilities; the flood of statutes that overencourage litigation by entitling winning plaintiffs but not winning defendants to recover their attorney's fees from the loser; and the creation of an intricate code of federal criminal procedure and its wholesale imposition on state criminal proceedings through the doctrine of incorporation.

Partly because of these developments, partly for reasons that are not understood (a testament to the shallow understanding that lawyers have—that anyone has—of the scientific laws that govern the legal system), there has been since 1960 an astonishing rise in the amount of litigation, especially but not only in the federal courts. The legal profession has responded with all the imagination of a traffic engineer whose only answer to highway congestion is to build more highways, or of a political establishment whose only answer to increased demands for government services is to print more money. Rather than raising court fees to dampen demand for court services, the powers that administer the judicial systems of this country (lawyers all) have lowered them in real terms, responding to the surge in litigation with more judges, more lawyers, more subsidies to litigation, more bureaucrats, more law clerks and other judicial adjuncts, and lately with novel settlement practices ("alternative dispute resolution") that raise substantial questions of both efficacy and legality. The fundamental reason the litigation explosion has continued unchecked is that nothing in a conventional legal education— nothing gleaned from the close reading of judicial opinions, statutes, and rules—equips a person to notice, let alone to measure, explain, temper, and adjust to, an increase in the demand for judicial services.

Bewildered by these developments, thoughtful members of the legal profession no longer feel on top of events. Looking back one realizes that the conventional methods of legal analysis in the 1950s were too *thin* to equip the legal profession to cope effectively with the troubles ahead (they may still be too thin). In particular, the lawyer's weak sense of fact—that lack of scientific spirit in law—was bound, sooner or later, to tell against the efficacy of legal reform. When one notes that the distinguished Harvard Law School professor of tort and agency law, Warren Seavey, thought it meaningful to state, in the Roscoe Pound Lectures that he delivered in 1953, "that the law of Torts is based on the principle that one who harms another has a duty of compensation whenever it is just that he should pay,"[10] without thinking it necessary to define what he meant by "just" or to indicate why he thought he was uttering something more than a tautology, one begins to sense how poorly equipped even the best of conventionally trained lawyers were to deal with questions that lay outside the narrow purlieus of legal-doctrinal analysis. Seavey must have believed law to be an autonomous department of thought in a strong sense, a field that rather than battening on other fields was adequately—indeed optimally—cultivated by the use of skills, knowledge, and experience that owed nothing to other fields. For the lectures go on to say "that in large measure the existing [tort] rules created by judges are just" and have produced "a system of law which meets the needs of the modern community" (pp. 45, 51). In fact, "on the whole our American courts have done a magnificent job in working out the intricate pattern needed for justice" (p. 70). The needs of the modern community are not specified, criteria of justice set forth, or the difficulty of determining the economic and social consequences of legal rules acknowledged. A few criticisms are offered, although diffidently, since Seavey has just expressed exaggerated respect for judicial abilities. Some of the criticisms have a quaint ring from the distance of thirty-five years: for example, "the increasing frequency of verdicts of one and two hundred thousand dollars, with the consequent drain upon productive funds, should at least cause us to be more careful with the machinery which leads to these" (p. 65). Above all, there is no recognition that evaluating the tort system might require more than legal learning and common sense—might require scientific skills and attitudes.

Another reason for the contemporary decline in a confident belief in the law's autonomy is internal to the enterprise of academic law. It is the same reason that led composers to write atonal music, painters to aban-

10. *Cogitations on Torts* 3 (1954). Subsequent page references to this book are in the text.

don representational art, English poets to tire of the heroic couplet. When a technique is perfected, the most imaginative practitioners become restless.[11] They want to be innovators rather than imitators, and this desire drives them to strike out in new directions. By 1960 the changes on the theme of the law's autonomy had been rung. Holmes had said most of the important things; Cardozo in *The Nature of the Judicial Process,* Hart and Sacks in their book on the legal process, and Edward Levi in *An Introduction to Legal Reasoning* (1949) had completed the edifice of classical legal thought. With law in constant flux there were (and are) always new cases, new doctrines—indeed entire new fields—to which to apply the classical techniques. But after a while this was bound to seem, at least in the higher reaches of the academy, and whether rightly or wrongly, work for followers rather than for leaders. Because of this perception and also because of the growth of collateral disciplines, a new type of legal scholarship emerged in the 1960s—the conscious application of other disciplines, such as economics and political and moral philosophy, to traditional legal problems. This growth of disciplines collateral to law was and continues to be part of an immense outpouring of academic research in America that has had the incidental but pertinent effect of blurring the boundaries between disciplines, making interdisciplinary work the norm rather than the exception in many fields. That a field should strive to remain autonomous has begun to seem anachronistic.

The continuing rise in the prestige, authority, and (underlying these) the achievements of the natural sciences (broadly defined to include mathematics, statistics, and medical and computer technology) may be another factor in the waning of faith in law's autonomy, quite apart from any direct applications of science to law. Advances in medicine, genetics, space exploration, weapons technology, computers, cosmology, and other areas of science and technology make traditional legal-doctrinal analysis—the heart of legal reasoning when law is conceived as an autonomous discipline—seem to many younger scholars, and to some older ones as well, old-fashioned, passé, tired. Fields in a similar plight, such as literary criticism, have not hesitated to borrow from trendier, arguably more rigorous fields (even using scientific jargon to rail against science); in retrospect it is obvious that academic law would do likewise. Although some classic works of traditional legal scholarship can still be read with profit and admiration, it is no longer easy for

---

11. See, for example, "Milton II," in T. S. Eliot, *On Poetry and Poets* 146, 150 (1957).

academic lawyers who want to be considered on the cutting edge of legal thought to imagine writing in the same vein. This point is distinct from my previous one, that the genre has been perfected (which is not to say completed). A purely verbal, purely lawyer's scholarship, in which the categories of analysis are the same, or very close to, those used by the judges or legislators whose work is being analyzed—a scholarship moreover in which political consensus is assumed and the insights of other disciplines ignored (Seavey's lectures illustrate both points)— does not fit today's scholarly *Zeitgeist*.

Then there is the fact that the student revolt of the late 1960s caused a diminution in law students' respect for law professors from which the self-assurance of law professors has never fully recovered. (A small token—and good example of the decline in authority noted in Chapter 2—is the advent of blind grading of law-school exams. Law students of my day would not have dreamed of distrusting their professors' commitment to grading exams "without respect to persons.") Gone for the most part is the Socratic bully, and with him some of the deference that earlier was so marked a characteristic of student-faculty relations. And with the dramatic rise in the average quality of law students at the elite law schools since about 1970, there is a growing suspicion that many students do not need a third year of legal-doctrinal analysis to equip them to practice law and that the requirement of three years of law school may reflect nothing more exalted than the legal profession's desire to limit the number of lawyers and the law schools' desire for more tuition income. Finally, the increasing importance of statute law and above all of constitutional law, the former resistant to conventional legal analysis for reasons discussed in Chapters 9 and 10, the latter a body of law almost nakedly political, has diminished the relevance of the conventional kit bag of lawyers' analytical tools.

The Neotraditionalist Response

The developments since the 1960s help explain and support the concept of law advanced here by exposing the bankruptcy of conventional legal thought in coping with the theoretical and institutional aspects of law. Yet not everyone is convinced that the most important techniques for understanding and improving the legal system lie outside the compass of the traditional lawyer's training and experience. In particular, a number of legal scholars steeped in philosophy[12] are trying to refurbish the idea that law can, after all, and should be left to lawyers trained in law and only in law. Most of these scholars recognize that autonomy is not an either-or proposition. No field is completely autonomous or, perhaps, completely parasitic; certainly law is not completely parasitic on other fields.[13] Modern economics is not independent of mathematics, but it does not draw its lifeblood from mathematics. The question is whether law is as independent from economics and moral and political philosophy as economics is from mathematics—whether, in other words, legal thought provides a unifying perspective that enables the legal analyst to place the other fields in a subordinate role when addressing legal issues. These scholars believe it does.

The neotraditionalists are a diverse lot. The common denominator is a desire to restore a strong sense of the law's autonomy, but the modes of restoration range from the ambitious theorizing of Anthony Kronman and Ernest Weinrib to what in some of Charles Fried's writings approaches (I am sure unintentionally) anti-intellectualism. Although most neotraditionalists are theorists, rather than practitioners of conventional legal-doctrinal analysis, they are responding to a demand created primarily by conventional analysts repelled by the academic movements—law and economics, law and philosophy, critical legal studies, feminist jurisprudence, and others—that have challenged the law's autonomy and sought to occupy the space created by the decline in faith in that autonomy. Such movements are politically radical, methodologically radical, or both; freighted with alien learning; often dismissive of conventional legal thought; sometimes deficient in lawyerly qualities.

What are the most important facets of neotraditionalism?

Antireductionism. I use this term to denote the idea that law is its own kind of thing and cannot be reduced to something else—to philosophy, or economics, or politics. ("So what is it that lawyers and judges know

---

12. And of course many not so steeped. See, for example, Peter R. Teachout, "The Burden of the Liberal Song," 62 *Indiana Law Journal* 1283 (1987); Teachout, "Chicago Exposition: The New American Jurisprudential Writing as a Cultural Literature," 39 *Mercer Law Review* 767 (1988); Harry H. Wellington, "Common Law Rules and Constitutional Double Standards: Some Notes on Adjudication," 83 *Yale Law Journal* 221 (1973). My focus is on the philosophical neotraditionalists—with whom, by the way, the rule-of-law conservatives (Hayek and others) mentioned briefly in Chapter 1 should be grouped. The debate between neotraditionalists and interdisciplinarians is well summarized in Donald H. Gjerdingen, "The Future of Legal Scholarship and the Search for a Modern Theory of Law," 35 *Buffalo Law Review* 381 (1986).

13. On disciplinary autonomy generally, see Francisco J. Ayala, "Biology as an Autonomous Science," 56 *American Scientist* 207 (1968).

that philosophers and economists do not? The answer is simple: law.")[14] Law is a collection of insights, procedures, and methods, of great antiquity and durability. Admittedly it is somewhat old-fashioned, somewhat slow-paced by the standards of the closing years of the twentieth century. The lawyer's role may therefore be a humble one—not that of a social architect or even a social engineer but of a social janitor,[15] tidying up in the wake of the policy sciences and the policy makers (the legislators and the constitution makers). But it is a role that only a person trained and experienced in law can play: a poor thing but mine own. If the lawyer becomes distracted by other disciplines he will lose his bearings and no longer be able to play his unique role well.

Stated differently, law is an art—the art of social governance by rules. The art can be practiced only by the artist, the person trained and experienced in law. As long as rules remain important, the lawyer has an important social role to play despite the rise of other disciplines and despite what appears to be the growing politicization of American society.

Law as a Via Media between Unacceptable Extremes. If law is an art, it is not a science; indeed it must stand in equal opposition to the two "scientific" schools of thought (as the neotraditionalists describe them)— critical legal studies, on the left, and law and economics, on the right.[16] Because most lawyers are uncomfortable with extreme positions, the

14. Charles Fried, "The Artificial Reason of the Law or: What Lawyers Know," 60 *Texas Law Review* 35, 57 (1981). Or as Weinrib has put it, "In realizing itself as an articulation of corrective justice, private law fulfills the only function it can have, which is simply to be private law." Ernest J. Weinrib, "Aristotle's Forms of Justice," in *Justice, Law, and Method in Plato and Aristotle* 133, 151 (Spiro Panagiotou ed. 1987). More succinctly, "the end of tort law is tort law." Weinrib, "Adjudication and Public Values: Fiss's Critique of Corrective Justice," 39 *University of Toronto Law Journal* 1, 12 (1989).

15. The metaphor is Charles Fried's. See "Jurisprudential Responses to Legal Realism," 73 *Cornell Law Review* 331, 333 (1988).

16. The bracketing of law and economics with critical legal studies has become a cliché of legal scholarship. See, for example, Owen M. Fiss, "The Death of the Law?" 72 *Cornell Law Review* 1 (1986); George P. Fletcher, "Why Kant," 87 *Columbia Law Review* 421, 424 (1987). I argue below that this bracketing is misleading. As for the suggestion that law and economics is inherently right-wing, this is both an error and an affront to its liberal practitioners (Calabresi, Polinsky, Ackerman, Cooter, Kaplow, Kornhauser, Donohue, others). What is true is that the study of economics instills in most students an appreciation of the social benefits of markets, an appreciation not shared by those who have never studied economics and who therefore have difficulty understanding how so decentralized an institution as a market can regulate complex economic activity in an efficient manner. But not everyone who appreciates the benefits of markets is a right-winger: most of the Communist world is at the moment pro-market.

opportunity to reject Left and Right in favor of a position safely centrist, both politically and methodologically, has powerful appeal.

Law as Practical Reason. Law is not a science even if it is described, less fancily than in the art metaphor though more so than in the janitor metaphor, as a branch of practical reason. The neotraditionalists emphasize three closely related, orthodox Aristotelian facets of this variegated concept: first, the centrality of deliberation, conceived as a mode of inquiry and judgment requiring qualities of character as well as intellect; second, the cautious, prudential, incremental character of Aristotelian practical reason in contrast to Platonic radical speculation, which produced the communistic utopia depicted in the *Republic*; third, the importance of tradition as a corrective to theoretical speculation. Law as practical reason in this account celebrates adherence to the traditional values, methods, and vocabulary of legal reasoning and is suspicious of systematic approaches.

Interpretive Communities. Building on Stanley Fish's idea of interpretive communities,[17] the neotraditionalist seeks to reclaim legal interpretation from indeterminacy by arguing that even if no text possesses objective meaning, the community of lawyers to which constitutional and statutory texts are addressed can impose determinate meaning on

17. See Stanley Fish, *Is There a Text in This Class? The Authority of Interpretive Communities* (1980); Fish, *Doing What Comes Naturally: Change, Rhetoric, and the Practice of Theory in Literary and Legal Studies* (1989). The idea of interpretive communities is not original with Fish. The term comes from Josiah Royce, *The Problem of Christianity* 211 (1913) ("a Community of Interpretation"), explicating Peirce's concept of a "community of inquirers." See Peirce, "Some Consequences of Four Incapacities," in *Collected Papers of Charles Sanders Peirce,* vol. 5, pp. 156, 186–187, 189 (Charles Hartshorne and Paul Weiss eds. 1934); Peirce, "Grounds of Validity of the Laws of Logic: Further Consequences of Four Incapacities," in id., vol. 5, pp. 193, 197–198; Margareta Bertilsson, *Towards a Social Reconstruction of Scientific Theory: Peirce's Theory of Inquiry, and Beyond,* chs. 4–5 (1978); Walter Benn Michaels, "The Interpreter's Self: Peirce on the Cartesian 'Subject,'" 31 *Georgia Review* 383 (1977). But the concept (as distinct from the term) as Fish uses it comes not from Royce or Peirce but from Wittgenstein's books *On Certainty* and *Philosophical Investigations.* Pears's summary of Wittgenstein's mature philosophy of mind could serve equally for Fish's philosophy of interpretation: "We all live in the unique common world from which it is impossible for each of us to cut out a minature world of our own." David Pears, *The False Prison: A Study of the Development of Wittgenstein's Philosophy,* vol. 1, p. 51 (1987). Cf. Saul A. Kripke, *Wittgenstein on Rules and Private Language* 91–92, 96–97 (1982). Fish's failure to acknowledge the provenance of his ruling idea has drawn comment. See Reed Way Dasenbrock, "Accounting for the Changing Certainties of Interpretive Communities," 101 *Modern Language Notes* 1023, 1027 (1985). For summary and criticism, respectively, of Fish's views, see Christopher Norris, *The Contest of Faculties: Philosophy and Theory after Deconstruction* 172–182 (1985); Brook Thomas, "Stanley Fish and the Uses of Baseball" (unpublished paper, University of California at Irvine, Department of English).

these texts by virtue of the shared outlook of the community's members.

The appeal of this four-faceted neotraditionalism is easy to see. It embodies attitudes both instinctual in lawyers of almost every ideological stripe except the radical Left and attractive to America's social and religious conservatives (as distinct from libertarians). These attitudes are: nostalgia for a time when law was law and was not infected by newfangled ideas, some of Continental origin; desire to free law from dependence on other disciplines, especially ones such as moral philosophy and economics that are abstruse, ideologically charged, or both; dislike of abstraction (the residue of traditional American anti-intellectualism, still a marked characteristic of many lawyers and of most other Americans); hostility to science and to systematic knowledge generally, or in other words to what is most characteristically and threateningly modern, love of stability, which is threatened if law is tied to rapidly changing fields of social thought, and, closely related, horror of indeterminacy and of the collapse of law into politics; relatedly, the natural desire of lawyers and legal academics to monopolize the practice and study of law; also their desire not to be thought the mere water bearers and hod carriers of theorists from other disciplines; and finally the fear that the legal profession will make a botch of its efforts to assimilate other disciplines.

These attitudes may explain the warm reception that neotraditionalism seems to be evoking from traditional legal scholars, the practicing bar, and social and religious conservatives, but they do not make an intellectual case for neotraditionalism. It is merely ironic that the theoretical grounds of neotraditionalism are derived from the same types of extralegal source that it is the whole purpose of the movement to escape dependence on. Let us forget that and proceed to an evaluation of the four props of the neotraditionalist argument, beginning with its antireductionism.

Lawyers are trained and experienced in, and some become highly skillful at, recognizing legal rules that are latent in difficult and ambiguous sources (such as a series of judicial opinions, or a carelessly drafted statute), discerning the applicability of those rules to new factual situations, determining the plasticity of the rules, making factual and legal arguments in a form persuasive to judges and other officials, and deploying other skills indispensable to maneuver in a rule-governed society. The training necessary to launch a person on a successful and socially productive legal career does not absolutely require exposing the student to any materials that are not legal in the narrowest sense—that is, that are neither statutes, broadly defined to include constitutional provisions, judicial rules, administrative regulations, and the like, nor cases. Conversely, virtually no one who lacks the minimum professional skills, whether acquired in law school or, less efficiently, by apprenticeship to a lawyer, can practice law successfully (even if allowed to) no matter how expert he is in the study of law from the perspective of other disciplines. In this sense law is indeed an autonomous discipline, irreducible to other disciplines.

The problem with stopping here is that the system of rules has gaps, and (only partly for that reason) the rules themselves are constantly undergoing creation, modification, and destruction. To determine what to do when the rules run out requires a judgment of policy, and nothing in a conventional legal education or in the experience of practicing law equips a lawyer to make policy judgments to which the community has compelling reasons to defer as it defers to scientists in matters of scientific judgment. If policy is a big component of law, Fried's triumphant tautology becomes problematic.

Even if a lawyer could get by today with the narrowest kind of legal training, it would not follow that legal training should be so circumscribed. Nor do the leading neotraditionalists advocate this. They recognize that what is minimally sufficient may not be optimal. Today no major law school and few minor ones fail to bring other disciplines into the law-school curriculum. Are they the deluded captives of weird ideologies, foreign or domestic? I think not. It is rather that other fields, notably economics, have worked their way so deeply into the fabric of law that a legal education seems incomplete without some instruction in them. Few neotraditionalists begrudge the borrowing of insights from other fields for service in those area of law conceded to involve economic (or statistical, or psychological) issues; few would argue that antitrust cases should be decided on the basis of lawyers' intuitions untutored by economic thinking on competition and monopoly. They concede that even if the lawyer is only a social janitor he should be allowed to use the latest brooms and sweepers; their objection is to the use of economic or moral philosophy to furnish overarching norms of legality.

But once the camel's nose is let in under the tent, the rest is sure to follow. If economics is conceded to be relevant to antitrust law, or to the computation of damages in personal-injury cases, then perhaps it must be conceded to have relevance, through the Hand formula, to the meaning of the negligence standard as well—which is also the reasonable-use standard of nuisance law. Maybe indeed it can be used to encapsulate the entire field of tort law—for maybe cost-benefit analysis is the basic logic not only of the negligence standard but also of the decision whether to make the rule of liability for a given class of accidents negligence or strict liability. It is not clear where the spiral ends. Like it or not, American legal reasoning is pervasively though not solely utilitarian and instrumentalist; and economics—in which the idea of balancing costs and benefits plays a leading role—is in one sense applied utilitarianism and in another the science of instrumental reasoning.[18] If expansion of the economic approach is to be resisted successfully, the resistance is more likely to be organized around philosophical ideas (for example, philosophical criticisms of utilitarianism), or around psychological or historical insights, than around ideas internal to law. Interdisciplinary legal theory is inescapable. One may even doubt whether opposition to economic thinking in law is consistent with the premises of neotraditionalism. For that thinking has been due in large part not to economists or even to economically minded lawyers but to the intuitions of conventionally trained, conventionally experienced lawyers such as Learned Hand, whose adoption of an economic approach to accident law would, one might have thought, have validated that approach for a neotraditionalist.

To switch from torts to contracts: if the relevance of economic analysis to contract law is accepted, its relevance to contracts of surrogate motherhood is not easily denied. And it is difficult to imagine countering the economic analysis of contracts of surrogate motherhood without bringing in theoretical ideas from the world of thought outside law—as Margaret Jane Radin did in her Marxist-feminist criticism of the economic approach to adoption and surrogate motherhood.[19] Similarly, if, as the Supreme Court has suggested, cost-benefit analysis supplies the proper algorithm for deciding how much due process a participant in an administrative proceeding is entitled to, why can't it be used to decide whether a preliminary injunction should be issued?[20] In both cases one is trying to figure out how much procedure (and therefore how accurate and how costly it will be) to require in advance of a governmental

---

18. See Frank H. Easterbrook, "Method, Result, and Authority: A Reply," 98 *Harvard Law Review* 622 (1985). And recall a point made in Chapter 12: usually the judge or lawyer when speaking in utilitarian terms actually means the corresponding economic (wealth-maximizing) terms.

19. See Margaret Jane Radin, "Market-Inalienability," 100 *Harvard Law Review* 1849 (1987).

20. On due process, see Mathews v. Eldridge, 424 U.S. 319, 335 (1976), discussed in my book *Economic Analysis of Law* 518 (3d ed. 1986); on preliminary injunctions see id. at 522.

action—whether denying welfare benefits or granting or denying a pre-liminary injunction—that may impose heavy costs on one or both parties, or on third parties.

And so with other disciplines. If philosophers mount cogent attacks on simple-minded ideas of textual determinacy—ideas that as it happens are the unexamined assumptions of many lawyers and judges engaged in interpreting statutory and constitutional texts—can the legal profession brush aside the attacks with the assertion that what lawyers and judges do when they interpret legal texts is its own sort of thing? The problems of interpreting such texts may well differ in vital respects from the problems of interpreting other kinds of text. But if the shoe happens to fit—if the philosophical criticism of methods of judicial interpretation is cogent—it is not responsive to point out that the criticism comes from outside the legal system or to assert that legal reasoning is a mystery whose premises may not be subjected to critical examination. That is an ostrich's tactic.

Charles Fried is reluctant to recognize that other disciplines can contribute to the understanding of legal problems. As examples of problems that he thinks economic analysis cannot solve because they involve entitlements, he puts forward the cases of (1) building a hotel across from another's restaurant, thereby causing the restaurant to prosper from the increased flow of potential patrons, and (2) building a new service station across from an existing one, thereby cutting into the profits of that station. In the first case there is no legal right to restitution for the benefit conferred and in the second no liability for the harm caused. Fried believes that this pattern can make no sense to an economist.[21] Economics does sometimes have problems with entitlements—but not in Fried's two cases. In both of them the external effect (that is, the harm to a nonparty to the transaction: the restaurant in the first example and the first service station in the second example) is pecuniary rather than real, meaning that there is no net social benefit or net social cost. Although the hotel causes the business of the restaurant across the street to increase, restaurants elsewhere suffer an offsetting diminution in their business, so there is no net increase in social wealth and legal intervention would not improve the allocation of resources—intervention would be all costs and no benefits. The service station causes its competitor's business to decrease, but its own business increases by an offsetting amount and consumers are better off; otherwise they would not switch. Again there is no basis for public intervention. Here the reasoning is the

---

21. See Fried, note 14 above, at 41, 44.

same as that used to show why the law does not equate "stealing" a competitor's business to stealing his car. The first "theft" produces a net increase in society's wealth, the second a net decrease measured by the cost of the resources consumed in committing and preventing thefts, as distinct from the transfer of wealth from victim to thief, which is a wash.

From what I have said about the incursions of law into economics at the practical level, it should be clear (turning now to the second ambition of neotraditionalism—to be the happy medium between law and economics at one end of the spectrum and critical legal studies at the other) that the twinning of law and economics and critical legal studies as symmetrically opposed extremes between which neotraditionalism can sail is untenable. Economics has been woven into the fabric of law at a number of places and cannot be removed without damaging the fabric. Critical legal studies has not yet penetrated a single area of law, partly because of the confrontational, *épater les bourgeois* style of many of its practitioners, partly because its politics are extremely left-wing, but mainly because of its all-encompassing negativism about the possibility of either coherent doctrine or constructive reform. This negativism acts as a damper on useful proposals for changing or reconceptualizing legal doctrines. The proponents of critical legal studies could reply that they have demonstrated the interweaving of law and politics as persuasively as the law and economics movement has demonstrated the interweaving of law and economics—even that they have demonstrated the law *is* politics. But critical legal studies has no lock on the study of politics in law, and I have tried to show that it exaggerates the political element, large as that element is, in law.

Law and economics and critical legal studies are sometimes thought to be contending for the mantle of legal realism. The affinity between critical legal studies and legal realism is undeniable. Both are debunking, predominantly left-of-center attacks on the legal establishment of their respective times, the difference in their politics reflecting the leftward shift of the political center in American universities since the 1930s. The relation between law and economics and legal realism, however, is equivocal. Many of the leading figures in law and economics are economists (like Gary Becker and Ronald Coase) who probably have never heard of legal realism. The law and economics movement is not left-wing or hostile to legal doctrine or, for that matter, to logic. The heavy reliance in economics on logical and mathematical reasoning, and the suggestion noted in Chapter 12 that economics points the way to a unification of legal doctrine around a handful of principles, explain the frequent charges that economic analysis of law is the new Langdellism. Economic analysis of law resembles legal realism primarily in claiming that legal rules and institutions have functional, social, explanations and not just an internal, lawyer's, logic; in this it is profoundly antiformalist. But in its emphasis on law's functionality the law and economics movement is closer to the father of legal realism, Holmes, than to the legal realists themselves with their emphasis on liberal meliorism.

Law and economics and critical legal studies resemble each other only in looking outside law for its springs and lifeblood. But that is something. With the law and economics aficionados implying that law is economics and the critical legal studies aficionados that it is politics—and with an increasingly influential feminist jurisprudence that, like law and economics and critical legal studies, is emphatically interdisciplinary— the door is open to the neotraditionalist, who wants to say that law is law. But as it is too late to remove economics from law, the reality is that law is no longer just law (if it ever was); it has been ravished by another discipline. The internal perspective has proved inadequate. To understand law as a system one needs an external perspective. The bane of professionalism is the professional's inability to gain distance and with it perspective.

The most interesting strand in neotraditionalism is the idea of law as practical reason in a sense distinct from that explored in Part I. I want to separate that strand into two threads, which I shall call prudentialism and epistemological traditionalism. The first draws mediately on the thought of Edmund Burke and of modern jurisprudential Burkeans such as Alexander Bickel, although ultimately on Aristotle. Burke is the key figure. Himself a lawyer, his political philosophy was shaped by habits of thought native to the English common law lawyer, and is derivative in part from the traditionalist legal philosophies of Coke and Hale.[22]

---

22. See J. G. A. Pocock, "Burke and the Ancient Constitution—A Problem in the History of Ideas," 3 *Historical Journal* 125 (1960). On Burke's prudentialism, see the interesting discussion in James Conniff, "Burke on Political Economy: The Nature and Extent of State Authority," 49 *Review of Politics* 490 (1987). Among contemporary English and American philosophers the closest to Burke may be Michael Oakeshott. See, for example, "On Being Conservative," in Oakeshott, *Rationalism in Politics, and Other Essays* 168 (1962)—a book that fairly breathes the neotraditionalist spirit. See also his rule-of-law piece, which I cited in note 38 of the Introduction, and Jeremy Rayner, "The Legend of Oakeshott's Conservatism: Sceptical Philosophy and Limited Politics," 18 *Canadian Journal of Political Science* 313 (1985). Russell Kirk, *The Conservative Mind from Burke to Eliot* 7-8 (6th ed. 1978), offers a six-point summary of conservatism at which some neotraditionalists will nod approvingly and others cringe: "Belief in a transcendent order, or body of natural law, which rules

The prudentialists emphasize human fallibility, urge humility, counsel adherence to immemorial custom, deplore breaking with the past, recommend prudence as the central principle of politics and judgment as the central principle of law, elevate the particularism and (apparent) lack of system of the common law over the generalizing tendencies of statutes and codes, and stress the limitedness of intellect as a tool of social reform. Prudence, or judgment, is a mixture of intellectual and temperamental qualities rather than an intellectual quality alone, and the prudentialist attitudes sum to a posture of caution about embracing theoretical solutions to practical problems. These attitudes are more likely to be held by social conservatives than by economic libertarians, and by advocates of judicial self-restraint than by advocates of judicial activism. They are the attitudes of conservatism in the sense of resistance to change rather than of preference for free markets or other "conservative" (actually, libertarian) social arrangements, although there may be some correlation.[23] They are well summarized in Hume's description of skeptical philosophers: "The academics [that is, skeptics] always talk of doubt and suspense of judgment, of danger in hasty determinations, of confining to very narrow bounds the enquiries of the understanding, and of renouncing all speculations which lie not within the limits of common life and practice."[24]

The problem with prudentialism is that it is a mood rather than a method of analysis. It is, though, the right mood in which to do law. If

---

society as well as conscience"; "Affection for the proliferating variety and mystery of human existence, as opposed to the narrowing uniformity, equalitarianism, and utilitarian aims of most radical systems"; "Conviction that civilized society requires orders and classes, as against the notion of a 'classless society'"; "Persuasion that freedom and property are closely linked"; "Faith in prescription and distrust of 'sophisters, calculators, and economists' who would reconstruct society upon abstract designs"; "Recognition that change may not be salutary reform."

23. Kirk makes the connection in his reference to property (see preceding footnote). And Hayek and his followers explicitly base their preference for economic and social regulation by markets, customs, and tradition, rather than by government, on the informational requirements of governmental control over the economy. See Barbara M. Rowland, "Beyond Hayek's Pessimism: Reason, Tradition, and Bounded Constructivist Rationalism," 18 *British Journal of Political Science* 221 (1988); Anna Elisabetta Galeotti, "Individualism, Social Rules, Tradition: The Case of Friedrich A. Hayek," 15 *Political Theory* 163 (1987); Russell Hardin, *Morality within the Limits of Reason* (1988) (index references under Hayek). A preference for a morality of custom and habit over one of systematic rationality is well defended in Gary Saul Morson, "Prosaics: An Approach to the Humanities," 57 *American Scholar* 515 (1988); and see generally Edward Shils, *Tradition* (1981).

24. *An Enquiry Concerning Human Understanding* 41 (3d ed., P. H. Nidditch ed., 1975) (§5, ¶34).

Blackstone is the common law's Aristotle, Bentham is its Plato. If forced, I would choose Blackstone,[25] but I would prefer not to have to choose, in view of the many respects in which Bentham's vision of law is superior to Blackstone's (see Introduction); and I do not think I have to choose. One strain in economic thought—call it the Aristotelian—emphasizes the resistance that reality puts up to ambitious efforts at social engineering. Another, however, regards society as a plastic medium easily shaped by altering incentives through governmental policy. That was Bentham's view, and it is reckless. Policy makers and advocates of policy changes should always bear in mind the propensity of social reform efforts to go awry and the destructive futility of measures that go against the grain of human nature.

But having stated and illustrated these lessons, the prudentialist may have run out of things to say. One cannot decide what to do about a concrete social problem simply by observing that such problems are often more difficult to solve than at first appears, that the solutions may engender further problems at present unforeseen, that (as Shakespeare's Troilus said) the will is infinite but the act a slave to limit. There is a deep irony in advancing caution as the solution to the problem of practical reason conceived of as the guide to what to *do*. Doing nothing is not *always* the right answer, as even Blackstone recognized. Let us not forget Burke's at times uncritical devotion to the status quo and his quickness to posit inarticulable grounds for absurd, even vicious, conventions and practices, not all of which we have outgrown.[26] Like eighteenth-century England, modern America is not entitled to congratulate itself on the perfection of its political, social, and legal arrangements. And many of our modern Burkeans are not defending the *current* status quo but urging a return to an earlier one, real or more commonly imagined. The merits of an earlier status quo cannot be defended on Burkean

---

25. See my book *The Economics of Justice,* ch. 2 (1981) ("Blackstone and Bentham").

26. On the arbitrariness—not to mention the cruelty—of such established conventions as the "unnaturalness" of hermaphroditism, see Clifford Geertz, *Local Knowledge: Further Essays in Interpretive Anthropology,* ch. 4 (1983) ("Common Sense as a Cultural System"). Burke was a reformer, not a reactionary; but among the institutions he defended were ecclesiastical establishment, hereditary monarchy, rotten boroughs, the aristocracy's hereditary privileges, and the *ancien régime* in France. For a useful sketch of the range of Burke's political views, see James G. Wilson, "Justice Diffused: A Comparison of Edmund Burke's Conservatism with the Views of Five Conservative, Academic Judges," 40 *University of Miami Law Review* 913, 917-941 (1986); also Gertrude Himmelfarb's two essays on Burke—the first hostile, the second friendly: "Edmund Burke: The Hero as Politician," in Himmelfarb, *Victorian Minds: A Study of Intellectuals in Crisis and of Ideologies in Transition* 4 (1970); "Edmund Burke: The Politician as Philosopher," in id. at 14.

grounds. It was itself the rejection of a still earlier status quo. And the fact that it did not survive calls for explanation. Burke's defense of the *ancien régime* overlooked the fact that the regime must have had grave weaknesses; it is rare otherwise for a political system to be overturned from within.

The traditionalist's emphasis on the finiteness of the human intellect may seem undeniably apt when considering the role of the judiciary. Partly because of the methods of selecting judges, partly because of the narrowness (even today) of legal training and experience, and partly because of the kind of person that is drawn to law, few judges possess the intellectual capacity, the vision, the courage, and the practical experience to be innovators of social policy. It is tempting to think that they will be better off, and the nation safer, if they stick to the tried and true and therefore stay in the narrow groove gouged by precedent. The problem is that the precedent they are asked to follow is apt to be the product of judges no more statesmanlike than they, responding to social conditions that no longer exist.

Moreover, legal prudentialism is a double-edged sword. If it is cautionary against judicial policy making, it is, or at least ought to be, equally cautionary against formalism. The formalist's battle cry—*ruat coelum ut fiat justitia* (let the heavens fall if necessary in order to do justice)—will strike a prudent person as moral fanaticism. He will want to leaven rules with—policy. Burke's own formulation of prudentialism is strongly antiformalist, indeed pragmatist: "All government, indeed every human benefit and enjoyment, every virtue and every prudent act, is founded on compromise and barter. We balance inconveniences; we give and take; we remit some rights, that we may enjoy others; and we choose rather to be happy citizens than subtle disputants."[27] He is talking about politics rather than about law, but our jurisprudential Burkeans want to transpose Burke's principle of political prudence to the legal arena. And law itself Burke regarded as a compromise between equity and utility.[28]

I hope I will not be thought to be disparaging Burke. He was a very great man; his prescience regarding the two great eighteenth-century revolutions was remarkable. But you cannot just admire Burke and think you have found a judicial philosophy. Prudentialism is the repeated sounding of a note of caution (repeated, not consistent—a consis-

27. "Speech on Conciliation with America," in *The Philosophy of Edmund Burke: A Selection from His Speeches and Writings* 37 (Louis I. Bredvold and Ralph G. Ross eds. 1960).
28. "Tract on the Popery Laws," in id. at 24.

tently cautious person would be cautious about caution as well as about everything else), and a tune with one note soon becomes tedious. So the neotraditionalists would be well advised to explore additional facets of practical reason, especially the epistemological. Kronman and Weinrib are beginning to do this, but as yet without much to show for the effort. Merely to point out that not all reliable knowledge is the product of exact inquiry and to infer from this that the lawyer need not be ashamed that his toolbox contains little else but the tools of practical reason will not advance the neotraditionalist program. Indeed, law as practical reason, far from putting up defenses against the inroads of other disciplines into law, implies openness to all methods by which justified true beliefs can be induced, including the methods of economic reasoning and political philosophy. Law as practical reason is not law as its own sort of thing.

Fried disagrees. He says "there is a distinct method [in law] . . . It is the method of analogy and precedent . . . Analogy is the application of a trained, disciplined intuition where the manifold of particulars is too extensive to allow our minds to work at it deductively."[29] This statement divides all of reasoning into just two departments, deduction and "trained, disciplined intuition," and allots the whole of the second department to the lawyer. This is an incomplete epistemology, and greatly exaggerates the cogency and significance of reasoning by analogy. One *could* say that reasoning by analogy triumphed when (for example) the principle forbidding racial discrimination was seen to instantiate a broader principle of equal protection that embraced aliens, women, and illegitimate children. But implicit in that recognition was a choice of the level of generality with which to state the rule, and that choice could not be determined by analogy but only by policy or ethics.

Weinrib, too, is assiduous in endeavoring to distinguish legal from policy reasoning. He examines a case in which a municipality through negligence caused a water main to break, forcing the plaintiff to vacate his home; squatters moved in and damaged it. The question was whether the municipality was liable for the damage. One judge thought the answer required a policy judgment based on such considerations as which party could insure against such damage more easily. Weinrib disapproves of this judge's approach but likes the approach of another judge, who

> made no reference to insurance or to loss-spreading. Instead, he drew attention to what is suggested by "the very features" of the act or event

29. Fried, note 14 above, at 57.

for which damages are claimed. This included such matters as the nature of the event, the time and place of its occurrence, the identity and intentions of the perpetrator, and the responsibility for taking measures to avoid the occurrence. These factors did not produce anything that could be a universal test, but [the judge] found that they yielded "the instinctive feeling" that the squatters' damage was too remote for the defendant's liability.[30]

The second judge's approach has no analytical content; it is a visceral mixing of incommensurables. Such surrender to uncabined judicial discretion in the face of problems of legal causation is a standard response to such problems,[31] and maybe this is the best one can do, but I think not. Economic and philosophical approaches to causation expose the poverty of conventional legal thinking on a matter of central concern to the legal system, that of the scope of liability for wrongful conduct, and point the way to a more satisfactory solution. Weinrib deploys an elaborate apparatus of Aristotelian and Kantian analysis to build the foundations for a neotraditionalist theory of law, but like the famous vise whose jaws didn't quite close, the apparatus fails when confronted with a specific legal question. And the apparatus itself is creaky, for reasons discussed in Chapter 11. Notice, too, the paradox that Weinrib's approach to the problem of causation in tort law, an approach overtly and proudly formalist, abjures rules and embraces uncanalized judicial discretion. Mired in an ambiguous rhetoric of fairness, justice, traditional pieties, and case-specific considerations, the traditional legalist subverts his own project of creating a system of *rules*. If "the end of tort law is tort law" (see note 14), we are staring at our navels.

Kronman has given us a sketch of the ideal Aristotelian judge.[32] The sketch properly emphasizes empathy, imagination, and an awareness of the rebarbative character of reality, against which reformers are constantly stubbing their toes. (To this could be added the importance of tacit knowledge.) Although I think Kronman gives too little weight to such mundane but important qualities in a judge as experience, self-restraint, and getting along with people, my main criticisms lie elsewhere. The first concerns Kronman's implicit belief that every judge

---

30. Ernest J. Weinrib, "Legal Formalism: On the Immanent Rationality of Law," 97 *Yale Law Journal* 949, 1006 (1988) (footnotes omitted). This is only a small part of his analysis: the concrete part.

31. See, for example, W. Page Keeton et al., *Prosser and Keeton on the Law of Torts* 263 (5th ed. 1984).

32. In "Practical Wisdom and Professional Character," 4 *Social Philosophy and Policy* 203 (1986); see also Kronman, "Living in the Law," 54 *University of Chicago Law Review* 835 (1987).

should have the *identical* mixture of qualities. This exaggerates the degree to which success in judging can be predicted from a handful of conventional traits associated with an Aristotelian aristocrat and is a clue to the latent authoritarian streak in neotraditionalism. The insistence on judicial uniformity also undermines the test of time—a mode of validation that a traditionalist could be expected to set a high value on; certainly Burke did.[33] The test is of limited validity if the "testing" community is homogeneous. There can be no surprise, and no great merit, in the fact that a community of like-thinking persons is likely to agree with a position taken by one of its members. A robust test of time requires a diverse community—in the present context, a diverse judiciary. A related point that might also be expected to appeal to a traditionalist is that diversity, in judges as in gene pools, operates as a hedge against risk and in doing so increases the organism's survivability. We ought to think of judging—appellate judging particularly—as teamwork rather than as individual heroics, and ask what qualities make for the best judicial *team*.

Second, Kronman does not show how any of the traits he associates with the ideal legal practitioner or judge is special to law—a product of legal training and experience rather than of other training and experi-

---

33. "It is a presumption in favor of any settled scheme of government against any untried project, that a nation has long existed and flourished under it. It is a better presumption even of the *choice* of a nation,—far better than any sudden and temporary arrangement by actual election. Because a nation is not an idea only of local extent and individual momentary aggregation, but it is an idea of continuity which extends in time as well as in numbers and in space. And this is a choice not of one day or one set of people, not a tumultuary and giddy choice; it is a deliberate election of ages and of generations; it is a constitution made by what is ten thousand times better than choice; it is made by the peculiar circumstances, occasions, tempers, dispositions, and moral, civil, and social habitudes of the people, which disclose themselves only in a long space of time. It is a vestment which accommodates itself to the body. Nor is prescription of government formed upon blind, unmeaning prejudices. For man is most unwise and a most wise being. The individual is foolish; the multitude, for the moment, is foolish, when they act without deliberation; but the species is wise, and, when time is given to it, as a species, it almost always acts right." "Speech on the Reform of Representation of the Commons in Parliament," in *The Philosophy of Edmund Burke*, note 27 above, at 211. This eloquent statement in defense of the extraordinarily restricted suffrage in eighteenth-century England illustrates the limitations of traditionalism as a political principle. It is not true that every practice that survives is good, especially when as in this case the practice is not the result, or subjected to the test, of unforced inquiry. Burke's belief in the suprarationality of established political institutions is highly questionable. (Himmelfarb, "Edmund Burke: The Hero as Politician," note 26 above, at 9, cites his ferocious opposition to a proposal to shorten the term of Parliament from seven years to three years.) Other criticisms of traditionalism may be found in the article by Rowland, note 23 above.

ence—or helps to distinguish legal reasoning from other practical reasoning. They are traits as important in a businessman or a politician as in a lawyer or a judge. One is left wondering, once again, whether lawyers have distinctive attributes besides familiarity with legal materials and skill at using logic critically (not that these are negligible attributes). And Kronman presents no evidence that judges possessing the qualities he thinks desirable in a judge have, as a matter of historical fact, rendered better decisions than other judges.

Third, we are given no clues to recognizing the Aristotelian judge. We cannot infer his qualities from his judicial opinions; the warrant of their quality is that *he* delivered them. Will he carry the badges of his authority in his face or bearing, his posture or voice? The problem is the old one with tacit knowledge. It is inarticulate. The proof of its possession is in the eating. This is fine when there is a feedback loop between the world and the deed, but there is none in the case of the judge. We have no way to pick the Aristotelian judge in advance and no way to determine after he takes office whether he really is an Aristotelian judge. One fears that in testing for such a judge Kronman will be looking not for particular judgments but for a diction suggestive of mature and weighty deliberation. That is easy to fake.

We should also be aware of the tension between the prudential and the epistemological versions of the neotraditionalist conception of law as practical reason. When law is believed to be independent of other disciplines, judges may be emboldened to try to solve profound social, economic, and political problems that are thrown up to them in cases. The result may be an imprudent activism, because legal learning and acumen do not equip people to solve such problems. A judge who realizes that he has no special source of insight into them—that the source, if any, lies in another discipline—may hesitate to try to solve them unless he has confidence in his ability to master other disciplines, a confidence few judges have. Neotraditionalism is potentially a complacent faith, a source of false humility.

There is the related danger of overselling practical reason, which, though indispensable, is also prone to error. Intuition, common sense, and many other heavily used methods of practical reason supported such persistent fallacies as the geocentric theory of the universe and Aristotle's laws of motion. They also supported belief in witchcraft and sorcery, and trial by battle and by ordeal—examples of the limits of common sense in legal reasoning. There are many other examples, including a host of antitrust doctrines that make common sense but not economic sense. Political establishments rich in practitioners of the conventional

wisdom have frequently come a cropper; one thinks of the British establishment in the 1930s and the American in the 1960s. Would a judicial
establishment similarly constituted respond well to the crises of the law?
Could a neotraditionalist ever challenge, let alone transcend, the conventional wisdom, the pieties, of his legal and social milieu?

The "interpretive communities" strand in neotraditionalism, well
articulated by Owen Fiss,[34] seeks to establish the determinacy of statutes
and the Constitution by showing that texts have objective meaning,
albeit meaning determined by the interpretive community rather than
by the text itself. The approach appears to rest on a misunderstanding
of Stanley Fish's use of the term. Fish uses it to explain how it is possible
that if, as he believes, no text has a determinate meaning—meaning is
in the eye of the beholder—there is substantial agreement on the meaning, or at least on the range of possible meanings, of even the most
complex texts. His explanation is that if through selection, training, or
hierarchy (professional or political), some like-thinking (perhaps coerced to
be like-thinking) group obtains a monopoly of interpretation, there will
be interpretive consensus—but not because the text itself compels agreement. How can it? To someone of a different language or culture, it is
just scribbles on a piece of paper.[35] Fish's concept of interpretive communities is thus a sociological generalization about how consensus is
created rather than a defense of objectivity or a guide to interpretation.
As Fish never tires of saying, nothing in his writings on theory provides
any reason why anyone—lawyer or literary critic—should prefer one
interpretation of a text to another. To observe that there are interpretive
communities in law, as in literature and other text-based disciplines, is
to say nothing that can be used to defend or attack particular interpretations of statutes or the Constitution.

We can fancy up Fiss's account of the interpretive community by
drawing more explicitly than he does on the pragmatist tradition of
Peirce, James, Dewey, Wittgenstein, Kuhn, Rorty, and Habermas. In
place of the idea that thought is disciplined, kept rational, by unmediated contact with reality (in interpretation, the idea that texts have an
objective meaning that we can discover if only we will read them carefully enough), the pragmatists substitute the idea of "*self-discipline* as a
control over the rationality of beliefs and favour discussion, argument,

---

34. In "Conventionalism," 58 *Southern California Law Review* 177 (1985).
35. Cf. W. V. Quine, "Indeterminacy of Translation Again," 84 *Journal of Philosophy* 5
(1987); Stig Alstrup Rasmussen, "The Intelligibility of Abortive Omniscience," 37 *Philosophical Quarterly* 315 (1987).

decision and judgment constrained by consistency and the limits of intelligible adjustment."[36] The difficulty is that, when applied to law, the "conversational" method and the limits of consistency and intelligible adjustment that constrain it leave a vast area in which opposite outcomes are equally rational. Consider, by way of contrast, the game of chess, viewed not (as in Chapter 1) as a set of rules more rigid and closed than the rules of law, but as a language like law when law is viewed conversationally. The statements in the language of chess consists of lawful moves. Although the reasons these particular moves are allowed and others forbidden would be clear only to a deep student of the game, no such study (corresponding to theoretical investigation of the fundamental norms of law) is necessary or even pertinent to whether a player is speaking the language of the game. If a player announces that he is going to move his rook diagonally, he is no longer playing the game of chess. We might similarly think of law as a set of conventions that are as arbitrary as the rules of chess or the vocabulary and surface grammar of Attic Greek, and the judge's task as being to condemn departures from them. The problem is that modern American law is not at all like chess. It is altogether more fluid—indeed more fluid than any "real" language. Some moves—for example, appealing to the judge's sense of class solidarity—are ruled out by the legal culture. (Or are they? Will a judge who, being a member of a historically disadvantaged minority group, leans a bit, in decisions, toward that group be criticized for partiality? I wonder.) But not many are. The conversational method may, as Fiss argues, show that *Brown v. Board of Education* was not decided incorrectly merely because the framers of the equal protection clause probably did not intend black children to have a constitutional right to attend public schools with white children. But it does not show that a decision in favor of the school board would have been incorrect, any more than Robert Bork was able to show this in his formalist analysis of the decision (see Chapter 10).

Neotraditionalism is mostly aspiration. In a plea for a return to traditional methods of legal analysis, Peter Teachout uses a brace of passages from Robert Jackson's opening statement at the Nuremberg Trial

---

36. R. W. Newell, *Objectivity, Empiricism, and Truth* 8 (1986); see also id. at 16-18. Such a view is implicit in James Boyd White's extensive writings on law (best illustrated perhaps by chapter 9 of his book *When Words Lose Their Meaning: Constitutions and Reconstitutions of Language, Character, and Community* [1984]), all of which (I now see) can be fitted within the neotraditionalist framework, "conversationally" conceived, and used to explain White's otherwise surprising antipathy to legal theory, as in his article "Judicial Criticism," 20 *Georgia Law Review* 835, 843-845 (1986).

to demonstrate that the Nazi leaders were rightly punished.[37] Jackson's statement is eloquent and moving, but as an exemplum of what lawyers can do on their own (so to speak) it fails. Interdisciplinary analytic methods were not necessary to demonstrate that the Nazi leaders were evil men who should be punished severely, whereas they are often necessary to resolve difficult legal issues intelligently in our domestic legal system. The passages quoted by Teachout do not discuss the problem of retroactivity, an obviously important issue and in the Nuremberg setting one of policy. With that issue out of the way Teachout is shooting fish in a barrel. It has yet to be shown that neotraditionalist methods can decide a *difficult* case.

Mention of Robert Jackson, a man of unusual intellectual breadth, should serve to remind us that the greatest figures in American law have been people who transcended the traditional conceptions of the lawyer's craft. Jackson did not graduate from law school, and Cardozo left before getting a degree. Learned Hand was a flop at the practice of law. Holmes was neither the most successful of lawyers nor the most lawyerly of judges. Greatness in law implies the transcending of law—when law is defined as narrowly as the neotraditionalists would define it. The greatest American judges have not been Aristotelians in the sense in which the neotraditionalists regard Aristotle. The significance of Aristotle for the modern world is not that he was an Athenian aristocrat but that he was an empiricist.

Daniel Farber and Philip Frickey argue that the futile quest for "foundations" for ethical, political, or legal norms turns aspiring foundationalists into skeptics, and offer in place of foundations practical reason in the neotraditionalist sense.[38] The specifics of their proposal are not reassuring: "a concern for history and context; a desire to avoid abstracting away the human component in judicial decisionmaking; an appreciation of the complexity of life; some faith in dialogue and deliberation; a tolerance for ambiguity, accommodation, and tentativeness, but a skepticism of rigid dichotomies; and an overall humility."[39] Give me these leeways and I will move the world.

There is a deeper reason why neotraditionalism cannot be the antidote to legal skepticism. The intellectual currents that feed the movement are

37. "The Burden of the Liberal Song," note 12 above, at 1326-1348.
38. "Practical Reason and the First Amendment," 34 *UCLA Law Review* 1615, 1644-1645 (1987).
39. Id. at 1646.

themselves rooted in skepticism—the skepticism of a Burke, an Oake-shott, or a Bickel, the skepticisim of such rebels against the Enlightenment as Hegel, Nietzsche, Heidegger, and Gadamer, and the skepticism of the pragmatists, of whom Fish perhaps is one.[40] The term "skepticism" may seem misplaced. Theirs is not the skepticism that doubts the existence of an external world or other minds. It is skepticism about the power of reason to deliver objective judgments on difficult questions of fact or value.[41] The neotraditionalist, being skeptical in this sense, insists that the judge approach his task with humility, with reverence for professional tradition, with faith in the wisdom of the past. Such a judge may employ a formalist rhetoric as an obeisance to tradition, just as a self-restrained judge might do in the hope of limiting his and other judges' power. But in either case the judge who knows what he is about will harbor no formalist illusions. This is not to say that a neotraditionalist judge and a pragmatist judge will be indistinguishable. The latter will be more innovative, more venturesome, and thus more inclined to be forward-looking where the neotraditionalist is backward-looking.[42] The contrast between forward-looking and backward-looking is the contrast between Bentham and Blackstone; so the pragmatist will be a bit of a Benthamite, though refusing—on pragmatist grounds—to go all the way. The pragmatist will also be less "professional," more policy-oriented, more candid; in short, less the traditional legalist.

The difference should not be exaggerated. I stressed in Chapter 4 the importance of "prejudice" (in Gadamer's sense) as a proper ground for resisting purely rational argumentation, and in this chapter the importance of caution and of realistic awareness of the pitfalls of reform. The temperamental difference between those inclined to emphasize our links with the past and those oriented to the challenge of the future is a significant one, but no more than the pragmatist will the neotraditionalist be able to rest securely on traditional certitudes. The foundations have been kicked away. Today we are all skeptics.

40. And recall the nonrational component in Aristotelian deliberation. See Martha C. Nussbaum, *The Fragility of Goodness: Luck and Ethics in Greek Tragedy and Philosophy* 307–310 (1986).

41. Hume distinguished between these two types of skepticism—the philosophical skepticism that is unanswerable but yields no conviction, and the practical skepticism that helps us negotiate the shoals of life, and in particular cautions against precipitate action. Compare Hume, note 24 above, at 155 n. 1 (§12, pt. 2, ¶122), with id. at 161 (§12, pt. 3, ¶129).

42. Cf. "The Development of American Pragmatism," in John Dewey, *Philosophy and Civilization* 13, 33 (1931).

15 ∽

A Pragmatist Manifesto

I have endeavored to use the methods of analytic philosophy to guide a critical appraisal of modern American law. My focus has been on the twin preoccupations of the legal establishment in its rationalizing moods. One is a preoccupation with the autonomy of legal reasoning as a methodology of decision making. The other is a preoccupation with objectivity—here used in the strong sense that persons with different political or ideological commitments can nevertheless be brought to agree on the answer to even the most testing, the most politically charged, legal question—as a goal of the legal enterprise. I have emphasized the precarious position of the judge, forced to make unpopular decisions—every judicial decision is unpopular with one of the parties and with those in the same position as that party—without the intrinsic authority of the more "organic" (popular, authentically sovereign) branches of government from which the judiciary has studiously and even ostentatiously separated itself in an effort to secure political independence. The creation of an independent judiciary involves a substitution of professionalism, of expertise, for political legitimacy and sets up the eternal tension between law and politics in the discharge of the judicial function, a tension mirrored on the jurisprudential plane in the age-old dispute between Legalists and Skeptics.

What I have just said is familiar enough. Any novelty is in the bill of particulars that I have drawn up against the defenders of law's autonomy and objectivity—the formalists, as one might call them, because the essence of formalism is to conceive of law as a system of relations among ideas rather than as a social practice. I do not reject formalism *tout court*; not only are there immensely worthwhile formal systems such as logic, mathematics, and art, but logic has an important role to play in legal decision making. I reject the exaggerated legal formalism that considers relations among legal ideas to be the essence of law and legal thought. Formalism in this sense is sometimes thought a discredited position in law. This is far from true. Many of the most powerful minds in the profession are formalists, whether or not they use the label; and at this writing the formalist style is resurgent in the Supreme Court and in the lower federal courts as well. Formalism is the official jurisprudence of lawyers and laypeople alike, and of both positivists and natural lawyers, although not of all individuals in either camp.

Let me review very briefly the main points of the analysis. I began with the epistemological and ontological dimensions of adjudication and searched for keys that might enable cogent answers, offered from within the conventions of legal argument and evidence, to be given to difficult questions, both legal and factual. No keys were found. The constructive as distinct from the critical role of logic in law (the critical role being to expose inconsistencies), though important, is limited. For while rules have a logical structure, *legal* rules are often vague, open-ended, tenuously grounded, highly contestable, and not only alterable but frequently altered. From the judge's standpoint they are more like guides or practices than like orders. The role of scientific inquiry in law is also limited, partly because of attitude and tradition but partly too because of essential characteristics of the legal enterprise, in particular the value rightly placed on the stability, certainty, and predictability of legal obligations.

Unable to base decision in the difficult cases on either logic or science, judges are compelled to fall back on the grab bag of informal methods of reasoning that I call "practical reason" (using the term in a slightly unorthodox sense). These methods often succeed but sometimes fail; in any event they owe less than one might think to legal training and experience. In particular, reasoning by analogy has been oversold as a method of reasoning at once cogent and distinctively legal. It is neither. The power of an analogy is as a stimulus to thinking. The law seeks a logic of justification rather than merely or primarily a logic of discovery. As a method of justification, reasoning by analogy is really either enthymematic (that is, deductive) or weakly inductive, rather than being its own kind of thing; and whatever it is, there is nothing distinctively legal about it. Precedents that are squarely on point do have authority in a court of law, but their authority is political—that is, rooted ultimately in force—rather than epistemic in character. Judges follow the previous decisions of their court when they agree with them or when they deem legal stability more important in the circumstances than getting the law right.[1] But a precedent's *analogical* significance means simply that the precedent contains information relevant to the decision of the present case.

Many changes of legal doctrine owe nothing either to analogies (except insofar as they operate as similes or metaphors—powerful though alogical modes of persuasion) or to logically or empirically powerful arguments or evidence. Instead they are the result of gestalt switches or religious-type conversions. Indeed, of such limited power are the tools of inquiry available to courts that the highest realistic aspiration of a judge faced with a difficult case is to make a "reasonable" (practical, sensible) decision, as distinct from a demonstrably correct one—the latter will usually be out of the question. The ingredients of reasonableness include, but are not exhausted in, conventional legal materials such as precedents and the principles for using precedents. Often the judge will have no choice but to reason to the outcome by nonlegal methods from nonlegal materials, and sometimes he will have to set inarticulable intuition against legal arguments.

I have emphasized the difficulties, in the forensic setting, of factual as well as of legal analysis and noted that often the legal system settles for "formal" rather than "substantive" accuracy—that is, settles for procedural rules (such as rules on burden of proof) that force determinacy on outcomes notwithstanding irresolvable factual uncertainties. Uncertainty about matters of fact pervades efforts not only to determine what happened in the dispute that gave rise to the litigation but also to measure the consequences of legal doctrines, and as a result the factual substrate of those doctrines often is tenuous. And, partly for evidentiary reasons, partly for deeper philosophical ones, the law's ostensible commitment to a rich mentalist ontology of free will, intent, and the like turns out to be superficial. As Holmes said, the law deals with externals. The operative model of human action in such fields as criminal law is a behaviorist (determinist) one; even the concept of a "voluntary" confession is seen to be determinist in character.

Law itself is best approached in behaviorist terms. It cannot accurately or usefully be described as a set of concepts, whether of positive law or of natural law. It is better, though not fully, described as the activity of

---

1. Obviously "rightness" here is being used in the second of two senses relevant to law: that is, with reference to substantive justice, justice in the individual case, rather than formal justice, which emphasizes systemic concerns such as adherence to precedent. The disvaluing of the second sense is a defining feature of critical legal studies and other radical theories of law.

the licensed professionals we call judges, the scope of their license being limited only by the diffuse outer bounds of professional propriety and moral consensus. Holmes was on the right track in proposing the prediction theory of law, which is an activity theory; his critics have been too quick to dismiss it. Redescribing law in activity terms tends to erase the distinction between natural law and positive law, and the distinction has indeed outlived its usefulness. Judges make rather than find law, and they use as inputs both the rules laid down by legislatures and previous courts ("positive law") and their own ethical and policy preferences. These preferences are all that remains of "natural law," now that so many of us have lost confidence that nature constitutes a normative order.

If epistemology and ontology will not save the law's objectivity and autonomy, neither will hermeneutics. Neither interpretive theory in the large nor the rich literature on legal interpretation (a real embarrassment of riches)[2] will underwrite objective interpretations of common law, statutes, or the Constitution. Of course one can go too far with interpretive skepticism. Communication works—verifiably so—and statutes and constitutional provisions are efforts at communication. But often in dealing with statutes and the Constitution the channels of communication are obstructed, and when that happens the concept of interpretation is altogether too loose and vague to discipline legal inquiry. We see this when we ask what the *goal* of legal interpretation is and discover that there is no agreed-upon answer to the question and no rational means of compelling agreement, that it all depends on the interpreter's political theory. We might do best to discard the term "interpretation" and focus directly on the consequences of proposed applications of statutory and constitutional provisions to specific disputes.

The situation for the defenders of law's autonomy and objectivity is not improved when the searchlight is trained on overarching principles that might organize and discipline legal inquiry. Natural law as the name for ethical and policy considerations that bear on the exercise of judicial discretion—considerations such as those encapsulated in the equity maxims (for example, no man shall profit from his wrongdoing and *pacta sunt servanda*)—is in fine shape. But natural law as a system of

---

2. And one mirrored on the practical level in the extraordinary diversity of interpretive approaches found in judicial opinions. It is difficult for even a supreme court to bring about uniformity of interpretive approach, because ordinarily the interpretive theory in a judicial opinion is just dictum. The case would, or at least plausibly could, have come out the same way on a different theory, making the particular theory articulated dispensable, and therefore dictum.

thought that generates definite answers to difficult moral and legal questions is hopeless in a society that is morally heterogeneous, as ours is. Distributive justice cannot replace natural law, for it too is riven by unbridgeable political disagreements. Although corrective justice, which is rooted in our deep-seated retributive emotions, and wealth maximization—especially, I think, the latter—have significant domains of application, particularly to common law, neither can provide a complete framework that will enable adjudication to be made determinate. Nor can the literary, feminist, and communitarian perspectives that are receiving increasing attention or the nostalgia-soaked movement to return to traditional legalism via philosophy that I call neotraditionalism provide comprehensive frameworks for adjudication. The cat is out of the bag. Efforts in this scientific and pluralistic age to regain a confident sense in the law's autonomy and objectivity seem futile. Yet the radical skepticism and vague communitarian yearnings of critical legal studies are a dead end too.

The underlying problem can be stated simply. Law uses a crude methodology to deal with extremely difficult questions. The crudeness is concealed when no other inquirers have a powerful methodology, and now they do, thanks to advances in natural and social science. The difficulty is concealed when the legal establishment is homogeneous, for then its priors and prejudices fix the necessary premises for confident decision. As a result of social and political changes, America no longer has a homogeneous legal establishment. The more diverse the judiciary, the more robust are the decisions that command strong support within it—but the less likely is a given decision to command such support and the more exposed, therefore, is the contingency of legal doctrine. Some lawyers and judges believe that a diverse judiciary is bad, because it makes law uncertain, unpredictable. They have a point. But from the standpoint not of order but of knowledge, they are wrong. A diverse judiciary exposes—yet at the same time reduces—the intellectual poverty of law, viewed as a method not just of settling disputes authoritatively but also of generating cogent answers to social questions.

A diverse judiciary must be distinguished from a judiciary selected on the basis of racial and sexual politics. Of course persons of a different race or sex from that of most judges may have relevant life experiences that contribute to the moral and intellectual diversity of the bench, but this is also true of individuals of different religious and professional background, different temperament, different health, and even different hobbies. A machinery of judicial selection that merely seeks a balance among clamoring, politically effective interest groups will not generate an optimally diverse judiciary.

The concept of law that has emerged here can be summarized in the following theses. First, there is no such thing as "legal reasoning." Lawyers and judges answer legal questions through the use of simple logic and the various methods of practical reasoning that everyday thinkers use. In part because of the law's (salutary) emphasis on stability, the scientific attitude and the methodology of science are not at home in law.

Second, partly for the reason just given, partly because many methods of practical reason are inarticulate (for example, tacit knowledge), partly because "prejudgment" in the sense of resistance to rational arguments that contradict strong priors often is itself rational, partly because there is little feedback in the legal process (that is, the consequences of judicial decisions are largely unknown), the *justification* (akin to scientific verification) of legal decisions—the demonstration that a decision is correct—often is impossible.

Third, a closely related point is that *difficult* legal cases can rarely be decided objectively if objectivity is taken to mean more than reasonableness. The more uniform the judiciary is, however, the more agreement there will be on the premises for decision, and therefore the fewer difficult cases there will be. I have stressed both the costs of this uniformity and the degree of disuniformity in the contemporary American judiciary. But it should be borne in mind that even within a judiciary as diverse as ours, there will be many shared intuitions (of course, it could be more diverse, and then there would be fewer), which will provide premises for objective decision making. Moral and legal nihilism is as untenable as moral realism or legal formalism.

Fourth, large changes in law often come about as a result of a non-rational process akin to conversion. Rhetoric in the sense of persuasion not necessarily addressed to the rational intellect (the sense famously criticized by Plato in *Gorgias*) may change the law as much as hard reality does.

Fifth, law is an activity rather than a concept or a group of concepts. No bounds can be fixed a priori on what shall be allowed to count as an argument in law. The modern significance of natural law is not as a body of objective norms that underwrite positive law but as a source of the ethical and political arguments that judges use to challenge, change, or elaborate positive law—in other words to produce new positive law. There are no moral "reals" (at least none available to decide difficult legal cases), but neither is there a body of positive law that somehow preexists the judicial decisions applying, and in the process confirming, modifying, extending, and rejecting, the "sovereign's" commands. The line between positive law and natural law is no longer interesting or important and the concepts themselves are jejune.

Sixth, there is no longer a useful sense in which law is interpretive. This is true of statutory and constitutional law as well as common law. Interpretation butters no parsnips; it is at best a reminder that there is a text in the picture (and there is not even that in common law fields). The essence of interpretive decision making is considering the consequences of alternative decisions. There are no "logically" correct interpretations; interpretation is not a logical process.

Seventh, there are no overarching concepts of justice that our legal system can seize upon to give direction to the enterprise. (This point is related to the earlier one about the absence of moral "reals.") Corrective justice and wealth maximization have important but limited domains of applicability, the former reflecting the residue of vengeance thinking in law and society, the latter the persistent utilitarian, instrumentalist, pragmatic spirit of American society. Distributive justice seems quite hopeless, however, and it has yet to be shown that the literary, feminist, or communitarian perspectives have much to contribute to the legal enterprise that is both new and useful. The prudentialism of a Burke has cautionary value in law, but that may be all.

And eighth, law is functional, not expressive or symbolic either in aspiration or—so far as yet appears—in effect. Hence in areas where the social function is the efficient allocation of resources, law appropriately takes its cue from economics. The law is not interested in the soul or even the mind. It has adopted a severely behaviorist concept of human activity as sufficient to its ends and tractable to its means. It has yet to be shown that law changes people's attitudes toward compliance with social norms, as distinct from altering their incentives.

All this is not to deny the indispensability of law or the importance of its contributions to civilized society. But it amounts to a less than thrilling vision of law. It is remote from "law day" rhetoric and even from most academic views of law.

Yet a pragmatist might ask what all this nay-saying, this carping, this harping on dubiety, this heaping on of wet blankets, is *good* for. I am not claiming that the condition of law spells a crisis for capitalism or the liberal state. I have not presented dramatic proposals for improvement. Although I can imagine radical changes in the legal system that would imbue legal institutions with greater respect for scientific methodology,

I am not sure they would be justified, given the competing social functions that law serves. Have I, therefore, ended at dead center, violating Voltaire's dictum (improving on Socrates) to be moderate in everything, including moderation?

My colleagues in the legal profession will not consider the picture of law that I have painted merely a dull monochrome; some of them will even say that I have announced "the death of law." And the approach has practical as well as conceptual or atmospheric implications, only a few of which I have tried to draw out in this book. A moment ago I remarked the pros and cons of a diverse judiciary, and the remark bears on the perennial proposal for an Intercircuit Tribunal that would on reference from the Supreme Court resolve conflicts among the federal courts of appeal that the Supreme Court lacks the time to resolve.[3] At first glance it might seem that the resolution of conflicts that generate legal uncertainty would be an unequivocal good, so that the only question about the proposal would be its cost (principally delay), the difficulties of staffing such a tribunal, and so forth. But from a pragmatic perspective the main concern is with the danger of premature closure of legal debate. Intercircuit conflict provides a method of unforced inquiry in the nation's most important judicial system. Of course debate continues after the judges have ruled, and sometimes their decision is overruled. But once a national precedent is laid down and begins to accrete reliance and interest-group support, it may be difficult to overrule, however powerful the criticisms of it. So intercircuit conflict has epistemic value that must be traded off against the undoubted loss in legal certainty from the absence of a method for prompt resolution of all intercircuit conflicts. My analysis also suggests a more hospitable attitude toward judicial dissents than is found in some circles. They are not only, as they so often seem to be, a nuisance (my frequent reaction as a judge). They compromise the authoritarian character of law, but in doing so they exemplify unforced inquiry, of which American law could perhaps use more. To quote William Blake, "without contraries is no progression."

I would stress the implications of my analysis for research—in the suggestions, for example, in Chapter 2 that a careful study would show that specialized courts are less rather than more attentive to precedent

---

3. See, for example, Federal Judicial Center, *Report of the Study Group on the Case Load of the Supreme Court* (1972); Note, "Of High Designs: A Compendium of Proposals to Reduce the Workload of the Supreme Court," 97 *Harvard Law Review* 307 (1983); Arthur D. Hellman, "Caseload, Conflicts, and Decisional Capacity: Does the Supreme Court Need Help?" 67 *Judicature* 28 (1983).

than generalist courts, in Chapter 3 that we ought to study the effects of an inefficient state legal system on the state's welfare and the feedback effect on the legal system, and in Chapter 6 that conviction of the innocent is less rather than, as one might think, more common in a society in which the crime rate is high. There are implications, too, for teaching (it is a scandal that law students are not instructed in the fundamentals of statistical inference), for practice (legal advocates should place much greater emphasis on facts and on policy than they do), and for judging (judges should at long last abandon the rhetoric, and the reality, of formalist adjudication). I have proposed a new explanation of the pattern of the coerced-confession cases—that under the rubric of "involuntariness" some voluntary confessions are excluded from evidence in criminal trials because they are unreliable and some reliable confessions are excluded because they are involuntary on a determinist account of "free will"—and a new approach to statutory interpretation. And I have embraced (or rejected, which comes to the same thing) both legal positivism and natural law.

But the most important implications have to do with attitudes. The traditional—and neotraditional, and liberal, and radical—pieties of jurisprudence should be discarded, and the legal enterprise reconceived in pragmatic terms. Once this is done the dichotomy between legal positivism and natural law collapses, with no loss. But I do not suggest that it is easy to change attitudes.

The attack on foundations, on certitudes, on tradition, on Grand Theories owes much, as I have emphasized throughout, to the pragmatist tradition. It is a pity that it is so hard to define the tradition, both generally and in relation to law. Conventional histories of pragmatism begin with Charles Sanders Peirce, although he himself gave credit for the basic idea to a lawyer friend, Nicholas St. John Green. From Peirce the baton was handed to William James, then to John Dewey, George Mead, and the British pragmatist, F. S. C. Schiller. The pragmatic movement gave legal realism much of its intellectual shape and content. But with the coming of World War II, both philosophical pragmatism and legal realism seemed to expire, the first superseded by logical positivism and other "hard" analytic philosophy, the second absorbed into the legal mainstream and particularly into the "legal process" school that was to reach its apogee in the 1950s. Then, beginning in the 1960s with the waning of logical positivism, pragmatism came charging back in the person of Richard Rorty, followed in the 1970s by critical legal studies— the radical child of legal realism—and in the 1980s by a school of legal neopragmatists, including some feminists. In this account pragmatism, whether of the paleo- or the neovariety, stands for a progressively more emphatic rejection of Enlightenment dualisms such as subject and object, mind and body, perception and reality, form and substance, these dualisms being regarded as the props of a conservative social, political, and legal order.

This picture is too simple by far. The triumphs of science, and particularly of Newtonian physics, in the seventeenth and eighteenth centuries persuaded most thinking people that the physical universe had a uniform structure accessible to human reason; and it began to seem that human nature and human social systems might have a similarly mechanical structure. This emerging worldview cast humankind in an observing mold. Through perception, measurement, and mathematics the human mind would uncover the secrets of nature—including the mind as a part of nature and the laws of social interactions: laws that decreed balanced government, economic behavior in accordance with the principles of supply and demand, and moral and legal principles based on immutable principles of psychology and human behavior. The mind was a camera, recording activities both natural and social and alike determined by natural laws.

This view, broadly scientific but flavored with a Platonic sense of a world of order behind the chaos of sense impressions, was challenged by the Romantic poets (such as Blake and Wordsworth) and Romantic philosophers. They emphasized the plasticity of the world, and especially the esemplastic power of the human imagination. Institutional constraints they despised along with all other limits on human aspiration, as merely contingent; science they found dreary; they celebrated the sense of community—of oneness with humankind and with nature—the sense of unlimited potential, that an infant feels. They were Prometheans. The principal American representative of this school was Emerson, and he left traces of his thought on Peirce and Holmes alike. Emerson's European counterpart (and admirer) was Nietzsche. It is not that Peirce, or Holmes, or even Nietzsche was a "Romantic" in a precise sense (if there is a precise sense). It is that they wished to shift attention from a passive, contemplative relation between an observing subject and an objective reality, whether natural or social, to an active, creative relation between striving human beings and the problems that beset them and that they seek to overcome. They believed that thought was an exertion of will instrumental to some human desire (and we see here the link between pragmatism and utilitarianism), and that social institutions—whether science, law, or religion—were the product of shifting human desires rather than the reflection of a reality external to those desires.

This account should help us see why "truth" is a problematic concept for a pragmatist. Its essential meaning, after all, is observer independence, which is just what the pragmatist is inclined to deny. It is no surprise, therefore, that the pragmatists' stabs at defining truth—truth is what is fated to be believed in the long run (Peirce), truth is what is good to believe (James), or truth is what survives in the competition among ideas (Holmes)—are riven by paradox. The pragmatist's real interest is not in truth at all but in belief justified by social need.

This need not make the pragmatist unfriendly to science—far from it—but it shifts the emphasis in the philosophy of science from the discovery of nature's laws by observation to the formulation of theories about nature (including man and society) on the basis of man's desire to predict and control his environment, both social and natural. The implication, later to become explicit in the writings of Thomas Kuhn, is that scientific theories are a function of human need and desire rather than of the way things are in nature, so that the succession of theories on a given topic need not produce a linear growth in scientific knowledge. Science in the pragmatic view is a social enterprise.

The spirit of pragmatism is not limited to the handful of philosophers who have called themselves pragmatists (and a tiny handful it is—Peirce himself, the founder, having renounced the term because he disagreed with William James's definition of it). Rival of pragmatism though it is thought to be, logical positivism, with its emphasis on verifiability and its consequent hostility to metaphysics, is pragmatic in demanding that theory make a difference in the world of fact, the empirical world. Popper's falsificationist philosophy of science is close to Peirce's view of science, for in both philosophies doubt is the engine of progress and truth an ever-receding goal rather than an attainment. Wittgenstein's emphasis on the "sociality" of knowledge marks him as pragmatist, while Habermas has acknowledged the influence of the pragmatists on his own theory of "conversational" rationality. Plainly we are dealing with an immensely diverse tradition rather than with a single, coherent school of thought.

Latterly pragmatism has come to be thought a left-wing ideology, a celebration of the plasticity of social institutions. The discussion in Chapter 12 of a recent article by Richard Rorty shows why, and Rorty is not even on the left of the neopragmatist movement. But the connection between pragmatism and socialism is adventitious. Rorty is a Romanticist, and this is only one of the flavors that pragmatism comes in. Pragmatism in the sense that I find congenial means looking at problems concretely, experimentally, without illusions, with full awareness of the limitations of human reason, with a sense of the "localness" of human knowledge, the difficulty of translations between cultures, the unattainability of "truth," the consequent importance of keeping diverse paths of inquiry open, the dependence of inquiry on culture and social institutions, and above all the insistence that social thought and action be evaluated as instruments to valued human goals rather than as ends in themselves. These dispositions, which are more characteristic of scientists than of lawyers (and in an important sense pragmatism is the ethics of scientific inquiry), have no political valence. They can, I believe, point the way to a clearer understanding of law. Law as currently conceived in the academy and the judiciary has too theocratic a cast. There is too much emphasis on authority, certitude, rhetoric, and tradition, too little on consequences and on social-scientific techniques for measuring consequences. There is too much confidence, too little curiosity, and insufficient regard for the contributions of other disciplines. Jurisprudence itself is much too solemn and self-important. Its votaries write too marmoreal, hieratic, and censorious a prose. Law and religion were long intertwined, and many parallels and overlaps remain.[4] Law, too, has its high priests, its sacred texts and sacred cows, its hermeneutic mysteries, its robes and temples, rituals and ceremonies.

Admittedly, much that I am complaining about is surface rather than substance, for on the whole the law *has* been shaped by practical needs (the same may be true of religion). Influential judicial decisions as diverse as *Farwell* (the fellow-servant case) and *Barnette* (the second flag-salute case)—one conservative, the other liberal, as these terms are used today; one common law, the other constitutional law; one decided in 1842, the other in 1943—are quintessentially pragmatic. Still, law needs more of the scientific spirit than it has—the spirit of inquiry, challenge, fallibilism, open-mindedness, respect for fact, and acceptance of change. I use "spirit" advisedly. I am not referring to the particulars of scientific

---

4. See generally Sanford Levinson, *Constitutional Faith* (1988). One potentially constructive overlap is the lawyer's and the theologian's common interest in practical reason. In Chapter 2 I cited Cardinal Newman's *Grammar of Assent*; here I add Nicholas Rescher, *Pascal's Wager: A Study of Practical Reasoning in Philosophical Theology* (1985).

discourse, although economics and other social sciences have a large role to play in any modern system of law.[5]

I find pragmatism bracing; others may find it paralyzing. Pragmatist skepticism about "truth" might, for example, be thought to undermine the nation's commitment to free speech. If there is no truth "out there," how can free speech be defended by reference to its efficacy in bringing us nearer to truth?[6] Actually that is not such a difficult question. If there is no truth out there, this should make us particularly wary of people who claim to have found the truth and who argue that further inquiry would be futile or subversive and therefore should be forbidden. If there is no objective truth, moreover, this makes it all the more important to maintain the conditions necessary for the unforced inquiry required to challenge and defeat all those false claims to have found the truth at last. There is knowledge if not ultimate truth,[7] and a fallibilist theory of knowledge emphasizes, as preconditions to the growth of scientific and other forms of knowledge, the continual testing and retesting of accepted "truths," the constant kicking over of sacred cows—in short, a commitment to robust and free-wheeling inquiry with no intellectual quarter asked or given.

Such a theory is wary of proposals to give less protection to scientific than to political freedom of expression on the ground that scientific truth is objectively determinable and therefore need not be left to the hurly-burly of the marketplace of ideas, or to limit protection of artistic expression on the superficially inconsistent ground that fiction is parasitic on and therefore less important than fact.[8] If, consistent with the

---

5. Holmes's prophecy of 1897 is in process of being fulfilled at long last: "For the rational study of the law the black-letter man may be the man of the present, but the man of the future is the man of statistics and the master of economics . . . I look forward to the time when the part played by history in the explanation of dogma shall be very small, and instead of ingenious [historical] research we shall spend our energy on a study of the ends sought to be attained and the reasons for desiring them. As a step toward that ideal it seems to me that every lawyer ought to seek an understanding of economics . . . In the present state of political economy . . . we are called on to consider and weigh the ends of legislation, the means of attaining them, and the cost. We learn that for everything we have to give up something else, and we are taught to set the advantage we gain against the other advantage we lose, and to know what we are doing when we elect." "The Path of the Law," 10 *Harvard Law Review* 457, 469, 474 (1897).

6. See C. Edwin Baker, "Scope of the First Amendment Freedom of Speech," 25 *UCLA Law Review* 964, 974–981 (1978).

7. As powerfully argued in Peter Munz, *Our Knowledge of the Growth of Knowledge: Popper or Wittgenstein?* (1985).

8. These are views propounded by Frederick Schauer. See *Free Speech: A Philosophical Inquiry* 32–33 (1982); "Liars, Novelists, and the Law of Defamation," 51 *Brooklyn Law*

skepticism of the pragmatist, we reject essentialist ideas of art and moral-realist ideas of offensiveness, we deny the competence of courts to condemn expressive works on the ground that their offensiveness outweighs their artistic value.[9] The emphasis in this book on the importance of metaphor and other forms of "warm" argument for legal change supplies a further argument against sharply distinguishing rational from emotive expression and can even be thought to argue for defining speech more broadly than courts have as yet done, so that it would encompass the burning of draft cards and other expressive activity now classified as "action" rather than as "speech."[10] The danger of warm rhetoric is that it will become hot—by which I refer not to burning one's draft card but to attacking one's opponents physically. Violence is a way of getting people to alter their perspectives, and despite all its emphasis on unforced inquiry pragmatism has difficulty drawing and defending the line between peaceable and forcible means of changing the way people think. But the pragmatist will not be insensitive to the costs of free speech, including the costs of providing police protection at public expense to speakers who desire to provoke violence.

Although American lawyers have made significant contributions to the theory of free speech, their attitude toward law itself is pious and reverential rather than inquiring and challenging. Law is not a sacred text, however, but a usually humdrum social practice vaguely bounded by ethical and political convictions. The soundness of legal interpretations and other legal propositions is best gauged, therefore, by an examination of their consequences in the world of fact. That is a central contention of this book. In making it I do not mean to deny that the legal tradition includes insights and sensitivities of great social value. The rule of law is a genuine, indeed an invaluable, public good, and one to which formalists like Coke have made great contributions. The refusal to acknowledge these contributions is one of the flaws of critical legal studies. But there is a tendency in law to look backward rather than forward—to search for essences rather than to embrace the experiential

---

Review 233, 266 (1985). Schauer does note with approval that fallibilist theories of science support the epistemic case for a free market in ideas. See *Free Speech: A Philosophical Inquiry,* above, at 25. But on the whole he is skeptical about that case.

9. This argument is developed in Richard A. Posner, "Art for Law's Sake," 58 *American Scholar* 513 (1989).

10. While adhering to its earlier ruling upholding punishment of draft-card burning, the Supreme Court has now ruled that flag burning is constitutionally protected. See Texas v. Johnson, 109 S. Ct. 2533 (1989).

flux. The consequences of law are what are least well known about law. The profession's indifference to studies that cast doubt on the lawyer's faith in the expressive, symbolic, and norm-reinforcing consequences of law is appalling.

The situation is unlikely to be changed (to continue the religious metaphor) by preaching. It is deeply rooted in the nature of legal education, which in turn reflects the age-old practices and traditions of the profession. Judges and lawyers do not have the leisure or the training to conduct systematic investigations of the causes and consequences of law. That is work for the academy. But the law schools conceive their function to be the training of legal professionals rather than legal scientists. (There are good economic reasons for this.) The emphasis is on imparting the skills, knowledge, and folkways most essential to the effective practice of law, and that means the skills of doctrinal analysis and legal argumentation, knowledge of legal doctrines, and the folkways of the judge and practicing lawyer.

I mentioned in the Introduction that the study of law is begun *in medias res,* and here I add that this procedure forestalls the emergence of a critical, an external, perspective. It presents law as something not to be questioned, as something that has always existed and in approximately its contemporary form. Within a few months of entering law school the law student has lost the external perspective. There is very little postgraduate legal education in this country other than for foreigners, and little effort is made to equip the law student who may one day become a law professor with the skills, knowledge, and attitudes requisite for studying the causes of law, the direct and indirect consequences of law on behavior, the experience of other nations with law, and the scientific laws of the legal system. Skills of mathematical modeling, statistical analysis, survey research, and experimentation; knowledge of legal institutions here and abroad and of the pertinent parts of the disciplines (economics, political science, statistics, philosophy, psychology) that bear on law; the scientific ethic—all these are for the most part ignored. This neglect is the obverse of the law schools' preoccupation with imparting skills of immediate use in the practice of law. It is no surprise that so much legal scholarship and judicial analysis is unoriginal, unempirical, conventional, and unworldly, overwhelmingly verbal and argumentative (indeed, verbose and polemical), narrowly focused on doctrinal questions, mesmerized by the latest Supreme Court decisions, and preoccupied with minute and ephemeral distinctions—rather than bold, scientific, and descriptive. The academy does not generate the knowledge that judges, lawyers, and legislators need in order to operate a modern legal system, yet there is no other institution capable of generating it. Unless these grave deficiencies of academic law are overcome, ambitious programs for improving law are unlikely to succeed.

Let us begin to recognize the problems by noting that a carapace of falsity and pretense surrounds law and is obscuring the enterprise. It is time we got rid of it. I end as I began with a quotation from William Butler Yeats—this one, from "A Coat," made apt by the importance of the robe as a judicial symbol: "there's more enterprise / In walking naked."

Index